TCHAIKOVSKY 19, A DIPLOMATIC LIFE BEHIND THE IRON CURTAIN

TCHAIKOVSKY 19, A DIPLOMATIC LIFE BEHIND THE IRON CURTAIN

ROBERT F. OBER, JR.

Library of Congress Control Number: 2007908744
ISBN: Hardcover   978-1-4257-7847-7
                  Softcover   978-1-4257-7846-0

This book was printed in the United States of America.

To order additional copies of this book, contact:
Xlibris Corporation
1-888-795-4274
www.Xlibris.com
Orders@Xlibris.com
40124

Contents

To Liz and the other wives who gave unstinting support to American diplomatic and consular communities during the Cold War

American Embassy, Tchaikovsky 19, Moscow (Corbis photograph)

Acknowledgments

Frederick Inman Sharp—a retired business executive, consultant, and classmate from Kent School—ploughed through and marked up at least two drafts of every chapter. Fred never hesitated to ask the hard question, suggest a better way of expressing a thought, or press for a more thorough explanation. I am grateful for his readiness to "enter" my career and make this memoir more understandable.

I could not have completed this project without my wife's strong support. Liz suggested additions, deletions, and improvements as I worked through it. Anticipating that I might write about my career some day, my mother had collected and preserved every letter that Liz and I sent home. My own letters were handwritten, brief, and no more frequent than biweekly; Liz's were typewritten (single-space), two or three pages long, and at least weekly.

Elise La Fosse, Abby Laible, and Robert Ober III—our children—have refreshed my recollection of incidents and events; and I thank them and their families for support. My late brother, David, his wife, Karen, and my cousin Sandra Harrison added details to chapter 2.

Foreign Service, State Department, and military friends and associates (some who prefer anonymity, a few on active duty) have generously contributed, volunteering their own recollections and responding to questions. Thank you, Ty Cobb, Dick Combs, Roger Diehl, David Fischer, George Griffin, Bob Haney, Mary Haney, Tom Huffaker, Herb Kaiser, Curt Kamman, Michael Klecheski, Kathy Kleiman, Mel Levitsky, Bill Manthorpe, Gary Matthews, Allan Mustard, John Parker, Mary Ann Peters, Jim Pettit, Robert Pringle, Dennis Reece, Jonathan Rickert, Jim Schumaker, Steven Steiner, Sandy Vershbow, Marty Wenick, Wade Williams, Bernie Woerz, Marie Yovanovitch, and Eugene Zajac. I apologize if I have forgotten a contributor.

I thank Cory Nishi at the American Foreign Service Association, Washington DC, for responding to several questions about the Foreign Service today.

Informed of my intention to write a memoir, my old friends in Poland and Russia have answered questions and filled in various blanks. I found Olga Michelson in the United States; we spoke by telephone and she clarified her parents' story. I apologize to my friends abroad if I have erred here and there; transatlantic communication, especially across languages, is not always easy.

I am grateful to Edmund Stevens Jr. for sharing his mother's memoir and clarifying questions about his family.

Thanks to David Clampitt at Yale University and Stanley Rabinowitz at Amherst College for responding promptly to inquiries and directing me to sources.

I thank Floor Kist, a retired Dutch diplomat, for his research and advice as reflected in chapter 6.

Don Connery and Murray Seeger, friends who once reported from the Soviet Union, also contributed. Don is a Sharon, Connecticut, neighbor; he kindly let me borrow whatever I needed from his extensive collection of publications on Russian and Soviet affairs, shelved in a barn silo he converted into library and office space, and located not far from where we live. Murray shared a report he prepared following a return visit to Moscow in 2003.

One doesn't complete a project of this scope without recourse to well-run libraries and capable librarians.

Four local libraries gave me support, including access to books obtained through interlibrary loans: the John G. Park Library at Kent School; the Kent Memorial Library in Kent; the Hotchkiss Library in Sharon, Connecticut; and the Public Library in Venice, Florida. Thanks in particular to the director of the John G. Park Library, Marel Rogers, and her assistants, Austi Brown, Rosemary Fax, and Sue McKenna; the director of the Hotchkiss Library, Louise Manteuffel; and the director of the Kent Memorial Library, Lorraine Faison, and her assistant, Catherine Sweet.

I thank the Slavic department at the New York Public Library for letting me peruse reference books and review microfilm copies of *Izvestiya*, and Mary George at Princeton's Firestone Library for making available information about Piotr Eristov and the eulogy delivered at his funeral by a colleague, whose name is not given.

I appreciate the excellent advice and support that the Xlibris team has furnished.

The professional memoirist, William Zinsser, concludes a description of an "insular" period (his own school days) with an apology: "But they were what they were, and I tried to be true to them as I remembered them" (*Writing About Your Life*. New York: Marlowe & Company, 2004, p. 27).

Some events described in this memoir are insular—but others are far from it, and will be recalled differently by different observers. As Zinnser writes, trying to be true to events as the memoirist remembers them is all that anyone "can hope to do."

Introduction

I became interested in the Soviet Union in 1945 when I was nine, living in Connecticut with my mother and younger brother. My father was commanding the U.S. Navy gunnery crew on a Merchant Marine Liberty ship when he sent a letter home about Murmansk, the Soviet open-water port above the Arctic Circle to which his and other ships were delivering supplies.

Because of German submarines, the "Murmansk run" cost many American lives; but the USSR was an ally at the time, and the supplies we delivered contributed importantly to victory in World War II.

Hardly had we celebrated this war's end, however, when a new, undeclared war began. It would pit the United States against its erstwhile ally and last ten times as long. Violent and fraught with danger at one extreme, diplomatic and sometimes covert at the other, it would be known as the Cold War and would end only with the Soviet Union's collapse in 1991.

As a boy growing up in Connecticut and Illinois, the Cold War fascinated me. The tensions it generated, including those resulting from Senator Joseph McCarthy's search for Communists in the United States, stirred my imagination. At Princeton University I studied Soviet affairs and began learning Russian. After graduating I entered Harvard Law School in Cambridge, Massachusetts, and set my sights on a diplomatic career. At the end of my first year, I married Elizabeth (Liz) Stone in Illinois; in my second year, I took and passed the Foreign Service examinations; and after receiving my JD in 1961, Liz and I went to Washington where I began a twenty-six-year career.

The Cold War was the major determiner of the events in my career, the assignments I received, and the places where we lived. We spent almost ten years behind the Iron Curtain, including three in Poland and seven in the Soviet Union. My first assignment in Moscow began in 1972, and I ended my career there in 1987.

There were many exhilarating moments during these Soviet years, and the pace was often frenetic. Families of diplomats bore a particularly heavy burden, yet the American embassy community was cohesive, its morale was usually high, and few ever questioned the impact and importance of their roles.

The embassy I left in 1987, however, was a far different place from the one I had joined fifteen years before. As the Soviet Union approached dissolution, the embassy itself neared collapse. The forced withdrawal of its Russian employees on the heels of Washington and Moscow's mutual expulsion of diplomats and spies, and exaggerated accounts of espionage by its marine guards (to which many in Washington subscribed) brought it to its knees.

The embassy was already reeling from the many changes that had occurred in American life and in the Foreign Service since the 1960s. Most were overdue and salutary; the Foreign Service, like other institutions, grew stronger as racial, religious, and gender barriers disappeared. But not all the changes I saw during my career have strengthened the service or served the country's interests.

Effective diplomacy has long been associated with language and area expertise. To be at all influential, diplomats often have to function across multiple cultures and different languages. Their degree of success depends directly upon the extent to which they acquire and efficiently use this expertise.

Language and area knowledge is also important in framing the national policies that diplomats carry out. Two Russian-speaking Foreign Service Officers (FSOs), Charles Bohlen and George Kennan, helped the United States navigate the Cold War's most dangerous years by contributing to policy making, not only from positions abroad but also assignments at home.

When I joined the Foreign Service in 1961, there were four functional "tracks" from which we could choose a career: political, economic, consular, and administrative. Only the first two readily supported officers in developing area and language expertise. Although another track, the managerial, has since replaced the administrative and although public diplomacy (informational work) has recently been added as a fifth, those pursuing the political and economic tracks continue to provide most of the Foreign Service's area experts.

By the time I retired, however, the Foreign Service was giving greater priority to the acquisition of managerial rather than area expertise, and fewer officers were committing themselves to the difficult task of mastering the culture, traditions, and languages of individual countries and the regions associated with them. At the same time, area experts were also fulfilling lesser roles in Washington. Officials with little or no diplomatic experience, often coming from the academic world, were dominating foreign-policy decision making, with little or no recourse to Foreign Service officers or other professionals who knew the affected areas from their personal experience.

The Foreign Service's reduced interest in developing language and area experts, and the sharply reduced role of such experts in policy making did not bear directly on the outcome of the Cold War. The USSR collapsed largely because of its internal contradictions and resistance from its non-Russian republics.

But there have been adverse consequences elsewhere, most obviously in the Middle East. More than two decades ago, the Carter administration was slow to grasp the potential harm lurking in a crisis in Iran because of a lack of Farsi-speaking experts at home and abroad and then, compounding the problem, set policy without regard to the experts who remained.

Similarly, the George W. Bush administration shunned the advice of Arab experts in setting its flawed policy on Iraq and has since seen its policy handicapped by a lack of experts to oversee its implementation abroad. As the American people have learned, to their dismay, there is a woeful lack of Foreign Service officers and professionals in other agencies who speak the Arabic language and understand the Arab world. The Iraq Study Group report, which former secretary of state James Baker and congressional leader Lee Hamilton gave to President Bush in December 2006, found that the embassy in Iraq, comprising one thousand Americans, contained only 33 speakers of Arabic of whom six were fluent.

Ambassador Monteagle Stearns, with whom I served in Greece, has written that "when policies are formulated without reference to the experts, the government may go in circles, because it does not know where it is or where it has been before."[1] As many of us learned from *Alice in Wonderland*, "If you don't know where you are going, any road will take you there." For most Middle East experts, the Bush administration's explanations for *where* it was heading when it undertook the second Iraq war, and *how* it would get there and out again, never made sense.

*   *   *

I joined the Foreign Service largely because of the Cold War; I wanted to play an active role, to be more than a mere spectator in public and world affairs.

George Kennan, President Harry Truman's ambassador to Moscow, once addressed the question of whether a young person should choose a Foreign Service career:

It would depend on him and on his expectations. If he was ambitious, if he wanted to get ahead, if it was going to cause him pain if anybody got promoted ahead of him, I would tell him not to go into it. If he wants to live abroad, keep his eyes open and broaden his horizons intellectually, then I would say go right ahead.[2]

The career I chose opened my eyes and stretched my horizons, provided many treasured friends (including behind the Iron Curtain), and enabled me to be deeply involved in the Cold War. While I can't point to sweeping policies I authored such as Kennan could with the policy of containment, and while I had few opportunities for heroics, my efforts and those of others with whom I served helped bring "our war" to a successful end.

Despite the passage of time, my recollection of life inside and around the embassy in Moscow remains vivid. It has been refreshed by return visits, reunions, and serendipitous meetings with one-time "Soviet hands."

In writing this memoir, I have drawn on a personal archive of material, including letters, memoranda, and media reports collected during and after my career. My wife is a conscientious and prolific correspondent, and I often refer to letters she sent back to the United States during our years abroad.[3]

For security reasons I, like others in the Foreign Service, did not keep a diary. After his expulsion from the Soviet Union in 1972, the Nobel laureate Joseph Brodsky was asked whether he ever had. "Yes," he responded, "as a boy, when I was fourteen and fifteen, I did attempt to keep something like a diary . . . Now all this is in the KGB archives." To keep a diary, the poet explained, "you need a life a la Leo Tolstoy . . . on your own estate. Where life flows evenly." [4]

Life rarely flowed evenly at embassies behind the Iron Curtain, and the KGB was always close at hand.[5]

I have not availed myself of the Freedom of Information Act to seek classified materials from Washington agencies. Others, including professional historians, will draw on these to provide additional perspectives on the events and persons I describe.

Communist regimes went to great lengths to control and limit their citizens' contacts with non-Communist diplomats and visitors, but none was ever completely successful. Behind the Iron Curtain, there were always strong-willed persons prepared to accept the risks in order to learn and share the truth.

Had Liz and I not made Russian friends, we probably wouldn't have returned to Moscow after completing our first assignment—few American families served there more than once. Russian friends helped us transcend the aggravations and politics that colored everyday routines; they also provided insights on which this memoir draws.

When writing a memoir, an author can reconstruct no more than his or her own knowledge and remembrances of the past. Leonard Woolf, the British politician and editor, once said, "The only point in an autobiography is to give, as far as one can, in the most simple, clear, and truthful way, a picture, first, of one's own personality and of the people whom one has known, and secondly of the society and age in which one lived."[6]

A reconstruction of the past will inevitably include inexactitudes, not only because of the elapse of time but because of the "divided nature" of the writer's consciousness, the tendency of later happenings to influence the memories of a past occurrence.[7] As I describe how I felt about certain events, intervening thoughts based on twenty-twenty hindsight will intrude.

Chapter 1 begins with a description of a reunion with friends in Moscow that took place in 2004 and of my visit to an embassy that is startlingly different from the one in which I served three times.

Chapter 2 describes my family background and preparation for the Foreign Service, including the teachers and events that drew me into the Russian field.

Chapters 3 through 14 describe my life and work as an FSO on assignments in Hamburg, Warsaw, Garmisch, Moscow, Delhi, and Athens; on missions to Kabul, Prague, and fourteen of the fifteen Soviet republics[8]; and on duty in Washington, New York, and Bloomington, Indiana.

Although I resisted assignments within the United States, this does not mean I didn't come to understand my own capital and the forces interacting there. As Kennan once noted, an FSO serving abroad "learns at least as much (and it is sometimes a harsh lesson) about the government he represents" as the government to which he is accredited.[9]

In an epilogue, I return to the question of the embassy in Moscow and the role that area and language expertise ought to play in diplomacy. I allude there to the making of policy toward Iran in the late 1970s and toward Iraq today—two countries sharing a region I came to know in a career that followed the Foreign Service.

1

Reunion in Peredelkino and Moscow

I had stood at the same gravesite more than three decades before. With my wife, Liz, and our three children, I had driven to Peredelkino and wandered about its cemetery in 1972. I remembered the visit because it had also occurred in October and the leaves were turning pale yellow. A Russian village doesn't have the bright colors of New England in autumn, but its leaves are as radiant when the sun bursts through.

Like other diplomatic families, we needed periodic breaks from the Soviet compounds in which we lived. However, there were only two villages to which we could go without being stopped by the militia: Tarasovka where the embassy had its dachas and Peredelkino where privileged Russians had theirs.

Russians go to Peredelkino to honor their poet Boris Pasternak, the author of *Doctor Zhivago*. He had died there in 1960 in a dacha where he had been living since 1936. When we first visited, three pine trees circled his gravestone; when we returned in October 2004, there were only two, but they towered above the cemetery. The sculpted relief of the poet, abraded by Russia's weather, had almost completely disappeared.

Lying twelve miles west of Moscow, the village seemed little different from the way it had appeared when we first came. But the Communists who had hounded the poet were no longer in power; in December 1991, their system had collapsed.

It was our friends who had made it easy to return for two additional assignments. It had been risky for them to be seen with Americans, yet we hadn't been shunned, and were in Russia again because we owed them a visit.

I hadn't seen Ludmila Vronski, my language teacher for a decade; Liz hadn't seen her for longer. We couldn't keep promising we'd come in a year or two and then not come.

We had already lost the opportunity of seeing her husband, Sergei. He had died in 2003 after a career as a director of photography at Mosfilm, the studio where the best films were made. He had reached the top because of talent, not Communist Party connections or patronage.

During the war, Sergei had flown American aircraft against the Nazis. It is said that Stalin favored aviators more than sailors and soldiers[10]; perhaps this is why Sergei was one Russian who didn't hesitate to express thanks for our wartime assistance. His close friends had called him "Count Vronski," as if he had stepped out of *Anna Karenina*, out of a different era.

We scheduled the trip for October and planned to spend all five days in Moscow. Mila was excited when we told her we were coming. She suggested that Alyosha drive us to Peredelkino to see the dacha where Pasternak had done most of his writing. Alyosha, or Alexei, is Mila and Sergei's only son and was a teenager when we met him first. Now in his forties, he is among Russia's leading restorers of Orthodox icons and frescoes. Moscow has more than two hundred churches today—only twenty were open in the 1970s—and Alyosha brought many of them back to life.

Mila said that we'd also visit the poet Andrei Voznesenski. After Pasternak's death, Andrei and Yevgeni Yevtushenko had vied for his mantle as Russia's leading poet, and both had soared to fame. Fourteen thousand fans once assembled in a Moscow stadium to hear Andrei recite poetry[11]; three hundred thousand copies of one of his collections had sold out in a single day[12].

In a famous poem about a dam in Siberia, Yevtushenko had once written that "a poet in Russia is more than a poet."[13] Until Liz and I lived in Moscow, we had no idea what this meant.

We had shaken hands with Voznesenski at embassy receptions but couldn't call him a friend. But we knew he was important to Mila. Her daughter Anya had once been his muse. A statuesque beauty, Anya had become his lover after they met at the embassy. She was now raising Arina, or Arisha, her daughter by him. Mila had learned about the affair when she read one of Andrei's poems in *Literary Gazette* (*Literaturnaya gazeta*) that described a hat that only Anya wore[14]. At the time, the story struck me as quintessentially Russian, something Tolstoy might have written.

Mila said she would take us to see Natalia Pasternak, the widow of Boris's second son, Leonid. Thanks to Natalia's perseverance, the poet's dacha is now a museum. Liz and I had walked its grounds during trips to Peredelkino, and our friend Igor had shared with us his photographs, including of the poet's stand-up desk; but we had never been inside.

I had discovered Pasternak myself while writing a senior thesis on Russian writers during my last year in college. He had just smuggled his long-awaited *Doctor Zhivago* out of Russia. A month after I entered law school, in October 1958, he was awarded the Nobel Prize for Literature. The award outraged the Communists, and they unleashed a vitriolic campaign, calling him an internal émigré, a parasite, a Judas. According to his mistress, Olga Ivinskaya, they "broke and then killed him."[15]

The prospect of meeting Natalia Pasternak and visiting the dacha while finally seeing our friends added to the excitement of returning.

*   *   *

The weather was unseasonably warm when we landed at Domodedyevo Airport on October 13, 2004. Each of our five days would turn out to be bright and crisp, the temperature above freezing, unlike any October week in Russia we ever recalled.

We flew direct from New York, arriving at Domodedyevo fifty miles south of the capital. The international passengers that Domodedyevo received during our Soviet years were mostly from the Communist bloc, apart from foreign dignitaries on special flights including from Washington. Regular traffic from abroad had been restricted to Sheremetyevo Airport, eighteen miles north of Moscow; that airport I knew like the back of my hand, having rescued scores of tourists stranded there.

We arrived in midafternoon on a Wednesday. The traffic was heavy as we were driven to a new hotel near Red Square. Even before rush hour, the four-lane highway was jammed, and the trip took twice as long as I remembered. It seems that every Russian now owns a car.

Individual houses are under construction in what were once farm fields. Closer in, sleek apartment houses are going up and some of the bleak high-rises are receiving new facades. Liz wondered whether the two compounds where we had lived were also being redone.

Billboards advertising Western and Russian goods line the highway. During our three assignments, a consumer goods industry barely existed and billboards carried Communist Party slogans. Foreign-made goods were desperately sought but impossible to find.

As we neared the Kremlin, traffic slowed to a crawl. A large banner stretching overhead announced the visit of an Israeli dance company. The Russia we knew had no contact with Israel. After the Six-Day War in 1967, diplomatic relations had been broken and Russian Jews by the tens of thousands began clamoring to leave.

The American ambassador, Sandy Vershbow, a career Foreign Service officer, had invited us to stop by the new embassy the day after we arrived.

A quarter century before, Sandy and I had worked together in the old embassy's political section at Tchaikovsky 19.

Both of us had been present in September 1979 when Ambassador Malcolm Toon broke ground for a new embassy complex, one that would include a chancery for offices and housing for staff. I remember that the weather was drizzly and raw, and the empty lot behind the old embassy where the new buildings would go up was a sea of mud. The Soviet authorities knew they couldn't have a new complex in Washington unless we had one in Moscow, and wanted a good ceremony. They arranged for a brigade of women—*babushkas* we called them—to work three days, smoothing out the mud with their brooms of twigs and branches (*veniki*). Little did we realize then that more than two decades would pass before the chancery would be completed and fully occupied.

The next morning, after breakfast in the hotel, Liz and I set out by foot for the embassy. In half an hour we were passing our old haunt at Tchaikovsky 19. Ten stories tall with a facade of yellow stucco, it had become the embassy in 1953. It was a new building at the time, with all the neoclassical features that Stalin's architects liked—thick cornices and pedestals, obelisks on the roof. The chief architect was later awarded the Lenin Prize for helping to design the Kremlin's Palace of Congresses.

When Stalin ordered the Americans to leave their first embassy at Mokhovaya 13 opposite Red Square, they were allowed to lease Tchaikovsky 19. Today it is vacant, except for the consular section on the building's ground floor. Its upper floors are used for storage. Steel gates block all but one of its three entrances (its full address was Tchaikovsky 19-21-23), and its windows are opaque. After the Soviet Union collapsed, the street reverted to the name it had before the Revolution—Novinski Boulevard.

As we passed the gates, I recalled that a CIA friend operating under the cover of the economic section had sometimes stood on my secretary's chair to peer out the *fortochka*, the little window that provides ventilation, to check the KGB's surveillance eight floors below. This was in 1986 when the Soviets were arresting the last of the Agency's Russian spies.

Liz and I turned the corner and headed down the side street that led to the new embassy. I was surprised to see the old wooden shack, "the beat-up box," where the militiamen working for the KGB used to interrogate Russians trying to visit us in the consular section. I spotted three burly militiamen standing in front of the gate of the new embassy. I couldn't imagine they were any different from those who had caused problems for us.

Taking a hard look, they decided we were tourists and waved us into a small guardhouse connecting the new complex's main steel gate and high brick wall. Through the gate we could see the new chancery, like the old one, ten stories tall.

A stocky American sitting behind a sheet of bulletproof glass took our passports and pointed to a telephone hanging off the wall. He looked older than any of the marines who used to guard the old embassy, obviously a contract employee doing the duty they had once done. I telephoned the FSO with whom we had arranged the visit.

While waiting, we looked through the guard's window into the compound and saw the town house where we had briefly lived. When the housing opened in 1986, Liz and I had been the first to move into a town house, one of eleven reserved for the embassy's senior officers. Although we knew we'd be leaving in a few months, we wanted a taste of the lifestyle our successors would have.

In October 1986, we moved out of our dingy Soviet apartment in Proletarsky District. It was located on the twelfth floor, and we could see most of the district's factories, but the windows were loose fitting and cold drafts were already making it unpleasant.

Each of the new town houses had a door of a different color; ours, at town house number 4, was a glossy black. They were all three stories tall with separate kitchens on the first two floors—one for formal diplomatic functions, the other for everyday use—and they were linked by a motorized dumb waiter. A crystal chandelier lit the main dining room. There were a maid's quarters, extra rooms for guests, and brand-new furniture—everything more luxurious than we had experienced in government housing before. A week after the move, searching for a closet on the third floor, I had stumbled into bathroom number 6.

What a contrast with the compound from which we had come! This one was antiseptic, its grounds manicured. It looked as if it had been designed for a Hollywood set. In fact, architects in California had designed it.

If Washington wanted its diplomats to enjoy an upscale lifestyle, it had succeeded. Probably there was nothing east of the Atlantic like town house number 4.

After a few days, however, we began to feel the disconnect. The sights, sounds, and smells that we had known in our old district had all disappeared. As I wrote at the time, I missed the atmosphere on the Metro (it was a half-hour ride to the station nearest Tchaikovsky 19), the delivery of *Pravda* to my mailbox, even the clang of buses and trucks rising to the twelfth floor.

Seeing the new complex in the making, Ada Louise Huxtable, the *New York Times* architectural critic, had called it "a ten-acre walled American Kremlin."[16] There was something to what she wrote. The atmosphere behind the brick wall was totally different from what lay outside—seductive but so far from reality. Could Americans do their job from inside a Kremlin?

The ambassador's aide arrived and arranged for Liz and me to receive temporary identification badges that were clipped to our coats. As I reclaimed our passports from the guard, I saw a half a dozen truncheons on a rack behind him. With the complex's wall, I couldn't imagine they'd ever be needed.

We passed through an electronic door and entered the courtyard. The complex covers almost a city block. The town houses and adjoining apartment buildings looked as attractive as when we had first seen them; the front door of our town house was still a glossy black.

A sidewalk dividing a lawn, as groomed as any in Connecticut, led us to the chancery at the center. The chancery itself looked different from the way I recalled it. In 1988, the *Times* had called it "an architectural blob, a block of red brick no grander than New York City's police headquarters, to which it bears a striking resemblance."[17] The criticism must have stung. Beige-colored slabs of limestone now covered the brick.

The layout of the ground floor was familiar. The ambassador with whom we last served, Arthur Hartman, had inaugurated it in January 1987, when he and his wife, Donna, gave a farewell reception two months before our own farewell. We had toured the swimming pool, bowling alley, saunas, as well as the squash, racquet, and basketball courts, and had looked at the areas that would later become a restaurant, a commissary, and a hairdressing salon.

The construction of the floors above had been halted in August 1985 when Soviet workers were ordered out of the complex because the KGB had infested the building with listening devices. Questions about the new complex's security and scandals involving the embassy's marines had coincided with the arrests of the Russians spying for the CIA. Believing that the arrests were related to the KGB's penetration of the old embassy, the Reagan administration cracked down on the Soviets. Scores of its officials were ousted from New York, San Francisco, and Washington. Having become the general secretary of the Communist Party only the year before and needing the Politburo's support, Gorbachev had retaliated and ordered the withdrawal of every Russian from Tchaikovsky 19.

Of course, it turned out that the spies doing the damage were Americans from the CIA and the FBI, and no one from the embassy.

With the withdrawal of the Russians, my final months at the embassy involved as much manual labor to keep it operating as dealing with Soviet officials and writing dispatches. Liz and the other American women substituted for the Russian janitorial staff.

The relocation of the Americans from Tchaikovsky 19 to offices in the new chancery was only accomplished in 2000, after its compromised upper floors had been entirely rebuilt. The embassy had begun hiring Russians again eight years earlier, in 1992, but Washington had barred any who had previously worked at Tchaikovsky 19, including my language teacher, Mila. Security officials in Washington apparently concluded that Russians associated with Tchaikovsky 19 had been tainted forever. Did they really think that the Russians hired to work in the new complex would remain beyond the reach of the organization that succeeded the KGB?

Our escort seated us at a table in the ground-floor restaurant while we awaited the ambassador's summons. It was midmorning and the restaurant was already busy, Russian and American employees mingling freely. Russians hadn't been permitted in Uncle Sam's, the snack bar in the courtyard behind Tchaikovsky 19 where we used to eat.

While we waited, the FSO and two of his colleagues took turns briefing us. They explained that the embassy's role is to provide support as Russia builds a market economy and develops democratic institutions. To carry out the task, the embassy employs four hundred Americans and more than one thousand Russians, and has consulates in St. Petersburg (formerly Leningrad), Yekaterinburg (formerly Sverdlovsk), and Vladivostok.

The embassy's mission didn't surprise me but the numbers did—400 Americans, 1000 Russians.[18] The embassy had a staff of about 125 Americans and 200 Russians when we arrived in 1972. Two decades earlier, in 1953, there were "about a hundred Americans and about the same number of Russian employees," according to Ambassador Bohlen[19].

Almost every officer, Bohlen said, could speak the Russian language, the situation Liz and I had found when we arrived in 1972.

Today, twenty Americans and fifty Russians work in the embassy's consular section. There had been four Americans and four Russians in the section when I took it over in 1972. Of course, since the Soviet Union's collapse, Russian travel and emigration have exploded.

One of the officers said that ten Americans and ten Russians work in Political/Internal, the unit in the political section that reports on internal Russian affairs; and the same number are assigned to Political/External, the unit that covers Russia's relations with other countries including the United States. A third unit covers military affairs.

During my second assignment between 1978 and 1981, when I ran the external and then the internal political units, each consisted of four Americans and no Russians, unless Oleg, who sometimes helped us with translations and appointments, was counted. We had no unit dealing with military affairs; an FSO in the political/external unit, and the defense attachés covered this.

No wonder everyone today wears an identification badge. Until my last year and a half, we used to walk into the embassy without having to identify ourselves; the militiamen knew us by face, the marines by name. But no one could memorize more than a thousand faces and names.

It was time to call on the ambassador. An elevator took us to the fifth floor where Sandy was located, beyond another electronic door and a post guarded by an American marine, the first we had seen.

Sandy was not surprised when I expressed astonishment at his mission's size. "The Soviet Union has disappeared," I said. "The borders have shrunk, yet the staff has dramatically increased."

He replied that sixteen agencies in Washington are presently represented in Moscow. Just one, the Agency for International Development, has more than one hundred employees. They have their own building inside the complex, behind the old embassy where the shacks for Uncle Sam's, the garage, the doctor's office, along with the garbage pit, used to stand.

I did a quick count. Besides the State Department, only the departments of agriculture, commerce, and defense, along with intelligence agencies, had been at Tchaikovsky 19.

"We actually lost a few positions recently—junior officers—because of the needs in Baghdad."

The reference to "junior officers" caught my ear; in my day, they hadn't been sent to the Soviet Union for security reasons.

"We even have a psychiatrist on the staff," he continued.

This was indeed a change; we used to take our "therapy" in Helsinki, accompanying diplomatic pouches to and from Finland once or twice a year, or spending a few days at one of the embassy's dachas.

I asked Sandy whether the dachas still existed.

"They do but are deteriorating. They're rarely used." Families have opportunities for recreation a few steps from their front doors, he explained.

The bowling alley I had seen in 1987 is closed; but the swimming pool, the basketball court, and other facilities remain open. Embassy families who aren't housed in the compound live in gated communities on Moscow's periphery that have their own facilities.

While sitting in the restaurant, Liz and I had let the FSOs briefing us know that we were going to Peredelkino the very next day, not having seen it for years. My comment hadn't elicited a response, and I thought at first I hadn't been heard. But Sandy's comments put matters in perspective.

Americans in Moscow no longer need the kind of break we required. Families don't need to go to Tarasovka for rest and recreation; they don't have to know Peredelkino. They can travel almost everywhere; the country is largely open.

Peredelkino, for us, had been almost sacred ground, more than just an escape from our dreary compounds. It put us in the midst of Russia's literary and cultural heritage. Its leading writers, poets, playwrights, and filmmakers had a presence there. From their anecdotes and tales we gained insights into the Communist system, its culture and its politics. It was no accident that twenty-five of Peredelkino's writers disappeared at the height of Stalin's purges[20].

Liz and I had once spent an afternoon at the Peredelkino dacha of a journalist known to be linked to the KGB. In a locked-down system, even this kind of Russian could be helpful.

*   *   *

I wanted to spend more time in Peredelkino's cemetery, but Mila said that we couldn't keep Natalia Pasternak waiting. Just before leaving, I read the name of a Party activist on a gravestone next to that of Natalia's father-in-law. *How ironic, I thought. A Communist in the presence of Russia's great writer, the writer whom the Party reviled most. The dead man's family probably paid dearly.*

The four of us walked back to Alyosha's small Ford. He had parked it near the Church of the Transfiguration. Like every church we had seen on our drive in from the airport, it had been freshly painted. The new Orthodox patriarch, Alexei II, has a summer home nearby and occasionally officiates at its services.

In 1960, the bells of the same church had panicked the officials overseeing Pasternak's burial. The mourners were extolling the poet when, suddenly and unexpectedly, the bells began pealing. The official in charge was outraged—the church's presumption.

"Close the coffin," he ordered. "This demonstration is undesirable," and he rushed the coffin into the ground[21].

Because of the muddy condition of the road, Alyosha drove us the short distance to Pasternak's dacha, which sits in a heavily wooded yard off a narrow stretch of macadam. He parked the car at the entrance to a pasture just opposite.

As we walked toward the dacha, Mila stopped suddenly and pulled me aside.

"Bob, don't mention Olga Ivinskaya, Pasternak's mistress, to Natasha."

I knew what was on Mila's mind.

A few years before, I had read that Olga had secretly informed on the poet to the KGB[22]. At the time, I was surprised but decided that, if it were true, she had probably revealed the minimum to "buy" a few more months before both were arrested. In fact, after his death the KGB arrested her anyway.

Andrei Voznesenski had reacted to the allegation with a statement that Pasternak had loved Olga and that it was "not for us to judge his muse."[23] Knowing the pressure that the KGB could bring to bear, I tended to agree. Of course, Andrei had a reason to be sympathetic to muses; Mila's daughter had once been his.

I hadn't planned to mention Olga's name and told Mila so.

We made our way past a few lilac bushes and scraggly birch trees to the back entrance of the two-story structure. As we mounted the wooden steps, I saw workers installing lightning rods on the dacha's metal roof. A ferocious storm had unleashed lightning above it a few weeks before, and Natalia had decided that the rods were necessary if the dacha were to survive. She didn't have the money herself but persuaded one of Moscow's newly rich entrepreneurs to fund the project.

Natalia—or Natasha, as Mila calls her—greeted us warmly as we entered the kitchen. She introduced a young woman, an actress from Moscow, who helps as a guide.

The dacha is furnished sparsely just as Pasternak had left it, and its windows let in abundant light. Through them were the poignant images that Liz and I had grown so fond of—birch trees springing up wherever their seeds had fallen, untended grass, and a pasture beyond the road. Had it been November instead of October, we could have made out the cemetery where the poet lies.

The hard iron bed on which Pasternak died is on the ground floor. The niece of Boris's brother Alexander had slept on it "in awed discomfort" after she and her father rushed from London to attend the funeral[24].

In a second room is Boris's writing desk and near it are shelves of books—a few in English—that writers from around the world had sent to demonstrate their solidarity when he was being persecuted.

Natalia invited us to the dining room, already filled with sunlight through its latticed windows. She served tea from an electric samovar and passed cookies and cake while she described her struggle to make the dacha a museum.

The struggle hadn't been unusual. The widow of Sergei Prokofiev, the composer who died on the same day as Stalin in 1953, had wanted to make a museum out of their apartment (a *muzey-kvartira*); but she hadn't been given permission by her own death fifteen years later.[25] In 1948, Party ideologues had charged Prokofiev with "formalism," with favoring form over content from an alleged preoccupation with the West; and they maintained their hostility for long after his death.

After Boris's widow died, Natalia was forced out of the dacha. Fearing that the authorities would toss out Boris's possessions, she dispersed them to his friends. Andrei Voznesenski and Yevgeni Yevtushenko had then joined her in a quiet campaign to create the museum.

The authorities didn't respond but tried to induce writers who toed the Party line to take the dacha over, but none would dare.

Finally in 1985, after Gorbachev came to power, the ideologues were forced to yield. In February 1990, on the one-hundredth anniversary of Pasternak's birth, the dacha officially became a museum. Another six years passed before it was brought back to its original state: floors refinished, furniture collected, and the sketches that Pasternak's father had drawn remounted on its walls.

As the tea drew to a close, I told Natalia that in 1974 a close friend had given Liz and me photographs of the dacha inside and out. She asked who, and I told her about Igor Palmin, whom we planned to see the following day.

"Igor? I've been trying to find him all these years."

Even now, it's not easy tracking someone down in Moscow.

A small group of girls in school uniforms arrived at the back door. It was time to leave. Natalia gave us a collection of Pasternak's letters and poems that she autographed. It had been published in Moscow in 1993, but no one in the West had shown interest in translating it.

With the Cold War over, few take an interest in Boris Pasternak. Even in Russia, poets and poetry no longer have the "symbolic value" they once enjoyed.[26] In 1960, a Soviet publisher had sold 1.7 million copies of the works of Anna Akhmatova, Pasternak's great contemporary; between 1998 and 2001, a prudent publisher put only fifteen thousand copies of her poetry on the Russian market.[27] I wondered whether Andrei Voznesenski could fill a stadium today.

As we rose to leave, we could hear the actress reciting a Pasternak poem as she led the school girls upstairs to the dacha's second floor. We returned to Alyosha's car, and he drove us slowly past the other dachas.

Mila pointed out Voznesenski's. We wouldn't see him after all. He had flown to Paris a few days earlier. Unshackled after years of control, Russia's writers and poets are taking advantage of the open borders. "Nor was Yevtushenko at his dacha," Mila said. "He's on a long-term teaching assignment in the U.S."[28]

*   *   *

I once spent an evening with Yevtushenko at Edmund and Nina Stevens's house, but I doubt he would have remembered. On a spring evening in 1986, Yevgeni had shown up for a dinner party at Ryleev 11.

Ed and Nina's house, fifteen minutes from the Kremlin, was *the* gathering place for diplomats, visitors fresh from abroad, as well as artists and others from Moscow's Communist-era intelligentsia. Behind its neoclassical façade and over good food and drink, one could talk more freely with writers, directors, and performers than at most other places. Yevtushenko would drop in from time to time.

Ed Stevens had gone to the Soviet Union from New York in 1934. Within a few months, he had married Nina Bondarenko, a young Russian who had migrated to Moscow from the Ural Mountains the year before. The Stevens had remained in the Soviet Union up to the beginning of World War II and then, after a break abroad, during most of the Cold War.

Ed had worked as a correspondent for American and British publications. While living abroad in 1950, he had written forty-four articles about the USSR for the *Christian Science Monitor* that had earned him a Pulitzer Prize. Naturally, the authorities weren't pleased about how he described their system (the articles were attacked as the "lowest and most stupid slander on Soviet reality and the Soviet people"[29]), but he resumed residence in Moscow with his family and, by the time of our arrival in 1972, knew as much as any Westerner about his adopted country.

When Liz and I first visited, we felt we had stumbled upon an early twentieth century salon, more Parisian than Soviet. The walls of Ryleev 11 were covered with marvelous artifacts of old Russia as well as works by local artists in a modernist style, works that Nina had collected when few others in Moscow had shown any interest.

Yevtushenko was in good form but had brought along a young actress who was clearly distraught. An autocratic director had humiliated her at a play rehearsal earlier in the day. Yevtushenko consoled her during dinner, then turned his attention to me, having just returned from a trip to the United States and wanting to share his impressions of Russia's cultural scene after one year of Gorbachev.

We must have talked and drank for two hours. At one point, I alluded to the gossip that he and Voznesenski saw themselves as rivals.

"My poetry is different from Andrei's", he explained. "We are friends; we travel together, but Andrei's work is colder than mine."

I knew that Yevtushenko had a reputation as an egotist. John Cheever, the American writer, had once said that his ego could crack crystal at twenty feet.[30] Of course, as Saul Bellow once observed through one of his characters, writing poetry is one of those professions "in which success depends on the opinion you hold of yourself."[31]

"Is Andrei more of a technician?" I asked.

"He has less feeling and uses cleverer metaphors."

"Is this because he is from Moscow while you are from Siberia?"

"No, not at all. Pasternak too came from Moscow."

Over six feet tall and looking fit, Yevtushenko was excited about the easing of censorship under Gorbachev's policy of *glasnost* (openness). "You must see the play *Brothers and Sisters* in Leningrad, and you must read my latest poem in the journal *Smena* (change). They wouldn't have been allowed before." "And be sure," he said, "to tell President Reagan that Gorbachev must be taken to an L.L.Bean store when he visits the United States."

Yevtushenko had visited an L.L.Bean store in Maine while reciting poetry at an American college. He was confident that the Soviet leader and Reagan would soon have a summit.

"Keep in mind that Gorbachev is from the country; when he sees all those saws, he will be a changed man."

I told Ambassador Hartman about the conversation, and we passed the poet's advice on to Washington. Yevtushenko turned out to be prescient about the summit, but a visit to L.L.Bean wasn't on the program that the White House arranged.

*   *   *

After our outing in Peredelkino, I telephoned Igor Palmin, a professional photographer whom we had met during our first assignment. Igor had graduated with a geology degree from a school in Voronezh, south of Moscow, in 1955. After a few expeditions to remote areas of the country, he decided he preferred working with film instead of geological formations. After further schooling, he joined Soviet television and learned how to make documentaries. In 1971, he set himself up as a "free photographer."

At the time, the Soviet regime viewed anyone who was self-employed with suspicion. By 1961, all fifteen Soviet republics had "antiparasite" laws under which citizens could be punished for performing work that wasn't "socially useful," work that didn't benefit the system. In 1964, the poet Joseph Brodsky, who had also spent time as a geologist, was exiled to a state farm near Arkhangelsk for five years under the Russian republic's law. He was later expelled from the USSR; he received the Nobel Prize for Literature while living in New York. Creative persons who didn't belong to one of the regime's officially sanctioned unions or associations were especially vulnerable.

Worse for Igor; he was drawn to recording Soviet life as it really was, not as the regime wanted it portrayed according to its theory of "socialist realism." He wasn't one to tell pictorial lies. He made black and white photographs of weddings in Orthodox churches, of poor people in Russian slums, of bleak villages depopulated by Stalin's deportations. He had visited

Pasternak's dacha when its future seemed in doubt, to ensure that it would at least survive photographically should it ever be destroyed.

Igor's subjects also included writers and artists in Moscow's creative elite, especially those like himself who dared to tread an independent path. A moral purpose underlay his work.

When I suggested that he come to our hotel, he replied, with his usual directness, "No, I'd rather we met somewhere else, perhaps at a small place on a nearby street." Igor spoke no English and I hadn't used my Russian for a decade, so I wasn't altogether sure about his concern.

Before I could react he asked, "Are you here on your own or for Washington?"

"On my own. I'm retired."

We used to meet at my apartment rather than his, which was located on the capital's outskirts. We'd appoint a time, and I'd wait for him on the street, to walk him past the militiaman in front of our compound. At the end of an evening of food and drink, I'd accompany him back out and walk with him for two or three blocks to be sure he wouldn't be detained. One time, after I had left him at a Metro station, he had been beaten up, his camera smashed. Neither of us knew for sure whether it had been local hooligans or the KGB.

Igor's reaction to my suggestion about meeting in the hotel caught me by surprise, transporting me back to Soviet times. Was he still cautious about being seen in public with an American? The post-Communist government has a security service much like the State Committee for Security, the KGB, although it operates under a different name, the Federal Security Service or FSB.

Igor had learned from childhood to be cautious. In 1937 when he was seven, his grandfather, who had once worked for a Soviet grain firm in London, was arrested and sent to the Gulag, never to return.

Or could our Western-style hotel be the problem? For Igor, pretension of every kind was abhorrent.

I told him I'd wait outside. It turned out that we missed one another and Igor went into the hotel, after all, and found Liz. Summoned from the street, I exchanged embraces with him, and we sat together and had tea in one of the hotel's restaurants.

He had gained weight. He had given up alcohol during our last assignment and looked better than I had ever seen him. He and his wife, Svetlana, were living in the same apartment that Liz and I knew from the 1970s. Svetlana had retired as a microbiologist a decade before and was visiting relatives outside Moscow. Igor still undertakes assignments for Russian and foreign publishers, but a bad leg keeps him from roaming Russia's far-flung corners, as he once did.

He explained that with all the privatization of property, it is almost as difficult to arrange "shoots" today as it had been under the Communists. "Everyone demands money."

I was reminded of Sergei Eisenstein's complaint about capitalism after he had cordoned off the famous steps in Odessa to film *The Battleship Potemkin*: "If we had to film a city street in Germany, we should have had to pay more money in bribes alone than the cost of the whole picture."[32]

Igor added, however, that his son Yuri, a photographer too, is thriving in the new economy.

Our friend had never failed to bring a gift when visiting. This time he brought a memoir in Russian by Georgi Costakis, the collector of avant-garde Russian art who emigrated from the Soviet Union with part of his collection in 1978.[33] I recognized the cover showing Costakis in his apartment as a photograph that Igor had taken.

In turn, I presented a book I had written. Igor brushed aside my suggestion that I make a further gift for the countless photographs he had given Liz, me, and the children.

Before the evening ended, I asked a question that had long been on my mind. Had the KGB ever interrogated him because of Liz and me? The Communists in Poland had jailed a close friend of ours because we had seen too much of him.

After a moment's reflection, Igor replied, "No, I was never asked about you." He had been "interviewed," he said, four or five times, but only because of contacts with dissidents, not with Liz and me. He said he would have told us had there been a problem.

Knowing Igor more than thirty years, I was sure he would have.

I had asked Mila the same question in Peredelkino. She replied that she had once been "invited" to a meeting to talk about an American at the embassy, but I wasn't the American. And she added, "But you shouldn't think about this kind of Russian," those who worked for the KGB, directly or indirectly.

How could I not *think about them?* I thought to myself. *They surrounded us whenever we traveled, intruded on us in restaurants, reported on us from the embassy.*

"Remember, Bob, the ones who worked at the embassy were victims themselves. They arrived in Moscow without family, without jobs, without housing. They ended up the way they did for reasons that are obvious."

I didn't pursue the conversation; for me, this was all history.

*   *   *

There was one more friend whom we needed to see, Valeriya Novikova, a seventy-five-year-old woman living alone with five cats in downtown Moscow.

We were a year too late for Mila's husband and a month too late for Nina
Stevens, and we had feared we might be too late for Valeriya, or Vava as
close friends knew her.

We had met Valeriya in 1986 at a Stevens' dinner party. Halfway
through the evening, Nina and Ed had encouraged her to sing, and she
had responded with a romantic Russian song.

We introduced ourselves and learned that she had graduated from the
Moscow Conservatory, Russia's preeminent school of music that dates back
to 1866 and the composer Tchaikovsky. Within a week, she asked us to her
apartment. When we arrived, she explained that we were the first Americans
to pay a visit in forty years. The fear that had discouraged ordinary Russians
from hosting Americans was beginning to disappear.

But it turned out that Valeriya was no ordinary Russian. Shortly after
World War II, she had met a navy enlisted man working in the embassy's
defense attachés office, Leon Patlach. As a student at Moscow's School of
Foreign Languages, as a seventeen-year-old, she had fallen madly in love
with him, and he, it seems, with her.

Walter Bedell Smith, a retired U.S. Army general, was the ambassador.
Valeriya said that Smith let Leon and her marry at Spaso House, where
American ambassadors have lived since U.S.-Soviet diplomatic relations
were established in 1933. Smith knew her, she said, because she had
interpreted for him at Spaso House receptions.

The wedding date was July 4, 1946. Moscow's Civil Registry Office (the
ZAGS, the acronym for "the department for documents of civil status")
made it official a day later, issuing a marriage certificate dated July 5, 1946.
As Valeriya spoke, she walked to an antique chest of drawers, picked up a
ruler, pried open a secret compartment, and extracted the certificate. The
date on it was just as she said, and the certificate (I had seen many during
my first assignment) was authentic. But marry at Spaso House on the day
of the ambassador's traditional reception?

According to Valeriya, for the first three weeks after the wedding, she and
Leon lived together in his tiny apartment at America House, a building not far
from her apartment, where most of the embassy's unmarried personnel, mainly
enlisted men, were then being housed. During the day, she and Leon spent
their time at the embassy itself, on Mokhovaya Street opposite Red Square.

Like Tchaikovsky 19, the embassy at Mokhovaya 13 contained both
office space and living quarters, so it was more than just a chancery.
The lower floors housed the consular section, several other sections, a
small library, and the communications (or code) room; the upper floors
contained twenty-five apartments for members of the American staff. (A
few Americans also lived in the Hotel National next door.) About thirty
Russians, mostly workers at the embassy, lived in the basement.

I asked Valeriya what she did at the embassy.

"There were parties almost every day." There were sandwiches and drinks available when conditions in the city were hard. Ambassador Smith appeared often as did a few American correspondents living in the capital and reporting for Western newspapers.

I knew that security in and around the first embassy had been lax both before and during the war. The Russians living in the basement were undoubtedly "reporting" on the Americans upstairs, and there were few, if any, restrictions on the Americans. Thomas Whitney, a young person who joined the economic section in 1944, wrote later how he managed to conduct "two lives, one during office hours in the embassy in an American world, the other outside the embassy after office hours in a Russian world."[34] A Russian woman "opened" Whitney's Russian world, and shortly after his arrival, he went to live with her in Soviet housing. By May 1945, when the war was ending, they were married. Judging from Whitney's account, neither the Americans nor the Soviets objected.

I knew that the Americans at Mokhovaya could invite Russian friends to their rooms. In his memoir, Ambassador Bohlen described the atmosphere in the middle and late 1930s (but not during the purges): "There were usually two or three ballerinas running around the embassy. They would go there for lunch and supper and would sit around talking and drinking until dawn."[35]

With the cementing of the alliance against Germany, the social whirl must have intensified. One of the embassy's code clerks even kept a Russian girl at a dacha.[36] (He was later convicted of passing secrets to Nazi Germany while working for the embassy in London, to which he was assigned after Moscow.)

Valeriya and Leon ended up living together in Valeriya's apartment a few blocks away. However, they weren't together for long. The warmth toward Americans that my father found in Murmansk during the war, the warmth that enabled Whitney to marry his girlfriend and Patlach to marry Valeriya was rapidly disappearing.

The foundation for worsening relations had been laid with Stalin's drive to communize Eastern Europe that began in earnest as the Red Army swept toward Berlin in late 1944. Stalin hosted Roosevelt at Yalta in February 1945 and their differences, though papered over in the name of alliance unity, couldn't be bridged. Roosevelt died in April, and Truman succeeded him. After Germany surrendered on May 7, the new president halted Lend-Lease shipments to the Soviet Union and to the United States' other allies.

Stalin reacted with the paranoia that would soon blacken the way he viewed everyone. Even the Russian official in Murmansk who used to welcome the Liberty ships was arrested and imprisoned.[37]

The marriage of Valeriya and Leon was probably the last allowed between a Russian and an American on Soviet territory. On February 15, 1947, the Soviet regime banned all marriages between its citizens and foreigners.

In the same month, Washington protested Moscow's failure to pay its Lend-Lease bills and its rigging of the January 19, 1947, election in Poland.[38]

In March and April 1947, Foreign Minister Vyacheslav Molotov hosted a conference of foreign ministers in Moscow. Secretary of State George Marshall headed the American delegation, and he, along with his special assistant Bohlen and Ambassador Smith, had a futile meeting with Stalin and Molotov in Stalin's Kremlin office.

After forty-three sessions in forty-five days, the conference broke up in failure. Bohlen later told Marshall's biographer that because of the failed meeting, it could be said that the Marshall Plan to rebuild Europe was "born in the Kremlin."[39]

For Russians, fraternizing with Americans became dangerous. Eddy Gilmore, the head of the Associated Press office in Moscow, was finishing up a final dispatch on the Moscow conference when he received a telephone call saying a young Russian woman who had seen him and his wife off at the airport a few months earlier had been arrested. He learned later that she had been sent to the Gulag. Fifteen or twenty of Gilmore's other friends also disappeared. [40]

"Their crime?" Gilmore asks rhetorically. "They knew and associated with foreigners, principally Americans. It was as simple as that."[41]

Stalin, even in the best of times, had little patience with romantic entanglements. When his daughter Svetlana became involved with a Jewish filmmaker in 1942, he ordered him sent to Stalingrad; when the filmmaker returned alive and the relationship resumed, Stalin had him imprisoned.[42]

Valeriya said she was ordered to dissolve her marriage. At the same time, Ambassador Smith, against the background of sharply worsening relations and concern about security, sent Patlach home.

However, Smith's economic officer Tom Whitney was determined to remain with his Russian wife. "The only way I could protect her was with my own person." "The Russians," he wrote, "had never molested the wife of a foreigner whose husband stayed with her so long as he was there with her."[43]

So Whitney resigned from the embassy on June 30, 1947, and became a journalist, an assistant to Eddy Gilmore. Another staff member, an army-enlisted man, deserted the embassy to stay with his Russian girlfriend.[44]

Valeriya felt she had no choice but to dissolve her marriage. To avoid arrest, she pleaded illness and remained inside her apartment until Stalin died in March 1953. She then enrolled in the conservatory (her mother was a well-known actress) and began studying music.

Valeriya's aunt, Klavdia Mikhailovna Novikova, may have helped her avoid prison. A singer of light opera, Klavdia was sometimes invited to perform at the Kremlin. (Light-opera connoisseurs say that her "laughing songs," still available in prewar recordings, are unmatched.)

For the Russian women who continued to see Americans, the consequences were far worse. When an American naval attaché was expelled from the USSR in 1948, his twenty-one-year-old girlfriend, a medical student, was interrogated for four months, charged with espionage, and sentenced to eight years in prison.[45] Others were also sent to the camps.

As for Patlach, he disappeared in the United States. Valeriya never heard from him again, and she never remarried. When Liz and I visited her apartment, we found his photograph mounted on the headboard of her sleigh bed, the bed they once so briefly shared.

Of Ambassador Smith, Valeriya said, "I don't blame him; I am even grateful to him. He ruined and saved my life at the same time." Smith went from Moscow to become the fourth director of the CIA in 1950.

During our final year at the embassy, we visited Valeriya several more times. Thereafter, we kept in touch by letters and calls.

It was especially important to see her in October 2004, as I frankly doubted that Liz and I would be in Russia ever again.

When I reached Valeriya by telephone, she said she couldn't invite us to her apartment.

"Could you come to our hotel?" I asked.

"I am old now, Bob. I want to, but . . . could I ask a friend to come along to help me on the walk?"

"Of course," I said.

Liz and I sat in the restaurant and waited until Valeriya, wearing carpet slippers and carrying a cake, arrived on the arm of her friend.

The friend turned out to be Anna Fedorovna, a Moscow dance instructor, an attractive woman in her sixties whom Liz and I had seen perform in *Swan Lake* at the Bolshoi Ballet a decade and a half earlier. Anna, it turned out, had grown up with Anastasia Stevens, Ed and Nina's daughter, who herself had appeared with the Bolshoi in the early 1960s, the first American to dance with that company.

Valeriya's English language was as proficient as I recalled it and as Ambassador Smith had found it in 1945, but the years had taken a toll. She had suffered a heart attack, and it had been her cats, she explained, that enabled her to survive. They had wandered about her bedcovers, "restoring the natural rhythm of my heart." Having seen my quizzical look,

Valeriya hastened to add that the doctors agreed—her cats had restored her health.

After two hours of reminiscing, our conversation turned to the Stevens. Anastasia had died in 1991, Edmund in 1992, and Nina had passed away in September 2004, a month before our trip.

"Where are they buried?" I asked.

"Peredelkino," Valeriya said.

"Really? Are you sure?"

In one of his books, Ed had spoken of the village as a "literary paradise."[46] Ed was a distinguished writer, but an American buried in Peredelkino?

The more I thought about it, however, the more sense it made. During the Cold War's most difficult years, the Stevens had kept a dialogue going between Russians and Americans, and this had meant a lot. Before most Americans or Soviets saw the need, they had provided the setting, issued the invitations, and encouraged the talk.

Through Ed's writing and Nina's collecting, they had also awakened Americans to the changes taking place in Russia after Stalin's death. In 1967, with permission from Russia's minister of culture, Nina had exhibited much of their art at a gallery in New York. Hilton Kramer, the *Times* critic, wrote that the exhibit gave New York its first "comprehensive glimpse of Russian achievements in pictorial art" in some forty years. He described the exhibit as "the first word" of an "artistic dialogue between Russia and Western countries" and confirmation that Russia was undergoing "drastic changes."[47]

After the exhibit closed, Kramer flew off to Moscow to see for himself what he called Russia's "new currents."

As our last day in Moscow drew to an end, Anna signed and gave Liz a pair of ballet shoes in which she had danced, and Valeriya implored us to return the very next year.

"You must come back. I am an old woman and don't have much time. You are my friends."

Before we left for Domodedyevo Airport early the next day, Valeriya telephoned again and, this time in tears, repeated her plea.

For the Russians we came to know, friendship was always the important thing.

2

In the Shadow of Conflict

I had a secure and tranquil childhood compared to many born in the middle 1930s. My younger brother David and I never lacked food or clothing; father always had a job, and mother didn't work outside the home until the war began. We lived in rented houses in rural parts of Connecticut. When Pearl Harbor was attacked, father was working for an insurance agency in New Haven, trying to save enough to buy his first house.

Because the elementary school in Cheshire, the nearest town, didn't provide for kindergarten and first grade was overcrowded due to a teacher shortage, I wasn't an early reader. However, mother and father subscribed to magazines like *Time* and *Life*, and we had a radio and telephone at home. Fewer than half of all American homes had telephones in the early 1940s[48]; ours was on a party line.

Like every American, David and I helped with the war effort. We brought small change to school to buy stamps for pasting in war bond booklets. I recall riding in the back of a platform truck while father collected scrap metal and rubber tires. We were proud that he spent some nights on a cot under a skylight in Cheshire's town hall spotting aircraft; no German aircraft approached Connecticut during World War II, but the threat was taken seriously up to 1943.

David and I participated in air raid drills at school and learned the usual ditties excoriating the country's enemies ("Whistle while you work, Hitler is a jerk, Mussolini is a meanie, and Tojo's even worse"). Because there were few children in the neighborhood, we'd often play "soldiers" together after the bus brought us home.

In April 1944, father enlisted in the navy and began basic training at Fort Schuyler on Long Island. One weekend, he reappeared and gave each of us a dummy rifle, adding excitement to our games. I probably fired as many rifles as David did while at the summer camps we attended during the war (an activity that the war department undoubtedly encouraged), but he had the better eye and enjoyed recreational shooting all his life. The last gun I held was an AK-47 assault rifle that a defecting Russian carried into our embassy in Afghanistan in 1980.

After being commissioned a lieutenant junior grade in June 1944, father was assigned to a Liberty ship, the SS *Robert Lowry*. The Lowry received orders to deliver Lend-Lease supplies to the Soviet Union. On December 7, 1944, on the third anniversary of Pearl Harbor, it docked in Murmansk. Five weeks later, after discharging its cargo, it sailed back to New York by way of a stopover in northern Scotland.

I read every letter my father wrote during the war, but the one he wrote about Murmansk influenced me most.

*   *   *

My father, Robert Fairchild Ober, was born in 1910 in Elgin, Illinois, a town west of Chicago. His paternal grandfather, Oliver Ober, had moved to Elgin from Watertown, Massachusetts; Oliver's parents had brought him to Massachusetts from Sweden in 1847 when he was three.

When Abraham Lincoln called for three hundred thousand volunteers to fight in the Union Army against the South in 1862, young Oliver joined the Massachusetts Fifth Regiment Infantry. As a new enlistee, he was described on its rolls as a "laborer." The regiment was sent to the Carolinas but saw little action; of its 1,115 men, only sixteen died, all from disease. Family lore says that Oliver served as the regiment's drummer boy. He was mustered out in August 1863.

After the war, Oliver relocated to Elgin, finding work with the Elgin Watch Company, the town's main employer. Judging from his obituary in 1913, he was a man-about-town, belonging to numerous civic organizations. Upon his death, the Elgin chapter of the Grand Army of the Republic, the Civil War veterans' organization, conducted services at his gravesite.

Oliver's wife, Anna Seested, my father's paternal grandmother, was also a child of immigrants, born of a family that had gone to Chicago from Norway in August 1871. The Great Fire broke out two months after their arrival, destroying seventeen thousand buildings in three days. Eleven-year-old Anna wrote in her diary that the fire burned itself out just short of where her family was living. Perhaps because of the fire, the family moved to the distant suburb of Elgin where, in 1881, Anna and Oliver met and married.

After Oliver's death on the eve of World War I, Anna supported herself and their only child, Oliver Victor (my father's father), by teaching music and selling landscapes she painted. She must have had a sharp memory; the paintings that survive portray lakes and streams amid dense, dark forests, scenes common enough in Norway but certainly not in Illinois. My father spoke of Anna almost reverently, as a strong-willed woman who held the family together despite the sparest of means.

My father's mother, Lois Fairchild, could also trace her immediate roots abroad. Her father James had migrated from London to Massachusetts in 1859. After the Civil War, he also settled in Elgin and found work at Elgin Watch, ultimately becoming the head of its gilding department. He was an ardent Methodist, traveling with a horse and buggy to proclaim the Gospel in towns near Elgin. He also conducted missions far afield, in California and New York. He met his wife, Mary Parkes, in Brooklyn; their marriage was registered there in 1880, but they made their home in Elgin. Because of his and Mary's religious parenting, Lois and her three sisters had their hair shaven until they reached fourteen. Lois was the family member who taught David and me how to say our prayers.

My father's parents, Lois Fairchild and Oliver Victor, met and married in Elgin. Their three sons, including my father, were born there before World War I. In a pattern of movement between the East and Middle West that reoccurs in the family, Oliver, Lois, and their three boys moved to New Haven in 1920. An advertising firm there had hired Oliver while he was marketing soap in Chicago.

Although self-educated, my father's father became a civic leader, including president of New Haven's Chamber of Commerce. In 1938, he was appointed to a committee of "first families" organizing the city's tercentennial.[49] Because his father had been a participant, he became a Civil War buff. His paneled study contained a collection of books about the war along with a set of Mathew Brady photographs. After retiring, when not playing golf, he would sit in a red Moroccan leather chair, sometimes smoking cigars, dividing his time between business publications and the Civil War. Whenever we visited, I would take a stereoscope and study Brady's photographs.

There must have been a radio in the study because Fulton Lewis Jr. was often mentioned. Lewis was an early supporter of Wisconsin's Senator Joseph McCarthy, first elected to the Senate in 1946; by the late 1940s, Lewis had a Mutual Broadcasting System audience of ten million, and McCarthy was gaining a national following.

Apparently, my father was not a good student. In 1926, his parents, affluent by New Haven's standards, sent him to Mount Hermon, a boarding school that Dwight Moody, the Methodist evangelist, had founded in western Massachusetts in 1881. As my father recounted, there he found his "salvation"; he earned passing grades, excelled in football and ice hockey, and was admitted to Wesleyan University, a college in Middletown not far from New Haven.

His admission to Wesleyan marked a turning point—no one in the family had attended college before. Still, my father never forgave himself for missing admission to Princeton, having flunked a French-language entrance exam by "a quarter point." When the time came for my brother and me to consider colleges and Princeton offered us admission in successive years, there was little doubt where we'd go.

*   *   *

Even before Wesleyan, my father had met the woman who would become his wife. When he was a fourteen-year-old Boy Scout, he fell in love with a thirteen-year-old Campfire Girl he met at a dance in New Haven. Her name was Celia Mahoney, and he told himself then and there they'd marry. My mother would dismiss this as an embroidered account of what really happened—"typical of your father's salesmanship."

Celia was linked even more closely than my father to the Old World but was never one to talk about it. "Never look back," she would say impatiently when, toward the end of her life, I pressed for more information. She acknowledged only that her father, Francis Mahoney, had come from somewhere in Ireland, probably County Kerry.

Perhaps Francis didn't know his own background or didn't want to share it. It appears he experienced a far-from-normal childhood—somewhat like the one he gave his children—and indulged in no sentimentality about the past.

Francis arrived in New York in 1882 as a two or three-year-old. It is unclear whether he came with his parents. Their marriage is recorded in a Catholic church in Brosna, County Kerry, so he was not an orphan in any true sense; but his father may have died before the voyage and his mother, from a nearby village, may have sailed alone with him, only to die herself within a year. Or did she entrust him to another family emigrating from County Kerry? A social security form prepared by Francis carries an entry, not in his own handwriting, that his mother was "unknown." However, his eyes by that time were failing, and a clerk might have made the entry. Francis had once spoken of a half brother, George Foley, and it may be that he was adopted, at least informally, by another family.

What is certain is that Francis's departure from Ireland and arrival in New York could not have been timed more providentially. In 1879, the so-called Land Wars broke out, engulfing southwest Ireland including

County Kerry; and in 1880, the City of New York elected William Grace, an immigrant, to be its first Irish mayor.

Francis had ambition and intelligence, attributes that figured in the success of new arrivals in what Henry Luce would later call "the American Century." He first worked as a journeyman carpenter, which was how his father's occupation had been described on the Brosna certificate, and then gained admission to Brooklyn's Pratt Institute, a newly founded college, in 1904. He worked days and studied evenings, excelling in "drawing, architecture and construction"; his transcript describes him as a "tireless worker, determined to succeed."

One year before his admission to Pratt, he married my maternal grandmother, Jennie Myers, in an Episcopal ceremony in Manhattan. Jennie was a native-born American, Scotch Irish by descent, with relatives in Massachusetts and Connecticut, some of whom were engaged in the tobacco trade and a few of whom died from the influenza of 1918.

Graduating from Pratt, Francis embarked upon a teaching and administrative career in New York City public schools. Mother suggested once that he rose to be a supervisor of night schools for the city's board of education. He always held two or three nonteaching jobs to supplement his salary. His writing skills appear in a thirteen-paragraph letter he published on behalf of one nonschool employer in the *New York Times* in 1925.[50]

Francis and Jennie lived in Brooklyn where their three children—my mother, her twin sister, and an older brother—were born; but in time, they established separate households. Francis purchased a house in New Haven for his wife and children while he stayed near his jobs.

One of my cousins speculates, on the basis of what she once heard her mother say, that Francis might have had a second family. Perhaps this is why my mother, who loved mystery novels, was always guarded about her father's life; could there have been a mystery in New York?

My mother and her siblings were raised in New Haven. When Jennie was away recuperating from bouts of tuberculosis, her Myers relatives assumed charge. Francis was said to have visited his family on weekends.

My mother's parents had little in common, and their marriage wasn't happy. Jennie became a Christian Scientist reader but developed few associations outside the home. My mother told me at the end of her life that she had never received as much as a hug from her mother, as she "didn't know how."

My brother and I didn't know what to make of Jennie, and probably Francis didn't either after their children were born, hence his decision to live apart. My mother saw little of her father but excused his absences. In turn, he saw that she received an education at Russell Sage College in Troy,

New York, where she studied French and acquired secretarial skills, suitable preparation at the time for smart girls from the middle class.

I came to know Francis slightly after he returned to New Haven to retire in the house he had bought for his family. (Until his death, he and Jennie coexisted rather coldly under the same roof.) I found him intriguing, more so than my paternal grandfather, the successful advertising executive who lived in a grander way in Hamden, an upscale New Haven suburb. Francis read everything that he could lay his hands on until his eyes gave out. Understanding that I too was a reader, he gave me biographies of Robert Moses—about whom he knew a great deal as a one-time New York City resident—and of the Rockefeller family. These were "used" books, probably scavenged from trash cans, as he scavenged (and repaired) the two lamps he gave my wife and me on the occasion of our wedding. His zany sense of humor also appealed to me. When father was in the navy, he once appeared outside the door of our house with a ball and chain around his leg. "This," he told David and me, "is what marriage is all about."

He was a freethinker with no interest in organized religion. Although she dabbled now and then in her mother's Christian Science, our mother acquired her father's earthbound ways of seeing things.

$$*\quad*\quad*$$

In February 1933, our parents eloped from New Haven to Brewster, New York. They pointed to the Great Depression as the reason, but something else may have been involved.

Before World War II, upper and middle classes in the United States tended to look down on the Irish. Even families that had sunk their roots in American soil a generation earlier recoiled from the Irish influx, stemmed only by an act of Congress in 1924. Did our parents elope because of reservations in our father's family? Our mother was a beautiful dark-haired Irish girl and had many suitors, but like her father, she came from an irregular situation. Could it be that the senior Obers hoped their oldest son would find a bride among more established families? Our two sets of grandparents never associated although their houses weren't far apart.

When I was born in 1935 and David a year later, we were living outside Hartford. After renting houses, father finally found one he could afford not far from Cheshire and a quarter mile from the closest neighbor. It had been a summer home for affluent New Yorkers and had an earthen basement that attracted small animals, including snakes. With the war beginning and finances tight, my parents set out to make the house habitable year-round. Their friends pitched in, and David and I did our part; I remember us working in the attic, rolling out asbestos.

Father worked long days and evenings as an insurance salesman. He joined New Haven's Junior Chamber of Commerce and became its president within a few years. His father was president of the senior chamber, and it was said that they were the first father-and-son team to head the senior-junior organizations in any American city at the same time.

Born with immense energy, father devoted weekend time to outdoor projects and to sports such as tennis and skiing. One of his close friends, John Chamberlain, lived nearby and owned a tennis court. Chamberlain had been in the thick of Manhattan's literary politics in the 1930s, a book critic with a leftist slant. Mary McCarthy made him a model for her "Portrait of the Intellectual as a Yale Man," a 1942 exposé of ex-Trotskyites who "sell out" to Henry Luce's *Time* and *Life*.[51] The novelist Robert Penn Warren described him as "the intellectual who made you think of Huckleberry Finn and Boy Scouts."[52]

I don't recall my parents talking literary or public affairs with the Chamberlains, but father became a fixture on their tennis court. In his memoir, Chamberlain describes playing tennis with Luce (and with Luce's guests, including a Lodge and a Bush) in Greenwich, Connecticut; perhaps he used Dad (whom he doesn't mention) to bring his game to Luce's standard. In 1984, inscribing a copy of his memoir to my parents, Chamberlain wrote that, "in Eric Johnston's words, [they] can't be Obersold."[53]

Johnston, the head of the United States Chamber of Commerce in the early 1940s, must have also played on Chamberlain's court. While serving as the president of the Motion Picture Association of America, he would later become known for creating, in 1947, the infamous Hollywood blacklist. Chamberlain ended his career writing for the *Wall Street Journal* and William Buckley's *National Review.*

In winter, father would take us to nearby ponds for skating and to New Hampshire and Vermont for skiing. My brother followed in father's athletic footsteps; I tried but usually lagged behind.

Like most Americans, we lived austerely through the 1940s. Father's parents didn't, and mother's parents couldn't provide support. The burden of raising my brother and me fell mostly on mother. Less energetic but more resourceful than her husband, she made most of what we had.

Although I was not raised amid talk about public affairs, the New Yorkers who once owned the house had left behind a trove of books, most from the late nineteenth century. I read a few, and mother helped me find others in Cheshire's library. Gradually, I filled my afternoons with more than "soldiers."

Thirty-four years old with a wife and two children, father wouldn't have been drafted under the regulations then in force but decided to volunteer. Was this an act of patriotism in the tradition of his drummer-boy grandfather, or something different?

I have no recollection of how mother received his decision, but it later became a point of contention. She would suggest that he had shirked his paternal responsibilities and had bowed to parental pressure. It is possible father's parents were embarrassed because their other sons, unmarried, had been declared unfit for service for reasons of health, although they looked robust enough (and one would outlive father by almost a decade); perhaps Oliver summoned his oldest son to uphold the family's honor.

Mother may not have been averse initially but grew resentful as she coped with two boys on her own in the country. Father was always more emotional than mother, and I'd like to believe his enlistment was patriotic. Whatever his motivation (and it was probably mixed as motivations are), we couldn't comfortably discuss most wartime experiences at home. David and I were never regaled with tales of shipboard adventures and out of prudence, rarely asked.

After basic training at Fort Schuyler and his commissioning, father was ordered to Gulfport, Mississippi, for advanced gunnery training. My brother and I were dropped off at a boys' camp in eastern Connecticut as our parents headed south. We had never been far from home before, and Camp Tohaci, even by wartime standards, was poorly administered. The counselors forced my brother and me to box against each other until a bloody nose ended the bout for me. The camp closed after a second summer. While it left me with no fond memories, it may have added a layer of toughness that would help me deal later with trying situations.

Liberty ships were manned by merchant marine sailors but also carried navy armed guard crews, each of approximately thirty men. The navy crews were responsible for the watches and battle stations. My father commanded the gunnery crews on two ships and was away from home—on duty in every ocean—for one and a half years.

In his absence, mother became strongly self-sufficient, running the household like her own tight ship. She planted and maintained a victory garden, and canned fruits and vegetables; assisted at United Service Organization functions in Manhattan; and taught French at Hamden Hall, a private school not far from her in-laws' house, to supplement the navy's meager paycheck.

My brother and I admired our father for his energy and business success, but mother's influence was dominant during a formative period, and it didn't really abate until after we established our own careers and families.

*   *   *

Father handwrote a dozen letters describing his navy experiences. After copying them on a typewriter, mother would forward them to family members and his former business associates.

On November 29, 1944, the SS *Robert Lowry* left Loch Ewe, Scotland, for Murmansk loaded with tanks, locomotives, trucks, machine tools, steel, and other materials. It sailed in a convoy of sixty-four ships, thirty of them carrying cargo, the others—including cruisers and destroyers—providing perimeter security.

In a report prepared for one of the embassy's navy attachés who was stationed in Murmansk, father wrote that U-boats and floating mines were in the area of the Kola Peninsula as the convoy passed. He could feel the reverberations as escorting ships dropped their depth charges.

Between 1942 and the war's end in 1945, 350 different American ships "ran the gauntlet" to Murmansk and Arkhangelsk, the two ports in European Russia that received Lend-Lease supplies. It was the war's most hazardous sea-lane; "more ships were sunk, and more seamen died there than anywhere else" (*Forgotten Heroes: The Heroic Story of the United States Merchant Marine*, Brian Herbert, 2004).[54]

At the beginning of the war, armed guard duty was described as the navy's "least coveted assignment."[55]

By December 1944, however, most U-boats had been cleared from the Atlantic and Arctic Oceans. Only seven of the nearly one hundred ships sunk during "the run" were lost in 1944.[56]

After a five-week stay in Murmansk, father wrote home:

> I'll admit that I was a bit scared leaving the barren fjord, because if ever we were going to get it, it would be on this last lap . . . I breathed a sigh of relief when the Russian pilot came on board to take us into port. [He goes on to describe how he took a shower after two weeks of sleeping in his clothes to maintain watches, and how, in "a dive for the bunk," he missed and injured himself.] I arrived in Russia, sleepy and with a broken nose.

> At the gangplank stood a Russian sentry. He was a nice-looking, rosy-cheeked lad of eighteen, with the usual fur coat that the soldiers wear and felt boots . . . The sentries are on duty twelve hours with no relief, carrying a sandwich in their pocket. We tried offering coffee and sandwiches, but they wouldn't accept them.

As I started uptown, a swarm of youngsters—hooligans, the Russians call them—saying "cigarette, thirty rubles; candy, chew gum," engulfed me and pushed me about. But I said, "Nya Nya," and shook my fist, and they moved on. Then, I got my first look at the town—it was really rather pathetic; everything I saw before me had been burned, bombed, or gutted . . . . Besides, these buildings were two-story log homes. The windows were all boarded off except for one pane of glass . . . . As I prowled up the street, I noticed a woman drawing water from pipelines, which ran along the surface. I learned later that she lived upon the hill and had to carry water for all her needs. Down the street came three barrage balloons manned by girl soldiers. They all looked splendid—not good looking but healthy, sturdy girls. The town boasted of five girl snipers who had won the Stalin medal.

[The American mission in Murmansk to which he reported sent him to a British hospital and, after a week's treatment, he was released to a Soviet "hotel"].

I had dinner at the American mission that night but went to the Seaman's Club for amusement. Refreshments consisted of tea, chocolate, vodka, and wine . . . . After a Russian movie depicting Nazi sadism, a tinny phonograph was turned on, and the seamen and girls danced . . . . Every nationality of merchant sailor was there, in every type of outfit, in rubber boots, in turtleneck sweaters. The girls dressed their best, but it was pathetic. Sleazy, cheap clothes; funny cotton socks; shoes with long, pointed toes, and lopsided heels. I believe I witnessed every type of dance step in the world that night . . . .

While in the hospital for a week, I had missed the welcome banquet but returned in time for the farewell dinner. Picture a big barren hall with a horseshoe table in the center. On the left side sits the Russian navy band, twenty shaved-topped boys. The band strikes up a tune, and the guests, British and American Navy officers, find their seats beside their hosts, Russian civilians. No sooner are we seated than the toastmaster arises and says in Russian, "Here's a toast to our excellent allies who have delivered successfully another convoy of supplies." When he is through, an interpreter restates the toast in English. This is the beginning of a long series of toasts by all . . . . On my left is a short fat Russian girl. On my right sits a fifteen-year-old Russian engineer. He says, "Watch me drink him"—nodding to the chief mate across the table—"under the table." Forty-five minutes later, we carried the chief mate out.

The first course consisted of cheeses, two types of cold fish, caviar, wine, mineral water, vodka. The next course consisted of more cheese and hot fish, chicken salad, and more of same liquors. The next course was chicken, french fries, and always refilling of glasses . . . finally, coffee and condensed milk ice cream. We danced between courses to dirgelike Russian music. In between, two accordionists played an old American jazz tune. By now, the vodka was beginning to show its effect [but] . . . I saw not one Russian under the influence . . . .

Next morning, I was back on my ship and had my last look at the town.

On January 11, 1945, the SS *Robert Lowry* weighed anchor and left Murmansk in a different convoy of twenty-three cargo and nineteen escort ships. A heavy rolling sea, snow, and fog made the outbound voyage more treacherous than the inbound one. A fire in an ammunition magazine had to be flooded, a storm blew the convoy apart, and the *Lowry* lost a life raft before it reached Scotland on January 20.

In a final report, Father complained about the dockworkers at Murmansk:

The Russians did not give a full weight measure of sand and ballast and did not trim it properly in the holds, but left it piled high in the center. The result was excessive rolling, shifting of ballast, creating a six-degree list . . . .

Father hadn't studied Russian history or the language but simply described what he saw. Because the winter sun never comes up in Murmansk and only glimmers on the horizon, it's a wonder he saw what he did.

Edmund Stevens, in Moscow at the same time, described the "vodka treatment" the *Lowry*'s chief mate experienced:

Whenever there was a party or a banquet, which was often, they [the Americans] found that their Russian colleagues expected them to drink toast after toast, bottoms up, to Stalin, Roosevelt, and Soviet-American friendship, tossing down the hatch whole

tumblerfuls of liquid fire. And anyone who didn't hold up his
end lost face. To deaden the effects and to protect the linings of
their stomachs, the Americans tried such time-tested stratagems
as swallowing chunks of butter or tablespoons of salad oil before
the ordeal.[57]

Years later, I saw bits and pieces of the Russia that father had observed.
The reception given the officers and sailors at the Seaman's Club was a little
different from that given American businessmen and diplomats at the height
of détente, and a few towns I visited looked no different from the Murmansk
he described. Workers' indiscipline has always been a Russian problem.

Father brought two souvenirs home, a traditional painted box from
the village of Palekh east of Moscow and two cloth dolls. He had wanted to
obtain Russian uniforms for David and me. But with Stalin in power, what
Russian would dare sell a uniform? How different from the late 1980s when
Soviet soldiers hawked their uniforms to tourists on Moscow's streets!

During service later on the SS *Chatterton Hill*, a Liberty ship that hauled
high-octane fuel around the Indian and Pacific oceans, father bought two
Indian army uniforms in Madras and had them sized to fit his boys. Thirty
years later, during my assignment in New Delhi, my son wore mine while
playing with Indian children.

Father was mustered out of the Navy in early 1946. Although he and
mother traveled abroad after the war, including to Warsaw when we were
posted there, he never returned to the USSR. For him, Murmansk had
been enough.

*   *   *

Just after father's demobilization, on March 5, 1946, Prime Minister
Winston Churchill delivered his landmark speech accusing the Soviet
Union of dividing Europe in two with an Iron Curtain. Like many families
in the United States, mine began to view the Soviet Union in a different
light, no longer as an ally but a threat.

In January 1947, within a year of leaving the service, father accepted an
offer to manage an insurance agency in Chicago. David and I were pulled
out of school, the house was sold, and after a two-day drive, we took up
residence in a one-bedroom apartment on Chicago's north side. David and
I shared the bedroom; mother and father a Murphy bed. I enjoyed walking
to and from Francis Parker, a nearby private school, but within days it was
clear that father couldn't tolerate apartment living.

In July 1947, we moved to a farmhouse fifty miles west of Chicago,
outside Geneva, not far from father's native Elgin.

The house was situated on a hilltop. From its spacious screened porch, one could see fields of alfalfa, corn, and wheat stretching for miles into the distance, up to a racetrack in Aurora, Illinois. The contrast with Chicago couldn't have been greater.

Forty acres, a barn, and two small ponds came with the house. Father called his place "Chartwell Farm" after Churchill's estate south of London, but by Midwestern standards, it was hardly a farm. It would be my parents' home for most of their lives.

From early morning to early evening, sometimes six days a week, father worked in Chicago, commuting more than one hour each way. Then, at home, following a cocktail (a shot of bourbon in a glass of orange juice, to which he also gave the name "Chartwell") and then dinner, he'd retreat to the barn. On summer weekends, if not playing tennis on a court we built, he'd ride his tractor about like a country squire. In winter, he'd toss bales of hay to his fifty heads of Angus cattle, and muck out the barn.

Father prospered in his business but had little aptitude for farming. His cattle and sheep strayed to neighboring farms, and David and I would have to chase them down and drive them home. He gave each of us fifty turkey chicks to raise; however, disease struck, and by summer's end all had died. He borrowed to buy a second farm an hour away as an "investment," but it proved unproductive and after three years was sold.

Mother would have preferred a suburb, but on matters of housing, father had the final word. She escaped to Geneva whenever she could but cared deeply for the animals and stayed involved. For her "sanity," she wrote and published articles under her maternal grandmother's maiden name; "Farming is for the Birds" was one. She also worked in area hospitals as a volunteer and helped organize the first mental health clinic in her husband's Elgin.

Chartwell helped father exorcise his business frustrations. In later years, we'd laugh together as he humorously recounted his mistakes. A failed farmer perhaps, but I attribute my feeling for country life—in Russia too—to his decisions about how and where to live.

My brother and I attended a public school in Geneva, forty minutes away by bus. My new classmates were delighted when I took on a playground bully; I had learned something from that camp after all.

My parents had no academic ambitions for themselves but wanted more for their sons. Before enlisting in the navy, father had written a Connecticut boarding school—as a kind of estate planning measure should he not return—expressing hope we could attend. In September 1949, I was sent to Kent School and, a year later, David was sent to South Kent School nearby.

Father Frederick H. Sill of the Episcopal Order of the Holy Cross (OHC) had founded Kent on the Housatonic River in Connecticut's rural northwest in 1906. Sill preached "simplicity of life, self-reliance, and directness of purpose," and modeled the school on his monastic years.

The school was poorly endowed (Sill didn't believe in endowments) and was struggling when I arrived. Food was sparse, and the dormitories were ill heated. Bill Armstrong—a favorite teacher ("master" in the school's lexicon) and the author later of *Sounder*, a popular book about a black boy and his dog that was made into a movie (and shown once at Spaso House)—told me that Kent couldn't even afford grass seed. In the summer before I arrived, he had threshed grain at the school farm in order to seed a new lawn.

The three hundred boys were each required to perform a job, take part in sports, and attend chapel daily, including twice on Sunday. We were barred from crossing the bridge that separated us from the town; only twice in five years, as a reward for good grades, I received "liberty" in Kent.

The senior class (sixth form) was in charge of everyday life. Paddling was permitted until several months after I arrived when a new headmaster from Wisconsin, Father John Oliver Patterson, imposed a ban. My first roommate did not return after a prefect (senior leader) meted out the customary three blows with a split baseball bat. George had flipped on a light after "lights out" at 9:30 PM to eat candy in bed (a double offense because food wasn't allowed in a room overnight).

Old masters, a few of whom had been at the school from the start, and new masters, some fresh from the war, accepted Sill's way of doing things, and Kent retained its original rigor almost up to his death in 1952.

With the United States caught up in the Cold War and then stalemated by a hot war in Korea, few Americans had tolerance for nonconformity. At Kent, an adolescent boy learned to be careful about sounding off or yielding to his natural instinct to rebel. In an ice hockey game my first year, I broke a collarbone. It wasn't diagnosed until months later, but I didn't complain and, in fact, it healed on its own, although tailors have since had to make an allowance for one of my shoulders.

Many boys did rebel, but mostly in surreptitious ways. Once after lights out, with the help of roommates Allen Clark and Beatty Collins, I created a document complaining about an abusive senior, crept out of bed after midnight in violation of the rules, and posted it on a bulletin board. This was probably my first experience with *samizdat*, furtively produced material daring to challenge authority. Looking back, I think Kent gave me an appetite—and perhaps the skills—for operating in a closed society.

Under Father Sill, Kent produced several graduates who made a mark in foreign affairs. Among those whose paths I crossed were Jacob Beam, my first ambassador in Moscow from Kent's class of 1924, and Cyrus Vance, the secretary of state from the class of 1935—well-intentioned, honest men. However, not everyone from Kent turned out so well; the embassy code clerk to whom I alluded in chapter 1, who was convicted of spying for Germany while serving at the American embassy in London, had been an under-former in 1924-25, and may have spied for Moscow while serving at the embassy there.

Kent's five-year program provided superb academic preparation. Latin, which readies the mind for foreign-language study, was required in my first two years.

I became involved in the debate society. On February 9, 1950, Senator McCarthy announced in Wheeling, West Virginia, that he had a list of 205 Communists working in the State Department. The "list" turned out to be fraudulent (he changed the number in later speeches), but this allegation, along with the Soviet explosion of an atomic bomb and the Communist takeover of China, generated fear across the United States and became grist for my own speeches.

Four months after McCarthy's announcement, the war in Korea broke out, and a young man from a family we knew in Geneva died in combat after China's intervention.

My father used to bring Colonel Robert McCormick's *Chicago Tribune* home after reading it on his morning commute. McCormick blamed President Truman and Secretary of State Dean Acheson for North Korea's aggression and for China's "loss," and this fueled my belief that misjudgments, if not rank disloyalty, were putting the United States at risk.

The Alger Hiss-Whittaker Chambers confrontation and Hiss's conviction for committing perjury at a congressional hearing also aroused my interest. I devoured *Witness*, Whitaker Chambers' best-selling memoir from 1952, as soon as it appeared in Geneva's only bookstore.

As president of the debate society in my senior year, I made speeches that today make me queasy. The write-up in my class's yearbook alludes to a cliché-ridden ("I hate Communism") rebuttal I delivered to fend off Graham Fuller, a more accomplished under-form debater; Fuller would later become a noted Middle East analyst for the CIA.

Fortunately, Father Patterson had earlier recruited Fuller's father as an English teacher. During my junior and senior years, Edmund Fuller steered me to Dostoyevsky and Tolstoy. While my interest in Cold War politics didn't flag, I began to appreciate the richness of Russian literature.

By 1954, I was more than ready for the freedom and variety that a liberal arts program provides. As a prefect with a strong academic record, I was admitted to Williams College and Princeton. I had seen Williams as a Kent debater but not Princeton; however, a last-minute telephone call from my father settled the matter.

Princeton required its freshmen to study a world language for two years. I was already planning to study German and Russian, the former because I was dating an exchange student from Germany whom I had met in Illinois, the latter because I was interested in the Cold War.

Russian did not qualify as a world language at the time so I took German to meet the requirement. (For some reason, I had no interest in resuming the Spanish I had studied at Kent.) The German class was full of beginning students, and the instructor was a native speaker; I met the requirement but I acquired no speaking knowledge.

In September 1955, at the start of my sophomore year, I began studying Russian. The class was small, unlike the German class, with no more than ten students, as I recall. Our teacher was Piotr Eristov. On the first day, he told us that he had been bound for a career in the Tsarist cavalry when the Revolution broke out, had eluded the Bolsheviks, and had made his way to Princeton.

Eristov brought us to understand the basics of the language. Without dwelling on his own experience, he gently stimulated our interest in the language and the culture. With his silver hair and gracious manner, he reminded me a bit of my mother's father.

Eristov didn't enjoy faculty status and wore a tired double-breasted brown suit to McCosh Hall almost every day. From his appearance, I judged he was impecunious, especially as compared with the tenured professors, and it bothered me because the university, even then, was manifestly wealthy.

Years later, Princeton let me know more about Pierre Sidamon-Eristoff, as he was known to friends. Born in St. Petersburg in 1889, he had received a bachelor's degree from Moscow University. He had served as a lieutenant in the Russian army in World War I and was "a veteran of the Crimean campaign." This meant that he had fought with General Anton Denikin against the Bolsheviks.

During my first assignment to Moscow, I saw Denikin's conqueror, Semyon Budienny, swagger through Red Square on a white horse to kick off the November 7 parade. Had I known of Eristov's military background (or been familiar then with Isaac Babel's *Red Cavalry* and its account of Budienny's campaign to seize and communize Poland in 1920, a campaign in which his Cossack troops perpetrated atrocities against Poles and Jews[58]), that scene would have galled me more than it did.

Eristov reached the United States in 1922, obtained a master's degree, and taught and tutored French and Russian before joining Princeton in 1937. He retired in 1958—the year I graduated—and died in 1970, never having married.

He was memorialized at services in Manhattan's Russian Orthodox Church at Ninety-third Street and Park Avenue. One of his friends from

Princeton described him as an "old world gentleman: kind, affable, timid, even shy, sincerely courteous but with a charming dash of malice, and cultured." It was said he had made his way out of Russia on foot and spent one winter in a Romanian barn. After his retirement, he sometimes could be seen sitting with Baron Wrangel on a bench "outside [Princeton's] Nassau Hall engaged in a lengthy but practically silent conversation."

This Wrangel must have been the great grandson of the Wrangel who was governor general of Alaska when the tsar sold it to the United States for $7 million in 1867, and the son of Piotr Wrangel who helped lead the anti-Bolshevik forces before their defeat in 1920.

How much more I would have learned had I befriended my first Russian teacher!

In my junior year, I was admitted to the undergraduate program at the Woodrow Wilson School for Public and International Affairs. Restricted to fifty students from each of the two upper classes, the program allowed me to choose courses from various departments instead of concentrating in one and to take seminars in foreign and public affairs.

Alexander Davit, an FSO assigned to Princeton by the State Department, directed a seminar on sub-Saharan Africa in which I participated. Davit was the first State Department employee I met, apart from Alger Hiss. I had heard Hiss speak at Princeton shortly after his release from forty-four months in the Lewisburg, Pennsylvania, penitentiary in November 1952. Hiss didn't impress me (in his autobiography he admits that his speech was "rather dull"[59]), but Davit did, and for the first time I began to consider the Foreign Service as a possible career.

On October 4, 1957, a month into my senior year, the Soviet Union launched a 184-pound satellite—Sputnik it was called—into space. It was followed by a half-ton satellite carrying a dog, the first living creature sent into orbit.

How would the United States respond?

We planned to put a four-pound satellite into space, but the Vanguard rocket that would deliver it blew up on its launching pad on December 6 of that same year.

Moscow's breakthrough in ballistic missile technology shocked every American who took an interest in foreign affairs. Almost overnight, the study of the Russian language and Soviet affairs became a priority.

Within a year, Congress enacted the National Defense Education Act, and Federal money for language study began pouring into public and private universities. Thirty thousand American students would soon be studying Russian. As a professor at the University of Chicago later wrote, we understood that "survival itself depended on better education for the best people . . . . For the first time, American students were really learning languages."[60]

I wrote my senior-year thesis on Soviet literature with the guidance of Princeton's other Russian language teacher, Ludmila Turkevich. Mrs. Turkevich was the first woman ever to teach at Princeton but, like Eristov, never received more than lecturer status, though she had a doctorate from Columbia and spent seventeen years at the university.[61]

Princeton prided itself on being "in the nation's service," but it could have done better by its Russian teachers. The Cold War was already a decade old, and they were demystifying a language and a culture of no little importance.

Before my senior year began, I spent six weeks in England caring for the children of an Illinois manufacturer of grain evacuators, James Dunbar. On weekends in London, I tracked down translations of the Soviet-era novels I needed for my thesis. While I was aware of the storm gathering around Pasternak, I did not read *Doctor Zhivago* until after graduation; but I worked hard on my paper, and Dr. Turkevich gave me an honors grade. Years later, in 1972, I encountered Dunbar's evacuators unloading grain in the Black Sea port of Odessa.

I was academically driven at Princeton and not especially "clubbable." A little athletic talent might have helped. I was not on any intercollegiate team, having been cut from the freshman hockey and from the 150-pound football. The football coach said I could stay if I was willing to be "scrimmage fodder," an unappealing prospect that I rejected. One of Kafka's diary entries would have chimed with me had I known of it at the time: "Nothing can be accomplished with a body like this."[62]

Had I more of a hail-fellow-well-met personality, I might have come to know Eristov and Turkevich better. I might even have come to know George Kennan. He was already famous for the "long telegram" he had sent from Moscow in 1946 advocating a policy of containment to deal with the USSR's "neurotic view" of the world. Kennan had graduated from Princeton in 1925 after having applied from the Middle West. When I read his description of his awkwardness in adapting to the university, I felt a twinge of recognition: "I could never find the casual tone . . . I was afflicted from the start . . . by a quality that has pursued me all my life: namely, of being the slowest and last to learn the ropes in any complicated organizational structure. Too shy to ask, I never found out."[63]

Frustrated by the militarization of thinking about the Cold War that he began to encounter in Washington, Kennan took leave of the Foreign Service in August 1950 and joined Princeton's Institute for Advanced Study. Two years later, Charles Bohlen, then counselor in the State Department, visited him at Secretary of State Acheson's behest to persuade him to resume his career, as ambassador to the Soviet Union. He agreed; but shortly after arriving in Moscow, he was PNG'ed (declared *persona non grata*) for a comment he had made to journalists in West Berlin that living in Moscow was reminiscent of living in Berlin at the time of the Nazis. With Eisenhower's election in November 1952, John Foster Dulles succeeded Acheson, and Kennan left the Foreign Service again, this time to be a full-time scholar at the institute.

Had I introduced myself (the institute was close to the campus), I might have gained an early understanding of the difficulties that professional diplomats experience while serving ideologically driven administrations.

The Foreign Service examination in the 1950s consisted of three parts: a day-long written test, an interview conducted by several FSOs and one outside person, and a security investigation carried out by State Department and FBI personnel. From the experience of others applying from the Woodrow Wilson School, I knew the competition would be stiff and that an Ivy League degree no longer assured success, as it usually did before the war.

Only a few in the class ahead of mine had surmounted all the hurdles. A fellow Midwesterner from my Tower eating club, Bill Shinn, later consul general in Leningrad, had been among them.

There was also the military draft. Volunteering for the navy as my father had done and as my brother would do held no appeal. If I had thought I might end up in the business world, then a three-year stint as a navy officer might make sense, but business was far from my mind. Besides, in my junior year, I had come to know Elizabeth Stone, a girl with a vivacious personality who was studying at DePauw University in Greencastle, Indiana, and I thought I might ask her to marry me. I had even dedicated my thesis to her.

Amid these uncertainties, I decided to apply to law school. There were no lawyers in the family, but my parents were willing to provide support. Were I admitted, my academic deferment from the draft would be extended.

I persuaded myself that I might like lawyering. If I found otherwise, at least I could apply to the Foreign Service with a greater prospect of success. If the draft remained a problem, I could apply for commissioning in the navy's Judge Advocate General's Corps.

In September 1958, I entered Harvard Law School. Of course, my father was delighted and entertained the belief I'd probably practice in Chicago. Breaking with nine years of dormitory living, I took a small apartment near Harvard Square and roomed with two Princeton graduates, Paul Hicks and Bill Balfour, the latter also a classmate from Kent.

Over five hundred bright, extremely competitive students comprised the law school's class of 1961. We were divided into four large groups for courses on agency, civil procedure, contracts, criminal law, property, and torts.

The reading assignments were heavy, mostly comprising federal and state appellate court decisions. The professors extracted lessons for us through intensive Socratic exchanges. As the philosopher Sidney Hook once pointed out, there are both "subtle and crude ways of using the Socratic method," subtly in the spirit of "let us reason together," crudely through "shock."[64] Both were employed at Harvard Law and, except for those who surged far ahead or fell far behind, there was little individual attention.

Examinations were usually for three hours at the end of the term, but a student could write more if the professor agreed, and some professors would. Success or failure was determined by a year-end ranking.

It was not too long, perhaps a few weeks, before I realized I had made a mistake. I knew that law school would require an immense commitment, and I had never shirked hard work, yet I hadn't expected this. I had trouble connecting the assignments to the practice of law and, in my reticence, failed to find out. I also discovered that I had little appetite for the material I was studying.

Looking around Austin and Langdell Halls, I could see that many of my classmates had come from backgrounds different from my own. They had grown up in urban areas and graduated from city and state universities. Many worked to one or two in the morning, sometimes all night, to stay abreast.

I was a kind of parvenu myself, but this kind of ferocious striving, especially after I had enjoyed the liberal arts, left me cold. The seven women in my class represented a healthy change from the all-male enrollments at Kent and Princeton, but their presence could hardly lighten the atmosphere.

Returning home for Christmas after the first term, I asked Liz to marry me. She'd be a perfect partner for whatever lay ahead. She had a zest for life that suited her for adventure, yet I knew that for her family would always come first.

Liz's parents lived in Glen Ellyn, Illinois. Her father, a graduate of Harvard too, commuted to Chicago to practice patent and copyright law. At home, he tinkered with inventions, including a flashlight he patented and profitably manufactured, until competition and a final illness brought that venture to an end. Liz's mother was of Pennsylvania-German background and had been educated at Missouri's Stephens College.

At the end of my first year, I was informed that my grades ranked me 269th in a class of 513. This was a shock as I had always ranked near the top, yet it was a fair appraisal, attesting to a simple lack of interest.

Most of my classmates would be successful in the law (Anthony Kennedy became a Supreme Court justice), but it wasn't for me. Probably out of a sense that I owed my parents something, I was determined, however, to stay the full three-year course.

Liz and I married in August 1959. She would finish her education at Boston University and support us in Cambridge my final year. The home she established in a bare-bones apartment near Harvard Square made the last two years more than bearable. We attended films at Cambridge's Brattle Theatre and concerts in Boston. We expanded our circle of friends to include those at Harvard's other graduate schools.

After paying rent, we lived on $135 a month, from our parents' assistance and, in the final year, Liz's paycheck from a nearby candy company. It was an idyllic time in the Boston area for many newly married couples, as captured in the novel *Love Story* written by a Yale professor who completed his years in Cambridge while I was finishing at Princeton.[65]

I had signed up for the written Foreign Service examination shortly after returning from our Bermuda honeymoon. I sat for it in December 1959. In January 1960, the State Department informed me that I had passed. I was invited to appear in Boston for an oral examination on April 14, 1960.

I arrived early and circled the block for an hour from sheer anxiety. When years later I read Bohlen's account of how he quaffed bootleg gin in anticipation of his "nerve-racking" oral exam, I wasn't surprised.

The FSOs conducting the exam tried to put me at ease, but I fumbled an early question about the Fourteenth Amendment, which puzzled them as they were quick to note. I regained my footing, and after two hours, they concluded their probing and retired to a back room to deliberate. I thought I had done rather well. They returned to confirm that I had. I am not sure how I would have reacted had they said otherwise.

I hurried back to Trowbridge Street and awaited Liz's return from the candy company. As she approached from Massachusetts Avenue, she could tell from my broad grin that the news was good. Only a security investigation and one more year lay between law school and a diplomatic career.

I immediately went to Dean Erwin Griswold and asked whether I could substitute Russian for one course of law my final year. Griswold was aware, from my record, that I'd select courses from among the school's international offerings whenever I had the opportunity. Without a moment's hesitation, he agreed. Reflecting the impact that federal funding was already having, I found many more students studying Russian in Harvard Yard than there had ever been in Eristov's classroom in McCosh Hall.

Two months into my final year of law, on November 8, 1960, Senator John F. Kennedy, a Harvard graduate, defeated Richard M. Nixon to become president-elect. Kennedy had begun his political career by gaining a seat in the House of Representatives from the district that included Cambridge.

Almost overnight, everyone at the law school was talking about an exodus of professors. Abram Chayes, who taught me corporate law, would be among the first to go, having been appointed legal advisor to the State Department. Stanley Surrey, who lectured us on the tax code, would become an assistant secretary of the Treasury. Then I heard that John McNaughton would be appointed an assistant secretary of defense. I hadn't encountered McNaughton in class, but he had given Liz and me advice after a Massachusetts state trooper impounded our car just after midnight on New Year's Eve 1960 while we were driving back from vacation in Illinois. Declaring that its Illinois license plate had expired (it hadn't), he seized the car and forced us to hitchhike to Cambridge with only a few dollars in our pockets. Perhaps he resented "Harvard" on the university's parking sticker.

Many expected Paul Freund, who taught me constitutional law, would be appointed to the Supreme Court. But Kennedy didn't include Freund in his first two choices, and the assassination deprived him of a third.[66]

Not everyone was pleased with Nixon's loss. W. Barton Leach, who had taught me property law, was a general in the Air Force Reserve. In postwar meetings at the Pentagon, he had participated in a conservative "cabal" that "was anti-Army, anti-Russian, and out to 'kill Oppenheimer' [then resisting pressure to develop the hydrogen bomb]." A military officer later remembered Leach "as a bald, emaciated professor who would be jotting down statistics about the number of Russians who could be wiped out by a single atomic bomb, all while sipping from a glass of milk for his ulcers."[67] Given my disaffection with the law, I probably would have found Leach's jottings at the Pentagon more to my liking than the tax-beating schemes he outlined in Austin Hall.

One course I took my final year dwelt on Soviet criminal law, especially the trial of Francis Gary Powers, who had been shot down in a U-2 aircraft while flying over the Ural Mountains on May Day 1960. Taught by Harold Berman who had been a consultant at Powers' Moscow trial, the course would prove helpful twelve years later when I headed the embassy's consular section.[68]

I couldn't imagine that Washington's security investigation would be a problem, but it seemed to take forever, despite the fact that I had once thought highly of Joe McCarthy. Only in February 1961, four months before graduation, did I receive a letter saying I had been cleared for appointment to the Foreign Service.

As soon as I finished my last exam in June, Liz and I packed our effects in a rented trailer and headed south.

3

Foreign Service Institute, Hamburg, and Warsaw

President John F. Kennedy was still generating excitement when Liz and I reached the State Department at the end of June 1961, five months after his inauguration.

Of course, we had our own reason to be excited; at last, the career was beginning.

We hadn't received notification in Cambridge as to when exactly I'd be hired. So when I strode into the department, Liz by my side, to announce our arrival, it wasn't without a degree of anxiety. Liz was pregnant, and money was running out.

After fumbling with some papers, an official in the Foreign Service personnel office told us that, like every fresh arrival, I'd be assigned first to an eight-week orientation course, the A-100 course. The course would begin on July 17 at an apartment complex in Arlington, Virginia, across the Potomac River from the department's main building.

It turned out that the course was located in the complex's basement, and the basement housed the entirety of the Foreign Service Institute (FSI), established as the department's training branch in 1947.

There were thirty-eight officers in my class. Two officers nearing the end of their careers conducted the course, inviting Foreign Service colleagues, civil servants, and academic experts to lecture us on foreign policy issues and the workings of U.S. agencies with overseas responsibilities. They also took us on field trips—to an agricultural research station in Beltsville, Maryland, the port of Baltimore, the mayor's office in Philadelphia, and the United Nations in New York.

One afternoon we were taken—for what we were told would be a classified briefing—to an unmarked building on a hilltop opposite the department. I had no idea that the building and the compound in which

it was located housed the headquarters of the CIA, which would move a
year later to permanent facilities in Langley, Virginia.

The briefer identified himself as Paul Chretien, a CIA "orientation
officer." He spoke a bit about Patrice Lumumba, who had been murdered
in the Congo shortly after the inauguration, and about Fidel Castro, who
had repulsed CIA-organized mercenaries at the Bay of Pigs in April.

Chretien made a passing reference to the agency's efforts to develop
poisons to assassinate foreign leaders. Notwithstanding his vagueness, we
were startled. "Did you hear what I think I heard," we muttered to one
another as we made our way back to Arlington. Several suggested that
"Chretien" was probably not the briefer's real name.

Fourteen years old, the CIA was already involved in much more than
intelligence gathering, although I (and most Americans) didn't realize the
full scope of its activities until much later. The National Security Act of 1947
had empowered it to carry out "services of common concern" and "such
other functions and duties" as the National Security Council (NSC) might
direct. It hadn't provided, however, explicit authority for or any prohibition
against paramilitary or other operations against foreign governments or
their leaders. The CIA had embarked on these on the basis of a secret
NSC directive that was only made public after the Cold War. The directive
expanded the agency's role to include "propaganda, economic warfare;
preventive direct action, including sabotage, anti-sabotage, demolition
and evacuation measures; subversion against hostile states, including
assistance to underground resistance movements"; and to other "elements
in threatened countries of the free world."[69]

When I joined the A-100 course, Allen Dulles, brother of the deceased
secretary of state John Foster Dulles, was the CIA director. In his wartime
work for the OSS (Office of Strategic Services, the agency's predecessor),
he had become intrigued by the attempts to assassinate Hitler.[70] In 1951,
he joined the CIA as a deputy to its director, Walter Bedell Smith, the
former ambassador in Moscow. Smith didn't care for covert actions (he
rejected a plan to assassinate Stalin in 1952) and was wary of his deputy's
more far-out schemes.

The idea of advancing American interests in third-world countries by
eliminating leaders or potential leaders with whom we didn't agree struck
me as a bit naïve and not at all comparable to eliminating the leader of
an industrial power waging a declared war. But I wasn't contemplating a
career in the third world and didn't think through the implications of what
Chretien had said. The full story of the agency's operations in the 1960s
only came to light during Senator Frank Church's Senate Intelligence
Committee hearings in 1975; it included a description of eight schemes to
kill Castro, hatched during Dulles' tenure.

The State Department was hiring about two hundred Foreign Service officers a year. Most of my thirty-seven colleagues were married and in their middle or late twenties. Nineteen had served in the military. We came from all parts of the country; most of us were middle class.

Seven of the class's thirty-eight had bachelor's degrees from Ivy League universities and colleges.[71] In 1961, many Americans still believed that an Ivy League diploma denoted membership in some kind of social elite; yet by the middle 1950s, these schools were admitting the vast majority of applicants on the basis of merit, not family connections, while still restricting the admission of minorities and Jews.

The relationship of the Foreign Service to society at large has always bristled with controversy. Critics of one or another foreign policy have suggested that FSOs are not really representative, that the problem really lies with the service's makeup. After all, what kind of red-blooded American would want to spend a career abroad?

During my years, the State Department did less than it ought to have done to dispel the notion of a Foreign Service-Ivy League nexus, of "an Ivy-League striped-pants outfit," as the Foreign Service's director general in 1988 claimed what "we once were."[72] James Baker, the secretary of state under George H. W. Bush, wrote in 1995 that FSOs "tend to come from the nation's top colleges, particularly the Ivy League."[73] In actuality, I encountered few with Ivy League degrees during the last decade of my career, and those having them certainly didn't constitute any social elite.

As I look back, what was far more relevant was that almost everyone in my A-100 class had majored in the liberal arts. We had pursued programs in the humanities, the social sciences, and the arts—programs that had opened our eyes to the outside world. We were curious about cultures and languages other than our own and had applied to the Foreign Service in large part to become more knowledgeable about them.

Surveying the United States' recent failures in foreign affairs, a *New York Times* columnist has cited the need for a generalist/humanist rather than a scientific approach to intelligence gathering: "I'll believe the intelligence community has really changed when I see analysts being sent to training academies where they study Thucydides, Tolstoy and Churchill to get a broad understanding of the full range of human behavior."[74]

Today, finding, recruiting, and retaining broad-gauged officers for overseas service is a challenge not only for agencies whose main focus is intelligence gathering but also for the State Department. The number of American college graduates who study the history and culture of peoples outside their country's borders, who study the likes of Thucydides, Tolstoy, and Churchill has dramatically declined. The portion of American youth studying liberal arts in the past half century has reportedly fallen to "fewer than 100,000 of the 14 million" now in higher education.[75]

Our class was far from representative in ethnicity or gender; we were all white males except for two women and a man of Chinese-American descent. The composition of the classes after ours began to change, slowly at first and then more rapidly.

When Cyrus Vance became secretary of state in 1977, he observed that "the white, male Foreign Service was already on its way out," but his goal would be "to hasten the transformation."[76] Vance did as promised, and his successors have taken up the cause.

No one uses the *quota* word, but diversity has become a mantra in the country's recruitment of diplomats. Beginning in the 1980s, department administrators began to devote extraordinary attention to it, adducing statistics in their public statements to demonstrate that the transformation is under way. The department's chief administrator in 1988, in a 4,500-word report on the state of the Foreign Service, noted that 34 percent of those joining at that time were women and 17 percent were minorities. The report made only passing reference to language training, saying it had been cut "to meet our budgetary challenge."[77] Pointing to that same year, the Foreign Service's director general announced that the service's total work force already encompassed 29 percent women and 13 percent minorities.[78]

The transformation that Vance called for would seem complete. In a valedictory statement in 2006, the director general reported that women account for "nearly 50 percent of our entering classes" and "minority hiring from exam passers" was "19 percent compared to 13 percent" in 2000.[79] (But not everyone may agree; a black woman ambassador who had preceded him as director general told Princeton's Woodrow Wilson School students in 2005 that "the Foreign Service should, but does not look [yet] like America.")[80]

In 2006, the director general made only passing reference to language proficiency, saying that "language, program management and crisis response drills will increasingly gain importance." The statement is odd not only because of the juxtaposition with other needs, but also because the Foreign Service, like other agencies with overseas responsibilities, has been coping with a critical deficit of language skills, especially Arabic.

Are administrators more interested in achieving a diverse Foreign Service than a Foreign Service rich in area and language experts, in Arabists, Asia hands, and others committed to mastering the world's varied languages and cultures? Statements from administrators over the past two decades suggest they have been focusing on developing diversity almost to the exclusion of language and area expertise.

A third of the officers in my course would leave the Foreign Service within their first ten years. One of the two women was required to resign after marrying a classmate. (She rejoined a few years later, after the rules were relaxed, but was made to repeat the course.) The other woman, Hanna Woods from Missouri, was killed in an automobile accident in Yugoslavia on her first overseas assignment; had Hanna lived, she surely would have been the first ambassador appointed from the class. The Chinese-American man left soon for a business career. The classmate with ostensibly the bluest blood, Gerry Studds, a graduate of Groton School ("the most aristocratic of New England's private schools"[81]) and Yale University, quit a year after the A-100 course ended and returned to Massachusetts, only to reappear as a congressman in Washington in 1973, the first congressman who acknowledged, a decade later, that he was gay.

*   *   *

As the course was winding down, the East Germans, on August 13, 1961, erected the wall that would divide Berlin for almost three decades. It was obvious to everyone in our class that Germany would remain in the thick of Cold War politics for years to come.

On the final day, the codirectors read aloud each officer's assignment. This was the climactic moment for which we had been waiting.

I knew that an assignment behind the Iron Curtain was unlikely. We would be on probation for our first or second assignment or until a promotion, and junior officers were deemed to pose a greater security risk than those who had already served abroad. To the applause of classmates, I received an assignment to the embassy in Bonn, the capital of the Federal Republic of Germany.

Seven in my class were assigned to European posts, but Bonn was a choice assignment, especially for someone who might want a career "behind the Curtain." As with most new officers, I would rotate between the embassy's four main sections: political, economic, consular, and administrative. This would enable me to decide which track or cone I'd want to pursue during my career. Before traveling, I was to receive intensive instruction in consular affairs and learn to speak the German I had only learned to read at Princeton.

An aptitude test that we were required to take confirmed that I could learn foreign languages, but it suggested I might not attain the highest speaking proficiency. Had I wanted to learn one of Asia's tonal languages, I would have been disappointed, but I had never thought of specializing in that region.

Wives could apply to join their husbands for language study, but most weren't able to because of children. Liz had given birth to our first child, Elise, in September and was busy being a mother in a grim furnished apartment (with robin's-egg-blue plastic furniture I will never forget) that we rented in Alexandria, a mile or so beyond National Airport, Reagan Airport today.

Languages were taught in dozens of windowless rooms at the FSI. There were four students in my German class, including one Foreign Service wife, Pam Fischer, whom we'd meet again with her husband, David, at the embassy in Warsaw. Each weekday for four months, native speakers bombarded us with sentences and phrases we'd repeat. One of our textbooks was from the defense department. Its vocabulary was more suited to occupation rather than diplomatic duty, but the department was only beginning to develop its own materials.

During ten-minute breaks every hour, we gleaned what we could from our instructors about life in Germany. Herr Hermann Lehmann gave colorful accounts of how he coped after the war, manufacturing an ersatz coffee extracted from grounds he wheedled from American soldiers.

When not in class, we used audio tapes to perfect our pronunciation. On evenings and weekends, I committed each day's work to memory; it was as if I were back in law school except this time I looked forward to "practicing."

Liz and I didn't have many possessions. We'd need only a trunk and several suitcases for the trip to Bonn. Liz found a German cruise ship on which I could use the language. (Restrictions on using foreign means of travel would later come into force.) We'd buy a used car after arriving.

Calamity comes when it is least expected. In December 1961, a few weeks before sailing, our plans collapsed. I fell ill from hepatitis, nervous exhaustion, or something else never diagnosed; it hit me just after the German program ended, and the consular course began. Apart from an enlarged liver, there seemed nothing physically wrong, yet I felt awful. Perhaps the stress of taking an intensive language course on top of law school had pushed me beyond a limit I didn't know existed.

I couldn't shake off the symptoms and was forced to take a prolonged break. The assignment was scuttled; and my parents let Liz, me, and Elise, soon to be joined by Abigail, live with them in Illinois. When the Cuban missile crisis flared in October 1962, I was stuck on a farm thousands of miles from Bonn. I lost two other assignments to Germany later in my career, because of decisions affecting the Foreign Service as a whole; but I could only blame myself for losing Bonn.

In December 1962, I returned to the department with a clean bill of health. My assignment was to prepare letters to Congress and the public defending the Kennedy administration's policies, especially in Vietnam. It was hardly comparable to an assignment abroad; but soon Walter Rostow, the director of policy planning, and Frederick Dutton, the assistant secretary for congressional relations, were singling out my work for praise.

After a few months, I learned that the head of my unit, not an FSO, was finagling the count of pro and anti-Vietnam letters, so it appeared that the war enjoyed more support than it did. A faraway war was corrupting a simple count.

Thanks to the FSO heading the office of which my unit was a part, I was included in meetings with Presidents Kennedy and Johnson. I don't recall Kennedy's remarks, but his sheer youth must have made me wonder why I was performing such a minor role. After Kennedy's assassination, one of my colleagues left the office and drank himself into a stupor; judging from his appearance a few years later, he hadn't yet recovered.

Three weeks after the assassination, President Johnson visited the department. Johnson tried to energize us for war. Eighteen thousand Americans are in Vietnam, he said, and we should "not go to bed any night without asking whether we have done everything that we could do that day to win the struggle there."[82] I had looked into the possibility of joining the Vietnam desk, mostly out of impatience with my writing duties, but nothing had come of it.

By the end of Johnson's presidency, five hundred thousand Americans would be involved in Vietnam. Only Undersecretary of State George Ball, who helped administer Lend-Lease during World War II, and a few FSOs who had survived the purges of the McCarthy era and knew the area firsthand from serving in it foresaw the quagmire it would become. The government and the country would pay a high price for denigrating and then ousting the service's Asia hands after Chiang Kai-shek was swept from power. Those who knew the region best were no longer in the career or were too removed from the Oval Office or the department's seventh floor (where senior officials have their offices) to influence policy.

After a year of letter writing, I finally received my assignment abroad, a posting for two years to the consulate general in Hamburg, Germany. Not as promising a start as Bonn, but it would put me back on track.

*   *   *

Liz and I flew into Hamburg with our infant daughters in January 1963. We were met by George Haselton, the head of the consulate's consular section to which I had been assigned. George took us to a government-furnished apartment in a beautiful old district not far from the canal that flows into Lake Alster at the city's center.

The Royal Air Force had laid waste to Hamburg's port and downtown areas in August 1943, causing a massive firestorm that killed and injured tens of thousands. Yet we rarely saw damage from the war (the sole reminders were several huge concrete bunkers that remained intact). The city's reconstruction, like all of West Germany's, had truly been a *Wirtschaftwunder,* an economic miracle.

The consulate occupies a white-columned neoclassical building overlooking the Alster. It had served as the headquarters of the Nazi *Gauleiter* Karl Otto Kaufmann. Having learned of a British ultimatum to deliver an even more devastating bombardment, Kaufmann resisted Hitler's order to defend the city to the last.[83] His decision probably saved the consulate building and the district where we lived.

George Haselton had entered the State Department after wartime navy duty. He had served at the San Francisco conference founding the United Nations in 1945. He joined the Foreign Service a decade later, but his career hadn't prospered. The fact that he had never married may have hurt.

By manner and dress, George struck me as an old-line diplomat. He probably owned a pair of those suspect striped pants. He seemed satisfied running a small section in a small consulate while playing tennis and circulating among friends in Hamburg's upper crust.

The American staff was divided among three or four FSOs like George nearing retirement, a few middle-aged officials representing Agriculture, the CIA, Commerce, and Defense, and five or six junior officers like me. I bought a used 1955 Opel for $200 and a bicycle that I rode to work when Hamburg's capricious weather allowed.

I began in the citizenship and welfare unit, working alongside five Germans and an American woman who had joined the Foreign Service after her husband's untimely death in Africa. The Germans were attractive, personable, and unmarried. One woman with a teenage daughter had lost her husband on the Eastern front a few days after their wedding; the other three women had never found husbands, a majority of the men their age and background having been killed.

As a vice consul in a large port, I learned to deal with all sorts of problems. My brother and I used to eye inmates wandering the sprawling grounds of an Elgin mental asylum whenever we drove by; now Americans suffering these illnesses appeared with surprising regularity in my waiting room.

Once I took the advice of a more experienced FSO and failed to disclose to Pan American Airways that a troubled indigent whom I had to place on a flight back to the United States was schizophrenic. Keep quiet, I was cautioned, lest we be stuck with caring for him indefinitely. Airborne and with a few drinks under his belt, he went berserk and had to be subdued; and I was properly reprimanded.

Another mentally ill American had been shoved into our district by East German border guards after arriving at one of their ports from St. John's, Newfoundland. The West Germans came to me for assistance, but the department instructed me not to get involved; our consulate in Newfoundland had found that the American had voted in a Canadian election, committing an expatriating act. Not knowing what to do, the city authorities imprisoned him as a vagrant. Once released, he made his way back to my office—unkempt, penniless, a hapless soul without a country. I interviewed him and found that he had served in the U.S. Navy. Assembling information from various sources, I learned that he had also spent time in a Canadian mental institution, information that the consulate in Newfoundland had ignored. I was able to reverse the department's finding and send the veteran to a hospital near his New York home.

These and other cases cured me of a temptation to defer to more experienced officers or to bow before seemingly authoritative no's. They also prompted me to write an article for the *Foreign Service Journal,* decrying a new policy assessing each consular section's performance by the number of "services" it rendered per hour, a consular "productivity index."[84] I cited the mentally ill veteran, pointing out that we had devoted more than one hundred hours to clarifying his situation. Had I adhered to the index, he might still be in Germany. At the article's end, I quoted the observation of the philosopher George Santayana that an "ideal not yet articulate in the American mind" is "to produce less in order that the product may be more choice and beautiful." Those who read the article applauded the sentiment, but Washington was beginning to apply the latest management tools to its operations abroad. The era of measuring progress by body counts, kill ratios, and targets hit would soon be upon us.

After a year, I was transferred to the consulate's visa unit. There I processed routine applications from Germans seeking to visit or immigrate to the United States. I adjudicated two applications from Ukrainian and Baltic nationals who had allegedly committed war crimes. The allegations in one case were flimsy (could spraying water on an inmate be adequate proof of a crime?), and I secured a visa for him and his family.

My father used to worry that my three years in Cambridge would go to waste. Now and then I described cases where my legal training had helped. This may not have been the lucrative "return" he expected from his investment, but I found the work satisfying, and in time, he came to understand my choice.

Liz's and my social life initially revolved around the consulate. It sponsored entertainment for George Szell and Cleveland's symphony orchestra returning from a successful tour of the USSR and the crew of the nuclear ship USS *Savannah* making a port call.

We soon fell into a circle of young Germans whose families owned ships and were politically or socially prominent. Most lived in the Blankenese suburb on the Elbe River, which extends from the North Sea through Hamburg into eastern Germany. Names like Binder, Schulte, Sieveking, and von Rosen still come to mind. One was a banker, Peter Claussen, married to a woman who had spent part of a summer on an exchange program at my parents' farm. Others we met through George. Liz and I grew fond of leisurely Sunday morning walks with our friends along the Elbe, followed by luncheons in their stylish homes. I regret we haven't seen them since.

The important reporting on West Germany was done from Bonn, and my work didn't require meeting local politicians, journalists, or academics. I knew I'd have this opportunity once I rotated upstairs into the political and economic sections. Still, my German was steadily improving, and Liz and I sensed that the relationships we were cementing would yield benefits for the country. A letter from an American search firm inviting me to explore careers in the United States didn't tempt me in the least.

George's mentoring had given me the start I needed. Yet mentoring is not an aptitude that the Foreign Service particularly values, and George soon faced retirement. Just before returning to Washington, he married the former wife of President Johnson's brother, Sam Houston Johnson. Thanks to the president, she was working at the consulate in Munich. John Kenneth Galbraith, when serving as an advisor to the president, had come to know Sam Johnson as "Lyndon's amusing, liberal, intelligent and highly unmotivated brother."[85] Had Galbraith known George, he could have written the same about him.

*   *   *

Without forewarning, during our sixteenth month in Hamburg, a telegram arrived from Washington ordering me to Poland. I was instructed to report to the embassy's consular section as a vice consul and third secretary. Probably I had written "Warsaw" on a preference report that I had filed earlier in Washington. Such reports were not taken too seriously; they were called "April Fool's Day" reports because they were due April 1 and rarely seemed to result in an assignment.

It turned out that another Princeton graduate was working in the department's personnel branch and needed to fill an opening in Warsaw created by the transfer of an officer to Rome. Seeing from my file that I had studied a Slavic language, he picked me out.

I hadn't known many Americans of Polish origin, but had read enough to know that the Poles were fiercely independent and, with few exceptions, hated the Soviet-imposed rule under which they were forced to live.

I also knew that World War II had devastated Warsaw, reducing its population from 1.3 million to fewer than two hundred thousand and destroying 90 percent of its buildings. The Nazis had herded Polish Jews into a ghetto they leveled in 1943; most of those who survived had then perished in concentration camps.[86] A year later, in 1944, the rest of Warsaw's population had risen; when the Soviet forces on the northern side of the Vistula River failed to come to their aid, they too were crushed. Hitler ordered that what remained of the city be razed. Shortly thereafter, the Soviets swept in and with a small number of Polish Communists established control.

Something told me that I would like the Poles; my Irish ancestors had suffered in fighting for their independence, if not so catastrophically. Liz and I realized also that the assignment would be an opportunity to decide whether we really wanted a career behind the Curtain.

There was a problem, however. Although I would be responsible for interviewing applicants for travel to the United States, I spoke no Polish, and no Pole in his right mind would want to use German or Russian, even if he knew them.

The consul general in Hamburg was E. Tomlin Bailey, who, like George, was nearing retirement. Unknown to me, Bailey had been posted to Warsaw in 1937 and had witnessed Germany's invasion in September 1939 shortly after returning from a leave in Connecticut, where he had married Mrs. Bailey.

Bailey hadn't paid much attention to me. The telegram piqued his interest, and he invited me to pay a call on him upstairs. After offering congratulations, he asked, "Do you know Polish?" I said I didn't. He handed me the textbook that he had taken with him to Warsaw[87]; he hadn't received language training either.

In the three weeks that remained, I created my own crash course. Because the textbook had been published in 1915—before Poland regained its independence—and was written to help Americans speak with Poles already in the United States, many of the stock expressions it recommended weren't particularly helpful. It made little sense to memorize, "For God's sake, do not send me away, please let me remain in the United States." Or, "Poland has been torn asunder by Russia, Austria, and Germany." One section dealt extensively with tuberculosis: "There are dangerous germs which you raise from your lungs . . . What you spit should be burned."

Polish uses Latin instead of Cyrillic letters, and I was able to extract a useful, if somewhat quaint, list of phrases. However, I could only guess at their pronunciation.

In June 1965, Liz and I set out for Warsaw in a new Volkswagen station wagon our parents helped us buy. At last, we would experience the real thing—Communism as it was being imposed on thirty million Poles.

We drove first to Nuremberg, West Germany, where we found a U.S. military hotel in which to stay. The next day we passed through the Czech border and reached Prague. Elise and Abby played or slept in the back amid the suitcases.

We had been unable to make a hotel reservation from Hamburg and upon entering the Czech capital were told to report to the Alcron, the single hotel accommodating Westerners. Judging from what we saw, it must have been glamorous when it opened in 1932; its interior bespoke the Modernist art deco style that had flourished in Central Europe before the war.

By 1965, however, the Alcron was a seedy wreck. The author Graham Greene happened to have been a guest when Prague fell under Communist control in 1948; he was en route to Rome to write the screen play for *The Third Man*.[88] The Alcron reminded me of the film's dark and spooky atmosphere.

From Prague we pushed northward to the Polish border. The roads were bad. One bridge was washed out, and we were forced to divert to back roads. Most of the villages we passed were wretchedly poor.

But people everywhere were friendly. Whenever we stopped, they'd gather to examine the car. When they saw the children in the back, their eyes would light up and they'd talk animatedly among themselves. How different from the Germans in our staid Hamburg neighborhood!

Once across the Polish border, we passed Soviet soldiers on field maneuvers, some of the several tens of thousands still based in Poland. We stayed overnight in the next large city, Wroclaw. It had been named "Breslau" before Poland's borders were shifted westward to the Oder-Neisse line in 1945. The German-born wife of a Foreign Service friend whom we would come to know in Warsaw persisted using the old name, to the chagrin of her husband as well as the embassy.

The Wroclaw hotel was even grimmer than the Alcron. We spent the night on straw pallets, and there was little to eat in the restaurant. One of our girls refused to use the bathroom because it looked so "dirty."

We entered Warsaw the next day, then a city of about a million. Although two decades had passed since the war, rubble lay on the outskirts and buildings were still pockmarked and scarred from the shelling. How different from the western part of Germany, where the Marshall Plan and private enterprise had erased almost every trace of war.

Low-lying apartment buildings, many of shoddy Soviet-style construction, had been erected to house Warsaw's homeless population. However, the two districts that had been reduced to rubble after the 1944 Uprising—the medieval Old Town and New Town—had been painstakingly restored. To ensure the authenticity of their work, Polish architects had studied paintings of Warsaw rendered by the Venetian artist Canaletto in the eighteenth century, paintings hidden from the Nazis.

Towering over the city as we drove toward the embassy was a huge thirty-story structure, the Palace of Culture and Science. The Russians had presented it to the Poles as Stalin's gift in the early 1950s. They had wanted to erect a statue of their leader in front, but even the Communist Poles balked at this.

The Palace dominates Warsaw today. Looking "like a gangster's wedding cake" (so it appeared to Graham Greene[89]), it contains 3,300 rooms and halls. In all likelihood, the Poles will some day tear it down. After World War I, they demolished a gift that Tsar Nicholas had made, an Orthodox cathedral that then dominated the skyline.[90]

We drove along a central avenue lined with trees and found the embassy, a four-story modern-style structure set some thirty yards behind a steel fence. The gates were open, and we drove up a half-circular drive and parked in front of the embassy's glass-paneled facade. As I strolled into the lobby, the door's lettering NIE PCHNAC DRZWI caught my eye. I was at the receptionist's desk before I figured it out—Don't push the door.

Whenever I passed through the lobby during the next three years, the lettering would remind me of how much more Polish I needed to learn.

Twice during the assignment, the Communist regime arranged for club-wielding demonstrators to destroy the embassy's façade. Accusing us of crimes in Vietnam, they ran up the driveway before the gates could be locked, invaded the lobby, and smashed everything in sight. We watched them perform their work from the other side of an interior gate that the marines had secured. The embassy billed the Foreign Ministry for the replacement glass and, as I recall, it paid.

*   *   *

The ambassador when we arrived was John Moors Cabot, from Boston's rarified circle where "the Lowells talk to the Cabots and the Cabots talk only to God." Cabot was a career diplomat and had previously served as ambassador to Finland, Sweden, and several countries in Latin America. He has also been consul general in Shanghai as the Communists were consolidating control; this made him a good choice to conduct meetings with the People's Republic envoy in Warsaw, through whom Washington was then communicating with the yet-unrecognized Communist regime.

The ambassador's father, Godfrey Lowell Cabot, had died just after his appointment to the embassy. When Cleveland Amory dissected *The Proper*

Bostonians in 1947, he had described the Cabots as "socially Boston's First of Firsts" and Godfrey as the city's wealthiest citizen.[91]

Introductory calls were still in fashion, but Cabot had added a special touch. He invited new officers (then almost always men) to meet him first in a sauna he had installed in the embassy basement. A day or two after my arrival, with a borrowed towel and robe, I made my way to the sauna where he was waiting with a satchel of beer, a bottle of Scotch, glasses, and ice.

Stripping down, I joined him on a tiered wooden bench next to the electric stove. The temperature approached two hundred degrees, and we alternated stints with cold showers. Cabot beat himself with birch branches that his old embassy in Helsinki supplied by diplomatic pouch, and afterward we drank and talked.

A week or two later, the ambassador and his wife invited us and several other couples to a picnic outside Warsaw. We drove in a caravan to a grassy field a mile or two beyond a tiny village. When we arrived, the Cabots were already ensconced on Oriental carpets, transplanted from their residence and spread under a grove of trees. They served drinks and sandwiches to us from picnic baskets their cook had prepared.

By the end of our first month, Liz and I felt we knew the Cabots as well as any of the ten ambassadorial couples with whom we would ultimately serve. The wives loved Mrs. Cabot; she would pay spur-of-the-moment visits to check on each family's welfare and look after its morale.

It wasn't too long before I heard about a testy encounter between Cabot and President Johnson's attorney general, Bobby Kennedy, which occurred a few months before we arrived.[92] The Poles deeply mourned President Kennedy and gave his brother a tumultuous reception.

Ambassador Cabot let Kennedy use his limousine for travel around the country, and then invited him to be his guest of honor at a farewell dinner at the residence. As the guests assembled, Cabot waited for Kennedy to appear. And waited and waited. Kennedy, it turned out, was outside, addressing Polish well-wishers from the roof of Cabot's car. After an hour's wait, Cabot announced that dinner would be served. After another fifteen minutes or so, in the middle of the first course, Kennedy finally appeared. In his welcoming toast, Cabot is reported to have said, "We started without you, Mr. Attorney General. Would you care to stand on the table and address the guests?"

After the visit, Cabot sent a telegram to Washington asking that his car be replaced as "Kennedy's hoofprints are all over the roof." Cabot received a new car.

How difficult it must have been for a Boston Brahmin to host an upstart Kennedy!

Cabot was sixty-four when we arrived; three months later, he and Mrs. Cabot left for retirement. They exemplified the noblesse oblige for which most American ambassadors then were known. They were classy but in a reserved way; they were also thoughtful about their staff as couples heading missions ought to be.

After sharing a residence with another family during the summer, we moved into our own house, one of four town houses that the embassy had acquired in Mokotow district. It was only twenty minutes by car from the embassy, off Aleje Niepodleglosci (Independence Avenue), which was known to the few at the embassy who didn't speak Polish as "New Pair of Galoshes" Avenue.

Each of the houses had a tiny yard enclosed by a chain-link fence that backed up to a Polish military base atop a munitions bunker. The neighborhood was known as the "ammunition dump." To our daughters' delight, a Polish soldier bearing a rifle would appear from time to time, patrolling the far end of our yard.

Mokotow district also contained a prison where Communists were jailed before the war. The Communists would incarcerate a Polish friend of ours there as the assignment was ending.

I interviewed forty to fifty Poles a day for immigrant visas. Most came from peasant farmsteads in the south, applying to join relatives who had left tsarist and Hapsburg-controlled Poland before World War I for northern industrial cities such as Chicago and Detroit.

The regime in Warsaw was not as hostile to emigration as its ally in Moscow. Nor were many Poles ineligible to receive American immigrant or nonimmigrant visas because of their political affiliations. As Roman Catholics, most had resisted pressure to become members of the Communist Party known as the Polish United Workers' Party (*Polska Zjednoczona Partia Robotnicza,* or PZPR) or its main affiliate, the United Peasants' Party (*Zjednoczone Stronnictwo Ludowe,* or ZSL). Some of those who had become members could be found eligible as "involuntary" members, if they could establish they had no real choice but to join in order to hold a job or otherwise survive.

With a heavy daily caseload, the work was onerous but not without rewards. I enjoyed reunifying long-separated families. There were amusing moments too. Now and then, an elderly Polish-American would lead a beautiful peasant girl into my office. "We're married, and I want to take her back." The regime's paperwork seemed to confirm the marriage, yet the man might be in his late seventies and the girl no more than eighteen. Because of American law, I had to determine, in my broken Polish, whether their relationship had, in fact, been consummated or was merely a dodge to expedite the girl's immigration.

Despite Poland's penurious conditions, many of the young women, including a few working in the consular section, were attractive. Their clothes might be homespun, but they were keenly aware of Western styles and made the most of what they had. More often than not, their personalities sparkled.

Each newly arrived FSO received a briefing from the security officer about the dangers of Communist entrapment. We were told about the embassy's general services officer who had fallen for a twenty-two-year old Polish woman five years before, and then had been inveigled by Polish intelligence to hand over secrets to avoid exposure. He had been caught, convicted in the United States, and sent to prison.

We knew that the regime didn't hesitate to pressure our Polish colleagues, and they knew they were vulnerable. Just after the war, an innocent woman working in the visa unit had been given ten years "for abetting espionage."[93] If she had agreed to spy against the embassy, she would have been spared.

I started each day with an hour of language lessons. The reading came easily but not the speaking. To supplement my lessons, I'd listen to Polish radio, including a morning calisthenics broadcast that helped me learn the verbs of motion. I was soon able to conduct interviews on my own, but I remained envious of colleagues like David Fischer and David Evans who had taken the full ten-month FSI course and could speak the language almost flawlessly.

Later in the USSR, I would be asked by Russians where I had learned my Russian: "You speak with a strange accent." I could never remove the Polish overlay. If a Soviet citizen mistook me as one of his own (as rarely happened), he would ask whether I had come from the western Ukraine where Poles had lived before their expulsion, or from Lithuania or another Baltic republic.

After a year and a half of immigration and citizenship work, Herb Kaiser, the political counselor, invited me to join his section, which included one officer besides himself and the CIA station chief. My assignment was extended to a third year.

My initial task was to manage an office outside the embassy, in a historic building on Jezuicka (Jesuit) Street in the Old Town. From 6:00 AM to early afternoon, I and a young officer from the British embassy (Ivor Rawlinson and later Margaret Thorn) would oversee an Anglo-American news service that published a daily *Polish News Bulletin,* a twenty or thirty-page translation of articles from newspapers and periodicals into English. It was modeled on a comparable service that the American and British embassies ran in Moscow in the 1940s.

There were ten Polish employees at the Bulletin: six translators, two secretaries, and two mimeograph machine operators. The British diplomat and I took turns arriving first. I'd leave Mokotow in my 1958 Chevrolet (I had acquired it from an outgoing FSO for $100 and sold it to the regime three years later for exactly $3.50) and race to the Old Town through the capital's deserted streets. In winter, I'd arrive long before daybreak. There I'd scan a score of Polish publications and identify articles for translation. The translators, arriving an hour later, would then do the articles. After editing their drafts, my colleague and I would print the report and distribute it to Western embassies in Warsaw for a fee, and to American, British, and other addressees abroad by pouch.

The translators worked on manual typewriters in a large room. Their personal politics ran the gamut from prewar rightist to leftist social democratic. In a way, each reflected a facet of their country's tumultuous history. Among themselves they could agree only on their hatred for the Soviet system and admiration for the United States.

One was a descendent of nobility, Stanislaw Tarnowski, a Polish count who had served with the government in exile in Britain, which inspired the 1944 revolt. He was little different, in personality, from the count that the Austrian novelist Joseph Roth portrayed, "a cavalry captain in the reserve, a bachelor, both happy-go-lucky and melancholy at once—loved horses, liquor, society, frivolity, and also seriousness."[94] It was a rare morning when Tarnowski, who in fact had an attractive wife, didn't arrive with an anti-Soviet joke.

Another translator was a woman in her forties—Pani (Mrs.) Wojkiewicz if memory serves, who had been a heroine in the Uprising; her colleagues treated her with special respect.

An elderly bespectacled gentleman, looking as if he had just walked out of a Warsaw coffeehouse in the 1930s, was the most erudite member of our staff. Kulerski by name, he had been traumatized by a stint in a Soviet prison. He labored painfully over each word to extract its most precise meaning and steered clear of the political banter. Out of fear of Polish security, he declined to visit my wife and me in Mokotow but invited us to visit his small apartment on the other side of the Vistula River, which we did as unobtrusively as possible.

Occasionally, a fierce argument would erupt among the six, and my British colleague or I would have to rush in from our shared office to break it up.

Around noon, I'd return to the political section, next to the ambassador's office, and draft telegrams and airgrams (the latter sent through the pouch rather than electronically) based on information gleaned from the controlled press and, later, from my own sources, Polish and diplomatic.

*   *   *

Before I joined Herb's section, President Johnson had named John Gronouski as Cabot's successor. During Kennedy's presidency, Gronouski had served as postmaster general, a reward for having helped defeat Kennedy's main rival, Senator Humphrey, in the 1960 Wisconsin primary. While barnstorming for Kennedy, Gronouski was said to have delivered 445 speeches in fourteen months, averaging more than one a day.[95] With a doctorate from the University of Wisconsin, Gronouski was bright and well prepared, unlike many nonprofessional appointees who end up in embassy front offices.

After Kennedy's assassination, Johnson wanted his own man in the postal position and persuaded Gronouski, whose father was of Polish origin, to succeed Cabot. Johnson was intent upon "building bridges" to the Iron Curtain, using that very metaphor in a 1964 speech, and Gronouski appeared to be an excellent choice. To make the assignment more palatable, he asked Gronouski to survey the performance of the region's other American embassies and report back to him.

The ambassador, his wife Mary, and their two daughters arrived in Warsaw by train from Vienna on a cold rainy evening in November 1965. Liz and I, along with other embassy families, assembled on the station's outdoor platform to give them a rousing welcome. Foreign Ministry protocol officials, Western ambassadors, and a few journalists were also present.

Radio stations abroad, including the Voice of America, had broadcast Gronouski's arrival time, and a few brave Poles with no connection to the regime stood with us. When the train came to a halt, the result was a melee as everyone pushed and shoved for a handshake. Gronouski, ever the politician, was delighted.

The new ambassador viewed himself as an emissary to "his" people as much as to the Communist regime to which he was accredited. This was far from the traditional understanding of an ambassador's role. Unfortunately, Gronouski spoke few words of Polish and few Poles knew English, so his opportunity to "barnstorm" as if in Wisconsin was limited. In addition, by the middle 1960s, relations between Washington and Warsaw were seriously strained, and Polish officials proved as standoffish to him as they had been to Cabot.

Had relations been better, the receptions that John and Mary hosted probably would have attracted sizeable turnouts. On one occasion they entertained Marlene Dietrich, Peter O'Toole, and Omar Sharif. Marlene was performing in a Warsaw theater. Sitting at her feet in Gronouski's residence, I thought she looked no older than the girl who had starred in *The Blue Angel* forty years before; I could understand why she had been pushed into filmmaking after modeling stockings. O'Toole and Sharif were making *The Night of the Generals,* and the film's director had wangled permission to bedeck Warsaw's Old Town with Nazi flags, for their first display in public since the occupation.

The Hollywood talk was a refreshing change from the usual conversation at diplomatic receptions, but no officials from the regime appeared. The only Poles who attended were a few writers and the members of a musical troupe heading for the United States. I met a young singing star, Anna German, whose voice was as powerful as Barbra Streisand's; had she not died in a road accident a few years later, she would have gained as devoted a following.

Gronouski's style was as far from Cabot's as could be imagined. Sometimes he would end dinner parties with his feet propped on the table and with a nail clipper in hand. It seemed to me that older Poles, including the intellectuals who had survived the war, didn't quite know what to make of him. Of course, they had no way of knowing that the Century of the Common Man had arrived too in the United States, and that more Gronouskis and fewer Cabots would henceforth head U.S. embassies.

Acting on President Johnson's instruction, Gronouski took senior officers with him to other posts in Eastern Europe. Several ambassadors from the ranks of the career service resented the intrusion of a political appointee and found excuses to be away.

Liz and I did advance work for Gronouski's trip to Katowice in Poland's coal-mining district. Edmund Gierek, the PZPR leader there, was beginning to attract attention as a potential successor to the regime's leader, Wlaydslaw Gomulka. (In fact, Gierek replaced Gomulka three years later). Gierek not only refused to receive the ambassador but also barred him from a coal mine. Gronouski had badly wanted to be photographed wearing a hard hat descending a shaft.

Liz and I took Gronouski to the two concentration camps nearby— Oswiecim (Auschwitz) and Birkenau. After visiting barracks filled with piles of women's hair, children's toys, and suitcases bearing the names of the dead, the ambassador laid a wreath "to the memory of the victims of man's inhumanity to man." Later I took a delegation of Polish-American mayors to the same camps. I returned from these trips somewhat shaken, and much less innocent about the human capacity for evil.

The Polish government was one of three governments—the Canadian and Indian governments the others—on the International Control Commission that had been established, pursuant to the Geneva Accords of 1954, to limit outside military involvement in Indochina. Warsaw's senior-most diplomats therefore enjoyed some standing in Communist

Vietnam. With opposition to the war growing at home, Gronouski cast about for a diplomatic approach that might lead to a settlement.

With Washington's approval, he opened a dialogue with Foreign Minister Adam Rapacki and other senior policy makers. In December 1966, he came close to establishing a direct channel of communication with an emissary whom Hanoi, at Rapacki's behest, had dispatched to Warsaw. But Washington wouldn't halt its bombing raids over North Vietnam, and the emissary was quickly recalled to Hanoi. In an eighth meeting with Gronouski amid the resumed bombing, Rapacki lost his temper and slammed his spectacles on the table, propelling a lens into the ambassador's face.

Gronouski probably believed that, had Johnson suspended bombing while he and the Poles were trying to engage the Vietnamese, his secret initiative, which Washington dubbed Marigold, might have produced a positive result.[96] Gronouski was determined and imaginative, but by 1966 the conflict was probably beyond his or the Poles' ability to influence. After the failure of Marigold, Washington looked to Moscow as a possible intermediary, but this also came to naught. Johnson's successor, Richard Nixon, then nourished the hope that Beijing would influence Hanoi. Although Nixon and Kissinger achieved the normalization of relations with Communist China, they too failed to secure pressure on Hanoi from the neighboring Communist state, pressure that might have paved the way for an earlier exit from the war.

*   *   *

Liz and I socialized mostly with Poles our own age. They were as attractive and personable as the friends we had made in Hamburg, and often livelier; but there the comparisons ended. They barely possessed a change of clothes and only one owned a car. Most resided with their parents in one or two rooms of large housing complexes, sharing a kitchen and bathroom with other families. They knew that conditions in the West were better, although it was impossible for them to leave the eastern bloc to find out for themselves. A strain of dark humor pervaded much of their conversation, which somehow made their lot more bearable.

We came to know Julek and Danuta, or Danka, Mierzejewski through Julek's mother who worked as a secretary at the elementary school operated by the American and British embassies. Pani Mierzejewska bore a tattooed number across her forearm from imprisonment in one of the German camps.

Liz and I would invite Julek and Danka for picnics in the countryside, and they took us to concerts at Chopin's home at Zelaznaya Wola just outside Warsaw. Sometimes they babysat for our daughters when we traveled.

Julek was tall and rangy and often absent while fulfilling compulsory military service in the northwest corner of the country, an area closed to diplomats. Danka had a Semitic kind of beauty; if Anna German's voice made us think of Barbra Streisand, Danka had her looks and manner.

We knew something of Julek's background but not of Danka's. She never mentioned her parents. Perhaps she was Jewish, but I never asked. She was always restless, yearning to go somewhere or do something, and I sensed that she had suffered greatly as a child.

Julek and Danka were fortunate in having their own room and bath. They'd play Polish and American records when we visited. Often we'd split a bottle of vodka we'd bring along. They took pleasure in the smallest things: a trip into the country, a little joke, an encounter with a friend on an Old Town street. Like most young Poles whom we came to know, they lived more in the present than the past or future.

It was the same elsewhere in the eastern bloc. Visiting an apartment in Budapest in 1967, the playwright Lillian Hellman was told by a young Communist, "Something new must come, Marxism must advance." But another tells her, "Lady foreigner, turn your ears away. Nothing new will come. There is nothing in this world but now for now." And the young Hungarians around her broke into song, "Shut your heart against the past and against the future. Now is for now."[97]

A few years after leaving Warsaw, we heard that Danka had taken her own life. Demons from the past, it was said. When I hear Barbra Streisand's voice today, my thoughts go back forty years to our Polish friends.

*   *   *

No one was closer to Liz and me than Bogdan Grzelonski. I first met Bogdan after he made his way past the Polish guards into the embassy's press and culture (P&C) section. (Communists found "press and culture" less offensive than "information service," hence the name that the U.S. Information Service used in bloc countries.) Bogdan was a graduate student specializing in American history, especially Jacksonian democracy; and materials for research were difficult to obtain except through the embassy and its modest library.

We would meet near my Old Town office or at Warsaw University, where he sometimes attended lectures, and discuss the culture and politics of our respective countries. Bogdan refused to be cowed by the fact that Polish security, then known by its initials UB (from "security office," *Urzad Bezpieczenstwa*), would sometimes watch me; he explained that the Old Town's winding streets made it easier for him to elude the agents who often lurked near my office.

Bogdan's parents invited Liz and me to their home, a small apartment on the north side of the Vistula River. His father worked in a meat market and provisioned his family well; his mother made the most splendid brandy-steeped desserts, what I imagined the best restaurants served before the war. We became friends too with Bogdan's teenage sister Jadwiga, who later married a Polish diplomat and served with him in Washington.

Tensions were rising when we arrived at the embassy, and they continued to rise during our three-year stay. Gomulka had taken over the leadership of the Communist Party almost a decade earlier. A revolt by workers in Poznan, a major industrial city, had precipitated a nationwide crisis that led to the collapse of the prior leadership, known for obsequious kowtowing to Stalin. The earlier regime had, in fact, imprisoned Gomulka and others for allegedly espousing a more national brand of Communism. Nikita Khrushchev grudgingly acquiesced in Gomulka's accession during a dramatic visit to Warsaw in 1956.

For a few years, Gomulka enjoyed a measure of support, even outside the Party. By calming the country, he had saved it from almost-certain Soviet military intervention. He had halted the collectivization of agriculture and freed the leader of the Catholic Church, Cardinal Stefan Wyszynski, from house arrest. For several years he tolerated a degree of openness in Warsaw's cultural life.

However, by 1965, Gomulka had squandered whatever popularity he once enjoyed. The economy was stagnant, his policies repressive. A junior philosophy professor at Warsaw University, Leszek Kolakowski, a PZPR member himself, took the lead in exposing the leadership's "neo-Stalinist" tendencies. Most educated Poles, including academics and intellectuals, agreed with Kolakowski, but few dared to sign petitions challenging the regime as he did. A year after we arrived, the Communist leadership condemned him as a "revisionist" and confiscated his membership card.

Bogdan alerted me to meetings at Warsaw University where Kolakowski spoke and where much of the ferment was centered. Once, wandering the campus, I slipped into a Communist Party meeting. It turned out that Professor Juliusz Katz-Suchy on whom I had just paid a call for the political section was speaking.

Katz-Suchy had been Poland's representative to the United Nations after the war. Jewish by origin, he was seen in the West as a pro-Soviet firebrand. In fact, he had few illusions about the USSR. The American Communist novelist Howard Fast relates how Katz-Suchy once exclaimed to a small private gathering in New York that the Polish people and its Party were "united forever in a holy hatred of Stalin and Russia." They could not forget, he asserted, that Stalin had put to death three thousand members of the

Polish Party before the war.[98] Of course, for most Americans during the Cold War, a Communist was a Communist regardless of what he thought about the Soviets.

I was in a back row, trying to remain out of sight so the professor wouldn't recognize me when shouts suddenly erupted and Party members began exchanging fierce polemics. I couldn't understand all the back-and-forth, but the drift was clear: orthodox and revisionist factions were at each others' throats. The meeting ended with everyone singing the "Internationale" in a mock show of unity (I pretended to know the words), but I felt that a 1956-like crisis was looming again.

As a backdrop to the intraparty ferment, Poland's Catholic church was celebrating its adoption of Christianity one thousand years before. Cardinal Wyszynski was organizing public marches and assemblies of the country's many million believers. Whenever the primate appeared, tens of thousands of Poles would join him. I attended a celebration in Warsaw, and the crush was so great I thought I might not make it out in one piece. But under Wyszynski's skillful leadership, the church knew how and when to draw the line, to control its flock without provoking mass arrests.

In June 1967, at the end of my second full year, Israel achieved a stunning victory against its Arab neighbors in the Six-Day War. Having armed and supported the Arab states, Moscow was humiliated, and this wasn't lost on the Poles. Reports of Polish intellectuals' exulting at the Soviet regime's embarrassment reached Gomulka, who reacted by warning of a "Zionist threat" to Poland.

No more than fifty thousand Jews were living in Poland at the time, the vast majority of them fully assimilated in the country's population of over thirty million.[99] Jewish cultural life was virtually extinct. Only a small synagogue existed in the capital, and it had no rabbi. Herb and his wife, Joy, knew of the Yiddish theater that a revered Jewish actress, Ida Kaminska, had founded in 1948, and they introduced Liz and me to it. During World War II, the troupe had performed in the Soviet Union, including in Poland's eastern territories, as Moscow cleared them of Germans and Poles and reduced them to its own control. One evening, we watched Ida and her husband perform *Mother Courage and Her Children*, even though the "theater" occupied a space no larger than a small living room, and the chairs were those we set up ourselves.

I had not grown up among many Jews. I had probably met more at Harvard Law than during all my previous schooling. Nor was I conversant with Jewish culture. I was therefore somewhat baffled by Polish anti-Semitism, especially when so few Jews remained in Warsaw. Yet it was apparent that Gomulka and a Party faction headed by his minister of interior, Mieczyslaw Moczar, were determined to revive the dangerous virus in order to turn ill-educated, susceptible Poles against the country's intellectuals and so-called revisionists.

Polish and Russian Jews had indeed held important positions in the first postwar regime.[100] A confidante of Beria, Stalin's security boss, while assigned to Warsaw in 1945, had warned Moscow that almost 20 percent of the employees of Poland's ministry of public security were Jewish and half of the ministry's directorships were held by Jews.[101] (Ironically, some of the children of these officials would later ally themselves with Kolakowski.)

Seizing on Gomulka's "anti-Zionist" line, Moczar pushed for a crackdown on Warsaw's educated elite. The objective was to isolate the country's disaffected intellectuals from its workers by suggesting that a disproportionate number of the former were Jewish. In particular, Moczar wanted to purge the Jews still remaining in Poland's cultural, academic, and government institutions.

Herb asked me to find out more about Moczar's faction. I knew an editor in Moczar's camp (I had met him through a young Polish girl); and during an evening at our home, in response to my questions, he put check marks by those in the Party's leadership—its Central Committee—who were allied with Moczar.

The tension burst open in February 1968 shortly after the regime closed the play *Dziady* (*Forefathers' Eve*). The country's revered poet and patriot Adam Mickiewicz (1798-1855) had written it to protest Russia's suppression of Poland's uprising against the tsar in 1830. It contains strong verses against Russian despotism; Poles imprisoned after the Soviet seizure of eastern Poland used to recite them from memory to insult their Russian guards.[102]

Rumors circulated that the Soviet embassy in Warsaw had demanded the play's closure. On March 8, 1968, protesting students began to demonstrate near the theater not far from their campus. One of the organizers was a Jewish acquaintance of Bogdan, eighteen-year-old Adam Michnik (whose older brother, interestingly, had served in Poland's first postwar regime). Soon the capital's main streets were flooded with thousands of protestors, and students in Krakow and other cities began to mount their own demonstrations.

Young Poles had been watching television pictures of Americans demonstrating against the war in Vietnam and had been reading about the Prague Spring to the south. They were now clamoring for a repeat of 1956 when their older brothers and sisters, and perhaps their parents, had forced the removal of the first postwar regime.

Gomulka and Moczar mobilized internal security troops and crushed the students in two days. Then they launched a vicious "anti-Zionist" campaign, adopting a tactic employed by Stalin when he attacked Russia's "rootless cosmopolitans" in 1948: Warsaw newspapers began exposing the birth names of Poles of Jewish origin, those who had adopted pseudonyms and noms de guerre or received them from their parents to escape persecution.

For several weeks, I was in the thick of reporting on the crackdown and its implications, not only for Poland and the USSR but also for U.S.-Polish relations. The crackdown hit close to home when Bogdan was arrested along with Michnik and thrown into Mokotow prison.

Personally, there was only minor harassment; after the play was closed, a smoke bomb was tossed through our front door. A military attaché at the embassy received a similar surprise.

Through the end of summer, officials and intellectuals allegedly tainted with revisionist tendencies or Jewish ancestry were dismissed from their posts and, if members of the PZPR, expelled. Two Jewish Communists in the Foreign Ministry who dealt with American affairs were barricaded in their offices by younger officials and forced to resign; nearly forty others were also expelled from the ministry.[103] Rapacki, not a Jew, resigned. Kolakowski was forced to go abroad. My one-time source Katz-Suchy and another Jewish law professor, who had also been a Polish diplomat, were ousted from the university.

The Yiddish theater was closed as Stalin closed Moscow's Jewish theater in 1949. Altogether twelve thousand Poles of Jewish origin left Poland, including Ida Kaminska and the remnants of her troupe. To secure an exit visa, Katz-Suchy, like the others, had to renounce his Polish citizenship and declare he was immigrating to Israel, according to the Soviet "model." In December 1969, he and his family found refuge in Denmark along with two thousand other Polish Jews. (The Danes saved almost seven thousand Danish-Jewish citizens during World War II, secretly evacuating them to neutral Sweden). Katz-Suchy died at age fifty-nine in Denmark three years later.

Liz and I were devastated by Bogdan's arrest. We could only imagine what he was undergoing. To what extent were we responsible? Perhaps we shouldn't have encouraged the friendship.

My assignment was coming to an end. Knowing we'd be leaving soon, Bogdan's mother and sister paid us a visit late one night. They had no more information about Bogdan than we had but affirmed their friendship and wished us well.

I used to take Elise and Abby, then seven and six years old, on walks past Mokotow prison. Elise reminds me that as we walked by it the last time, I told her that we had a friend inside.

We were in the United States when Bogdan was finally released. He was held for three months and accused of cooperating with the CIA. Some of the interrogations were "tough," he said, while omitting details.[104]

Upon his release, he was put on a blacklist, meaning that he could only work as a laborer. After Gierek succeeded Gomulka in 1971, he was rearrested and held again. In 1972, he was allowed to resume his academic career. A year later, he was permitted to go abroad to the Netherlands where his wife was studying. Security officials were upset when he returned; they had wanted him to stay abroad.

Bogdan was not one to abandon Poland's cause. He obtained a doctorate in American history and began a teaching career at Warsaw Economic University.

In June 1979, Pope John Paul II, who—as Cardinal Karol Wojtyla—had succeeded Wyszynski, spent nine days visiting Poland. The visit led to the rise of the Workers Solidarity Movement. This marked the beginning of the end for Communism in Poland and Eastern Europe, and ultimately, the Soviet Union. A decade later, Europe's entire Communist system fell.

The way was open for Bogdan and many other Poles who had always rejected the Soviet system to enter public life. In 1997, Bogdan was appointed Poland's ambassador to Canada. "I remained there," he told me, until "I achieved my goal. Canada was the first country to ratify Poland's membership in the North Atlantic Treaty Organization," the organization created in 1949 to halt the spread of Communism into Western Europe.

Bogdan is back in Poland today, the president of a university in Plock. He is writing books, the two most recent entitled (as translated from Polish) *US Diplomats* and *Polish Diplomacy in the XX Century.*

Were three months in prison and years of harassment a price worth paying? By all means, he declares. His conversations with Liz and me helped convince him that the system under which he and his family were living was bad. "Meeting you was for me and my sister and my parents very important. You were the people that gave us hope that one day Communism will fall apart. Meeting you in Warsaw and in your Washington house [in 1978] gave me a feeling of true America."

Actually, Bogdan must have held his strong beliefs before we met. Otherwise, he wouldn't have risked having us as friends.

Did he ever reconnect with Adam Michnik, the leader of the 1968 revolt who has since become a prominent editor? "No, I didn't believe in socialism with a 'human face' as administered by Communists."

*   *   *

No socialism had ever appealed to me, yet I had wondered sometimes whether there might be some middle way for the East, a kind of sunlit *via media* incorporating democracy with state control of an economy's "commanding heights." Graham Greene had once made fun of "the great American dream" of finding a "third force," a dream that bedeviled American affairs in the Far East, including in Vietnam.[105] The "dream" probably derived from the despair many felt about the Cold War's seeming intractability.

In 1965, before we left Hamburg for Warsaw, Rusty Latta, a CIA friend, had recommended that I read *The Captive Mind* by Czeslaw Milosz, a Polish intellectual then not widely known. Milosz had witnessed Poland's uprisings against the Nazis in 1943 and 1944 as well as its transformation into a Communist state. In 1951, while serving as an attaché at the Polish embassy in Paris, he had defected to the West.

I found an English-language translation and read the book as we drove east. I must have been struck by Milosc's prefatory words: "There are only two sides . . . the only choice lies between absolute conformity to the one system or absolute conformity to the other."[106]

The words were Manichaean and harsh, but three years in Warsaw left no doubt with me that they were true. It was a war of ideas, and one had to decide whether to submit or resist. Bogdan was among those who chose to resist.

In 1980, Milosz received the Nobel Prize for Literature. He returned to Poland and settled in Krakow after the collapse of Communism (and the collapse of most talk about "third ways" and "socialism with a human face").

The three years in Warsaw had taught me how to probe the vulnerabilities of a Communist system; they had also given me skills I wanted to use again. I was therefore delighted when the department, in December 1967, indicated I would be assigned next to the American mission in Berlin as a political officer. I would be responsible for dealing with East German and Soviet officials in the four-power governed city.

It was unusual to receive three consecutive assignments in Europe, but north central Europe was where the interests of the Soviet Union and the Western powers continued to collide, and Berlin remained the likeliest flash point.

Foreign Service officers skilled in the affairs of Germany, Poland, and the Soviet Union, and proficient in their languages, were not in great supply; and the assignment made sense, not only to me but to my superiors.

However, the assignment disappeared before it was put in official orders. The United States was making huge outlays for its armed forces in Europe and Vietnam, and the dollar was rapidly losing value relative to other currencies. President Johnson decided that the State Department needed to "reduce the total number of American personnel overseas by 10 percent."[107] The promised position in Berlin and many others were eliminated.

So the department told me it would give me more education, as if Kent, Princeton, and Harvard hadn't given me enough.

4

Tchaikovsky 19 and Leninsky Prospect 45

Approximately four hundred Foreign Service officers were "balpa'd," the verb coined from "balance of payments," to describe the abrupt change of assignments following President Johnson's decision. Of course, the impact of removing several hundred positions on the payments deficit was more symbolic than real; the savings realized could hardly offset the huge sums then being spent on the country's military engagements, especially in Vietnam.

I wasn't looking for any further education (I had already lost the year in Illinois) but was told that I had qualified for midcareer training, although the career, in my view, was only just beginning.

I had no idea that I would end up spending two and one-half of the next four years in classrooms, both in the United States and abroad.

The Foreign Service initiated training for officers after the enactment of the Rogers Act in 1924, which professionalized the career. Signed by President Calvin Coolidge, it amalgamated diplomatic and consular officers into a single service; made merit, not politics, the basis for recruitment and promotion; and prompted the department to establish the Foreign Service School, the forerunner of the Foreign Service Institute.[108]

For certain languages, the training could be overseas. Officers could be assigned for as long as three years to a country or area where the language was taught and spoken, not only to learn the language but to study the history and culture corresponding to it. The thinking was that FSOs with a thorough knowledge of the countries and areas in which they served would understand events better and make sounder recommendations. Officers steeped in the language and the culture of a given country might even reach the service's top ranks and be in a position to make policy.

Two Foreign Service careers, if no other, vindicated the department's decision to invest in overseas training. In the late 1920s, the department sent George Kennan to the university in Berlin for two years and Charles Bohlen to an institute in Paris (Ecole des Langues Orientales Vivantes) for two and one-half years in order to learn Russian and to study Russian and Soviet affairs. In view of the fact that the United States didn't recognize the Soviet state until 1933, the decision demonstrated unusually astute planning by the department's office of personnel.

Berlin and Paris contained sizeable colonies of Russian émigrés—refugees from the Bolsheviks—with whom Kennan and Bohlen were able to associate. With Washington's encouragement, they also spent time in other Russian-speaking areas: Kennan stayed in a Russian monastery near the Soviet border in Estonia; Bohlen lived in a *pension* in a former Russian resort not far from Tallinn, Estonia's capital.

The United States realized huge dividends from both investments. After two Soviet assignments in the 1930s, Kennan returned to Moscow for a third time in 1944 and drafted the telegram that conceptualized the policy of containment, the policy that governed American strategy during most of the Cold War. From positions in the department, including as head of the policy planning staff, he then helped apply the policy, albeit in some ways he later regretted.

Like Kennan, Bohlen served twice in Moscow during the 1930s. With the outbreak of war, he was selected to interpret for Roosevelt's emissary Harry Hopkins and Ambassador Averell Harriman at their meetings with Stalin. This led to his role as advisor and interpreter for Roosevelt and Truman at the summit meetings in Tehran, Yalta, and Potsdam. It also resulted in his receiving an office in the White House close to the Oval Office. With this, Bohlen, in his own words, "leaped over the barrier that insulated the State Department from decision-making at the White House,"[109] a barrier that has since proven insurmountable for all but few FSOs.

Bohlen and Kennan subsequently advised Truman and Secretary Marshall on establishing the Marshall Plan in 1947 and countering Moscow's Berlin Blockade in 1948-49. After an assignment as ambassador to Moscow, Bohlen ended his career advising Kennedy and Johnson on the crises that erupted abroad during their administrations.

*   *   *

My orders were to report to Bloomington, Indiana, for an academic year of "East European study." Just before we left Warsaw, Liz had given birth to Robert III. When she brought the baby back to Warsaw from the air force hospital in Wiesbaden, West Germany (I had to return to the embassy earlier), half of the staff welcomed them at Okecie Airport. Such was the community's closeness, the high level of embassy morale.

I had never been to Indiana University, but friends assured me that its East European program was among the country's best. I was already thinking about Moscow, however, and told personnel that I planned to choose courses covering the entire Communist bloc, since studying East Europe to the exclusion of the USSR seemed to make little sense. Perhaps the distinction had been valid before World War II, but I felt it didn't pertain once Moscow had installed its satellite regimes.

"Oh no," came back the reply, "restrict yourself to East Europe. The department's university training program makes a distinction between the two." This was probably because of a budgetary rule. By identifying several courses with ambiguous titles, I was able to develop a program that would serve me no matter where I went.

From August 1968 through June 1969, Liz, the three children, and I lived in a two-bedroom apartment in graduate housing on the Bloomington campus. Southern Indiana is covered with lakes and woods, and sometimes I felt as if we were in New England, or back at the Mazurian Lakes north of Warsaw where we had camped.

Because of Vietnam, however, Bloomington wasn't as quiet as I thought it would be. Antiwar demonstrations were common, and a few older students were propagating Marxist ideas. Radicals in one class to whom I spoke argued that capitalist America was only interested in Eastern Europe because of its potential for trade, ignoring the fact that millions of Americans traced their ancestry there.

One of my history professors told me that he had served as an analyst in the CIA before joining the university. Fearing student retaliation, he asked me not to breathe a word about it. His anxiety was probably justified in view of stories then beginning to circulate about the agency's operations in Vietnam. I encountered no unpleasantness myself, but our four and a half years in Europe hadn't prepared us for the anger mounting among young people because of the war and the draft.

In August 1968, a few weeks before classes began, the Warsaw Pact countries, except for Romania, invaded Czechoslovakia, dashing its people's hopes for creating a socialist system "with a human face." Vaclav Benes, one of my teachers and a nephew of the co-founder of Czechoslovakia, Eduard Benes, was delighted to have me report on the repression I had seen up close in Warsaw.

Thanks largely to my advisor Barbara Jelavich, I was able to obtain a master's degree in history before we returned to Washington.

I was assigned to the State Department office responsible for exchange programs with Eastern Europe and the Soviet Union. I wasn't particularly pleased with the assignment, but I hadn't made an effort to lobby for something more challenging. Like Kennan, I tended to be slow "to learn the ropes,"[110] even with a career at stake.

The exchange office's task was to help place Communist-origin scholars and scientists in institutions in the United States without jeopardizing national security, while assisting American scholars and scientists in gaining reciprocal access to corresponding institutions in the Communist countries. We wanted to expose as many of their scholars and scientists as possible to the West while expanding opportunities for our scholars and scientists in the East. The work involved liaison with the CIA, the FBI, and other agencies, as well as with universities and private organizations.

Of course, it was impossible to prevent Communist regimes from placing spies among their nominees. Of the first group of Soviet students sent to American institutions in 1958 under the U.S.-Soviet exchange agreement signed in January that year, half were connected with either the KGB or the GRU, Soviet military intelligence.[111] The "student" who later publicized this fact, Oleg Kulagin, said he had been sent to Columbia with a fabricated cover story attesting to his preparation at Leningrad University.[112] Before retiring from the KGB in 1990, he became its chief of counterintelligence.

Another student in the same group, Alexander Yakovlev, ended his Party career as an advisor to Mikhail Gorbachev, ultimately helping him dismantle the worst features of the Soviet system.

Many in the United States opposed exchanges, believing that a society like ours couldn't compete with a closed society on this kind of "playing field." According to their thinking, we shouldn't engage in such arrangements unless there is absolute certainty about complete reciprocity both in the quality of the participants and the extent of access they're granted. Of course, no one dealing with a Soviet-type system could be assured of such certainty. By the same token, however, no closed system could survive for long if more and more of its people, even those involved in its inner circle, were exposed to the West. Those in the United States who made a fetish of reciprocity were never comfortable with exchanges, but history has proved them wrong.

The office also oversaw the exchange of exhibitions and performing arts groups, some sponsored by the United States Information Agency (USIA). In the performing arts area, there were five major exchanges with the USSR during my first year. Holiday on Ice and the Alvin Ailey Dance Theatre went to the USSR, while the Moscow Circus on Ice, the Moiseyev Dancers, and the Moscow Philharmonic came to the United States. Because of the invasion of Czechoslovakia, the overall number of exchanges didn't grow as rapidly as everyone had expected.

We had no official responsibility for tourism but did track the numbers to the extent we could. An estimated fifty thousand Americans visited the Soviet Union in 1970; this was more than twice the number of visitors before the invasion. Despite setbacks, the flow of Americans behind the Curtain kept increasing, and tourism turned out to be another way of influencing attitudes. The welfare of Americans traveling in the USSR turned out to be my responsibility when I finally reached Moscow.

*   *   *

In November 1970, the Soviet Union Affairs Office, the largest country office in the department's Bureau of European Affairs and colloquially known as the Soviet desk, informed me that I had been selected for a two-year assignment to Moscow. It would be preceded by a one-year assignment at the U.S. Army Advanced Russian Institute (USAARI) in Garmisch, West Germany.

The USAARI was the government's premier facility for training military officers in Soviet affairs. The uniformed officers were assigned for two years after a year of language training in the United States; the department selected three or four FSOs every year to study alongside them for one year.

I had asked for a Soviet assignment and was delighted to be chosen. I don't recall asking specifically for Garmisch, but Olaf Grobel, with whom I had served in Warsaw, was on the Soviet desk and had put my name forward.

I first needed six months at the Foreign Service Institute to bring my Russian to an intermediate level, as required by Garmisch. I found that the FSI had changed its premises in the decade since I had studied German, and its classrooms were less grim, a few even with views of the Potomac River. Our teachers were Russian-speaking immigrants, mostly from families who had settled in the Russian communities that had sprung up in China, Europe, and Latin America after the Bolsheviks took over. Mrs. Nina Delacruz, the senior teacher, was from a distinguished Russian family; she had come to the FSI from Latin America where she had been married to a Brazilian diplomat. In her classroom, she kept a wooden model of the Kremlin and Red Square where, with miniature cars and pedestrians, we practiced the language's complicated verbs of motion.

On Friday afternoons, we received our reward—the showing of a Soviet film, including one so recent as Sergei Bondarchuk's 1967 epic, *War and Peace.* We did our best to make out the dialogue, but it was often a trial. Liz wasn't able to study the language with me because of the children but often attended the films.

Our teachers were capable linguists but, not having lived in Communist Russia, couldn't explain what life there was really like. In most classes, I was with two other FSOs—Steve Steiner, a Yale graduate who had served in Yugoslavia and had also been assigned to Moscow by way of Garmisch, and Jim Leach, a younger Princeton graduate. Shortly after the program ended, Leach resigned from the Foreign Service and returned to Iowa where he was elected to the House of Representatives, the second person who won a seat in the Congress after leaving one of my FSI classes.

In July 1971, after meeting the institute's language requirement, I took my family to West Germany. Garmisch is located seventy miles south of Munich in the Bavarian Alps under the country's tallest mountain, the Zugspitze. Along with neighboring Partenkirchen, it had been the site of the 1936 Winter Olympics at which Hitler presided.

The USAARI is located on a former *Wehrmacht* base at the edge of the village. The U.S. Army had converted it into a prison camp for German officers in 1945. After their release, it was retained as a training center. The institute continues today as the George C. Marshall Center for European Security Studies. The Russian language is still taught, but the department no longer trains its Russia-bound FSOs there, or indeed anywhere overseas.

When we arrived, the Pentagon was assigning about fifteen military officers a year to Garmisch, mostly to prepare them to serve as defense attachés in the Soviet Union and Eastern Europe. Most had begun their language study at a defense department school in Monterey, California; a few arrived in Garmisch by way of Vietnam. By rank, the uniformed officers were majors or lieutenant colonels.

Three FSOs and an officer from the U.S. Information Agency comprised the department's contingent. A few others, from the CIA and the National Security Agency (NSA), completed the civilian roster.

Classes were conducted exclusively in Russian and most of the instructors—Russian, Polish, Estonian, or Yugoslav by nationality—lived among us. Their politics were hard-line and fiercely anti-Communist, like those of the Poles I had supervised in Warsaw. Most had been brought up in the Soviet Union; one was a former military officer who, after capture by the Germans, joined the anti-Communist Vlasov movement to fight against his countrymen. There were two other defectors, one from the forces occupying East Germany, another from a border guard unit. The only full-time woman on the teaching staff had been in a German labor camp during the war, and then had eluded the forced repatriations that Moscow, with the West's connivance, engineered after the war.

Ivana Rebet, a pretty red-haired woman of Ukrainian origin, directed the library. In 1957, in Munich, the KGB had assassinated her father, Lev

Rebet, in one of its last so-called "wet" actions in Western Europe. He had been the chief ideologist of a Ukrainian émigré organization.

One of the USAARI teachers redefected to the Soviet Union after I reached Moscow. The KGB had "planted" him at the institute; the teachers were wary of him from the moment he arrived.

Virtually the entire non-American staff had worked at one time or another with American or British intelligence or anti-Communist front organizations. Unsurprisingly, Moscow viewed the institute as "a spy school," and its media portrayed it this way. In actuality, no one at the institute received instruction in espionage tradecraft.

We studied hard, acquired a good speaking ability, and sharpened our understanding of the Soviet Union and, no less importantly, Russia and its culture and history.

Before Kennan went to Berlin to study, he had asked the head of the department's Russian division whether he should take "strictly Soviet subjects." "No," he was told, "get the essentials of a good Russian cultural background; the rest can come later."[113] By sponsoring us at Garmisch, the department was saying the same.

One of the courses dealt with Russian literature. We heard lectures about Pasternak and other writers and poets, both pro and anti-Soviet. We read excerpts from the works of the author of *The Master and Margarita*, Mikhail Bulgakov, whom Bohlen came to know during his first Moscow assignment. One of the essays I wrote in Russian concerned the *samizdat* work of the dissidents Yuri Daniel and Andrei Sinyavsky; both had been prosecuted and imprisoned in the crackdown on culture that began with the persecution of Pasternak.

We also played hard, ending weeks of intensive study with riotous partying in Munich or on the base. At a celebration just before graduating, the more adventuresome husbands and wives, including Liz and me, rappelled down the side of a three-and-a-half-story housing barrack.

The institute and its students were a breath of fresh air after Washington's staid corridors and its very isolation contributed to our approaching mastery of Russian.

*   *   *

Twelve of us from the institute made a five-day visit to Moscow in April 1972, organized by the official Soviet travel agency, Intourist. It came as a surprise to the USAARI director, an earnest lieutenant colonel with a talent for languages, that we received Soviet entry visas. Moscow's embassy in Bonn had refused to grant them to six prior classes, viewing every institute student as a spy. Ironically, the CIA and NSA barred their students, the real spies, from the trip.

Perhaps not fully understood by the director, détente was beginning to affect Soviet decision-making, even in such mundane matters as official travel. Not long after our classes had begun, Moscow and Washington had announced that Leonid Brezhnev, the head of the Communist Party, had invited President Nixon to Moscow. The summit was scheduled to occur in May 1972, one month after our trip.

There had never been a U.S.-Soviet summit in the Soviet capital, and there had been only one summit during the previous ten years—the meeting in Glassboro, New Jersey, in 1967 that brought the chairman of the Council of Ministers Alexei Kosygin together with President Johnson. Kosygin was still the nominal head of government, but Brezhnev had since consolidated virtually full control as the head of the Communist Party.

An Intourist bus and a Russian guide met us at Sheremetyevo Airport, and we were shepherded to the Hotel Ukraina. Situated a few blocks from the embassy, the Ukraina is one of seven "wedding-cake" buildings erected in the early 1950s. I knew the style—Stalinist Gothic—from their stepsister in Warsaw.

I would become well acquainted with three of seven high-rises during my first assignment. One is the shared home of the Ministry of Foreign Affairs, where we conducted most of our consular business, and of the Ministry of Foreign Trade. Another is an apartment house two blocks from the embassy; we used to meet Russians whom we needed to escort past the Soviet guards into the embassy at a park in front, on Vosstaniya (Uprising) Square.

A third high-rise is the main building of Moscow State University (MGU). It stands on a hill at a bend in the Moscow River overlooking Lenin Stadium. The Soviet authorities went to great lengths to keep diplomats out of school buildings; but shortly after reaching the embassy on permanent assignment, I was asked by Spike Dubs, the deputy chief of mission, to deliver a confidential message to an Afghan student residing in one of them. (His parents opposed Moscow's growing influence in Kabul.) After Garmisch, I had no trouble talking my way in.

Excited to be in Moscow at last, we dropped off our suitcases, got back on the bus, and raced down to Red Square. To reach it, we were taken past two—and three-story stucco buildings as well as a few of plain wood, either unfinished or falling apart. A few had roofs of metal. Most were situated on the quaint streets that radiated off Moscow's broad Stalin-era boulevards.

Despite the high-rises on Kalinin Prospect, I liked what I saw. Much of Moscow's downtown was cut to a human scale, not radically different from Warsaw's, and I knew that Liz and I would adjust easily once we settled in.

With Nixon's visit a month away, Red Square was in picture-perfect form. The air was crisp and cold; there was no snow on the ground, but the cobblestones glistened. The whole area was lit by powerful klieg lights installed high on the department store GUM opposite the Kremlin wall. St. Basil's domes looked freshly painted, probably just for Nixon's visit; their twirled colors dazzled the eye.

We strolled around the square. It was filled with knots of tourists huddled around Intourist guides. A few militiamen patrolling in pairs looked on with apparent unconcern.

The atmosphere had been different two decades before. Toward the end of Stalin's rule, pedestrians had been barred from the square. An officer new to the embassy had carelessly wandered across it. "Then, suddenly, I realized I was all alone . . . there was nobody within a quarter mile of me."

A "big Russian militiaman in a long blue coat" ordered him to leave.[114] He was lucky not to have been expelled. The square reverted to its historic role as a place to stroll upon Stalin's death in March 1953.

On the morning after our arrival, Robin Porter, who had been a member of my A-100 course and had been at the embassy for a year already, showed up in the hotel's cavernous lobby to take three of us on a tour of the Metro system.

It was a beautiful day coming after a typically hard winter, and a *subbotnik* (from the Russian word for "Saturday") was underway, the one day a year when citizens "volunteered" their labor to clean up public places. The Garmisch visit couldn't have come at a better time; we'd see half of Moscow out on the streets.

A score of stout middle-aged women, several with *veniki*, were tidying up a tiny park in front of the hotel. They were working briskly, but savoring the sun. As we passed, Robin joked with them in his already accomplished Russian. These were the *babushka*s, literally, the grandmothers; a few may have been under forty, but they looked beat from the winter.

The next morning, two FSO colleagues and I set out on our own for the embassy. As we were late for an appointment, we cut across the park—more mud than grass—instead of using the sidewalk. A ruddy-faced woman looking no different from one of the *babushka*s the previous day confronted us, "How dare you walk here instead of on the sidewalk? Such uncultured (*nekulturniye*) behavior!"

In the early 1950s, Harrison Salisbury had encountered a similar *babushka* in front of the Hotel Metropol. She was hosing down a sidewalk when suddenly she turned the hose on him and other Americans with whom he was standing. "We were in her way," he said, and she "gave us an angry squirt."[115]

One learned to be wary of the *babushkas*.

During World War II, a seaman in Murmansk was heard to say, "I've dated all kinds of women in the world except Russians," and "I'd like to date one of them." He then watched as a woman stevedore picked up a length of piling weighing over a hundred pounds and tossed it nonchalantly out of her way. "On second thought," he said, "I don't believe I care to meet those women."[116]

In 1972, the *babushkas* could be seen everywhere in Moscow performing the heaviest and dirtiest work. By my last assignment, however, virtually all of them had disappeared. The women of the war generation were no longer extant, and their successors preferred working in factories and offices.

Not only had the demographics changed but also the attitudes; there weren't many Muscovites left who took an interest in the city's public places. By 1987, the Soviet Union was so demoralized that the *subbotniks* were poorly attended and few took notice if others misbehaved. The last time I walked by the park in front of the Ukraina it was filled with debris.

*   *   *

My two-year assignment began on June 28, 1972, five weeks after Nixon's visit. I had been appointed head of the consular section.

We arrived at Tchaikovsky 19 after a five-day drive (and two ferry rides) that took us through Hamburg, Copenhagen, Stockholm, Helsinki, and Leningrad.

The uniformed Soviet officers at the Finnish-Soviet border scrutinized the underside of our Volvo station wagon with a mirror, something I hadn't seen before. Having diplomatic passports, we weren't required to open our suitcases, but they studied them nonetheless through the vehicle's back windows. Few words were exchanged, and our children attracted no interest. The process took about an hour.

A uniformed soldier with a rifle over his shoulder patrolled a small bridge that we crossed ten or so miles after the border. It spanned a brook no wider than a few yards. There was no village in sight—the bridge was contiguous to nothing, yet a soldier stood guard.

There is a story, perhaps apocryphal, about a soldier outside a tsarist residence.[117] Nicholas I inquired as to what he was doing; no one knew, so they tracked down a retired general who explained that Catherine the Great had asked that a flower be protected in an adjoining garden, and a guard was posted. A half a century later, a guard was still there.

Perhaps the soldier on the bridge we crossed hadn't been told the war had ended.

I knew better than to take photographs once we reached Soviet territory. Before the trip, the embassy had sent me a list of dos and don'ts concerning photography, advising us against taking photographs of bridges, railroad crossings, the Metro subway, and the like. Later, in my consular role, I found I could do little but commiserate with tourists whose film had been confiscated, sometimes by genuinely irate Soviet citizens.

Truck traffic was continuous on the four-hundred-mile, two-lane road between Leningrad and Moscow. Passing was almost impossible, and passenger cars were rare.

Westerners traveling on their own were required to overnight at designated sites. We stopped in Novgorod, an ancient city, and located the hotel in a crumbling building. It was as decrepit inside as out.

When we reached Moscow and located the embassy, we were directed to the consular section in the north wing. Everyone was busy, and there wasn't much of a welcome; my predecessor was scheduled to leave in a few days and insisted we take advantage of the overlap. Liz and the children drove alone to our new home, an apartment thirty minutes away at Leninsky Prospect 45.

Leninsky 45 is a nine-story compound with twenty or so entryways off an interior courtyard. Altogether it would be our home for two assignments and five of the nearly seven years we lived in the Soviet Union.

Our apartment was on the top floor of an entryway that was taken up entirely by embassy families. Diplomats and businessmen from other countries resided with their families in five or six other entryways on either side of ours. Russian families occupied the others.

The courtyard covered about four acres and included an unkempt playground and a boarded-in area that could be flooded for ice hockey. Around the perimeter was a narrow roadway packed with cars with diplomatic plates. Few Russians owned cars in 1972, but by the end of the decade, we would have to compete for parking in the courtyard.

If you parked on the street outside, you risked losing your wipers, side mirrors, and costlier items. Liz once saw a woman at the Bolshoi Theatre powder her nose with the help of a mirror yanked off a Western car.

Inside the courtyard, opposite our entryway, was a small booth in which a militiaman stood. He kept an eye on everyone who entered the compound through the pedestrian and vehicle passageway next to our entryway. Any Soviet-appearing citizen who approached might be stopped and questioned. The telephone in the booth rang constantly as the militiaman, and those with whom he spoke, monitored incoming and outgoing traffic, pedestrian and vehicular. The militiaman was uniformed like a regular policeman but obviously worked with the KGB.

Our apartment contained six small rooms and two bathrooms, having been created out of two Soviet apartments. The embassy had furnished it with basic Scandinavian furniture, but the fixtures were mostly Russian. The three bedrooms had views of the courtyard, and when traffic subsided at night on Leninsky's eight lanes, we could hear the ringing of the guard's telephone.

A wood-framed elevator accommodating no more than four operated to the eighth floor. It shimmied its way up and down, sometimes stopping abruptly between the floors. The wives claimed that it was only out of order on days when the diplomatic pouch arrived at the embassy and they had to haul packages home.

The elevator ended its ascent before the ninth floor. A few speculated that the KGB needed the extra space in the room containing the hoisting machine—outside our apartment—for listening devices; but spy technology in the Soviet Union was never as backward as its elevators.

Because we were on the top floor, we had views of similar compounds. We could see the top floor of a Young Communist (Komsomol) hotel, the Sputnik, across Leninsky Prospect. Neon lights on commercial buildings were rare in the 1970s, but *Sputnik* was spelled out in bright red Cyrillic letters.

We settled into the apartment as fires were breaking out in the dry bog fields to Moscow's east. By the end of July 1972, smoke permeated the city. Liz woke in the middle of one night and, seeing the glare of Sputnik's neon through the smoke, cried out half-asleep, "The city's on fire." An image of Moscow aflame from a film we had seen must have flashed through a nightmare.

*   *   *

Jacob Beam was the ambassador when we arrived. By 1972 he had been in the Foreign Service forty years. His career had intersected with Kennan's at various junctures. He had first been sent to Moscow in December 1952 as the chargé d'affaires after the Foreign Ministry declared Kennan *persona non grata*. Kennan had arrived in May that year, but as previously noted, had compared conditions for diplomats in Moscow with those in wartime Germany while speaking with journalists during a stopover at Berlin's Tempelhof Airport in September. His comments had infuriated the regime, and it barred his return.

Beam's assignment lasted only until May 1953, but from a career standpoint, the timing couldn't have been better. Stalin died in March that year, and in April, at a reception at Moscow's Aragvi Restaurant, the acting head of the Foreign Ministry press department, Kartsev, took Beam aside to say, "There have been many mistakes in the past. The important thing is that we must forget the past and start out anew." Later in the evening, Kartsev proposed a toast to the health and success of President Dwight D. Eisenhower.[118] Clearly, changes were under way.

Beam was among the first to move into Tchaikovsky 19, located a mile and a half from Red Square. The Foreign Ministry had ordered the Americans and the British to vacate their embassies downtown by January 1, 1953.[119] Stalin had reportedly become obsessed by the presence of "enemies" near the Kremlin, although Mokhovaya 13 was hardly visible from his office. However, it had been designed by Ivan Zholtovsky, an architect to whom Stalin had given a Stalin Prize in 1950; perhaps the dictator couldn't tolerate Americans in a building designed by an architect whom he had honored.

The Americans complied with the order. The Britons, occupying an embassy on the other side of the Moscow River opposite the Kremlin, stalled. After Stalin's death, the order to vacate was withdrawn. The Britons still have their embassy opposite the Kremlin.

Beam's office was located on the ninth floor of Tchaikovsky 19's central wing, along with the office of his deputy and a smaller office in between shared by their two secretaries. The offices fronted on Tchaikovsky; but having been carved from space intended to be a Soviet apartment (or perhaps two), they were cramped.

The seventh and eighth floors of the central wing contained the political, economic, agricultural, science, and press and culture (P&C) sections. P&C also had a downstairs office in the north wing fronting on Tchaikovsky Street, a less secure area but readily accessible to outside visitors without security clearances.

The defense attaché office and those involved in electronic intelligence operated on the tenth floor and in the attic above. The CIA's quarters were on the seventh floor near the political section. Some CIA officers operated undercover from other sections, but not from the consular section when I was in charge. The communications center, or central processing unit (CPU), was a few steps from the ambassador's office on the ninth. Behind a closed door, opposite the center, was "the tank," as most officers in the embassy knew it, or "the bubble," as visitors from Washington tended to call it—the secure room where conversations could be conducted by twenty or so without fear of eavesdropping. It was a transparent room inside a windowless room, a structure of double-wall Plexiglas elevated from the floor that was effective as an acoustic barrier.

The consular section was in the north wing on the ground floor where it could be reached by Soviet citizens intending to emigrate, by third-country citizens, and by Americans. It shared a waiting room with "P&C down"; by the end of the 70s, it would have taken over the entirety of the wing's ground-floor space, and the downstairs office of P&C would have been relocated to the south wing.

Administrative offices were on the central wing's ground floor, also accessible. Apartments for senior officers and some staff members filled the middle floors of the central wing and the middle and upper floors of the north and south wings, which were six and seven stories in height, respectively.

In the central wing basement there was a small single-aisle commissary with basic foodstuffs imported from a military base in West Germany. Once or twice during an assignment, families bulk-shipped food in from abroad and stored it wherever they could—under their beds, in closets, in bathrooms. How much should one order? One family I knew kept a detailed yearlong record of its food and toilet paper needs in the United States and, before it reached Moscow, ordered accordingly. The commissary served as a backup source for essentials.

Behind the embassy building was a walled compound no larger than a half an acre. Within it stood several one and two-story wooden annexes, including a garage where official vehicles were parked and serviced, a small medical office directed by an American military doctor, and a cafeteria known as Uncle Sam's, managed by a German when we arrived, later by an Italian. The compound was American controlled, but Soviet citizens employed at the embassy could walk freely in and out of most of the ground-floor offices and annexes.

Beam's office, like all those on the upper floors, could be reached only through a heavy door off the ninth-floor landing behind which was the marine guard post. With few exceptions, the marine would only permit security-cleared Americans as well as diplomats and officials from other Western countries to proceed beyond the post.

Once beyond, the visitor would come to a narrow internal staircase that led upstairs to the suite of defense attaché offices and downstairs to the political, economic, science, agricultural as well as the press and culture (P&C Up) sections. The internal staircase was the vital link, the connector between the embassy's three upstairs floors, where most of the substantive reporting was done. Its risers were not evenly spaced, and it wasn't unusual to stumble when charging up or down to attend a meeting, secure a clearance from a colleague, or collect or send a telegram.

The upper-floor spaces allotted to communications, CIA, NSA, and defense personnel were controlled by additional locks and alarms. The CIA office on the eighth floor resembled a minisubmarine with a hatchlike entrance and interior walls packed with electronic gear. During my time, I never saw the NSA operation, having "no need to know," one of security's venerable rules.

One either climbed the central wing's main staircase or took one of two elevators on the ground floor to reach the entrance to the ninth. A Soviet-made wooden elevator operated inside a glass shaft fixed to the central wing's exterior. From its small cage, during its tortoiselike ascent, splendid views of the courtyard opened up; but it was bitterly cold in winter. An American-made Otis elevator occupied a shaft inside the central wing, accessible a half a flight up from the courtyard entrance. The ride was comfortable for four, less for five; but, alas, the elevator was out of commission more often than its rudimentary twin and required periodic attention from a West German mechanic whose arrival would invariably be delayed because of his need for a Soviet entry visa. Sometimes out of frustration, sometimes out of a need to exercise, we simply climbed the nine flights. If a congressional or official delegation bound for the ambassador's office was waiting outside the elevators, the climb was inevitable.

With one exception, Soviet citizens could not get beyond the ninth-floor marine into the embassy's upper floors. Every few nights, the marines would accompany one or two Russian char women (*babushkas*, hired by way of the Foreign Ministry) through the offices, but not through those occupied by communication, CIA, NSA, or defense-attache personnel who did their own cleaning. Rushing through their tasks under the marines' control, the char force removed the unclassified material that had piled up in wastebaskets during the day and did light dusting and vacuuming. It was a perfunctory exercise at best, and no office in Tchaikovsky 19 ever looked clean.

*   *   *

A day or so after our arrival, Ambassador Beam invited me to his office. Mrs. Margaret Beam—warm, outgoing, and known by everyone as Peggy—invited Liz to join her at Spaso House for tea.

Beam had attended Princeton after graduating from Kent School. His father was a professor of German at the university at the time; Beam spoke German but no Russian. He had served in Berlin from 1934 to 1940, doing political reporting as Hitler was consolidating power and preparing for war. When leaving Berlin for the last time, the American diarist William Shirer wrote that he was glad to leave behind "Nazi fanaticism, sadism, persecution, regimentation, terror" but would miss friends like Jake Beam.[120]

Beam then went to London as a staff aide to Ambassador John Winant. Beam gave one American journalist the impression "of being frightened of his job . . . . He would open the door to Winant's huge office and vanish."[121] Winant doesn't mention Beam in his memoir.

I had written Beam from Garmisch to introduce myself. He was gracious during our meeting but didn't allude to any of the associations we shared. In

1958, when he was serving as the ambassador to Poland, he had inaugurated the first American negotiation with the Communist Chinese. The sessions took place every few months in a small palace in Lazienki Park opposite the embassy. Early in my Warsaw assignment, I had served as the note-taker on the American side opposite the Chinese, who were led by the same ambassador with whom Beam had conducted the talks.

I was struck by how shy and self-effacing Beam was. When speaking at the weekly country-team meeting in the tank, he would often lift his hand and cup it over his mouth, making himself almost inaudible. I could understand why the journalist in London had concluded he was "frightened" of his job. As a young FSO, he must have been painfully diffident. I wasn't surprised when I learned later that he had roomed by himself at Princeton.

*   *   *

The consular section consisted of three Foreign Service officers.

Steve Steiner handled applications from Soviet citizens to immigrate to the United States; fewer than three hundred had done so in 1971, but the number had increased to five hundred in 1972 and more by the time Steve and I had left in 1974.

Jon Glassman, who had been in the section a year, processed applications from Soviet and third-country citizens seeking to visit the United States. The Foreign Ministry delivered the nonimmigrant applications to us, and we waived the interviews because of a bilateral understanding. Most of these applicants were Soviet officials, but every year a few hundred ordinary (but trusted) Russians were permitted to visit the United States in large delegations, usually as a reward for surpassing a plan or contributing to the Communist Party at their workplace. Virtually every applicant required a waiver under American law because of a Party connection.

I supervised the office and with Steve and Jon's help coped with the myriad of problems that American tourists, even officials, would encounter. Appeals for assistance reached us from almost every corner of the USSR, from entry and exit points, customs offices, militia stations, hotels, and so forth. Many visiting for the first time were fearful; in my first year, two Americans—one a member of an official delegation, the other a tourist—suffered nervous breakdowns while standing on Red Square.

Often we had to appear in person to deal with a problem. Jon and I were once informed that an American woman was being detained at Moscow's Kashchenko Psychiatric Hospital. We arranged for one of the embassy's Russian drivers to take us there. He talked his way past the guards (it wasn't always easy) and drove us around the hospital's extensive grounds and buildings until we found the section where the woman was housed. From conversations with her and her doctors, we surmised she was receiving adequate care. Displaced from Ukraine during World War II, she had suffered a breakdown while seeing her native village after an absence of many years.

As we were leaving, we passed a group of inmates in pajamas marching in a circle under a guard's watchful eye. The hospital was already known for "treating" Soviet troublemakers; in 1982, a Russian émigré would mention the hospital in *The First Guidebook to Prisons and Concentration Camps of the Soviet Union*.[122] The report that Jon forwarded to Washington dealt with more than the patient.

Steve, Jon, and I were in the Foreign Service's political track, having made this choice after our first assignments abroad. There had been a long tradition of initially assigning political officers in Moscow to the consular section; diplomats doing consular work tend to learn quickly what life in a country is really like. Harold Nicolson, author of a classic study, *Diplomacy*, observed that he would have learned more about Turkey had he started as a vice consul in Adana than as a diplomatic third secretary in Constantinople.[123] Nicolson was writing about the Ottoman Empire before World War I, but his observation is just as valid today. A diplomat doesn't gain deep insights into a culture from associating with a capital's officials and third-country diplomats.

By the middle 1970s, the State Department was beginning to restrict officers to jobs and functions corresponding to their tracks; and Steve, Jon, and I were probably the last political officers to serve in Moscow's consular section. Most FSOs today select their track *before* embarking on their first assignment, which deprives them of the opportunity to experience the full range of work in consulates and embassies and to make an enlightened choice of a track.

An American Foreign Service secretary and four Soviet women completed our section. The Soviet women, Russian and Ukrainian by background, performed routine tasks such as preparing visas and making passports, but we signed every document ourselves and kept control of the instrument to impress the seal over our signatures, whether written on visas, passports or sworn statements. The women knew their way around the Soviet bureaucracy and often helped us connect with the correct authority.

Physically, the consular section was divided into three areas: a room where visitors—at least those who managed to get by the Soviet guards—could wait for service; a narrow, desk-jammed room where the Soviet staff worked; and a secure area behind a Dutch door where the four of us worked. Our area was subdivided into four offices and a back area with a tiny conference room, a miniature of the ninth floor tank where we could hold confidential discussions. A hallway on our side of the Dutch door contained safes and cabinets with classified material. The only Soviet citizens permitted beyond the door were those applying to emigrate or those with whom we needed to speak in private, and, of course, the char force that breezed through at night.

The senior woman was Mary Litvinenko. She had returned to Moscow from the United States as a child before the war and spoke perfect English. During the overlap I had with my predecessor, he warned me that Mary worked for the KGB. "Are you sure?" I asked.

He said that only six months earlier, he had handed an American passport to a former embassy employee, Alexander Dolgun, enabling him to return to the United States after almost four decades in the Soviet Union, including a term in various prisons. Dolgun had come to Moscow from the United States in 1933, when he too was a child and had been forced to become a Soviet citizen. He was working in a clerical job in the embassy's consular section in December 1948 when he was arrested on a trumped-up charge of espionage and sent to prison for twenty-five years.[124] When Dolgun received his American passport in 1971, he apparently identified Mary as one of those implicated in his arrest.

Had Mary been compelled to cooperate with the Soviet authorities, or did she volunteer? Years had passed and no one but Mary could say, and of course, Mary wouldn't say. Interestingly, during his years in the Gulag, Dolgun had crossed paths with two other prisoners who had worked at the embassy until denounced by colleagues.

There was little the embassy could have done for Dolgun in 1948. Soviet officials would have claimed that he was a Soviet citizen, and therefore the embassy had no right to intervene. Even if they had conceded his possible claim to American citizenship, we had no consular agreement with Moscow that would have helped us press for access.

In 1956, Khrushchev arranged a general amnesty under which Dolgun and millions of other prisoners from Stalin's camps were released. Dolgun was instructed never to go near the embassy.

In 1964, an agreement that gave consular officers the right to visit and communicate with Americans under arrest or detention came into force, a few months before Khrushchev was ousted. I kept a copy, in Russian and English, on top of my desk and carried it with me wherever I went, even if only to a ministry or an airport.

Because a KGB-dominated branch (UPDK) of the Foreign Ministry supplied the Soviet citizens who worked at embassies and consulates, there was no practical way to avoid a KGB presence in one's midst.[125] An embassy could try to operate without Soviet employees, as the embassy was forced to do after Gorbachev withdrew them in 1986; but this created manifold problems, as will be seen.

The second-ranking Russian in our section was Maya. Grey-haired and reserved, Maya did not seem the kind of person who would denounce a colleague, yet she took her orders from Mary, and I never doubted she was loyal to the state.

The third woman in the office, Tamara, made no pretense of being amiable to us or her own people, the latter visiting usually in connection with emigrating.

Finally, there was Svetlana, an attractive married woman in her early thirties, soft-spoken with a ready smile. Once in a conversation at a Christmas party, when we exchanged token gifts, she told me that a relative of hers had been sent to a labor camp for arriving late to work during "Stalin's time." We may have been talking about punctuality, and the other three Soviet women were out of earshot, but the comment was unusual: Russians rarely used the dictator's name in the 1970s, especially with foreigners.

Khrushchev had denounced Stalin for his crimes at the Party Congress in 1956, but then had been ousted, and Leonid Brezhnev had maintained a stony public silence about the dictator since. As a result, Russians were uncomfortable using the name; by the early 1970s, Stalin was almost as much of a non-person as those of his allies whom he had ordered shot.

When the section's workload became heavier during my second year, we asked the Foreign Ministry for a fifth employee, and a personable young woman with fluent English appeared. Mary introduced her. After a few days, we could see that she would fit in nicely; unlike the others, she bantered with us in a relaxed way. After a third week, however, she stopped coming. Mary offered no explanation, but it was obvious that the newcomer's friendliness had displeased her. Mary probably feared that the new employee would end up reporting on her, and not on us.

The Soviet employees were efficient, but our relationship with them was more formal than friendly, far different from the way it had been in Warsaw.

*　　*　　*

A few days after Liz and I arrived, we were invited to the Fourth of July celebration at Spaso House, the ambassador's residence. Spaso House is a handsome neoclassical two-story building set on a spacious lawn behind a wrought-iron fence, a fifteen-minute walk from the embassy. It lies almost in the shadow of the Stalin-era high-rise that houses the Foreign Ministry. Built on the eve of World War I, it has been the residence of American ambassadors from shortly after the United States and the Soviet Union established diplomatic relations in 1933.[126]

The main floor includes a grand reception area under a huge crystal chandelier, a ballroom, and a dining room, and a few rooms radiating off them, including a kitchen and a switchboard. The second floor contains the ambassador's private quarters and two guestrooms. Although several hundred guests could be accommodated at functions on the main floor, ambassadors would bank on having their July 4 reception outdoors, and during my three assignments the weather always cooperated.

For our first Independence Day, it was sunny, the sky not yet dimmed by the bog fires to the east. Because I was a Russian-speaking FSO, I was instructed to appear early, which I did with Liz.

Spaso House's regular staff had been augmented for the occasion. Tables with plates of sandwiches, apples, and deviled eggs topped with caviar had been set up about the lawn. Heaped on every table were packages of American cigarettes. Bartenders stood in readiness behind rows of open bottles of vodka and whiskey. Waiters armed with trays of prepoured drinks were poised to circulate as soon as the guests arrived.

A diminutive Chinese native, Tang Yu-lin, was Spaso House's head waiter and its oldest employee. Tang had come to the USSR in 1933 as the servant of an American correspondent. In 1939, he had gone to work for Ambassador Laurence Steinhardt and had served every ambassador since.

After the war, Tang had married a Russian woman. When they tried to emigrate, the Soviet authorities said *nyet*, and they had no choice but to adapt. They obtained an apartment and raised a family. But Tang considered the residence his real home; when the ambassador was present, he spent nights in a basement cubicle, awaiting summons from above.

A cheery Italian majordomo, Clemente, oversaw the receptions and dinner parties. He and his Italian wife, Maria, who often worked as a waitress alongside Tang, lived in a carriage house behind the residence. Ambassador Foy Kohler had hired Clemente in 1965. Kohler had been succeeded by Llewellyn Thompson (serving as ambassador to Moscow for a second time) in December 1967; Beam had succeeded Thompson in April 1969. It was rare for a majordomo to survive successive ambassadorial couples, but each had found Clemente capable and to their liking. Maria was as quiet as Clemente was voluble, but worked with a gracious style that suited the residence.

Clemente was murdered in 1991. By then, he had served eight ambassadors and countless American visitors, including two presidents who had stayed at Spaso House while attending summits or funerals. By the time of his death, there was probably no one in the Foreign Service who remembered Spaso House as it had been before him.

In the aftermath of the Nixon-Brezhnev summit, the Beams sent Independence Day invitations to several hundred Soviet officials, cultural figures, and journalists, as well as guests from the United States and other countries, including diplomats, businesspersons, and journalists. During the worst years of the Cold War, only a small fraction of Soviet invitees would ever appear. In 1947, Ambassador Smith had invited three hundred Soviets, and twenty-five had turned up; this, he wrote, was better than usual.[127]

During periods when U.S.-Soviet relations seemed to be improving, Soviet leaders themselves had attended. In 1955, the Party's First Secretary Khrushchev, Foreign Minister Molotov, Chairman of the Council of Ministers Bulganin, and a deputy chairman from the council, Malenkov (who had lost the chairman's post to Bulganin five months earlier), arrived together.

The May 1972 summit had achieved a major breakthrough in U.S.-Soviet relations. Eight agreements had been signed, including two limiting strategic arms and antiballistic missiles. Brezhnev and Nixon had also agreed on a set of twelve "Basic Principles of Relations" that would henceforth govern relations. The first proclaimed that "there is no alternative to conducting their mutual relations on the basis of peaceful coexistence"; the second affirmed that "discussions and negotiations on outstanding issues will be conducted in a spirit of reciprocity, mutual accommodation and mutual benefit."

Attaining "reciprocity" between states with such radically different systems would be a challenge, but everything said and written at the summit pointed to improving relations.

Against this background, many expected a large turnout, including Foreign Minister Andrei Gromyko and perhaps even Kosygin or, less likely, Brezhnev.

The turnout was large indeed, and the guests arrived punctually. A few Foreign Ministry officials came in the black dress uniform with gold braid that Stalin had introduced during the war. Defense Ministry officials appeared in their dress uniforms bedecked with the usual profusion of medals.

Within a few minutes, all the cigarettes had disappeared, and the waiters couldn't keep up.

To my surprise, however, none of the leaders appeared, not Gromyko, not Kosygin, nor any other. The ranking official was Vladimir Kirillin, one of Kosygin's thirteen deputies in the Council of Ministers, a member of the Party's Central Committee but by no means one who could be deemed a leader.

As I recall, Gromyko's seventy-one-year-old deputy, Vasili Kuznetsov, led the contingent from the Foreign Ministry. Kuznetsov had done graduate work in metallurgy at Pittsburgh's Carnegie Tech in the early 1930s and then had worked briefly for the Ford Motor Company before returning in 1933. He spoke English fluently and had helped host Richard Nixon when he visited as Eisenhower's vice president in 1959.

The absence of leaders puzzled me, but as I learned more about Beam's relationship with Nixon and his national security advisor Kissinger, I would come to understand.

The officials responsible for consular affairs, from the ministry's consular administration, had arrived as a team. They said they were delighted to meet Steve and me, the embassy's newest officers, and allowed that our Russian would do. I knew from my predecessor that a majority of them had been involved at one time or another in intelligence or counterintelligence work. Not that I was surprised; since they dealt with travel in and out of the Soviet Union, it was a logical place for those who had worked in the KGB, the GRU, or a related or predecessor organization, if indeed they weren't still working for one or another under the ministry's cover. Perhaps a telltale sign was that none of those we met, except the distinguished former ambassador who headed the consular administration, wore the ministry's formal uniform.

From our own sources, we knew that one official, Ivan Ivanovich Vasilyev, had worked in the GRU in the eastern zone of Germany. Now in his late fifties or early sixties, he was dressed in a baggy suit instead of a uniform, but stood erect like an officer. His face was deeply lined, his manner sardonic, and it occurred to me that his kind had probably been involved in the kidnappings from Berlin's western zones that had marked the Cold War's start. With Nixon and Brezhnev's successful summit, however, no one at the reception was focusing on things like this.

The consular officials drank heavily. Periodically Steve, Jon, or I would raise the need for making progress on our family reunification cases, but they'd drown out any effort at serious talk by offering another toast.

By late afternoon, five of them were drunk. Locked together arm to arm, they staggered from one end of the lawn to the other. Other guests had imbibed heavily, but they weren't careening about in a comradely embrace.

Finally, the entire consular team lurched down Spaso House's driveway, passed the guards at the gate, and disappeared into the late-afternoon crush, heading back to their offices in the ministry or to a Metro station.

The next morning, the heads of sections gathered with Beam to share the information we had gleaned from the event. It was my first meeting in the ninth-floor tank, my first as a member of the country team. The ambassador sat at the head of the table with the deputy chief of mission at his left. The heads of the political, economic, P&C, agricultural, administrative, and defense attaché sections sat along the sides as did the station chief, while I took a chair at the far end. It would be the first of countless country-team meetings I'd attend during my career.

Beam said little as each section head spoke. As the meeting drew to an end, however, he looked in my direction and, citing the ministry's consular officials, said we couldn't tolerate this kind of behavior again.

Of course, it hadn't only been the consular types who had done the drinking. A deputy director of the ministry's American department, Konstantin Fedoseyev, a slightly built man well into his sixties, was notoriously fond of alcohol and had also stumbled out of the yard. But Fedoseyev was one of the embassy's more sophisticated interlocutors, as were a several others in the ministry's geographic departments, and I would find him good company as I came to know him from conversations at other diplomatic functions. Fedoseyev also had a good relationship with Ambassador Anatoli Dobrynin, having served with him in Washington in the early 1950s.

It was clear from the reception that I would be working with a different type of Russian than my colleagues upstairs. It was not the type ambassadors liked, but it was the type we as consular officers had been dealt.

The thrust of the postmortem was that U.S.-Soviet relations were on the upswing. Although none of the Soviet leaders had appeared, the officials who did appear seemed ready to move forward.

From all the effusive toasting we had done, I felt that our new consular contacts wouldn't dare lag behind. It might take time, and it might take cajoling from the ministry's political level and even from the Kremlin, but I was confident that our counterparts would come around. It would be the embassy's responsibility, and the responsibility of Kissinger and his people, to impress on the Soviet political level that détente was also needed in the consular sphere. Without Moscow's cooperation, we couldn't solve our most pressing problem—securing exit visas for American and Soviet citizens who had been blocked from joining their American families, often for years.

*   *   *

By the middle of 1972, an increasing number of Soviet citizens wanted to get out. A few were native-born Americans—like Dolgun (who did get out) and Litvinenko (who had no interest in doing so)—who had been brought to the Soviet Union as children.

Jobs had been scarce in the United States during the Depression, and many Americans had headed overseas looking for work, including in the USSR. Other Americans, out of naïveté, had been lured by Soviet propaganda, seeking their support in building Lenin and Stalin's vaunted "paradise." Having been induced or forced to obtain Soviet citizenship before the war, many now wanted to return, often with Soviet spouses and children.

In the Soviet Armenian republic alone, there were scores of persons who had close relatives in the United States or elsewhere in the West. Many had been drawn to Armenia after the war because it seemed to be the homeland about which they had been dreaming since their forbears were expelled from the Ottoman Empire. Edmund Stevens's wife, Nina, writes of how, in 1945, Stalin had diverted the Soviet ship on which she and her children were returning to the Soviet Union from its mid-Atlantic course in order to pick up five thousand Armenians in Lebanon.[128] The Soviet regime had ordered the captain to collect and deliver them to Batumi in the Black Sea from which they could make the overland trip to Yerevan, the Armenian capital.

Upon arriving and seeing the conditions, many had tried to return to the communities from which they had come, but virtually all were refused.

Writing in 1953, the embassy's navy attaché told the story of an Armenian-American girl whom a colleague met on a train traveling back to Yerevan from Moscow. The girl was in tears, having failed to contact an American consular officer, as her parents—trapped in Armenia—had asked her to do. Soviet guards had blocked the girl from entering the embassy. In fact, had she made it past the guards, "there was little the embassy could have done but protest," as the attaché noted.[129]

The State Department and the embassy maintained a list of scores of residents of the USSR who wanted to leave for the United States, who either had close relatives with American citizenship or had claims themselves to citizenship. My predecessor had handed me a copy of the list—Representation List XIV it was called—as soon as I walked through the Dutch door. If the Armenian girl and her parents were alive, they were probably on the list, still waiting for exit visas after thirty years.

Others seeking to leave for the United States included Russian Jews or Jews from non-Russian parts of the Soviet empire. Some had American relatives who had made their way out before or during the war. The Soviet authorities had blocked their emigration under various pretexts, one being that if the would-be emigrant had once held a white-collar job, he or she probably knew Soviet "secrets." In the early 1970s, Western journalists gave the name "refusenik" to any educated Jew whose application to leave had been repeatedly denied.

For those having no claim to American citizenship or no American relative, the possibility of securing an exit visa to immigrate to the United States was nonexistent. In 1948, the USSR had abstained from signing the

Universal Declaration of Human Rights that recognized everyone's "right to freedom of movement" and "to leave any country, including his own." But the declaration was adopted anyway, and although the Soviet regime denied the right to leave to the vast majority of its citizens, I never encountered a Soviet official who rejected my assertion that "freedom of movement" was an internationally recognized right. It was just that there were always extenuating circumstances arising from "the needs of the state."

In 1949, the embassy had sent the ministry an aide-mémoire listing "groups of American citizens . . . estimated to total 2,000 persons" who had been denied permission to leave.[130] At the time, over a score were being detained in Stalin's camps. After the collapse of the Soviet Union, it was confirmed that one of them, Isaac Oggins, had been executed by the NKVD[131], the ministry from which the KGB emerged.

Oggins was an American Communist who had been living in the USSR since 1937. An embassy officer had interviewed him in a Moscow prison at the request of his wife, who had made her way to the United States before the war. Stalin and Molotov feared that Oggins, if released, "would talk," perhaps reveal information about the American Communist Party to the House Un-American Activities Committee. So in 1947, he was summoned for a routine medical exam in Ulyanovsk—Lenin's birthplace—and given a lethal dose of poison.[132]

Only one American was in prison when I arrived, and we learned about him toward the end of my assignment, as I relate in chapter 6.

Representation List XIV, which I received, contained the names of about two hundred families desperate to emigrate. One American in the United States had been waiting for his wife and daughter since 1956.

A Soviet citizen could not simply appear at the embassy and ask for help. Guards stood in front of its two main entrances day and night.[133] They patrolled the corners of the block and adjoining buildings. Russians managed to climb the walls behind the annexes several times to reach the consular section during my first assignment, but we couldn't create an exit visa where none existed; and an American immigration visa counted for nothing if exit permission hadn't been granted. Our "visitors" would usually leave after a few hours, to be arrested by the guards upon departing. Soviet citizens going into the embassy without permission were aware of the risk.

Through prearrangement, Steve, John, or I would sometimes meet an intending visitor outside, usually in the park in front of the nearby high-rise, and escort him or her in. If we flanked the visitor and made it difficult for the guards to interfere, we usually succeeded. The guards were generally shrewd enough not to manhandle a diplomat, and of course, they could grab any visitor upon his or her departure.

If we heard a ruckus outside, we sometimes ran out to help. If an intending visitor had been subdued and removed to the beat-up box, there was little to be done except argue. If we had the name of the visitor, we could complain to the Foreign Ministry, but this yielded the standard response, "The guards are here to protect you from unauthorized visitors."

Securing the telephone number of the embassy to speak with a consular officer was also a challenge; there was no public telephone book listing the number.

Because mail reaching the embassy through the domestic system was monitored, it was impossible for a Soviet citizen to inquire about immigrating without drawing attention. And anyone who inquired could put his job and housing at risk.

Consular work in Moscow involved dealing with the underside of Soviet reality. As will be seen, during the height of détente from 1972 to 1975, not everyone in Washington wanted to be reminded that the underside still existed.

5

Venturing Outside the Embassy

The head of the embassy's security office (SY) briefed Liz and me in the tank a day or so after we arrived. He cautioned against currency dealings, sexual misconduct, and other misbehavior, and provided graphic accounts of how Americans had been compromised by the KGB. I recall being told to steer clear of the bar in the Hotel Intourist, three blocks from the old embassy building at Mokhovaya. "That's where the British defectors Donald Maclean and Harold Philby hang out." Maclean had fled to Moscow in 1951 with Guy Burgess; Philby, having warned them about their likely arrest, fled in 1963. All three had once belonged to the British Foreign Service.

Security tailored its warnings to the nature of one's job. Communications and secretarial personnel were discouraged from associating with any Russians outside the embassy; those responsible for meeting with Soviet officials obviously were not. From time to time, a technician from security would electronically sweep the offices to locate listening devices; he didn't bother with the apartments—everyone assumed they were bugged.

The FSI's A-100 course had included warnings about the KGB, and the vast majority of FSOs sent to Moscow and Leningrad had previously served in Eastern Europe. No new arrival could have been surprised by SY's "welcome."

At first I was cautious about meeting unofficial Russians outside the embassy, but I was on the Foreign Service's political track and had no intention of confining my Russian experience to Soviet officials.

Within a month or two, most of us had been the object of at least one probe to ascertain our vulnerability. On one of my first mornings, standing outside Leninsky 45 waiting for an embassy van to take me to work, an attractive dark-haired woman dashed up. "I need to speak with you urgently," she whispered to me in Russian. "Can you come with me around the corner?" She seemed near tears as she beckoned me away from the courtyard entrance that the militiaman kept in sight.

It might have been an innocent appeal, from someone desperate to emigrate, and my initial instinct was to follow. But I had just received my briefing, and my colleagues would be arriving any moment to catch the van. So I waved her off. Had she approached me a month later, I would have gone, at least to hear her story.

Six months later, while Liz, the children, and I were enjoying a break in Tarasovka with David Evans and his family (we had served together in Warsaw), we heard of a less subtle approach made the year before. Late one evening, David heard insistent knocking on the door of his apartment at the Vavilova compound not far from ours. David's wife—Stephanie—and their two children had left the previous evening for Helsinki on the Soviet wagon-lit to purchase winter supplies.

Rousing himself, David went to the door, opened it a crack, and found a partially clad young woman pleading to be admitted. Half a landing below, over her bare shoulder, he happened to see the shadow of a man. The shadow was reason enough to slam the door.

Militiamen were posted near all the diplomatic entryways, and one of their tasks was to keep Russians away. The appearance of an unknown Russian outside one's door put one on alert; he or she would have been extremely clever to have eluded the guard, or been in cahoots with him.

Of course, we could be approached anytime and anywhere: on the street, in the theater, on the Metro. Our foreign-made clothes were readily identifiable. Occasionally, a Russian in a pedestrian underpass (there was one a block from the embassy, under Tchaikovsky Street) would thrust a letter or message in one's hand before melting away. Security warned us against accepting anything from someone we didn't know. "You might be photographed as part of a provocation. Let it drop to the ground."

CIA officers had, in fact, followed up a few of these letters with good results. The longer one stayed in Moscow, the more one relied on one's own good instincts rather than rules.

Apparently, the operative belief on Dzerzhinskaya Square, where the KGB's Moscow headquarters stood, was that most Westerners couldn't resist sex, money, or alcohol, or a combination of the three. Probably officials at the FBI and the CIA trolling for recruits saw its Russian targets the same way. At least before learning of Aldrich Ames and Robert Hanssen, I would have said that the most successful spies were motivated by ideology, and they tended to work for the Americans.

Until the late 1980s, the security office didn't insist we go around the capital in pairs. Had we been required to do so, we would have drawn more attention to ourselves than we already did. Nor would our Russian acquaintances have understood. During most of my time in Moscow, Foreign Service personnel seemed to enjoy security's confidence.

Everyone understood that traveling alone outside the capital wouldn't be advisable. From the onset of the Cold War, the Soviets had paid special attention to foreigners traveling by themselves far from their posts. In 1947, the embassy's navy attaché let one of his noncommissioned officers ride an overnight train to Odessa alone; a young Russian woman appeared in the twin compartment and "started removing her clothes for bed as soon as the journey began." Not without pride in his service branch, the attaché noted that his colleague had "kept his distance."[134] Around the same time, a Turkish official couriering a diplomatic pouch alone on a Soviet train was found shot in the back of the head.[135]

Everyone assigned to an embassy or a consulate in the USSR was sure to come into contact with the KGB if only because it had agents among the locally hired staff. It was a rare foreign mission without a single Soviet or third-country employee.

If a Russian working at an embassy did not belong to the KGB, he or she would at least be expected to comply with its "request" for an interview. Self-preservation dictated as much.

Speculation about the KGB's "representation" at Tchaikovsky 19 was daily fare, especially in Uncle Sam's, but the opinions aired were only that; no one ever knew for sure. Valentina, the garrulous blonde hairdresser in the basement, plied Americans with questions about the community, but she didn't seem to take umbrage if no one responded. Perhaps she was just a busybody, a universal type such as inhabit hair salons, yet she ranked high on everyone's list.

A Russian maintenance worker once tackled a Soviet citizen as he broke past the guards and entered the courtyard to see an American. The maintenance man was fired; overtly hostile behavior wasn't allowed.

I embarked on relationships with Soviet citizens knowing that they were probably involved with the KGB.

Liz and I first met Viktor Louis at Ambassador Beam's Independence Day affair. Born in the Soviet Union in 1928 as Vitali Lui, he had Westernized his name after beginning work as a translator for foreign journalists. This was after his release from a labor camp where he had been incarcerated for petty corruption.

Viktor soon established himself as a journalist. He was working for a London newspaper in October 1964 when he telephoned Roger Provencher, an FSO at the embassy, to say that Khrushchev's portrait had been removed from its usual places of display in downtown Moscow. Roger promptly notified Washington. Viktor then broke the story of

Khrushchev's downfall for the *London Evening Standard*. Roger was still talking about "his" scoop when I met him on his second Moscow tour in 1972.

Among the stories Viktor sent abroad in the early 1970s were several aimed at discrediting Moscow's dissidents, including Alexandr Solzhenitsyn and Andrei Sakharov. By then, few had any doubt about his KGB connection.

Some prisoners released from the camps yielded more easily than others to official pressure, and Viktor may have been one. A report published after his death suggests that he first became involved with the NKVD, the ministry from which the KGB emerged, while running errands for Western embassies.[136] A Russian woman who was interpreting for the French embassy at that time claimed that his informing cost her ten years of imprisonment.[137] Viktor himself denied the relationship. "Did I collaborate with the KGB? Nonsense," he declared in 1991. "They didn't touch me simply because I had already done my term."[138] As if completing a term would have protected him.

In the early 1960s, Viktor married a British woman, Jennifer Statham, while she was working in Moscow as a nanny for a British family. Jennifer would bring their three children to the Protestant church services when they were held at the British embassy, more frequently the site than Spaso House or Uncle Sam's.

When President Roosevelt and Foreign Minister Maxim Litvinov exchanged letters formalizing diplomatic relations in 1933, one from Roosevelt stipulated that Americans serving in the Soviet Union would "have their spiritual needs ministered to by clergymen, priests, rabbis, or other ecclesiastical functionaries who are nationals of the United States."[139] In the early 1970s, an American Episcopalian, Ray Oppenheim, was ministering to the Protestants in Moscow's foreign community, and Father Joseph Richard, an American, was doing the same for the Roman Catholics. As there were few Jews then in the foreign community, there was no American rabbi. There were, however, two synagogues in the capital that officers could attend.

Elise, our oldest daughter, and Viktor and Jennifer Louis's oldest son, Nicholas, attended confirmation lessons together. For the service itself, an Anglican bishop, Kenneth Howell, came from London to officiate. The ceremony took place at the British embassy in a room connected to an exterior courtyard. During World War II, the British ambassador had used the room as his office and the courtyard as a garden to raise vegetables to supplement his staff's rations. According to Harrison Salisbury, he would "dig in his garden between callers and sometimes walked back into his office, his hands grimy, sweat pouring off his chest and trailing a shirt, to shake hands with some protocol-punctilious Russian from the Foreign Office."[140]

Viktor and Jennifer attended the service along with the thirty or so others who usually made up our Sunday congregation. Afterwards, they invited Bishop Howell, Father Ray and his wife, Liz, me, and our children to their dacha in Peredelkino for a celebratory "tea."

Viktor's Mercedes stood in front when we found the dacha, situated not far from Pasternak's. At the time, few Russians could afford an automobile, even the domestically manufactured *Zhiguli.*

The dacha was fully modernized and, by Soviet standards, luxuriously furnished, with ancient icons and works by Russia's "unofficial" artists adorning its walls. Viktor's bookshelves included publications few Russians dared possess, including English translations of works by Solzhenitsyn, who had been exiled to Western Europe a few months earlier. Elise, Nicholas, and the other children watched home movies of Viktor's world travels (for him, exit visas weren't much of a problem) while we enjoyed tea, cakes, French cognac, and Cuban cigars.

Before the afternoon ended, Viktor lined us up for group photographs. The bishop and Ray were invited to take chairs in front while Liz and I stood behind. From somewhere Viktor pulled out a tsarist military banner with the double-headed Romanov eagle and placed it in the bishop's hand.

I never received a copy of any of the photographs, but a set certainly landed at the KGB's Moscow headquarters. Years later, it emerged that Viktor had a warm relationship with Yuri Andropov, who became the spy agency's chairman in 1967 and the Party leader in 1983. (If Khrushchev's son Sergei is to be believed, Andropov didn't stand in the way when Viktor let him know he was smuggling Khrushchev's memoirs abroad.[141])

Liz and I would see Viktor and Jennifer at numerous diplomatic functions but weren't invited back to their dacha. When we returned to Moscow in 1978, I found that Ambassador Toon had declared Viktor off-limits. Toon's decision struck me as odd; his own embassy was the prime-paying customer of an annual English-language directory carrying indispensable telephone numbers that Viktor and Jennifer published, and Toon knew as well as anyone that foreigners living in the USSR all operated in a sea of agents.

Viktor died in 1992, shortly after the collapse of the system he had faithfully served. In 2000, Elise briefly visited Nicholas in England, where his mother and his siblings now reside. Nicholas and his wife use the family dacha when they pay visits to Moscow.

*   *   *

Early in the evening on November 29, 1972, as I was starting my sixth month, tragedy struck at Sheremetyevo Airport. A Japanese airline DC-8 carrying seventy-five passengers and crew crashed just after take-off. Bound for Tokyo on a nonstop flight, it had taken on thousands of gallons of fuel. It fell from about a thousand feet and landed beyond the runway in a ball of fire.

Soviet media were initially silent, in keeping with their practice of not reporting catastrophes until the authorities had developed an official line, but a Western journalist got wind of the accident and called Jon Glassman. Jon raced to the embassy (the three of us took turns covering off-hour consular problems) and confirmed the report through one of the Western airline representatives based in the capital. Within a few hours, the State Department was sending us telegrams, saying that Americans might have been on board.

We telephoned Botkin Hospital, a complex of sixty buildings a half-hour away, where ill or injured foreigners were usually taken (and were sometimes treated with Old Wives' remedies, such as cupping glasses that bring a patient's blood to the surface of the skin[142]). A spokesperson there told us that two Americans had been badly injured and were already under the hospital's care. (Readers of *Doctor Zhivago* will recall that Pasternak's hero was hurrying to Botkin when he suffered the fatal heart attack that ended the novel.)

It was difficult to gain access to hospitalized Americans (guards were present at every Soviet institution), but Steve got an embassy car and driver and headed out to Botkin. With another car, I went to the airport to track down the passenger list. As I neared the terminal, I could see that troops had cordoned off an area where the wreckage was still smoldering.

I had already been to the airport a half-dozen times to aid tourists and was confident I could get what we needed. This time, however, my contacts were unhelpful. One denied there had been an accident, although smoke was rising not far outside his window.

Telephoning back to the embassy, I asked that political counselor Tom Buchanan weigh in with the Foreign Ministry and insist that we be given access to the list and to any injured Americans in keeping with the consular agreement. The demarche was made, and the Soviets relented an hour later. I was escorted to a deputy minister of civil aviation at a command center that had been set up inside a guarded building opposite the terminal, from which I had already once been ousted.

The minister refused to make the list available but said two Americans had died. In the meantime, Steve had determined from the hospital that no Americans had been admitted there despite what the spokesman had earlier said.

Amid a welter of telegrams from Washington, I learned that three Americans had, in fact, been on board and none could be accounted for. The consular section then received a tip that a temporary morgue had been set up at the Sklifosovsky Institute of Emergency Medical Care, only a few blocks from Tchaikovsky 19. The embassy's doctor, Colonel Ron Walker, an air force attaché, and I rushed to the institute and talked our way in.

There we found a dimly lit hall filled with thirty or so metal tables. On each of them lay the blackened remains of two or more of the flight's passengers and crew, none with facial features and few with extremities. As we wound our way around the tables, we realized that visually identifying anyone would be impossible. The attending Soviet doctor told us that due to the fire (and, left unsaid, perhaps a lack of technology), even blood types were unascertainable.

Glassman, the doctor, and I made several other visits to the morgue but the experts could only identify a few remains, none of which were Caucasian. For public health reasons, they ordered a mass cremation. The Japanese embassy and the Japanese airline agreed.

We sent a report to Washington; and the department replied that two of the three Americans were Jewish and that cremation, for religious reasons, wouldn't be acceptable. The families in the United States were adamant that the remains of their loved ones be returned.

The department secured dental records from the families and sent them by telegram.

A week before the accident, I had been flattered to receive my first dinner invitation from Ambassador Beam, to join him for a black-tie dinner, a male-only event, with the French, Greek, and Turkish ambassadors, and the British minister. Although worn down from racing between the airport, the morgue, and the embassy, I couldn't renege on my acceptance. Exchanging a business suit reeking of the morgue for a tuxedo, I went to Spaso House. It turned out that the conversation mostly revolved around the accident, and Beam's guests were delighted to have all the grisly details.

The next day, an American businessman arrived at Sheremetyevo looking for his missing partner. Having no entry visa, the airport authorities locked him up in a facility maintained for "illegal" entrants. Somehow word leaked out that an American was being held near Sheremetyevo. Glassman, from his first year of consular duty, had acquired skill in extracting incarcerated tourists; after twenty hours and with the help of an entry and exit visa we cajoled from the Foreign Ministry, the American was sprung.

A Japanese forensic team had flown in from Tokyo after the accident to join the Russians at the morgue. Under instructions from Washington, we pressed the Soviets for an extension of the deadline for cremation. Aided by dental records, the two teams began to make progress, and the Soviets let the deadline slip.

By the sixth day after the crash, the three Americans had been identified. On the seventh day, we were able to collect their remains in boxes and prepare the required death certificates for dispatch to New York on a Pan-Am flight.

In a letter I wrote my parents a day or so later, I mentioned that I hadn't had much experience dealing with death. I didn't elaborate but had in mind that David and I had been largely shielded from morbid events while growing up. Mother was a Victorian at heart, and we weren't even allowed to attend funerals. When a Jersey cow that father had purchased before leaving for Murmansk died, she lowered the shades facing the barn to spare us the sight.

But Moscow was no place for squeamishness about death. One of our responsibilities was witnessing the cremation of American tourists who died while visiting, and authenticating their ashes for shipment to the United States. Every few months, Steve, Jon, and I took turns at the Donskoi crematorium, next to the monastery of the same name (which the Communists had converted to a museum decades before). For those of us on the political track, the crematorium had historical interest; it was where Stalin's henchman, Lavrenti Beria, had gone up in smoke in December 1953, and where ashes from thousands of Beria's victims, along with those from other purges, were buried.

*   *   *

As soon as I arrived in Moscow, I asked the administrative section whether I could join one of the Russian language classes. They were held a flight of stairs above the consular section in two small rooms. Because I spoke the language fairly well, I wasn't assigned immediately but, after a few months, was told to report to a class that Ludmila Vronski conducted.

Of course, I wanted to do more than simply improve my Russian. Mila had grown up in and around Moscow, and I wanted to learn as much as I could about what life for a Russian was really like.

There were seven women teaching at the embassy, all with excellent English skills. Like other locally hired employees, a Foreign Ministry branch, UPDK, had arranged their employment. Undoubtedly, one or more of them was tasked with reporting to an agency besides the ministry.

I started in a twice-weekly class with two or three others, but it wasn't too long before I arranged to study alone. There was a standard Russian textbook for English-speakers, *Russian As We Speak It*, by a Professor Khavronina. With Mila's encouragement, I supplemented it by translating and discussing articles taken from the weekly Writer's Union publication—*Literary Gazette* (*Literaturnaya gazeta*)—and other periodicals.

Mila had a wide range of interesting friends, not only because of her outgoing personality but because she was married to Sergei, one of the directors of cameramen at Mosfilm. After wartime service, Sergei had entered the Institute of Cinematography (GIK) in 1948. This was the premier film school in the Soviet Union; the renowned director Sergei Eisenstein was a longtime member of the faculty, although he had died just before Sergei enrolled.

Upon graduating in 1953, Sergei joined Mosfilm. In 1960, he married Mila, thirteen years his junior.

Mila was finishing up at the Institute of Foreign Languages at the time. She had been sent to Sokolniki Park in 1959 to help at the exhibit where Nixon and Khrushchev engaged in their "kitchen debate," which Nixon portrayed as "one of the major personal crises" (of six he described) marking his ascent to the presidency. After graduating from the institute, Mila found work translating documents at a foreign trade company. Then UPDK offered her a position at the embassy.

It was no secret that the Foreign Ministry was interested in having us improve our language skills (it insisted we speak Russian, not English, when we paid calls to discuss consular and diplomatic business), and it, of course, wanted us to become more sympathetic to the peoples comprising the multinational Soviet state. Accordingly, the teachers assigned to the embassy were well educated and self-confident. They were even given some slack in how and what to teach.

In her middle thirties when we first met, Mila was dark-haired and attractive, and initially I eyed her with a certain reserve. But it wasn't too long before I noticed that she avoided the usual cant when I edged conversation into sensitive areas. After a few weeks, I realized that her love of Russia, its literature, and its culture far transcended the obligation she felt to justify the Soviet system. It became obvious as months passed that the Orthodox Church had been important in her upbringing, that she had absorbed its humane values from her mother and grandmother.

Mila and Sergei lived on the fourth floor of a five-story walk-up apartment complex that Mosfilm had built, as a cooperative, in 1959. It was located in a picturesque wooded enclave close to the studio, not far from Moscow University in Lenin Hills, the city's high ground overlooking a horseshoe bend in the river.

As at Leninsky 45, the co-op's entryways faced away from the avenue on which it fronted. A narrow road branched off the avenue, passed between the entryways and a line of freestanding garages (Sergei owned a *Zhiguli* when we arrived), and ended in front of a seventeenth century building that had once been a church—Holy Trinity ("Life-giving Holy Trinity")—but was serving as a warehouse.

Outside the entryways were a scattering of trees, patches of grass on which children could play, and a few wooden benches on which old-timers could spend their days. Peering into the yard from the Vronski apartment while standing near Sergei's icons mounted on one of its walls, I felt I could make out the paths that years before had led to the church.

Sergei had been raised in Rostov-on-Don. His father had served in World War I as a military doctor but had died before he knew his wife had given birth to a son. Sergei's grandfather, a tsarist general, had been a bureaucrat in a St. Petersburg's ministry.

Seven members of Sergei's family had been lost to Stalin's purges. Perhaps for this reason, Sergei didn't like looking back. He had little use for genealogy, as Mila told me when I asked more about his background in 2004. "Let my children deal with that," he said when she suggested, after the Soviet Union collapsed, that he take stock of his family history.

About the same time, the film director Elem Klimov, a good friend, had urged Sergei to claim his grandfather's post in the Assembly of Nobility, the revival of which was then being discussed in St. Petersburg, the former Leningrad.

Klimov had always been interested in Russia's prerevolutionary history. Like Sergei, a graduate of the Institute of Cinematography, he had made a film in the middle 1970s about Rasputin's influence at Tsar Nicholas's court. The film portrayed the tsar in a more sympathetic light, however, than the Communists would permit, and it sat on the shelves until Gorbachev took power. In 1986, the film was finally released, and in the same year, Klimov became the head of the Cinematographers' Union.

"Why should I join an assembly of nobles (*dvoriane sobraniye*)?" Sergei retorted. "I already have a *dvor* [the co-op's yard and the adjoining garage] where you, I, and our friends assemble to drink after we finish a film."

Liz and I first met Sergei at one of Beam's film showings. From almost the moment Americans moved into Spaso House, they made it a showplace for Hollywood films.

Eisenstein himself attended a few. The playwright Lillian Hellman, staying at Spaso House with Ambassador Harriman during the last months of the war, once suggested that the filmmaker stop by for a visit, but he begged off, saying it would be dangerous for him to be seen there alone.

Eisenstein did attend Hellman's farewell party; when seeing Americans, most Russians preferred to be in a crowd.

Sergei enjoyed Spaso House's whiskey as much as its films but never lost control like the Soviet consular officials. Mila explained that the war was to blame; Sergei and other aviators were given shots of pure alcohol for the obligatory toast "to Stalin and victory" before each flight.

In 1980, Ambassador Thomas J. Watson Jr. invited the Vronskis to one of his film showings. As a U.S. Army lieutenant in 1942, Watson had been in the Soviet capital as a member of a delegation negotiating arrangements for the delivery of A-20 bombers and P-39 and P-40 pursuit aircraft under Lend-Lease.[143] The aircraft were already being shipped by sea to Murmansk (Sergei used to fly them from there to airfields near the front); but because American and British convoys were under pressure from the submarines, the Allies were looking for an air route from the U.S. mainland to a base in Fairbanks, Alaska, from where Russian pilots (Stalin wanted no Americans flying over "his" territory) could navigate them across Siberia. (Agreement was finally reached, but the bulk of Lend-Lease aircraft continued to arrive by sea, through Murmansk or an Iranian port.)

When Sergei met Watson at Spaso House, he recognized him as an officer in the American delegation with whom he had shaken hands at Moscow's Central Aerodrome thirty-eight years before.

We visited Mila and Sergei several times during our first assignment and met their teenage son Alyosha and their daughter Anya, a pupil in elementary school. Alyosha was struggling with his studies, and his parents made no secret of their concern; could he only be interested in sports?

By our last assignment, Alyosha had developed into a different person. He had immersed himself in religion and art, and had become an apprentice to Savva Yamshchikov, an expert on ecclesiastical art and architecture, whom we had met through Mila.

In the early 1990s, Alyosha began to restore Russian icons and religious murals, and the Orthodox Patriarchate took an interest in his work. His first major project was to return the "warehouse" behind his parents' apartment to its sacred purpose. Mila and Sergei hadn't expected Holy Trinity to be restored in their lifetimes, and hardly by their son.

In the years since, Alyosha has restored numerous Orthodox churches in and around Moscow and across Russia. During an assignment in the United States, he repaired and restored church iconostases in New York State, both in the metropolitan area and at Holy Trinity Monastery in upstate Jordanville.

A History of Icon Painting published in Moscow in 2005 appraises three "masters" painting icons in Russia today, and Alyosha is one of them. The book's coauthors—the chairwoman of the Department of Christian Culture of St. Andrew's Theological College in Moscow and the head of the School of Icon Painting at the Theological Academy, also in Moscow—describe his work this way:

> A. Vronsky consciously follows the canonical tradition, but at the same time he makes use of artistic freedom. In some works by masters in this circle, weightless, immaterial images seem to acquire a material heaviness, and there is occasionally a touch of mannerism. Yet they often manage to combine the austerity of icon painting with remarkably warm feeling, which is found in the faces of the saints on their icons. All three [masters] have a distinctive, interesting manner.[144]

Yamshchikov considers Alyosha one of Russia's most talented iconographers, not only because of his technique but because of the "soul" he inherited from Mila and Sergei.

*   *   *

In December 1972, I took a flight to Odessa, the main Black Sea port, with David Evans from the economic section. David had a master's degree in Russian studies from Harvard, acquired while I had been slogging through law school.

Foreign Ministry approval was needed for travel beyond a twenty-five-mile zone around Moscow (it had been sixty miles prior to 1947), and a diplomatic note requesting approval had to be filed at least forty-eight hours in advance. In an atmosphere of improving relations, the ministry approved more requests than were denied; and travel related to consular business, including visits to American ships, was generally not viewed with suspicion.

If the Foreign Ministry refused a request, as it would do at the KGB's behest, the State Department would retaliate and refuse travel to an official at the Soviet embassy in Washington, in keeping with the principle of reciprocity.

David and I intended to welcome the first American ship to visit a Black Sea port in several years. It was hauling wheat from the Middle West, the first of many shipments pursuant to a $1.2 billion grain agreement signed shortly after Nixon and Brezhnev's summit. It was grain exported from tsarist Russia that had made Odessa rich; now grain was being imported into Odessa to keep Communist Russia fed.

We stayed at a hotel a few blocks from the steps that Eisenstein had made famous with *The Battleship Potemkin,* and walked down them to reach the ship's berth. With the captain, we watched as the kind of evacuator that I had helped manufacture during a summer job in Illinois unload the grain at a record tempo, a detail that Mike McGuire, a *Chicago Tribune* correspondent also visiting from Moscow, highlighted in his dispatch.

A few months later, it became clear that the Soviet regime had "outmaneuvered" Washington (to use Kissinger's word) to obtain the grain on exceptionally favorable terms.[145] I still have a vial of it from the Odessa shipment; it doesn't rank with the vial of Boston Tea Party leaves that Herman Melville's grandfather used to carry around[146], but it does remind me of a dividend—albeit a tarnished one—from that first Moscow summit.

Shortly after returning, the five Obers and the four Evans took a five-day vacation at Tarasovka. The embassy had two dachas there—a "big dacha" with five bedrooms and a "little dacha" with two bedrooms—within yards of each other on a fenced lot of several acres. The big dacha had been in the embassy's possession since at least the late 1940s; the little one, reserved for the ambassador and his guests, was added later. The lot also encompassed a macadam tennis court, a stand of pine trees, and at the base of a steep hill, a small brook. A Russian couple living in a tiny cottage at the lot's gated entrance maintained the property.

On arriving in Moscow, Liz and I had reserved the big dacha for the first week it was available, which turned out to be the week after Christmas. By December, the clouds in central Russia are thick and leaden, and daylight is limited; but after six months of compound living, we needed a break, even if we wouldn't see much sun.

When we left Leninsky Prospect—the car packed with a week's worth of food—the sidewalks were covered with piles of snow that were already turning black from Moscow's pollution.

Together we explored Tarasovka, tramping its frozen roads and trails. Several times we stopped at its only church, a late nineteenth century building made entirely of brick except for its cupolas, and without much charm. "Today was Orthodox Christmas . . . and the entire congregation was filled with *babushkas*, very old, but also a few young families waiting to christen their babies," Liz wrote.

When we visited an older, truly beautiful church just outside the village, I thought I was being duly reverent by clasping my hands behind my back. A *babushka* approached me noiselessly from behind, however, and with a single chop separated my hands. I was being disrespectful, she said as she walked off.

The *babushkas* gave us little peace. Several months later, at the start of an Aeroflot flight, a stewardess brusquely knocked one of my legs off the other, warning me that legs were not to be crossed.

We ate a meal at Tarasovka's only restaurant. The cook was Georgian and was famed for his bread. Slipping into the kitchen to buy loaves to take home and freeze, one couldn't help noticing Stalin's portrait next to the sink. Apparently, he was still a hero to some from his native region.

The food was uninspiring, the restaurant unheated. "I could barely bend my fingers to cut the meat," Liz wrote. "And it wasn't really meat."

Every week, seven or eight films were pouched to the defense attachés from a base in West Germany, and families would sometimes take one to the dacha along with a projector. Liz and I never did, though we screened films for friends at the apartment.

The dacha had a fireplace, and we kept a fire roaring with wood split by the Russian caretakers. The week passed too quickly. After returning to the compound, Liz wrote my parents:

> Going out to the country was the best rest any of us could have had. All beds were in use, and your puzzle was made and re-made four times! We played card games, checkers, read books, hiked in the woods, skated every morning at a nearby frozen reservoir, had a fire going all day.

Tarasovka filled a crucial need for the community. A day before or after every July 4 reception, everyone would converge on the dachas for a daylong picnic. Then, during the rest of the summer, until the Anglo-American elementary school opened in September, the big dacha and the yard surrounding it would serve as a camp—Camp Wocsom ("Moscow" spelled backwards)—for the embassy's children. Volunteers from among the wives and student-nannies organized and ran the camp.

*   *   *

In the course of winter 1972-73, we were included in our first dinner party at Ed and Nina Stevens's house, a two-story building at Ryleev 11 Street, a few steps off the city's inner ring, and a short walk to the Kremlin in one direction and Spaso House in the other.[147]

Edmund had arrived in Moscow in 1934. Though born in the United States, he was accustomed to living abroad. His mother, a young widow, had taken him to Italy just before the outbreak of World War I. After the war, in 1919, she brought him home, and they settled in New York City.

Edmund was enrolled in the charter class of Connecticut's South Kent School. I knew the school because this is where my brother had been sent in 1950, the year after I started Kent School. Father Sill had helped Sam Bartlett, one of his first graduates, establish the school in 1924.

But after the freedom he had enjoyed in Italy, Edmund didn't find a strict boarding school to his liking. He lasted a year before his mother enrolled him in Browning, a day school in Manhattan. Upon graduating, he matriculated at Columbia University on the upper West Side.

By the time Ed reached Columbia, the country was experiencing its worst-ever depression, with unemployment approaching 25 percent. Disenchanted by what he saw around him, Ed took up student politics and joined the National Student League, which was associated with the Communist Party. "We held demonstrations in support of various left-wing causes, joining picket lines during strikes and organizing an expedition to support striking Kentucky coal miners."[148]

According to Ed's account, he was "a Red student leader" by 1932, "even though I attended white-tie debutante balls" at night.[149] Whether he became a full-fledged Party member is in dispute. Ed's son declares that he didn't[150], but a Soviet document released after the Cold War suggests he did[151].

Scholars say that "during the 1930s, about 250,000 Americans affiliated themselves with the CPUSA [Communist Party of the United States] for at least a short time."[152]

Before going to Moscow, Ed posed for Diego Rivera, the Mexican artist, after the Rockefellers had commissioned him to paint a mural in Fifth Avenue's Rockefeller Center. Rivera had visited Moscow in 1927-28; although the experience soured him (Stalin exiled his hero Trotsky while he was there), he remained an outspoken Communist. Broad-shouldered and husky, Ed probably fulfilled Rivera's notion of an American worker, though Ed, by background, was no proletarian. Rivera's politics became a public issue after he slipped a small portrait of Lenin into the mural, which covered a space sixty-three feet long and seventeen feet high, and the Rockefellers ordered it destroyed. Workers wielding axes pulverized it in the course of a single night.[153]

Radical students thronged American colleges and universities in the 1930s. When Thomas Merton—later to become a celebrated Trappist monk—arrived at Columbia in 1935, he found that "most of the smartest students were Reds."[154]

Writing after World War II, the New York critic Malcolm Cowley described the early 1930s as "a madly hopeful time": Russia "didn't impress us as a despotism or as the great antagonist in a struggle for world power; it was busier within its own boundaries trying to create what promised to be a happier future."[155] Just before U.S.-Soviet diplomatic relations were established, the trading firm Amtorg, incorporated in New York in 1922, processed, as Moscow's de facto consulate, "350 applications a day from Americans eager to work for the Five Year Plan."[156]

In 1933, a play about Americans living in the USSR, *They All Come to Moscow*, had twenty Broadway performances.[157] One of its actors was Clifford Odets. Odets's own play two years later, *Waiting for Lefty*, would be a sensation in New York and Moscow (it quoted from Marx's *The Communist Manifesto*) and would become the most frequently performed play in theatrical history.

Ed met Nina shortly after he reached Moscow. Nina believed that if they hadn't met, he would have gone off to fight in the Spanish civil war. (It's fortunate he didn't; almost half of the American volunteers perished.) They married in 1935.

Nina came from the southern Urals, from Cossack families who had settled in Orenburg. Her father, of Ukrainian descent, had trained to be an Orthodox priest. Her mother, of Russian origin, refused to marry a priest, so he became a schoolmaster.

Nina, their oldest child, was born in 1912 near Chelyabinsk, in a town where her father was then teaching—Fadushino. While growing up, Nina was influenced by her mother's mother, another strong-willed *babushka* who, as a stout Christian, had sheltered nuns from the Bolsheviks. She taught Nina how to pray before the family's icons.

For three years, the Reds and Whites fought to control the southern Urals. Nina and her family saw the Revolution at first hand, and suffered from the famine that then followed. Nina recalled seeing its victims—frozen and stripped of clothes—lying by the roadside as she and the family made their way to one of the centers where Herbert Hoover's American Relief Administration offered assistance. Later, as a teacher herself in an elementary school, she witnessed the arrest and deportation of "wealthier" peasants, those whom the Communists labeled "kulaks." From loyalty to her family and her own experiences, she resolved to avoid all politics, even the Komsomol.

She made her way to Moscow on her own. After a stint at Moscow University and a failed relationship with a Russian, she moved to Leningrad to study but didn't remain long. Having ill health, being out of money, and being far from her family whom she had already brought to Moscow, she returned and took a factory job grinding metal. At the back of her mind was the hope that her employer would provide a stipend so she could complete her degree. She met Ed before the stipend materialized.

Fresh from the United States, Ed found work with the Cooperative Publishing Society of Foreign Workers, a Moscow firm that published books and pamphlets for Westerners beginning to congregate in the USSR. Visiting a bookstore in Massachusetts in 2001, Liz and I came upon a *Guide to the City of Moscow: A Handbook for Tourists*, one of the books Ed had edited. The guide came out in July 1937 in a run of 10,100 copies; it had been submitted for approval more than a year before, but Stalin's Great Purge that would destroy millions of lives had begun, and the censors were not about to approve any publication without vetting every one of its words.

Ed had actually been released by the publisher before the guide's appearance. Years later, he noted that senior officials in almost all of the co-op's different language sections were "repressed," that is, imprisoned or liquidated.[158]

Liz and I liked the Stevens. From Ed's size, I assumed he had had an athletic career in school, but he was more cerebral and easygoing than athletic and, according to Nina, could hardly dance a step. Even though Ed had no Slavic ancestry, he had the broad face of someone from the old intelligentsia, before it was largely scattered and destroyed.

From my vantage in the embassy, what impressed me most was that Ed seemed to know more about Moscow than most other foreign journalists. He spoke excellent Russian, knew French and Italian, and circulated widely.

Nina was good-looking and stylish. Admiral Leslie Stevens, the navy attaché in 1947, had described her as "attractive in a light, almost delicate sort of way with the marked slant of her blue eyes to give her an exotic touch."[159] Nina would fix a steely gaze on those with whom she spoke. Thornton Wilder, who frequented salons at the height of his writing career, aptly wrote that "the soul of a salon is conversation, and the soul of *that* is the hostess' undivided attention [italics original]."[160]

I wasn't surprised to read in Nina's memoir that, after Ed brought her to the United States in 1939, his mother tried to steer her into modeling. Nina rejected the idea after a bad experience with a Manhattan couturier and went to study English instead. She enrolled in Wellesley College near Boston; Ed was working for the *Christian Science Monitor* at the time.

It wasn't long after we met that I heard several American correspondents, new to Moscow, speculate about the Stevens' situation. How did Ed and Nina manage to have a beautiful house in downtown Moscow, the only freestanding house occupied by foreigners? Why was Nina able to travel back and forth between Moscow and New York? "They must have a special relationship with the authorities."

I didn't know what to make of the talk, but it puzzled me and persisted.

Probably some of the correspondents weren't aware that it had been Ed who secured the lifting of Soviet censorship, enabling them to dispatch their reports without interference. Censors of the Main Administration for Safeguarding State Secrets in the Press (Glavlit), located at the Central Telegraph Office near Red Square, used to examine each outbound report before allowing its transmission. If the report wasn't turned down by the censors (in a single month in 1950, Harrison Salisbury had thirteen rejected[161]), it would likely be mangled with deletions.

While serving as a *Time* correspondent in 1961, Ed had sent Khrushchev a letter on behalf of his colleagues seeking approval for reporting without censorship. In March 1961, they were advised that henceforth they would *not* have to submit their reports to the censors. At the July 4 reception at Spaso House that year, Khrushchev approached Ed and acknowledged his letter.[162]

I knew that Ed's politics had been leftist before the war, but I also knew that during the war he had helped U.S. officials. He had served as a "technical advisor" to Ambassador Harriman during the latter's negotiations with Stalin in 1942 and had aided couriers from the State Department, bringing diplomatic pouches from Tehran.

Ed's Pulitzer Prize winning book of 1950, *This is Russia: UnCensored*, was as hostile to the Soviet system as any book published in the United States at the beginning of the Cold War. It opened with a description of how Ed and his family were "constantly being spied upon." It exposed the USSR's "rubber-stamp parliament" and ended with a recommendation that the United States "proffer the hand of friendship to the Russian people over the head of the Soviet government" using Russian-language broadcasts on the Voice of America.[163] Former Ambassador Walter Bedell Smith wrote the introduction (and was appointed the head of the CIA the year the book was published). I wondered if the correspondents doing the speculating had read the book.

Ed had written an earlier book, *Russia Is No Riddle*, and this may have been the problem. Reflecting the Zeitgeist of the wartime alliance, it had glossed over the Soviet system's abuses. It had also been dismissive of the Polish people's aspiration to have a government of its own choosing.

If Ed had revisited his first book in a final memoir, he probably would have echoed Harrison Salisbury's words when he looked at the first book he wrote about the Soviet Union:

> A lot of it isn't worth the paper I wrote it on. I understood that the Soviet Union and the United States were in for a long, long period of quarreling, but I did not foresee the polarization nor its depth. I kissed off Poland and the Balkans.[164]

In his introduction to Ed's second book, Ambassador Smith alluded to his first, noting that "years of disillusionment" had intervened. But still, Ed has demonstrated "an understanding of the Russian people which few Westerners have attained."[165]

I knew that Nina had become an American citizen after the war and thus could travel freely between the United States and the Soviet Union, so long as the Soviet authorities issued an exit visa. When Foreign Minister Litvinov was honoring Ambassador Joseph Davies before his final departure for the United States in 1938, Davies had turned to Litvinov and, introducing Nina, asked whether she, as the wife of an American correspondent, could not, as a final favor to him (Davies), be given an exit visa. After a moment's consideration, Litvinov said he'd try. A few weeks later, the visa was approved.

A Democratic Party politician and lawyer, Davies didn't accomplish much else during his tour. Kennan describes how he and other FSOs gathered secretly at the end of Davies's first day to decide whether or not to "resign in a body from the service." They decided to stay, and alas, Kennan found himself interpreting for Davies at the notorious show trials. "Davies," he wrote, "placed considerable credence in the fantastic charges leveled" at Stalin's victims.[166] Davies published a memoir, *Mission to Moscow*, in 1941, and then hired the team responsible for *Casablanca* (a favorite at Spaso House in 1944) to do a film version. He screened it for Stalin when visiting Moscow in 1943. The dictator found Davies's "vision of a happy, prosperous, and friendly Russia" so appealing that he approved its release to Soviet theaters, the first American film approved for distribution in the USSR in more than a decade.[167]

The Russian wives of three other American correspondents (the marriages had taken place after Ed and Nina's) were not so fortunate; they had to wait until after Stalin's death to receive their exit visas. Shortly after arriving to replace Jake Beam, Ambassador Bohlen raised the wives' plight with Molotov, and Molotov sanctioned their issuance. One of those who benefited was Julie Whitney, the woman who had married the embassy's economic officer. The Whitneys left the Soviet Union together in July 1953. But the long delay between the issuance of Nina's exit visa and that of the other wives must have rankled.

Only a handful in the American community apparently knew that Nina had become a naturalized American during the war. Beam's wife, Peggy, expressed surprise when I told her in 1995. Perhaps it was because the Stevens were associating more with West Europeans and Russians than with Americans by the early 1970s.

Ed and Nina acquired their house at Ryleev 11 in 1966 in an exchange for a log house beyond the city center that they had purchased before the war. (The Communists named the street "Ryleev" to honor a minor poet who participated in the Decembrist uprising against Tsar Nicholas I.) The authorities forced the Stevens out of their first house when the Soviet military claimed the lot on which it stood. The Foreign Ministry's diplomatic services branch took up the Stevens' complaint and offered them Ryleev 11 instead, but as tenants, not owners. The Stevens were miffed by the seizure of their house, yet had no choice but to accept the exchange.

When they took Ryleev 11 over, it was in shambles, without a kitchen or bathroom. They set to work, tearing out its infrastructure—including a heating system dating from before World War I—and stripping it down. Then using their own funds, rebuilt it, restoring many of its prerevolutionary features, including parquet floors and wrought-iron hardware.

Adding to the house's charm was the art that Nina and Ed had begun collecting in the 1950s. When Liz and I arrived, we knew little of Soviet-era art. Moreover, we had come two years too late for an exhibit of unofficial artists that they mounted in their backyard on July 22, 1970. The one-day exhibit, *in plein air* as if along the Seine, featured the works of Masterkova, Plavinski, Rukhin, Kozlov, and other artists who are now considered the founders of Russia's postwar avant-garde movement.

Ed and Nina had been hosting unofficial exhibits since the late 1950s, but their 1970 exhibit is the one the art historians remember.[168]

Liz and I would come to know a few artists, but didn't become collectors. Igor Palmin introduced our daughter Abby and me to Dima Plavinski, who had a studio near the Stevens; and he gave Abby an etching. I once spent an evening with Boris Kozlov and his wife; their apartment walls were covered with practice brushstrokes. We met other artists at diplomatic residences, including that of Venezuelan Ambassador Burelli Rivas, an avid collector whom we had known in Warsaw.

In 1967, three years before their exhibit, the Stevens had sent a major part of their collection to the Gallery of Modern Art in Manhattan's Edward Durrell Stone-designed building at 2 Columbus Circle. The show ran from June to September and was entitled A Survey of Russian Painting from the 15th through the 20th Centuries. It was deemed New York's most complete survey of Russian art since 1923, embracing ancient icons at one extreme and post-Stalin avant-garde art at the other, including twenty-two works by Plavinski.

Writing in the *New York Times*, Hilton Kramer considered the exhibit, as previously noted, "the first word in this new artistic dialogue between Russia and the Western countries."[169] The works awakened American critics to the fact that a growing number of Soviet artists were working outside the tenets of socialist realism.

After the exhibit closed, Alfred Barr, the founding director of the Museum of Modern Art (who had gone on "an icon-hunting expedition" in Moscow with Diego Rivera in 1928[170]), and Norton Dodge, who was beginning to assemble what is today the West's largest collection of Soviet nonconformist art, bought most of the Stevens' collection.

Some wondered how the Stevens obtained permission; had they smuggled their art abroad? It turned out that the Russian Republic's Ministry of Culture had approved its export. N. A. Kuznetsov had taken over the ministry in

1965, after having been transferred from the Moscow City Party organization, where he had served as a second secretary.[171] By this and other personnel shifts, the Party was reasserting control over ministries that had gained too much influence, in its view, under the now-ousted Khrushchev.

Kuznetsov must have approved the art's export without securing permission from either the all-union Ministry of Culture or the Party's Central Committee. He may have misjudged the extent of his own power as the new head of a republic-level ministry, for as soon as rumors of smuggling began to circulate, he was removed from office, and a successor was named. Nina "petitioned" the successor to explain that no smuggling had occurred, but it was already too late for Kuznetsov. Nina was told that he was "ill," then that he had "died."

Control of Soviet cultural policy was in flux in 1967, the jubilee year marking the fiftieth anniversary of the Revolution. In May, Andropov had taken over the KGB from Vladimir Semichastny, a notorious hard-liner who had led the assault on Pasternak. Andropov was known to have ties with artistic circles. There were even hints that the authorities might let Solzhenitsyn publish parts of *Cancer Ward.*

The number one man in the Moscow City Party organization was Piotr Demichev, and he was the Party's watchdog for culture when Kuznetsov took over the republic ministry. Perhaps Kuznetsov didn't check with Demichev before sanctioning the export, or perhaps he thought a new cultural thaw was beginning. No one knows for sure.

The American journalist who gave currency to the smuggling story, Stanley Johnson of the Associated Press, had committed an earlier mistake in reporting from Moscow, claiming that Stalin's image had been removed from a painting in the Hotel Metropol when it hadn't.[172] Johnson lost his job too.

A few years later, in 1973, the all-union Ministry of Culture let George Costakis, a Greek citizen who had spent his entire life in the USSR, take nonconformist works abroad in connection with lectures he was delivering. Costakis was working as a clerk at the Canadian Embassy at the time and was allowed to export two boxes of works along with slides; before returning to Moscow, he deposited six of his works at a gallery in London.[173] The Costakis collection included Kandinsky's and Chagall's, and its value far surpassed that of the Stevens'. In his memoir, Costakis wrote that "it was not at all difficult to receive permission to export paintings of the Russian avant-garde" so long as they didn't have political content.[174] Before the 1980s, most of Moscow's unofficial artists steered clear of political themes.

However, collecting art generated endless speculation about smuggling, illegally obtained rubles, and KGB involvement. Not surprisingly, when Costakis visited Ottawa during his lecture tour, he was accosted by two

Canadian security officials who accused him of working for the KGB.[175] Now and then, the Soviet authorities cracked down on diplomats who were heavily involved with art; they reportedly asked Venezuela to withdraw Ambassador Rivas in 1978. In view of the prices the works of Russia's "second wave" avant-garde now command, some would say Liz and I were foolish *not* to have become involved. Our son Rob, who runs a gallery in Kent, Connecticut, specializing in this art, might agree.

Ed and Nina made Ryleev 11 into a place where one could socialize with Russians and Europeans in an informal setting. Guests could count on superb food—sometimes prepared by Nina's mother—and an open bar. American journalists were not part of the scene during our visits; had they been, interesting Russians wouldn't have come.

The Stevens had also been hurt by several journalist colleagues. When we first visited, they were still upset by how the Schecters—a *Time* magazine correspondent and his wife—had portrayed Nina. The Stevens had entertained the couple, yet they described Nina in their memoir as someone who operated as an illegal middleman in the art market, apparently holding her to the norms of the Soviet system, including its notion of what was acceptable art.[176] If this is how your colleagues treat you, why go to the trouble of hosting them.

As the decade of the 1970s wound down, Ed did less and less reporting. The topics he addressed were those to which he devoted attention during his first decades: Soviet foreign policy, politics in the Kremlin, the complexities of everyday life. By the early '70s, a new generation of correspondents was descending on the capital—more interested in reporting on ethnic issues, human rights, dissidents, refuseniks, and U.S.-Soviet trade. The new correspondents were also traveling far beyond the capital, covering parts of the sprawling Soviet empire that had once been closed or difficult to reach.

*   *   *

The embassy staff in the early 1970s consisted of about 125 Americans, excluding children and wives not working full-time. About twenty-five were Foreign Service officers from the State Department and Information Agency (USIA). The rest were clerical, communications, and secretarial personnel, and officers and support personnel from other agencies. The staff also included eleven young marines; they manned the ninth-floor post, patrolled the embassy building and its annexes, supervised the char force, and otherwise provided security.

The American community also encompassed twenty-five or so journalists and reporters from newspapers, periodicals, and television networks; seven or eight businessmen; two clergymen; and a score or more students and scholars on short and long-term stays. Virtually every nontransient American in the Soviet capital had access to the diplomatic pouch for unclassified mail; they were also allowed to visit Uncle Sam's and the bar that the marines opened evenings in their quarters at Tchaikovsky 19.

The embassy staff had been about the same size during the early years of the Cold War (also 125 Americans in 1948[177]), although there were few journalists (no more than seven in the early 1950s) and a negligible number of businesspersons and scholars.

Everyone who stayed at least a year came to know everyone else, usually by first name. Until the middle 1970s, the American community was small and tight-knit.

Ambassador Beam described the attraction of an assignment to Moscow:

> The embassy staff were all handpicked volunteers, most of them with Russian language training. The rewards were mostly personal: an attachment to Russian culture and the Russian language; a liking for the people despite their perversities and despite the Soviet regime's cavalier disinterest in foreigners except for gainful exploitation; as well as vivid memories of the Russian landscape and the harsh but invigorating climate.[178]

With the exception of the marines, most of the Americans were married. The vast majority of wives spent their days looking after their families, running households, and volunteering in the community. Securing food (nothing like a supermarket existed), caring for children, and entertaining diplomatic and official guests as well as friends added up to long and exhausting days. The wives seemed no less committed to being in the USSR and performing their tasks than did the husbands.

But changes were taking place in the United States, and they would soon have a profound impact on the embassy community and its families.

I had an inkling of what was to come shortly after we arrived in 1972. An administrative officer took me aside and said that certain remarks would have to be deleted from the performance evaluation prepared on me by the commanding officer in Garmisch. Complimentary remarks about Liz had been included, as they had been included in reports prepared by my Foreign Service supervisors in Hamburg and Warsaw. She had been praised for her contributions to the communities involved and for her representational work.

I was told that all remarks bearing on her would have to be "blanked out." The Foreign Service's director general had issued a "Directive on

TCHAIKOVSKY 19, A DIPLOMATIC LIFE BEHIND THE IRON CURTAIN   139

Wives" the preceding March—eliminating requirements for employees' spouses except the most minimal—"that she comport herself in a manner which will not reflect discredit on the United States."[179] The effect of the ruling was that spouses could no longer be mentioned in an evaluation.

It turned out that most officers on their first assignments at the embassy in the early 1970s would not return for a second or third assignment. Some didn't find the rewards that Beam described; others discovered that their wives aspired to have careers of their own, even in the Foreign Service. ("Tandem" couples with both spouses engaging in a diplomatic career and having their assignments synchronized at the same post or with periods of separation soon became common.) To our dismay, a few marriages among the couples we knew well broke up after the assignment.

*   *   *

It was shortly after returning from Tarasovka on New Year's Day, January 1, 1973, that we learned that Ambassador and Mrs. Beam would retire at the end of the month. No one was surprised by the announcement; a few had thought it would come earlier.

Beginning with the preparations for the May 1972 summit, the Nixon administration had largely ignored the ambassador. This was surprising in that Beam had gone to Moscow as "Nixon's man." In the run-up to the 1968 election, Nixon had visited Prague and had been hosted by Beam, then serving as ambassador there. Beam had impressed the candidate with his graciousness, and after Nixon's election he was awarded the Moscow post.

Henry Kissinger, Nixon's national security advisor, began preparing for the Moscow summit in the second half of 1971. Using Ambassador Dobrynin in Washington as his channel of communication, Kissinger roughed out the modalities and the agenda with top officials in the Foreign Ministry and the Kremlin. According to Dobrynin's count, in the course of 1972, both before and after the summit, he and Kissinger engaged in more than 130 confidential discussions.[180]

What was striking about the preparations was that both Nixon's secretary of state William Rogers and Ambassador Beam were kept entirely in the dark.[181]

Kissinger's back-channel diplomacy culminated in an advance visit to Moscow, on April 21-24, 1972, ahead of the summit. Kissinger brought along Ambassador Dobrynin and an NSC delegation of eight on a special flight. No one at the embassy was made aware of the visit.

Negotiating with Brezhnev, Gromyko, and other Soviet officials, Kissinger wrapped up the summit's details, including most of the agreements that Nixon and Brezhnev would later sign.

On the final day, a Soviet official summoned Beam to the Foreign Ministry. Surmising that the summons might be related to a crisis in Cambodia, the unsuspecting Beam planned to bring along a political officer, but the ministry called again and asked him to come alone. On reaching the ministry, Beam was told that Kissinger and his team had been meeting in Moscow during the preceding four days. Beam was taken to one of the Kremlin's guesthouses on Lenin Hills and introduced to Kissinger.

Kissinger praises Beam in his memoir for conducting himself "with dignity and the attitude that stressed the word *Service* in his title of Foreign Service Officer [Kissinger's italics]." Kissinger distances himself from responsibility for the slight to Beam, artfully explaining that Beam "deserved better than this apparent vote of no confidence that our strange system of government imposed on him."[182]

Strange indeed!

It got stranger as Nixon's advisor prepared to leave. Beam was instructed not to provide any confirmation of the visit until *after* the White House released a statement upon Kissinger's departure.

Beam was hosting a dinner that night in honor of the widow of Llewellyn Thompson, who had preceded him as ambassador. The dinner was repeatedly interrupted by telephone calls from Western journalists who had gotten wind of the visit and wanted to break the story. Beam's staff aide, who was seated at the table, took the calls and, having no knowledge himself of the visit, could honestly say he knew nothing about it. Beam finally suggested that he stop taking the calls.

Beam's unflappability must have been severely tested, but he remained a good host. He never mentioned the snub at any meeting I attended and alluded to it only indirectly in his memoir.

Of course, presidents and their top aides had ignored ambassadors in Moscow before. Roosevelt had bypassed Ambassador William Standley in sending messages to Stalin.[183] Yet Roosevelt bypassed the Soviet ambassador in Washington at the same time, which gave Standley a measure of comfort when writing his memoir. It took the arrival of Nixon and Kissinger in the White House, however, before a Soviet ambassador rather than an American ambassador became the exclusive conduit for bilateral negotiations.

To assure that the department remained in the dark, Kissinger even used Soviet rather than American interpreters during his visit.[184]

Kissinger would justify his and Nixon's approach by arguing that the administration's major successes "had proved unattainable by conventional procedures."[185] The diplomat-scholar Raymond Garthoff, from his contemporaneous involvement with the strategic arms negotiations and his service in six administrations, comes to a different conclusion: studying the altogether short life of these "successes" and of détente itself, Ambassador Garthoff makes the point that, had they been accomplished "through more conventional procedures and less by sleight of hand, they might have had greater staying power."[186]

The snub to Ambassador Beam didn't pass unnoticed. Soviet officials owed their careers to identifying where power lay, and the American system was never as opaque as their own. After April 1972, it was obvious to everyone in Moscow that Beam enjoyed no influence whatsoever in his own capital. Why would any Soviet leader bother to show up at Spaso House? Before leaving for retirement, Ambassador and Mrs. Beam gave a farewell reception. Because of the consular administration's debauch at the July 4 reception, we forwarded the name of only one of our ministry contacts—a gentleman known for sobriety—for inclusion in Beam's last guest list. The overall turnout was meager; I don't recall that anyone of significance from the Soviet side attended, even our contact.

It may have been for the best that Jake Beam left when he did. An ambassador so steeped in traditional diplomacy would have been uncomfortable with at least one issue coming to the fore in U.S.-Soviet relations—human rights.

In Congress and among the American public, Moscow's repression of dissidents was receiving increasing attention. In Washington, the expectation that the embassy would provide more reporting and more moral, if not material, support to Soviet citizens challenging their regime was growing.

As ambassador, Beam thought it wise "to avoid direct contacts with dissenters which might embarrass us and cause them serious trouble,"[187] and he authorized only one or two political officers to meet with them under the most discreet circumstances. By his own account, he once warned a congressman visiting Moscow to steer clear of one group of dissidents. The congressman ignored Beam's advice, and the Soviets promptly expelled him. The lesson that Beam drew was that embassy officers and official visitors should keep a respectful distance from dissidents.

When I arrived in 1972, no one in the embassy was permitted to visit Sakharov and Solzhenitsyn, the regime's most vocal opponents. At the time, both were more interested in communicating with Western correspondents than with embassies, so the question of their involvement with the embassy was probably not high on their own agendas.

But under Beam's successor, the embassy would become directly involved. Beam sarcastically observes in his memoir that "in line with the Carter administration's emphasis on human rights, officers in our embassy now compete in claiming the number of 'house dissidents' each of them cultivates."[188] This is an exaggeration, yet it is true that Washington by the mid-1970s was pressing the embassy to cover the dissident scene more aggressively, and it did so.

After Beam's retirement, the top post in the embassy remained unfilled for thirteen months. With Dobrynin remaining in Washington and Kissinger continuing as the NSC advisor, this suited the White House fine.

The deputy chief of mission at the time of Beam's departure was a career FSO, Adolph Dubs, and Dubs would lead the embassy as its chargé d'affaires.

Dubs's background was about as far from Beam's as could be imagined.[189] His parents, members of the Volga German community, had left tsarist Russia before World War I and settled in the American Midwest where his father took a job as a machinist. Dubs attended high school in Chicago and then matriculated at Beloit College in Wisconsin. His mother scrubbed floors to help pay the bills.

Dubs's college classmates gave him the nickname, "Spike"; Adolph didn't ring particularly American during the war.

After a tour in the navy, Spike joined the Foreign Service in 1949. With the exception of a posting to Liberia, his entire career had been spent in Canada and Europe, including one stint in Moscow. Spike was fifty-two when he took charge of the embassy.

Spike wouldn't receive an ambassadorial appointment until 1978, and it wouldn't be to Moscow or to any capital where he had previously served. It would be to Kabul, Afghanistan, a country Spike knew only from serving in Washington as a deputy assistant secretary of state for the region to which it belonged, and not from professional experience.

In February 1979, shortly after arriving in Kabul, Spike was abducted by a radical Islamic group. The local police mounted a rescue attempt with Soviet guidance, but bungled the job, and Spike was killed. The State Department protested the Soviet role to Dobrynin, but he denied responsibility. In the memoir he wrote after retiring, however, he conceded that the Soviets had "failed to control" the Afghans.[190]

The reason why Spike was sent to South Asia and not to a region where he had previously served is a story for later telling, a story that also involves Kissinger and a decision he took to "reform" the Foreign Service.

6

Kissinger, Détente, and the Soviet Underside

By the time of Ambassador Beam's retirement in January 1973, we knew that a second summit would occur in June and its main venue would be Washington. Beam had represented the embassy at the first summit, but no one from the embassy would be at the second. Ambassadorial-rank diplomats typically participate in summits; but Spike Dubs was the chargé d'affaires, not the ambassador. A successor to Beam would not be named until shortly before Nixon's final summit with Brezhnev in 1974.

After the Beams left, and in anticipation of the summit, the embassy began preparing reports on Moscow's foreign and domestic policies as they affected American interests. This mainly involved the political and economic sections. Over Spike's name and in telegraphic form, the reports received wide distribution in the department, the White House, and other agencies.

Our task in the consular section was simpler but no less important, at least for the families involved. We needed to furnish the Soviet desk in the Bureau of European Affairs (EUR/SOV) the names of dual-national and Soviet-only citizens who had been denied permission to join their families in the United States. The desk would combine them into a new representation list that would be handed to Soviet officials at the highest possible level.

The list deserved maximum attention from two ministries—the Ministry of Foreign Affairs and the Ministry of Internal Affairs. In collaboration with the KGB, the Offices of Visas and Registration (OVIRs) of the latter ministry were responsible for processing emigration applications from persons residing on Soviet territory. OVIRs existed in each of the fifteen republics.

The new list would be called Representation List XV. Both the desk and the embassy recognized that it would receive the attention it deserved only if it were linked to the summit. Otherwise, it would simply disappear in the bowels of Soviet bureaucracy, to languish there with most of the diplomatic notes and less formal papers ("non-papers") that we delivered when making our demarches.

The first representation list grew out of the exchange of visits between Vice President Nixon and Party leader Khrushchev in 1959. During the six years between Stalin's death in 1953 and Nixon's visit, Moscow granted exit visas to a mere fifty-five persons seeking to join their families in the United States, most of them wives joining husbands. When Nixon visited Moscow in August 1959, he brought along a list of more than one hundred persons wanting to emigrate. In his letter enclosing the list, he asked Khrushchev to solve the cases in the interest of the "principles of nonseparation of families" and the need to avoid "irritants to larger solutions." When Khrushchev paid his reciprocal visit in September 1959, he told a few families in the United States that their relatives would soon be released. In November 1959, four Soviet citizens whose names were on Nixon's list received exit permission.[191]

It seemed that intervention at a high level would be required, from time to time at least, to secure the release of such families.

The State Department followed up Khrushchev's gesture by preparing a single comprehensive list that included more than two hundred names. This was probably the first representation list that the embassy delivered to the Soviets in the post-Stalin era.

The final list prepared for the second Nixon-Brezhnev summit, List XV, contained the names and addresses of 221 families. One or more persons from at least 12 of them were entitled to receive an American passport. The others were close relatives of Americans—spouses, parents, and children; several had been waiting for exit visas for more than a quarter century.

The new list was substantially larger than the one I received on my arrival, and it was larger than any previous list in the consular section's files. Perhaps emboldened by the atmospherics surrounding the first summit, an increasing number of Soviet citizens were prepared to run the risk of applying to emigrate.

At the same time, a much larger number of Soviet citizens—tens of thousands—were seeking permission to leave for Israel. The Jewish state was willing to accept any family claiming a Jewish heritage, whether or not a relative could be found within its borders. Grudgingly, Moscow was beginning to respond, but on its own schedule and on its own terms.

The Nixon administration was saying little in public about Soviet restrictions. While studying in Garmisch, I had seen several complaints voiced by midlevel department officials at hearings before committees at the United Nations and on Capitol Hill, but nothing at all from Secretary Rogers or National Security Advisor Kissinger.

It took me a few months to realize that Kissinger was conducting the administration's Soviet business through what he called his "special channel"—that is, Ambassador Dobrynin.[192] It took me a bit longer to understand that he didn't want any Washington officials questioning the Soviet regime's behavior except on issues he considered important and, then, only in ways he approved. His attitude seemed to be, "Let's not embarrass the Soviet leaders while I'm talking with them about important matters, and by the way, emigration from the Soviet Union to the United States isn't one of them."

Kissinger states in his memoir that beginning in 1969, he did raise the question of Soviet emigration to Israel in the special channel and that the channel could be credited with increasing Jewish emigration from four hundred in 1968 to nearly thirty-five thousand in 1973.[193] He makes no reference, however, to persons on Soviet territory—of whatever ancestry—separated from their families in the United States.

Perhaps the back channel was operating as Kissinger claimed, but the beneficiaries were Soviet citizens of Jewish background leaving for Israel, not Soviet citizens of Jewish, Armenian, Ukrainian, Russian, and other backgrounds desiring to join families in the United States.

The Israeli embassy stood vacant on Bolshaya Ordynka Street, not far from Leninsky 45. Diplomatic relations between the USSR and Israel had been broken in June 1967 during the Six-Day War; they wouldn't be reestablished until January 1991.

Our son Rob and a classmate from the Anglo-American School once sneaked over a wall into the empty embassy's courtyard. When spotted by Soviet guards, they fled over a second wall only to land in a militia station. Somehow, the boys scampered away; I didn't hear about their adventure until years later.

The Israeli diplomats in Moscow and Warsaw were said to be the most knowledgeable of all the non-Communist diplomats. To my regret, I never had the opportunity of working with them; I was too junior in Warsaw, and they were no longer around when I arrived in Moscow.

The Dutch looked after Israeli interests following the Six-Day War. Steve Steiner had a good relationship with successive Dutch consuls, and together they examined the backgrounds of the Jews allowed to emigrate. They found that the authorities were, in fact, "purging" their border areas of Jews, especially in Moldavia and the Transcarpathian district of Ukraine, while maintaining tight restrictions on those residing in Moscow, Leningrad, and other major cities where the more educated applicants lived. Obsessed with the security of their borderlands, the Soviets could wow the West with annual healthy increases in the number of Jews going abroad while blocking the emigration of those who were still contributing to Soviet science, technology, and industry (and, correspondingly, who would be in a position to help Israel). Raising the gross number of Jews who received exit visas was never the success that Kissinger suggested it had been.

Western journalists covering the first summit in June 1972 had asked the national security advisor about Jewish emigration, and he had responded only that the president had "mentioned the problem."[194] But Dobrynin states in his memoir that, before that first summit, Kissinger "had delivered an assurance from Nixon to the Soviet leadership that the president would not make any appeals on behalf of Jewish and Zionist organizations during his Moscow visit."[195] It is doubtful that Kissinger himself ever raised the subject; the now-available transcript of a meeting he had with Brezhnev and Gromyko in the Kremlin more than two years later, in October 1974, reports him saying, "Nor had I ever mentioned Jewish emigration [to you before]."[196]

In August 1972, after I had been on the job for two months, Moscow suddenly made conditions more onerous for all would-be emigrants. It enacted a decree imposing a heavy tax, the equivalent of $10,000 or more, on each adult receiving an exit visa. The regime justified the tax as "compensation" for the free education the would-be emigrants had received during their years in the USSR. Already it was depriving emigrants of much of their personal property and documentation, now it was imposing an "education tax."

For those leaving for the United States, we dealt with the document problem by pouching irreplaceable personal papers (such as certificates of marriage and academic degrees) to their American families. But what to do about the tax? The applicants for immigration visas whom Steve was interviewing made clear it was causing considerable hardship, especially for their sponsoring relatives. For those lining up outside the Dutch embassy seeking approval to go to Israel, the tax was an even more serious problem; the vast majority of Israeli-bound emigrants were extremely poor, few having access to families with resources.

As word about the tax spread, Jewish organizations and families in the United States complained, and Congressional representatives—some with large Jewish constituencies—took notice. Many outside the Nixon administration became vocal in denouncing the latest obstruction.

Kissinger was aware of the tax but withheld public comment. On September 6, 1972, Leonard Garment, White House counsel and Nixon's special advisor on Jewish affairs, complained to Kissinger that the issue "is flooding my desk." According to the White House tape that Robert Dallek audited, Kissinger responded, "Is there any more self-serving group of people than the Jewish community?" To Garment's "None in the world," Kissinger added, "You can't even tell the bastards anything in confidence because they'll leak it."[197]

Later in the same month, Kissinger paid another visit to Moscow. Meeting with senior officials, he wrapped up two sets of negotiations—one for settling the debt that Moscow owed Washington for its Lend-Lease assistance, the other for extending most-favored-nation (MFN) status to the Soviet Union as part of a comprehensive trade agreement. The Lend-Lease agreement was conditioned on the Congress's approval of the latter.

For many outside the administration, however, the education tax had been the final straw. On the day that the administration announced the visit of the Soviet foreign trade minister to Washington to sign the trade agreement, Senator Henry Jackson offered an amendment conditioning the grant of MFN on Moscow's removal of *all* obstacles to emigration. Charles Vanik of the House of Representatives lent his name to the amendment, and seventy-two senators and most House members endorsed it.

Kissinger states in his memoir that he was flabbergasted by the education tax. "Why the Soviet Union interrupted the process [of allowing Dobrynin and me to work the emigration problem] right after the Moscow summit will have to be left to the publication of the Soviet archives or the memoirs of Soviet leaders."[198]

The very fact that the Soviet leadership adopted the tax on the heels of the first summit suggests that Nixon and his team had soft-pedaled the emigration issue, if they had mentioned it at all. Ambassador Beam didn't brief us about any discussion concerning emigration; of course, with Nixon and Kissinger in charge, it is possible that Beam had been excluded.

Late in 1972, Israel Prime Minister Golda Meir (interestingly, her country's first diplomatic representative in the USSR) asked American businessman Armand Hammer to raise the tax issue with Brezhnev.[199] Hammer enjoyed special standing in Moscow, having met with Lenin in his Kremlin office in 1921; Hammer's company, Occidental Petroleum, had also signed a five-year scientific and technical agreement with Moscow just after the summit, an agreement that was hailed as one of détente's first successes.

Hammer agreed and met with Brezhnev in February 1973. In March, three months before the second summit, the Soviet tax was suspended. Kissinger's representations through the back channel, and during his September visit, undoubtedly helped, but his and Nixon's policy had taken a serious blow on Capitol Hill, a blow from which it would never recover.

*   *   *

We knew that the summit in Washington would be dominated by issues such as strategic arms, European security, Vietnam, and the Middle East, issues impinging on war and peace; and it was unrealistic to expect Nixon to hand Representation List XV to Brezhnev, even though the first list had grown out of the visit he had made as vice president. Yet we hoped that a high-ranking official would present the new list, if not at the summit, at least at the presummit planning meeting that we knew Kissinger would hold. We could be sure that Foreign Minister Gromyko and Brezhnev's personal aide Andrei Alexandrov (who occupied a position comparable to Kissinger's) would be involved at both sets of meetings.

With the education tax lifted, Kissinger and his delegation arrived in Moscow on May 4, 1973, for the presummit meeting. Spike Dubs welcomed them at Domodedyevo Airport; as a chargé d'affaires, however, Spike would not be added to the delegation. I was present as consul, responsible for passport and registration formalities, which were obviously pro forma with a delegation of this rank.

Kissinger's deputy for Soviet affairs, Helmut Sonnenfeldt (known, quite unofficially, as "Kissinger's Kissinger"), had received Representation List XV from the State Department just before the trip, and brought it with him.

However, the list was never presented. It turned out that Kissinger had brought another list, one provided by an American Jewish organization, and it contained the names of some one thousand Soviet Jews seeking to leave for Israel. The embassy knew nothing in advance about Kissinger's list, but it was this list that he handed over in the Kremlin.

After Kissinger and his delegation left for Washington, Spike let me know that Sonnenfeldt had instructed him to deliver Representation List XV only after the delegation had left Moscow. According to Sonnenfeldt's explanation, this would avoid confusing the Kremlin about the delegation having brought two lists—one dealing with immigration to Israel, the other immigration to the United States.

A week later, Spike delivered Representation List XV to Kuznetsov, Gromyko's first deputy. In protocol terms, Kuznetsov would have been the correct interlocutor, a chargé d'affaires being a step below an ambassador. Yet the elderly Kuznetsov could hardly give "our" list the visibility and clout it needed. Gromyko was a full member of the ruling Politburo, the Party's top body, and was in weekly, if not daily, contact with Brezhnev; Kuznetsov was a relatively new "candidate" (deputy) member, and his influence was less than that of Secretary of State Rogers (whose influence on U.S. policy toward the Soviet Union was probably less than that of Dobrynin).

In a setting where the level of attention to a request correlates closely to the level from which it comes, Kissinger had preordained disappointment for the families on Representation List XV. The White House's decision not to send an ambassador to replace Beam served no one's interest but Kissinger's.

We all understood the logic of encouraging a greater flow of Soviet Jews to Israel, but there was no overlap between List XV and the Israeli list, and there was no reason to ignore altogether the 221 families—some of whom were Jewish—on the American list.

Kissinger and Sonnenfeldt themselves had immigrated to the United States—having both fled Nazi Germany in 1938 and having become naturalized American citizens. As biographers have noted, Kissinger retained, however, a "very special feeling for the survival" of Israel.[200] This would only have been natural.

The enormity of Hitler's crimes against Jewry and the importance of Israel to the survivors of the Holocaust and their families had registered with me, a non-Jew, after three years in Poland. However, I couldn't understand, and will never understand, why Kissinger and Sonnenfeldt wouldn't also espouse the cause of those in the USSR—Jews and non-Jews alike—who wanted to begin life anew with loved ones in the United States.

On the day that Spike delivered List XV to Gromyko's deputy, the ambassador of Canada, Robert Ford, delivered his country's list—much smaller than ours—to Gromyko.

*   *   *

Whenever Steve, Jon, or I raised our emigration cases at the Foreign Ministry, its response was that we were "interfering" in the Soviet Union's "internal affairs." Officials like Vasilyev, our main interlocutor, argued that we had no right to mention those we named—they were "Soviet citizens"—whether or not we considered them American, whether or not their parents or their children living in the United States had sought our help in securing their release.

One of the agreements reached at the first summit had been a description of the "Basic Principles" that Nixon and Brezhnev decided would henceforth govern U.S.-Soviet relations. Twelve principles were enumerated (the first highlighted two longtime Soviet favorites—"peaceful coexistence" and "non-interference in internal affairs"), but none cited the importance of resolving the humanitarian issues plaguing U.S.-Soviet relations.

Moscow had pushed for the principles' adoption. Nixon apparently had little interest in them (he may not have read them),[201] and Kissinger and Sonnenfeldt had viewed them as a sop to the Soviets so they could secure concessions in other areas.

In May 1973, a few weeks before the second summit in Washington, Steve and I learned from our West German colleagues that Brezhnev and Willy Brandt, the German chancellor, had signed a joint communiqué committing their governments to "contribute to a settlement of humanitarian questions." The phrase caught our attention.

Like us, West German consular officers were dealing with numerous families trying to get out of the USSR. In particular, they were being bombarded with appeals from ethnic Germans living along the Volga River and in Kazakhstan and Siberia.

Germans had begun migrating to Russia two centuries before, after the German-born tsarina Catherine promised them land and cultural freedom in 1763. The *Russlanddeutschen* prospered, but Catherine's successors began to withdraw their privileges; and toward the end of the 1800s, they began looking westward, toward Germany and even beyond including the United States.

At the start of World War II, Stalin exiled the Volga Germans further east. George Feifer, an American exchange student at Moscow University in the 1960s and now a neighbor in Connecticut, would come to know a Russian German student whose father had died during the mass round-up and whose mother, before dying a year later, had to build "a hut with her bare hands in the wilderness" of Siberia in order to save her children.[202]

Of course, we at the embassy had reason too to know of the Volga Germans; before World War I, Spike Dubs's parents had come to the United States from one of these communities.

In extracting explicit language from the Soviets about the importance of solving humanitarian questions, the West German government had given their consular officers an opening (and a juridical basis) for pressing the Foreign Ministry and the OVIRs for a resolution of their consular cases. We promptly telegraphed the Soviet-German language to Washington and suggested that similar wording be included in a Soviet-American document at the second summit.

We didn't know that Nixon and Kissinger were skeptical about Willy Brandt's Ostpolitik and that Brandt's just-concluded meetings in Washington with both of them hadn't gone particularly well, at least from their perspective. Yet if the West Germans could extract a concession from Soviet officials, an explicit acknowledgement of the need to address humanitarian problems such as the plight of the Germans on Soviet territory, then surely Nixon and Kissinger could.

The second summit took place in the United States from June 18 to June 25, 1973. It proved to be another missed opportunity. Representation List XV wasn't presented to anyone on the Soviet side; and neither the joint communiqué nor any other document alluded to the existence of humanitarian problems in U.S.-Soviet relations. We learned later that an assistant secretary of state, Walter J. Stoessel, had passed a copy of List XV to Dobrynin three weeks *before* the summit. If it hadn't already been buried in Dobrynin's office, it would certainly be interred in the Foreign Ministry should it ever reach Moscow through Dobrynin's diplomatic pouch. Obviously, the White House attached no importance whatsoever to the divided families on our list.

A few days after the summit, a French journalist in Moscow alerted us to the fact that Brezhnev, paying an official visit to Paris en route back from Washington, had referred at a press conference to a list he had received while visiting the United States. According to the journalist, Brezhnev said that 177 persons named on it had not even applied for exit permission, and another 149 had been refused exit for reasons of security.

Representation List XV contained only 221 names. What Brezhnev had received in Washington—from Kissinger or Sonnenfeldt—was not any American representation list but another list of Soviet Jews trying to leave for Israel.

It was clear to us that Washington's indifference was as much of an obstacle to solving our cases as the obstructionism we encountered every time we visited the ministry or an OVIR.

At the end of the second summit it was announced that Nixon would travel to the USSR for a third summit in 1974. For the next twelve months, we would have to devote at least as much energy to changing attitudes in Washington as to making our demarches.

*   *   *

The publicity generated by the first two summits softened the attitudes of many Americans about the Soviet Union. The curiosity of many others was aroused. The flow eastward of American tourists and businesspersons, and scholars and students studying within the framework of the educational, scientific, and cultural exchanges that Nixon and Brezhnev had approved, steadily increased.

Looking back at the 1970s, Robert Gates—the one-time CIA director and President George W. Bush's secretary of defense—concluded that "détente's greatest achievement was the opening of consistent contact between the United States and the USSR in the early 1970s—a gradually intensifying engagement on many levels and in many areas that . . . would . . . open the Soviet Union to information, contacts, and ideas from the West and . . . would influence the thinking of many Soviet officials and citizens."[203]

Yet the popularization of détente through summitry also raised expectations that simply couldn't be met. The principle one was that the Soviet system itself was changing for the better and repression was easing. In fact, this didn't begin to occur until Gorbachev became Party leader in 1985.

As 1973 wound down after the second summit, there were, in fact, signs that the regime was retrenching, that the authorities were tightening control and digging in against what many were hoping to gain from the summits.

In September 1973, I sent a long report to Washington describing the problems that Americans were encountering when they sought to marry Russians or Soviet citizens of other nationality. Over the preceding year, beginning after the first summit in 1972, the consular section had received some fifty inquiries from Americans about the rules and regulations governing marriages. Some came from those who had already taken the plunge; others were simply planning.

Stalin had banned all his citizens from marrying foreigners in 1947. Although permitted again after his death, such marriages were abhorrent to many Soviet bureaucrats still influenced by Russia's historic xenophobia.

Whenever a Soviet citizen inquired about the possibility of marrying an American at a local civil registry office (ZAGS), he or she was instructed to have the interested American provide a written assurance from the embassy to the effect that it knew of no impediment to the marriage. During my first year, we took oaths from about twenty Americans affirming that they were single or divorced, and put our name and seal on a Russian and English-language form that they, or their intending spouse, would present at the ZAGS.

Even with the embassy's form, however, Soviet officials generally looked for a way to block a marriage between one of their citizens and one of ours.

Toward the end of my first year, just after the first summit, an American woman was expelled for becoming romantically involved with a Moscow resident. Then the Russian fiancé of another American was unexpectedly conscripted into the Soviet army. Another Russian was committed to a psychiatric institute upon registering his intention to marry an American.

In the latter case, the KGB and the parents of the young man probably colluded; under Soviet regulations, parents were within their rights to disapprove the marriage of their offspring no matter how old.

The KGB tried to talk one girl's parents into withholding permission by advising that "it would be better for your daughter to be dead and buried here than to live married in America."

If an American managed to schedule a marriage date at the ZAGS, where a waiting period of thirty days was required, the authorities at the corresponding OVIR might refuse to extend his or her period of stay to include the date. If the marriage had already taken place, the OVIR might simply refuse an exit visa to the Soviet spouse. We knew of ten to fifteen Soviet citizens married to Americans who had been refused permission to leave.

In November 1973, a young woman clutching a Russian-language "invitation letter" made it past the guards into the consular section. The guards generally blocked visitors who didn't have exit visas, but now and then, at the behest of a family member in the United States, we would invite a Soviet citizen to the embassy by letter. Sometimes the letter wouldn't be intercepted or the guards wouldn't interfere.

Our visitor had long blonde hair, wasn't attired like most Russians, and knew some English; perhaps the militiamen believed she was an American. She introduced herself as Olga Michelson, an art student in Moscow. I recognized the name immediately; the folder bearing the Michelson name was among the oldest, certainly the thickest, in our files.

Olga described her mother's long and unsuccessful struggle to join her husband, Anatoli Michelson, in the United States. When Olga was eight, in June 1956, he had gone to Vienna with one of the first groups of Soviet tourists permitted to travel outside the bloc after Stalin's death. At the time, Anatoli was the director of an engineering office at a Moscow institute and a member of the Communist Party.

Anatoli decided not to return, and the authorities promptly declared him "an enemy of the state." He was sentenced to a twenty-five-year term in absentia. The prosecutor threatened Olga's mother, Galina, with imprisonment for half the term because she hadn't warned the authorities of her husband's intention; but a court decided she couldn't be held responsible, even if the family's property could be confiscated. From Austria, Anatoli immigrated to the United States and became a citizen.

Galina and Olga began applying for exit visas soon thereafter, but year after year, their applications were rejected. The State Department and members of Congress pressed the embassy to raise the case, and it did so repeatedly. The Michelson name was on every representation list.

By the time Olga walked into my office, seventeen years had elapsed since Anatoli's decision not to return from Vienna, and the watchword in U.S.-Soviet relations was supposed to be détente. Yet whenever Steve, Jon, or I mentioned the case at the ministry or the Moscow OVIR, the conversation stopped. "Michelson has nothing to do with détente," Vasilyev would say, and his gorge would rise if we pressed on, as we would.

After a fruitless representation, I would return to the embassy and scour the file once again. Could Anatoli have been connected with the KGB before his trip, hence the intransigence we're encountering? But nothing pointed in this direction; his only "offense" had been to bolt from a tourist group and then to have made several broadcasts into the Soviet Union on a Western radio station.

It was clear to me that a representation from a much higher level would be needed before Galina and Olga would ever gain their freedom.

In 1986, thirteen years after I first raised the case, Anatoli mounted a demonstration in front of the Soviet embassy in Washington. In reporting it, American journalists noted that his family was still waiting in Moscow, his wife having become blind, and his own health precarious in the intervening years. President Reagan, as his published diaries confirm, took a deep interest in families separated by Soviet restrictions. Just before his summit meeting in Washington with Gorbachev December 8-10, 1987, he met privately with "5 individuals who have wives, husbands or fiancés in Soviet U[nion] who've been held there for years" [December 3 entry]. Reagan told them he'd appeal on their behalf to Gorbachev.[204] Olga and I haven't confirmed that Anatoli attended the meeting, but his plight was certainly brought to Gorbachev's attention because Olga and her mother's exit visas were issued just after the summit. After thirty-one years of waiting, the family was reunited.

The Michelsons settled in Florida for the last months of Mr. Michelson's life. He died there in 1990. Olga currently lives with her mother in North Carolina. Galleries in the southeast display her paintings, some of which—generously, it seems to me—include themes from her involuntary years in Russia.

*   *   *

American media was well represented in Moscow in the early 1970s. Among the twenty-five or so print and electronic reporters were Hedrick Smith of the *New York Times*, Robert Kaiser of the *Washington Post*, Murray Seeger of the *Los Angeles Times*, and Michael McGuire of the *Chicago Tribune*.

From time to time, a journalist would stop by our section to be briefed on a particular case or on overall trends. Despite Kissinger's attachment to "quiet diplomacy," we were glad to publicize our cases, which spoke to the heartbreak of families trapped by the Communist system. The more publicity abroad a long-refused applicant for an exit visa received, the more likely that someone high-up in the United States might take notice; and someone at Dobrynin's embassy might be prompted to flag the "irritant" to superiors back home.

Steve Steiner once told the *Times's* Smith about an Armenian who phoned regularly from the Armenian republic. The man's parents had brought him to Yerevan after World War II, and he had been repeatedly denied exit. Still, he considered the United States *his* country. He would periodically ask Steve how many more home runs Henry Aaron needed to hit before he set a new record. The plight of the Armenian made it into the *Times*.

Censorship of Western dispatches had ended during the Khrushchev era, but if the authorities took umbrage at a particular story, they didn't hesitate to bring it to the offending journalist's attention. The Foreign Ministry's press department that accredited foreign journalists would issue an official rebuke. If the story was deemed especially obnoxious, "others" would become involved, and the journalist might find his telephone out of order or a tire slashed. We experienced occasional harassment as consular officers, but generally less than the journalists whose work, unlike ours, was always in view.

In July 1973, as my final year began, Leonard Willems, an FSO specializing in consular affairs, succeeded Jon. In June 1974, Len would take over from me as consular head.

In September 1973, Nixon appointed Kissinger his new secretary of state, while letting him retain his NSC position. Kissinger was now in charge of the State Department, but it wasn't clear what this would mean. Would he take an interest in the divided American families, using the bully pulpit of a cabinet post to encourage Moscow to ease its restrictions? Would he begin dealing with the Soviet leadership through the embassy instead of his back channel?

As summer slipped into autumn, the KGB became more aggressive. In Leningrad, it subjected a sixty-seven-year old woman who had been typing the first copy of Solzhenitsyn's *The Gulag Archipelago* to remorseless questioning.[205] A decade earlier, she had volunteered to help the writer after reading *One Day in the Life of Ivan Denisovich*, the book that had propelled him to fame. After five days of interrogation, she revealed where she had hidden her copy, and then went home and hanged herself.

Expecting the worst, Solzhenitsyn left his apartment and took refuge in the Peredelkino dacha of Lidia Chukovskaya, a writer who had already spoken out against the persecution of dissidents. Chukovskaya came by her courage naturally; her father, a well-known writer of children's stories, was the first to congratulate Pasternak after he won the Nobel Prize.

On October 18, 1973, the KGB invaded the Moscow apartment of Sakharov and his wife, Elena Bonner, in the guise of two "Arabs" claiming to represent Black September, a terrorist organization.[206] The "Arabs" warned them to steer clear of Middle East affairs in their human rights work or risk harm to their children and grandchildren. Shortly thereafter, the KGB summoned Bonner for a round of "interviews."

In December 1973, the first copies of *The Gulag Archipelago* appeared in the West. In January 1974, Chukovskaya was expelled from the Writers' Union. On February 13, after being arrested and charged with treason, Solzhenitsyn was put on an Aeroflot flight and exiled to Frankfurt, West

Germany. Moscow's human rights abuses quickly moved to center stage in the embassy's reporting.

Foreign Ministry and OVIR officials continued to be unyielding on Representation List XV, brushing aside our appeals from behind their leather-padded doors. An OVIR representative in Yerevan was delighted to take a few bottles of whiskey off my hands while promising to review a few refusals, but the bottles were handed back to me in Moscow after a superior objected. With few exceptions, our Armenian cases remained unsolved.

In mid-January 1974, shortly before Solzhenitsyn's expulsion, an American dancer studying with the Kirov Ballet in Leningrad, Martin Fredmann, showed up in my office. Fredmann escorted a Russian woman whom he had married two weeks earlier, on January 2.

The woman turned out to be Kaleria Fedicheva. She had been dancing with the Kirov since 1955 and was considered one of the leading ballerinas. A few years earlier, she had been made a People's Artist, entitling her to special treatment in housing, medical care, and the kind of funeral she'd receive should she die in the USSR, a fate she was determined to avoid.[207] Valeri Panov, when writing about his own defection from the Kirov a few years later, would describe Fedicheva as not only having "sultry good looks" but a "blazing temperament."[208]

Fedicheva had met Fredmann while dancing in the United States on exchange visits in 1961 and 1964. Their relationship had rekindled after Fredmann went to Leningrad to study under a further exchange.

The authorities in Leningrad were known to be difficult (the KGB treated Americans at the consulate much more harshly than we were treated in Moscow), and I was surprised that the local ZAGS had allowed the marriage. A Leningrad consular officer had even participated as one of the required witnesses.

According to Fedicheva, the Kirov administrators were already ratcheting up the pressure. They told her that she could no longer dance; if she began to behave, she might be able to teach.

Beginning with Rudolf Nureyev in 1961, the Kirov Ballet had suffered the defection of five leading dancers. I couldn't imagine that an American would be able to carry off a sixth.

Fredmann told me that the authorities had already refused Kaleria's application for an exit visa and were claiming that their marriage was void; a "procedural defect" in a divorce she had earlier obtained required that it be annulled. Complicating matters, she had a child from her first marriage. It was obvious to me that the Leningrad ZAGS, before registering the marriage, hadn't checked with the local OVIR or the Ministry of Internal Affairs in Moscow to which it reported, or with the KGB.

We brought the case to the attention of the consular administration as soon as we learned of it, but it refused to intervene. It was another "internal affair" about which we had no right to complain. Fredmann was forced to return to the United States without his bride, and we added Fedicheva and her child to the representation list, then being readied for the third summit in June.

In the meantime, the consular officer who witnessed the marriage fell into a trap. A few days after the ceremony, the KGB pounced on him while he was trying to meet a contact. He was beaten badly during the arrest and was expelled. Liz and I liked the officer and his family (they had spent a few weeks in Moscow before moving to Leningrad), but the consular position was being used as a cover for "other work." With American tourism and commercial activity in the consulate's district (which included the Baltic republics) rapidly increasing, Washington's decision to let the CIA have the consulate's single consular position hadn't been wise.

No Western newspaper could resist a story involving a Russian ballerina and an American suitor, and it began circulating widely abroad. Although Fedicheva had been led to believe she might be able to teach, the authorities soon took away her students.

The Soviet authorities then overreached. Two "strangers" attacked and beat Fedicheva outside her apartment. Like the "Arabs" who threatened Sakharov in "accented but correct" Russian, the strangers were probably from the KGB. This made the story even more interesting abroad.

With bad publicity mounting, higher-ups in Moscow came to their senses. The KGB and the OVIR were ordered to retreat; and in February 1975, a year after the marriage, Kaleria and her son from the "rescinded" marriage received exit visas and left for the United States.

Reunited with Fredmann, Fedicheva embarked on a second career—staging and choreographing ballets, classical and new. In 1982, she established the Fedicheva Ballet Company in Glen Cove, New York. Four years after her arrival, she and Martin divorced; not all ballet stories end happily.

Since 1987, Martin has been the artistic director of the Colorado Ballet. Kaleria died of cancer in 1994.[209]

*   *   *

In December 1973, just before the Fedicheva marriage, Steve and I had read that the White House used a German-type formulation in a statement that President Nixon and Romanian President Nicolae Ceausescu had signed in Washington. The two leaders, in a joint communiqué, committed themselves to "contribute to the solution of humanitarian problems on the basis of mutual confidence and good will."[210] Nixon also assured Ceausescu that he would seek most-favored-nation treatment for Romania, as he was seeking it for the Soviet Union.

If Nixon and Kissinger acquiesced in the use of the West German-Soviet formulation in their dealings with the Romanians, they had no reason to shun it at their third summit in Moscow. We were more hopeful than ever we could gain a reference in the June documents to the importance of solving our own "humanitarian problems."

As the date approached, Soviet officials downplayed the Jackson-Vanik problem—the conditioning of Washington's grant of most-favored-nation treatment to Moscow's loosening of travel restrictions. Perhaps they believed their government could "buy off" the president's critics by stepping up the outflow of Soviet Jews after the summit, enabling the president to overcome Capitol Hill's resistance. Or perhaps they were taken in by Kissinger's confidence that the administration would ultimately prevail.

American businessmen in Moscow naturally looked forward to having the Soviets receive MFN treatment and the credits promised with it. Now and then, they would express frustration that the embassy was highlighting its family reunification cases. Talk about human rights was only complicating the prospect for greater trade.

At the start of 1974, I developed—with Steve's help—a telegram that argued it was time to address Moscow's restrictions in a public way. Kissinger's back-channel diplomacy had accomplished nothing for those trying to leave for the United States, even if it might be contributing to a rising number of Soviet Jews heading to Israel.

We knew that there were elements sensitive to Western opinion inside the Soviet regime. Some were in the Foreign Ministry. Others were in the USA and Canada Institute, which had its own channels into the leadership, mostly through the International Department of the Party's Central Committee. It was no secret that the institute's director, Georgi Arbatov, a member of the Central Committee, gave advice to Brezhnev as to how to deal with Washington.

The problem was that those connected with the regime who were well positioned to argue for relaxing Moscow's restrictions were being deprived of ammunition because of the administration's posture. If the White House and the State Department began to treat the Soviet restrictions more openly, then more pragmatic elements inside the regime might come to recognize the issue's importance and exert influence on their colleagues. As Steve and I viewed the situation, hard-liners in the Soviet bureaucracy were delighted with Washington's back-channel diplomacy; in the absence of condemnatory statements coming out of the administration, it was easy for the Soviets to remain intransigent. Someone high up in the executive branch needed to say clearly that no one in Moscow should misconstrue silence for acquiescence. A strong statement by a senior administration official before a Congressional committee would dramatize Washington's commitment to the right to travel—as provided for in the Declaration of Human Rights—and it might slow, if not finally derail, the Congressional drive to link trade with emigration, and forestall détente's looming wreck.

If Dubs were not willing to sign the telegram, I was prepared to send it through the so-called dissent channel, which Dean Rusk had established in 1968 when FSOs assigned abroad were clamoring to register reservations about the war in Vietnam, but were blocked by superiors.

I was reflecting on when to dispatch the telegram when we were told that the president had finally selected an ambassador to replace Beam. Spike had covered the yearlong gap in an exemplary manner, but it had become obvious that only someone enjoying full ambassadorial standing could expect to have clout in Moscow and, indeed, in Washington.

The president's appointee was Walter J. Stoessel, a career FSO. Stoessel had been a consular officer in Moscow in the late 1940s when Soviet behavior was at its worst, when one of his own staffers, Dolgun, had been arrested and imprisoned. Stoessel had returned to serve as the embassy's deputy chief of mission in 1963. After an intervening assignment in Washington, he had succeeded Gronouski in Warsaw, remaining there for nearly four years.

With Stoessel's background in consular affairs, I was sure he would know how to frame our concern in a way that would gain Kissinger's attention. I set my telegram aside.

Ambassador Stoessel and his wife, Mary Ann, arrived at Sheremetyevo Airport on February 21, 1974. Senior members of the embassy, including heads of sections and their wives as well as Foreign Ministry protocol officials, were on hand to greet them. Liz described the scene in the airport's VIP lounge:

> Everyone lined up according to protocol and the Stoessels made their grand entrance. Very elegant, well dressed people, both with silver-gray hair, she wearing a black mink coat with mink hat and black boots. Obviously both were once very blonde. And both are petite and short—he is only my height, she about the same. They were introduced to each of us.

Born in Kansas, the son of a U.S. Army cavalry officer stationed at Fort Hood, Stoessel had been raised in Beverly Hills, California. After graduating from Stanford University, he had served as a navy intelligence officer during

World War II. It was rumored at the embassy—but never confirmed—that
he had once appeared in a Hollywood film.

Stoessel looked the part of an old-line diplomat even if he wasn't from
Cabot's milieu. He never failed to wear a round-collar shirt with a collar
pin behind his tie—such shirts figured in Ivy League wardrobes through
the 1950s but had vanished since. The new ambassador's sport of choice
was paddle tennis. He had installed a court at the residence in Warsaw,
and as soon as he and Mrs. Stoessel settled in Spaso House, he arranged
for a court to be built next to the carriage house. When the court was up,
he organized the first of what would be annual competition between the
embassies, alternating home matches between Moscow and Warsaw.

The chairman of the Presidium of the Supreme Soviet, Nikolai
Podgorny (whose career would abruptly end in 1977 when Brezhnev took
over the largely ceremonial post), presided at the ceremony where Stoessel
handed over his credentials. The ceremony gave me my first look at one
of the Kremlin's most closely guarded buildings.

With an ambassador finally in place, the embassy awaited another visit
by Kissinger, this time as secretary of state, to set the stage for the third
summit.

*   *   *

On March 20, 1974, three days before Kissinger's arrival, we received a
visit from Sergei Kovalev, one of the leaders of the Soviet Union's nascent
human rights movement. A biologist by profession, Kovalev was a close
friend of Andrei Sakharov. In 1970, he had helped the physicist found the
capital's Human Rights Committee, and it had cost him his career.

Kovalev telephoned and asked us to meet him and a woman companion,
whose name he didn't mention, in front of the Stalinist high-rise. Steve
and I strolled out of the embassy without arousing attention and found
them sitting together on a bench in Uprising Park. After introductions,
we led them back to Tchaikovsky 19, four of us abreast, Steve on one side,
I on the other. Once inside, Kovalev asked for a telephone and dialed up
Sakharov to tell him he had safely arrived.

Kovalev's companion turned out to be Marija Sulskis, the sixty-eight-
year-old mother of a Lithuanian seaman, Simas Kudirka. Three and a half
years earlier, in November 1970, Kudirka had leapt from a Soviet trawler
off the coast of Martha's Vineyard on to the deck of an American coast
guard cutter to request asylum. However, the U.S. captain and crew allowed
Soviet crewmen to board the cutter and to drag Kudirka back. Returned
to Lithuania in chains, he was interrogated, convicted of treason, and
sentenced to ten years in prison.

Kudirka's seizure off an American vessel unleashed a storm of protest in the United States. Lithuanian-Americans and others with families in Eastern Europe and the USSR took to the streets and demonstrated against coast guard and Soviet offices, including Dobrynin's embassy. Not wanting to seem too complacent while promoting détente, Nixon protested the behavior of both the coast guard and the Soviets.

Mrs. Sulskis lived in a village in the Lithuanian republic but had been born in New York City. The purpose of her visit was to determine whether she retained a claim to American citizenship. If so, perhaps she and the Americans could help her son. Unknown to us, she had been blocked from visiting the embassy the previous day. One of the Soviet guards had "yelled at her and refused to let her in," and she had left in tears.[211] Thwarted, she had gone to the apartment of a dissident in Moscow and there had met Kovalev. Coordinating with Sakharov, he agreed to attempt to enter the embassy on his own with her documents. However, he too was stopped by the guards and was dragged off to Dzerzhinskaya Square. After an interrogation and a warning, he was released. It was at this point that he telephoned and asked for our help.

We made copies of Mrs. Sulskis's documents and pouched them to Washington. We knew we'd have to wait a few weeks before we received guidance, confirming or denying her citizenship claim.

In the meantime, on March 24, 1974, Kissinger, his counselor Sonnenfeldt (who Kissinger had brought with him from the White House to the department), two assistant secretaries of state, and others from the department and the NSC arrived for their presummit meeting with Brezhnev, Gromyko, Alexandrov, and other high-ranking Soviet officials. As in the past, Kissinger brought Dobrynin with him on his special flight.

The agenda was full of weighty issues, including arms control and European security. With an ambassador finally in charge, the embassy would be represented at all the meetings.

Sitting in Brezhnev's Kremlin office, Kissinger exuded confidence that the administration could manage the challenge mounted on Capitol Hill to its effort to secure most-favored-nation treatment for the Soviets.

He also employed the flattery and wit for which he was already known. At the March 25 session, Gromyko alluded to the fact that Stoessel's successor in Washington—Assistant Secretary for European Affairs Arthur J. Hartman, an FSO—had briefly stepped out of Brezhnev's office to look for a missing member of Kissinger's team. Gromyko jocularly assured the secretary that the Soviets didn't engage in "kidnapping."

In reply, Kissinger noted that an FSO had, in fact, just been kidnapped in Mexico and that the kidnappers were demanding a half million dollars in ransom, "but I don't know one that's worth $500,000, so we're refusing to pay. We're prepared to proceed without him." Although the transcript doesn't report a Soviet reaction, one presumes that Nixon's advisor at least elicited a smile.

The kidnapped vice consul was later found dead, killed by an American ex-convict living in Mexico.[212]

The delegation had brought with it a new representation list, List XVI, on which the Soviet desk, Steve, Len, and I had worked. It had grown to 300 family units from the 221 on List XV. More Soviet and American families had brought their tragic situations to our attention since the second summit.

Because Kissinger now headed the cabinet department responsible for protecting American citizens abroad, we were hoping his attitude toward the lists had changed. He and his staff couldn't have been unaware of their importance; we had stepped up our reporting about divided families, and our journalist friends had done the same.

I can't say I was shocked, however, when a member of the delegation (I don't recall who) told me that Kissinger had no intention of delivering the list, whether to Brezhnev, Gromyko, or anyone else on the Soviet side. Sonnenfeldt's instruction from the year before remained in force: the embassy can deliver the American list *after* the secretary has left.

Shortly before Kissinger's arrival, Stoessel had sent me a lengthy list of Soviet Jews seeking to immigrate to Israel. Stoessel had received it by pouch from Washington without an accompanying explanation. I surmised from it that Kissinger had been talking with Senator Jackson and other members of Congress as well as with American-Jewish organizations in an attempt to head off the Jackson-Vanik Amendment, and had passed the original of the list to Dobrynin before emplaning for Moscow.

After Kissinger and his delegation left, Stoessel took the American list and delivered it to the Foreign Ministry.[213] I didn't hear to whom he gave it and may not have asked; Kissinger had refused to present it to anyone on the Soviet side, and the new list would probably be buried. I should have sent my telegram after all.

A few days after Kissinger's departure, the department confirmed that Kudirka's mother was indeed an American citizen. On April 27, she set out from her village in the Lithuanian republic to return to the embassy. We intended to hand her an American passport and discuss how we could help her son. She evaded detection until she reached the railroad station in Vilnius; there the KGB stopped her and ordered her home.

After careful planning by Kovalev and other rights activists, she set out again on May 15, and this time was successful. Steve and I met her along with Kovalev in the park and walked them past the guards into the embassy. Len Willems handed her an American passport and confirmed that her son, Simas, could claim American citizenship by derivation because of the nationality law in force when she was born in New York.

On July 13, 1974, Len met with Mrs. Sulskis in Vilnius, and shortly thereafter, the embassy registered Simas as a citizen. He was still a prisoner in a strict-regime prison in the Ural Mountains; but under the U.S.-Soviet Consular Convention, an American consular officer was now entitled to see him.

On July 22, back in Washington, Senators Jackson and Jacob Javits drew Kissinger's attention to the case, asking him to secure Simas's earliest release and his immigration to the United States. Dobrynin was vacationing in the USSR, but Kissinger promised he would raise the case with the Soviet chargé d'affaires. According to Simas's biographer, Kissinger didn't follow through, but a deputy did.[214]

On August 14, 1974, President Gerald Ford, in his first official get-together with Dobrynin after Nixon's resignation, asked Dobrynin to permit Kudirka's immigration.[215] On August 23, two months after my departure, the Soviet authorities freed Simas (they certainly didn't want an American consular officer visiting a prison camp); and in October, he appeared at the consular section and received his American passport. In November, after securing Soviet exit visas, Simas, his wife, and their three children, along with Mrs. Sulskis, flew to New York.

After Kudirka left, the Soviet authorities struck back in the only way they knew. In December 1974, they arrested Sergei Kovalev. One year later, they tried him in Vilnius for "anti-Soviet agitation." Sakharov was at the courthouse for the trial but was barred from entering; his wife, Elena Bonner, was in Oslo, Norway, accepting the Nobel Peace Prize he had been awarded. Kovalev was convicted and sent to a strict-regime prison in the Ural Mountains—Perm Camp number 36. It was probably no coincidence that this was the camp where Kudirka had been held.

Shortly before he was freed seven years later, the Soviet regime went after his son Ivan. Ivan had assumed responsibility for the "Chronicle of Current Events," an important *samizdat* publication that had begun appearing in 1968 with Sergei's support.[216] Ivan was arrested and imprisoned, then Ivan's wife was arrested and imprisoned.

Sergei Kovalev was allowed to return to Moscow at the end of 1987. Upon Andrei Sakharov's death in 1989, he became the leader of the human rights movement in the USSR. Since the collapse of the Soviet system, he has worked for the attainment of human rights in post-Communist Russia, including in embattled Chechnya.

*   *   *

Two weeks after Kissinger's visit, I renewed the effort that Steve and I had made the previous year to have at least one summit document cite the need to address the humanitarian problems besetting U.S.-Soviet relations. With Stoessel's support, I informed the department that such language would help us negotiate our cases with working-level officials. I called attention to the fact that similar language had been used both in the Nixon-Ceausescu statement in December 1973 and the Brandt-Brezhnev statement in May 1973.

Liz worked part-time as a receptionist during my final months. She had earlier helped Chase Manhattan Bank open a Moscow branch, including arranging a grand reception for its chief executive, David Rockefeller, at the Hotel Metropol. But as our workload grew and as Soviet officials became more recalcitrant, her skills were more important to the consular operation than the bank.

In the course of a single week after Kissinger's visit, she helped me sort out a rash of problems:

- A tour leader of an American high school group "whispered" in her ear that one of his students was having a nervous breakdown. After further discussion, she ferreted out the fact that drugs acquired by the student from a Soviet source were the problem.
- An elderly couple claimed that the KGB had stolen their luggage because they had met with a Soviet Jew trying to emigrate.
- A businessman raced in to say that the vice president of his company, associated with Armand Hammer's Occidental Petroleum, had died while negotiating with Soviet trade officials.
- Three tourists from New York City expressed outrage they had been denied access to the Kremlin gold collection despite the agreement they thought they had with their tour group, and they demanded the embassy's intervention.
- A woman in tears displayed a passport defaced at a hotel in Kiev and expressed concern that she would be kept forever in the Soviet Union.
- A distraught American demanded that a Catholic priest be summoned to the embassy to "confess" her.

Americans visiting the USSR in 1974 were encountering no fewer problems and experiencing no less anxiety than those who had preceded them. Détente was on everyone's lips but the Soviet environment remained intimidating. Despite two summits and a multitude of written agreements, little had changed.

Just before the final summit, Steve and I prepared a confidential telegram describing the behavior of the guards in front of the embassy. Someone in the administration, also skeptical about détente's accomplishments, leaked it to the Washington journalists Rowland Evans and Robert Novak.

Under a headline "A Tightened Fist in Moscow,"[217] they reported how the guards were interfering with our work, detaining visitors (even those with invitation letters), and going so far as to block a West German diplomat from picking up a visa for a trip to the United States. The article reported that our protests to the guards and to the Foreign Ministry had gone unheeded, and we had recommended that Washington raise the situation with Dobrynin's embassy.

The two journalists included a personal comment: the embassy's telegram contradicts the "Nixon administration claims that détente is relaxing repression in the Soviet Union." No one in the administration, they added, had acted on the embassy's recommendation for a demarche to the Soviet embassy.

I don't recall how I reacted when I read that our telegram had leaked (leaks weren't unusual as the Watergate scandal was unfolding), but the fact that the administration didn't want to raise something unpleasant with Dobrynin's embassy—something having to do with human rights—didn't tell me something I didn't already know.

*   *   *

The main events of the third summit took place in Moscow from June 27 to July 3, 1974, shortly after Len Willems succeeded me. Nixon and Brezhnev formalized a new array of agreements and issued a communiqué that affirmed, in the fulsome language of the era, that the summit "results represent a new and important milestone along the road of improving relations between the USA and the USSR to the benefit of the peoples of both countries, and a significant contribution to their efforts aimed at strengthening world peace and security."[218]

The Nixon administration was of course in its final days. The Watergate scandal was nearing a climax and détente was under full attack, within and outside the administration. There had been no summit agreement on strategic arms: The Pentagon had adopted "an unyielding hard line against any SALT agreement [that is, strategic arms limitation treaty] that did not ensure an overwhelming American advantage."[219] According to Nixon's recollection, Jewish emigration did come up once; Brezhnev, traveling to

Domodedyevo Airport with the departing president, allowed that, "As far as I am concerned, I say let all the Jews go and let God go with them."[220]

Although the number of divided American families kept increasing, the final communiqué was silent about the existence of any humanitarian problems. Nor did any other summit document provide language that could be used by my successors at the ministry and the OVIRs. Nixon and Brezhnev's last meeting did nothing to improve the prospects of the three hundred families on our list.

It would take another Republican administration—that of President Reagan—before Washington treated the American list at least as well as the Israeli list. In 1985, the Soviets were given a list containing the names of twenty American citizens, twenty Soviet citizen spouses of American citizens, and over one hundred other families who had been prevented leaving for the United States. Within the matter of two years, most of the cases were solved.

The Reagan administration continued Kissinger's practice of handing over lists of Soviet Jews desiring to go to Israel. In 1985, the Israeli list contained the names of 3,400 families.

From the Six-Day War in 1967 to the reestablishment of diplomatic relations between the USSR and Israel in 1991, the Netherlands, as previously mentioned, served as Israel's "protecting power." A friend in the Dutch Foreign Service, Floor Kist, has found no indication, however, that the Foreign Ministry at The Hague or the Dutch embassy in Moscow was ever informed of Kissinger's practice of handing over Israeli lists to the Soviets. Observance of the proprieties was never one of Kissinger's strong points.

After the final Nixon-Brezhnev summit, Kissinger intensified his dialogue with Senator Jackson and others on Capitol Hill in a determined effort to break the trade and emigration link. By this time, however, Jackson wanted more. He pressed for an annual quota of one hundred thousand exit visas for those seeking to leave for Israel. He also raised Moscow's policy of granting visas "preferentially to Jews living in the provinces, to Jews of a lower educational and cultural level than those living in Moscow"[221]—the concern that Steve had earlier flagged to Washington.

Just before the final Nixon-Brezhnev summit, Senators Stevenson, Jackson, and eighteen others had compounded the administration's problem by adding a further amendment to the proposed trade bill to bar the extension of credit unless the Soviets lifted their emigration restrictions. In December 1974, the trade bill with both the Jackson-Vanik and the Stevenson Amendments became U.S. law, and less than a month later, in January 1975, the Soviet Union abrogated the trade agreement as it appeared in that form. It also stopped further payments on its Lend-Lease debt.

Had Nixon and Kissinger spoken out on behalf of the divided American and Soviet families in the early 1970s, it's just possible that the Kremlin would have moved, even if modestly at the start, toward reducing its emigration barriers. Certainly the Kremlin wouldn't have adopted the education tax that so poisoned the atmosphere on Capitol Hill. As it was, the Soviet leaders dug in their heels, Congress blocked the grant of most-favored-nation treatment and credits; and Nixon and Kissinger's policy collapsed.

*   *   *

From the time of his arrival in February 1974, Ambassador Stoessel encouraged officers to report matters as they saw them, without any soft-pedaling in deference to an administration uncomfortable about protecting human rights. As a former consular officer, Stoessel was especially sympathetic to the problems we had downstairs. Looking over Representation List XVI, he told me he saw the name of one woman who had been waiting for an exit visa since 1948.

The embassy's coverage of unofficial cultural trends and dissident activities increased markedly during his three years, as the American public and the Congress focused ever more on the Soviet regime's treatment of its people.

Many Americans reacted strongly when the Ford administration decided, with Kissinger's concurrence, not to invite Solzhenitsyn to the White House in July 1975. This occurred shortly before the United States, the Soviet Union, and thirty-three other governments signed the Helsinki Final Act that included extensive language supporting human rights, language that would embolden dissidents throughout the bloc.

With the election of President Jimmy Carter in November 1976, human rights became an explicit plank in American foreign policy. The State Department established a bureau for human rights and began issuing annual human rights reports on individual countries.

Stoessel opened Spaso House to Soviet citizens whom previous ambassadors had shunned, including refuseniks and others out of favor with the regime. He even invited Russians to see the film based on the still-banned *Doctor Zhivago*. For the first time, a Soviet jazz group that enjoyed no official standing was invited to perform at the residence.

The Soviet regime's view of jazz had always fluctuated in sync with its attitude toward different American administrations. As S. Frederick Starr's comprehensive study explains, although this kind of music was well known in Western Europe and as far afield as China by the time of the Bolshevik Revolution, it didn't reach Russia and take root until the early 1920s when

Lenin introduced his less militant, more accommodating New Economic Policy.[222]

Then, as Stalin consolidated power, reaction set in. Maxim Gorky, one of the dictator's favorite writers, published an article in *Pravda* in 1928 entitled "On the Music of the Gross": "The monstrous bass belches out English words; a wild horn wails piercingly, calling to mind the cries of a raving camel; a drum pounds monotonously."[223]

With the establishment of U.S.-Soviet relations in 1933, the pendulum swung again toward tolerance. In 1935, a Russian woman, Vera Dneprova, who used to party with Bohlen and others at the Mokhovaya embassy (according to Starr, she became the mistress of the American diplomat Elbridge Dubrow), organized a women's jazz orchestra that the regime's concert agency let perform at Black Sea ports.[224]

As the Great Terror began, so did another crackdown; Dneprova was arrested in 1937 and sentenced to ten years hard labor (she was released after five years of felling trees on the Kola Peninsula).

But American culture again came into favor with the start of the war; General Kliment Voroshilov and Lazar Kaganovich, from Stalin's coterie, were among jazz's protectors.

The Cold War brought renewed hostility. Jazz was forbidden, and its performers were imprisoned. One day in 1949, saxophonists in Moscow were ordered to bring their instruments to the regime's music agency; the word *saxophonist* was struck from each performer's identification card, and their instruments were confiscated.

After Stalin's death, American diplomats noted that jazz was enjoying another renaissance, especially among the young. Bohlen, then ambassador, recommended that the VOA, which had been beaming programs into the USSR since 1949, develop a program that would appeal to youth. A year later, in 1955, Willis Conover, in *Music USA*, began broadcasting the music of Louis Armstrong, Oscar Peterson, John Coltrane, Miles Davis, among others. Despite jamming, bits and pieces of his broadcasts could be heard; Conover became "more effective than a fleet of B-29s" in reaching the Soviet heartland. Jamming was suspended at the height of détente.[225]

Melvin Levitsky, a political officer from Sioux City, Iowa, reported on dissident and refusenik affairs in Stoessel's first year. Mel came to know artists and performers who worked outside the official canon. He arranged two concerts for Soviet jazz groups at Spaso House. Arsenal, one of the groups, put on a combined jazz-rock version of *Jesus Christ Superstar*. Its leader, Alexei Kozlov, a saxophonist, had been monitoring foreign broadcasts since the early 1950s; he worked as an industrial designer while developing his musicianship on the side. By the 1970s, Kozlov and Arsenal were being invited to perform at fifteen or twenty closed events a year. In

1974, Rick Smith of the *Times* heard them perform before a group of four hundred young persons in an unmarked hall in Moscow's Achievements of National Economy Park.[226]

Since the collapse of the Soviet Union, Kozlov and his colleagues have represented Russia at numerous jazz festivals abroad. Almost thirty years after Arsenal's Spaso House performance, Kozlov told Mel that its appearance there had helped protect it from the KGB.

Stoessel's confidence in his Foreign Service officers was confirmed for me when I became entangled in a prank involving Kremlinology, the arcane method by which analysts in Washington and its embassies in the Communist bloc extracted information from "tea leaves" in the tightly controlled media.

On Sundays, I would often wander in different Moscow neighborhoods, hoping to learn something from casual conversations with ordinary Russians. During one outing, I found a discarded reel of film sitting in an uncovered trash bin outside a church that had been converted into a research institute. Looking at a few frames, I was astounded to see Fidel Castro on a yacht entertaining a Soviet delegation in what must have been Cuban waters. I turned it over to one of the CIA officers who lived in our compound. He rushed back to search for something I might have missed, but I had found the only item of value.

A few days after Stoessel arrived, I came upon a cache of newspapers piled in a bin outside a nearby housing compound. It was a gloomy Sunday morning, and no one else was out. Looking more closely, I saw that the papers covered the pivotal events of winter 1953, from *Pravda*'s January 13 announcement of the alleged "doctors' plot" against Stalin to the dictator's death and burial in March. Many of the articles were marked up in pencil and ink.

It struck me that I could have some fun with the embassy's political officers. I grabbed what I could and hurried back to Leninsky 45. Over the next few days, I added cryptic comments in Russian to various articles and slipped the papers into my colleagues' mailboxes.

I had put the prank totally out of mind when two weeks later, at a country-team meeting, a political officer began describing the bizarre receipt of marked-up newspapers from random dates in 1953. Were rogue elements in the regime trying to convey some kind of message to Washington through the embassy? Could the items reporting Stalin's death and burial be related to rumors of Brezhnev's declining health?

Stoessel listened intently as the officer applied his analytic skills to unraveling the mystery. Finally, the ambassador was informed that a telegram would go out to Washington with the political section's considered interpretation.

I was dumbfounded. The third summit was fast approaching, and the embassy couldn't dispatch a frivolous analysis. I may have inherited my Irish grandfather's penchant for scavenging, and maybe his humor, but this I couldn't afford.

There were a few seconds of silence after I admitted the prank. Fortunately, Stoessel laughed it off, and we worked together on real problems in the weeks that remained. And I resisted the temptation to "dumpster dive" during the balance of my career.

*   *   *

By the end of two years, I knew that I wanted a second tour in the USSR. Consular work had kept me too close to my desk. I hadn't been to the Central Asian republics; I hadn't experienced all the Soviet Union's twelve time zones. Problems of nationalism among the USSR's non-Russian peoples were looming, yet I had barely scratched the huge empire's surface.

I had seen signs of restiveness during the few trips I had taken. I could not forget the pretty Lithuanian girl in Vilnius who had gone out of her way to hand me and my traveling companion a bouquet of flowers. We were checking prices in a shop when she heard our American accents.

I had agreed to travel to Lithuania and the other Baltic republics after a colleague working with Mel had suggested it, not realizing that he was with the CIA and that we would be followed constantly. The girl was probably detained as soon as we left her; thereafter, I would choose my traveling companions more carefully.

Nor could Liz and I forget the toast of a young Georgian as we mingled with him and his friends in a Tbilisi nightclub. "Please, when you return to freedom in the United States, remember we Georgians want freedom too." The farther one traveled from Moscow, the easier it was to strike up conversations with real people, outside the control of the KGB.

Work in the consular section had been satisfying, especially when we succeeded in reuniting long-separated families and extricating Americans from difficult situations. But the Foreign Service had assigned me to the political track, and this was how I wanted to spend the career.

Liz told me she'd be glad to return, although the burden of maintaining a household had fallen disproportionately on her. The wives in Moscow encountered more day-to-day hardships than the husbands, having to wait in lines, scour markets for decent fruit and vegetables, make two or three trips a week to the hard-currency stores and the one-aisle basement commissary. Fortunately for me, I had married a woman whose interests centered on family and community, but stinted nothing when representing the country.

We had found compensations for many of the hardships. The Anglo-American School provided a good education for the children. There were opportunities—winter and summer—to escape compound living, in the city's parks, theaters, and rinks, and in the two villages beyond, Peredelkino and Tarasovka.

We had even discovered a swimming hole to which we could travel without official permission, a stream a few yards wide at the edge of a farm field near the village of Uspenskoye. There were beautiful birch groves nearby. On Sunday afternoons, diplomats in the know and Soviet bureaucrats would retreat to the muddy "diplomatic beach," stretch out blankets, and have their picnics. The militia monitored vehicles, especially those with diplomatic plates, but the beach lay in an open zone even if near the leaders' dachas in Barvikha; and not once were we stopped. We became better acquainted with a Foreign Ministry official Igor Bubnov from the American department and his wife when we met there by chance.

Shortly before the assignment ended, Mel introduced us to Igor Palmin, a self-employed photographer. Slightly built, Igor arrived one evening with a knapsack on his back, camera and film inside, just after visiting the Levitsky's across the hall. We had arranged for him to photograph the children. Film and processing chemicals were difficult to obtain and were expensive, but I knew from Mel that Igor was a serious photographer. Before he set to work, we had a drink and chatted about our vastly different lives.

Igor had been in the forefront of a post-Stalin era trend to portray ordinary citizens in their everyday routines. In 1966, he and a few friends had been acclaimed at a landmark exhibition organized by one of the capital's photography clubs. Their "search for new forms" included photographs of people without the backdrops of socialist construction that had seemed to define earlier Soviet photography.[227]

Igor returned to the apartment several weeks later. This time I met him outside and accompanied him past the guard. The photographs were superb. Children's faces are not easy to capture—it takes time for character to form—yet Igor had caught the personalities of ours.

I had assumed that Igor was Jewish but then saw a portrait he had taken of himself on a mountainside near an abandoned Chechen village showing a cross around his neck. He explained that a forebear, before the Revolution, had converted to the Orthodox Church. Palmin might have come from the palm trees seen on a pilgrimage to Jerusalem's Holy Places, such as Russians took by the thousands before World War I.[228]

I knew that a Jew in tsarist times had little choice but to convert if he wished to hold an imperial post or to marry a Christian. Pasternak had come from a Jewish family, and his father was supposed to have converted after becoming a professor at an art school under tsarist patronage, but he had ignored the order. A nurse, however, arranged for Boris's baptism in a neighborhood church. Because of his nurse, Pasternak's works are suffused with Christian beliefs, although his enemies never let him forget he was born a Jew.

Igor struck me as no less independent and no less Russian than the poet. He told me that he had never considered leaving his country, as some of his acquaintances urged.

Pasternak once told Khrushchev—after the Writers' Union voted to exile him—he was "tied to Russia by birth, by life, and by work" and couldn't imagine living outside.[229] For Igor, too, living outside would have been unthinkable.

Years later, I asked Igor what prompted him to embark on such an independent path in face of all the pressures to conform. I knew that his parents—long since dead—had been associated with a provincial theater, but what had been the other influences?

He said that the satiric writings of Ilf and Petrov, the coauthors of *The Twelve Chairs*[230], had made an impression. Published first in 1928, the novel describes the comic adventures of a crook and rogue, Ostap Bender, as he outwits pretentious and stupid Soviet officials and pursues various schemes, even including a political conspiracy. The Bender character proved so endearing to readers that the regime dared not ban the book; despite criticism from the ultra-orthodox *Literary Gazette*, it had been republished during Stalin's last years.[231]

Friends like Igor had spent all their lives under a ruthless Communist regime, yet they impressed Liz and me as being as free in spirit and as courageous as our friends in Warsaw. If given the opportunity, we knew we'd have to return.

7

New Delhi, Foggy Bottom, Brzezinski, and Vance

In March 1974, while still in Moscow, I received a telephone call from the department indicating that my next assignment would be to the American mission in Berlin, where I would be the political section's "eastern affairs officer," responsible for dealing with Soviet and East German officials.

The United States did not yet recognize the so-called German Democratic Republic but considered the Soviet Union to be East Germany's governing power. Recognition wouldn't be granted until several months later.

Personnel had earlier suggested I return to Poland to head the consulate in Poznan, but my Russian had progressed to a near-professional level, and I was concerned about losing what I had acquired by again using Polish. Also, I wanted to do political work in Germany, having lost that opportunity twice before. Now, at last, I'd be involved with Germany, or at least its spurious "twin" in the east.

I figured that the assignment was all but mine. Within a few days, however, it had fallen through. Secretary of State Kissinger had different plans for FSOs awaiting assignment in 1974.

According to the story that reached Moscow, a senior FSO had angered him as they were traveling together to Mexico the month before, in February 1974. Kissinger had asked the officer about some aspect of East-West relations, and the officer had responded to the effect: "Sorry, Mr. Secretary, I know little about these matters. I'm a specialist in Latin American affairs."

I later heard a second story: While briefing East-West issues to American ambassadors who had gathered in Mexico from our Latin American embassies for a treaty-signing ceremony, Kissinger realized that few understood what he was talking about. Only a handful of the career professionals in attendance had ever served outside the Bureau of American Republics Affairs (ARA) or the Latin American region it covers.

Whatever the reason, Kissinger decided that all FSOs would henceforth be assigned to bureaus and regions outside their area of expertise. This would ensure they'd acquire the "global outlook" that he deemed they needed.

Almost overnight, the department adopted the Global Outlook Program, GLOP as it became known, for its more than four thousand FSOs. In the parlance of the day, I was "glopped" out of Berlin as I had been "balpa'd" from that post six years before.

I was told my fate in April. I received a two-year assignment as a political officer to the embassy in New Delhi, India. Since I had no background in Asian affairs, the assignment appeared in line with the secretary's thinking, although his program, as far as I recall, wasn't officially explained.

I wasn't the only one affected in Moscow. Upon Ambassador Stoessel's arrival, Spike Dubs had reverted to his role as deputy chief of mission. When that assignment ended, he was ordered back to the department as a deputy assistant secretary of state in the Bureau of Near Eastern and South Asian Affairs (NEA). Spike hadn't served in that bureau before, or in any of the countries for which it was responsible. He too had been "glopped."

Reflecting on Kissinger's new personnel policy during my final weeks in Moscow, I couldn't help but see a parallel with the decision he and Nixon had made to deny us an ambassador for thirteen months. When framing policy toward the Soviet Union, both had found it expedient not to have a top-ranking ambassador in charge of Tchaikovsky 19, someone who might challenge their policy or tactics on the basis of in-country experience and area expertise. By keeping area experts out of embassies and geographic bureaus that corresponded to their expertise, Nixon and his national security advisor were replicating what they had done in Moscow, assuring a freer hand for themselves and protecting themselves from well-informed second-guessing. As will be seen in chapter 11, Kissinger in particular didn't like the advice he was then receiving from the service's Africa hands.

The Global Outlook Program remained in effect until early 1977 when Kissinger left the department toward the end of the Ford administration. In the final volume of his memoir, he refers to it:

> Until I became Secretary, the majority of Foreign Service officers spent their entire careers in the bureau to which they had been assigned early on. Thus they tended to reflect the point of view of the regions with which they had been associated most of their professional lives as well as the conventional wisdom of academicians and other savants in their areas of responsibility.

> For officers dealing with Europe or Asia or the Middle East, this regional perspective was inevitably related to America's broad Cold War strategy; since each of these regions contained major powers and was affected by Soviet policies, they were obliged to consider their problems from a global outlook. But the backwaters of policy—Latin America to some extent and Africa in very large measure—did not encourage geopolitical perspectives.[232]

In fact, Kissinger applied his Global Outlook Program to every region—not simply to Latin America and Africa—and to every FSO awaiting assignment. Moreover, as will be seen, the program was more East-West in spirit than truly global. Kissinger's use of *backwaters* to describe policy making toward Latin American and Africa reveals more about himself than he probably intended.

Kissinger complains in his memoir that his "successors" abandoned the GLOP program before it could accomplish the "20 percent rotation out of each regional bureau every year" that he wanted.[233] Had his program remained in force after 1977, it would have been even more disruptive than it was. Perhaps the one-time professor didn't understand that assignments in the Foreign Service are generally for two, three, or four years and that a requirement that personnel in the geographic bureaus "turn over" every five years would have exacerbated the discontinuities already built into managing policy toward individual countries and managing a career. Or perhaps he did understand, and this for him was the point.

The loosening of officers' connections with areas and languages continues today, albeit in a different way. Middle-ranking officers are encouraged to seek ever more challenging supervisory assignments; focusing on one or two countries and developing area expertise no longer enhances a career.

When the Foreign Service was professionalized in the middle 1920s, the FSOs who studied the hard languages were expected to use them for long periods in the regions where they were spoken. "In all cases of language study at Government expense it was understood that the Foreign Service Officers benefiting thereby would undertake to serve at least 7 years at posts in countries where the languages of their specialization were spoken, and one out of three years thereafter." (*The Foreign Service of the United States, Origins, Development, and Functions*[234]).

Charles Bohlen described the Foreign Service as it was *before* it became professional:

> One of the difficulties of the Foreign Service in those days was that an officer would spend two, three, or even four years in one

country and then be transferred to another without really having much opportunity to acquire a serious knowledge of the first country's customs, institutions, and history. This skipping around like a water bug from one country to another had produced a certain superficiality in our career officers. To increase the knowledge of certain countries and areas, a program of regional specialization had been established.[235]

The Foreign Service ought to return to its professional roots and once again encourage officers to specialize and develop area expertise. The failures of American policy in recent years, including in the Middle East, underscore the importance of having experts rather than dilettantes hold the positions that bear importantly on foreign-policy making.

*   *   *

Paul Kreisberg, the embassy's political counselor, met us at Delhi's Palam Airport on August 8, 1974, which was also Nixon's final day as president. The weather was brutally hot, and our daughter Elise fell to the floor in a faint just after we entered the terminal.

Paul took us to our housing, an apartment on the ground floor of a two-story white stucco bungalow in a New Delhi neighborhood known as Golf Links. A CIA officer and his Congolese wife (a tribal princess, we were told) lived upstairs, and affluent Indian families occupied all the nearby houses. The Ashoka Hotel and its beautiful golf course were a few minutes away.

Paul had already arranged for a staff, and they lined up to welcome us as we pulled into the parking area: Ali, a Muslim, was to be our cook; Harry, a Hindu, the laundryman; and George, a Christian with children of his own, the houseboy. Within a few days, Liz had organized them into an effective multicultural team. However, George didn't last; when items of clothing kept disappearing from the girls' bureaus, we confronted him and he admitted he was taking several a week.

To complete the team, we hired Ram, an Indian expelled from Burma, to be our *mali*, the gardener. Ram would hunker on his haunches and with marvelously dexterous fingers produce a beautiful lawn. He had no family and no property, and we let him live in an empty room above the garage; his kind was surely in St. Matthew's mind when he said that the meek would inherit the earth.

A short drive away, behind a formidable wall, was the embassy's chancery. The driveway leading to its front steps was paved with strips of white marble and pebbles from the Ganges River. The front door sat atop a staircase of marble from which gilded metal columns rose to support the roof. The façade consisted of a latticework of marble and concrete tile; behind the lattice were glass walls, and behind them were the offices.

The chancery's architect, Edward Durrell Stone, had taken ideas from the Taj Mahal and other South Asian structures, and adapted them to his Modernist style. From the front gate, the effect was beautiful. When Prime Minister Jawaharlal Nehru attended the chancery's opening in January 1959, he said he was "enchanted."[236]

Conditions inside, however, were not so enchanting.

The chancery was built around a large central atrium at the center of which sits a pool of water under a latticed aluminum roof. Indigenous vegetation cared for by the Indian staff grows on concrete islands in the pool. Our offices were dispersed around the pool on two levels. Because suffocating heat comes often to central India, the offices were air-conditioned; but the walkways outside, from June through August during the monsoon season, were often soaked with rain and oppressively humid.

What an Irish statesman once said about architects working in Africa may be to the point: "European architects designing buildings for tropical Africa had a tendency to think more about how a building would look in photographs circulated in Europe than in how they might suit the people who had to live and/or work there in a tropical climate."[237]

The New Delhi chancery was situated at one end of a compound that covers sixteen acres. The compound encompassed the ambassador's residence, or Franklin D. Roosevelt House (also designed by Stone); several rows of town houses and apartments to accommodate the American staff; and extensive facilities for recreation, including a theater, restaurant, bar, bowling alley, swimming pool, baseball field, and tennis courts.

An underground network of tunnels facilitated movement around the compound. Harvard Law School had a similar system, and it was said that the students with the best marks, the ones with the telltale pallor, never saw daylight. As I acclimated myself to the embassy, I wondered whether there were Americans who had never left the compound to see India.

When we arrived, the ambassador was Daniel Patrick Moynihan, who would later serve as ambassador to the United Nations and a senator from New York. By the time we left in June 1976, William B. Saxbe, Nixon's last attorney general and an ex-senator from Ohio, had succeeded Moynihan.

The embassy had a large support staff numbering in the hundreds, both American and Indian nationals. Moynihan's staff at Roosevelt House included three waiters ("bearers"), two cooks, two laundrymen, two inside sweepers, and countless outside sweepers, gardeners, and guards.

The embassy was also full of senior officers, most within one or two assignments from retirement. There were seven Foreign Service counselor-level officers and ten senior-level attachés (both categories ranking higher than the embassy's first, second, and third secretaries). The comparable figures in Moscow had been five and four. As a first secretary, I was number 44 on the protocol list.

The political section to which I was assigned was about the size of Moscow's. When Paul first evaluated my performance, he described the section as having eight members of whom six were FSOs. At the conclusion of my second year, however, he wrote that there were twelve of us of whom five were FSOs. Ambassador Saxbe brought three aides with him from Washington, and although they didn't participate in the section's meetings, Paul probably included two of them in his second head count. (How the three kept busy intrigued us at first, but they were avid golfers and frequently slipped away to play golf with Saxbe.) A CIA officer or a labor attaché may have been included too; supervisors sometimes hike the number of those supervised to exaggerate their managerial responsibilities.

I had been assigned to the section's "Communist affairs" position. Even embassies remote from the Cold War's front lines organized themselves to appear in the thick of it, to be "global" in the way Kissinger used the word. My position, therefore, kept me involved in Soviet and Communist affairs, which wasn't the point of GLOP as the anecdotes had described it.

John Kenneth Galbraith, Kennedy's ambassador to India and Roosevelt House's first occupant, found that "the necessary tasks . . . could be accomplished in around two hours of official work a day." In Galbraith's opinion, "any more time involved ill-concealed idleness."[238] Galbraith was speaking about his own work, but it wasn't long before I concluded that the embassy itself suffered from an excess of hours relative to tasks.

I was given a grab bag of responsibilities besides the Soviet Union, Eastern Europe, and "international communism," including reporting on India's interests and relations with East and Southeast Asia (excluding Burma); the UN and its specialized agencies; the nonaligned group—Tibet, Bhutan, and Sikkim; and Law-of-the-Sea matters. I don't remember why Burma was excluded, but Paul was a China hand (I met him first when he was visiting in Warsaw in connection with the China talks), and perhaps he reserved the area to himself, not that there was much happening in Indo-Burmese relations. My tasks remained the same the second year except for the addition of the Middle East, North Africa, and the rapidly-emerging field of human rights.

The subjects for which I was responsible weren't central to Washington's interests in South Asia. My colleagues, several of who had lived in the region before (in the Peace Corps or in school), had the weightier portfolios, tracking India's internal situation, its relations with neighbors like Pakistan, China, Bangladesh, Nepal, and Sri Lanka, and—after India's explosion of a "peaceful device" in the Rajasthan desert in May 1974—its nuclear ambitions. India wasn't a signatory to the Nuclear Non-Proliferation Treaty of 1968.

I hadn't traveled in any of the non-European countries for which I was responsible, and the embassy didn't have the funds to send me. In retrospect, I shouldn't have acquiesced in Kissinger's scheme but should have gone back to Washington to take my chances on a department assignment.

Seeing that I was underemployed, Moynihan put me to work on Sikkim, the remote protectorate in the Himalayan Mountains that the Indian government was bent on controlling. The ruling Chogyal, or prince, had married an American citizen, Hope Cooke, in 1963 (at a ceremony that Galbraith attended), and Moynihan figured there had to be someone in Washington interested in knowing what was happening. I researched the history of the protectorate in India's colonial and postcolonial eras, and wrote a lengthy report that Moynihan liked. The marriage between the Chogyal and the American girl ended, but my report likely molders in a Washington pigeonhole still.

Moynihan asked me to ghostwrite an article for him on the occasion of the twenty-fifth anniversary of India's independence. At the time, the country was undergoing terrible turmoil, including daily demonstrations against Prime Minister Indira Gandhi. Over Moynihan's name, I informed the readers of *Yojana*, the Indian Planning Commission's publication (in the Assamese, Bengali, Gujarati, Hindi, Malayalam, Marathi, Tamil, Telugu, and English languages) that they shouldn't despair. The United States had found itself in similar straits a quarter century after its Constitution was promulgated: "The enemy [the British, of course] marched on the capital city Washington and burned public buildings, not even sparing the White House."[239] Moynihan didn't let me know of reactions to the article if there were any, but I'm sure he would have arranged other diverting tasks from which I would have profited had he not ended his assignment and returned to Cambridge the month it appeared.

*   *   *

My predecessor in the political section had become acquainted with a Soviet diplomat, Andrei Fialkovski, and I telephoned Andrei and introduced myself shortly after arriving. Andrei lived with his wife, Tanya, in a Soviet compound not far from us. As he was not comfortable hosting me there, we'd meet every few weeks at a hotel or at my apartment for a meal prepared by Ali.

The USSR and India had signed an elaborate twenty-year Friendship and Cooperation Treaty on August 9, 1971. Just before the signing, Kissinger had paid a visit to India en route to Pakistan from where, on July 9, he would launch his secret visit to Beijing. At the time, India was supporting the Bengali movement, which would soon lead to the breakaway of eastern Pakistan and the establishment of Bangladesh. Kissinger warned Mrs. Gandhi that the United States would not help her if she took India to war against Pakistan.

Nixon and Kissinger had been "tilting" American policy toward Pakistan while feigning a policy of balance between that country and India, the two dominant powers in South Asia. They were cultivating Islamabad to set the stage for normalizing relations with China, its longtime ally. So Kissinger deliberately arranged his schedule to show "roughly equal" stays in Islamabad and Delhi to help conceal the tilt; as he wrote in his memoir, "to stay a day longer in Pakistan than in India would have been interpreted as favoritism to Pakistan, with repercussions in New Delhi, our bureaucracy, the media, and above all the Congress."[240]

In Kissinger's word, the announcement of the Indo-Soviet treaty came as a "bombshell," threatening to embroil the Soviet Union in a war against Pakistan and disrupt American policy.[241] Nixon's advisor took it as a personal affront.

Nixon didn't care for Mrs. Gandhi, as the record shows, and Kissinger didn't enjoy dialoguing with Indians, no matter with whom.[242] When I later headed the India desk, it took almost a year of memo writing before he agreed to see a new Indian ambassador.

Against the background of the Indo-Soviet Treaty and a "makeup" visit by Kissinger to India in October 1974, Andrei Fialkovski and I spent hours discussing South Asian events. I tried to assess the range and depth of the Indo-Soviet relationship, and he tried to determine if the Indo-U.S. relationship was as bad as it appeared.

As far as I could tell, Andrei was a regular diplomat, not KGB, and we spoke as much about our prior diplomatic experiences and our families as about India, neither of us having information of particular importance to share.

Our association did lead to a transient "détente" between the embassies. One of the agreements signed at the first Nixon-Brezhnev summit provided for U.S.-Soviet cooperation in the exploration and use of outer space. The governments agreed to develop compatible "rendezvous and docking systems of [their] manned space craft and stations in order to enhance the safety of manned flights," and then to conduct joint experiments.[243] Not long thereafter, they announced they would test the compatibility of their systems by docking their respective Apollo and Soyuz spacecrafts in 1975.

When I learned that the docking was scheduled for July that year and that television would carry it worldwide, I suggested to Paul that the American and Soviet ambassadors and their aides mark the occasion with a small reception at Roosevelt House. Moynihan had already left, and Saxbe was just beginning. Why not have Saxbe do something for détente, already in trouble due to Nixon's resignation and Moscow's abrogation of the trade treaty.

Generally, the American and Soviet ambassadors in New Delhi had little contact, seeing one another occasionally at National Day receptions where they would converse mostly with colleagues from embassies representing governments allied with their own. When Ambassador Galbraith served in India, he was once invited to the Soviet embassy to greet Yuri Gagarin, who was on a round-the-world propaganda tour as the world's first man in space. Galbraith relates how he had to overcome opposition from the "more militant NATO ambassadors" who favored a boycott.[244]

I wasn't sure how my proposal would be received. Saxbe was a conservative Republican, and the deputy chief of mission, David Schneider, was a cautious FSO who had spent his career—except for an African assignment—in South Asia. Yet Paul, seeing no harm himself, obtained Schneider and Saxbe's approval.

I brought the idea to Andrei, and he carried it to his ambassador, Viktor Maltsev. Maltsev also had no objection, and on July 17, 1975, he and Andrei and a few other Soviets trooped over to Roosevelt House. Toasts were exchanged, and the event transpired without any controversy but also without much warmth. Saxbe and Maltsev were probably unaware that, at the same time in Washington, President Ford, Kissinger, and others from Ford's Cabinet were hosting Dobrynin and his staff at a comparable event.

Two years later, Maltsev was recalled to Moscow and succeeded the aged Kuznetsov as one of Gromyko's two first deputies. I can't say my attempt to soften his feelings toward the United States had the slightest impact. After the Soviet invasion of Afghanistan in 1979, Ambassador Watson, who had just taken up his post, was instructed to deliver Washington's protest at the highest level. Gromyko was unavailable, and Watson had to meet with Maltsev. Watson's impression was negative: "I nicknamed him Mr. No, because he was a rude and taciturn man, a real throwback to the worst days of the Cold War."[245] Of course, by their invasion, the Soviets had just ruined Watson's dream of salvaging détente, and anything Maltsev had said would have been upsetting.

When I returned to Moscow in 1978, I tried to reconnect with Andrei. I saw him once in the lobby of the Foreign Ministry while I was waiting for an escort to take me to the American Department, but, eyes averted, he pretended not to see me and quickly walked by. My subsequent telephone calls to the ministry's South Asia department yielded no information about where he worked or whether he existed.

This wasn't surprising. When Ambassador Beam returned to Moscow after assignments in London, Prague, Warsaw, and other major capitals, he noted that he had "no particular friends among Soviet officialdom."[246] Beam was shy, but the real problem was that it was nearly impossible to maintain a relationship with a Soviet diplomat through several assignments. Unless the official was a KGB officer with a specific assignment, he would be reluctant to resume an interrupted relationship with a Western diplomat for fear of his counterintelligence people.

In order to gain a better sense of India and its foreign policies, I associated with other Communist diplomats besides Andrei, including one other Russian and several East Europeans.

I met the Russian, Viktor Mizin, at a National Day reception held by one of the several Asian countries for which I was responsible. Mizin was known to be KGB and had spent his entire career in the developing world. He invited me to lunch at several high-priced restaurants.

After one such get-together, a CIA officer in the embassy asked me to stop by. His office happened to adjoin mine, but the common door, by longstanding practice, was kept locked from both sides (which of course made it easy for the Indian employees to distinguish the "spooks" from the diplomats).

I entered the steamy atrium and wandered into my colleague's office.

"Don't you know that Mizin is KGB?" he and another Agency officer standing by his side asked.

I replied that I did know, but it didn't make much difference to me—I was used to dealing with all sorts of Russians.

This was not the point, they replied. I shouldn't be associating with the KGB. This was *their* responsibility.

In truth, there wasn't enough happening to keep the CIA fully employed, and they thought I was poaching on their territory, although I didn't see my role as so constricted.

The irony is that, apart from the Apollo-Soyuz event, the time I invested in cultivating and maintaining Soviet contacts was largely a waste. Unknown to me and probably unknown to everyone in the embassy except the CIA station chief, the senior attaché at the Soviet embassy, Major General Dmitri Polyakov, was already on the Agency's payroll, having begun working for the United States more than a decade earlier. There was nothing of value that Fialkovski or Mizin could provide that Polyakov hadn't already passed to his handler, electronically or otherwise. Had I been posted to India to serve as a "screen" to protect Polyakov's relationship with the CIA? Since the relationship was so tightly held, I doubt this had figured into Washington's decision.

I learned about Polyakov long after I left India. He was the GRU *rezident* at the Soviet embassy. After the collapse of the Soviet system, a senior KGB official, Viktor Cherkashin, wrote that Polyakov "hardly ever mingled with KGB personnel or others in the diplomatic community, even though he lived on [sic] the [Soviet] embassy compound."[247] I don't' recall meeting him.

The KGB confirmed Polyakov's double dealing following his execution two years after Edward Lee Howard defected to Moscow. Howard was the officer whom the CIA dismissed for drug use, theft, and cheating on a lie detector test while he was being prepared for assignment to the station at Tchaikovsky 19. During his training, he acquired critical information about its operations and was happy to turn everything he knew over to the Soviets once the CIA fired him. The Agency's top officials had forgotten, or never learned, the old British adage that "a discarded spy, like a discarded mistress, is dangerous."[248]

*   *   *

Although I was frustrated from a career standpoint, my family and I enjoyed many aspects of India. Liz involved herself in community activities and was named president of the American Women's Association.

We frequented the embassy's tennis courts that were presided over by Abdul—a middle-aged Muslim originally from Pakistan—and "Mr. Lal," an elderly Indian. For a pittance, they would give lessons or simply hit with us. We reveled in the unaccustomed luxury of ball boys and a playing season that lasted almost year-round.

Elise, Abby, and Rob attended a well-run American community school not far from our neighborhood and had many friends in the foreign community. Rob played with the Indian children on the *maidan*, the greensward in front of our apartment. Wearing the Indian military uniform that my father had given me in 1945, he would disappear for hours in the hovels behind the private houses where the servants lived. He learned firsthand what Rudyard Kipling taught the readers of his *Kim* and other stories set in South Asia, namely, that lives lived "outside the notions of orderliness, success, and gentility" that we so esteem in the West are no less important than our own.[249]

Amoebic dysentery was one of the discomforts intruding on our routines. Ambassador Moynihan claimed the record with over twenty bouts, and Liz and I each suffered a few.

Indian newspapers, uncensored and freewheeling, were also a problem. Under a front page headline—"Is Diplomat Ober CIA Man?"—an English-language newspaper *New Wave* cast doubt on my *bona fides* a few months after we arrived:

> Suspicion of Indian authorities have [sic] been aroused by the recent transfer of a man named Ober to the U.S. diplomatic mission in New Delhi. This name came up recently in connection with the *New York Times* exposure of the CIA's espionage activities within the USA.[250]

The article claimed that my wife and son also worked for American intelligence. Evidently, a Richard Ober, an authentic "CIA man," had served at the embassy a few years earlier, and his name had resurfaced in the United States in connection with Nixon's domestic spying operations.

The *New Wave* was a Communist newspaper. My given name was different; Rob was only six in 1975; and other discrepancies suggested that someone was working hard to discredit me. I wondered whether one of my contacts at the Soviet embassy could have floated the story to discourage Indians from seeing me, or could someone from my own embassy have been intent upon keeping Soviets away from me? A slightly different version of the exposé appeared a month later in a Bengali language paper in Calcutta, but neither seemed to affect the attitudes of those with whom I met.

Despite the comfortable lifestyle, I was anxious to return to the Soviet or East European area. I suggested to my superiors that, in the larger scheme of things, my contribution wasn't particularly vital. I also noted, in the appropriate box for comments in Paul's first evaluation, that the embassy was "generously staffed."

When I added a comment to his final report a year later, I was more direct: "I continue to feel that the mission has a disproportionately large number of senior as compared with middle and junior-grade officers, and is probably oversized, especially considering the reduced level of our activity in India and the redefinition of U.S. priorities since the early 1970s."

It was an honest opinion but not wisely stated, and as a result my next promotion was held up, even though the Soviet affairs position, among others at the embassy, was soon eliminated.

In April 1976, I received orders to return to Washington for a two-year assignment as the India desk officer. To prepare myself, I spent a few days at the consulates in Bombay, Calcutta, and Madras before leaving. I understood the reason for the assignment; the department wanted to make full use of my familiarity with the embassy and the consulates and the sticking points in Indo-U.S. relations.

We had been abroad five years when we reached home in June 1976. The office to which I was assigned oversaw India, Pakistan, and the other South Asian countries. Its director was an experienced South Asia hand, Dennis Kux, and he reported to Spike Dubs, the former number two in Moscow who was fulfilling his Global Outlook Program requirement in the Bureau of Near Eastern and South Asian Affairs (NEA).

If there was a high point during my stint on the India desk, it was gaining an education in nuclear issues, one that helped me better understand the Chernobyl disaster when it occurred during my final assignment in the USSR. I worked closely with officials at the Nuclear Regulatory Commission, the Arms Control and Disarmament Agency, and other organizations inside the department and out to deal with the fallout from an American transfer of heavy water to India in the late 1950s that contributed to the 1974 explosion of its "peaceful device." A memorandum I co-authored relating to India's nuclear program evidently landed on President Jimmy Carter's desk after my assignment ended.

Kissinger had let the world know a month after the explosion that it "occurred with material that was diverted not from an American reactor under American safeguards but from a Canadian reactor that did not have appropriate safeguards."[251] Two years later, however, he conceded that there was "a high probability" that heavy water supplied by the United States had been used in the reactor that produced the plutonium required for the explosion.[252]

India didn't violate the Non-proliferation Treaty because it wasn't a signatory, but it did misuse technologies and materials that had been supplied for civilian purposes. It has since exploded four more nuclear weapons and assembled a stockpile of at least fifty. This didn't deter the George W. Bush administration from making a treaty with India in 2006 that would reopen the American nuclear supply line—a treaty that flies in the face of its avowed interest in blocking Iran and North Korea from pursuing their nuclear ambitions, but is consistent with its refusal to seek ratification of the Comprehensive Test-Ban Treaty.[253]

A year into my India desk assignment, Mark Garrison, the director of the Soviet desk, asked if I would like to return to Soviet affairs. We knew each other from Moscow where Mark had headed the political section's external unit, Pol/Ext, whose responsibilities included covering U.S.-Soviet relations. Mark had served with Ambassador Beam in Prague, and it was expected he would return to Moscow as the next deputy chief of mission once he completed his desk assignment.

Of course, this is what I wanted. Spike arranged for my release from NEA a year early, and he and Dennis joined in writing the kind of enthusiastic evaluation that helped my career recover the momentum it had lost in India.

The election of Jimmy Carter in November 1976 ended the Kissinger era. Détente was spoken of less and less, and the Global Outlook Program disappeared. In fact, Nixon's appointee had never viewed the world in a truly global way. A major country like India figured in his *Realpolitik* only because of the impact it might have on what he was trying to achieve with the Soviet Union and the People's Republic of China, not for other reasons.

During the Kennedy years, Ambassador Galbraith used to assure the Indians that Washington's struggle against Communism was *not* "the only reality." "We sought friendship with other countries for its own sake," he would explain.[254] Within a decade, Kissinger had shifted the focus to strategic relations among five blocs—the United States, the Soviet Union, China, Western Europe, and Japan—while paying little heed to the rest of the world. When a new Indian ambassador arrived in Washington, the architect of the Global Outlook Program had no time to see him. When I finally succeeded in arranging the call, their get-together was no warmer than that between Saxbe and Maltsev.

As Cyrus Vance wrote of Kissinger, he was late to recognize that there was a "need to look at Third World problems on their own terms and not through the prism of East-West competition."[255]

Alas, the person whom President Carter selected to be his national security advisor turned out to be even less deft than the one chosen by Nixon. Carter's choice would surpass Nixon's in terms of his fixation on the Soviets. The Cold War not only reignited with Moscow's invasion of Afghanistan in December 1979, but spread to the world's outermost corners.

*   *   *

President Carter's choice to head the National Security Council was Zbigniew Brzezinski. Like Kissinger, Brzezinski is a naturalized American whose worldview bears the imprint of a European upbringing. His father had been a diplomat for the prewar Polish government and had taken his family to Canada on the eve of World War II. Brzezinski went on to New York to study in 1953 and married into the family of one of Czechoslovakia's founders, Eduard Benes.

Benes had been the country's president when the Communists, with a combination of constitutional and unlawful means, seized power. I had been exposed to the fierce anti-Communism of a branch of the family in Bloomington.

Brzezinski was a professor at Columbia University when Carter made the appointment. As an academic, he had written extensively on the Communist system, including Soviet "totalitarianism" and Soviet rule in

Eastern Europe. His career had included a stint on the State Department's policy planning staff in the 1960s.

The Soviet regime entertained no illusions about Brzezinski. Dobrynin indicates that he appraised Carter's appointee as "notoriously anti-Communist"[256]; undoubtedly, he warned his superiors in Moscow about what to expect.

It was no accident that President Carter took his first major trip abroad to Poland. Brzezinski relates in his memoir how he overrode concern in Foggy Bottom that the Soviet leadership might view the trip as provocative, and organized it to play to Polish nationalism, including having the president lay a wreath at the monument honoring the Poles who rose against the Germans in 1944 while the Red Army tarried on the other side of the Vistula.[257]

When Carter was elected in November 1976, there was no one who was not aware of Kissinger's dominance as national security advisor. Carter indicated *his* awareness when he organized his foreign-policy team. Before naming Brzezinski as his White House advisor, he gave Secretary of State-designate Cyrus Vance an opportunity to reject his choice. Mindful of Kissinger's record, Vance told Carter that he would not object so long as he would be the president's spokesman on foreign policy and could present "his own unfiltered views" to him before final decisions were taken.[258] On the basis of this understanding with Vance, Carter put Brzezinski in the White House.

The National Security Council had come into existence in 1947 at the Congress's behest, in reaction to President Roosevelt's style of managing foreign policy from his vest pocket. The legislation it enacted ensured that the secretaries of state and defense, the director of central intelligence, and an executive director would henceforth be involved in framing and coordinating foreign and defense policy, along with the president and—as the legislation was later amended—the vice president. At the time, it was believed that the statutorily responsible cabinet members would loom large in these deliberations; it would have been inconceivable to the lawmakers that a secretary of state might be excluded.

The notion of an advisor in the White House contributing to the coordination of policy for a president grew out of the founding statute's arrangement for an executive directorship. With Kissinger performing the role, the incumbent soon became more powerful than either the secretary of state or secretary of defense. Kissinger bypassed or ignored both when it suited his purposes ("I tried to bypass him [Rogers] as much as possible"[259]).

Kissinger's lateral move to the department as secretary in August 1973 changed little. He retained his position at the NSC and left day-to-day operations in the hands of Brent Scowcroft, a loyal assistant. Only when President Ford reorganized his staff in October 1975 did Kissinger yield his White House position, and then to the self-effacing Scowcroft.

Vance probably anticipated that if differences arose with Brzezinski, they would be most acute in relation to Soviet policy, so he brought his own Soviet expert into the department. He appointed Marshall Shulman, another professor from Columbia, to be his special advisor, installing him two doors from his suite of offices on the seventh floor. He also arranged for Marshall to receive full ambassadorial rank in July 1977.

Like Brzezinski, Shulman was a scholar of East-West relations. He had written extensively about Soviet foreign policy, and his curriculum vitae included a stint as a special assistant and speechwriter for Secretary of State Dean Acheson in 1950-51.

The new administration was still taking shape when I transferred to the Soviet desk in June 1977. Mark Garrison explained that my assignment would be to serve as the executive secretary of a new interagency committee established to deal with U.S.-Soviet relations.

Brzezinski had brought the committee into being on July 15, 1977, with a signed three-paragraph unclassified memorandum on White House stationery. Copies were circulated to offices in the White House and in every department and agency with foreign affairs responsibilities.[260]

The committee's full name was the Interagency Coordinating Committee for U.S.-Soviet Affairs, ICCUSA for short. As the memorandum explained, its mandate was "monitoring and coordinating U.S. Government activities with respect to the Soviet Union." Shulman and George Vest, the assistant secretary of state for the Bureau of European Affairs under which the Soviet Affairs Office fell, were named joint chairmen, but Shulman was actually in charge.

I felt honored to be asked to work with Garrison and Shulman, thoughtful men steeped in Soviet affairs. Only later, however, did I gain a full picture of ICCUSA's genesis.

During the administration's first months in office, Shulman and Brzezinski shared a house that W. Averell Harriman, Roosevelt's ambassador to Moscow and a longtime presidential advisor, owned in Georgetown next to his personal residence. As the two appointees walked to work one morning—Brzezinski to the White House, Shulman to Foggy Bottom—"we lamented," in Brzezinski's words, "the absence of effective coordination within the U.S. government of the various cooperative U.S.-Soviet links."[261] Brzezinski recalls that he suggested to Shulman that an interagency committee be created that Marshall would chair.

Within days, the *New York Times* front-paged the existence of the committee and appended an interpretation, one that deeply annoyed Brzezinski:

> In the past, the National Security Council, particularly under Henry A. Kissinger, had been responsible for coordinating policy. Officials said that now, with the size of the council and its responsibilities reduced, it was believed more practical to let the State Department take the lead.[262]

The article went on to assert that Shulman, while not condoning Soviet human rights violations, was urging the administration to give priority to seeking arms control agreements and reducing U.S.-Soviet tensions.

In his memoir, Brzezinski professes to be amazed that ICCUSA's establishment was taken as a "public signal" that "the Administration was moving toward a more conciliatory attitude toward the Soviet Union, with policy influence allegedly passing from the NSC to Vance and Shulman."[263]

Brzezinski believed that someone in the State Department—probably Vance or Shulman (he doesn't use a name)—had leaked his memo to the *Times* and encouraged an interpretation that denigrated him as the new president's advisor. Brzezinski had no intention of yielding any of the power that Kissinger had wielded at the height of his influence.

My assignment as the committee's executive secretary was to arrange meetings, prepare agendas, and ensure the attendance of administration officials (at the assistant secretary level) from the concerned departments and agencies. I was charged with recording the substance of the discussions, tracking follow-up actions that might be required, and serving as ICCUSA's spokesperson to the press, public, or any others who might inquire.

I participated in three or four ICCUSA meetings during the nine months that remained before I reported to the FSI for a refresher course in Russian. During the meetings, we discussed some forty agenda items, ranging from arms control and trade to cultural and scientific exchanges. Brzezinski did not appear for any of them but rather assigned a holdover from President Ford's NSC staff, William Hyland, to be present.

Shulman did most of the talking. I don't recall that any of the topics that later became a source of significant disagreement within the administration was aired. ICCUSA was useful for me personally, setting the stage for my return to Moscow, but it didn't turn out to be a viable forum for bridging substantive differences.

Six months before ICCUSA's creation, Brzezinski had established two far more important committees within the framework of the NSC: the

Policy Review Committee (PRC) that Vance would chair and the Special Coordination Committee (SCC) that he (Brzezinski) would chair. Carter approved both committees on inauguration day, and these were where the battles were fought.

The differences between Brzezinski and Vance were substantive in nature, relating to their different perspectives about the scope of Moscow's ambitions and capabilities, and they are described at length in the memoirs that each wrote. Disagreements about process magnified the differences, as they tend to do. Vance objected to Brzezinski's claim that he was entitled to interpret, frame, and forward recommendations to Carter based on PRC and SCC discussions without returning to him for further consultation. This, Vance believed, violated the original understanding he had reached with the president.

But propinquity counts for much—as Kissinger once observed—and Brzezinski was much closer to Carter's ear than Vance. Even in petty matters, this made a difference. Whenever the man whom Vance considered his mentor, Averell Harriman, showed up to see the president, he would be intercepted by Brzezinski who, in the words of Harriman's biographer, "would stroll into the Oval Office with him uninvited."[264]

In his memoir, Brzezinski gleefully recounts how, in one dispute, he outwitted Vance "and his more dovish State Department associates, including . . . Shulman" by arranging for the surprise entry of the president into a meeting that Vance was chairing.[265] There are parts of Brzezinski's memoir that read more like the minutes of a Columbia faculty meeting, with department chairs squabbling over classroom space, rather than war-or-peace deliberations in the capital. But as Robert Gates, then a senior CIA official assigned to the NSC, later wrote, "Brzezinski relished outmaneuvering others."[266]

The Vance and Brezinski conflict ebbed and flowed, and the result was that the United States' policy toward the Soviet Union zigged and zagged, to the dismay of not only the leaders of the Soviet Union but also of our allies.

Brzezinski's memoir mentions ICCUSA in passing as an instrument for coordinating "various cooperative U.S.-Soviet links."[267] He justifies its creation by explaining that agencies in Washington had developed numerous "bilateral contacts with their Soviet counterparts" as well as "official and unofficial exchanges" during the era of détente, and these needed to be coordinated. The memorandum that Brzezinski signed, however, spoke of a broader mandate, "coordinating U.S. Government activities with respect to the Soviet Union," not simply of activities "cooperative" in nature. Was there a misunderstanding from the start about ICCUSA's role, or did Brzezinski curtail the committee as soon as he saw it might be an instrument for propagating the "more dovish" views he imputed to Vance and Shulman? Was this why he only assigned a Ford administration holdover to attend its meetings?

Vance does not refer to ICCUSA in his memoir, and Shulman did not write about his service with the Carter administration.

*   *   *

If there were outside inquiries about ICCUSA's responsibilities that required an explanation, only one ever reached me. It came from a well-known KGB officer at the Soviet embassy, Boris Davydov. As soon as Davydov ascertained I was ICCUSA's executive secretary, he invited me to lunch. We had met before at a Soviet embassy reception in December 1977.

As Ambassador Dobrynin observes, regular Soviet diplomats assigned to Washington "were limited at the time to twenty or twenty-five dollars for the whole meal" and would have to cover the balance out of pocket, while a KGB officer's expenses were covered in full.[268] Davydov could afford to be a good host and took me to a fancy Virginia restaurant, the Lido di Venezia, where he was welcomed as a regular.

I knew that Davydov's name had surfaced in a book-length exposé of the KGB published in 1974, *KGB: The Secret Work of Soviet Secret Agents*. Author John Barron had reported that when Sino-Soviet border clashes broke out in 1969, Davydov, then a second secretary at Dobrynin's embassy, told an American outside of government that Moscow was contemplating a preemptive strike against China, possibly including the use of nuclear weapons. How did the American think Washington would react? Instead of trying to respond, Davydov's guest prudently passed the comment to the authorities. It came to President Nixon's attention, and at that level, it was decided to say nothing.[269] A fuller account of the Soviet probe, including the fact that the American was a Soviet specialist assigned to the department's Vietnam desk and that U.S. strategic bombers were placed on alert as a consequence of Davydov's question, appeared in 1999.[270]

Not surprisingly, Davydov was seeking information about ICCUSA, the role of the cochairmen, and its relationship to the NSC. Because I knew his reputation and because the committee had just come into being, I was not particularly obliging. However, I may have conveyed an exaggerated picture of the ICCUSA's importance, not realizing then that Brzezinski's reservations about it and differences with Vance and Shulman had already doomed its prospects and, more significantly, the prospects for any coherence in American policy toward Moscow.

Davydov was a fixture in Washington for years. He had been among the first students permitted by Khrushchev's regime to study at an American university and was on his fourth assignment at the Soviet embassy when he took me to lunch. I saw him two years later at a Spaso House reception, where he told me that he was returning to Washington for yet another tour.

Unlike their counterparts in Washington, the Soviets making personnel decisions didn't hesitate to exploit an officer's area expertise. Ambassador Dobrynin served in Washington for twenty-four years, from 1962 to 1986. I doubt that anyone headed any American embassy during the Cold War for a quarter as long.

*　　*　　*

One small dividend from my association with Marshall was an invitation extended to the department's Soviet hands to meet with Harriman in Georgetown. As candidate Carter's unofficial emissary, Harriman had held talks with Brezhnev and Gromyko shortly before the election.

Shulman arranged the get-together in May 1978. I arrived a few minutes late and took the only seat available, next to Harriman himself. As I was the first officer scheduled to leave for the Soviet capital, Harriman asked for my background. Then he held forth for an hour and a half on U.S.-Soviet relations, largely uninterrupted because his deafness made it difficult for him to hear questions.

Harriman had gone to the Soviet Union first in 1926, when he was a businessman in his thirties. He had returned in 1941 to work out arrangements for Lend-Lease deliveries. In 1943, Roosevelt had named him ambassador, and he stayed in Moscow until his appointment to the Court of St. James in 1946.

Harriman had advised a succession of American presidents—Carter being but the latest—about how to deal with Moscow. At President Kennedy's behest, he had negotiated the Limited Test Ban Treaty with Khrushchev in 1963.

Harriman began by describing all the changes he had seen in the USSR. He was convinced that the Soviet leaders would never again resort to the kind of terror that prevailed under Stalin. "Even they understand they are living in a different epoch." George Kennan would make the same point in 1981 in a meeting with embassy officers at Tchaikovsky 19.

While supportive of President Carter, Harriman was wary of the attention his administration was already giving human rights. The president shouldn't be making statements in public, he said, that the Kremlin interprets as interference in its internal affairs.

I wasn't surprised by Harriman's remark. He was known for strictly prioritizing his objectives when dealing with the Soviets, focusing first on the ones that he considered most important. During the war, he had refused to intercede with the Kremlin to secure exit visas for the Russians married to American correspondents. Ed Stevens reported him saying in 1945 that he had "too many requests of major military and political importance to make use of his influence on trivial personal cases."[271] Nina Stevens was in the United States at the time, and Ed was seeking Harriman's intercession on behalf of colleagues.

Harriman told us that he was concerned that Vance would not have sufficient influence with the president. He reminded us that Brzezinski had supported candidate Carter when few others had. He said that Brzezinski had arranged for Carter to join the Trilateral Commission in the early 1970s when he (Brzezinski) was serving as the executive secretary of its North American branch. Carter, Harriman judged, had always been extremely loyal to his friends.

Harriman made clear that he was already aware of the problems that Vance was encountering in the White House. Harriman had a close relationship with Vance going back to the Johnson administration when they were in Paris together negotiating with the North Vietnamese. From what Harriman said, I judged that he didn't have a high opinion of Brzezinski.

Harriman also commented about the White House's neglect of the Foreign Service—especially its officers with Soviet expertise—and said that the State Department is "too cautious" in registering its views. It should "stand up to those who don't favor improved relations."

Harriman was prescient about Carter's loyalty to Brzezinski and what it would mean for U.S.-Soviet relations. When Harriman heard of Vance's resignation in April 1980 to protest the plan espoused by Brzezinski and others to rescue the hostages in Iran (the plan that ended in disaster outside Tehran), Harriman was so upset that he told Dobrynin that his "first impulse was to take the earliest flight to Fiji or somewhere far away from Washington."[272]

Harriman died in 1986 at the age of ninety-four. He had devoted more than sixty years to building a constructive relationship with the Russians. One didn't need to agree with everything he said or did; but old-timers like Kennan and he were able to provide the kind of straight talk—grounded in experience and bereft of ideology—that presidents, regardless of their politics, ought to hear.

8

Political Reporting from Moscow

On July 1, 1978, our Pan American flight landed at Sheremetyevo Airport. I had been assigned to head the political/external unit—Pol/Ext, as it was called—responsible for analyzing and reporting on Soviet foreign policy, especially issues and trends important to the United States. Supervising three FSOs, two of whom had been at the embassy for a year, I would work with political counselor Bob German, an FSO with extensive experience in European affairs. Trained as a lawyer, Bob had begun his career with an assignment to Moscow in 1948.

Before I left Washington, Mark Garrison, the head of the Soviet desk, told me I'd have the position for one year. An officer with Middle East and West European experience, Edward Djerejian would then take over, and I'd assume charge of political/internal—Pol/Int—the political section's second unit. Ed was senior in rank but had no prior experience in the USSR.

Having headed the consular section, I probably knew the domestic Soviet scene as well as anyone. However, my work in Western Europe had been limited to a stint in Hamburg's consular section, which hadn't prepared me for reporting on the relations between the Soviet Union and our European allies. The switchover would be in the embassy's interest as well as mine.

Sheremetyevo brought back a flood of memories. How many times I had butted heads with officials there, including in connection with the air crash.

The main terminal dated from the early 1960s. For security reasons, most of its windows were sealed shut. There was little ventilation, and the air was always thick with fumes from stale tobacco, vodka, and sweat. As Liz and I approached Passport Control, we could hear our girls say, "It smells just the same."

Lawrence Durrell once said that a person could "smell the whole of London in one pub, or the whole of Paris on the crowded terrace of a little student-quarter cafe."[273] For me, Moscow was my first whiff of Sheremetyevo.

A few months earlier, the foundation for a new terminal, Sheremetyevo II, had been poured. It was scheduled to open in January 1980, six months before Moscow's first Olympics. Designed by German architects and built with imported materials, it would turn out to be as antiseptic and efficient as almost any Western terminal. Eighteen months after our return, however, in December 1979, the Soviet Union would send its troops into Afghanistan, and President Carter would respond by organizing an Olympic boycott. For most of its first year, Sheremetyevo II would be empty.

An embassy driver took us to the compound where we had lived before, Leninsky Prospect 45. We were being temporarily housed in an apartment across the hall from our old apartment. The place permanently assigned to us, on the fifth floor, was being repainted and refurnished.

Liz's reaction to the old neighborhood was that little had changed; her reaction to the compound was that it had "deteriorated enormously."

The neighborhood did look the same. The bread store was a block away in the same location with the usual line of customers waiting for it to open at 11:00 AM. At the far end of the block, the House of Fabric, the city's largest retail outlet for textiles, stood in the same spot, its display windows hardly changed from when we had seen them last. Opposite it stood the wooden kiosk where on Sundays I'd buy my Russian newspapers.

Liz said that the women shopping on Leninsky Prospect were better dressed, with styles less provincial and colors brighter. Moreover, the younger women had discovered the miniskirt, the fashion that had already come and gone in the West.

The compound didn't seem different to me except for its courtyard now packed with cars. During our absence, Russian families had been madly buying the *Zhiguli*, the Soviet-built Fiat. The traffic going toward Red Square on Leninsky was two or three times heavier than I recalled. At the same time, the avenue's militiamen were more relaxed; they no longer stopped drivers for using their full beams at night. During our first assignment, they had waved their batons and pulled us to the curb several times. Dimmed lights had been required in New York and other East Coast cities at the start of World War II[274], but Moscow had maintained them into the early 1970s.

Night driving was still hazardous. With all the traffic, gaping holes would appear in the roadways and remain for weeks. And because of thieves, covers for manholes would sometimes disappear.

No sooner had we unpacked than we found that the hot water had been turned off. The authorities had started their annual "cleaning" of the Leninsky District water pipes. We knew the routine from before; for several weeks we'd have to boil water on the stove.

*   *   *

We arrived on July 1 because I wanted to attend the Independence Day reception at Spaso House, to see old friends and make new contacts. Unfortunately, the turnout was poor. Liz and I enjoyed seeing the residence's staff—Clemente, Maria, and Tang—as well as colleagues at the embassy whom we already knew; but few Russians appeared, and those who did were mostly from the Foreign Ministry. On top of this, only a few "unofficial" Russians—from the capital's artists, refuseniks, and dissidents—showed up. I knew they had thronged the residence during Stoessel's tour.

I wasn't the only one to notice their absence. Reporting on the reception a day later, the *New York Times* suggested there had been "a shift in embassy policy, a step away from the cordial and relatively free and frequent association between dissidents and diplomats" that had existed before.[275]

Were dissidents no longer welcome at Spaso House? Obviously, some couldn't attend because they were no longer in circulation. Anatoli Shcharansky, a friend of several officers in the middle 1970s, was behind bars awaiting trial.

The ambassador was Malcolm Toon, Mac to his friends. Ford had named him ambassador in early January 1977 as President-elect Carter prepared to take over. Toon wasted no time getting to Moscow; he presented his credentials on January 19, the day before the inauguration.

However, four weeks later, on February 18, Carter withdrew Toon's nomination along with that of forty-seven other ambassadors whom Ford had appointed. Carter then dallied until April 25 before announcing he would retain Toon after all.[276] On the same day, he appointed a career FSO, Arthur J. Hartman, to be ambassador to France, the first nonpolitical appointee to that post since Kennedy selected Bohlen. Obviously, Carter wasn't ill disposed toward professional diplomats, but why leave Tchaikovsky 19 in such limbo?

Toon was a career FSO with a wealth of experience in Soviet and East European affairs. He had worked as a consular officer in Moscow in the early 1950s (surviving "an unjustly negative fitness report" written by Ambassador Kennan[277]), and then as political counselor in the middle 1960s. Before returning as ambassador, he had headed American embassies in Prague, Belgrade, and Tel-Aviv.

Liz and I met Mac and Betty Toon at the reception. Then a few days later, we chatted with them at the traditional picnic at the dachas in Tarasovka. Toon asked why we had decided to return. I told him that I had enjoyed working with Russians. Then I must have alluded to the Nixon-Brezhnev summits and the gift-giving accompanying them; I probably said, "the Russians could be cultivated," or something like this. I recall Toon giving me a quizzical look and letting me know that he didn't think Russians deserved this kind of attention. I left the picnic with the impression that he viewed the Soviets differently than Beam and Stoessel, and certainly Shulman and Vance. This should be an interesting assignment, I thought to myself.

Toon had the reputation of being a hard-liner. Dobrynin would later call him "a belligerent career diplomat."[278] Probably Dobrynin had in mind a widely circulated statement that Toon made in August 1977, ten months before we arrived.

A fire had broken out on Tchaikovsky's upper floors where the substantive reporting sections were located. The marines fought it for an hour before Toon, coming back from a dinner party, agreed to let the Russian firemen enter. The plan called for a marine to accompany each fireman, but the fire spread so rapidly that the marines were in no position to provide coverage; and Toon had no choice but to let the Russians fight it by themselves.

After it was quelled, Toon held a press conference for American correspondents. He praised the Soviet firemen but noted that "petty looting" had occurred. Rubber stamps for franking mail and classifying documents, a few address books, and a silver medallion from his office had been taken. Because the fire had occurred at night when the safes were secured, apparently no classified material was lost.[279]

When Toon's "looting" remark found its way back to Moscow from the correspondents' reports in the American press, Soviet officials were livid. There was grumbling in Washington too, and I recall someone on the seventh floor saying that Dobrynin had registered a complaint.

But Toon was the right person to head the embassy in 1978. When we arrived, U.S.-Soviet relations were at their lowest point in more than a decade. On June 12, three weeks before Toon's reception, an American businessman—Jay Crawford, the representative of International Harvester—had been dragged out of his car on a Moscow street and arrested. The KGB was retaliating because, a few weeks earlier, the FBI had arrested two KGB officers in New York—employees of the United Nations Secretariat and therefore without diplomatic immunity.

Then on June 27, a week before the reception, two journalists—Craig Whitney of the *Times* and Hal Piper of the *Baltimore Sun*—were ordered to appear in a local court to face slander charges. The Soviets claimed they had suggested that a Georgian dissident's confession at a trial they had been covering in Tbilisi had been fabricated. In fact, it was the dissident's friends who had questioned the confession, and the Americans reported what they had said. It was unprecedented for the Soviets to haul accredited foreign correspondents into court.

On the same day, seven Soviet citizens from two families of Pentecostal believers had rushed past the militia guards into Tchaikovsky 19. They refused to leave and were living in the consular section when we arrived.

After the reception, there were other incidents. On July 20, a guard intruded a few feet inside the entrance at the far end of the north wing in order to grab Ray Smith, a Pol/Int officer, as he was returning to the embassy. Ray wrestled free, but his jacket was torn. The embassy filed a protest, but it was immediately rejected, with the ministry saying that Ray hadn't identified himself.

Ray had been at the embassy for two years and was known to the guards. His duties included contacts with dissidents and refuseniks. He had just spent five days standing outside a courtroom (from which embassy officers were barred) where Shcharansky was being tried. The embassy rejected the notion that we had to identify ourselves before entering the embassy.

The KGB was harassing families too. Liz was driving on Leninsky Prospect with the three children when a man and woman tailing her sped alongside on the passenger side, forcing her to swerve to the left to avoid a collision. Then they moved to the front, forcing her to brake. It was unusual for the KGB to harass families, and we wondered whether the FBI was "playing games" with Russian families in the United States, perhaps in connection with the New York arrests.

Reading the memoir of the CIA's representative to Carter's NSC, Robert Gates, two decades later, I was startled to see a reference to the interception of "a KGB order sent to its officers in Moscow to humiliate U.S. citizens there."[280] The order was related to the arrests of the KGB officers and obviously accounted for Liz's harassment. Washington didn't share the intercept with Toon, or Toon didn't share it with us, though I would have liked to have known.

Puzzled by the poor turnout on July 4, I inquired and learned that the ambassador had instructed officers to seek his approval before seeing dissidents. It was said that he had already withheld permission several times. Speaking anonymously, one staffer told the *Times* that "Toon runs a very tight ship."[281]

*   *   *

The political section was located on the seventh floor of the central wing. Most of the offices looked out on Tchaikovsky Street. Because of the building's layout, to reach my office I had to take an elevator to the ninth floor—where Toon's office was—and after passing the marine guard descend two flights on the internal staircase.

The building looked more decrepit than I recalled. A team of Seabees—members of the U.S. Navy construction corps—had been rebuilding the upper floors since the 1977 fire; but reminders of it were still everywhere. One of the first letters I sent home was on scorched stationery I inherited with my office.

The façade of the embassy reflected its overall condition. The winter of 1978-79 would turn out to be one of Moscow's worst. Whenever there was a slight thaw, chunks of stucco would fall onto the sidewalk in front and the courtyard behind. Several members of the community suffered abrasions (and a broken bone) from falling debris, and the Seabees were forced to remove the building's more vulnerable ornamentation, including the obelisks at the edge of the roof that Stalin's architects liked. Their removal prompted a Foreign Ministry complaint on "aesthetic" grounds.

The KGB directed operations against the embassy from neighboring buildings, including one opposite it across Tchaikovsky Street's eight lanes. The embassy's windows in front were all shrouded in curtains to shield the classified material lying on our desks.

For a few weeks after I arrived, the fluorescent lights overhead in my office kept flickering. Then in mid-July, a power panel in the basement exploded and caught fire. A Seabee was injured, and for several days we worked in the dark.

Boxes of Russian-language books and pamphlets that had been pouched to the embassy from émigré publishing houses cluttered the corridor outside my office. A few of the boxes were strewn on the old rug in front of my desk; now and then I'd trip on a box while rushing to a meeting upstairs. I hadn't noticed the boxes when visiting the section during my first assignment. Again, Gates's memoir, years later, provided the answer: An NSC committee that Brzezinski chaired had approved an "enhanced clandestine distribution in the USSR of Russian-language books and periodicals by dissident authors and of Soviet *samizdat* [italics added]"[282] so boxes with these materials kept pouring in. The problem was that, in the late 1970s, political officers had fewer contacts than their predecessors, and those with them were more cautious because of the arrests, trials, and Toon's admonitions. As the boxes arrived, they kept piling up. A fire marshal would have complained; but the embassy had no fire marshal, and the work was so absorbing that no one really cared.

There was one condition, however, about which we did care: The KGB had been bombarding the upper floors with microwaves since May 1975, sometimes for three hours a day, apparently in an effort to disrupt eavesdropping on Soviet communications from equipment on the embassy's top floor. It was bruited about that Ambassador Stoessel had abbreviated his tour because of eye problems resulting from the bombardment. Staffers with technical knowledge said that the microwaves could sap one's energy, even scramble one's mind.

Screening had already been installed on every window facing Tchaikovsky Street, and it was said to have reduced the microwaves by 90 percent. Washington said there was nothing for us to worry about, yet it kept sending out medical teams to run tests on us and ask how we were feeling. A few months after our arrival, we heard that some staff members had abnormally high white blood cell counts because of "an undetermined microbe" allegedly unconnected with the microwaves.

Occasionally, I missed my consular office, which was larger than any other embassy office including the ambassador's and had windows opening to the courtyard; but I wouldn't have traded jobs.

The first weeks were hectic. No sooner had I arrived than I was asked to brief a group of lawyers visiting from New York and Washington. They wanted to help us solve the standoff resulting from the arrest of Crawford in Moscow and the KGB officers in New York; one of them was a Kent classmate from a New York firm, Edward Hughes.

Ambassador Toon needed a speech for a conference in Philadelphia, and I and another new Pol/Ext officer, Dale Herspring, were asked to prepare the draft. This required us to dig into the strategic arms negotiations with which I hadn't previously been involved.

President Carter had come into the White House with unrealistic expectations for achieving a breakthrough in these talks. He wanted "to leapfrog over the unfinished" understanding that President Ford and Kissinger had reached with Brezhnev and Gromyko at the summit in Vladivostok in November 1974.[283] Senator Jackson—a Democrat—and other members of Congress had long been critical of Republican administrations for limiting the growth rather than actually reducing the number of Soviet intercontinental ballistic missiles (ICBMs), and Carter wanted to be responsive to the critics.

Secretary of State Vance knew there would be difficulties negotiating a breakthrough and favored a graduated, step-by-step approach but was overruled as soon as the administration took office. In his second month, in March 1977, he therefore went to Moscow with a proposal calling for deep cuts in Soviet ICBMs.

Angry because of Carter's human rights criticism, Brezhnev and Gromyko gave Vance and his team, which included Toon, a sharp rebuff. Brezhnev told Vance,

> If the United States wants to reopen questions that have already been solved, then the Soviet Union will again raise such problems as the American Forward-Based Systems in Europe and the transfer

of American strategic weapons to its allies. The principal demand of the American administration is for half of Soviet heavy land-based missiles to be liquidated, and that is utterly unacceptable.[284]

Toon's confidence in the capacity of the new administration to manage Soviet affairs must have been shaken from the start. Not since Kennedy and the Bay of Pigs had a White House begun so badly.

Reflecting on Vance's failed mission when writing his memoir a few years later, Brzezinski suggests that "it might have been wiser to prepare the ground through confidential discussions with Dobrynin in Washington and with the Soviet leaders through our Ambassador in Moscow."[285] But this wouldn't have suited Carter and Brzezinski just after moving into the White House. Reviving the back channel would have raised questions about their willingness to distance themselves from Kissinger's secretive style (Brzezinski initially "sought . . . to distinguish his style, his approach, his policies from Kissinger's," as noted in Strobe Talbott's history of the SALT II negotiations[286]); and using an ambassador in Moscow about whom they apparently had doubts would have risked losing control of a process new to them both.

After Brezhnev's rebuff, the administration revived the Dobrynin back channel and began to make use of Toon to supplement the work of its standing delegation in Geneva, Switzerland, where for several years experts from both sides had been trying to contain the strategic arms race. On July 5, 1977, the day after Toon's first Spaso House reception, he and his deputy Jack Matlock were invited to the Kremlin to receive from Brezhnev and Kuznetsov, Gromyko's first deputy, a response to a letter that President Carter had arranged for Toon to deliver. Toon was told that the summit meeting, which Carter wanted, would have to await the attainment of an arms agreement.

During the remaining months of 1977, the administration managed to put the March rebuff behind it and renew the arduous talks.

As I was refreshing my Russian at the FSI in the spring of 1978, however, the Soviets were stepping up their activities in Africa; and Brzezinski was becoming more vocal about the need for countermeasures. As Vance later explained, Soviet and Cuban activities in the Horn of Africa and the nature of Washington's response opened the first serious disagreement over foreign policy among Carter's advisors, "primarily between Brzezinski and me."[287]

Vance "did not believe Soviet actions in Africa were part of a grand Soviet plan," but ought to be dealt with "in the local context in which they had their roots."[288] Seeing the entire world as an East-West battlefield, Brzezinski argued for a more aggressive approach.

Brzezinski was also forcing the pace of normalizing relations with China to use the Chinese as a counterbalance to the Soviets. In May 1978, a few weeks before our return to Moscow, he had visited Beijing and had spoken of the United States' new strategic partnership with the USSR's Communist rival.[289] He also briefed his hosts about the SALT talks. Vance had opposed Brzezinski's visit (unbeknown to Vance, Brzezinski had solicited the invitation[290]) and deplored "loose talk" about playing "a China card" against the USSR.[291] According to one account, as Carter began his presidency, Brzezinski had bypassed Vance in urging the president to reaffirm Nixon's commitment to the Chinese to push rapidly ahead on normalization.[292]

Vance bracketed Brzezinski's Beijing trip with two sets of meetings with Gromyko, in Moscow in April and in Washington in May 1978. At the latter meeting, Gromyko let Vance know that "the Chinese had 'no legitimate interest' in SALT and therefore 'no right' to an official briefing" such as Brzezinski had just provided. As Talbott writes, "for the first time—but not for the last—the Carter administration's China policy had complicated SALT."[293]

In the context of the White House's repudiation of the Vladivostok understanding, its stepped-up diplomacy toward China, and its heightened attention to Soviet human rights abuses, the modest turnout at Toon's reception at Spaso House in July 1978 was hardly surprising.

Vance was supposed to meet again with Gromyko in Geneva on July 12-13. However, the trial of Shcharansky was scheduled to begin on July 10. In light of the trial and of the threatened prosecution of Crawford and the two journalists, Toon recommended that the meeting be cancelled.[294] Senator Jackson also called for its cancellation, and Brzezinski argued for its postponement. Vance insisted on the original schedule, however; and this time, Carter agreed with his secretary. In fact, the meeting turned out to be useful; it opened the way to a serious and ultimately successful discussion of the problem of restricting the modernization of ICBMs, thereby reducing the danger that whatever new balance was struck in an arms agreement, it wouldn't be undermined by subsequent breakthroughs in technology.

A day after the Moscow meeting, Shcharansky was convicted of espionage and sentenced to thirteen years. A week later, on July 18, 1978, Whitney and Piper were found guilty of slandering Soviet State Television and Radio and were ordered to pay a token fine.

The signs were not auspicious as my second Moscow assignment began.

*   *   *

In late August I was asked to escort a visiting American Law-of-the-Sea (LOS) negotiator to several Soviet ministries. The discussions turned out to be constructive, confirming that even when the U.S.-Soviet atmospherics were highly "charged," working-level officials could have useful exchanges.

I invited four of the ministry officials to our temporary apartment for dinner, and they surprised me by accepting. For Liz, the challenge was to secure adequate food. The regime kept promising to upgrade its people's diet, yet there was less food available, and it was of poorer quality than during our first assignment.

Liz found the peasant markets mostly bare. The only decent vegetables to be had were carrots and potatoes. The strawberries offered were ridiculously priced, the equivalent of $8 a pound at the rate of exchange we were obliged to observe.

Meat and poultry were also scarce. Because the Soviets had delayed a special U.S. Air Force flight to Sheremetyevo, the commissary was rationing its inventory of frozen chicken. Liz had no choice but to go to the *Gastronom*, the hard-currency store near the embassy reserved for privileged Soviet citizens and foreigners. There, the shelves were mainly filled with canned goods, alcoholic beverages, and tobacco products—imported and Soviet, but sometimes meat and poultry from Eastern Europe could also be found. In the early 1970s, several American wives, including Liz, had taught the butcher how to make hamburger from Polish and Hungarian beef.

A day after the dinner, I arranged for the American negotiator to visit the fourteenth century Trinity-St. Sergius Monastery at Zagorsk, forty miles north of Moscow. Six months before we arrived, the Foreign Ministry had opened a few more areas to which we could drive without obtaining advance approval, but Zagorsk hadn't been among them. Even with permission, one couldn't stop along the route; the traffic militia had once ordered an embassy couple to return to Moscow when they were found picnicking by the side of the road.

Because the ministry officials didn't feel comfortable taking the American negotiator to a monastery, Liz and I went with him in an embassy car. We had seen its extraordinary collection of icons in the early '70s and were happy to see them again.

By September, we were in our "permanent" apartment, this time with the elevator three paces away instead of a floor below. Because of the summer turnover of staff, the general services unit couldn't provide the labor needed to finish the apartment's painting. Liz resorted to the usual bribe to keep the embassy's workers after hours. A bottle of vodka from the *Gastronom* cost us $1.25 in ruble coupons, a fraction of what Russians paid, and this was what the workers always wanted. "To get as much mowed as possible" before the sun set, Levin had ordered the foreman overseeing the harvest in *Anna Karenina* to give the peasants vodka.[295] Little had changed in a hundred years.

We celebrated the move with a dinner party and the film *Casablanca*. We invited Peter Tomsen, the Asia hand with whom we had served in New Delhi (it was his apartment in which we had stayed while he and his family were on home leave); Judi Mandel, a science section officer who would join me in Pol/Int the following year; the *Christian Science Monitor* correspondent David Willis; and their spouses.

I also invited Leonid Shcherbakov, an officer known to be with the KGB, who was fond of American movies. Steve Steiner had introduced us when Leonid was serving as a "consular officer" at Dobrynin's embassy. He had since joined the international department of the Council for Religious Affairs—the KGB-controlled agency responsible for supervising the Orthodox Patriarchate and other religious bodies permitted in the USSR—and had been helpful in arranging the visit to Zagorsk. I don't recall how Leonid reacted to *Casablanca,* a movie that draws attention to Vichy France's unforgiving exit visa controls.

Leonid and I would meet several more times during my second assignment, usually in the second-story restaurant of the National Hotel that overlooks Red Square. It was considered one of the capital's best restaurants, yet only a few dishes on its menu would ever be available. Cabbage soup (*shchi*), boiled buckwheat (*kasha*), and chicken Kiev were among the certainties. Although Leonid liked his food, the restaurant was more a place to drink. Waiters kept customers supplied with glass beakers holding one hundred grams (*sto gram*), or about three ounces, of first-class vodka.

We typically discussed U.S.-Soviet issues. At what turned out to be our last meal together, Leonid probed for a formula that would resolve the plight of the Pentecostal families housed in Tchaikovsky 19's basement. But he couldn't suggest anything that would guarantee they'd be permitted to leave the Soviet Union if they walked out. Until President Reagan appealed directly to Dobrynin in 1983, the Soviets remained unyielding.[296]

Leonid was nowhere to be found when I returned for my last assignment in 1985. An official at the Council for Religious Affairs with whom I spoke said he had left two years before. I didn't expect a KGB-controlled organization to let me know the whereabouts of one of its officers, but I left my name anyway.

Leonid never called, but I remembered him saying at our last luncheon that he suffered from high blood pressure. Sweating profusely (the vodka didn't help), he said he was looking forward to a month at a sanatorium on the Volga, one of many that the KGB controlled. It's possible he never made it back.

Reading Maya Plisetskaya's memoir in 2001, I was struck by her description of a KGB agent of the same surname who accompanied the Bolshoi Ballet on its tour of India in 1954. This Shcherbakov made the dancer's first trip abroad miserable, "bringing his sweaty face right up close to mine" with his overbearing instructions "in good manners."[297] The reports he subsequently filed kept her from traveling abroad for another six years. Could her Shcherbakov have been the same as mine?

At the end of that first summer, our two daughters returned to Kent School. (The Anglo-American School provided no classes beyond eighth grade.) We hired Sarah Heyer, a student from Wyoming who was enrolled in an advanced Russian language course in Moscow, as a live-in nanny to take care of Rob when we were traveling or otherwise out.

At the end of summer, Liz and I, along with Rob, ventured out to visit Peredelkino. Making a wrong turn, I got lost and stopped for directions at a wooden shack that looked as if it might be occupied. Behind it I found a toothless old woman and her middle-aged son harvesting fruit from several trees. They followed me back to the car and, before answering my question, began pouring apples and plums into the back. Within a few moments Rob was buried in fruit. The generosity of ordinary Russians never failed to amaze us; unfortunately, we could only reciprocate with the chewing gum Rob had brought along, not that they would have expected anything in return.

Later in the fall, when a Russian truck driver and his girlfriend pulled our car out of a snow bank (we were on our way to Tarasovka), we handed them the only alcohol we had—two bottles of imported French wine. They stared uncomprehendingly at the labels before agreeing to take them. A few colleagues at the embassy wouldn't drive without being sure that they had a bottle of vodka in their trunk to deal with such contingencies.

We strolled around Peredelkino for several hours. This time we wouldn't call on Viktor and Jennifer Louis; at one of my first meetings, Toon made clear that none of his officers was to talk with Viktor.

*   *   *

The number of Americans working in and around the embassy compound had been about 125 in 1972, nearly the same as in the 1950s, but the staff was much larger by the late 1970s. The number of FSOs had actually increased only slightly; agencies other than State accounted for most of the growth.

There were also more officials coming from Washington on "temporary duty" (TDY), staying a week or two or even longer in connection with specific projects, including some related to the agreements that Nixon and Brezhnev had signed.

Socializing *within* the community had dropped off from the early 1970s. The city excursions, collective shopping, and casual gatherings that had enlivened the wives' daytimes in the compounds had mostly disappeared. By 1978, more than half the spouses worked in full or part-time jobs, almost all at the embassy. Liz had not expected to work, but with the absence of wives from Leninsky 45, she decided to join the science section for twenty hours a week. (More working time would have required the embassy to provide benefits, so it limited her hours.) In the four years since we had left, the science section had grown from one officer and a shared secretary to three officers and two secretaries.

Sitting in my office in late September 1978, I was startled to hear fluent Russian being spoken within earshot. Concerned about a security breach, I leapt from my desk and rushed to the end of the corridor. I expected to encounter a tightly secured door that blocked access to the south wing's upstairs apartments, but it was ajar, and I strode in.

Several persons were chattering in Russian. It turned out they represented the department's Foreign Buildings Operations (FBO) office.[298] They were no less American than me, with security clearances probably matching mine, but were of Russian origin. They had been recruited in the United States to help build a new chancery-and-housing complex on a ten-acre vacant lot behind Tchaikovsky 19, beyond the shack that housed the garage and a three-story Soviet apartment house beyond it. I hadn't realized that the Seabees had already converted what once had been south-wing apartments into space for FBO's engineers.

I knew of the project. In 1969, the two governments had signed an agreement providing that each could build a new embassy on leased land in the other's capital. I recalled a briefing in Beam's office in 1973 when we were told what Washington had in mind. However, no one outside FBO and a few senior officers knew the schedule. Liz and I only knew that should we return for a third assignment (an unlikely prospect), we'd live in American housing.

The expansion of the staff was felt most acutely in Uncle Sam's. It was no larger than a midsized Starbucks, with a small kitchen separated by a counter and fifteen or so tables closely clustered together. No Russians were given access except for the two *babushka*s who worked in the kitchen and the counter woman Tanya, who took orders and marked up the Community Association chit cards we bought from the budget and fiscal unit. Almost every American in Moscow, including correspondents and businesspersons, ate several lunches a week at Uncle Sam's. A few even appeared for breakfast. In the early 1970s, friends from other Western embassies were delighted to be invited; it was sufficiently quiet that, sitting at a corner table, one could conduct a conversation with a Western diplomat that might yield a telegram.

By 1978, however, the tables had multiplied, chairs were pressed hard against one another, and the din was continuous. Alfredo, the snack bar's Italian manager; his colleague Piero; and the Russians who helped them couldn't keep up with the orders. Nonworking wives, children, and nannies—familiar sights during our first tour—were excluded until 2:00 PM. A young Russian woman with a face like a Madonna, also named Tanya, was now working at the counter alongside "old" Tanya.

The steady stream of visitors and the expansion of staff were taking a toll, but only those on second tours could possibly know. The sense of belonging to a single community was eroding. Staff members socialized more with their immediate colleagues—FSOs more with FSOs, communicators more with communicators, secretaries more with secretaries, etc., etc., up and down the line of a burgeoning roster.[299]

The community still came together twice a year, at Tarasovka for the July picnic and at Spaso House for the November Marine Ball. And the Marine Bar in the north wing remained a kind of social center for the single set, including unattached persons from other embassies, a larger number of marines, and the now-permanent Seabees. The community had expanded so much, and some of its members stayed for such short periods that it was no longer possible to know every name.

*   *   *

On October 21, 1978, Secretary of State Vance returned to Moscow for a further round of talks with Brezhnev, Gromyko, and other senior officials. As I recall, expectations on the United States side were high.

Vance again let the Soviet side know that President Carter wanted a summit, and Brezhnev responded, not surprisingly, that Vance and Gromyko should first settle their negotiating differences. According to the history that Strobe Talbott published a year later, the meeting "was marked by a large and awkward Soviet step backward" from what the American side thought it had secured a few days before at the talks in Geneva, a step having to do with Soviet encryption of ICBM telemetry.[300]

Ambassador Toon participated in Vance's meetings, but the embassy's contribution was mostly logistical. Still, three of us from the political section were invited to the luncheon that Gromyko hosted at the Foreign Ministry's guesthouse on Alexei Tolstoy Street.

In 1928, the Foreign Ministry (then the People's Commissariat of Foreign Affairs) had converted a private home that a rich merchant had built in 1894 into an official guesthouse, enabling it to host foreign dignitaries in the kind of bourgeois setting (with prerevolutionary trappings like Faberge silver and nineteenth-century paintings) to which they were accustomed.

The ministry served caviar, consommé with *pelmeni* (dumplings), sturgeon a la Moscovienne, and filet with mushrooms, the kind of fare not easily found at the National or other hotels. Those holding the regime's top positions didn't stint on their guests, or for that matter, themselves.

I joined others from the embassy in seeing Vance and his team off at Domodedyevo Airport. It was clear from the tight lips around us that the talks had been disappointing.

Arms issues monopolized the U.S.-Soviet agenda for the nine months left to me as the head of Pol/Ext. Now and then, Ambassador Toon would be the intermediary in delivering or receiving high-level messages to further the dialogue; but the embassy's influence was limited, not because Toon wasn't Carter's "man" but because the White House's back channel, its interagency committees, and the two sides' experts in Geneva monopolized the important business. The embassy could report on what the Soviets were saying or writing in their set speeches and carefully controlled media, and at their ministries and institutes, but no one at the embassy, not even an experienced hand like Toon, could influence a process that involved maneuvering among powerful foreign-affairs, defense, and intelligence-community personalities in each of the capitals as well as a thicket of highly technical questions.

My Pol/Ext colleagues did produce important reporting and analysis of non-arms-control issues, especially those having to do with Moscow's involvement in third-world trouble spots. Peter Tomsen and Dick Miles initiated wide-ranging conversations at ministries, institutes, and foreign embassies based in Moscow; and the information they adduced and interpretations they provided sharpened Washington's "reading" of the Kremlin's intentions, and undoubtedly contributed to policy making.

But it was the political section's Pol/Int unit that impressed me most. Its officers were providing information and insights largely unattainable outside the USSR, far beyond the capability of Soviet "watchers" in Washington or elsewhere abroad. Keeping their ears to the ground, collecting the gossip and scuttlebutt that circulated constantly, Pol/Int officers were able to shed light on debates inside the Party, on individual leaders, and on long-term political and social trends. The conditions and viewpoints they unearthed were rarely found in the media but could be picked up from their interlocutors at ministries, think tanks, and newspaper and journal offices, as well as from conversations with ordinary Soviet citizens, including dissidents and refuseniks. Their firsthand accounts yielded a comprehensive picture of the system's ills.

It didn't take me long to realize that Washington's craving for information about conditions outside Moscow itself was nearly insatiable. The State Department and CIA welcomed every tidbit of fact and plausible rumor, especially from those areas where non-Russian peoples predominated.

Dick Combs headed the Pol/Int unit when I arrived. Dick had earned a PhD in Soviet affairs from the University of California, Berkeley, and had taught there before joining the Foreign Service in 1966. While growing up, he had been steeped in Communist affairs; his father had been involved in exposing Communist influences in California during and after World War II. Working as a lawyer for a state legislative committee analogous to the House Un-American Activities Committee, the senior Combs had led an investigation of Berkeley's radiation lab where the physicist Robert Oppenheimer was employed.

When I entered the Foreign Service, few officers were sent behind the Iron Curtain for their first overseas assignment, but an exception had been made in Dick's case, and he went to Communist Bulgaria. After fulfilling consular and political duties there and after a subsequent year at the institute in Garmisch, he was posted to Moscow in 1969, first as a consular officer (which was how most of us began) and then as an economic officer.

Dick had returned to Moscow to head Pol/Int in 1976. In 1977, he had received a Superior Honor Award for working with the Russian firemen extinguishing the upper-floor fire.

Obviously, these were big shoes to fill, and I set out to prepare myself by working hard on improving my Russian and traveling outside the capital whenever possible.[301]

*   *   *

I had made arrangements for language lessons with Mila Vronski as soon as I returned. As compared with the early 1970s, there were many more persons needing lessons, which meant that I could only arrange an hour a week. But even one hour would help; Mila and I could chat about developments in the cultural sphere while she improved my language.

Toward the end of Liz's and my first tour, she had arranged for us to see *Hamlet* at the Taganka Theatre. The Taganka Company had burst into prominence a decade earlier. Its director, Yuri Lyubimov, had taken over and renovated an empty theater in a part of the city I didn't know and staged a succession of bold productions. Although the censors had closed a few, Lyubimov wasn't one who was easily daunted.

Theater tickets were difficult to obtain. Diplomats seeking them had to apply to the Foreign Ministry's diplomatic services branch. At the time, the American embassy was one of more than one hundred embassies in Moscow; although it was the largest by far, it obviously couldn't monopolize the ministry's ticket allotment.

Playing Hamlet was Vladimir Vysotsky, an actor and singer already well known for composing and performing songs deploring the hardships ordinary citizens endured, including food lines and crowded apartments. Some of his lyrics targeted the privileges of the ruling elite, the Party's *nomenklatura* (its list of members deemed sufficiently trustworthy to hold the regime's important posts). Vysotsky's songs had spread throughout the Soviet Union via homemade publications (*samizdat*) and cassette recordings (*magnitizdat*). By the early 1970s, he enjoyed cult standing among many Russians, especially the young. (Writing years later, Gorbachev noted that even Andropov had been "particularly fond" of Vysotsky.[302])

Pasternak had translated *Hamlet* into Russian in the late 1930s, and Vsevolod Meyerhold, the great Jewish director, was planning to produce it in Leningrad. But in 1939, Meyerhold was arrested and shot. At the start of the war, there was again talk that Pasternak's version might be staged. Pasternak told the widow of a Georgian poet (who had been executed in 1937) that the Moscow Art Theatre would perform it[303], but word got out that Stalin considered the character of Hamlet pessimistic and reactionary; and then no one would touch it.

After Stalin's death, Pasternak's version was produced in Leningrad. Pasternak's cousin, Olga Freidenberg, saw it in 1954 but exclaimed in a letter to the poet, "How much is deleted!"[304] It is impossible to know whether Freidenberg was complaining about Pasternak's deletions from Shakespeare or the censors' deletions from Pasternak; probably the latter, but one had to be careful what one wrote.

Somehow Mila obtained tickets for us. When the curtain rose, Vysotsky was dressed in black and was standing at an open grave. Accompanying himself on a guitar, he sang in his distinctive voice ("that could sandpaper sandpaper," as was said once of Lotte Lenya's[305]) the lines from the *Hamlet* poem that Pasternak included in the still-banned *Doctor Zhivago*. In the foreground to one side, a coarsely woven curtain hanging from the ceiling above the stage swung back and forth. A wooden cross hung off the stage's back wall. The curtain was in motion throughout, enveloping and exposing the performers as the plot proceeded. A Western critic would later describe the curtain as "a giant monster . . . setting the pace, and holding within its folds the symbols and tools of power—black armbands, swords, goblets, thrones edged with knives"—all of which appeared in Lyubimov's production. At the end, the curtain "sweeps the stage clean and moves toward the audience as though to destroy it too."[306]

The visual impact was powerful. For older Russians, the atmosphere on stage must have been evocative of life with Stalin. What extraordinary theater!

Yet we were at a loss to understand much of the dialogue. The actors delivered their lines with a fiery intensity, and only someone highly proficient in Russian—and perhaps knowing Pasternak's translation cold—could understand them all; and I wasn't one.

Mila arranged another theatrical treat when we returned in 1978. She secured tickets to *The Master and Margarita,* also at the Taganka. Mikhail Bulgakov wrote the novel on which the play is based in the 1930s. It satirized the corruption and insecurity that pervaded the capital between the wars, a daring subject with Stalin ruling.

Bulgakov's writings had been banned in 1930. The novel first appeared, in a heavily censored form, in successive issues of a literary journal, *Moscow* (*Moskva*), in 1966 and 1967, as the thaw that Khrushchev had launched was nearing an end. The full text was circulating in a *tamizdat* (published "there," outside the USSR) in the early 1970s, and I had read an English translation in Garmisch.

Lyubimov broke further Soviet conventions with this production. Not only was a cross displayed throughout the play but the initials "XB," for the Orthodox Easter greeting "Christ Is Risen!" (*Khristos Voskrese*!), were inscribed on a plaque at the front of the stage. The actress playing Margarita made a brief appearance in the nude, and the performance ended with the company holding up photographs of Bulgakov.

Vysotsky's fame continued to spread, but we wouldn't see him again. He was a heavy drinker, and in 1980, at the age of forty-two, he suddenly died. There was no announcement in the press, but thousands of Moscovites, learning from word of mouth, gathered in front of the theater. When the crowd grew too large, the authorities whisked away the body for burial in Moscow's Vagankovskoye Cemetery.

Vysotsky's grave, like Pasternak's, is a kind of shrine today.

Russians have a way of choosing their own heroes; and whenever one dies, their outpouring of grief is genuine, and the regime is put on edge. It had been no different under the tsars; when the poet Alexander Pushkin died in 1837, such was the tsar's fear of disorder that he deployed troops to the streets and ordered St. Petersburg's students and professors to remain in their classrooms during the funeral.[307]

In 1984, just before we returned to Moscow for the third time, the Party's watchdogs banned a play that Lyubimov was producing to honor Vysotsky himself. Then they closed two plays in the theater's repertory and demanded he stop rehearsing two others. At this, Lyubimov decided he had had enough and exiled himself, first to England, then to Israel. In turn, the regime stripped him of his citizenship. After Gorbachev dismantled censorship in 1988, Lyubimov returned to Moscow and began afresh.[308]

*   *   *

Several weeks after visiting Zagorsk, I persuaded Liz to travel with me to Ulyanovsk, an industrial city on the Volga River where Lenin himself had been born. It had been known as Simbirsk but received the revolutionist's family name after his death in 1924.

Ulyanovsk was one of the few open cities along the Volga to which we could travel; but no one had been there for a few years, and it had the reputation of being tightly controlled. (It was one of the last Russian cities to accede to Gorbachev's reforms.) The Foreign Ministry had turned down my request to visit Kazan, a more interesting city to the north, saying there were no rooms available except during the period of Vance's visit, when it knew I couldn't leave the embassy. After an exchange of telephone calls, the ministry approved three days in Ulyanovsk.

It was mid-October, and the temperature was hovering around freezing when our flight touched down. The Intourist guide assigned to us, Margaret by name, met us at the terminal.

After a perfunctory welcome, she led us to a black Volga, a sedan manufactured in the closed city of Gorky just north of Ulyanovsk, and ordered her driver to take us to the hotel to which we had been assigned, also named the Volga.

At the hotel, she directed us to a semi-lit room off the main lobby. The room was furnished austerely with a table and four chairs and had just been painted. (By our departure, it had reverted to its function as just another hotel room.) On the table stood miniature Soviet and American flags. Margaret seated herself and began reading a lengthy formal statement describing the program Intourist had arranged. It included every sight connected with Lenin (his parents' house, the school where he had studied, the museum honoring his life) but little else. After some minutes, I interrupted to note that the program included none of the calls I had requested through the ministry and through telexes that Oleg, the political section's single Russian employee, had sent. Among the visits I wanted was one to the city's industrial island where a popular jeep-style vehicle was being manufactured. Margaret said she'd look into my requests.

We were conducted upstairs and along a dingy corridor to our room. It turned out that it too had just been painted, and the door was still sticky. The fumes were bothersome as we unpacked, and I tracked Margaret down to ask if a different room were available. No, this wouldn't be possible.

Beginning with the boom in foreign tourism in the early '70s, Intourist had been hiring attractive, well-educated young women and men to fill its ranks, but I quickly sensed that Margaret, heavyset with thick ankles, was a throwback to the old tradition.

For the first evening, we were driven to a small theater for a musical based on *The Three Musketeers*. It was located on the main floor inside a new hotel that also belonged to Intourist. The hotel was spacious and mostly unoccupied; obviously there were reasons for housing us in the Volga, and perhaps in the room to which we were assigned.

We were directed to a private box situated on a balcony overlooking an already assembled audience, mostly comprised of school children wearing the Red neckties and kerchiefs associated with membership in the *Pioneers*, the Soviet cub scouts, and accompanied by their parents.

The play must have been written during Stalin's time. At one point, eight "nuns" performed a lascivious cancan dance to entertain a red-robed "cardinal." The cardinal was later shown torturing a captive "spy" with a branding iron. The children were delighted, though the performers lip-synched all their songs.

Years before, I had read a novel by Igor Gouzenko, one of the first defectors from a Soviet embassy after the war, and it included a scene with a play portraying Father Christmas as a spy. I had thought Gouzenko might be exaggerating, but here was the same propaganda a quarter-century later. A theater in Moscow wouldn't stoop so low, but they could get away with it in Lenin's birthplace.

We tried to leave during the intermission but found we had been locked in the private box. Margaret had turned the key when she deposited us.

Driven back to the hotel, we found a table reserved for us at the Volga's only restaurant, already crowded with diners. An attractive young couple approached and asked if they could join us. Since there were no other places available and the point of the trip was to talk with as many Russians as possible, we agreed.

They introduced themselves as Tanya and Mikhail Dryzlov. Mike, tall and good-looking, worked at the local power station; Tanya, attractive with dark hair and dark eyes, probably in her twenties, said she was studying at an engineering institute. It turned out they both spoke good English and that Mike took occasional trips to Moscow in connection with his job.

Our new acquaintances ordered cognac, and we exchanged toasts and small talk until the meal appeared an hour later.

After a convivial evening, Mike and Tanya suggested we go to another place. The day had been long, however, and we suggested exchanging addresses and telephone numbers instead. Tanya gave us her mother's

ROBERT F. OBER, JR.

address in Pyatigorsk, north of the Caucasian Mountains, where she said she spends her summers. "Perhaps we could meet there," she said.

Liz and I had exchanged addresses with Russians before, but no one could get by the guard at the compound unless we arranged to meet them outside in advance. Few Russians would venture alone into an entryway guarded by a militiaman.

The next morning, Margaret confirmed that none of the meetings I requested, including calls on local officials, were possible to arrange. Liz and I took in some of the official program but broke away to walk the streets on our own.

Ulyanovsk was a demoralized city. Drunks stumbled about during the day; antialcohol clinics and a venereal disease center operated not far from the hotel. A taxi driver with whom we rode complained that gasoline would run out before December as it had in previous years. A native-born Aeroflot employee told us he regretted he hadn't married his girlfriend in Moscow to gain a residency permit there. A single Orthodox church existed (of twenty-one that had served Simbirsk before the Revolution), but it was outside the city limit, beyond where we could go. I visited the municipal building to see if I could make an appointment on my own but was told everyone was traveling or sick.

The next day, Liz and I continued to prowl the streets. Several men in dark suits, usually a block or two away, didn't let us out of their sight. Margaret's black Volga cruised slowly beside us, sometimes a block behind, sometimes a block ahead. Every so often she'd have her driver bring the car abreast and remind us with a glare that we had missed another stop on the official program.

In the evening, at the same table where we had met Mike and Tanya, two of the men, whom we recognized as having shadowed us, plopped down uninvited. After we pointed to empty tables elsewhere, they slunk off without a word.

The experience we had in Ulyanovsk was not unusual, at least for cities we visited in the Russian republic outside of Moscow. One's requests were usually brushed aside, and the programs were touristic. Margaret would have made Prince Potemkin proud, making every effort to shield us from the real Russia.

Two months later, we were surprised to find Tanya standing outside our door in Moscow. We invited her in for a drink. She explained that she just happened to be visiting the capital and wanted to remind us of her invitation to visit Pyatigorsk. In fact, I did want to travel through the Caucuses after I transferred to Pol/Int.

In July 1979, she showed up again. By then there was no doubt she was working for the KGB.

Tanya and I did have a final meeting, described in due course, but it didn't turn out the way she wanted and probably didn't help her career.

Mike also got in contact with us. He arrived at our apartment in February 1981 as my assignment was nearing an end. Tanya, he explained, had run off with an engineer at the jeep factory, but he had been promoted to head a department at the local power station. Wouldn't we visit him again?

With a casual aside, he added that he was on his way to see his brother in Leningrad. "Didn't I tell you that he was stationed at a submarine base there? Our father is a retired submariner."

Mike and Tanya were playing carefully scripted roles.

A few years after the end of my second Moscow assignment, in January 1985, I received a Russian-language season's greeting card from Mike that had been addressed to our home in Maryland. It had been forwarded from there to the embassy in Athens where I was then serving. Could I have shared my home address with him?

More interestingly, could he have known even before I knew that the embassy in Moscow would telephone me two or three weeks later and ask me to return for a third assignment? Had the KGB picked up hints of the plan to send me back to Moscow, perhaps from monitoring the embassy's open-line to Washington? There were always mysteries in the USSR I couldn't crack. In fact, I never saw or heard from Mike again. Perhaps he was engaged in another project by the time we returned.

*   *   *

In November 1978, while still heading Pol/Ext, I persuaded Liz to take another trip with me, this time to Vilnius, the capital of the Lithuanian republic. I had traveled there in 1973 and felt the population's longing for independence. The young woman who greeted me and my colleague with a bouquet of flowers remained fixed in mind.

Lithuania was one of three Baltic countries whose independence had been quashed in 1940. Because the United States never recognized the takeover, Moscow barred us from traveling in the republic except to its two main cities—Vilnius, which had belonged to Poland between the two world wars, and Kaunas.

An American diplomat could visit Kaunas but only under Intourist auspices and during daylight hours; and the drive from Vilnius would take more than an hour if Intourist agreed to provide a guide, a car, and a driver. I knew that Poland's national poet Mickiewicz, a ferocious opponent of tsarist oppression, had taught in Kaunas in the 1820s. More importantly, the only seminary training Roman Catholic priests in the USSR was situated near the city's main square, and I wanted to visit it if possible.

The Vilnius KGB was subordinate to Moscow, and we experienced the usual surveillance; but the local Intourist office, comprised mainly of Lithuanians, was more than happy to arrange a visit to Kaunas. On the drive up, I suggested to our young guide that she have lunch with Liz while I call on the seminary. Unlike Margaret in Ulyanovsk, she had no problem with an American breaking away to pay a visit on his own.

The priest who received me at the seminary was wary at first. Was I an *agent provocateur*, a Russian pretending to be an American? But a warm, even if somewhat guarded conversation, ensued; and I learned about the seminary's work under the onerous conditions set by the Council of Religious Affairs, where my acquaintance Leonid worked.

Returning to Vilnius, Liz and I visited several Roman Catholic churches (they were as crowded as the ones in Warsaw), and we called on several families who were on the embassy's representation list. We invited one woman and her fifteen-year-old daughter to join us for dinner. We heard how her husband, the conductor of a Vilnius orchestra, had slipped away from a Soviet tour in Yugoslavia five years before and made his way to Chicago. Her story brought to mind the many family separations I had dealt with as a consular officer; how long would this family have to wait?

The authorities rarely blocked visits to Russian Orthodox bishops and priests. They liked foreigners to see the "freedom" that "their" church enjoyed. In fact, through the Council of Religious Affairs, the KGB exercised "near-total control of the Orthodox Church, both at home and abroad," as a one-time KGB official later admitted.[309] A sizable number of the Orthodox priests were homosexual—the official explained—and that served to strengthen the KGB's hand since homosexuality remained a crime under Soviet law.[310]

I don't recall asking to see the Orthodox archbishop of Vilnius, but someone, probably in the Intourist office, suggested we call on him. Upon arriving at the cathedral, we found that he and three other priests, attired in the church's splendid regalia, had arranged for us a veritable feast. We were taken to a table covered with plates of caviar, salmon, liver pate, preserved mushrooms, and the like, with three or four empty glasses set at every place.

Tall, stately, and fully bearded, the archbishop welcomed us warmly. After a relaxed exchange of banter and toasts, serious eating and drinking commenced. Waiters kept the glasses full not only with vodka and wine but also with cognac and champagne. The conversation wasn't particularly edifying—there weren't many believers among the Russians who had taken up residence in Vilnius after 1940—and the assistant priests were subdued in the archbishop's presence.

After more than an hour of this, I thanked our hosts and explained we would have to be on our way. If we missed our flight at Vilnius Airport, the Foreign Ministry would complain. "Don't worry," the archbishop replied, brushing crumbs from his beard, "my limousine and driver will get you there."

It took several more reminders before the archbishop released us. Like good shepherds, he and his entourage led us to the cobblestone courtyard in front of the cathedral where his limousine was parked. While the driver helped Liz into the backseat, the archbishop, already tottering from drink, gave me an affectionate hug and followed me around to the other side. Wresting the back door open, I tried to slip inside without further ado, but he forced me against the car and landed his mouth square on my lips. I don't think this was any liturgical "kiss of peace."

After Lithuania regained its independence, one of our host's successors, Archbishop Chrysostom, acknowledged that he, like other priests, had worked with the KGB, but "had also "tried to maintain the position of my church, and, yes, to act as a patriot . . . in collaboration with these organs."[311] Throughout the Soviet period, the Orthodox Church was in a terrible state; but after Stalin's death, not many of its priests were sent to prison, and none was executed. It retained just enough authenticity during its prolonged purgatory that it was able to recover its health once the system collapsed.

*   *   *

For many Americans, December was always a favorite month. The Anglo-American School let its pupils out for vacation, and their siblings, studying abroad in boarding schools and colleges, began streaming back. Christmas was in the air, even if there was no hint of it on any Moscow street. Orthodox Russians, the many who still believed, wouldn't celebrate it themselves—in accordance with their calendar—until thirteen days after December 25.

Elise and Abby arrived from New York around December 20. The fact that the month turned out to be one of the coldest in Moscow's history would make no difference to them.

The city was experiencing a blizzard when we reached Sheremetyevo, and the girls' flight was diverted, at the last moment to Vnukovo Airport an hour away. Obtaining accurate arrival and departure information at Soviet airports was always a challenge, but our driver managed to learn about the diversion a half hour before the aircraft's scheduled landing. He raced us around the capital's outer ring road in blinding snow to reach Vnukovo just as the girls were clearing customs.

Elise, Abby, and Rob were soon out, skating together in the compound courtyard in eight-degrees-below-zero weather. There was no one else present, but they lasted almost an hour.

Three days before Christmas, we all watched the Czechs and the Russians battle it out at the hockey rink near Lenin Stadium. The police were out in force. The previous August, the Soviet Union and Czechoslovakia had "marked" the tenth anniversary of the Soviet suppression of the Prague Spring and Brezhnev's enunciation of the doctrine "justifying" it, so the match had political overtones. Surrounded by Russian fans, we discreetly rooted for the Czechs. They led into the final period when the Soviet team scored two goals, and the game ended in a 3-3 tie.

A Protestant Christmas Eve service at the British embassy—in a wood-paneled room overlooking the Kremlin and its golden domes across the river—lifted our spirits.

By December 29, the temperature had fallen to thirty degrees below zero. The car battery, only six months old, refused to turn the engine over, and Rob and I pulled it out and brought it upstairs to thaw.

We had signed up for *The Turning Point,* a film about ballet to show on New Year's Eve. We had invited British friends to join us, the Maddens whom we'd see again during an assignment in Athens; but they were forced to cancel. Their battery too had failed.

The five of us had just seen *Swan Lake* at the Bolshoi; and Elise, a ballet enthusiast, was determined to see Mikhail Baryshnikov, a defector from the Kirov Ballet and the one of the film's stars. So Elise and I donned several extra layers of clothing (she wore her mother's sheepskin coat, I wore mine), and set out for the nearest Metro station three blocks from the compound.

There was no one else out as far as we could tell. The temperature was still thirty below. The gust of hot air that greets riders as they enter each Metro station was never more welcome!

The platform for the trains heading downtown was almost deserted, and we found ourselves riding an empty car to Oktyabskaya Station. There we transferred to the ring line and a train to Barrikadnaya Station. Riding the escalator up, bracing ourselves again, we made the fifteen minute trek to the embassy. We got the key to the film cabinet from the marine, secured the film, and made our way home. There were few cars on the streets and no Russians on the sidewalks, not even the drunks.

The next day, as others had reserved the film, we lugged it back. The weather was the same.

Diplomats in India often quoted Noel Coward's doggerel that only "mad dogs and Englishmen go out in the midday sun." There was no comparable doggerel at Tchaikovsky 19, but it seemed to me that the Americans were the only ones to challenge that memorable cold.

9

From Carter's Summit to Brezhnev's Afghanistan

The pendulum of the Cold War swung its widest arc in 1979, from President Carter's summit meeting with Brezhnev in June to the Soviet intervention in Afghanistan in December. At its midpoint in October, Thomas J. Watson Jr., IBM's former chief executive officer, succeeded Malcolm Toon as ambassador to Moscow.

On May 7, 1979, Secretary of State Vance informed President Carter that the two governments had finally reached an agreement on strategic arms. At the end of 1978, Vance and Gromyko had narrowed their differences in meetings in Geneva. Then Vance, Brzezinski, and Carter, talking with Dobrynin in Washington and being backstopped by their delegation in Geneva, had overcome the ones that remained. Between January 1 and May 7, 1979, Vance and Dobrynin met twenty-five times in the secretary's seventh-floor suite of offices.[312]

At last, Carter could have his summit. The meeting ought to have taken place in the United States, the previous one having occurred in Vladivostok in the USSR's Far East; but Brezhnev's health was failing, and his medical team urged that Moscow be the venue. The administration couldn't be seen, however, as too accommodating (the Senate would have to ratify the agreement and key senators were already expressing doubts), so the two governments settled on neutral Vienna.

The summit took place June 15-18. It would be the last summit until Gorbachev and Reagan met in 1985. The agreement that Brezhnev and Carter signed on June 18 would be known as the Strategic Arms Limitation Agreement, or SALT II.

The embassy couldn't contribute much to the summit's preparation. The USSR was no longer the *terra incognita* it had been in the early 1970s, and the officials on the Soviet side were virtually the same as those with whom Nixon, Kissinger, and Ford had dealt.

As soon as the summit ended, I handed over responsibility for Pol/Ext to the newly arrived Ed Djerejian and replaced Combs as head of Pol/Int.

A major development six months before the summit was the establishment of full diplomatic relations with the People's Republic of China (PRC). Overriding Vance's objections, Brzezinski had secured the president's approval for fast-tracking normalization.[313] As the SALT II negotiations dragged on, Brzezinski had pushed the idea of a relationship that would move "beyond just diplomatic normalization"[314] to that of "strategic partnership."[315]

Brzezinski had established his own relationship with Vice Premier Deng Xiaoping and other PRC leaders on his trip to Beijing in May 1978, the trip that Vance had opposed. Brzezinski had told the Chinese that the two countries had been "allies before"[316] despite their near-quarter century of animosity and that their new relationship "has long-term strategic importance."[317]

After his return, Brzezinski launched a public attack on Moscow, alleging it was "engaged in a sustained and massive effort to build up its conventional forces" in Europe and "on the frontiers of China."[318]

Brzezinski intended to please the Chinese, but his language had the effect of reinforcing the impression, in Moscow and other capitals, of divisions among Carter's chief policymakers.

Once formal relations were established on January 1, 1979, the Chinese embassy wasted no time approaching the American embassy. In mid-January, the Chinese invited the entire political section, including secretaries and nonworking wives, to their compound for dinner. It was clear they wanted every Russian official in Moscow to be acutely aware of the nascent "partnership."

Chinese diplomats had been off-limits to American officials from the time of the Communist takeover in 1949. I had dealt with them only once before, as a note-taker at the Warsaw talks, but even then we weren't allowed to shake their hands as I recall. I had also spoken Russian with several PRC trade officials in the lobby of a Bucharest hotel in 1971 when our Garmisch class was in Romania sightseeing; the institute director hadn't been pleased with such impromptu diplomacy, though it consisted of no more than a pleasantry. In India, I had been the embassy's contact with the Taiwanese government's representative; Paul Kreisberg spoke Chinese but wanted to keep his "hands clean" should he seek an assignment in Beijing.

Nine of us in the political section accepted the invitation. We were open about it, arriving in vehicles chauffeured by the embassy's Russian drivers. As they did in most foreign capitals, the Chinese lived and worked in a large compound. It encompassed everything that assured their day-to-day independence of the Soviets, including recreational facilities, greenhouses, gardens, as well as offices and apartments. I don't believe they allowed Russian workers in their compound.

Three of our hosts were waiting outside when we arrived. They helped our wives and secretaries out of the vehicles and led them across an icy threshold into a reception hall. With their attentiveness to the women, they had already set themselves apart from the Russians; our Soviet contacts rarely included wives in their functions and were often awkward around them.

Our Chinese hosts numbered about ten, and they all spoke Russian. A few had studied in the USSR in the 1960s, before worsening Sino-Soviet relations ended student and scholarly exchanges. Several spoke passable English.

Chinese art and handicrafts—including silk tapestries, porcelain vases, stone sculptures, and enamel and lacquer ware—decorated the hall through which we passed. We ended up in an intimate reception area next to a dining room. Liz noted that the pillows resting on our chairs were silk covered with exquisitely hand-embroidered designs.

For almost five hours we sat together conversing, eating, and drinking. We were served seven courses, including the traditional age-blackened eggs, bamboo shoots, shark fin soup, and other delicacies. The *mao-tai* liquor was stronger than any vodka I had ever encountered, even the homemade kind. Toasts were drunk. The evening had been carefully planned, and the Chinese made sure it was suffused with camaraderie. It was unlike any evening I had spent with Soviet officials.

The Chinese didn't have an easy lot in Moscow. Most had been assigned without family, and their assignments were for four or more years, without provision for any break back home. The hardships we experienced were minor compared to theirs.

Three weeks passed, and before we could reciprocate, the Chinese invited Liz and me along with several other embassy couples to a second dinner, this time an elaborate buffet in the company of West European diplomats and spouses. Vice Premier Deng Xiaoping had just concluded a visit to Washington, and Brzezinski had hosted him at his home in Virginia.[319] Brzezinski had included Vance, but by this time, the Chinese understood that the NSC advisor, not the secretary, was the driving force behind the new relationship.

The entire Chinese embassy was involved in the second dinner. Liz was running a household and was holding a part-time science job (perhaps the Chinese knew this), but they didn't hesitate to seek her views on Sino-American and Sino-Soviet relations. A young woman who specialized in the Soviet media cornered her for much of the evening. The woman explained that she systematically added up the number of anti-PRC articles appearing in each month's Soviet press in order to gauge the trends in Moscow's thinking. She reported that Deng's visit to Washington had gone especially well, and this had gladdened everyone at their embassy.

It happened that, at the very end of his stay in Washington, on January 30, 1979, Deng had told President Carter that the Chinese intended to teach Vietnam a "lesson" for having sent its forces into Cambodia[320], the action that had unseated the murderous Pol Pot regime. The lesson turned out to be the invasion of Vietnam on February 17. In the first month of the war, twenty thousand Chinese reportedly died; undoubtedly, Vietnamese losses were higher.

Only Chinese archives will reveal to what extent, if at all, Brzezinski's "forcing" of the pace of normalization encouraged the PRC to move ahead with its short-lived and costly invasion.

Naturally, the Soviets detected a degree of Chinese-American collusion in the assault on their ally. According to Dobrynin, Brezhnev queried Carter on the hotline, "Is it a mere coincidence" that the invasion came on the heels of Deng's visit?[321] Vance complains in his memoir that when "American calm and prudence were essential to avoid any misinterpretation . . . by Moscow that we were colluding with the Chinese, we in the State Department were told by reporters that they were being briefed in the White House about a Soviet buildup taking place on the Sino-Soviet border." Vance adds, almost as an aside, that there was no evidence of a Soviet build-up.[322]

The secretary's efforts to keep the Soviets calm as he worked toward achieving the strategic arms agreement were periodically derailed by words and actions emanating from the White House.

It was not as if Brzezinski was unmindful of the effects of his approach. Immediately after the United States announced its agreement to establish diplomatic relations with Beijing, the Soviets had cautioned Washington not to sell arms to the Chinese. The appearance of U.S.-Chinese collusion was reigniting Russia's historic preoccupation with encirclement. (After the Soviet invasion of Afghanistan, I sent Ambassador Watson a copy of an old statement made by Khrushchev in the context of Afghanistan that the United States was trying to "encircle us with military bases."[323] I thought this might help the ambassador, who had no background in Russian history, be somewhat more conversant with the Soviet mindset when discussing issues with his ambassadorial colleagues.)

I later became well acquainted with several Chinese diplomats, particularly Wang Houli, a Pol/Int officer whose responsibilities were analogous to mine. Because Wang had studied in Moscow in the early

1960s, our common language was Russian. When he brought his team to our apartment, however, he included an attractive young woman who could effortlessly interpret in and out of three languages—Russian, English, and Chinese.

*   *   *

In a letter home in February 1979, I described a typical day as head of Pol/Ext. I prefaced my description with a comment that "we had a busy Washington Birthday weekend because of the Chinese invasion . . . the China/Asian expert on my staff [Tomsen] worked all three days and our Middle East expert [Miles] was busy because of Washington's interest in Moscow's policy toward Iran." A few days earlier, Iranian radicals had stormed the American embassy in Tehran, rehearsing their seizure of our diplomats later in the year.

My schedule looked like this on the day I wrote:

8:20 AM—Liz and I reach the embassy from Leninsky 45.

9:00 AM—After reviewing the main articles in *Pravda* and *Izvestiya* and scanning incoming telegrams, I begin drafting a telegram reporting a French protest delivered to the Foreign Ministry about which Toon had learned from his French counterpart.

9:30 AM—My three colleagues and I meet and, on the basis of our review of the media and the incoming telegrams, decide on the day's work.

10:00 AM—Meet with the ambassador, the deputy chief of mission [Garrison], the political counselor [German], and section heads at the country-team meeting to receive an account of the ambassador's meeting with the British, French, and German ambassadors at their weekly "quadripartite" gathering.

11:00 AM—Complete my telegram and review and clear telegrams prepared by my colleagues or brought to me by officers from other sections.

12:00 NN—Receive the Yugoslav political counselor for an exchange of views.

1:00 PM—Lunch in Uncle Sam's with an American graduate student working as a translator at the Soviet press agency Novosti.

2:00 PM—Complete the section's reporting to Washington and other posts; begin drafting two telegrams drawing on

information obtained at lunch and at meetings earlier in
the day, and from the media and other sources.
6:00 PM—Drive home with Liz, if she works to the end of the day,
otherwise in a van.
7:30 PM—Leave for dinner party hosted by the Japanese political
counselor.

My letter doesn't refer to the strategic arms negotiations then nearing
conclusion in Washington and Geneva, but the endgame didn't involve
the embassy at all.

*   *   *

While the White House was dealing with Brezhnev's hotline message
about the Chinese invasion, telegrams from the American embassy in
Kabul were monopolizing our attention. Islamic radicals had abducted
Ambassador Dubs; and the Afghan police, advised by Soviet officials in
Kabul, had in turn cornered them.

Most of us knew Spike personally, if not from his tour at the embassy
in the early '70s then from his prior assignment as head of the Soviet desk.
He was one of the rare senior officers who wouldn't hesitate to leave a
front-office perch to visit subordinates at their own desks. By the late 1970s,
he was among a small number of Soviet hands from whom we thought the
White House might select a successor to Toon.

As the P&C news ticker spewed out foreign press reports and embassy
Kabul's telegrams piled up, voices fell to a hush, and the atmosphere
turned somber.

It was Marshall Shulman who announced Spike's death in a telegram
he sent to every diplomatic and consular mission on February 14.[324] The
Afghans had foolishly tried to force Spike's rescue, and he had been killed
in the cross fire.

Marshall praised Spike for combining "high professional competence
with human warmth and compassion," while adding a comment that FSOs
like Spike meet their responsibilities despite a lack of recognition. The
telegram made me aware that Spike had been one of Marshall's students
during his midcareer assignment to Columbia.

Spike's body was sent to Washington, and his funeral took place on
February 20. Shulman delivered a eulogy in the presence of Mrs. Carter,
Vice President Mondale, Secretary Vance, and Spike's wife and daughter
(the latter from his first marriage that had ended after his last Moscow
assignment).

Winter 1979 was grim for other reasons too.

The bitter cold that swept into Moscow in December refused to release its grip. The temperature dropped to twenty degrees below zero (Fahrenheit) for several days in January. In the middle of the month, twenty-five fire trucks converged on the building opposite Tchaikovsky 19 to put out a blaze that threatened its upper floors. This led to speculation among the staff that the equipment transmitting the microwaves had been damaged, but the embassy's technicians provided no confirmation, and the bombardment continued.

Mark Garrison flew off to West Germany in February to have his eyes checked, reviving the stories that Stoessel's assignment had been shortened because of eye problems due to the microwaves. I began to notice a falloff in my hearing around the same time; I'd miss words at staff meetings inside the tank, where there was no background noise to blame. There was no history of hearing loss in my family, and my parents and Liz decided that the microwaves were responsible. The State Department informed me later, however, that no studies had ever found a hearing loss from microwaves.

The Soviets suspended their bombardment in May 1979. In July that year and in July 1980, I underwent minor procedures during three-week leaves in Illinois that dealt with the problem, although my mother, to her death, maintained that the Russians were responsible.

In March 1979, the department sent a psychologist to Moscow for a weeklong visit—said to be the first such visit in the embassy's history. At a meeting Liz attended, he reported that the department had found from a study of five hundred FSOs that they rank high for resiliency and adventurousness, yet it was possible that Moscow wouldn't be a suitable post for everyone. "Foreign Service personnel in Moscow work too hard; staying late and spending weekends in one's office could actually be a sign of depression." This must have elicited bemused, if not nervous, laughter. (Today the department employs seventeen psychiatrists and four psychologists, of whom fourteen are abroad, including one permanently posted to Moscow[325]; it hired its first psychiatrist in 1971.)

Later in March, Liz wrote home:

> The weather is unbelievably bad. Everyone feels they are living on another planet. The ground is covered black over the snow—solidly—from the terrible pollution in this city . . . . They have no sewer system . . . so the melting snow and the black soot sit in rivers everywhere with no place to go . . . . There hasn't been any sun since the girls arrived, [for their spring vacations] three weeks ago.

Moscow has storm sewers; they simply weren't adequate to cope with snowfalls averaging fifty a year and intermittent thaws. Not to be entirely downbeat, Liz assured my parents that the children were back in Moscow enjoying their spring vacations.

On the last Friday in April, a demented Russian with two sawed-off shotguns and a bomb made it past the militiamen into the consular section. The staff got out safely (probably through the windows in my old office), and the Russian ended up killing himself. In the absence of Ambassador Toon—who was at the dacha—I was summoned to the Foreign Ministry late Saturday afternoon to receive its "regrets."

How the visitor managed to get by the guards remained a mystery. The guards in Warsaw had once let a crazed Pole enter the consular section; he wounded my boss Al Harding—who happened to be sitting in my office—on the forehead with the brass eagle on the mast of the flag under which I took oaths.

In other respects, the weekend was restful. The sun came out briefly, the temperature reached sixty degrees, and Liz and I received word from the diplomatic services branch that we would be given access to an outdoor tennis court, not far from Lenin Stadium, for three hours a week beginning in June.

*   *   *

With the talk of a possible summit at which a new arms agreement would be signed, members of the Congress decided it was time to become better acquainted with the Soviet leaders.

Ambassador Toon put Liz and me in charge of two congressional delegations—CODELS they were called—the first to arrive in January, the second in April 1979. I was asked to negotiate the details of their programs, greet them at the airport, escort them to meetings, and accompany them whenever they traveled outside Moscow. Liz was asked to escort the wives when separate programs for them were arranged.

The Soviet leadership understood the Senate's importance for the ratification of any arms treaty, and it assigned responsibility for arranging and hosting the CODELs to officials in the Kremlin, those associated with the Supreme Soviet—the highest legislative body, and not to those in the Foreign Ministry. The chairman of the executive body of the Supreme Soviet, its presidium, was Leonid Ilych Brezhnev, the leader himself.

Being chauffeured into the Kremlin past the checkpoint at Borovitsky Gate and then negotiating in the Presidium building was a refreshing change from embassy routines. The Presidium building stands next to the building of the Council of Ministers where Russian leaders—from

Vladimir Lenin to Vladimir Putin—have kept their principal offices. During the Soviet era, most also had offices in the Party's Central Committee building on Old Square (*Staraya Ploshchad*), a fifteen-minute walk from the Kremlin; but they wouldn't meet there with any high-level foreigner who was *not* a Communist until, as will be seen, Gorbachev became leader.

Senate Minority Leader Howard Baker led the first delegation of twenty-nine persons. Six Republican senators, including John Tower of Texas and Jack Danforth of Missouri (a Princeton classmate) along with their wives, staff members, and other aides, flew into Leningrad in early January 1979.

The Toons and I took the overnight Red Arrow train to the prerevolutionary capital and met the special flight. After calls on the mayor and largely ceremonial events—including an evening at the Kirov Ballet—we all flew back to Moscow on the senators' plane. They then met with the leadership. Everything ran like clockwork, without the complications that events involving visiting Americans usually entailed. One evening, we were taken to a performance of *Swan Lake* at the Kremlin's Palace of Congresses, where Communist Party congresses were held. When Liz and I reached home, we discovered she had left her purse behind, and we ordered the driver to return to Borovitsky Gate. After making a few phone calls and examining the vehicle, the guards let us drive to the hall, but it was locked. Early the next day, we reached one of the Presidium officials with whom I was coordinating the visit and had the purse back within the hour. Had it been left at a theater outside the Kremlin, including the Bolshoi, it might not have been seen again.

After the CODEL's return to Washington, Baker let Toon know that Liz and I had done our part; but this didn't mean that the Senate's Republicans would be any more receptive to the arms agreement, the final details of which were being worked out in Washington and Geneva.

Not to be outdone, the House of Representatives then sent a delegation of fifty-two persons headed by the Majority Whip John Brademas of Indiana and the Minority Whip Bob Michel of Illinois. Charles Vanik, who had helped spike Kissinger's trade bill, was one of its members. Ornate rooms in the Grand Kremlin Palace were the site of most meetings, but for a session with the chairman of the Council of Ministers Alexei Kosygin, the head of government, we trooped over to the Council of Ministers building. As Soviet aides led the congressmen into Kosygin's office, Toon intercepted me and said it would be best if only one from the embassy attended; and he would be the one.

I found myself sitting outside Kosygin's and Brezhnev's offices drinking tea with Soviet security types more than once during 1979. More out of boredom initially than design, I began taking notes about the location and layout of the leaders' offices.

After Moscow, the Brademas delegation went to Tbilisi, the capital of the Georgian republic. There it met Eduard Shevardnadze, the leader of the Georgian Party who later would be Gorbachev's foreign minister. The Georgians, with a tradition of extravagant entertainment more ancient than even that of the Russians, arranged an extraordinary welcome. One highlight was an excursion into the mountains of eastern Georgia for a feast that lasted four hours. To reach the event, we were driven for almost two hours on harrowing rain-slicked roads in fifty ZIL limousines (ZIL denoting *Zavod imeni Lenina,* the "factory in the name of Lenin" from which they came). Ours bore number 49, suggesting where diplomats rank protocol-wise when congressmen, spouses, and hangers-on converge on embassies. (Years later, I read the report of the *Times* Beijing bureau chief that Brzezinski "ensured that Holbrooke's car was placed at the end of every motorcade" during his China visit in 1978. Holbrooke was Vance's senior assistant for Asian affairs and no minor diplomat, but Brzezinski was then waging his "poisonous competition" with Vance[326]).

When Senator Robert Byrd of West Virginia, the Democratic majority leader, arrived in July 1979, Combs was put in charge. By this time, the SALT II agreement had been formally signed, and the question of when it would be submitted for ratification was on the agenda. Byrd's program included a walk through Lenin's Mausoleum on Red Square that my two delegations had pointedly avoided. It was bruited about that Byrd was the first senator to pay such homage to Lenin.

A delegation of six senators, led by Joe Biden of Delaware, completed the upper chamber's visits in 1979. Had I not embarked on a grueling trip through the Caucasian region, I would have been involved. The embassy called on Liz while I was traveling, and Biden later wrote Garrison, the chargé d'affaires in Toon's absence, that "although Liz is not an FSO, perhaps she should be." [327]

The year ended with the visit of six governors and their wives. Liz and I were again put in charge, and accompanied them to Leningrad and Minsk, the capital of the Belorussian republic. In the former city, we were taken to a model old people's home where I interpreted for Governor Dick Thornburgh. He queried an elderly woman, obviously from the old intelligentsia, about whether "workers" were among the home's other residents. "God forbid!" ("*Nye dai Bog!*") she replied.

After working sessions in various Moscow ministries, we were taken to the Council of Ministers building to see Lenin's apartment and the office where he and Stalin met their top officials. The apartment had been opened to foreign heads of state in 1955 (Ho Chih Minh was among the first to see it), but few Americans had been inside.

One of the governors, Babbitt of Arizona, sought the Democratic Party nomination for president in 1980. Among others contending for the nomination was Gebhardt of Missouri, who had traveled with Congressman Brademas. It seemed that every American entertaining a presidential ambition wanted to be photographed inside the Kremlin in 1979.

The *apparatchiki* with whom I negotiated the agendas and itineraries were straightforward and good-humored. Serious disagreements rarely arose, unlike at most Foreign Ministry meetings. However, a wall as formidable as the Kremlin's would rise if I strayed too far from the agenda. An exception was Dmitri Marushenko, the official in the presidium's department of international relations who helped Liz recover her purse. Marushenko traveled with us outside Moscow several times and was not afraid to exchange talk about work or family. He and his wife had two teenage daughters; later, Liz and I found decorative pocket mirrors for them in Helsinki.

Marushenko's career had begun in Minsk in the Belorussian republic. His most telling characteristic was a steel-hard handshake that made one wince, but he was agreeable as a traveling companion. When I think of him, de Gaulle's comment about a Soviet ambassador in Paris comes to mind: "While Soviet rule encased the personality of its servants in an iron mask without a chink, it was unable to prevent there being still a man underneath."[328]

Marushenko was dead from natural causes when I returned to Moscow in 1985. He couldn't have been more than fifty in 1979; but life expectancies in the USSR were far short of ours (male life expectancy in Russia is less than fifty-nine today, probably about what it was back then), and I got used to the sudden disappearances of contacts.

It was around the time of Senator Baker's meeting with Brezhnev that *Time* journalist Strobe Talbott reacted testily when I asked at a dinner party hosted by the magazine's local representative Bruce Nelan, "In which room in the Kremlin did you meet with Brezhnev?" Talbott had just come from interviewing the Soviet leader with *Time*'s managing editor, Henry Grunwald.

"Why do you want to know? Are you with the CIA?"

No, I wasn't with the CIA, but I was becoming more curious about the Kremlin and the interactions among those leaders privileged to have their offices there.

At the time, Western Sovietologists were pursuing their craft without much sense of place. Anticipating that I'd be spending more time in the

Kremlin, I decided that if I found the opportunity, I'd write an article and try to fill in the blanks.

*   *   *

It was no secret that the health of the seventy-year-old Brezhnev was failing. Under Combs's leadership, Pol/Int had done extensive reporting about his condition.

Toon must have let Washington know about the Kremlin meeting during which Brezhnev toyed with a red felt pen while everyone else focused on important bilateral issues. As Toon related the story, the Party leader was intent upon reddening each of his fingertips. When he finished, he lifted his hand, splayed his fingers, and with a silly grin showed his handiwork off to the astonished Americans.

In advance of the June 1979 summit, Dobrynin told the White House that Brezhnev's health would be a factor. He recommended that the sessions be brief and focus on disarmament issues. However, Brzezinski believed that Carter should "engage Brezhnev in a discussion of the state of the relationship as a whole . . . ," including the Soviet Union's military buildup and its "activities, directly or by proxy, in the Indian Ocean area." In his view, the summit would be "worthless unless we could make the Soviets understand how sensitive these matters were to the American public." Brzezinski "hinted to the President that it would be useful for him to use me [Brzezinski] in that context."[329]

Vance went to Vienna with more realistic expectations. "Too much had happened since January 20, 1977 [inauguration day], for any of us to expect much at Vienna aside from the practical business at hand: to sign the SALT II Treaty and associated agreements."[330] In his memoir, Vance recalls his uncertainty about Brezhnev's mental capacity.

Except for SALT II and the related understandings, the summit proved unproductive. In Brzezinski's words, "the exchanges on global-strategic problems, both in the plenary sessions and at the informal dinners, were perfunctory." Worse, there was no agreement on any follow-up consultations. "I doubt that any dent was made in Soviet thinking."[331]

Brzezinski describes the Brezhnev he saw in Vienna as a "genuinely pitiful figure."[332] Brezhnev's interpreter, Viktor Sukhodrev, wrote later that the leader could barely understand what Carter was saying. Sukhodrev had prepared ready-made answers in advance—several on each sheet of paper—and would mark the correct one and cross out the others before handing it to him. The befuddled Brezhnev once read the correct answer and then asked aloud for everyone to hear, "I shouldn't read on, should I?"[333] According to Dobrynin, despite his interpreter's *nyet*, he read on.[334]

It is difficult to understand why the president went to Vienna thinking he could engage Brezhnev in a real discussion; but by the time of the meeting, Vance and Brzezinski were wide apart, and Brzezinski's influence was paramount.

Shortly after the summit, in September 1979, Vance cautioned Carter that a "tilt" toward China rather than a balance between China and the Soviet Union was emerging in U.S. policy, and it threatened to increase tension with the Soviets to the detriment of American interests. Carter rejected Vance's concern and approved a visit by Secretary of Defense Brown to Beijing (which, for other reasons, never occurred). Vance writes in his memoir that in regard to military cooperation, "it became apparent that I was alone in my desire to maintain our longstanding policy of evenhandedness between the USSR and the PRC."[335]

Although SALT II was never formally ratified, both governments observed its ceilings, and it contributed to stabilizing the arms race until Gorbachev and Reagan's historic breakthroughs.

*   *   *

Because many families had children at the Anglo-American School and few were at the embassy for more than three years, the staff underwent its typically heavy turnover during the summer 1979.

Ambassador Toon was scheduled to retire but wanted to be on hand for the groundbreaking of the decade-old new embassy project in September, and therefore delayed his and Mrs. Toon's final departure until October. In July, both left for the United States for a few weeks' leave. An American television network suggested that the ambassador appear to discuss the Vienna summit; but Vance, perhaps recalling Toon's telegram urging postponement of a meeting with Gromyko the year before, withheld approval.

As Combs's successor, I was now heading the team responsible for discerning, at least in theory, in which directions Brezhnev and his colleagues—those in the Central Committee's Politburo and Secretariat—were taking the country. Were they shifting resources away from their ongoing build-up of the Soviet military to meet the growing needs of their people, including the many millions who weren't Russian or weren't Christian? What priorities were the central planning organs and ministries pushing?

Every leader publicly conformed to the Party line as enunciated at the twice or thrice-yearly meetings of the full Central Committee that had "elected" them, and at the weekly Politburo or Secretariat meetings. Lenin had proscribed deviations from the Party line in 1921, and everyone holding top positions in the Party and the government maintained at least a façade of unity. Toward the end of Khrushchev's rule, the façade had broken down; but since his ouster in 1964, it had remained largely intact. This didn't mean, however, that individual politicians based in Moscow or in the republic capitals didn't have their own priorities, reflecting the interests of their varied constituencies and personal experiences. One of Pol/Int's tasks was to identify these priorities, assess their significance in the larger scheme of things, and discern the implications, if any, for American interests.

With Brezhnev in decline, who would succeed him and what might this mean for the United States? Because of the age and health of most of his colleagues, change could come quickly and have far-reaching consequences.

We kept a close eye on Brezhnev; but unlike Khrushchev, he rarely appeared at functions where Western diplomats and journalists were present. If the ambassador gave us his invitation to attend a Supreme Soviet session where the leaders did appear, we'd seize the opportunity. From the diplomatic box in the Grand Kremlin Palace, one could observe the leaders moving papers among themselves, sometimes in intriguing sequences, as "legislators" from the provinces and other officials intoned their preapproved speeches. Even with a discreet use of opera glasses, however, it was difficult to draw conclusions as to how the leaders lined up and interacted, or who was healthy and who was not.

In the final analysis, television afforded the best view. Whenever Brezhnev or another leader was scheduled to appear, we'd gather in front of my office's television—a Soviet-made model with perhaps a thirty-inch screen, the largest on the market—and track the speaker's every word and gesture. Often the speeches would last more than an hour. Sitting cross-legged or sprawled amid piles of newspapers and émigré publications, on a rug mottled by years of coffee stains, we'd say little until the telecast ended, then pool our reactions and divide up the work. Although the telegraphic agency TASS provided a near-contemporaneous English-language version and the next morning's newspapers carried the full Russian text (occasionally with cryptic emendations), Washington expected an immediate synopsis of the salient points and the embassy's impressions.

It was disconcerting to watch Brezhnev in the late 1970s. He suffered from heart ailments and high-blood pressure. Because his lips were frequently dry from all the medications he was taking, he'd smack them repeatedly as he spoke. His health seemed so precarious that at one point the CIA conducted a study of photographs to determine whether he used a "double" to spare him appearances far from Moscow; by an analysis of the shape of his ears, the analysts decided no double was involved.

My deputy in Pol/Int was John Parker, an accomplished Sovietologist with a PhD from Yale who had joined the department in 1974. John had visited the USSR as a student in 1965 and had returned several times since to accompany official exchanges and exhibits.

As the unit's chief Kremlinologist, John collected and analyzed every snippet of information that came our way. After he ended his assignment, he returned to Washington and wrote a detailed, comprehensive study, *Kremlin in Transition: From Brezhnev to Chernenko 1978 to 1985*, that incorporated much of the work he did while reporting to Combs and me.[336]

Kosygin, the chairman of the Council of Ministers, had suffered a stroke in 1976, revealed first to the West by Viktor Louis. Kosygin's city apartment was located in a small building overlooking the Moscow River, a ten-minute walk from our apartment. On weekends, Liz or Rob and I often walked by it to sightsee at the river. I once sighted Kosygin, in what was obviously a medically prescribed therapy, making his way slowly up the mile-long incline toward Moscow University as his limousine and a security vehicle slowly trailed behind.

The more frequently we roamed the streets, the more likely we found the telltale bits and pieces of information that substantiated our—and Washington's—hypotheses.

Fedor Kulakov, a Politburo member touted as one of Brezhnev's most likely successors, had died suddenly at the age of sixty on July 17, 1978, two weeks after Liz and I arrived. By tradition, Brezhnev should have attended the funeral on Red Square but instead stayed away. Was he too enfeebled to travel back to Moscow from the Crimea where he was vacationing, or was something else involved?

John began to pick up rumors that Kulakov had actually committed suicide. As a member of the Central Committee's Secretariat with responsibility for agriculture, had he chosen this way out after becoming enmeshed in corruption, in what John would later call "the great caviar scandal"?

Kulakov probably died of natural causes, but his sudden demise had important consequences for the Soviet Union and, indeed, the world; it opened the way for Gorbachev to leave his post as the Party leader of a regional subdivision (*kray*) in the northern Caucasus and to assume Kulakov's duties in the capital.

Unlike Brezhnev, Gorbachev attended Kulakov's funeral and spoke a few words. It was the first time, he said, he had stood atop the mausoleum. In his memoir, he acknowledged that the top leadership's absence struck him as strange; it also made him aware—"for the first time"—of how remote the leaders were from each other. Gorbachev found it odd that he had to submit his brief eulogy to the Central Committee staff for advance approval.[337]

The main speaker at Kulakov's funeral was Andrei Kirilenko, who—some Kremlin watchers had decided—was the leading candidate to succeed Brezhnev. But John discovered anomalies in the media suggesting that Kirilenko was losing favor, and that Andropov and Chernenko, the latter a longtime personal aide to Brezhnev, were on the rise. As I was about to take over from Combs, John's supposition gained credence when a Moscow newspaper cropped Kirilenko from its photograph of the leaders standing atop the mausoleum on May Day.

We didn't always agree with the Kremlinologists. Sometimes their conclusions jumped too far ahead of the evidence at hand. In September 1979, we received an analysis from Washington that drew conclusions about the ranking of the leaders from language that appeared in an unsigned lead article in the Party's main ideological journal "Communist" (*Kommunist*). The language immediately struck me as too obscure to support any judgment about "who was up and who was down" in the Party hierarchy.

Gaining access to Communist ideologists for help in deciphering their articles was near impossible. Usually the best we could do was to talk with an East European diplomat or journalist, someone steeped in Marxist-Leninist jargon who might have gleaned an insight from a meeting at the Central Committee, or with a Soviet correspondent at one of the Party's newspapers. Or perhaps with someone like Ed Stevens whose connections went back years.

I decided to go to the horse's mouth, Richard Kosolapov, the chief editor of *Kommunist.* Kosolapov had long been touted as a possible successor to the aging Mikhail Suslov, the Politburo and Secretariat member who, from Stalin's final years, had fought to keep ideology pure.

I had exchanged a few words with Kosolapov when he, along with Arbatov of the USA Institute and several Foreign Ministry officials, traveled with the Brademas CODEL. Although he had mostly kept to himself, he had sounded reasonable in one toast he offered for improved U.S.-Soviet relations. Having nothing to lose, I telephoned and asked whether he'd see me. To my surprise, he agreed and invited me to his office in downtown Moscow, in what once had been a handsome private home. Perhaps he wasn't the ideological ogre others had made him out to be.

Kosolapov offered tea, and we were soon discussing the article. The editor's Russian was no problem (by this time I knew most of the ponderous language); but like many self-important officials, he dropped his voice to a near whisper when making crucial points. It turned out that the explanation he gave for the article ran counter to the gloss that the Washington analyst had given it; and as it seemed much more plausible as he explained it and not self-servingly so, I reported it in full.

After the Soviet invasion of Afghanistan, I visited Kosolapov again. He was still friendly, but U.S.-Soviet relations had greatly worsened. He defended the invasion by citing incursions by armed Afghan groups into Tadzhikistan, the neighboring Soviet republic. During a final meeting, as my second assignment was ending, he inscribed and gave me a collection of articles he and others had published in *Kommunist*; and I gave him a collection of materials bearing on U.S.-Russian relations between 1765 and 1815[338], when they hadn't been so bad.

My successors in Pol/Int paid visits to Kosolapov up to the middle of 1986 when he was ousted for resisting Gorbachev's reforms. In August that year, *Pravda* front-paged a Central Committee resolution exhorting his journal to improve its performance, including taking into account Lenin's "last years" when his New Economic Policy sanctioned private entrepreneurial activity. Kosolapov wasn't criticized by name, but he was already thoroughly compromised, though we didn't know it at the time. At the Central Committee meeting in 1985 that made Gorbachev the Party leader, he had tried instead to rally support for the hard-line head of Moscow's Party organization, Viktor Grishin.

Kosolapov has since become the ideologist for the Russian Communist Party, which emerged from the wreckage of the all-union Communist Party. In 1998, he completed the final volume of the collected *Works of J. Stalin*, a project on which he had been quietly working since its suspension after the dictator's death. Undoubtedly, the elderly ideologist now waits for another turn of the dialectic, or a new Stalin, to restore him and his kind to power.[339]

*   *   *

Russia was the dominant republic of the fifteen comprising the Soviet Union. During my years in Moscow, the Russians controlled every important lever of power. In a much-publicized toast at a 1945 dinner celebrating victory over Germany, Stalin, of Caucasian origin, had acclaimed the Russians as "the most remarkable of all the nations of the Soviet Union."[340] This sentiment lay at the heart of the system up to the day of its demise.

During my time, it was no secret that demographic trends were shifting to the advantage of the non-Russian peoples, including the Muslims of the Caucuses and Central Asia.

We subscribed to the main newspapers in each of the non-Russian republics and paid visits to their capitals and outlying areas to the extent the Foreign Ministry, the KGB, and the embassy's travel budget allowed. We'd prepare full reports recounting our experiences, including what we learned from interviews and conversations we managed to arrange at offices and restaurants, churches, mosques, or synagogues, or on sidewalks and in parks. Thanks to these reports, the State Department and other agencies in Washington had a wealth of information about the non-Russian republics when they became sovereign and independent in 1991.

I initially put myself in charge of Tadzhikistan, Uzbekistan, and Kirgizia—three of the Muslim republics in Central Asia; and my three colleagues assumed responsibility for reporting on the other eleven. We all covered the Russian republic.

While heading Pol/Ext, I had visited Tadzhikistan and Uzbekistan with Ed McGaffigan, a young FSO from the science section. With degrees in physics from Harvard and Caltech, Ed was interested in the civil defense arrangements the regime was making far from the capital (we didn't find much, undercutting those in Washington who believed the Kremlin might be planning "a first strike"); and I wanted to learn more about the ethnic and religious relationships between the native populations and the Slavs.

We tramped for five days through the two republics' capitals and several towns. Menachem Begin, the Israeli prime minister, had briefly lived in one of them—Dzhizak—after being exiled following his release from a Soviet prison during World War II; the NKVD had arrested him for Zionist activities after Moscow's seizure of Vilnius in 1940. In a memoir, Begin had described his housing as "a wretched mud hut."[341]

Four decades later, the hotels weren't much better, and we returned home hungry and dirty. Liz said she could smell me before I came through the door.

In August 1979, two months after joining Pol/Int, I set out to explore Muslim towns in Russia's southern Caucuses, a mountainous region between the Black and Caspian seas, north of the two predominantly Christian republics—Armenia and Georgia—which I had already visited. Jim Mandel, who had a doctorate in history from Yale and was the husband of Judi in Pol/Int, agreed to accompany me. Jim was not in the Foreign Service but was working with the Foreign Buildings engineers, preparing to build the new embassy.

Chechnya was one area I badly wanted to see. The embassy's travel reports went back years, but only one covered the so-called Chechen-Ingush Autonomous Republic, and it had been drafted two decades before by an officer (perhaps TDY from Washington) who was only interested in its oil and gas reserves.

The embassy subscribed to newspapers through an arrangement with an official Soviet agency but could never secure anything published in Chechnya or Dagestan, the other "autonomous" region we planned to visit. The attitude in Moscow seemed to be, the less the Americans know about the Russian republic's Muslim areas, the better.

Moscow's reluctance to have us travel to Chechnya was understandable. The native people had been fighting for their independence since the tsarist empire first encroached on their territory at the end of the eighteenth century. That war lasted almost fifty years to the middle of the nineteenth century; thereafter, uprisings against the Russians occurred in 1877 and 1918-1920. *The Cossacks*, one of Tolstoy's greatest works, contains a graphic description of the warfare, including the execution of a wounded Chechen prisoner by a Russian Cossack.

In 1942, with the German army driving northward into the Caucasus, the NKVD had rounded up a half million Chechens in twenty-four hours and deported them in boxcars to Kazakhstan. Thousands had died along the way. After the war, many of the survivors had returned to their villages, but others could still be found in Central Asia and Siberia, eking out a bare existence peddling fruit and vegetables in local markets.

I asked the embassy's travel officer to submit a diplomatic note to the ministry outlining the trip we proposed: by air to Makhachkala, the capital of Dagestan; by rail from Makhachkala to Grozny, the capital of Chechnya; by rail from Grozny to Mineralniye Vodi; and finally by air back to Moscow. The stopover in Mineralniye Vodi would permit me to visit Pyatigorsk, the resort area nearby where Soviet leaders (notably Andropov) vacationed (perhaps I'd pick up some leadership rumors), and where Tanya, the young woman whom Liz and I had met in Ulyanovsk, claimed to spend her summers.

I was skeptical that the KGB would permit the trip, but the note elicited no reaction, which was tantamount to approval. The summit's good atmospherics had carried over into September, or Dzerzhinskaya Square was simply undermanned because of August vacations. Or did the KGB expect a payoff from Tanya?

We were on our own with regard to appointments, the usual state of affairs; the ministry refused to help, and local officials to whom Oleg sent telexes didn't reply.

On the flight down, Jim and I met a young Dagestani woman who, with the warmth for which the Caucasian peoples are known, insisted we visit her and her parents. She gave us the address of an apartment on Makhachkala's outskirts, and we promised to come by.

After settling in our hotel a few blocks from the Caspian Sea, Jim and I set out for the address. We quickly discovered that the KGB was tracking our every step. We changed streetcars twice, but couldn't elude them. About a block from the entrance to the apartment house, I decided not to complicate the family's life, and we retreated back to the hotel. In retrospect, I should have pushed ahead; a promise is a promise, and the KGB wouldn't punish a family for a single meeting. This was Brezhnev's, and not Stalin's Russia.

On our second day, we arranged to see an administrator at the Dagestan Academy of Sciences. No sooner had we entered his office than he told us he'd have nothing to do with us. He had just heard, he said, that New York authorities had "kidnapped" a Russian dancer performing there with the Bolshoi Ballet. Now "we" were trying to get our hands on the dancer's wife, one Vlasova. She was on an Aeroflot plane that he claimed we wouldn't let depart Kennedy Airport.

"I will not talk to you while you are kidnapping our dancers," he yelled as he put an arm on my shoulder and pushed me out his door.

After we returned to the embassy, we learned that Alexander Godunov, a Bolshoi dancer, had defected in New York and that State Department and Immigration Service officials had insisted on interviewing his wife before permitting her to leave. Someone, probably from the Makhachkala KGB, had passed the Soviet version of the incident to the academy official just before we reached his office. The interview in New York, in fact, established that Vlasova was returning of her own free will; Godunov later divorced his wife and remained in the United States, where he danced until he died in 1995.

Jim and I took a taxi to Buynaksk, a town nearby that was also on our itinerary. The townspeople were all native Dagestanis; Stalin had promised them "autonomy" during a visit in 1920. The only Slavs we saw were KGB, conspicuous by their Western dress.

Two teenagers gave us a walking tour of the main street before dropping us off in front of a gated mosque. A mullah stuck his head out and invited us in.

We were greeted warmly; the first Americans to ever visit his mosque, he said. We removed our shoes, and he gave us a full tour, including of a minaret of concrete blocks that had just been completed. The mullah was so proud of the addition that he insisted we join him in climbing to the top to a small balcony from which he could call believers to prayer.

After the tour, he invited us to hunker down on an antique rug, spread over an earthen floor, for lunch. His wife emerged from an adjoining room with a pilaf dish. The mullah related stories about his and his people's devotion to Islam. If the mosque experienced Russian harassment, he never mentioned it. For dessert we were served slices of watermelon on which a cloud of flies also eagerly gorged.

We spent more than an hour with the mullah. After we bid farewell and emerged from the mosque to find a taxi, several KGB types fell in behind us. They remained on our heels, on foot and in vehicles, until we returned to Makhachkala and boarded the train for Chechnya.

The surveillance grew more aggressive when we reached Grozny. Jim and I boarded a streetcar on our first evening to travel to the outskirts where a small Baptist church, about which I had read in an émigré publication, was located. A motorcycle and sidecar, with its lights extinguished, followed us until the road paralleling the track ended. Then another streetcar, its passengers ousted, took up pursuit, traveling the same track through open fields and thinly populated neighborhoods.

When we reached the vicinity of the church, we disembarked and walked on dirt roads and paths before locating the address. Both ends of the street on which the house stood suddenly filled with agents. We spoke with the Baptist minister at the threshold of his house but broke off after a minute or two, not wanting to complicate his situation more than we already had.

On our second day, a young Chechen woman, Zarya, waited on us as we lunched in a restaurant on the main street. Ascertaining that we were Americans—the first she had met—she insisted on showing us the city as soon as her workday ended. We warned her that we were being closely observed, but she dismissed our concern.

With her dark hair covered by a green kerchief, Zarya met us outside our hotel at 7:00 PM. For three hours she led us around Grozny, politely answering questions and relating her people's history.

Part of the time we sat on a bench in the city's darkened park. Every ten minutes or so, a stocky Russian would approach, stop short of the bench, take a menacing look (and sometimes a photograph), and then back off before repeating his routine.

Zarya was unmarried and had five brothers. Discussing Chechen mores, she said her "brothers would kill anyone who touches me," and left no doubt this included the Russians.

Walking us back to the hotel, Zarya insisted upon seeing us off the next day. As the KGB continued to buzz about, we urged her to stay away. But she showed up anyway as we were boarding the train, handing us a bouquet of flowers. It wouldn't have been right, she told us, not to say good-bye.

We watched through the train window as she walked through a throng of passengers to a dusty lot where taxis were waiting. Just as she reached the lot, she was accosted by a tall Russian. She pointed to herself as if surprised. She turned and followed the man to a vehicle, entered the backseat, and through a lowered window waved vigorously in our direction as she was driven away.

As we proceeded north toward Mineralniye Vodi, we scanned the newspapers we had picked up at Grozny's kiosks. They were shot through with reports of conflicts between Chechens and Russians; it was clear why the embassy never could arrange a subscription. And it was clear why Zarya had been detained; the Russians didn't want Chechens meeting with Americans.

I had brought Tanya's telephone number along with me. After checking into the Intourist hotel in nearby Pyatigorsk, I made the call. Tanya encouraged me to come by; she said her mother in whose apartment she was staying was out.

The apartment was on the third floor of a new building. When Tanya opened the door, she was dressed in a bra and panties and was startled to see Jim; hadn't I mentioned my traveling companion?

With embarrassment that seemed feigned, she invited us to sit in the living room while she went to her room. We waited and waited. After ten minutes, thinking I might have misunderstood, I quietly crept to the back of the apartment. The first room I reached was the kitchen. Tanya, already dressed, was standing on a small balcony off it, signaling to a man standing in the yard below.

Pyatigorsk, meaning "five mountains," is a town of spas nestled among five hills. Russians seeking health cures have gone to it for years. Tanya knew the town; perhaps the apartment really belonged to her mother. It was a sunny day, and she guided Jim and me along a pedestrian path on a hill offering splendid views. She wore a dress that turned diaphanous whenever the sun landed, and *babushka*s hissed at her whenever they passed.

Periodically we'd pause at a spring (they are placed every several hundred yards) to try the sulphur water for which the area is known. The water is said to cure digestive problems. William Allen White, the newspaperman, had once described the "quantities of terrible sulphur water" he imbibed to his regret while honeymooning in Las Vegas[342]; I had no digestive problems when I arrived in Pyatigorsk, but they were with me when I left.

We brought a trove of local newspapers as well as many anecdotes back to the embassy. I never heard from Tanya again, but Jim and I did hear from the KGB. Four weeks after we returned, *Literaturnaya gazeta* carried an exposé of our trip.[343]

The editor of *LitGaz*, as we called it, was Alexander Chakovski, a frequent guest at diplomatic functions. In the late 1950s, the writer Alfred Kazin, on an exchange visit to the Soviet Union, had described him as a "watchdog of literary orthodoxy."[344] By the late 1970s, he had become something worse, an avid collaborator with the KGB.

Oleg Kalugin, the KGB's former head of counterintelligence, characterized *LitGaz* as the "prime conduit in the Soviet press for propaganda and disinformation." "Whenever we [the KGB] called the editor Alexander Chakovsky, and asked him to print an article, he complied." Kalugin added that the KGB also employed *LitGaz* for its "nonexistent authors" too.[345]

When the weekly made its Friday appearance in the newspaper bin next to the switchboard downstairs, we'd rush for a copy to see who would be the latest target. This time it was Jim, although I received a glancing blow. The author was one "Valentynov," probably with the KGB.

Under the headline "Mister Mandel in Various Faces," Jim was accused of having introduced himself to the Buynaksk mullah as "a Muslim from America." He and I allegedly told our host that we knew that the Soviet authorities were repressing Muslims but wanted to find out for ourselves, hence the trip. The article claimed we had refused to remove our shoes while tramping around the mosque, "scandalizing" Islam.

Obviously, the KGB was incensed that we had been warmly welcomed and that its agents had failed to intimidate the mullah and the Chechens.

The article ended with a reminder to Jim that he was staying in the USSR as "the spouse of an American diplomat" and ought to observe Soviet "etiquette."

At the time, Jim's wife, Judi, was seeing a number of dissidents and refuseniks in connection with her work with me in Pol/Int. A few weeks earlier, Judi and I had met with Andrei Sakharov. The human rights activist had come to the embassy to expedite an American visa for an imprisoned dissident's son, but had asked whether we could also arrange to forward his Order of Lenin and a few personal papers to his wife's daughter in Boston. He was concerned about the regime's mounting crackdown.

Had Ambassador Beam been in charge, we probably would have had to say no, but the embassy was now helping dissidents however it could.

Sakharov's sense that the KGB was "closing in" proved prescient; six months later, in January 1980, he was arrested and exiled to Gorky (Nizhni Novgorod today), a city closed to foreigners. At the same time, the Presidium of the Supreme Soviet stripped him of his Order of Lenin "for systematic acts that defile him" in the eyes of the Soviet people.[346] By that time, the medal was across the ocean.

Soon after the Caucasus trip, Judi introduced Liz and me to Lev and Raisa Kopelev. Lev had been imprisoned with Solzhenitsyn in 1945, and this had led to a close friendship; Solzhenitsyn used him as the model for Rubin in his novel *The First Circle*. Kopelev remained a believer in the system until 1968 when he was expelled from the Party for protesting the invasion of Czechoslovakia. Shortly after Judi introduced us, Lev and his wife were deprived of their Soviet citizenship and forced to live abroad.

Through *LitGaz*'s article, the KGB was warning Judi and Jim that they were being closely monitored. Probably because I was dealing with senior officials at the Kremlin and the Foreign Ministry (and wasn't Jewish), the KGB pulled the punch it threw at me, casting me only as Jim's "strange traveling companion."

A month later, I wrote a former teacher of mine at the Garmisch institute—Dr. Kunta (originally, Abdulrakhman Avtokhanov)—about the trip. Kunta, a Chechen, had been arrested in 1937 while serving as a professor in Moscow but had managed to flee during the war. I told him that our visit to his native land had "brought home to me that potentially the most troublesome problem for Moscow in coming decades will be 'managing' its nationalities." I was mistaken with regard to "coming decades"; little more than one decade would pass before the most numerous and well-organized of the nationalities threw off the Russian yoke.

Alas, the Chechens weren't among them and are still resisting Russian control. The post-Communist regime of Vladimir Putin continues to assault their land. Tens of thousands have died, some say, as many as 10 percent of Chechnya's total population.[347] If still alive, Zarya and her brothers are paying a terrible price.

And what about neighboring Dagestan? Muslim militants swept into Buynaksk in 1999 and blew up a building that was housing Russian troops.[348] The Russians undoubtedly retaliated with full fury. It's hard to imagine that the mosque, the minaret, and the mullah survive today.

*   *   *

Despite the summit meeting, tensions in U.S.-Soviet relations were rising as 1979 was winding down. The repressive organs were tightening their screws as Party and government officials were becoming more agitated about Afghanistan, Poland, and the prospect of increased dissident activity and anti-Russian nationalism.

Muslim insurgents in Afghanistan were stepping up their actions against Kabul's pro-Soviet regime, which had come to power in a bloody coup in April 1978. As resistance grew, the regime began appealing to Moscow for military assistance. The Kremlin turned a deaf ear to its approach in March 1979, several weeks after Spike was killed; but the Politburo agreed in June to send a token contingent—fewer than a thousand soldiers—to bolster security at Kabul's main airfield and at the Soviet embassy.[349]

In September 1979, Nur Mohammad Taraki, the leader of the regime, was overthrown by Hafizullah Amin, a one-time exchange student at Columbia University about whom some Soviet *apparatchiki* entertained doubts, believing he might be involved with the CIA. In November 1979, Amin demanded the ouster of the Soviet ambassador. The Kremlin complied and appointed Fikryat Tabeyev, Muslim Tatar by origin and the Communist Party leader in the Tatar autonomous republic, to be the ambassador's successor.

Ten months later, I would find myself negotiating the fate of a Soviet soldier with Tabeyev.

In September 1979, shortly after my trip through the Caucasus, Liz and I received a surprise visit from Bogdan Grzelonski, our friend from Warsaw. Bogdan and his wife Urszula, whom we hadn't met before, were in Moscow conducting research. One year earlier, Bogdan had stayed with us in Maryland while studying Washington's policy toward Poland between the two world wars under a grant from the Kosciuszko Foundation. Before leaving Washington, Bogdan had given Liz a copy of Olga Ivinskaya's *A Captive of Time,* a book that had reawakened my interest in Pasternak.

Pope John Paul II had visited Poland a few months earlier, in June 1979, and his presence had contributed to a further weakening of the Polish regime. We sensed from what Bogdan told us that his country might be on the threshold of important change.

A week or two later, Igor came to the apartment for a drink. I met him outside and shepherded him past the guard. The persecution of dissidents was increasing, and rumors about the arrest of Sakharov were already circulating. Igor was as pessimistic about prospects for the future as Bogdan had been optimistic. It appeared that a grim winter awaited us, that the pendulum in U.S.-Soviet relations was again about to swing.

In early October we were busy saying good-bye to Ambassador and Mrs. Toon. On October 7, a Sunday evening, fifteen couples assembled in Uncle Sam's to honor them at a dinner dance. A few wore costumes. Tom Buchanan, traveling with his wife Nancy from Leningrad where he was consul general, came dressed as a Georgian, sporting a white jacket dripping with odds and ends of fake medals. Helen Semler, wife of the economic counselor, wore a *kokoshnik,* a decorative headpiece, along with a *sarafan,* a colorful frock and blouse such as Russian and Ukrainian women wear to celebrate harvests.

Liz and I had been wondering how to mark the occasion when we spotted a caravan of trucks on Leninsky Prospect hauling cabbage. Every September, outlying *kolkhozes* would send trucks loaded with cabbages and potatoes to the city's peasant markets. Was there anything more emblematic of life here than these vegetables, so indispensable to tiding the populace through Moscow's interminable winter?

Liz and I ordered a can of spray paint through an embassy couple visiting Helsinki and gilded a huge cabbage that we presented the Toons along with a poem we recited.

The party lasted until 2:30 AM. Liz commented in a letter home that "it was just like the old days when we used to do such things often in the Foreign Service." That *esprit* "is, for some reason, no more."

We admired the Toons for their professionalism and tenacious good humor, especially at a time when Soviet officials were mostly unaccommodating and ill-humored.

The ambassador had done his best to keep the embassy in the thick of U.S.-Soviet affairs, pressing officials in Washington to use it no less than the Soviet embassy to conduct business. But Dobrynin remained a frequent guest at the White House while Toon was rarely invited to the Kremlin. If invited, it was to present his credentials, to accompany high-level visitors from the United States, or to receive replies to Washington's messages.

Before our return to Moscow for a second assignment, Toon had suggested to the Foreign Ministry, under instructions from the department, that it might be useful for Secretary of Defense Brown to meet with his counterpart Dmitri Ustinov. Toon evidently stretched the instruction to include the suggestion that he also be permitted to meet the defense minister. Recounting Toon's approach, Ambassador Garthoff notes that Toon was "irked by the long-standard Soviet practice of limiting access by the American ambassador to the foreign minister and trade ministers."[350]

Perhaps because of Toon's linkage, nothing came of the department's proposal, but Toon wasn't shy about trying to level a playing field that Washington persisted in tilting. Vance never took up Toon's cause, and Brzezinski and he would end up using the back channel no less than Kissinger. As a result, Toon achieved no greater access to the Soviet leaders than Stoessel or Beam.

*   *   *

The Toons flew off to retirement on October 16, 1979; and Ambassador Thomas J. Watson Jr., who had been waiting impatiently for Toon's departure, arrived the next day. Watson had asked the staff not to turn out to greet him at Sheremetyevo's VIP lounge, as had been the tradition when new ambassadors arrived. A day later, Watson's wife, Olive, a one-time model (she had appeared on the covers of *Vogue* and other fashion magazines), arrived on a separate flight along with her personal secretary and the ambassador's new Foreign Service secretary.

The two cabinet secretaries, Vance and Brown, knew Watson from their service together on IBM's board of directors when Watson was the CEO. They had suggested to President Carter in 1977 that he appoint Watson to chair the General Advisory Committee on Arms Control and Disarmament (GAC), a prestigious group whose purpose was to provide outside advice on nuclear strategy. Vance and Brown thought Carter could look over Watson this way as a potential successor to Toon.

Watson recalled that he first met Toon while chairing the Advisory Committee. He found him to have "an odd, abrasive style." When Toon talked about Russians, Watson wrote, "He usually had reasonable ideas, but he'd lead off with a hostile aside like, 'Well, of course, I hate the sons of bitches.'"[351] Toon was tough-minded and sometimes did talk like this, and Watson correctly surmised that Toon was skeptical about détente.

Watson's service on the Advisory Committee reinforced his commitment to nuclear disarmament, and he didn't hesitate to challenge its members' thinking. He arranged for a private screening of *Dr. Strangelove* "to confront the professionals with a radically different viewpoint on the bomb." By his own telling, his action startled at least one member, Brent Scowcroft, Ford's NSC advisor.[352]

As we would find out, Watson often did the unexpected, and perhaps this explained his success at IBM. In the early 1960s, he had made a five-billion dollar gamble on a family of computers (System/360), and it had paid off with IBM's dominance of the then-infant industry.[353] Perhaps Carter felt that Watson could achieve comparable success with the Soviets.

Watson had been in the USSR twice before. As a young man, he had passed through Moscow en route to Tokyo in 1937. Stopping at the embassy, he found that "everyone damned the Russians to some degree." He met Kennan and noted that even he spoke about Communism's "utter failure." Describing these attitudes to his father, he received a quick response, a reminder that each country is in a position "to figure out what is best for its own people" and that it is "not our duty either to criticize or advise them in these matters." Watson said he then "toned down" his own criticism.[354]

Watson had also spent four months in the Soviet capital in 1942 as an aide to the American general arranging the delivery of Lend-Lease aircraft. Watson was proud of the fact that nearly eight thousand American aircraft had been delivered to the USSR by war's end, and he mentioned his own role at staff meetings more than once.

Unfortunately, Watson was preceded by bad press. Two journalists interviewing him at the time of the Carter-Brezhnev summit had seen "t-o-o-n" written on his thumb; Watson explained that he wanted to remind himself to look for Toon at the opera scheduled that evening, but the journalists' story led to speculation that the sixty-five-year-old Watson had a bad memory.

Rumors also circulated that he believed he had become ambassador as soon as the president announced the appointment. It was said that he wasn't aware, or had forgotten, that ambassadorial appointments needed to be confirmed by the Senate.

Nonetheless, many of us were ready for a change, even if the ambassador's experience with the USSR had been limited to arms control issues and visits more than three decades before. Bilateral relations had resumed a downward drift; at least, someone who enjoyed the administration's full confidence would now be in charge.

On their second day, the ambassador and Mrs. Watson dropped into Uncle Sam's. This was an auspicious beginning; ambassadors rarely visited Uncle Sam's but ate lunch at the residence. Noticing that borsch was listed on the blackboard menu, the ambassador told Tanya he'd have borsch. Mrs. Watson, evidently unfamiliar with Russian cuisine, announced that she would have "a borsch sandwich." I was standing nearby and decided to introduce myself later.

The Soviet Union launched its invasion of Afghanistan during Christmas week 1979. The decision to intervene must have been taken within days of Watson's arrival, probably just after we joined him at the Kremlin on October 29 for his presentation of credentials to the ageless Kuznetsov. (A Politburo meeting on October 31 may have been "a turning point," according to Ambassador Garthoff.[355]) After the ceremony, the Watsons invited us to the residence for champagne.

SALT II was in serious trouble before the invasion. A majority of the members of the Senate Foreign Relations Committee but not a single member of the Armed Services Committee (some of whom had been hosted by the Kremlin) had voted for it.

On January 3, 1980, in the wake of Moscow's move, President Carter asked Majority Leader Byrd to defer action on the treaty's ratification. A day later, Carter announced his administration's retaliatory measures. Not surprisingly, the decrepit Brezhnev regime was incapable of reversing course. It was Watson's fate to be the ambassador as détente finally expired.

Peredelkino, dacha of Boris Pasternak
(Palmin's photo)

Family outing, Red Square, 1978 (passerby's photo)

**Governors Babbitt, Thornburgh, and Ray, with wives and Liz,
Red Square, November 1979 (*Soviet Life*)**

Ambassador Stoessel presents credentials, Kremlin, March 4, 1974. Dubs behind the ambassador; US department head Korniyenko and his deputy Fedoseyev, in their Foreign Ministry uniforms, left of Dubs; author back row, far left, next to Zimmerman (Kremlin photo)

Spaso House (author's photo)

Igor Palmin, mountainside, Chechnya (self-portrait)

Igor and Svetlana at home, 1995 (author's photo)

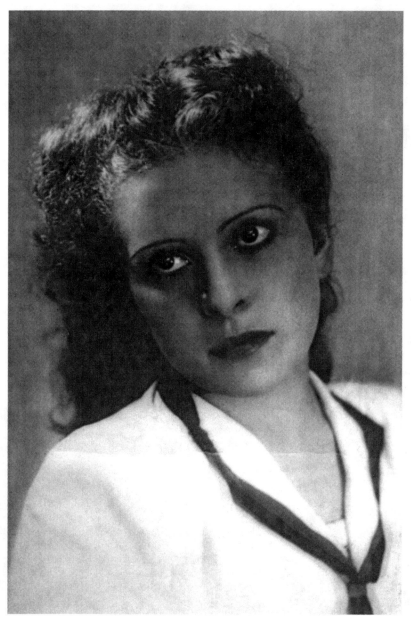

Valeriya Novikova, 1945

Valeriya Novikova at home, next to her sleigh bed,
1995 (author's photo)

Tanya in her diaphanous dress in Pyatigorsk,
August 1979—a KGB surveillant having hidden his face
as I snapped the photo

Author on Leninsky Prospect 45 apartment balcony
(Liz's photo)

Sergei and Mila Vronski, with Rob III and author,
1995 (Anya's photo)

Anya Vronski (author's photo)

Anya and Andrei Voznesenski (Anya's photo)

Nina Stevens at home, with author's son, 1995
(author's photo)

**Ambassador Watson presents award for dealing with
Kruglov in Kabul, January 1981 (embassy photo)**

**New embassy compound, townhouses left, chancery right,
October 1986 (author's photo)**

10

Cold War Reignited, Embassy Challenged

Our daughter Elise—a freshman at Georgetown University—and Abby, a senior at Kent School, reached Moscow a week before Christmas. After attending the Protestant service on Christmas Eve and exchanging gifts the next morning, we packed the car with food and drove to Tarasovka. This was our first opportunity to overnight at the dacha since returning—the waiting list had grown so long—and we looked forward to spending three days together. We had no idea that Soviet forces were about to invade Afghanistan.

The snow was deep, and the temperature hovered between fifteen and twenty degrees above zero. Shortly after arriving, Elise and I tramped to the village restaurant and bought freshly baked Georgian bread, including loaves to freeze at home. Later, Rob and I joined the caretaker to chop wood. Before noon, a CIA friend arrived with his wife and two children for cross-country skiing and Liz's lunch.

After a day and a half, Rob and Abby were anxious to return to the apartment. Rob wanted to skate on the rink in the compound, and Abby wanted to see more of Pavel and Zoran, boys from the Polish and Yugoslav embassies whose families lived in an entryway close to ours.

We drove back late morning December 27. There was an extra militiaman on duty when we reached the compound. It turned out that the CIA's new station chief was being temporarily housed in our entryway; it didn't take the KGB long to figure him out.

On the same day, President Carter penned the following in his diary:

> The Soviets have begun to move their forces in to overthrow the existing government . . . . 215 flights in the last 24 hours or so. They've moved in a couple of regiments and now have

maybe a total of 8,000 to 10,000 people in Afghanistan—both advisers and military. We consider this to be an extremely serious development.[356]

On December 28, the Soviet people were officially informed of the "intervention." Ambassador Dobrynin recalls that he was awakened by a radio announcement at the hospital in Moscow where he was awaiting his annual physical. When he saw Brezhnev a few days later, the leader confided, "It'll be over in three to four weeks."[357]

Eight years would pass before the Kremlin began withdrawing its troops.

The Soviet action generated a storm of activity at Tchaikovsky 19. My colleagues and I began reporting local reactions, both official and man in the street. We also responded to inquiries from colleagues at other embassies and Western journalists. On New Year's Eve, Tony Austin, a writer from the *New York Times* visiting Moscow, stopped by to interview me on the state of Islam in the Soviet Muslim republics. I brought Igor into the apartment to have the girls photographed, before they returned to school, and to hear what some Muscovites were thinking.

On January 2, Ambassador Watson left for Washington, recalled by President Carter to underscore the administration's displeasure. He met with the president on January 4, and the president spoke to the country later that day, announcing that the administration would postpone the ratification of SALT II, impose an embargo on further grain sales to the USSR, suspend the visits of delegations and others under U.S.-Soviet bilateral agreements (of which there were ten alone in science and technology), and tighten technology transfers.

Even before the president's speech, Liz had noted a shortage of flour in a local store. Some citizens had begun hoarding. She went to the bread store two days after Carter spoke, and the line was longer than usual; for a half hour she was "pushed and shoved" by *babushkas* as she jockeyed for bread. Onions and potatoes had disappeared from the nearby vegetable store.

Carter's announcement on January 20 that the United States would boycott the Olympics seemed to have the most telling impact.[358] Soviet media responded with stepped-up attacks on all the retaliatory measures, and the Foreign Ministry began turning down requests for travel, including one I submitted for a trip to Central Asia. It became more difficult than usual to make appointments. The vehicle of one of the defense attachés was trashed.

Ambassador Watson held a community-wide meeting in Uncle Sam's on January 22, shortly after he returned. As I was out of the embassy, Liz gave me a summary. He began in his usual self-deprecating way, saying he had no particular qualifications for his job and depended on us all for advice.

He said he had been in Berlin for the 1936 Olympics as German Jews were being dragged off the streets; because there had been no response from the West, Germany proceeded to invade Poland. According to the ambassador, we had no choice but to boycott Moscow's Olympics. We should expect increased harassment, and everyone needs to stand together.

Liz found Watson charming and old-fashioned.

Watson's memoir indicates he visited Berlin in 1937 with his father, who was involved in a conference there as president of the International Chamber of Commerce; and his father met Hitler and received a medal from his economics minister. According to the ambassador, "Dad's optimism" blinded him to the German menace.[359] In 1940, the senior Watson returned the medal.

On the day the ambassador spoke, Sakharov was arrested and exiled to Gorky, the closed city on the Volga River. Then we heard that Vladimir Kirillin, the director of the state committee for science and technology (and Sakharov's colleague at the Academy of Sciences), had resigned in protest. A French delegation abbreviated its stay in Moscow and returned to Paris.

Sakharov had been meeting with foreign correspondents and, through them, encouraging Western governments to move the Olympics out of Moscow. His statements, broadcast back into the Soviet Union, had outraged the regime.

Altogether, some fifteen Western correspondents sought interviews with different Pol/Int officers to discuss the invasion's political ramifications and Sakharov's plight.

At the end of January, the press attaché Phil Brown and I filed a request to fly to Odessa and from there to take a train north to Lvov before returning to Moscow by air. This time the ministry didn't object, probably because we wouldn't be traveling in Muslim areas.

On our first evening in the port city, after attending a concert, we set out by taxi to visit two Russian Jews who had been trying for years to secure permission to immigrate to Israel. Their apartment lay on the outskirts of Odessa. When we arrived at their door around 10:00 PM, we found that the couple (whom I hadn't met before) and two friends were talking about Sakharov's arrest. At first, they weren't sure they wanted to see us, but then decided that the KGB wouldn't intrude with diplomats present, and encouraged us to stay. They were scientists by profession and were more upset by Sakharov's arrest than the invasion, foreseeing their emigration would be pushed back further.

On the train ride north, several young Ukrainian women in the compartment next to ours invited us to share their homemade vodka (*samogon*). Intent upon protecting an important source of revenue, the government frequently publicized deaths from *samogon*, but the brew turned out to be as good as the state product.

Lvov belonged to Poland before World War II. During my Warsaw assignment, I had met a few older Poles who dreamt of reclaiming it. When we arrived at the railroad station, I felt as if I were back in Poland. The streets looked more central European than Soviet, many of the prewar buildings were still intact, and the pedestrians bustled about the sidewalks in ways that made me think of Warsaw. There were no taxis waiting outside the railroad station when we arrived, but an ambulance driver moonlighting from a hospital pulled up and asked if he could help. We explained where our hotel was located, and he opened the ambulance's back gate and shoved us in.

Washington had asked Pol/Int to check Lvov's newspapers for information about the trial of a Ukrainian nationalist who had reportedly been convicted of sabotage. While Phil checked out bookstores, I dropped into a local library and asked for its back issues. The librarian gave me a bunch bound together by string, and after an hour of searching, I found the article. Since the library had no copying machine (few did), I copied the article out by hand. My accented Russian seemed to go unnoticed.

On the flight back to Moscow, I found myself sitting next to a Soviet army officer of Kazakh origin who said he had just completed an academic course in Lvov. I introduced myself, and he was soon railing about "capitalists" who yearned for war and "American pornography." He wasn't responsive when I asked about Kazakh attitudes toward the invasion of a neighboring Muslim country, although he must have been born a Muslim. By the time the two-and-one-half-hour flight was over, I decided that I had been placed next to him for a reason; I reported his comments but included a caveat.

Ambassador Watson wasn't comfortable working in a tense environment and showed his irritation at staff meetings. At one, he warned about rumor mongering in the embassy.

In February, *Newsweek* had carried an article challenging his suitability: "Is Watson out of Tune?"[360] Around the same time, United Press International (UPI) quoted an unnamed officer saying that Watson "seems to have regretted taking the post."[361] The UPI correspondent claimed that Watson had stated at a meeting, "I feel like a chameleon, now I've got to change my spots." I hadn't heard the comment, but the ambassador made little secret of the fact that he didn't enjoy being a hard-liner.

*   *   *

As winter moved into spring, Soviet media stepped up their attacks on the president. The White House was called "rabid" and "schizophrenic," the latter because of the now-open differences between Vance and Brzezinski.

The consulate in Leningrad reported that local KGB agents tailing staff members had forced several off the road. They were also intimidating the consulate's joggers, driving toward them before slamming on their brakes. A few American tourists visiting refuseniks there had been roughed up.

The head of the consular section, Tom Hutson, resigned from the Foreign Service while on home leave, publicly berating the administration for its policies.

I needed an excuse to get into the Kremlin in order to secure a copy of the latest version of the *Deputaty*, a thick book published by the Presidium of the Supreme Soviet that contained the biographies of the deputies "elected" to it from the ranks of Party organization types, national and regional officials, and citizen-activists. The book couldn't be found elsewhere and Washington needed it.

I telephoned a contact at the Presidium whom I knew from the CODEL visits and said I wanted to learn more about the Soviet legislative process. I knew that the Supreme Soviet was a sham; in its long history, no deputy had been known to oppose a government bill. (It had been different in Communist Poland; the Sejm, the parliament, had occasionally modified regime-sponsored legislation, and non-Communist deputies had even cast negative votes.) Somewhat to my surprise, the contact agreed to set up an appointment with the appropriate officials; despite worsening relations, not every official was hostile.

Little came of the discussion about the Supreme Soviet and its committee system, but I got the *Deputaty*. I pouched it to Washington where it was copied, distributed to various agencies, and pouched back to the embassy in multiple copies. I also fattened my file of Kremlin notes.

In March, the science counselor Bob Houston and I received permission to visit two Central Asian capitals—Alma Ata in Kazakhstan and Ashkhabad in Turkmenia. Turkmenia borders Iran where our diplomatic colleagues were in their fifth month of captivity; on a clear day in Ashkhabad, you can see the Iranian border.

We were given no official appointments. However, the Intourist guide recommended that we visit the ruins of a fifteenth century mosque that had a reputation as a holy place. All of Ashkhabad's mosques had been destroyed during Russia's takeover in the 1920s, and none had been rebuilt.

We were driven to a barren rocky site ten miles east of the city. We came upon a heavily damaged complex of towers and tombs. The guide claimed that an earthquake in 1948 had done most of the damage.

A few pilgrims were milling about. One tomb was covered with cakes and sweets wrapped in paper, with bits of white and colored pieces of cloth also attached. According to the guide, the tombs belonged to ancient sheiks, and the local people believe they receive their "spirit" if they attach something of their own—a piece of clothing or a token gift—to their resting places. An old man wandering about the site told us that there were still a million believers in the republic's population of three million. Despite half a century of propaganda, most native Turkmen retained their Muslim beliefs.

Intourist guides may report to the KGB, but they could still be helpful.

There was little food in the hotels, and the plumbing was primitive. In the lounge at the airport in Tashkent, where we were forced to spend one night, the men's room had been awkwardly designed; the urinals were so close together that any two "customers" would have had to overlap their legs.

*   *   *

Ambassador Watson did what he could to lift morale. He arranged for Lowell Thomas, renowned from radio ("So long, until tomorrow"), to be his guest at a dinner dance at Spaso House. Thomas had been a friend of Watson's father and was eighty-eight years old, yet he performed with the energy of a much younger man, sharing stories about Herbert Hoover, Lawrence of Arabia (whom he helped catapult to fame in 1918), and other figures from the distant past.

After returning to New York, Thomas sent the ambassador a brochure entitled *Into Forbidden Afghanistan* that described a trip (sponsored by General Motors) that he had taken into Afghanistan from British-controlled India in 1924 in a Buick touring car. After my trip to Kabul in September, Watson inscribed the brochure over to me. The Moscow visit was Thomas's last before his death in 1981.

The Watsons invited Liz and me to a small dinner party and a movie. Among the guests was Metropolitan Yuvenali, the Orthodox Church's senior priest responsible for international relations. The movie turned out to be a professionally made account of a Watson family skiing holiday in British Columbia. During dinner at my end of the table, we discussed the Orthodox tradition of having worshippers stand during services, some of which could last two or more hours. Mrs. Watson suggested to the Metropolitan, at her right, that the church equip its believers with collapsible shooting sticks, portable seats such as hunters use; Yuvenali, the good diplomat that he was, wasn't fazed in the least.

In 1990, Yuvenali came in fourth in the first round of voting by the Orthodox Church's bishops to select a new patriarch.[362] In the last round, the current patriarch, Alexei II, was elected.

A week later, the ambassador summoned me to complain about Judi Mandel's coverage of the domestic scene. From her wide range of contacts, Judi would assemble detailed information about food prices and shortages in areas of the Russian republic that were difficult to reach. "Why is this necessary?" Watson demanded, after handing me a telegram I had approved and sent.[363]

Pol/Int was creating the impression, he said, that the Soviet Union was in a state of crisis, unable to manage its affairs. I tried to explain that the experts, including some in the CIA, found this kind of reporting useful, but the ambassador seemed not to understand. He said he didn't want us encouraging people back in Washington who were demanding that the administration bring more pressure to bear on the Soviet regime.

Several months later, in June, when we picked up rumors about work stoppages at the Togliatti and Gorky automobile plants because of food shortages[364], he cautioned me again. Watson said that we needed hard information before reporting and shouldn't send in rumors.

One of my officers, Louis Sell, had made contact in Moscow with someone from a fledgling free trade union (Free Inter-professional Association of Workers, or SMOT[365]), and we were beginning to see signs of a genuine workers' movement.

Hard information about sensitive developments far from the capital was not easily obtained, and Watson thought we were hyping the notion of a crisis: "We shouldn't distract Washington from important issues like the nuclear threat, and we shouldn't create the impression that the Soviet Union can't compete with the United States because of its problems."

It turned out that the food shortages and work stoppages had substance, and the reports we forwarded helped analysts develop a better picture of the system's ills.

Afghanistan and signs of worker unrest were not the regime's only concerns. In July 1980, the Polish government was forced to raise food prices drastically. Strikes erupted, and in August it was forced to recognize Solidarity (*Solidarnosc*), the first genuine union in the Communist bloc. Bogdan's optimism was being vindicated.

I missed the July 4, 1980, reception due to a virus. The girls were back in Moscow for summer vacation (Abby would work as a counselor at Camp Wocsom, Elise at the embassy), and Liz took them with her to Spaso House. The turnout was poor, and apparently I didn't miss much.

The Olympics were about to begin, with eighty countries attending, sixty-four boycotting. I asked the girls not to attend: "If you do attend, don't tell me." Abby told me later that she watched several boxing matches with her East European friends.

The Watsons hosted Bob and Dolores Hope in September, inviting the entire community to Spaso House. Somewhat to my surprise, Carter was the butt of several of Hope's one-liners: "We shouldn't pick on Carter because he hasn't done anything." Of himself, Hope said he had gone into the Kremlin because he thought it was his dressing room: "I saw a red star on the door." Hope also entertained at the British embassy and the Anglo-American School. A nine-year-old pupil reportedly asked a series of personal questions, and Hope quipped, "Say, are you from the FBI."

With little happening in U.S.-Soviet relations and with Moscow locked down because of Olympic-related security concerns, Elise and I flew off to two Central Asian republics, Tadzhikistan and Kirgizia.

Kirgizia lies on the Chinese border. Its population is 50 percent Kirgiz and 25 percent Russian, with other nationalities making up the balance. Its capital, Frunze (Bishkek today), is one of the prettiest Central Asian cities—situated under snowcapped mountains, its streets lined with trees.

In the restaurant at Intourist's Ala-Too Hotel, Elise and I met Misha Kuznetsov and Tanya Shcherbakova. They sat down at the table next to ours just after we were seated in the nearly empty room. When it emerged that both spoke English, we pushed the tables together. Misha told us he was a twenty-year-old first year student at Kirgiz University; Tanya introduced herself as a twenty-one-year-old student from the same university and said they were both studying English.

We spent a pleasant evening drinking Moldavian champagne, eating lamb dishes, and discussing our respective countries. I was interested in how the Kirgiz were reacting to the war. For a new acquaintance, Misha was voluble; only a noisy orchestra playing mostly Western music could drown him out. The next morning, I met them again as Elise slept, and together we strolled about the city.

Like Mike and Tanya in Ulyanovsk, they just "happened" to be dining at the Ala-Too. It turned out that six years later, Misha would have sufficient skill to entrap an experienced American correspondent, Nick Daniloff. The entrapment, as will be seen, had serious consequences for the embassy and U.S.-Soviet relations.

Supreme Court Justice William Douglas had stayed in the same hotel thirty years before, in 1955, and had found a man in his room when he returned to it unexpectedly. The man explained that he was looking for a friend. Before Douglas left Frunze, the manager of the hotel told him that the man had been "arrested." Douglas was appalled—believing a terrible mistake had been made—and wrote the prisoner an apologetic note. Back in Moscow, a more sophisticated American told Douglas that it was likely that the man was working for the authorities.[366]

The KGB operated much more skillfully in the 1980s.

Elise and I made our way back to Moscow by way of the Tadzhik capital, Dushanbe, a dusty sun-drenched city an hour's drive from the Afghan border. I looked for but couldn't find wounded or injured Soviet soldiers on the grounds of a large hospital on the city's main avenue that the defense attachés had mentioned to me; they were probably being airlifted to the Russian republic from Afghanistan. Our stay was uneventful, but I filed the usual reports on my return.

In August 1980, the Soviet authorities resumed jamming foreign radio broadcasts for the first time since 1973. They also rejected proposals I made for two other trips: a flight to Lvov (I wanted to assess reactions to the unrest in Poland) and a drive to a medieval battlefield five hours south of Moscow that one of the embassy's drivers said he'd be willing to undertake.

Six hundred years before, in September 1380, the Russians had defeated the Tatars at the battle of Kulikovo, a victory for Christians over an Islamic tide that had submerged Russia for more than a century and threatened Europe. During July and August 1980, the daily newspaper *Sovetskaya Rossiya*, which catered to more nationalistic Russians, was playing up the approaching event.

In Stalinist Russia, the anniversary had been an occasion for promoting patriotic feelings. The composer Yuri Shaporin had been awarded a Stalin Prize in 1941 for his cantata "On the Field of Kulikovo."[367] I was intrigued whether Brezhnev and his people would acknowledge the historic victory. Could it be done without offending Muslims, those in the Middle East and South Asia including Afghanistan, and its own?

I was not too surprised, though disappointed, when the ministry withheld approval. Soviet officials in Moscow let the anniversary pass without any notice.

We invited Ed and Nina Stevens to dinner and watched *The Turning Point*. Nina brought Liz two small metal icons like the ones Orthodox believers carried before the Revolution when traveling. Ed passed on the latest anecdotes, including several about the Olympics. He said that the authorities had deployed anti-aircraft batteries along the river embankment opposite Lenin Stadium, concealed under trees and targeting the airspace above. Because the airspace was closed during Brezhnev's appearance at the opening ceremony and insufficient notice had been given abroad, several inbound foreign flights were forced to divert to Helsinki.

*   *   *

Late Monday evening, September 15, 1980, the acting deputy chief of mission Sherrod McCall (who had succeeded Bob German as political counselor a few weeks earlier) asked if he could stop by. The girls had already left for the United States, and Liz had gone to bed; it was an unusual time for a call.

Sherrod explained that the White House and the department wanted me to deal with a Soviet soldier who had entered the embassy in Kabul carrying an AK-47.[368] None of that embassy's sixteen staff members or the six marines spoke Russian. I could say no if I wished.

The number of Soviet troops in Afghanistan had grown to eighty-five thousand, yet the department hadn't assigned a Russian-speaking officer to Kabul.

Of course, I said I'd go.

There were Aeroflot flights from Moscow to Kabul, but the Soviets refused to make a ticket available. On September 17, I flew to New Delhi to pick up an Indian Airlines flight to Kabul. I stayed overnight at a posh hotel while my old embassy tried to secure an Afghan entry visa. I thought there was a Bond-like moment when a sultry Indian girl knocked on my door late in the evening and asked if she could tender a service; I had to remind myself that I was no longer in the Soviet Union, and she probably wasn't KGB.

The embassy told me around midnight that it had secured an Afghan entry visa. Early the next morning I flew into Kabul. George Griffin, an FSO, met me on the tarmac. On the drive to the embassy, we passed Afghan soldiers patrolling the streets and saw helicopters overhead. In the distance could be heard the *thump-thump* of artillery batteries.

Soviet and Afghan soldiers had sealed off the embassy compound as soon as they learned a Russian soldier had gone inside. They installed concrete barriers around the main gate and were stopping and searching every vehicle going in and out. They ordered George's driver to stop when he reached the barriers. George instructed him not to open the doors despite the soldiers' demand; after an exchange of words, they let us enter.

The Soviet ambassador, Fikryat Tabeyev, was demanding the soldier's return, claiming he had been drugged and kidnapped and was being held against his will. The U.S.-Soviet Consular Agreement provided for access by Soviet consular officers to their citizens, but only if they were being detained, and Kruglov wasn't being detained. As the embassy had told the Soviets, he could walk out anytime he wished.

In no event would he be turned over to a Soviet consular officer against his will. For three years, we had been protecting the Pentecostal families in the basement of Tchaikovsky 19. After the furor surrounding the Kudirka case, it was inconceivable that we wouldn't protect a possible asylum seeker.

George introduced me to the chargé d'affaires Hawthorne (Hawk) Mills and the staff. A few expressed concern that the Soviets, in their determination to recover the soldier, might arrange for the Afghans to occupy the embassy, as Khomeini's people had done in neighboring Iran.

The Russian turned out to be Private Alexander Kruglov from Kemerovo in the Ural Mountains, an area closed to Westerners. The staff had already determined that he was partly ethnic German; the chargé d'affaires of the West German embassy had visited him and found that the only German he knew were nursery rhymes.

George took me to Kruglov, and the two of us began a series of meetings. We discussed his background, family situation, and the reasons for his flight into the compound. Every so often I'd take a break, and Hawk and George would report my findings to Washington. After two days of talking, it was clear that Kruglov had fled to escape mistreatment at the hands of his unit's noncommissioned officers, not for larger political reasons.

Hazing was common in the Soviet military, beatings almost an expected part of service. Kruglov had been beaten several times. He had acted on impulse in entering the embassy, without thinking about asylum and all its implications.

The marines had found some Russian-language materials, including a Bible and Solzhenitsyn's *The Gulag Archipelago*, in a local market, and had given them to him. Another Marine played chess with him. Only the whiskey he asked for had been refused.

The situation outside the embassy was tense. As George later recounted:

> We were surrounded by tanks and [Soviet] sharpshooters perched on our perimeter walls. They wouldn't let us take vehicles in or out, so we camped in the embassy. We kept cars parked outside and went out only to get food. They allowed us to walk out but didn't want us to smuggle out the soldier in the trunk of a car.

Because of the sharpshooters, Kruglov was kept in interior rooms away from windows and was moved to a different room every few hours.

It took me four sessions before I decided that he had little, if any, interest in politics. Kruglov was no Kudirka; he simply wanted to escape the beatings.

I told him he could stay as long as he wanted; we wouldn't force him out. Should he decide to stay, however, he would probably have a long wait. The Soviets controlled Kabul, and they certainly wouldn't let us take a Russian out of Afghanistan.

I had studied the criminal and civil codes before I left Moscow. Under Soviet law, Kruglov could be tried and executed as a deserter.

The State Department telegraphed the same provisions to Kabul, and I went through them carefully with Kruglov so he understood the risks of returning. I told him that should he want to stay, he might want to meet Soviet representatives, though he was entitled to refuse. If he intended to remain in the embassy, it would probably be best if he let them know face-to-face.

Most of the staff spent the first night on mattresses. Just before midnight, all the lights went out, including those at the compound's perimeter. Because of background noise, including the occasional din of artillery, the marines thought they might have been shot out. One marine reported that an intruder had gone over the wall into the compound.

Mills sent flash messages to Washington and Moscow, and the department and the embassy in Moscow delivered warnings to the Soviets. By 1:00 AM, the power was back on; the Russians were playing a game of nerves. (Viktor Cherkashin, a senior KGB official, confirmed this later in a memoir, writing that the Soviet troops "surrounded the building and cut off [its] electricity and telephone lines."[369])

On the third day, Kruglov decided he would meet with the Soviet officials. Hawk, George, and I went to the Soviet compound to inform Ambassador Tabeyev and to explain that the meeting would take place in our embassy under our rules. He could bring along two officers if he wished. Hosting us with cognac and tea, Tabeyev agreed without any quibbling.

Six days after Kruglov entered the embassy, we held the "confrontation meeting." Tabeyev arrived with an officer from his consular section and a KGB official. Kruglov sat with Hawk, George, and me on our side of the table. Several marines stood guard, and I interpreted.

The Soviet side brought letters from Kruglov's family and friends in Kemerovo. Addressing the young recruit as Sasha, Tabeyev did most of the talking. He told Kruglov there would be no punishment if he returned; he would be mustered out of the army and allowed back in school.

After two hours, Kruglov made a decision to leave with the Soviets. We secured Tabeyev's oral guarantees in writing, handed him Kruglov's assault rifle, and the affair ended.

I returned to Moscow on an Aeroflot flight. Around me were a dozen uniformed Soviet soldiers wounded from the fighting, a few with bandaged legs propped up on the folded seats in front of them.

There was skepticism that the Soviet regime would honor Tabeyev's promises, and I had told Kruglov in Kabul that we would follow up with the Foreign Ministry in Moscow. I made an appointment at the American Department and was received by Trifonov, a short, rotund man whom I knew from my consular days and who bore an uncanny resemblance to Khrushchev. Not surprisingly, Trifonov responded the way he used to when rebuffing representations on consular cases: This was "an internal matter," and I had no right to ask. Had U.S.-Soviet relations been better, he would have been less blunt, but the answer would have been the same.

My gut feeling was that Kruglov wasn't being punished and was already back in Kemerovo and out of the military. Had Stalin been in power, he would have been shot, but the system under Brezhnev was losing whatever rigor remained; there weren't many Russian Communists left who believed in the "heavy hammer of revolutionary justice." Kruglov would probably lead a normal life, at least as normal as any closed city far from Moscow could provide.

Tabeyev later told Americans in Kabul that Kruglov had, in fact, been released and was back in school. Perhaps an enterprising journalist will track the one-time soldier (or his family) down someday and confirm, or belie, that assurance.

Before leaving Afghanistan, I visited a small monument on the embassy's front lawn erected to the memory of Spike Dubs.

In January 1989, almost a decade later, Washington, in view of deteriorating conditions in Kabul and the removal of the last Soviet troops, withdrew all the Americans from the embassy and entrusted it to its Afghan staff. After Al Qaeda's attacks on September 11, 2001, and Washington's response, a Taliban mob uttering "God is great" and "Death to America" temporarily seized the compound.

In 2005, a new embassy was opened, and the memorial to Spike was restored. Bernie Woerz, an FSO on temporary duty in Kabul, a friend with whom we had served in Warsaw, tells me that the American flag will henceforth fly at half-staff to mark the anniversary of the ambassador's death.[370]

*   *   *

Cyrus Vance resigned as secretary of state in May because of his opposition to the plan to rescue our hostages in Iran by military force. It wasn't long before his successor, the former senator from Maine Edmund Muskie, ran into Vance's problem: the NSC's tendency to keep the department's seventh floor at bay.

Muskie was frozen out of deliberations on nuclear arms strategy. Retired Ambassador Toon was quoted in the *U.S. News & World Report* saying that "Muskie should have threatened to resign on the spot if this sort of thing happens again."[371]

The same article pointed to problems in the Foreign Service, including the fact that American diplomats "earn 25% less than counterparts in the civil service." Pay disparity was never much of an issue in Moscow; we received an additional allowance (usually 15-20%) because Washington viewed it as a hardship post. We also received *per diem* when we traveled; I received $271 for the trip to Kabul.

The article noted that "America's social revolution" was playing havoc with diplomatic careers. "Foreign-service wives—and in some cases, husbands—no longer are automatically content to accompany spouses overseas at the expense of their own career opportunities at home." The result, the article claimed, is increased divorce, discord, and stress.

From the families Liz and I personally knew, we could vouch for this.

Correspondingly, the number of single people at Tchaikovsky 19 had grown to almost three times as many as during our first tour.

U.S. News further reported that standards for admission to the Foreign Service had been lowered "to enable more women and minority applicants to qualify." Department officials denied the report, saying that only "perceived cultural biases" had been eliminated. I wasn't sure what biases had persisted into the late '70s, but clearly young persons with backgrounds like mine were finding it more difficult to join.

The article also cited a decline in language requirements for those joining the Foreign Service, but it failed to mention management's lessened attention to developing language and area expertise in those already in the career. Vance's new Foreign Service law was just coming into force, and few understood its implications for the long term.

In October 1980, I took a seven-hour flight to Irkutsk, Russia's gateway to Siberia, with Geoffrey Wolfe, an economic officer. The weather was bitterly cold, and the local authorities refused to see us. We spent two days wandering in and out of stores, and up and down the city's quaint streets. Three or four-hundred-year-old log cabins stood near our hotel. Like those surviving in Moscow, they were picturesque, but only the hardiest would choose to live in one. They had no indoor plumbing—a hand pump and a spigot on a street nearby supplied their water.

The Communists had seized Irkutsk's main cathedral, Holy Trinity, during their early drive against religion and had removed its Christian symbols and punched holes in its domes to accommodate telescopes. As our Intourist guide stood with us and surveyed what was now a planetarium, he denied there had been any religious desecration.

Like the church of the same name near to where Mila lives, the cathedral has since been restored and reconsecrated.

We flew north to Bratsk, a city on the Angara River whose source is Lake Baikal. During Khrushchev's first years, fifty thousand workers—many of them young volunteers—had gone to Bratsk, then a small town in the wilderness, to build one of the world's largest hydroelectric dams.

Yevtushenko made the dam famous with a lengthy poem in 1965 that included stanzas about workers coming from Moscow:

Rise, O Siberia, brightest of the bright,
Rejoice
And bring joy!
You who were once a punishment
Make of yourself
A reward!

They have composed an orchestral chorus,
These Moscow boys and girls.
The Bratsk Hydroelectric Station moves along,
With the girls' red pigtails bobbing:

"I lived on [Moscow's] Sretenka Street—
I am taking my leave of it.
I used to drink sodas—
The Angara River tastes better,
My knapsack is full of
Mama's little barankas [Moscow rolls] . . .
Taiga, my new mama,
Receive me into the family."

"You have no idea, my girl,
How in the rigors of the first year
Your smart little skirt
Will be used for leg wrappings;
How in your tiny tent,
The minute the thermometer drops below 45 degrees [C],
Your little red pigtails
Will freeze to your folding cot."[372]

The dam began producing power in 1961. It was completed five years ahead of the aluminum plant for which the power was intended, a mistake not unusual in Soviet planning.

Bratsk was preparing to celebrate its twenty-fifth anniversary when we arrived in the middle of a blizzard. A guide met us at the airport with a car and drove us past row after row of identical-looking apartment blocks, each five stories tall, to an Intourist hotel. These were the infamous *Khrushchoby*, buildings slapped together from concrete panels during Khrushchev's era when more than one hundred million Soviet citizens received new housing.[373] (*Khrushchoby* is an amalgam of the Russian words for slum—*trushchoba*—and Khrushchev.) The theory behind the five stories was that buildings of this height wouldn't need elevators.

Even in a blizzard, Bratsk looked bleak. It seemed that every tree had been uprooted as the housing went up. The workers who moved out of log cabins into walk-up apartments must have been delighted (they'd have electricity and plumbing, at last); but the planners could have done better. As Ada Louise Huxtable wrote in 1968 after seeing Bratsk and Norilsk, another new Siberian city, "If the engineering challenge was accepted, the design challenge was not."[374]

The director in charge of the hydroelectric dam agreed to give Geoff and me a tour, and for a Soviet official he was candid. When I mentioned that I hadn't encountered his kind of openness in Moscow, he proudly said that "this is the Siberian way." Years later, Yegor Ligachev, who helped Gorbachev launch his reforms (before falling out of favor), would write that he preferred Siberia to Moscow because there "people tell you what they think to your face."[375]

At night, we sat in the hotel bar with two military attachés from the embassy, one a classmate from Garmisch, Jeff Barrie, who would have a business career in Moscow after retiring from the military, and would die there in a taxi accident in 2007.

Unknown to Geoff and me, they were visiting Bratsk too and had rounded up two Tatar women with whom they were drinking. I was in a less-than-ebullient mood because of an incident I had witnessed in the hotel lobby earlier in the day. A Russian boy about Rob's age had sneaked in to look at the cheap combs and other everyday items on display in a glass case. (Probably there were no stores in his neighborhood.) A husky doorman charged out of nowhere—like a Gogol character—grabbed the boy, beat him over the head, and threw him out the front door into the snow.

George Kennan once wrote that "the overwhelming majority" of the Soviet people "have no greater fondness for cruelty than people anywhere else in the world."[376] Sometimes it didn't seem this way.

*   *   *

As the 1980 presidential election approached, American politics became *the* topic in Uncle Sam's. Ambassador Watson was away when the results came in, but P&C arranged an "Election Day breakfast" at Spaso House to which Soviet journalists and members of the American community were invited. The ballroom was decorated like a convention hall, and Rob's seventh-grade class came from school to share in the excitement.

By the time the breakfast began, Governor Reagan's victory was clear. Thanks to P&C, the window cases in front of the embassy carried photographs of the beaming president-elect with an accompanying Cyrillic text the very next day. Pedestrians, many of who stepped up their pace when they passed the militiamen, slowed to take a look.

"Just two months to go, and I can get out," Ambassador Watson remembered thinking as he listened to the results in Brussels where he was attending a North Atlantic Treaty Organization conference.[377]

The ambassador wasn't in good form during his final weeks. He kept confounding the names of past and present Afghan leaders. At one meeting, he asked whether Italy was a member of NATO.

Mark Garrison announced that he too intended to leave. Mark was fifty-one, and he and Betty had held the community together during a difficult year. Mark said he was disappointed with Washington's failure to conduct a coherent policy and with the department's and the Foreign Service's diminished role.

On November 15, the Garrisons hosted a large farewell party in their apartment above the consular section in the north wing. They invited Americans, Russians, and others they knew from their two Moscow assignments.

Mila and Sergei Vronski brought Anya, their nineteen-year-old daughter, whose marriage to a Russian artist had earlier failed. She was a dark-eyed beauty who had inherited her mother's warm personality and her father's aristocratic bearing. Among the Garrisons' other guests was the poet Andrei Voznesenski who, it seems, couldn't help noticing Anya. She would soon become his *femme inspiratrice,* a muse for his poetry.

After retiring from the Foreign Service, Mark became the head of the Watson Institute for International Studies at Brown University. Ambassador Watson, a Brown alumnus, funded the think tank after leaving Moscow. Upon Watson's death, the institute received a bequest of $21 million, part of which went to support the Olive C. Watson Professorship honoring Mrs. Watson.[378]

Mark was closely identified with the Carter administration, having advised Shulman, Vance, and then the novice ambassador. Had Mark continued in the service, he probably wouldn't have received an ambassadorship—which many believed he deserved—from the Republican administrations that followed.

*　　*　　*

As with every December at the embassy, December 1980 was booked heavily with social events, and it was especially memorable for twelve-year-old Rob.

On December 7, as he and a schoolmate, Eddie, were walking back to Leninsky 45 from skating on a frozen pond near Kosygin's compound, they were jumped by two adult Russians who stole all their hockey equipment, including a new pair of Finnish skates we had just received from Helsinki. Neither boy was hurt. Eddie's father, from the defense attachés' office, raced to the pond with a baseball bat, looking for the thieves; but by then they had escaped. Liz and I took the boys to the nearest militia station and filed a report, and the embassy sent a diplomatic note to the ministry. The equipment was never recovered, the culprits never found.

Then a few days later, as Rob and Abby were disembarking from a bus bound for Red Square, Rob accidentally dislodged a bottle of vodka a drunk was holding, and it smashed to the pavement. The enraged Russian grabbed Rob and was about to throw him to the pavement too when Abby pulled out her loose change, the equivalent of $8 in rubles, and threw it at him. Other Russians at the stop then intervened and told her this was enough. Ranting, the drunk wandered off, looking for another bottle.

The days before Christmas were busy. We invited an Indian and a Singaporean diplomat and their wives to dinner and to see a Bogart and Bacall film, *The Maltese Falcon*. Liz and I accepted ten invitations between December 7 and Christmas Day, a few more than needed. Igor came by and, anticipating we'd be leaving the following summer, I arranged for American friends to meet him.

Ambassador and Mrs. Watson flew a square-dance "caller" in from the United States and invited the community to Spaso House. Seventy-five accepted, and Liz recalls the evening as enjoyable. Two days earlier, a colleague and I planned to fly to Odessa to check on rumors of a labor stoppage: "Watson insists that we make on-the-spot checks" before doing this kind of reporting. However, the trip never took place; the ministry withheld approval. Still I didn't attend the dance, and it turned out that only thirty did.

The next morning the ambassador expressed his irritation. I learned later that square-dancing was an important annual event at Watson's posh compound on an island in Maine.

Morale at the embassy was at low ebb, and staff members were more interested in being with their own families. When planning the marine ball in Spaso House in November, Mrs. Watson had told several wives that she didn't want the marines dancing with her daughter when she visited from the United States, and her comment had ricocheted around the community.[379]

At noon on Saturday, December 20, the press agency TASS announced that Alexei Kosygin, who had resigned as chairman of the Council of Ministers in October, had died two days earlier. Kosygin had long been a ranking official; he represented the regime at the 1967 Glassboro Summit before Brezhnev consolidated power. Would Moscow invite delegations from abroad to attend the funeral? Washington wanted to know.

The Foreign Ministry had no answer for us on Saturday. On Sunday morning, *Pravda* announced that Kosygin's body would lie in state for viewing on Monday, from 10:00 AM to 6:00 PM, at the Central House of the Soviet Army. A few hours later, a duty officer in the ministry's protocol department let us know that the diplomatic corps would receive an invitation, but a slot hadn't yet been set for Ambassador Watson. The funeral itself would be held on Red Square at 11:30 AM on Tuesday, but there was still no decision whether any foreign delegations would be invited.

I sent a telegram to Washington late Sunday reporting what we knew. It included my supposition that the Kremlin would not invite delegations from abroad, except perhaps from Communist allies.

On Monday, we were told that Ambassador Watson could view the body at 3:00 PM. We arranged a wreath to be sent in advance; and shortly before 3:00 PM, the ambassador, his staff aide Bill Montgomery, and I left in the ambassador's limousine for the Central Army House, a building I didn't know. Thousands of Soviet citizens, five abreast in a line a mile long, were patiently waiting to enter when we arrived.

The Central Army House turned out to be a former palace that had been confiscated after the Revolution by the Red Army. When the Mexican muralist Diego Rivera visited Moscow in 1927, he signed a contract to paint a mural on one of its walls, but insisted that all its Empire-style features be removed first. The Soviets balked at this and lost interest in Rivera.[380]

It was a gray, wet day with the temperature below freezing. I wore a khaki-colored storm jacket, the coat I had worn to work. As we disembarked, Watson, believing khaki wasn't suitable for a lying in state, suggested we all remove our coats. Bareheaded and coatless, we walked the one hundred or so paces to the entrance where a *babushka* pinned a black and red mourning band on our sleeves and a protocol official directed us up a flight of marble stairs. An honor guard stood at Kosygin's open casket, surrounded by flowers and wreaths draped with ribbons. A table at the base of the casket displayed his awards and medals. The three of us were invited to sit, which we did for about five minutes, then returned to the car.

Three hours earlier, the entire leadership, including Kosygin's successor Nikolai Tikhonov, had been officially photographed standing stiffly next to the casket. Brezhnev headed one row, Gromyko the other. Gorbachev, who had been elevated to the Politburo in October, apparently attended but wasn't shown.

A UPI newsman standing outside took a good photograph of Watson and me as we were walking back to the limousine. A friend clipped it from a newspaper and sent it to my father. Impressed that I was in the company of a business legend, he carried it around in his wallet the rest of his life.

On Tuesday, the ambassador, his aide, and I stood on Red Square for the funeral itself. (Phil Brown kindly lent me his dark coat, one sleeve of which hung by no more than a few threads.) The weather was cold and somber. No foreign delegations were present. To the sound of mournful music, an armored personnel carrier accompanied by goose-stepping soldiers and members of Kosygin's family transported his ashes across the square to a point in front of the mausoleum, on which the leaders were standing. After Tikhonov read the deceased's biography and others delivered short eulogies, they descended the mausoleum's steps, received the box of ashes, and symbolically as a single body delivered it to a niche in the Kremlin wall. Then they climbed back up the stairs, observed the march-by of different military units (KGB troops taking up the rear), and the funeral ended, having lasted about thirty minutes.

I was glad to have experienced the stark liturgy of at least one Red Square funeral.

On Christmas Eve, a Romanian and a French diplomat paid separate calls on me to discuss the internal scene, and my colleagues in Pol/Int and I collaborated on a report summarizing all the high-level personnel changes (twenty-one) that had occurred since Kosygin's resignation. Almost half of the deputy chairmen of the Council of Ministers had been replaced. Kosygin's successor was trying to rejuvenate government, but there was no sign yet of any policy change.

Later the same afternoon, I walked to Spaso House to join Liz and the children for the Christmas service. Afterwards, Elise and I took an embassy vehicle to Sheremetyevo Airport to find her missing suitcase.

The day after Christmas, the ambassador's secretary called to say that his driver would be stopping by with a gift. The ambassador gave me a tie clip with *faux* whalebone and a framed photograph he had taken of his family skiing in Zermatt. Perhaps he recalled me saying that my parents had skied there once. For the prior Christmas, he had arranged fresh produce from Helsinki for every family in the community; and Liz and I received a bunch of celery, an especially thoughtful gift during a Moscow winter.

Probably no ambassador worked harder and had less success maintaining staff morale.

*   *   *

On January 15, 1981, the ambassador concluded his "short, unhappy tour as a diplomat"—as he would later describe it—and left for the United States.[381] A week before, he had pinned a Superior Honor award on me in Uncle Sam's for having helped in Kabul; the consular section and I had received the same award from Spike in 1973.

At his final meeting with the country team, Watson reminisced about his tour and took photographs of us around the table. No one had the heart to remind him of the rule against photography inside the embassy and, even more so, inside the tank.

Two days before the ambassador's departure, the KGB entrapped two American military attachés in a hotel in Rovno, a city close to the Polish border where they had been checking reports of Soviet military movements. After imbibing cognac and vodka in the bar, the officers ended up with girls in their room, whereupon the KGB broke in and took the predictable photographs.[382]

The attachés rejected the KGB's proposal that they make a deal, and reported the situation as soon as they returned to the embassy. The attachés lived with their families in our entryway, one in the apartment opposite ours; within a week of leaving Rovno, they were packing up to leave. It took the Western press corps another three weeks to discover their absence and to report the story. Until the incident, one of the officers was on the short list (of four officers) to be the military advisor to Vice President-elect George H. W. Bush.

*   *   *

It seemed to me that most Americans at the embassy welcomed the inauguration of President Ronald Reagan on January 20, 1981. I at least looked forward to a more coherent policy, one without the disarray that had dogged the Carter administration. The fact that the inauguration coincided with the release of the hostages in Iran after 444 days of confinement added to the optimism.

However, the administration got off to a clumsy start. In his first press conference after the inauguration, the president accused the Soviet leaders of reserving "unto themselves the right to commit any crime, to lie, to cheat." Reagan apparently wanted the world to know that détente was dead, but this kind of talk wouldn't help us meet our responsibilities.

A day earlier, on January 28, Alexander Haig, the new secretary of state, had accused the Soviet Union of promoting "international terrorism."[383]

Thanks to an invitation from the Moynihans for a cocktail at Roosevelt House, Liz and I had met Claire Sterling, the correspondent in Rome who was popularizing the notion of Soviet state terrorism. I hadn't been impressed with her arguments, including those in the book she wrote, *The Terror Network: The Secret World of International Terrorism*.

Unless Haig's definition of terrorism encompassed Soviet military threats or aggression (it wasn't being defined this way), the charge seemed off the mark.

We know now that he spoke before he sought the evidence. Only afterwards did he ask the CIA for its judgment. According to Robert Gates, then the chief of staff to CIA Director William Casey, "Everyone knew he [Haig] wanted an answer that would support what he had said." The CIA subsequently found some "thin and contradictory" information that Moscow's "friends and allies" had supported some purely terrorist groups, but this hardly confirmed a decision made by the Kremlin to promote international terrorism.[384]

No one expected an early improvement in U.S.-Soviet relations, but the new administration focused more on arousing anti-Soviet feeling in its first months than developing any fresh approaches.

Then we read that Ambassador Dobrynin could no longer use the State Department garage to reach the elevator to take him to the seventh floor for meetings with Haig and senior officials. Instead, for the first time during his stay in Washington, he was told he would have to enter the department through its C Street pedestrian entrance. On his first visit to see Haig, his driver had been forced to back out of the basement garage.[385]

The department's press office would later explain that the change had to do with reciprocity, since the American ambassador in Moscow was only allowed to enter the Foreign Ministry through its front entrance.[386] I couldn't imagine that any ambassador in Moscow would want to enter the ministry through its basement; I wasn't even sure it had a garage underground with access to elevators.

Haig wrote in his memoir that the new head of the Soviet desk, Bob German, the former political counselor, had suggested turning Dobrynin's limousine back.[387] Like the rest of us, Bob resented the disparity between the hospitality shown Dobrynin and the cold shoulder his American counterparts received.

Yet the disparity couldn't be overcome through gambits like this. Unless Washington sent out ambassadors who knew Russia inside and out, spoke the language, and stayed long enough to gain credibility, I couldn't imagine it would ever disappear.

In early February, my Pol/Int colleagues and I prepared to report on the Communist Party's twenty-sixth Congress. Delegates from all fifteen Soviet republics would receive the Party line for the next five years. Most of the reporting burden would fall on Steve Coffey, who had replaced John Parker the previous summer.

On February 23, the Congress opened in the Kremlin's Palace of Congresses, with Brezhnev delivering the usual numbingly long report. But he was in bad shape; after ten minutes, live television coverage ceased, and a studio announcer read the balance of the speech.

A closed event, the Congress ran for nine days without a break. Like our colleagues at other embassies, we raced about the capital to pick up whatever insights we could garner; however, not much seeped out of the Kremlin or the Central Committee building, and we drew heavily on *Pravda*'s daily reporting. On March 3, 1981, a very ill Brezhnev was unanimously reelected Party general secretary for a successive five-year term.

The department sent out Jack Matlock to be the chargé d'affaires until a new ambassador was appointed. Matlock had served twice before in Moscow and was awaiting confirmation as the next ambassador to Prague.

Matlock's Russian language capability and understanding of the Soviet system were unmatched. However, he was not known for his easy congeniality and would insist that the embassy "pull up its socks," but this is what was needed after Watson's tour.

Matlock would pay special attention to Soviet policy toward Poland. By April, there were twelve Soviet divisions in a state of readiness along the Soviet-Polish border. Would the Kremlin send them in? Fighting was intensifying in Afghanistan, and I couldn't imagine the Kremlin would risk a second front; it couldn't be unmindful of the Poles' readiness to take up arms whatever the odds.

As Matlock wrote later, the embassy "sent several messages every day, relaying every scrap of information . . . bearing on the Soviet attitude toward Poland."[388] He looked mainly to Pol/Ext, one of whose officers, Dale Herspring, knew Polish and had a good contact in the Polish embassy.

Matlock was probably unaware that the White House was already receiving information from a colonel attached to Warsaw's General Staff. David Forden, who was the CIA station chief in Warsaw when I moved to the political section there, had helped develop the operation, which generated thousands of important documents during the crisis.

At an early meeting, Matlock suggested that the embassy needed a redeployment of personnel. After thinking a bit about it, I sent him a memorandum suggesting that a reduction rather than redeployment was needed. The embassy had grown too large, and a leaner and more-focused staff could improve morale and better serve Washington.

By 1981, many at the embassy seemed disconnected from what was going on outside, in Moscow and in the rest of the USSR. Many were involved in pure support functions, including communications, maintenance, construction, and so forth, with no reason to be "connected"; but if fewer officers were assigned to the embassy, perhaps the support staff could be reduced, even with the new embassy project starting.

At one meeting, Matlock suggested that the embassy might be better off dismissing its Soviet employees and replacing them with American graduate students or others with a talent for the language. I don't recall any follow-up discussion, but I couldn't imagine that substituting Americans for Russians would improve the operation, even in terms of security.

The Russians worked within a tight web of constraints woven over many years; if one of them took a step—deliberate or inadvertent—beyond the web, he or she would be removed. We could do our jobs more efficiently and better, I believed, with the Russians around.

Matlock asked Pol/Int to examine the extent to which the two embassies—the American in Moscow and the Soviet in Washington—enjoyed comparable rights and privileges. Was there full reciprocity with regard to each embassy's operations? The answer was of course no, due to the vastly different political and cultural systems in which the two embassies operated.

I asked Don Johnson, who had been trained as a lawyer and succeeded Louis Sell, to undertake the project. Don prepared a lengthy telegram (more than one hundred pages as I recall) detailing all the differences, from major to minor. Among the latter: Soviet diplomats could obtain theater tickets without going through any kind of diplomatic services branch as we were required to do in Moscow, although now and then some of us were able to circumvent the procedure using Russian friends.

Matlock was prescient in seeing that reciprocity would become a major theme for the new administration. In the back of my mind, however, was a concern that those with no experience in the Soviet Union, those driven more by hostility toward the Russians than knowledge of their culture, their system, and how the embassy in Moscow operated would push it to an extreme. A worrisome sign had been the barring of Dobrynin's car. I can't say, however, that I articulated my concern in any official way.

With the swelling of staff, the embassy had become a different place from what it had been in the early 1970s. "The attachment to Russian culture" and the engagement with language and landscape that Beam had found among his officers were no longer much in evidence.

American movies had become a huge distraction. A library of videotape cassettes was now maintained near the commissary in the basement, and every staffer soon owned a videotape player/recorder (VCR). A few apartments in the central wing were wired to receive video broadcasting. Attending a defense attaché's reception just before my assignment ended, I was amazed to find that a central station set up somewhere inside the central wing was beaming movies into Tchaikovsky's apartments.

Frequenting Russian cultural events had once set American officers apart from their colleagues in the diplomatic community. Leslie Stevens, an attaché from 1947 through 1949, described some forty plays, ballets, and concerts he and his wife attended.[389] The head of the embassy's wartime Lend-Lease office let it be known that he had seen thirty-five ballets.[390]

Bohlen, who began his career at Mokhovaya 13 in 1934, surmised that he had seen *Swan Lake* fifty times ("I think I could dance every step").[391]

During and immediately after the war, there had been few other diversions, and theater and concert tickets were easy to come by. Family entertainment mostly revolved around record players, card playing, occasional movies at Spaso House, and sports like cross-country skiing.

In the early 1970s, FSOs were still attending Russian plays, ballets, and movies; but by the end of the decade only a handful did. By then, the Marine Bar had become a popular attraction, especially for the single set and a growing number of students and nannies in the unofficial community. Similar bars and clubs existed at other embassies, including the British, Canadian, and Yugoslav.

Access to the diplomatic bars wasn't well controlled. A Harvard graduate student, in Moscow on an exchange program in 1980, described how she and her American boyfriend helped walk their Russian friend Valeri "passing as an American" by the Soviet guards into the Marine Bar. Valeri, she explained, was "a young man with two lives," a Moscow University philology student in love with the West.[392]

I met a middle-aged Russian during my last assignment who claimed he had been visiting the Marine Bar since 1975. He had just completed two years at a labor camp near Tomsk; he said that his father had been imprisoned for eight years under Stalin. He gave me the names of the marines he knew, and the security office confirmed they were genuine.

I doubt many Russians were able to sneak past the embassy's Soviet guards. However, there were probably a few whom the KGB recruited to go in—Russians living "two lives" of a different sort.

Preparing for departure in June, Liz and Rob's nanny Sarah decided to take advantage of the flea market that the embassy sponsored every spring. Families whose assignments were ending were allowed to sell televisions and electronic equipment (items adapted to 220 volts or 50 cycles), worn-out clothing, and other items they no longer needed. Diplomats from other embassies, mostly from the third world, would flock to the event, sometimes held in Spaso House, sometimes in Uncle Sam's.

Occasionally, sales occurred away from the market; an African diplomat, a Mr. Ba, haunted our Leninsky Prospect entryway in May to make deals with outbound families, and I disposed of an old coat I no longer needed.

The flea market was a relatively small affair in the early 1970s, but it had expanded into a large operation by 1981. A few staffers purchased VCRs and hi-fidelity systems abroad for quick sale at ruble prices. They could convert the rubles into dollars at the embassy at the official exchange rate and reap a profit.

Because it took place on embassy territory, the flea market lay beyond Soviet control. Many of the non-Americans attending would arrive with wads of "soft" rubles obtained outside official channels where the ruble was not pegged to the regime's artificial exchange rate but floated.

The administrative section did its best to control the event, to ensure that no one sold anything above cost, but the scale of activity soon overwhelmed its ability to enforce the rules. An investigative reporter later claimed that "many diplomats made tens of thousands of dollars by selling cars and other expensive items."[393] This seems improbable, even for the period of the middle 1980s which he was describing, yet controls were clearly eroding as the staff and the market grew.

My main concern was to find a buyer for our beat-up Ford. We would be able to recover its purchase price (but nothing more) if we could make a deal with a third-world diplomat on the diplomatic list who had a bundle of unofficial rubles. Just before I sent fliers to other embassies advertising the car, a Soviet truck backed into it while it was parked in Leninsky's courtyard, and I had to round up replacement parts from Helsinki. With the help of workers in the embassy garage, I got it fixed and circulated the ad.

An Iraqi soon showed up with a bag of rubles, but the administrative section couldn't find his name on the diplomatic list and blocked the sale. He then brought an Iraqi friend around who *was* on the list, and my car was sold.

*   *   *

A visiting British bishop, John Drumm, and the Lutheran minister accredited to Moscow presided at the Easter service at Spaso House. Afterwards, Liz and I took Rob and Elise (she was working on Armenian immigration cases in the consular section while on leave from Georgetown) to the Stevens for a luncheon reception. Nina served the traditional Russian Orthodox *kulich* cake. Among their guests were the Japanese and Turkish ambassadors and their spouses. Liz and I then dropped the children off at the apartment and attended a party at the British dacha in Moscow's Silver Woods (*Serebryanny Bor*) area near the river.

It was during the following week that Mila told me about Anya's, relationship with Voznesenski. She had just found out herself. Another language teacher in the embassy had telephoned her at home.

"Have you seen the latest Voznesenski poem in *Literaturnaya gazeta*? Go look at it. I think he's describing Anya. Doesn't she wear a gray tweed cap, one with red and navy blue threads?"

Mila ran out and bought a copy. There it was, a poem entitled "Kepochka," the little cap.

In English it read:

> Your hair is surprisingly long.
> You are not yet a girl friend, but no longer a sister.
> Give me
> Three kilometers
> Of your enchanting time
> From the Arbat up to 2 AM.
>
> You belong to the club of the planet's best women.
> Everything in life has moved.
> There are no limits.
> Between our shoulders blaze beams of light—
> From centimeters up to a thousand years.
>
> Your gray tweed cap—like a roasted pistachio,
> Slightly cracked,
> Like a beak,
> A shell . . .
> The way your life chirps for the distance
> From Dante to Kievski Bridge![394]

Mila knew that Anya had met the poet at the Garrisons' reception. She recalled that on several occasions, a man had called their apartment where Anya was then living without leaving his name. The calls had been puzzling.

Mila was stunned when she read the poem.

When she told me about the tweed cap, I thought of the purse with which Tolstoy identifies his *Anna Karenina*. Fortunately, Anya's affair would end more happily.

*   *   *

In late May 1981, four weeks before the end of my assignment, Liz and the children packed up to precede me to Washington. Shortly before leaving, Rob suffered a scorpion bite on an Anglo-American School outing to Central Asia. He and his classmates were exploring an ancient ruin outside Samarkhand when the insect bit. The hotel where they were staying summoned a doctor who pumped multiple shots of some antidote into him, and Rob was still reeling when he and his class made it back to Moscow.

The Soviets complicated our final weeks. The Foreign Ministry refused to extend Sarah's stay beyond April despite the embassy's representations. She had made too many friends among young Russians, and the authorities wanted her out. Liz accompanied her to Sheremetyevo to be sure there were no last-minute hitches.

The authorities also obstructed the clearance of our effects for shipment home. There had been some incident at Dulles Airport involving U.S. customs, the FBI, and an Aeroflot plane; and we surmised that the Soviets were retaliating.

On May 14, a few staff members received threatening phone calls related to the incident. Anti-American placards were glued to the windshields of several cars parked in front of Tchaikovsky 19. Our effects were already packed in a van sent from West Germany, but Soviet customs refused to clear them without further inspection. I never found out whether the incident at Dulles was connected with the administration's fixation on reciprocity, but this was "a card" the Soviets too could play.

The shipment was ultimately cleared. When it was unpacked in Washington, however, all the silver from our wedding was missing. The embassy told us that two other staff members had also lost their silver in shipments home; ours was never recovered, and insurance covered but a fraction of the loss.

I stayed behind for an additional three weeks to ensure coverage in the political section during the turnover of its officers. I spent a few sunny hours crouched on our balcony, pad of paper in hand, composing a tale for children set in the Kremlin.

None of the balconies would meet an American code, and an East European diplomat had fallen to his death off one of them a few weeks before. They were a bit more than three feet wide with a low iron railing, yet a sturdy girder exposed in the crumbling floor of ours assured me it was safe.

I was just getting into the story when a Kabul-like incident was reported at another embassy. The department asked me to deal with an eighteen-year-old soldier who had wandered onto the grounds of the American embassy in Prague and was refusing to leave. So on May 26, 1981, I paid my first visit to the Czech capital since staying at the Alcron sixteen years before.

*   *   *

The embassy in Prague occupies a beautiful seventeenth-century building, the Schoenborn Palace, which the United States acquired in 1925. It contains more than one hundred rooms; for a few months in 1917, Franz Kafka had lived in two of them. Behind the palace is a seven-acre grassy courtyard.

George Kennan had served at the embassy on the eve of World War II. He recounts how he was forced by American policy to expel two German Social Democrats and a Jewish acquaintance when they sought asylum as

German troops were marching in.[395] Fortunately, Washington's policy on asylum had since become more enlightened.

For me, it would be the same drill as in Kabul: If the soldier wanted asylum, we would not force him out; if he wanted to talk with his countrymen, we would organize a meeting with the Soviet embassy.

I began a series of meetings with the soldier, Private Anishchenko by name. He was from a small town south of Moscow. His father was a coal miner, his mother a metallurgical worker. His parents were divorced, and he had no brothers or sisters. He had failed admission to two institutes after finishing elementary school, and then had been conscripted. He was serving in Czechoslovakia as a telegraph operator.

He said there were difficulties in his unit ("mutual bad relations") and there had been some hazing, but from his description I could tell it didn't compare with what Kruglov had described.

It didn't take me long to determine that Anishchenko was but one part of the problem.

The embassy itself was in disarray. Matlock hadn't arrived (he was still in Moscow), and the FSO in charge seemed at a loss. He complained that the Americans on his staff, who numbered about twenty, had conflicting opinions about the soldier. The marine guards considered him a deserter and wanted nothing to do with a deserter, even from the other side. On the other hand, a young woman from P&C felt sorry for him and had already arranged guitar lessons and a guitar. She had also installed a television set in the room in which he was living. Her colleagues speculated she was becoming emotionally involved.

Further, the communications unit closed down promptly at 7:00 PM, whether or not there was a telegram waiting to be sent, and whether or not the front office liked it.

Wringing his hands, the officer spoke of a generation gap. The fact that almost every American at the embassy was scheduled to leave Prague for a new assignment compounded his problems.

After several days of conversation, it was clear that Anishchenko had no ideological convictions. While on leave from a Soviet base outside Prague, he had simply decided he wanted to meet a foreigner. When he saw the American flag flying over a building, he wandered into that building's backyard. It turned out to be the American embassy, separated from Czech territory by an easily scalable wall.

He told me that he was ready to meet with Soviet officials but wouldn't say what he'd decide.

We organized a confrontation meeting on June 5, and three officers from the Soviet embassy appeared: Zhuravlev, the political counselor (who spoke passable English); Zamyatin, an attaché; and Yegorov, a "consular officer." Yegorov's face was scarred, and his left hand was mangled; if he wasn't KGB, he at least looked the part.

We hadn't met with the Soviets in advance as we had in Kabul, and this proved to be a mistake. We explained the rules as soon as they arrived, but they still began badly. Yegorov exuded hostility from the moment he opened his mouth, and he did most of the talking. He told the soldier that thanks to his thoughtlessness, his mother had suffered a heart attack. He played a tape of the mother's voice, and then described for the soldier various offenses of which he was guilty.

The Soviets seemed to be mounting a trial; Kafka would have understood.

We called a halt to the meeting; the point was not to heap on blame on Anishchenko but to explain what choices he had and the consequences of each. The meeting resumed and became more workmanlike, and the Soviets offered the guarantees that Tabeyev had provided in Kabul. After about two hours of back and forth, Anishchenko decided to leave with his countrymen.

In January 2005, fourteen years later, I was reminded of the Prague incident when I read an article in the *National Review* describing the earlier incident in Kabul "as a symbol of the cluelessness and impotence of the Carter administration" because "astoundingly . . . , nine months into the Soviet occupation . . . there was no one at the embassy who could understand Russian."[396]

But why single out the Kabul incident, I said to myself, when there was one that came right on its heels in Prague!

Soviet forces had been occupying Czechoslovakia for much longer than nine months, indeed, from their invasion in 1968, yet there was also no one in Prague who knew Russian.

The Prague incident had occurred five months after the Reagan administration was inaugurated. Shouldn't it be faulted too for failing to have a Russian speaker in a country with a significant Soviet military presence?

The difference between the two incidents was that Reagan's people covered up "their" oversight, and the *National Review* writer, giving him the benefit of the doubt, had never heard of it. Fearing the kind of criticism that had been meted out to Carter during the 1980 election campaign, Haig had slapped a secret label on everything having to do with the second soldier.[397]

Of course, the real secret lay elsewhere; by the late 1970s, the State Department and the Foreign Service had largely lost interest in training and developing Russian-speaking FSOs, and there weren't many around who could have been assigned to Kabul or Prague. It's fortunate that the Cold War ended when it did, for this reason and, of course, for many, many others.

11

New York, Athens, A Career's Twists and Turns

Shortly before I was summoned to Prague, I received an appointment to the Council on Foreign Relations for 1981-82.

The council is a private institution in the heart of Manhattan, occupying adjoining town houses on the Upper East Side. From the 1920s to the present, it has been bringing officials, businesspersons, journalists, lawyers, and scholars together for daylong, weeklong, and even yearlong seminars having to do with foreign affairs. I was the eighth State Department officer to be appointed a "senior fellow" under a program that the council had inaugurated in 1974.

Elihu Root, Hamilton Fish Armstrong, W. Averell Harriman, and Allen Dulles are among those who shaped the council's early history. Dulles had gone directly from its presidency to the number two position at the CIA, from which he became director. The Council's patrician origins find ample reflection in the oil portraits, leather upholstery, and dark paneling that mark its library and meeting rooms.

Almost two thousand persons were regular or honorary members at the time I was appointed. Many of them, along with most of the council's in-house scholars, had spent time in government, often in important positions. Seventy percent of them came from the Boston-New York-Washington corridor. Winston Lord, a former aide to Kissinger at the NSC and the State Department, was the council's president, David Rockefeller the chairman of its board.

I recognized that the council was a prestigious place, but the assignment left me far from excited. I hadn't sought another year "off-line," but wanted my own post, perhaps a consulate in Eastern Europe. I had asked for Zagreb, Yugoslavia. The personnel officer responsible for assignments at my level took it for himself, however, and apparently no other post suiting my background was available.

In back of my mind was a concern that an association with the council while Reagan and his fellow Californians were consolidating power might not be the wisest move. Vice President George H.W. Bush, on the council's board from 1977 to 1979, had pointedly resigned his council membership after entering the presidential race. Bush "was about as eastern establishment as an American can be without being named Adams"[398] (or one might say, Cabot or Lowell), yet he had positioned himself as a Texan, as far from New York as plausibly possibly, to improve his electoral chances.

My two degrees from Ivy League schools had already raised an eyebrow. In 1968, a department personnel officer had warned me *not* to try to substitute Columbia for Indiana University for my midcareer training; my education, he said, already made me seem "too Eastern."

At the time of my appointment, the council was trying to shed its reputation as a bastion of Northeasterners. Lord and his people were holding conferences elsewhere in the country and were selecting new members from locations far from the East as old members departed. But "rebranding" a storied institution can take years, especially if the size of its membership is fixed and almost everyone is appointed for life, as the council's charter provided.

I had been promoted in September 1980 as I entered the final year of my second Moscow assignment. Earlier in the year, Secretary Vance had overseen the introduction of a new promotion system under the Foreign Service Act of 1980, replacing the system that had come into effect in 1946 when the Congress modernized the Rogers Act. The new system provided that those who wanted to serve in the service's senior-most ranks would have "a window" of six years in which to apply. The conundrum was that, by *not* applying, an FSO would not attain the highest ranks but would be assured of longevity in his or her career, perhaps into his or her sixties.

Instead of waiting a few years as was permitted, I had jumped right in, or—as the parlance of the day put it—"opened my window immediately." Even if the new law was designed, as some suspected, to "hasten the [the Foreign Service's] transformation" from the "white, male Foreign Service"[399] which Vance had set as his goal, I didn't anticipate a problem. The Foreign Service's director general had assured everyone that there would be a "regular and predictable flow upward through the ranks and into the senior Foreign Service."[400] If I had to wait more than six years for a promotion, then it would be best to embark on a second career anyway, and I'd have a modest pension with which to begin.

The new system was cleverly designed; the department could argue that an FSO, by choosing or not choosing to apply for admission to the senior ranks, assumed "ownership" for the duration *and* nature of his or her career.

When the telegram confirming the senior fellowship arrived in Moscow, Jack Matlock, still the acting head, encouraged me to take it. He told me that the council's president personally reviewed each nomination before making a selection. Moreover, the council had turned out to be a "fast track" for some. Without further ado, I accepted the appointment, packed my suitcase, and caught up with my family on leave in Illinois.

While at my parents' farm, I received a surprising call from personnel. Would I rather go to Reykjavik, Iceland, as the embassy's deputy chief of mission instead? The man who had just been named ambassador, Marshall Brement, had put forth my name. I recalled that I had met Brement once, when he was passing through Moscow while serving on Brzezinski's staff at the NSC.

My first reaction was, would it be fair to drag Liz to Iceland after three years in arctic-like Moscow?

Twenty years before, just after we reached Washington, she had surprised me with a caricature she had drawn of the State Department, the FSI, and a hypothetical embassy, portraying me as the "diplomat" (written in Cyrillic letters no less) traipsing among the three buildings with an oversized briefcase. Emblazoned along the top edge were the names of three world capitals—Rome, Paris, and London; along the left edge, eight other capitals including Warsaw, Moscow, and Athens; and along the right edge, twelve others including New Delhi.

Mulling over personnel's proposal, I didn't think I could ask her to go to Iceland, especially after almost ten years in northern Europe, though she would have gone had I asked.

I was concerned about chemistry too. Brement was considered a hard-liner, which by itself didn't bother me (I had enjoyed working with Toon); but he had struck me also as a bit bombastic when we met, someone for whom bashing the Russians was a kind of sport, and this had left me cold. Perhaps I misread him, but I told personnel I'd stick with New York.

I didn't fully understand at the time that administrators were not only streamlining the Foreign Service's upper ranks but were also re-engineering its members' skills.

They had come to the conclusion that "there are too many foreign policy experts but not enough officials with managerial experience." As a result, FSOs aspiring to join the service's senior ranks would soon be "desperate to show" managerial experience. "Instead of jumping at the opportunity to serve overseas for three years in a post like Manila or Moscow, these officers are seeking assignments as deputy chiefs of mission in smaller, less exciting posts, so that they can have it noted on their personnel files that they have 'managerial experience.'"

That was how the *New York Times* analyzed the situation in 1986 (in an article entitled "Of Retirement, Morale and the Senior Diplomats"[401]) when the Foreign Service's upper ranks were beginning to change their character due to the new criteria. Had I been roaming the department's corridors in 1981, I might have understood what was happening and seized the opportunity personnel offered; in hindsight, Reykjavik would have been the perfect post.

Liz and I reestablished residence in Maryland at summer's end. I planned to commute, spending weekdays in New York and weekends with the family. Thanks to Peter Semler—Moscow's economic counselor—and his daughter's Russian connections, I was able to find a furnished room in the apartment of an émigré, Xenia Schidlovsky, on Ninety-fifth Street off Madison Avenue. I learned later that Mrs. Schidlovsky, a widow, was related to the wife of Serge Schmemann, the *Times*'s correspondent whom I knew from Moscow.

With Elise and Abby at college and Rob in boarding school (in anticipation of our plan to go overseas as soon as possible), it would not be an easy year. The department provided only a modest stipend: $50 per day for my first twenty-one days in Manhattan, $25 for the succeeding ninety-nine days, and $12.50 for the balance of the assignment.

Liz joined me for my first visit to the council. Within minutes of entering its main town house on the corner of Sixty-eighth Street and Park Avenue, I received a surprise—Paul Kreisberg would oversee my program.

With the change from a Democratic to a Republican administration, Paul was leaving the department's policy planning staff—where he had been the deputy—for a sabbatical as head of the council's studies program. Reagan's secretary of state, Alexander Haig, had installed Paul Wolfowitz (of later notoriety as an architect of the second Iraq war, as George W. Bush's deputy secretary of defense) to be his director of planning. Kreisberg had leapt at the opportunity to have his own sabbatical.

It had taken two strongly positive evaluations to get me back on track after India, in part because Paul's background and mine had been so disparate. I was from small-town America, most recently the Midwest, while Paul was thoroughly urban, 100 percent New Yorker. He had graduated from Bronx High School of Science just after turning seventeen in 1946.

His school had been founded eight years earlier, in 1938, but it was already one of the country's best. New England boarding schools with histories often going back a century or more would crave having one Nobel Prize winner among their alumni; by 2006, Bronx Science had six.

Paul had earned his bachelor's degree from the City College of New York and a master's from Columbia. After joining the department in 1952, he had studied Chinese and served mostly in Asia. Virtually all the social barriers that afflicted the old Foreign Service had disappeared by the start of the Cold War; and Paul, hardworking as he was, moved rapidly to the top of the career.

Pondering the background of Leonard Woolf—Virginia's husband—Harold Nicolson once reflected on the British Foreign Office's deep-seated prejudice against Jewish applicants. After all, he wrote, they "are far more interested in international life than Englishmen."[402] To its credit, the American Foreign Service acknowledged this fact long before its European counterparts.

The senior scholar at the council specializing in Soviet affairs was Bob Legvold. Bob was also associated with Columbia's Harriman Institute, the Russian studies institute to which Shulman, after serving as Vance's advisor, had returned as director. Paul would supervise me, but Bob would be my academic advisor.

I decided to pursue two projects: a study of decision-making in and around the Kremlin, based in part on what I had seen and learned in Moscow, and a book-length story—the one I had begun on the balcony—to help young Americans understand what life in the USSR was really like. I also planned to take advantage of the council's discussion groups and seminars, not all of which were fixated on Soviet and Communist affairs, as the new administration in Washington appeared to be.

*   *   *

My weekdays revolved around the council's programs, my own research and writing from an office overlooking Park Avenue, and my daily "commute" by foot between Sixty-eighth and Ninety-fifth Streets along Madison Avenue. As the *Times*'s architectural critic wrote at the time, Madison Avenue, with its "boutiques and bakeries, drugstores and chocolatiers, restaurants and coffee shops, fine food and wine stores and omnipresent Gristede's, antique shops and art galleries, delis, and designers," is one of the world's urban delights.[403] It wasn't long before I was under its spell, and the images of dingy store fronts, begrimed windows, and empty shelves I carried with me from Moscow had disappeared.

Few Russians, other than my landlady, crossed my path. I recall one meeting, probably a lunch, with a Soviet official, a diplomat assigned to the Soviet Mission to the United Nations. An FBI agent was sufficiently intrigued that he asked whether he could see me to find out what had transpired. The agent was low-key, but his curiosity brought to mind how the KGB would pursue any Russian who dared speak with an American. When I told Bob Legvold about the request, he reminded me that I was free to say no, but I saw little point in not sharing an innocuous exchange.

In December 1981, four months into my appointment, the Communist regime in Poland—finally yielding to Moscow's relentless pressure—imposed martial law. Reagan, in turn, announced a series of retaliatory measures against the Soviet Union, including the suspension of Aeroflot flights and U.S. licenses for the export of oil and gas equipment, including pipe-laying machines that would assist it in extending a pipeline into energy-starved Western Europe.

The council quickly pulled together a "Polish crisis" group. Brzezinski, a longtime council member back at Columbia, told participants that the United States might be witnessing the reigniting of the Cold War. In fact, the Cold War had already reignited with the Soviet invasion of Afghanistan and the countermeasures that Brzezinski had helped design. Among those who participated were Madeleine Albright, another émigré from Europe whom Brzezinski had brought into the NSC (and who would be secretary of state during the Clinton administration); Sonnenfeldt, Kissinger's one-time aide; and Scowcroft, Ford's NSC advisor. I don't recall that Vance and Shulman participated in any council discussions during the year, though both were members.

The council takes great pride in its nonpartisanship, yet provides a platform for almost any guest should a group of like-minded members ask. Jonas Savimbi, the founder and leader of UNITA, the Portuguese acronym for National Union for the Total Independence of Angola, had been waging an armed insurgency against the government of Angola since 1975, when Portugal had given the colony its independence. Savimbi had been educated in Protestant and Catholic mission schools and had then gone off to Portugal and Switzerland to pursue medical studies. He claimed to have earned an MD although it was never confirmed; still, as a British correspondent observed, "it was always wise to address him as 'Doctor.'"[404]

Because the Angolan regime based in Luanda was receiving military assistance from Cuba and professed to be Marxist-Leninist, council members associated with the Reagan administration identified with the guerrilla operations that Savimbi was conducting. He had delivered a talk at the council two years before, on November 5, 1979, the year before Reagan's election; in its report summarizing that year's activities, the council had euphemistically described the insurgent as a member of Angola's "opposition front."[405] Reagan's supporters, finding him charismatic and worthy of support, asked that he be invited back.

Because African issues had played such havoc with détente and seemed to have preoccupied Brzezinski even more than Kissinger, I decided to attend the luncheon arranged in Savimbi's honor, scheduled for December 11, after he returned from meeting in Washington with officials in the new administration.

Savimbi arrived at the town house with a small entourage. He was stocky and full-bearded, someone who appeared capable of sustaining an insurgency in the African bush. He was conducted to one of the council's round tables (bedecked, as always, with fine linen) to sit, as I recall, with Congressman Jack Kemp from upstate New York, a fervent supporter. I recall thinking that Savimbi, dressed in combat fatigues, was probably as incongruous a figure to grace an East Side town house since Leonard Bernstein had hosted the Black Panthers.

Kissinger had justified the Global Outlook Program in terms of the "failure" of the department's Africa hands to embrace Savimbi. FSOs who were making careers on the continent believed that the Angolan government had only turned to Cuba because of armed attacks against it from Savimbi's forces and those of apartheid South Africa, not because of any meaningful commitment to Marxism-Leninism. The Africa hands believed that Washington should address Africa's political and economic ills in the context of the continent's colonial and tribal history, instead of attaching significance to every move made in the region by Moscow or Havana.

When Kissinger was in charge, he had approved a CIA program of covert assistance to Savimbi. He knew that his backing for the program would precipitate the resignation of the top Foreign Service officer in the Bureau of African affairs (AF), Ambassador Nathaniel Davis. As Kissinger told President Ford in July 1975, "we'll have a resignation from Davis, then I'll clean out the AF bureau."[406] Davis was not unsophisticated about the Soviet Union. He had served in Moscow and had been President Johnson's advisor on Soviet affairs; but Kissinger wouldn't brook any nay-saying, and in four months Davis was out of the job. Kissinger had dismissed Davis's predecessor—Ambassador Donald Easum, another FSO—after nine months for essentially the same reason.[407]

But Kissinger had less success with the Congress. In late 1975, it banned granting assistance, covert or otherwise, to Savimbi and his insurgents.

Brzezinski decided to circumvent Capitol Hill. Visiting the People's Republic of China, the visit that Vance had opposed, he urged the Chinese to support Savimbi because his own government couldn't. (If the Chinese ever provided support, it didn't amount to much.)

When the Cubans then showed up in Ethiopia, Brzezinski urged that the Joint Chiefs of Staff deploy a U.S. Navy carrier task force off the Horn of Africa. Because Vance, Defense Secretary Brown, and the Joint Chiefs disagreed, this suggestion went nowhere.

I don't recall Savimbi's comments at the luncheon (the council forbade quoting outside speakers unless they issued a text, and note-taking wouldn't have been seemly); but with Reagan in the White House, his hopes were running high. They would be fulfilled only in part, however, and at that, mostly ceremonially; he would receive red-carpet treatment at the White House (Reagan considered him "a freedom fighter") and at the Departments of State and Defense.[408]

Dobrynin writes in his memoir that the Cubans were, in fact, operating on their own when they established themselves in Angola. The Foreign Ministry "had nothing to do with our initial involvement," but the ideologues in the International Department of the Communist Party—the "morally righteous" ones Dobrynin calls them—warmed to the idea of embarrassing the West, and arranged support for Cuba's policy.[409]

Kissinger acknowledges in his memoir that Dobrynin is right, although "at the time we thought he [Castro] was operating as a Soviet surrogate."[410]

Dobrynin expresses revulsion "at the amount of energy and effort spent almost entirely in vain by Moscow and Washington on these so-called African affairs. Twenty years later no one (except historians) could as much as remember them."[411]

I haven't seen a comparable acknowledgment from Kissinger.

Carter's Vance and Reagan's Shultz, like the Foreign Service's Africa hands, believed that the best way to blunt Soviet influence and achieve the removal of Cubans from the continent was to focus on the conflicts that had drawn them in. Vance wasn't able to make much headway because of Brzezinski, but Shultz succeeded. His memoir gives a lively account of the resistance he encountered along the way—from the CIA, from "right-wing fringes of the [Reagan] administration and Congress," and from "right-wing staffers from Congress" and South African lobbyists. Shultz describes "a stinging set-to" with Congressman Kemp in Reagan's presence and notes that Kemp "called for my resignation because I opposed open assistance to Savimbi."[412]

Washington established full diplomatic relations with the Angolan government in 1993, but Savimbi, undaunted, fought on.[413] Rumors of cannibalism committed by his forces spread as many more thousands died. The twenty-seven-year war, which perhaps cost the lives of a half million Angolans, finally ended with Savimbi's death in a hail of bullets in 2002. By then, even the most "morally righteous" of his supporters, presumably including those belonging to the council, had come to understand that he was more psychotic than charismatic.

Looking back, what is amazing is for how long Savimbi held his American supporters in thrall. For some reason he "had the power to charm or frighten rudimentary souls into an aggravated witch-dance in his honor," to borrow Conrad's description of Kurtz who also shed a lot of African blood, albeit only in a novel.[414]

It would be my and Liz's lot to live alongside Angolans—those against whom Kissinger and Brzezinski had fought—during our last assignment in Moscow.

*   *   *

As my main project at the council, I prepared a report on the Kremlin, the seventy-acre fortress from which Soviet leaders ruled after they left Petrograd (Leningrad) in March 1918. "Who rules the Kremlin rules Russia," the Russian people had always said; and it was the Bolsheviks who honored the aphorism by abandoning Peter's capital.

Something that Kissinger had written about his years in the White House encouraged me to undertake the project: "Propinquity counts for much; the opportunity to confer with the President several times a day is often of decisive importance."[415]

Alexander Haig, Reagan's first secretary of state, would later describe his frustration at not being able to gain "direct, regular access" to Reagan from the seventh-floor in Foggy Bottom.

"No route at all had been pointed out to me, no arrangement made for regular contact." He saw himself as "mortally handicapped" by a lack of direct access to the Oval Office.[416]

It made sense to look at the Kremlin's working areas to determine whether and how "propinquity" counted there, whether one could learn something about the importance and role of individual Party and government leaders by the location of the offices from which they ruled.

Of course, Soviet leaders deliberately shrouded their workplaces in secrecy. Access to the Kremlin's nontourist area was strictly limited and controlled. It was not until the third edition of the *Large Soviet Encyclopedia* and the publication of its *K* volume in 1973 that these buildings were even shown, and then graphically, not photographically. I remembered how alarmed the Soviet handlers of Congressman Brademas had been when, in 1979, he abruptly pulled a camera out of his overcoat and began snapping photographs as we walked away from the Council of Ministers building.

I had many notes from meetings in the Kremlin by the time I reached the council. Just before leaving Moscow, I had added to them, spending an hour or two observing officials pass in and out of the fortress's pedestrian entrances, at its Spassky, Borovitsky and Troitsky Towers; I was probably observed in turn, though I was never challenged.

Vladimir Nabokov's *Lectures on Russian Literature* had just come out, and I seized on one of his ideas too. Nabokov noted that Dostoyevsky placed readers at a disadvantage by failing to provide physical descriptions of the landscapes and personalities dotting his fiction.[417]

By the same token, those practicing Kremlinology, especially American scholars, lacked an understanding of the Kremlin's layout and other attributes, or neglected to take them into account. Their readers too were disadvantaged.

As I was writing, the leadership in Moscow was changing. In November 1981, Brezhnev died, and Andropov succeeded him as general secretary, only to survive until February 1984 when Chernenko succeeded him.

My article contained some sociology about decision-making in large organizations, including the idea that the optimum group size for face-to-face contact is between two and seven persons. When a leadership circle expands beyond this, it is difficult to sustain mutual contact, and the group has a tendency to fracture. Reports about Stalin's practice of ruling through groups of five to nine colleagues, exclusive of the Party's formally constituted bodies, lent support to the idea, as have revelations about the small number in Brezhnev's Politburo (five of a total of thirteen full members), who actually decided on the invasion of Afghanistan.

I developed enough interesting material that *Orbis*, a journal sponsored by the Foreign Policy Research Institute in Philadelphia, published it in 1983.[418] Included is a graphic showing the Kremlin's work areas. Possibly with an eye to setting a story inside the fortress, the spy novelist Charles McCarry asked for a copy, but I don't believe he ever wrote the story.

With Gorbachev's arrival, the Kremlin became a less forbidding place, and my article less a tool for analysis. Still, the White House's secret service agents relied on it during a visit with which I was involved in 1985; and embassy officers told me in 2004 that the Kremlin, under Putin, was becoming as opaque as it had been during Soviet times.

My attempt to publish a children's story set in the Kremlin failed. If Russia reverts wholly to Soviet ways, perhaps I'll try again.

*   *   *

I visited the department to determine what onward assignments might be available after New York, but Reagan's ambassadorial appointees had already selected their deputies, and there were no openings in the Soviet Union or Eastern Europe for which I would be a logical candidate.

However, a three-year assignment as chief of the political-military (Pol-Mil) section in Athens would be available in a year. Liz and I had

ROBERT F. OBER, JR.

visited Athens on a weekend excursion from Moscow and had liked what we saw.

Until the 1960s, the curriculums at the best American high schools reflected Britain's nineteenth-century fascination with the classical world. Kent School had required the study of Latin and "ancient history" for first-year pupils and had taught Latin and Greek as electives in its upper-class curriculum. I had gone no further than Cicero in my second year, but something had sunk in, and I was drawn to the idea of serving at least once in southern Europe. I also believed that a stint doing political-military work would help my career.

Greece had been caught up in a fierce civil war at the start of the Cold War, pitting its native Communists against a pro-Western royalist government. With Great Britain nearly prostrate and unable to defend its interests in the eastern Mediterranean, President Truman committed the United States, in the doctrine that bears his name, to preventing a Communist takeover of both Greece and Turkey. In 1952, not long after the Greek Communists were defeated, a pro-Western government brought Greece into the North Atlantic Treaty Organization.

The American military maintained facilities on the Greek mainland and on the island of Crete, which provided a homeport for the navy's Sixth Fleet. Some of the facilities supported communications, surveillance, and intelligence-gathering activities; others included storage depots for conventional and nuclear weapons. The main U.S. Air Force base was at Hellenikon next to Athens's international airport.

I had not served in the military but had enjoyed working with its attachés. As chief of Pol-Mil, I would be the principal point of contact for some twelve defense department bases and detachments as well as the commands outside Greece to which they reported. I would also be dealing with the Greek Ministries of Foreign Affairs and Defense in assuring the smooth operation of the bases and the implementation of the bilateral Defense and Economic Cooperation Agreement (DECA), the so-called bases agreement then being renegotiated.

I had no doubt I would find Greece's Orthodox Christian culture congenial. After all, it had been two Greek monks—Cyril and Methodius—who had given Russia its alphabet. Modern Greek, however, would be a challenge. I am not a natural linguist nor was I growing younger, yet personnel insisted that the head of Pol-Mil be language qualified, even though everyone knew the officials with whom the incumbent would deal spoke adequate English.

It would require ten months of study to acquire the level of Greek I was told I needed. As my assignment in New York was nearing an end, I could see only one other possibility—take a job in Washington pending the availability of another position abroad. But the idea of working in the bureaucracy even for a short period had never appealed to me. Jack Matlock, when invited to leave Prague and join the NSC in 1983, had reacted the way I would have had a Washington assignment been suggested: "I like to work in embassies, and like to deal with other countries. That's why I joined the foreign service."

So I applied for the Athens position. The embassy probably had its own Greek-speaking area specialist in mind for the job, but if the department wanted FSOs to move out of their areas of expertise, to move from area to area like Bohlen's "water bug," then it would be difficult to dismiss a bid from someone like myself with nary a day of Mediterranean experience under his belt.

Personnel gave me the assignment, and I embarked upon studying my third language at the FSI. It turned out to be a dreary slog, alleviated only by the companionship of classmates, including a fighter pilot bound for the embassy's defense attaché office and a Japanese-language speaker who would end up in the embassy's political section.

A few months into the program, I received a copy of the evaluation of my performance in Manhattan. Paul had prepared it over Winston Lord's signature. While it did no harm, it was not calculated to win a promotion; but an evaluation based on a sabbatical away from the Foreign Service rarely would.

*   *   *

Liz and I reached Athens in June 1983. We were temporarily lodged in a small furnished apartment next to the embassy. Liz spent the first weeks searching for permanent housing and arranging a school for Rob, now fifteen.

She soon found a house in a northern suburb, Palio Psychico, a few blocks from a bus line serving the embassy area. After a year coping with persistent plumbing and electrical problems, we were offered an American-leased residence closer to the embassy, and it turned out to be the best housing we had up to that point in my career.

We grew fond of several families in the neighborhood, spending leisurely evenings with a young banker Manthos Anagnostou with whom I rode a bus to work and Costas Filippas, the editor of "Hearth" (*Estia*), a conservative newspaper. I also became friendly with a Greek army general stationed in the prime minister's office and responsible for U.S. bases issues.

While dining *alfresco* at private homes, or at downtown restaurants, or on Greek islands with the sun hovering above the horizon, Liz and I came to understand why colleagues had made a specialty of serving in countries on the Mediterranean rim. How sweet it would have been, I must have mused, had I discovered the writings of Seferis and Cavafys before those of Pasternak and chosen assignments accordingly.

But it did not take me long to see that Athens, by itself, was not the place I had imagined it to be:

> Today, Athens is a small and frugal city surrounded by barren hills, with a second-rate port, Piraeus, ten miles away. Its physical monuments and buildings on a central hill in the city—the Acropolis—are now closed to tourists, so decayed are the structures, above all the great Parthenon. No one today thinks of Athens as an important, or wealthy, or beautiful city.[419]

Norman Cantor, a teacher of mine at Princeton, wrote these words a few years ago when contemplating classical Greece's gift to the West. There is no connection, he affirmed, between the Athens of today and the Athens of one's schooling, the Athens of 400 BC.

Greece's capital is choked with traffic. Except on weekends, a purplish cloud of pollution hangs over the downtown area, above its classical ruins and above the embassy.

Walter Gropius, the Bauhaus architect who emigrated from Germany to New York, had designed the embassy (officially, the chancery) with the Parthenon in mind.[420] It is a two-story building with walls of glass and a colonnade of marble piers. When it opened in 1961, Gropius probably envisioned its interior courtyard as a kind of *agora*, an area where Americans and Greeks could mingle freely, perhaps sharing lunch over a bottle of *retsina* wine.

But it didn't turn out this way. Greece has been prone to violence, and terrorism against Americans has been a problem. The embassy now sits sequestered behind a high steel fence. Its front entrances are usually closed—back and side doors provide access—and its interior courtyard is inaccessible. Cipher locks inside the building keep Greeks and Americans apart. In one of her first letters home, Liz wrote that it took her ten minutes to get into the embassy: "It is sort of like Sing-Sing prison."

Security was tight for good reason.

In 1967, Greek military officers seized control of the government and, because of Greece's strategic importance, Washington felt it had no choice but to recognize and deal with them. However, when democratic forces returned to power in 1974 amid a crisis with Turkey over Cyprus, anti-American feelings, mostly dormant since the civil war, surged to the fore. They found one outlet in a terrorist movement called "November

17," the date coming from a student demonstration in 1973 that the Greek military had bloodily suppressed.

When we arrived, Andreas Papandreou was ruling the country through the Panhellenic Socialist Movement (PASOK). Papandreou had spent most of the 1960s at the University of California, Berkeley and had observed, if not relished, the tumultuous protests and marches against the war in Vietnam. As prime minister, he freely criticized U.S. and Western policy. When the Soviets shot down the Korean airliner in August 1983, killing 269 passengers and crew, he initially gave credence to Moscow's accusation that it had been on a spy mission and had his foreign minister block the European community's attempt to condemn the shootdown.[421] Whenever it suited his purposes, he tapped into the anti-Americanism that was also animating "November 17."

The terrorist group had shed its first American blood by assassinating the embassy's CIA station chief in 1975. Assassinations of other foreign nationals and pro-Western politicians followed.

Six months after we arrived, "November 17" killed a navy attaché at the embassy, Captain George Tsantes. Two men on a motor scooter, traveling the main thoroughfare that passes by the embassy, raced up behind George's car, and the man on the pillion let loose the shots. "November 17" had used the same *modus operandi* and the same revolver in assassinating others. A letter mailed to Athens newspapers explained that the killing was to protest the Greek government's renewal of the bases agreement.

I had been in frequent contact with George, who left behind a widow and two children. The killing shocked us all.

Not long thereafter, another American was targeted and wounded, a sergeant at one of the bases. Again, a scooter was used. The fact that the Greek authorities seemed incapable of ending the violence after almost a decade added to the anger most of us felt.

Although I was in charge of the office responsible for the bases agreement, I was not a likely target, being a civilian and not from the CIA. Besides, to and from work I rode a crowded bus where it would be difficult for the group to carry out the kind of "clean" killing for which it was known. Still, the embassy suggested I wear body armor, and gave me a bulletproof vest.

Carrying it home in my briefcase, I tried it on, intending to wear it under my jacket, but its bulk made me look ridiculous. I was sure that no right-minded driver would let me board his bus.

I did wear it once in the privacy of our home to show to David and Anthea Madden, a couple at the British embassy whom we knew from Moscow. They joined Liz in laughing at the figure I cut. The four of us agreed that it wouldn't do.

A decade later, the Maddens returned to Athens, David as Her Majesty's ambassador. In 2000, "November 17," using the same *modus operandi* and the same .45 caliber pistol with which it had begun its rampage, assassinated David's senior military attaché, for its victim number 23.

I returned the vest to the embassy, and it gave me instead a quarter-inch steel plate, something that I could install in my briefcase, the theory being that I could duck behind the briefcase as soon as the firing began.

Taking a more practical approach, my brother sent me a set of license plates from Illinois with which I replaced the Greek diplomatic plates that advertised us as American; at least, Liz and I would have some peace of mind when driving.

Our ambassador was Monteagle Stearns, a sixty-one-year old career diplomat who knew the eastern Mediterranean region from previous assignments, including in Greece and Turkey. Monty had a good personal relationship with Papandreou and was able to put his more outrageous behavior in context, helping Washington make sense of Greece's convoluted politics.

Stearns would acknowledge privately that the Greek leader was a challenge. More than once I heard him say to American generals (with whom he, as a former marine, had credibility), "You can't fly on automatic pilot with Papandreou, but must constantly be on alert, as if flying a helicopter."

After retiring from the Foreign Service, Stearns elaborated his philosophy about dealing with populist leaders like Papandreou: "Diplomacy . . . cannot await the appearance of ideal leaders operating in the most propitious of political climates. It must work with conditions as they are."[422]

As ambassador from 1991 to 1995, Stearns dealt with Papandreou *as he was,* not as we wanted him to be. His *sangfroid* was so marked that a book he later published (under the auspices of the Council on Foreign Relations) about our two allies in the eastern Mediterranean refers not once to "November 17" or its assassinations. Perhaps professionals specializing in the Mediterranean area are inured to this kind of violence.

There were frequent demonstrations against the embassy and the military bases, especially the base at Hellenikon. The day after the new bases agreement was signed, tens of thousands of protestors descended upon the embassy, opposite the temporary quarters where we were then living.

There had been eighteen strikes at the different U.S. bases during the two years before we arrived. A year into my assignment, Greek workers at Hellenikon blocked its gates to the American military personnel working there. The workers claimed that the American officers in charge had failed to fulfill promises for more pay and shorter work-weeks agreed to during an earlier strike. Actually, the "promises" had come from the Greek government claiming to speak for the Americans and desiring to entice the workers back to work to avoid another angry reaction from Washington.

I enjoyed working with the Greek officers, especially with General Nikolas Andrikos in Papandreou's office, but the gap between what they would promise and what they were able to produce was maddeningly wide, unlike anything I had encountered before. Arthur Miller's description of Spyros Skouras, the Greek movie producer who immigrated to Hollywood, seemed to apply:

> You could hate Spyros, but you had to like him, if only for the naïveté of his disregard for truth, which was at least not surgical and dry but had a certain ardor; he always meant what he said when he was saying it.[423]

But this way of operating infuriated the American military commands, seething anyway because of Athens's inability to stamp out the terrorists targeting their people. When I visited the headquarters of the air force command at Ramstein, Germany, to deliver a speech about Greece's strategic importance, the general in charge dismissed Papandreou as a "duplicitous bastard" with whom no self-respecting American ought to deal.

At the end of March 1984, Secretary of Defense Weinberger arrived from Washington with a delegation of more than twenty officials. Among them were the assistant secretary of defense Richard Perle (who as Senator Jackson's aide helped undermine the U.S.-Soviet trade agreement); his deputy Ronald Lauder, the scion of the Estee Lauder Company; and Weinberger's military assistant, Major General Colin Powell. I was in the thick of the three-day negotiation as the note-taker, but little of substance came from it; the Papandreou government wouldn't change its ways, and the American military wasn't prepared to reduce its presence, giving up bases or withdrawing its nuclear weapons. After Weinberger met with Papandreou, I rushed back to the embassy to do a report to Washington, only to find that twenty thousand Communist demonstrators had blocked all its entrances. Powell uttered not a word during the meetings, which I recalled with unease when I heard that George W. Bush had appointed him secretary of state.[424]

As welcome relief two days later, Colonel John Sloan, with whom I had studied Greek, flew the general in charge of the bases and me to a conference in Garmisch, which I hadn't seen since leaving the institute in 1972.

When conditions at the bases grew no better, Secretary Weinberger sent Lauder back for further talks. The perfume magnate met with Yiannis Kapsis, the deputy foreign minister. Looking at a map of the Aegean Sea where, to the dismay of NATO planners, Greek-Turkish maritime and air conflicts periodically erupted, the two officials traded acerbic barbs as I took notes. Lauder told Kapsis that Greece did not have a "real minister of defense" with whom the Americans could work (Papandreou held this portfolio in addition to being prime minister, as Lauder well knew) and that the Greek islands a few miles off the Anatolian coast (at which Lauder wagged a finger) ought really to belong to Turkey. I doubt that Lauder knew the history of the islands, but at the start of Greece's War of Independence in 1822, the Turks had massacred twenty thousand Greeks on just one of them.

The exchange went downhill from there, with Lauder finally telling Kapsis that he shouldn't have kissed visiting Archbishop Iakovos of the North and South American Greek Orthodox Church, an act for which Kapsis was being pilloried in the left-wing press, traditionally hostile to ecclesiastical authorities.

Anticipating problems with Lauder's visit, Stearns had told me ahead of his arrival not to bother arranging a formal luncheon. Of course, Lauder complained; but I couldn't blame the ambassador for trying to keep a novice at bay, particularly one practicing the kind of surreal diplomacy he did.

My impression that Papandreou's government didn't take terrorism seriously deepened during my second year. A major problem was Athens international airport; terrorists would pass through it with impunity. The Israeli embassy occupied a building a few houses from ours. One day, the police nabbed a terrorist loitering outside. He and two companions had walked through the airport after arriving from Beirut, each carrying a weapon. For once, with police swarming all over the street, we felt safe.

Seven bombs went off downtown during one week in December 1984. One was tossed into a café at the Hilton Hotel near the embassy, another killed a Greek guard at the Iraqi embassy. The deputy chief of mission at the Jordanian embassy was fired at, and a bomb was defused at the British Council. Our embassy only suffered the desecration of a flag.

Several months later, an Arab passed through a Greek-guarded gate at Hellenikon and fired a bazooka shell at a 727 airliner. Fortunately, it didn't explode.

For a few years after leaving Greece, I couldn't put "November 17" out of my mind. Whenever I drove, I'd routinely check the mirror for onrushing scooters and motorcycles.

A conservative government finally rounded up and prosecuted the gang after I left the Foreign Service. But don't count on an end to leftist violence in Greece; in January 2007, a new terrorist group, Revolutionary Struggle, launched an antitank grenade at the American embassy.

*   *   *

Seven months into my three-year posting, on January 20, 1984, I received a call from Moscow. Warren Zimmerman, the deputy chief of mission, came on line.

Liz and I first met Warren and his family when they arrived at the embassy and moved into Leninsky Prospect 45 in summer 1973. Warren was taking over Pol/Ext at the time. He was the one, I believe, who drafted the telegram explaining why Stalin-era newspapers kept appearing in officers' mailboxes; always equable, Warren wasn't disturbed in the least when I acknowledged the prank, although he probably had worked hard making sense of the affair.

Warren was in the tradition of the old Foreign Service; he and his wife Teeny, from the Roosevelt family, were the last of a kind. With the exception of a posting to Venezuela, they had spent all their years overseas in Europe—in Austria, France, Spain, Switzerland, and Yugoslavia, a pattern of assignments that, given the service's diminished interest in area expertise, would be difficult to replicate today. Warren was the last American ambassador to serve in Belgrade before Yugoslavia broke up.

"Would you like to return to Moscow as economic counselor a year and a half from now? Ambassador Hartman and I would like you to take the job."

I had no forewarning of the call and didn't know Hartman. "I appreciate the suggestion, Warren, but I've never done any economic reporting, not anywhere."

"Think about it, and give me a call. We need someone who knows the Soviet Union."

The position was graded one rank higher than the one I was holding, and returning to Moscow would mean curtailing the Athens assignment by a year. Evidently the department was having trouble identifying a capable Russian-speaking candidate, so the embassy had come up with its own. Not a testimonial to good planning, but flattering for me.

It wasn't clear that the embassy in Athens or the department, which had invested ten months in teaching me Greek, would agree, but Warren told me that if I said yes, Hartman would see that the assignment was made.

Liz was beginning to enjoy aspects of Greece (she had just been named a board member of the embassy's community association), but she agreed that the move made sense. The Greeks were complicated, especially with Papandreou in charge—more complicated than even the Russians—but the embassy would have no difficulty finding a replacement for me. Any FSO knowing the Mediterranean would relish the job.

Many of the Soviet officials with whom I had dealt were still on the scene, especially in the Foreign Ministry and Kremlin (Gorbachev hadn't taken over yet). Liz and I probably knew our way around the Soviet system as well as anyone. Moreover, our friends would welcome us back.

Ambassador Stearns and Alan Berlind, the deputy chief of mission, told me they wouldn't stand in the way, and I told Warren we'd be happy to return. (Three years later, I had the pleasure of escorting Stearns, visiting Moscow after his retirement, to a Taganka production of *Three Sisters*; he didn't know Russian but appreciated serious theater.)

Although I wouldn't receive the department's decision for several months, I arranged for a subscription to *Pravda* and began reviving my Russian. My Greek had faded almost from the moment I arrived; every official I worked with spoke English and preferred doing so. In April 1984, the department approved my assignment to Moscow effective August 1985.

During the fifteen months that remained for me in Athens, the Papandreou government continued to let U.S.-Greek problems fester. After my departure, the George H. W. Bush administration in 1990 signed a new agreement with a conservative Greek government. The agreement provided for closing the two bases that caused the most problems—Hellenikon next to the airport and Nea Makri on the Aegean.

Because I was involved in Pol-Mil work, I had no reason to meet with Soviet officials in Athens, and it would have alarmed security had I done so. Just after I left, a new CIA station chief, David Forden, orchestrated the defection of a Soviet diplomat. I was glad I was far from Greece and in no way involved; I had no interest in reawakening the KGB's interest in me.

In June 1985, Liz and I went back to the United States for a short home leave and consultations in Washington. I spent several weeks visiting the department and other agencies involved with Soviet affairs, including the CIA and the National Security Agency (NSA). I also brushed up my Russian at the FSI. There I met Dick Combs and Mark Ramee, who were preparing to go to Moscow as the deputy chief of mission and political counselor respectively.

Mikhail Gorbachev had been elected Party leader in March 1985 upon the death of Chernenko. Studying *Pravda* in Athens, I had already filled a notebook with the themes on which he was harping. One of his statements was to the effect that Soviet officials were staying too long in office; from this I inferred that he would shake up the system, removing Brezhnev-era *apparatchiki* and bureaucrats from positions in which they had become entrenched. Gorbachev hadn't yet "charged" the Soviet era of "stagnation" to Brezhnev's account, but he was clear about the importance of change.

The analysts on whom I paid calls in Washington were poring over his speeches to figure out what lay ahead. They sensed that he understood better than his predecessors what the problems were. A few suggested that in order to avoid bureaucratic resistance, he was deliberately concealing his plans; others felt he had little or no idea of how to proceed. Of course, the latter school of analysts proved to be correct.

Serious arms negotiations had resumed when Secretary Shultz and Foreign Minister Gromyko met in Geneva during January 1985. A month earlier, in December, Prime Minister Margaret Thatcher had met with Gorbachev (while Chernenko was still leader) and had come away with a strongly favorable impression ("this was a man with whom I could do business"). A few days later, she shared her impression with President Reagan at Camp David.

Even earlier, Secretary Shultz had let Dobrynin know that the administration would welcome a visit by Gorbachev, but Gromyko had sat on Dobrynin's telegrams, depriving Reagan of the opportunity to meet the up-and-coming politician. An old-timer like Gromyko, who had taken charge of the Soviet embassy in Washington as a thirty-four-year-old and had negotiated with Roosevelt in the White House (in his bedroom, no less[125]), still wielded enormous power and was not about to let an energetic newcomer invade his turf.

Publicly, little was happening in U.S.-Soviet relations. This was especially true in the economic sphere for which I would have responsibility. Moscow had encouraged West European and Japanese suppliers to step in after Washington imposed its sanctions following the invasion of Afghanistan, and they were doing just this. Under both Carter and Reagan, Washington had been unable to forge a common policy with its key allies on East-West trade, especially with regard to technology and equipment bound for the Soviet oil and gas sector. The differences became acute after the Polish regime cracked down on Solidarity, and the Reagan administration prohibited the fulfillment of oil and gas contracts by licensees and subsidiaries of U.S. companies operating abroad. This infuriated the West Europeans, even friends like Mrs. Thatcher.

By the beginning of 1985, with Secretary Shultz's influence increasing and with an expert on Soviet affairs working in the White House, the Reagan administration had begun modifying its controls. However, Soviet officials remained bitter due to the damage already inflicted because of all the disrupted contracts and withdrawn licenses. Many hadn't forgotten the imposition of the Jackson-Vanik and Stevenson Amendments a decade before. How could they forget? The system was so calcified that the officials dealing with foreign trade in the middle 1980s, including Foreign Trade

Minister Nikolai Patolichev, were virtually the same as those who had staked their careers on détente.

In May 1985, while I was winding up in Athens, Secretary of Commerce Malcolm Baldridge met with Patolichev in Moscow. The two officials presided over the first meeting of the U.S.-Soviet Joint Commercial Commission since 1978, and Gorbachev welcomed Baldridge in the Kremlin.[426]

Baldridge also took the opportunity to witness the renewal of Pepsico's barter arrangement with the Soviet trading company that controlled the export of Stolichnaya vodka. Khrushchev had sipped his first Pepsi at the company's stand at the Sokolniki exhibit in 1959. With years of work, Pepsico had parlayed that moment into a series of bilateral agreements providing for the importation of vodka into the United States in exchange for the right to build Pepsi bottling plants in the USSR. The first such agreement was signed in 1972, and others followed.

It was fortunate for Pepsico that Khrushchev hadn't reacted like Stalin when Truman sent him a few bottles of Coca-Cola: "Stalin reacted angrily and ordered [his] food scientist . . . to develop a superior pear-based fizzy drink to send in return."[427] For those of us who traveled, it was always a relief to find a Pepsi; perhaps because of Stalin's reaction, we never found a Coke.

Twenty-six American companies were accredited to conduct business in the Soviet Union as Liz and I prepared to return. One of them had contracted to sell fifty-two pipe-laying machines to a Soviet buyer at the start of 1985; another had signed a $12 million contract to modernize an ethylene plant. These were small transactions compared to what the European and Japanese companies were doing, but at least the Americans and the Russians were again "talking trade."

In terms of agriculture, Reagan had lifted Carter's prohibition on Soviet purchases of grain (beyond the quantity stipulated in the existing agreement) as soon as he became president. After the crackdown in Poland, however, he put a halt to negotiating a new agreement. Before the Soviet invasion of Afghanistan, the United States had provided two-thirds of Moscow's annual grain imports; after the introduction of sanctions related to the invasion and the imposition of martial law in Poland, the American share of Moscow's grain imports had shrunk to one-third, with Argentina, Australia, Canada, and the European community making up the difference. In 1983, a new U.S.-Soviet grain agreement was finally reached.

Amid all the perturbations in bilateral relations during the first half of the 1980s, American tourists had lost their appetite for traveling on Soviet territory. Only fifty thousand Americans visited in 1984, half the number that had traveled there in 1974 when I was completing my consular assignment. In contrast, two hundred thousand Americans were traveling to China every year.

Although I focused on Gorbachev and his plans for the economy, several of my interlocutors in Washington mentioned conditions at Tchaikovsky 19. I knew that the project for the new embassy was moving ahead and that the number of Seabees and contract workers had increased many times over. While in Athens, I had received a letter from the administrative counselor saying that we would not receive an apartment in the north or south wing, where counselor-level officers customarily resided, because the embassy had to house "increasing numbers of Seabees." Liz and I had wanted to live at the embassy this time, and the letter came as a disappointment. On a positive note, Curt Kamman, Zimmerman's successor as deputy chief of mission, wrote to say that "the chances are good that at some point during your stay, you could and indeed should move into one of the counselor apartments in the new compound."

I sensed an undercurrent of concern about embassy security during my consultations. The arrest in Washington of John Walker, a navy employee, and his three associates in May had heightened the government's concern about Soviet espionage. I wasn't involved in security matters and never raised the subject myself, but an NSA official on whom I called told me that the Soviets had managed to compromise the embassy's electric typewriters, enabling them to "read" classified reporting. The discovery had been made in 1984. Apparently, the KGB had gained access to the typewriters before they were installed on the upper floors, perhaps as they passed through Soviet customs. The KGB had added sensors that would be activated as soon as their keys—each of which had its own sound characteristic—were struck. "We found that their technology was three to five years ahead of ours," I remember the official saying.

It was difficult for me to believe that security had let the typewriters pass through Russian hands, but because I had always used a manual typewriter, I was confident that my own reporting hadn't been compromised. I rarely used the names of individual sources, although the KGB could probably figure some of them out.

No one suggested that the Russian workers inside the embassy had been involved, but their presence, along with that of scores of Russians at the construction site, was also on the minds of the NSA official and others with whom I spoke. Personally, I had never seen any Russian on any of the upper floors except one or two closely-watched babushkas in the cleaning force. At most, a Soviet might drop off an envelope or a newspaper for an American at the ninth-floor marine post; to my knowledge, none—apart from the firemen in 1977—had ever stepped beyond.

With regard to the Russians working on the new embassy project, I assumed that the necessary safeguards had been taken from the start. And if it turned out that the KGB had still managed to compromise the shell of one or more of the new structures, security could certainly deploy the usual "tanks" to thwart eavesdropping.

I can't say I paid much attention to what was being said. Once the Cold War was underway, there had never been a time when security in Moscow was *not* of paramount concern. This is why a security office with specialized equipment and know-how and security officers who provided frequent briefings were always on hand, and why the State Department and other agencies in Washington filled their positions at the embassy with trustworthy, well-trained professionals.

I couldn't imagine that conditions at the embassy—and not Soviet politics, economics, or trade—would end up dominating my assignment. That these conditions, attributable as much to misjudgments in Washington as to Soviet actions, would bring the embassy to its knees was simply beyond my belief.

12

Spy Dust, Spies, and Reporting on a State Economy

On August 11, 1985, Liz and I reached Moscow for a third assignment, this time without children. Elise was in Paris studying at the Institut d'Etudes Politiques, Abby was in Washington pursuing graphic arts at the Corcoran Gallery, and Rob was in Bradenton, Florida, completing high school while boarding and playing tennis at Bollettieri Tennis Academy.

A van from the embassy met us at Sheremetyevo II and took us to a twelve-story compound on Krutitsky Val Street. A chain-link fence surrounded the site, which included a parking lot at the rear of building. At the fence's opening in front stood the usual militia box.

We were told that the apartments, seventy-five or so, were occupied by foreigners with either diplomatic, business, or media accreditation. Our apartment was on the top floor. As we dragged our suitcases toward the entryway, I noticed a flag draped over a balcony just above, a flag I didn't recognize with a yellow star and sword against a field of red and black.

Krutitsky Val is in the Proletarsky District in southwest Moscow, a district filled with large industrial plants. The Metro stations bear names like Automobile Factory (*Avtozavodskaya*) and Textile Workers (*Tekstil'shchiki*).

I knew immediately we'd miss our old neighborhood in the Leninsky District. It had sprung up during Stalin's final years and included numerous Academy of Sciences buildings. Educated families with deep roots in the city occupied its housing. The apartments, even if smaller, were well built, often due to the forced labor of Germans taken prisoner during the war.

Proletarsky's housing had gone up in the Khrushchev and Brezhnev eras when rural migrants were pouring into the city. The apartments were

larger but the buildings shabbier, as if first-generation Muscovites wouldn't
have cared.

As my first letter home suggests, we were taken aback by what we saw:

> The apartment is fairly spacious by Moscow standards, but poorly
> furnished. We will have to do battle with the general services
> section to get decent unstained sofas, chairs, etc . . . . We are
> on the top floor of a ten-year-old building that is already falling
> apart. The entrance on the ground floor is completely exposed
> to the elements because a store-size plate glass window had
> been smashed to smithereens: glass shards lay in the foyer as we
> crunched our way to the two elevators . . . . As we went up . . .
> two African children, about three feet tall, rode with us wielding
> plastic swords . . . After one slashed at my briefcase, I raised my
> hand and they backed off. Probably an African diplomat lives in
> the entryway.

It turned out that the entire staff of the Angolan embassy, with the
exception of the ambassador, took up the first few floors of the entryway. It
was their government that the Reagan administration was trying to topple,
and their flag I failed to recognize.

A few officials from other developing countries and four American
couples occupied the remaining apartments. The Americans included an
army colonel in the defense attachés' office, a Foreign Service "tandem
couple" (he was assigned to Pol/Int, she to the consular section), and
a communicator. The colonel's wife worked in the Foreign Buildings
Operations (FBO) office, the communicator's in the science section.

A contract worker involved with the embassy construction project lived
with his wife across the hall, in the other apartment on our floor. After
introductory handshakes, we rarely saw them again. Every weekend, they'd
pump up the temperature of their apartment with a variety of space heaters,
take off their clothes, and pretend they were back in their native Arizona.

The Foreign Ministry's diplomatic services branch (UPDK) was
neglecting the compound. Perhaps by the mid-1980s, it was neglecting all
of them. Even the militiaman disappeared from time to time.

One of the Angolan families kept hens and roosters on its balcony. At
odd hours, we would hear them cluck and crow.

The Angolan children, including the two with swords, had scribbled
graffiti on every wall. Their indoor games included pushing the buttons in
the two elevators and setting fires on the landings. Descent from the twelfth
floor often took several minutes. Because of the smashed plate glass, the
ground floor remained open until winter.

The American embassy was so consumed with administrative problems that I didn't have the heart to ask about relocating. As for the Soviet officials working in the ministry's diplomatic services branch, they must have enjoyed locating U.S. and Angolan apartments in the same entryway.

Until our car arrived from the United States, Liz and I commuted on the Metro between the Proletarskaya and the Barrikadnaya Stations, the latter the closest to the embassy. (The station after Proletarskaya is Taganskaya, which is on Taganka Square where Lyubimov's theater is located.) The trains came every few minutes, but seats were difficult to find at rush hour. Those who found them usually read books—their titles concealed by homemade covers for privacy—instead of newspapers, at least through December 1985 when Boris Yeltsin took over Moscow's Party organization and the local papers, almost overnight, became lively. Because the Metro system carried eight million passengers a day, just short of Moscow's total population, I knew we'd have some interesting experiences even on a thirty-minute ride.

On occasion, I took the van to work. Jumping into it one morning, I groused that a second flag had appeared on another Krutitsky balcony.

"The Foreign Ministry used to complain if diplomats displayed their flags," I noted to my colleagues, slouched in their seats and only half-awake. "Now it didn't seem to care. The flag looks Cuban to me."

"That's no Cuban flag, Bob, but the flag of Texas," Colonel Dick Naab replied. Thus I learned that another contract employee had joined the entryway.

Because every American in the compound was employed, Liz took a part-time job in the embassy's personnel office. After our car arrived and until we moved into the new embassy compound in October 1986, she usually drove to work (her hours were irregular, fixed beneath the limit so benefits wouldn't be triggered) while I took the Metro.

I supervised three officers in the economic section (a fourth was with the CIA). Although each was on a first Moscow tour, they had arrived the year before and spoke good Russian. They wasted no time introducing me to colleagues at other embassies and in the foreign business community.

The Russians at the embassy greeted us warmly, but less so than when we had arrived for the second assignment. It couldn't have been the state of relations (U.S.-Soviet tension had been higher in 1978), but everyone was more reserved. As Liz reported in a letter home, rumors were already circulating that the department planned to "get rid of all the Soviet employees." Obviously, this was on their minds, though no one mentioned it to us. In the same letter, Liz asked rhetorically, "Who will do the services they provide?"

The rumors gained credence a month later when Dick Combs told the country team that the department was advertising in the United States for sixty persons to work in Moscow. Dick wasn't able to say whether the jobs would be in the embassy or at the construction site. If we were asked about the advertisement, we were supposed to say nothing.

In fact, removing the employees had already been adopted as policy. On August 7, 1985, President Reagan entered the following into his diary (only published in 2007):

> At 11AM we had an NSPG [National Security Planning Group] meeting on coming up with a new directive & new program for counterespionage. It will involve replacing a lot of Russian employees in our Moscow embassy with Americans & getting a reduction in the number of Soviets who are in our country on one pretext or another but who are in reality KGB.[428]

That the administration had taken this decision was not immediately revealed to us, and perhaps not even to the ambassador, but it dribbled out in bits and pieces, rather haphazardly as I look back, in the course of late 1985 and most of 1986.

For our first Saturday evening back, Liz and I went to Red Square. Little had changed in four years except that we saw fewer drunks. Gorbachev had launched his anti-alcohol campaign in May, shortly after becoming the Party's general secretary. Yet appearances could be deceiving. When Liz visited a bread store in our neighborhood a few days later, a knot of men stood outside with empty bottles into which a *babushka* poured vodka—probably *samogon*—from a jug. The woman cackled with delight as she doled out portions, and the men slugged it down on the spot.

Gorbachev hadn't displayed political acumen by starting out with a drive against drinking, one of the few pleasures remaining for ordinary Russians. The lines outside liquor stores were long, and there was universal grumbling. He would later blame two others in the central leadership—Ligachev and Solomentsev—for implementing his policy "to the point of absurdity." [429]

We stopped at the Hotel Metropol near Red Square to have a bowl of ice cream. The headwaiter refused to admit us until I showed my Foreign Ministry-issued identification card (*kartochka*). There was no reason for him to be accommodating unless a customer, Russian or foreign, helped him meet his plan; serving two bowls of ice cream without a full meal wasn't worth his trouble.

On our first Sunday, we took the subway to Spaso House to attend the Protestant service. Tang had retired, but Clemente and Maria looked as cheery as when we had last seen them. Ambassador and Mrs. Hartman, whom we hadn't met yet, were abroad on vacation.

Spaso House had undergone a major redecoration. Modern-style sofas with bright blue upholstery, with matching pillows piled high, dominated the ground-floor rooms. The gilded wooden chairs with purple-shade velvet seats that I liked were no longer in the ballroom; for the service, we sat instead on chrome-legged chairs with bright blue seats. The new chairs were comfortable (the old ones lacked arms) but far less elegant. The gilded ones had dated at least back to 1951, having been mentioned by the wife of Ambassador Kirk in her published diary.[430]

When Ambassador Robert Strauss arrived at Spaso House in 1991, he complained that its décor resembled that "of a Marriott hotel."[431] His reaction struck a chord when I read it.

Mila and Sergei Vronski welcomed us back with a dinner on August 30. Alyosha was living in a village not far from Moscow, painting icons and studying the Bible; but Anya was able to attend, bringing along her two-year-old daughter Arina, or Arisha. Anya was living in an apartment that Andrei Voznesenski, Arisha's father, had arranged not far from Leninsky Prospect. Sergei was crazy about Arisha and had become more comfortable with Anya's situation. Andrei wasn't present, but we talked about his call on President Reagan during his visit to Washington the prior June. The call had been kept private, and Andrei had suggested to Reagan an exchange of poets.[432]

A few months later, Anya invited Liz, me, and her mother to her place for dinner. With beef, cauliflower, and cabbage that she had found in the Cheremushki market (where Liz used to shop), she outdid any restaurant we knew. She served Georgian wine and gave us baked apples, wild berries, and preserved cherries for dessert.

Anya was radiant throughout the evening. Years later, Francine du Plessix Gray would write that the women of Russia's intelligentsia were always interested in being "the muse of a famous poet."[433] Gray knew of what she wrote; in the early 1930s her mother had been Vladimir Mayakovsky's muse.

*   *   *

Ten days after our return, the American staff was told that the construction site would henceforth be closed to Russians. If asked about the ban, we were to reply "no comment." Washington and the embassy were finally addressing the site's rumored security problems.

A day later, we were told that Combs and an official from Washington would hold important briefings "on a matter of community-wide interest" at Spaso House. Because the staff had grown so large, three sessions were scheduled.

Liz and I went to the evening session and heard that the KGB was using microscopic chemical agents to identify Soviet citizens with whom embassy officers were meeting. It was "dusting" doorknobs, car handles, and other objects associated with the Americans to establish who among its own people dared be in contact with them. The department and the embassy had already protested. We surmised that CIA officers and military attaches were the targets, but no one would say so directly at the briefing. A team from Washington, including environmental and health experts, would arrive shortly to assess the scope of the problem, including whether the dust was harmful. The staff asked numerous questions but the answers were few.

Apart from making calls on other diplomats and businesspersons around the city, I was talking with the Foreign Ministry about an agreement on air safety in the northern Pacific, an agreement that grew out of Moscow's downing of the Korean airliner. Direct air service between Moscow and New York by Pan American Airways and Aeroflot wouldn't be restored until the agreement came into force.

The embassy switchboard caught fire on September 12, knocking out every telephone except two on the ground floor, one right next to a copying machine. I was summoned downstairs to take a call from the ministry and had to negotiate a knotty issue relating to the agreement against the din of the machine going full blast. The fire was extinguished before it spread, and no one was hurt; but Garmisch hadn't prepared me for this.

I was busy with meetings outside the embassy. I took Senator Byrd and seven others to meet a deputy minister of foreign trade, Vladimir Sushkov (whose career would abruptly end four months later). The commercial counselor Bob Krause and I spent two hours with a second deputy minister, describing the problems that American businessmen were having. I paid an introductory call on Valeri Pekshev, the deputy chairman of the state bank (Gosbank). Pekshev began by lauding our countries' cooperation during World War II. I responded that I was well aware of it since my own father had delivered Lend-Lease supplies to Murmansk. "Is your father still alive?" When I said yes, he dug a silver ruble—struck to commemorate the fortieth anniversary of the war's end—out from a desk drawer and asked me to send it to him. The Russians hadn't forgotten those who made that dangerous run.

The pace picked up as the first summit between Reagan and Gorbachev—scheduled for Geneva on November 19, 20, and 21, 1985—approached. We were told that Shultz would visit on November 2-3 to meet with Shevardnadze, the Georgian Party leader who had succeeded Gromyko. Shevardnadze had extended the invitation to Shultz at a meeting in New York. One day before, a Russian seaman had jumped ship in U.S. waters and sought asylum, and the U.S. Immigration Service had turned him over to Soviet custody.[434] It was the Kudirka situation again, this time with immigration officials instead of the coast guard to blame. The controversy ended when the Soviets agreed, under pressure from Shultz, to a consular interview; and the seaman decided to return.

Then on October 31, I was told that I might have to go to Kabul again to deal with a Soviet soldier who had fled into the embassy.[435] As in 1980, Soviet troops had surrounded the compound. It turned out, however, that a Pol/Int "alumnus" fluent in Russian, Ed Hurwitz, was now stationed in Kabul. The department didn't intend to repeat its earlier oversight.

My workload was heavier than it had been in Athens. The Reagan administration was finally addressing the important issues in U.S.-Soviet relations. It had indulged in political rhetoric during its first two years, culminating in the president's speech to evangelical Christians berating "the aggressive impulses of an evil empire," but there hadn't been an effort to engage the Soviet regime in serious talks.

The rhetoric had been accompanied by the department's establishment of the Office of Foreign Missions (OFM) to tighten the rules of reciprocity, but this didn't contribute to reducing the danger of a nuclear-armed Soviet Union.

Under the new reciprocity rules, Soviet and other Communist diplomats would be subjected to the same petty controls imposed on us. Henceforth, they would have to secure their tickets, hotel reservations, and services through the OFM, as we were required to do through the diplomatic services branch. If the Soviet embassy needed an outside repairman, it would have to submit to the bureaucratic rigmarole that the ministry levied on us. An FBI official with a counterintelligence background was put in charge of the office.

By the middle of 1983, the administration had achieved one real success, apart from keeping Dobrynin's car out of the Foggy Bottom's basement and tightening reciprocity rules. Reagan had asked Dobrynin to let the two Pentecostal families leave the embassy basement where they had been living for five years and to emigrate. Moscow had finally relented, allowing them to immigrate to Israel in July 1983 from where they flew to the United States.

Shultz called it "the first successful negotiation with the Soviets in the Reagan administration."[436]

David Rothkopf, a scholar of White House decision-making, blames the people around the Oval Office for the bad start. After taking over, they had "downgraded" the National Security Council. The result was "an undersupervised, underproductive, ingrown system that collapsed on itself and almost brought the administration down with it."[437] (The "collapse" refers to the Iran-Contra affair.)

Reagan's first set of advisors didn't believe that a president, or even the NSC, needed anyone with real-world experience dealing with Moscow in the White House. Their choice to be the president's Soviet expert fell instead on an academic expert, the Harvard scholar Richard Pipes.

Pipes had fled occupied Warsaw as a teenager during World War II, had served in the American military, and had begun teaching Russian history in 1958. He had worked on military issues for Senator Jackson and for the Ford administration but had never dealt with the Soviets face-to-face. When George Kennan spoke to us at the embassy in April 1981, shortly after the administration's takeover, he warned that Pipes was someone who writes from documents, an "exterior historian," and not from personal knowledge. Some of Pipes' academic colleagues considered him "Russophobic."[438]

A comment that Reagan had made on March 10, 1983, alerted Shultz to the fact that even Reagan was uncomfortable with the kind of advice he was receiving. Shultz wrote in his memoir:

> 'I don't want these people to know about Dobrynin,' the president
> said to me, referring to his private meeting with Ambassador
> Dobrynin and our subsequent effort to allow the Pentecostals . . .
> to gain the freedom to emigrate.[439]

The private meeting had occurred three weeks before, on February 15, when Shultz "sneaked Ambassador Dobrynin into the W.H [White House]," as Reagan's diary described his and Shultz's ploy to circumvent the negativity extant in the NSC.[440] "These people," in Shultz's view, included Pipes to whom Shultz was subsequently introduced. Shultz left the Oval Office with the impression that "the president was a prisoner of his own staff."

Soon thereafter, Pipes returned to Cambridge, and the White House recruited someone with first-hand knowledge of the USSR, Ambassador Matlock. Matlock left Prague and arrived at the NSC in June 1983. Steve Steiner, with whom I had worked in the consular section, became the second FSO to join the NSC staff, and Judi Mandel, a colleague of mine from Pol/Int, arrived soon thereafter.

Back in Cambridge, Pipes wrote his own memoir[441], replete with complaints about Secretaries Haig and Shultz (who was accused of presenting "a distorted picture" of the above-described meeting with

Reagan) and fellow scholars like Bob Legvold who had helped me in New York (and has since become Shulman's successor as head of the Harriman Institute.) Pipes rejected the suggestion that he was Russophobic, but did allow that he drew a sharp distinction between "educated Russians and the population at large." The population," he wrote, requires "'a strong hand' to regulate their public lives"—an attribute, he said, he didn't like.[442]

*   *   *

The American staff at the embassy had doubled, perhaps tripled, during our absence. It was difficult to know how large it had become. The contract workers and others involved with the construction project kept changing, and their work sites were dispersed—around the embassy, in the courtyard outbuildings, and at the walled construction site.

It used to be easy to know who was performing the security function; there were three or four professionals in the SY office on the ninth floor, and they remained for full tours. Other offices with security functions had since come into being. The embassy's telephone directory listed a "new office building (NOB)" security office, a warehouse security office, and a Foreign Office Building (FOB) security office. There was also an engineering service office that may have been involved, although its function wasn't apparent, and I didn't try to find out.

The team in the ninth-floor security office had more than doubled to nine from what it had been when we arrived in 1972. It now supervised the marine guard detachment, the Seabees, and everyone else at Tchaikovsky 19 and the construction site involved with security. It also hosted a steady stream of long and short-term visitors (TDYs) from security as well as counterintelligence agencies in Washington. During our final months, there were at least one hundred such visitors.

Altogether, the embassy staff on two or three-year assignments numbered about three hundred, and almost all the spouses worked. Even the wife of the deputy chief of mission had a job in the science section. In the past, the deputy's wife was fully engaged coordinating volunteer and morale-building activities, but there was a dearth of these in the embassy's new (and, to my mind, bloated) configuration.

The marine complement had expanded to more than thirty from the eleven in 1972, again enlistees just out of high school. Like their predecessors, they had gone through an eight-week training course at Quantico, Virginia; in a six-hour segment, they had been taught how to steer clear of Russians and to avoid entrapment. At some embassies, marine officers led the marine detachment; but apparently, Washington judged that the embassy's security office, together with a noncommissioned officer (a marine gunnery sergeant), would ensure adequate supervision.

On October 4, the marines invited Liz and me to lunch in the Marine Bar. As we entered, those not on duty were lined up smartly. At the end of the meal, I gave a short toast, thanking them and their service branch for providing such good support, not only in Moscow but at every post where we had served.

FSOs might complain about a particular marine, especially if he had meted out a security violation when the offense seemed more technical than substantive (e.g., leaving a classified document on one's unattended desk in an upper-floor area to which no Russian had access), but no one I knew ever questioned the marines' importance; they had been protecting embassies and consulates, sometimes at considerable personal risk, since 1949.

The marines in 1985 struck me as less confident, however, than those we had known in previous assignments. The Harvard exchange scholar who visited the Marine Bar in 1978-79 wrote about "their unfailingly healthy faces" and "polite Southern and Midwestern accents"[443]; the healthy faces and politeness were still there, but more of the marines seemed to have come from inner-city rather than small-town America, and from families or circumstances that had ill prepared them for living in an isolated but close-knit overseas community.

The Foreign Service—including officers, specialists, communicators and secretaries—probably accounted for no more than sixty persons of the total embassy complement in 1985. Only five or six had served in the Soviet Union before, and as far as I could tell, only three had been at the embassy more than twice. The investigative journalist Ron Kessler would later claim that "for the most part, the same diplomats populated the embassy year after year. They would do a tour in Moscow, return to work on the Soviet desk, then do another tour in Moscow."[444]

This may have been true in the 1950s and '60s, but it wasn't at all true in the '70s and '80s. In fact, the embassy had a glaring deficit of officers with Soviet experience; no wonder Hartman had turned to a political-track officer like me to head his economic section. If the "back-and-forth" pattern had been as Kessler described, the Soviet desk itself would have been staffed with FSOs who would have foreseen the danger of trying to apply rigid rules of reciprocity to such starkly different embassies as ours in Moscow and the Soviets' in Washington. But the department was no longer developing a cadre of Russian area experts.

Another "watering hole" had come into being at Tchaikovsky 19. A navy Seabee club was functioning in what once was a north-wing apartment. Just after we arrived, the Seabees advertised a "casino night" with beer and tacos. Liz and I went to the Marine Bar for the luncheon, but never made it to the second club.

Kessler noted that the Seabees "could have girls in their rooms" and that this had irked the marines who could not.[445] The Seabees were also permitted to visit hotel bars as the marines were not; and they did so often, particularly a bar at the International (*Mezhdunarodnaya*) Hotel a short walk from the embassy.

Many more security-related devices had been installed on the upper floors. The ceiling of the eighth-floor corridor outside the economic section bristled with electronic gear, including motion detectors, television monitors, and alarms. The marine guard on duty on the ninth floor could observe us entering and leaving our suite of four offices.

Because the fire risk had increased with the addition of new equipment and many more staffers, the administrative section organized a building-wide drill a few months after we arrived. When the bells went off, the five of us in the economic section raced to the door at the end of our corridor as instructed, wrested it open (it was normally locked), and made our way down on a darkened staircase. Upon reaching the ground floor, we were stopped by a locked steel door and forced to retreat back upstairs. Problems were encountered elsewhere too. In a postmortem, the fire warden, on a TDY assignment from Washington, reported that had there been a real fire, 40 percent of the staff would not have survived.

On my first day, a stack of official-looking blank forms (about five by eight inches), with a place for a signature at the bottom, occupied a corner of my desk. I was supposed to write in the name and address of any Soviet citizen on whom I planned to call, and the name of the embassy person who would accompany me. The form was to be submitted to the security office in advance of any visit.

The form was new to me. I hadn't seen anything like it before at any post, including Moscow.

I didn't care for the idea of seeking advance approval for meetings with Russians, whether at a ministry, an apartment, or anywhere else. Sometimes I met my contacts on the spur of the moment, when a friend was visiting the neighborhood and asked to see me, or when I placed a telephone call during an evening or a weekend, usually from a public phone far from our apartment.

Perhaps my predecessor had filled out such forms, but I didn't intend to; their existence suggested that an FSO assigned to Moscow could no longer be trusted. Obviously, the form would especially inhibit officers on first Russian assignments (the large majority of all embassy officers), discouraging them from roaming the city's streets and taking advantage of random opportunities.

And how could I explain to a Russian acquaintance the presence of another person, someone he or she didn't know? Hosting one person from the embassy was risk enough.

I had asked for a manual typewriter as soon as I arrived, and general services promptly provided one. For officers and secretaries who used electric typewriters, the Seabees were building a special room on the sixth floor with an independent source of power, making it impossible for the Soviets to collect electromagnetic signals from their typewriters (and then to feed them into a typewriter of the same make and model to reproduce the text).

Security examined and approved my new typewriter, but asked me to stash it away at night in the safe next to my desk, despite the fact that no Russians (except the *babushkas*) was ever allowed on the upper floors. I was glad to have a manual typewriter and didn't argue.

The wife of Harrison Salisbury, the longtime *Times* correspondent, had once written about the futility of arguing with Russians about *their* rules when they made no sense: "There is never any point in arguing," she said. "A mere human being can't win against the rigidity of their insane way of doing things."[446] I hoped Tchaikovsky 19 wasn't coming to this.

*   *   *

Liz and I gradually made peace with the neighborhood. I went out on the balcony and was happy to see Kremlin spires in the distance, above the rows of housing blocks. Two former monasteries, their monks long since departed, were within easy walking distance. Novospassky Monastery, Moscow's oldest, overlooks the Moscow River, three blocks from Krutitsky Val. A pond, allegedly a dumping place for victims of Stalin's purges, lies in front of its forbidding wall. The monastery itself, with its bolted-shut front gate, looked unoccupied when I circled it the first few times, but Mila later arranged for Liz to enter and visit a studio where icons were being restored. It turned out that Saveli Yamschikov, a scholar of Russian ecclesiastical art whom Mila had introduced us to in 1974, was in charge. Not long after we left Moscow in 1987, Saveli arranged for Mila's son, Alyosha, to apprentice at his studio.

When Liz and I wanted a more challenging outing, we'd stroll along the river to the more distant Simonov Monastery. It sits on a knoll close to the sprawling grounds of the ZIL automotive factory (*Zavod imeni Lenina*). I had wandered through the monastery's destroyed buildings during my second assignment, but a fortresslike wall had since been built around them, and I could only guess as to what was going on inside.

On a walk one Saturday morning, I followed a truck hauling live cattle to a plant which turned out to be a slaughterhouse, a meat *kombinat*. It explained the odors that sometimes wafted through the apartment, reminding me of my six months as a boy in Chicago when the stockyards reeked of slaughtered cattle.

On September 21, Liz described the view from one window:

> I have a great view as I type this: rain, mud, a crane, an unfinished building, a vegetable stand (that means beets, potatoes, and cabbage) with a line of a hundred miserable looking people in front of it, all dragging their bags filled with the things they have already bought. The unfinished building will be unfinished two years from now, and the crane will still be there.

> I went out to the store to get my week's supply of bread, which I cut in half and put in the freezer, and I never saw so many beaten-down people. Boy, after 35 or 40 years, everybody looks terrible here . . . . The local bar next to the bread store was in full operation at noon, jammed with people, women too. They never sit down when they drink, so they can get a lot of people into the bar.

Moscow contained more uncompleted buildings than we had seen during the first two assignments, and the quality of the work seemed to have declined. A member of a Housing and Urban Development (HUD) delegation, whom I briefed the same week, told me that a colleague of his, a builder from California, had been taken to a new building in Leningrad. Upon viewing it, he told his host, "If one of my contractors had put it up, I'd tell him to tear the goddamn thing down and start over."

Liz's letter went on to describe how we were preparing for winter. Since the apartment was on the twelfth floor, neighbors had warned us we'd freeze ("You will never get above fifty degrees"). Because the district's steam heat wouldn't be turned on until mid-October, we ordered electric heaters from Helsinki and sealed up the windows. They were double-pane but only a few would tightly close; I worked a Saturday afternoon stuffing wet newspapers around the frames and securing them with duct tape. My timing was good; the first snow fell on September 30.

It didn't take long before we had seen our old friends. I brought Igor Palmin into the apartment in early October after having met him at the Proletarskaya Station. Having renounced all alcohol, he looked wonderful. Then Ed and Nina Stevens hosted a dinner party. They had celebrated their fiftieth wedding anniversary just before we returned; Ed was full of interesting stories, but was suffering from a debilitating spinal condition.

We were also making new contacts. A Greek journalist based in Moscow, whom we had met in Athens, invited us to join him and his Russian wife on a boat trip down the river organized by a group of California peaceniks. It was a blustery cold day, the first Saturday in September. Among the guests were a Russian actress, a Russian film director, a Kazakh actor (who told Liz she looked like Bette Davis), the Maltese ambassador, and a group of third-world journalists. A Russian Dixieland band played, vodka flowed, and the Californians gave everyone a small crystal rock—a keepsake, they explained—to symbolize mankind's enduring hope for peace. A Russian scholar from the academy's Oriental institute brought an editor from a Moscow literary journal as his date, and they expressed skepticism about Gorbachev. Later, the woman invited us to her apartment where we saw a chest of drawers that had once belonged to Beria.

The Maltese ambassador invited me to several receptions where I met unofficial artists whose work he exhibited (and sold) from his apartment. I heard later that he was forced to abbreviate his tour; the KGB was displeased by his choice of friends.

For the first time ever, I was conscious of overt surveillance in Moscow. During the first two assignments, Liz and I had been followed but usually by car, and rather discreetly. Now two agents—one cadaverous in appearance (resembling the actor Jack Palance), the other husky and wearing tennis shoes—tracked me from the Proletarskaya Station to work. It was obvious they wanted me to see them, to know that I was being watched; they made no pretense of hiding behind other passengers. They weren't a bother but brought to mind the "misshapen peasants" (*urodliviye muzhiki*) who haunt Anna Karenina.[447]

When I approached Tchaikovsky 19's main pedestrian entrance on my second day (the entrance had served as a vehicle entrance during my first two tours, but the Seabees had since converted it to a narrow passageway with a booth where a marine now stood), I was stopped by a militia guard who asked me to identify myself. I rejected his demand and walked right in. I didn't realize that the British had just "exfiltrated" a KGB officer who had been spying for them, and that the guards at every NATO-country embassy in Moscow had heightened their vigilance. A few months later, two militiamen blocked me from attending a meeting of economic officers at the British embassy after I refused to identify myself (this time they didn't yield), and I missed the meeting, although colleagues from other embassies, apparently less committed to principle of unrestricted access, didn't.

After a few weeks, the overt surveillance ceased. It didn't resume until we moved into the new embassy compound.

In October, I sent my first note to the Foreign Ministry requesting permission to travel. I wanted to visit the Tyumen oil and gas fields in western Siberia. A Soviet delegation to the United States had just visited Alaska, and a Soviet energy official had assured me there would be no problem as my trip would be "reciprocal."

Yet the Foreign Ministry denied my request, as it denied every travel request I submitted during my final assignment. Apparently the KGB wanted to keep me in Moscow under its nose.

*   *   *

Ambassador Arthur Hartman and his wife, Donna, returned on October 1, 1985. A career FSO, Hartman had spent most of his overseas years in Western Europe, including a tour in Paris as ambassador. He had earlier headed the department's Bureau of European Affairs, accompanying Kissinger on several of his détente-promoting trips to the USSR.

Participating in Harvard's commencement in 1947, Hartman had heard Secretary Marshall describe what would soon be the Marshall Plan. (Also in the audience was Richard Pipes; he found "nothing but commonplaces" in Marshall's address at the time, but later judged it to be "one of the most important public speeches of the century.")[448]

Hartman spoke little Russian and had not served at the embassy before his arrival in 1981, just after Liz and I had completed our second tour. He did not claim to be a Soviet expert but was naturally curious and intelligent. Before taking up the assignment, he had gone to George Kennan in Princeton who told him, "Don't worry about any studies of what has happened since 1917 and the Russian Revolution. Go get yourself a couple of good nineteenth century memoirs."[449] I have no doubt that this is what Hartman did.

We shook hands on October 2. Looking younger than his fifty-nine years, he was over six feet tall, with a gracious manner. The next morning, he summoned me to join a meeting he was having with Donald Kendall, Pepsico's CEO, who was in Moscow seeing Soviet officials. Kendall had been the driving force behind Pepsico's entry into the Soviet market.

Kendall told the ambassador that his company was planning to build ten more bottling plants in addition to the sixteen already operating. In exchange, the Soviets were pressing to have a second brand of vodka distributed in the United States. (Pepsico was already distributing Stolichnaya). They hinted that Edgar Bronfman, representing Seagram's, might be given the business if Kendall didn't oblige. Bronfman was president of the World Jewish Congress and was someone whom Moscow wanted to cultivate. Kendall explained that he had offered Bronfman part of the Soviet deal fifteen years before, but Bronfman had declined out of concern for the Jewish lobby.

Kendall told the ambassador that he was optimistic about Pepsico's Soviet business because of Gorbachev's plans. The chairman of Gosbank, Vladimir Alkhimov, had just told him that in order to revive the economy, Gorbachev would be guided by the New Economic Policy, which Lenin had adopted in the early 1920s. Enterprises would be more independent; proposals for joint ventures with Western companies would be expedited.

When I walked Kendall out of Hartman's office, he took a moment to survey the photographs of ambassadors hanging in the corridor near the marine post. "Thompson and Bohlen had been your best ambassadors," he said; "Beam the weakest, Stoessel all right, and Toon all right but belligerent." He passed over Watson's photograph without comment. His favorite, he said, had been Spike Dubs; the chargé for thirteen months, although Spike, as I recall, wasn't pictured.

Unknown to me at the time, Kendall may have been in the running to replace Hartman. After his Moscow trip, Kendall told Dobrynin that Robert McFarlane, Reagan's second NSC advisor, had sounded him out about the position, but he had declined because of the press of business.[450] If Dobrynin's report is accurate, the White House was considering replacing Hartman as Liz and I were settling in.

A few days later, the ambassador and Donna hosted a reception for newcomers. They had been in Moscow for five years already, at a time when relations were badly strained; yet they struck me as no less enthusiastic about the challenge than those of us who had just arrived.

Then they flew off to Helsinki to attend a performance of the violinist Isaac Stern, a personal friend. The embassy staff knew Helsinki more for shopping than high culture, but the Hartmans were interested in classical music. They brought back 250 lemons, something rare in Moscow, which the commissary distributed as gifts.

Secretary of State and Mrs. Shultz arrived for their two-day visit on Monday, November 4. Following the Kissinger tradition, they came with two aircraft, twenty-four journalists, and dozens of officials, including department administrative and security personnel. They had been preceded by a large advance party. As Liz wrote, "The embassy was turned upside down for at least ten days before Shultz got here."

The Shultzes stayed at Spaso House. The secretary was scheduled to meet twice with Shevardnadze at the ministry's guesthouse on Alexei Tolstoi Street and once with Gorbachev. According to the ministry's diplomatic note, the latter meeting would take place in the leader's "private study" at the Kremlin at 10:00 AM on Tuesday. One of my assignments was to escort members of Shultz's security detail to the fortress before the secretary arrived himself, a not unusual role for an FSO since Washington began sending huge delegations to Moscow.

I hadn't previously encountered the term *private study* to describe an office in the Kremlin, but Gorbachev was doing things differently. Two KGB officers, including Captain Vladimir Sovkin from the ninth directorate (which was responsible for protecting Soviet leaders), drove me and two of Shultz's security men to the Kremlin. It took all of four minutes from Spaso House, with the militia waving us through every light. Entering the vehicle gate at Borovitsky Tower, we disembarked at the Council of Ministers building. Welcoming us, the commandant of the Kremlin led us three flights upstairs through entrance 2 (*pod'ezd 2*), which I knew well from earlier visits, to the top floor.

The secretary's security agents quickly found that their radio devices couldn't bring in their colleagues still waiting with Shultz at Spaso House. Unless Soviet countermeasures were involved, the Kremlin's walls were trumping American technology.

We sat in an anteroom off the main corridor. We were not given any official word but figured that Shultz, Hartman, and NSC Advisor McFarlane, along with their American interpreter, had made their way to the study by a different route and that the meeting was underway.

We sat and sat as the Soviets served tea. One of Shultz's agents read a paperback copy of *The Hunt for Red October*, and I occasionally chatted with our hosts. After almost three hours, one of the Russians finally said it was time to leave. Upon reaching the embassy, I was dumbfounded to hear that Shultz hadn't gone to the Kremlin after all; Gorbachev had met with him at the Central Committee building on Moscow's Old Square, at the Party's headquarters. Gorbachev hadn't informed the Foreign Ministry, the KGB, or the Kremlin's commandant.

I knew that the embassy's role, apart from Hartman, would be limited, mostly providing logistical support; but still, what a waste.

Few Americans had been inside the Party's Old Square building. It turned out that Matlock had been one. An *apparatchik* had invited him there in 1984 when he was in Moscow with Vice President Bush for Andropov's funeral. Matlock wrote later: "Now, after twenty-three years of trying [from his first assignment in Moscow in 1961], I was entering that inner sanctum of the Communist system."[451]

I could understand his reaction. The building's only other visitors from the United States had been top officials from the Communist Party of the United States (CPUSA) and several scholars. It was daring for the new leader to open the Party's hallowed building to a name capitalist like Shultz.

Gorbachev's decision to do so may have grown out of his feeling that "it was time for foreign affairs to be managed directly by the party," the words that Dobrynin used to explain why Gorbachev had selected Shevardnadze—a republic Party leader and not one of Gromyko's longtime aides—as foreign minister.[452] For Dobrynin, the setting accentuated the "businesslike character"[453] of the Shultz meeting, but it must have appalled Gromyko.

In his memoir, Shultz describes the meeting in a chapter entitled "Classroom in the Kremlin."[454] But the Kremlin was where the meeting did not occur. One day later, *Pravda* also reported that the meeting occurred in the Kremlin. Shultz's confusion could be forgiven, but confusion in the daily "Organ of the Central Committee of the CPSU"? This was unusual, but symptomatic of the turmoil Gorbachev was creating.

Shultz flew back to Washington on November 5 and invited Dobrynin to his office two days later. He then briefed Reagan at the White House. Of his meetings in Moscow and Washington, Shultz would write: "I was feeling good. We were on to something."[455]

Gorbachev's presentation would have daunted a less determined secretary. According to Hartman's account, Gorbachev was argumentative and belligerent, especially targeting Reagan's Strategic Defense Initiative (SDI): "If you want superiority through your SDI, we will not help you . . . . But we will also not reduce our offensive missiles. We will engage in a buildup that will break your shield."

Dobrynin was sufficiently disturbed that he delivered "something of an apology" when he saw Shultz on November 7.[456]

At the time of that meeting, I was on Red Square for the Revolution's celebration. As on May Day, access was strictly controlled. Among diplomats, only heads of mission, their spouses, and senior military attachés were invited.

NATO ambassadors had been boycotting the celebration since the invasion of Afghanistan, and Hartman had passed his two invitations to Mark Ramee and me. For two and one-half hours, we stood in the diplomatic section (the mausoleum to our right) amid Communist and third-world representatives as well as security types in plainclothes and uniform.

The embassy's defense attachés working with NATO colleagues had earlier scouted out the hardware, pre-positioned at sites around the city, which the Soviets intended to show. The attachés had even determined its order of appearance, from motorized antitank missile batteries and armored personnel carriers at the beginning to nuclear weapon-capable SCUD rockets at the end.

It was a raw drizzly day, the temperature a few degrees above freezing. Above the dome of Sverdlov Hall beyond the wall behind us, the Soviet red flag waved continuously, the wind machine going full blast. The troops' hurrahs resounded as they marched by. "'Hu-ra-a-ah!' the prolonged shout echoed down the line," exactly as Tolstoy had described them a century before.[457]

While waiting in vain for Shultz two days earlier, I had heard the same hurrahs. Stepping up to the third-floor window and peering over the wall, I could see that the square was empty except for the usual snakelike throng leading to the mausoleum. Thanks to modern sound technology, the hurrahs on Red Square were always robust.

My colleagues from the economic section and I spent all day Saturday, November 9, analyzing the "guidelines" for the USSR's twelfth five-year plan ("for 1986-1990 and for the period up to 2000"). That morning's *Pravda* had devoted more than five pages to summarizing them, and we converged on Tchaikovsky 19 to develop the embassy's telegraphic report.

The guidelines reflected ideas that Gorbachev had been promoting, including ones that had set analysts abuzz when I was in Washington. The plan itself would be adopted by the Communist Party at its Congress in February 1986.

In one of his first speeches as leader, Gorbachev had not only bewailed the country's uncompleted construction projects but also its wasteful use of labor. Accusing managers at the ZIL automotive plant of planning to hire twenty-five thousand additional workers, he had ordered them to look for growth instead through science and technology, not increases in labor or material inputs on which they, and most other managers, had come to depend.

However, neither Gorbachev in his speeches nor the plan as foreshadowed in the guidelines called for the truly fundamental reform the system needed. But how could the regime dismantle central planning and supply, as controlled by Moscow's huge Gosplan and Gossnab organizations (the State Committee for Planning and the State Committee for Material and Technical Supply) without risking crippling dislocations? This would remain an impossible challenge, and the dislocations that ensued in the wake of Gorbachev's partial reforms would contribute importantly to bringing both Gorbachev and his successor, Yeltsin, down.

I don't recall that we made any dire predictions in our November 9 report, but we must have let Washington know that the numbers didn't add up and that exhortations from even a vigorous leader couldn't guarantee reform. The thrust of our reporting throughout 1985-86 was that managers no longer heeded Moscow's directives, workers no longer stood in awe of managers, statistics were becoming less reliable, and corruption was spreading. Moreover, the technology that might have increased productivity was nowhere to be seen. A leader like Gorbachev could break with protocol, but he didn't have the knowledge or the power (and the Stalinist personality) to transform the economy.

I reached home in time to don a tuxedo and join Liz at Spaso House for the marine ball. The ballroom was jammed (I hadn't seen many of the faces before), and we danced until early morning.

Sergeant Clayton Lonetree, one of those with whom we had lunched, spent the evening with Violetta Seina, a Russian employee with whom I had chatted when she was serving as a telephone operator at the residence. Only a few days before the ball, Liz had baked a cake for Lonetree, as the wives did for the marines when they celebrated their birthdays.

Seina had struck me as a bit saucy and sly, and I wasn't surprised when I heard that Mrs. Hartman had asked general services to reassign her to Tchaikovsky 19.

The switchboard at Spaso House had long been an issue. When Lillian Hellman stayed at the residence toward the end of the war, she found that the operator "listened in on all conversations, even in languages he said he didn't understand, and sometimes he made a point of coughing into the phone to let you know he was there."[458]

Four months after the ball, in March 1986, Lonetree would be posted to Vienna, where Ron Lauder, rewarded for his Pentagon work, was serving as ambassador. In December 1986, Lonetree confessed to having had an affair with Violetta, and a month later, the "spy scandal" burst upon us.

On November 13, the Hartmans hosted a performance of the Manhattan String Quartet. It was the ensemble's first tour of the Soviet Union, and Shostakovich was on the program. At a candlelit dinner in the ballroom following the performance, I sat with the German ambassador, the wife of the Belgian ambassador, and an Italian correspondent; Liz sat with the Canadian deputy chief of mission, a British diplomat, and the British wife of a Russian refusenik. Spaso House shone at times like this.

*   *   *

A week later, Hartman flew off to Geneva to take part in the first Reagan-Gorbachev summit, from November 19 to 25, 1985. On his return he briefed the country team. By his description, Gorbachev continued to be preoccupied by SDI, seeing it as the prelude to Washington's deployment of offensive weapons in space. The president's promise to share the technology wasn't believed (including by some on his own staff), and there were no breakthroughs at the summit, but the tone was at least civil. I was pleased to hear that Reagan had mentioned family-reunification cases to Gorbachev and that Gorbachev and his wife, at one dinner, had acknowledged that religion in Russia was experiencing resurgence. In one toast, Gorbachev had quoted from the Bible.

By the end of the three-day event, the Soviet leader had decided *not* to allow Reagan's insistence on SDI be a stumbling block to further negotiations. He had come to understand that if he wanted to achieve progress, he would have to set aside his blanket opposition.

Shultz described the climactic moment. Gorbachev was haranguing Reagan about SDI when the president "exploded." Angry words went back and forth until Reagan "got the floor." The president spoke "passionately about how much better the world would be if we were able to defend ourselves against nuclear weapons . . . . We must do better, and we can."

After Reagan finished, "there was total silence."

Finally, Gorbachev said, "Mr. President, I don't agree with you, but I can see that you really mean what you say."

Shultz concluded that Reagan had "nailed into place an essential plank" of the American position.[459]

The summit confirmed the conclusion of two agreements with which the economic section was marginally involved: air safety in the northern Pacific and air service between the United States and the USSR. The negotiations had been carried out by aviation experts, and we had helped expedite their completion.

Other summits would be held before the Cold War ended; had the ice not been broken at Geneva, however, it wouldn't have ended as soon, and perhaps as quietly, as it did.

*   *   *

Security was on the ambassador's mind when he returned from Geneva. The subject kept coming up at meetings. He warned that he and Combs would check all outgoing telegrams classified confidential or above to confirm they had been typed in the special room.

For the first time, I heard him mention the name "David Major." Major was an FBI official assigned to the NSC; he had been promoting the idea that the embassy should operate without Russians. Matlock had suggested the same in 1981, and he was at the NSC too.

Major headed the NSC's counterintelligence unit. During a visit to the embassy, he had taken photographs showing the Soviet employees—some of whom were undoubtedly KGB—working alongside Americans in the ground floor offices and the courtyard shacks. For Major, who hadn't worked at an embassy before, this was apparently proof that the KGB had control of Tchaikovsky 19.

With his photographs, he made a slideshow for Reagan because, as Kessler later explained, "the President responded better to pictures than to words."[460] Hartman said that Major was a spellbinding speaker and had also impressed Reagan's NSC advisor (McFarlane) and CIA director (Casey).

It was probably Major, in a briefing on "Soviet espionage within our embassy in Moscow," who prompted the president to record in his diary, "I was overwhelmed by the evidence of high tech alterations in our typewriters which have delivered our top most papers & messages to the Soviets."[461] Reagan had been told earlier of different staffing arrangements at the U.S. and Soviet embassies ("We haven't one Am. employee in the Soviet embassy in Wash. They have 209 in our embassy in Wash. [sic—Moscow]."[462]

I surmised that Hartman had received an earful about security from Shultz and others in Vienna. A great deal of misinformation about how the embassy operated, he said, was now circulating in Washingtgon.

The ambassador let us know that the embassy would begin reducing the number of its Soviet employees; the first group had already been identified and their dismissal would occur soon ("the cuts won't be deep")—and discussions would begin shortly about a second group ("these cuts will hurt"). He said that Reagan had already approved a decision to reduce the size of the Soviet Mission to the UN (from which the KGB and GRU had long spied) from 275 to 170.

On December 12, Charles Redman, the department's press spokesman, made a brief comment that the embassy would replace "a substantial number" of its Soviet employees with Americans, but he gave no timetable. He assured that "no national [Soviet] employees are employed in sensitive jobs and none have access to any area of the embassy where classified work is performed."[463]

Redman also said that Reagan had signed a classified directive mandating lie detector tests of government employees to improve the country's "counter-espionage and counterintelligence" capabilities. On December 17, the administrative section duly circulated a memorandum entitled "Polygraphing State Department employees and contractors," alerting us to the directive and reporting that each agency would select its own method for carrying it out.[464]

Someone back in Washington might have reminded Reagan that when the Senate was considering Bohlen's nomination to be ambassador to the Soviet Union, Senator McCarthy had asked that he be required to take a lie detector test, and even conservative Republicans, including Bob Taft of Ohio and William Knowland of California (not to mention Secretary of State John Foster Dulles), had recoiled at the idea. At the time, McCarthy was doing the dirty work of Scott McLeod, a former FBI agent who, as head of the department's security office, had already purged a number of FSOs, including Bohlen's brother-in-law, Charles Thayer.[465]

Would the president have changed his mind? Probably not. The "unhistorical Reagan," to use the phrase of historian Fritz Stern, had already visited the Bitburg cemetery where members of the notorious Waffen-SS were buried, over the objections of Shultz and others that this was not a good way to commemorate the Allied landings at Normandy.[466]

Shultz was queried two days later, on December 19, whether he would take a lie detector test were he asked to do so. "Once," he answered. "The minute in this government I am told that I'm not trusted is the day I leave."[467] I didn't learn of Shultz's reaction until years later, but it conveyed how many of us felt when we saw the administrative memorandum.

However, this didn't end the "polygraph affair" In April 1987, four months after the marine scandal broke, Shultz had to overrule a recommendation by an ambassadorial-rank FSO, William Brown, that personnel at the embassy be subjected to the test. After observing that the test is not reliable and probably can be beaten by professional spies (as Aldrich Ames would later do), Shultz wrote in his memoir: "If the security experts felt that the only way to deal with the security challenge was to transform the American system into one resembling the Soviet system, then they'd lose me for good."[468]

The FSO making the recommendation ought to have known better; he had seen the Soviet system close at hand, having served at Tchaikovsky 19 twice during his own career.

*   *   *

The economic section was fully engaged during the month of December. The U.S.-USSR Trade and Economic Council (USTEC) opened its ninth annual meeting on December 9, and 450 American business executives flew in to participate and, if possible, make deals. Secretary of Commerce Malcolm Baldridge represented the administration.

The main social event was a dinner that Gorbachev and Hartman attended in the ornate Faceted Hall of the Kremlin's Granite Palace. I represented the embassy at a second dinner, in the Kremlin's far less august Palace of Congresses.

Baldridge met with Gorbachev for an hour and a half and found him more positive than when they had met the prior May. Gorbachev suggested that the two sides stop arguing about their differences. "Our systems are different. We think we have democracy, you think otherwise. But let's look for practical solutions." Gorbachev made no reference to SDI, lending support to the belief that Moscow was de-linking SDI from negotiations about strategic and tactical nuclear arms.

I escorted one of USTEC's guests, Mayor Dianne Feinstein of San Francisco, on calls to various officials, including Vladimir Promyslov, Moscow's mayor since 1963 (he would be dismissed shortly after our meeting), and the Minister of Culture Piotr Demichev, a Politburo member.

Brezhnev had made Demichev the Central Committee's cultural watchdog in 1965 and then, a decade later, had given him the ministerial portfolio. I had seen him close at hand at a luncheon that Toon gave in Spaso House. By reputation, he was two-faced—socially most agreeable but privately uncompromising.

Solzhenitsyn had seen both faces in 1965, shortly after Brezhnev had toppled Khrushchev. Because Khrushchev had authorized *Novy Mir*'s publication of *One Day in the Life of Ivan Denisovich*, the first literary exposé in the USSR of the camps, Solzhenitsyn was concerned as to what the change would mean. He had already smuggled a copy of his *First Circle* abroad and secreted a second copy with friends; and he had begun working on what would later become *The Gulag Archipelago*. When Tvardovsky, *Novy Mir*'s editor, suggested a meeting with Demichev, Solzhenitsyn agreed.

To all appearances, the meeting went quite well. "I can see you really are an honest, straightforward Russian," Demichev said to the writer. A bit later, "I can see that you really are a very modest man." As the meeting concluded, Demichev told the writer, with seeming satisfaction, "*They* [the Soviet authorities] have not been given a second Pasternak [italics in original]."

Yet, several weeks later, the KGB raided the apartment of Solzhenitsyn's friends and seized *The First Circle* manuscript. According to Solzhenitsyn, the KGB had probably wired his friends' apartment and overheard the version of the Demichev meeting that he had passed along.[469] Around the same time, the authorities began prosecuting the literary critic Andrei Sinyavsky, kicking off Brezhnev's all-out assault on dissidents.

It is difficult to believe that Demichev wasn't aware of the looming crackdown when he met Solzhenitsyn.

The mayor of San Francisco, two of her aides, and I called on Demichev on December 10. Feinstein began with praise for Moscow's sights, saying she wished more Americans could see them. The minister in turn spoke highly of San Francisco. "We have no Golden Gate or ocean, but Moscow has its strong points, and perhaps more Americans will come and visit us after the successful summit."

The minister and the mayor then explored possible exchanges, including art, antique cars, streetcars, ballet troupes, and symphony orchestras. Demichev had just met with Armand Hammer, also attending the USTEC meeting, and they had agreed on an art exchange involving Leningrad's

Hermitage. Feinstein encouraged Demichev to travel to San Francisco for the opening of the show. It would be a "dream," he replied.

The meeting ended after fifty minutes. Not an unpleasant word was spoken. Perhaps naïvely, I had hoped that the mayor (who became a senator in 1992) would allude to Demichev's "other" cultural interests, including the repression of writers and closing of plays.

Two days later, Demichev attended the Congress of Russian Writers in the company of his Politburo colleagues, including Gorbachev. Yevtushenko delivered a strong speech that referred favorably to Pasternak, called for an end to silence about Stalin's purges, and praised Gorbachev's policy of openness.[470] *Pravda* and *Literaturnaya gazeta* carried only a few lines from his speech, and nothing about Pasternak or the purges.

The USTEC chairman on the Soviet side was Vladimir Sushkov, a deputy minister of foreign trade. Not long after the American business leaders left for the United States—a few with deals—Sushkov was arrested and charged with taking a $50,000 bribe from a Japanese firm. According to Kulagin, Sushkov had been buying "vast quantities" of consumer items during trips to Italy and shipping them back to his cronies. The Soviet ambassador in Rome had even complained to the KGB.[471]

There was no reference to Sushkov's arrest in the media until August 1986 when *Izvestiya* cited his name in a back-page report on the ministry's corruption.[472] But I had an inkling that something was awry when my copy of the *USTEC Journal,* edited and published in New York, arrived in January 1986, a month after the meeting; Sushkov was missing from all the events and the photographs.[473] Although edited by an American, the *Journal,* at Moscow's behest, had already made him a nonperson. Sushkov would later receive a ten-year sentence for bribe-taking.

Beria's disappearance in 1954 had at least been announced; subscribers to the *Large Soviet Encyclopedia* received instructions to excise the entry about him and to paste in a new one, an essay about the Bering Sea. As Gorbachev's first year ended, his policy of openness hadn't sunk deep roots.

*   *   *

Socially, December was always a hectic month. Before Christmas, the economic section hosted a large dinner party at one of the new dachas at Serebryanny Bor, a twenty-minute drive from Tchaikovsky 19. We invited members of the Western community and diplomatic colleagues. Our wives prepared food at home, and we hauled it, along with the makings of a bar, to the dacha. While the party was a success, the dachas had been built from kits purchased in Finland and lacked the ambiance, not to mention the memories, of the ones we knew at Tarasovka.

Igor and his wife Svetlana had hosted us earlier in the month. The temperature was fifteen degrees above zero; and the car wouldn't start, so we set out for their place the Russian way, riding a Metro line to its last stop, riding a bus another mile, and then trudging through ten inches of snow. Svetlana served chicken and rice with two vegetables we had never tasted, grass shoots from the Caucasus and from Siberia she had marinated. A Hungarian brandy and coffee topped off the evening.

On December 15, just before Liz and I flew home for Christmas to be with the children, Ed Stevens had us over for dinner. Ed was celebrating the signing of a contract he and a London impresario had negotiated for the Bolshoi Ballet's appearance in Britain. The day before the dinner, Ed had telephoned to ask Liz whether she would bake a cake in honor of the birthday of the impresario's wife. Nina was away in the United States, and Alfredo, at Uncle Sam's, was now too busy to fill outside orders.

Yuri Grigorovich, the director of the Bolshoi Ballet (he held the position from 1964 to 1995, well past the system's collapse) and the prima ballerina Natalia Bessmertnova were among Ed's guests. Liz and I spent much of the evening talking with Saveli Yamshchikov, the icon scholar, and the British ambassador and his wife, Sir Bryan and Lady Cartledge, whom we knew from the 1970s when he had served as head of chancery. Bryan had taken a double first in history and Russian at Cambridge University before serving as a don at Oxford. He had helped Sir Anthony Eden on his memoirs and had been Prime Minister Thatcher's private secretary for overseas affairs before his appointment. Lady Cartledge matched her husband in attractiveness and wit.

The Stevens' dining room was located in the basement of Ryleev 11. Designed by their architect son, it resembled the interior of a peasant lodging, an *izba*, with expanses of rustic-looking logs and brick as well as a hearth. The walls were hung with Russian icons and wood figurines.

Halfway through dinner, the director of Moscow's swimming pools, Ed's friend for more than twenty years, announced that he would be toastmaster. In a stentorian voice he launched into a lavish eulogy. "Edmund builds bridges between peoples . . . He's America's unofficial ambassador . . . We are gathered at America's unofficial embassy to celebrate Ed." Others added comments praising Ed and, in the spirit of the evening, Sir Bryan's wife, apparently not a student of Russian, interjected a few that were barely comprehensible.

We were seated together. Knowing that I had studied in Cambridge, Massachusetts, she told me about the year that she and Bryan had spent there on a Foreign Office sabbatical. She was nostalgic about the Brattle Theatre. "You know, *Casablanca* is my favorite film."

I couldn't resist Bogart's apocryphal line, "Here's looking at you, kid." At this, she broke up in laughter, and we drank a glass of vodka in honor of Cambridge—America's and England's.

As the dinner progressed, Lady Cartledge turned maudlin. She explained that her husband, sitting at another table, was leaving for London the next day for consultations and that the Foreign Office had refused to pay her way. She had wanted to see her daughter whose adolescence had been affected by their many absences. Separations from loved ones, we agreed, defined the lives of our families.

"Here's looking at you," I said again, and she downed another vodka.

"I'll collapse if you say this again," she said.

I don't believe I said it, but not long thereafter Lady Cartledge collapsed. Bryan rushed to her side, wrapped his arms about her, and carried her up the stone staircase and out of Ryleev into the night.

The party continued until early morning. Had it occurred before 1917, I know it would have ended with us flinging glasses into the smoldering hearth.

*　　*　　*

Liz and I returned to Moscow from Illinois on January 5, 1986.

I hadn't found my name on the promotion list the previous October (the Foreign Service was promoting fewer officers at my level, reportedly 30 percent fewer as compared with the prior decade). I wasn't terribly surprised (the time I had spent in New York and at the FSI hadn't helped). If my name wasn't on the next list, however, I'd have to look for a job.

During my absence, security had confiscated my typewriter. "What's going on?" I asked one of its officers. The response was that the Soviets could also pick up signals from a manual typewriter. This made no sense to me, but there was no point arguing in view of the rising drumbeat about security. Henceforth I'd prepare my classified reports by hand for my secretary to type two flights below.

At the country-team meeting on January 6, Combs reported that samples taken by the spy dust team had turned out "positive" and that further tests would have to be conducted. A few days later, the Hartmans returned from leave in Washington.

Winters in Moscow are difficult, but January and February 1986 were especially harsh. The wind was so fierce one morning that Liz and I had to cling to each other to reach the Metro. Russians don't like midseason thaws, but there was a major one at the end of January, which was followed by a hard freeze. The city authorities no longer cleared sidewalks the way they had, and on February 1 I took a dive on slick ice and sprained a wrist. Two weeks earlier, I had fallen and jammed a thumb. Hartman warned everyone to be careful. He said he knew of three serious injuries due to falls, including a concussion and a broken bone. I remarked in a letter home that the *babushka*s now preferred factory work to clearing sidewalks.

The cars of staff members also took a beating. Although our Ford was parked inside a guarded compound, I found the driver's side door bashed in one morning. Another car had likely slid into it, although deliberately inflicted damage could never be excluded.

I spent the evening of February 1 at the district militia station. A thirteen-year-old Russian boy had sneaked into the compound and smashed a neighbor's car window to steal two videotapes. The militiaman had caught the boy, and the neighbor summoned me to be the interpreter.

Liz was also involved with cars. In mid-January, the spy dust team returned from Washington to conduct more tests. Liz volunteered to sit in the ambassador's unheated garage while the experts examined officers' cars. On February 20, she was summoned again to help two staffers from the medical office take further samples, including from the ambassador's personal vehicle. We had been told the week before, however, that the KGB was using its tracking agent selectively, and it didn't pose a health hazard.

While we were away in December, the Soviet employees who worked on the ground floor of the central wing had been moved to the courtyard outbuildings. The embassy was now able to inform Washington that no Russians worked in the central wing.

The Americans in the administration section, including the personnel office, were moved upstairs to the sixth floor. After passing the marine desk on the ninth floor, Liz had to descend three flights on the internal staircase, two more than me. Debris and dust lay about as the Seabees set to work installing a bathroom.

Beginning in January, the head of security Fred Mecke, who had arrived with us in August 1985, required everyone to wear a photo ID badge. According to his memorandum, "Cleared U.S. citizen employees and long-term TDYers" would receive blue badges; "non-cleared U.S. citizen employees" white badges; nannies, journalists, teachers, contractors, etc., white badges with an overprinted black V; and Soviet employees, pink badges. The color determined the extent of one's access inside Tchaikovsky 19.

There was some grousing ("If Russians are now barred from the central wing, what's the point of having badges?"), and a few argued with security or the marines. One wag circulated a spoof memorandum identical to Fred's requiring employees to wear smocks of a different color, the Soviets receiving pink smocks. "These smocks," according to the hoax, will also enable the staff "to keep your work clothes much cleaner and dust-free."[474]

The Russian char force whom the marines used to escort around the upper floors at night—to collect unclassified waste and vacuum carpets—was no longer on the job. Every officer and secretary was made responsible for keeping his or her work area in good condition; vacuum cleaners were distributed.

Administrative officers began issuing a stream of memoranda. Because of the staff's rapid expansion and its relative inexperience, and perhaps pressure from Washington, they probably believed they had no choice but to spell things out in meticulous detail. Thus, those who used correction tape when typing were warned to destroy it or store it as classified material should it include a "recognizable portion of a classified word, phrase, or sentence"—an obvious precaution.

We were informed on March 11 that light bulbs in the embassy's secure areas were now the responsibility of "the cleaning contractor, Robert Stufflebeam":

> If a lightbulb [sic] in your work area needs to be replaced, fill out a work order addressed to the GSO [general services unit]. Please specify where the burned-out bulb is located and what kind of bulb it is (i.e., regular incandescent with wattage stated, or 4 foot fluorescent tube, etc.).

Stufflebeam was a tall good-looking marine. He and several other marines were being paid to do the work of the charwomen. Previously the Seabees or someone in the office concerned replaced the light bulbs. Now the marines were in charge.

The general services unit was so overwhelmed that families living in outlying compounds were instructed not to submit requests for repairs at their apartments. We were also told not to bring our cars into the courtyard for any reason—including inflating tires—without security's approval.

Because air could not be easily obtained at the few garages available in Moscow, this was more of a hardship than appeared.

Liz wrote home that the place was "going berserk" with security. "We are nearly locked into the embassy now, and the Soviets are completely out." Cipher locks had appeared on every door. "I have already memorized four combinations to safes . . . The doors are now so heavy that I have to drop everything and use both hands, shoulder muscles and feet solid to the ground, to get them open." By midwinter 1986, at least as much of our energy was going to security and to maintenance as to meeting our usual diplomatic responsibilities.

At the end of January, Combs reported that the department was about to inform the Soviets that they had to reduce their United Nations Mission (SMUN) by one hundred positions; it would begin to affect SMUN during the summer. I don't recall any follow-up discussions about the possibility of Soviet retaliation. Perhaps the front office didn't want to distract us.

Liz and I continued to see our Russian friends. I escorted several into Krutitsky Val to watch the film *An Officer and a Gentleman*. They were skeptical that Gorbachev would succeed in his campaign against corruption; the question for them was whether he would resort to "administrative measures" once he ran out of patience.

Western economists were flocking to Moscow to collect insights about Gorbachev's reforms. In December, we had hosted Arthur Burns, President Nixon's Federal Reserve chairman, a scholar of the business cycle. Burns suffered from the cold, and I gave him a pair of bright red wool socks that made him look downright revolutionary when he visited Soviet institutes.

On January 21, we invited several Russian economists to dinner to continue discussions they had been having with Professor Marshall Goldman and his wife, who were visiting from Harvard's Russian Research Center.

A few evenings earlier, I had met a near-namesake of mine, Mats Oberg, the Swedish commercial counselor, at a party hosted at the Donskoi compound by Dr. Anders Aslund, that embassy's economic expert. Mats told me that had my forbears not emigrated from Sweden, my name would be spelled the same as his. "Do the genealogical research," he urged. He said I would find that when Sweden's King Charles XII defeated the Russians in 1700, making the Baltic Sea a Swedish lake, one of his fearless warriors had been an Ober.

Did my heredity ordain me to deal with these people?

On February 9, to celebrate their thirty-seventh wedding anniversary, the Hartmans hosted a piano concert by Vladimir Feltsman, a long-time refusenik whom they had befriended. When Feltsman applied for an exit visa in 1979, the authorities had not only turned his application down but purged his recordings from music stores and cancelled his engagements. For two years, he was not allowed to perform publicly. Then because of negative publicity, they grudgingly let him play in provincial towns. When he was finally permitted to perform in Moscow, they gave him a concert hall on the city's outskirts notorious for its bad acoustics; the only advertisement was a poster outside the hall that misspelled his name.

Liz and I arrived at Spaso House to find a flurry of activity around its grand piano. A friend of Feltsman had tuned and checked it earlier in the day; but moments before the concert, Feltsman checked it again and found that one string had been cut and two others were damaged in an attempt to cut them. It was an inside job, a case of KGB sabotage. Donna speculated that one of her cooks had been involved.

The Hartmans had invited thirty Russian friends, a few other ambassadors, and Americans from the embassy who knew Feltsman and his family or were known to be interested in serious music. The Soviet authorities had posted extra militiamen in front of Spaso House to scrutinize every guest.

An American correspondent, just before leaving his office for the concert, had received an anonymous telephone call (probably as a KGB joke) suggesting that he bring tools for repairs. The piano was, in fact, repaired by a friend of Feltsman, and he played compositions by Liszt. Afterwards, we were treated to a sit-down dinner and dancing.

Two months later, the Hartmans hosted Vladimir Horowitz, who was returning to Russia with his wife (Toscanini's daughter) after decades of living abroad. I failed to respond to Hartman's offer of tickets to Horowitz's performance at the conservatory, out of a belief that there were others who were more deserving—in retrospect, a mistake.

On February 22, Mike Einik and his wife, Sarah, invited Liz and me to visit their apartment in our former compound to hear a refusenik musical group perform Israeli songs. Six of the performers had been waiting to emigrate more than a decade.

Administrative and security issues continued to dog the embassy. A week after Feltsman's concert, the embassy school bus lost two rear wheels on the same day; probably the garage had overtorqued them, a further sign of Soviet pique.

In early March at a country-team meeting, the ambassador spoke of a "nonfraternization policy." I had never heard a head of mission use the phrase when talking to section heads, at Tchaikovsky 19 or other posts. Hartman also reminded us that one's social involvement with Soviet citizens shouldn't lead to any emotional involvement. This was so obvious, why say it? I thought to myself. Who did he suspect?

"Those officers with experience in the country and with a specific task", he continued, "can see people alone, others not. It was important that the embassy not cut itself off." The ambassador asked us to deliver the message to our staffs.

I assumed that Hartman had the marines and those with no reason to deal with Russians uppermost in his mind, but the fact that he felt he had to say it bothered me. Was the embassy so depleted of experience? From all the warnings issued and the measures taken, I felt that the embassy was already cutting itself off.

Not long thereafter, the ambassador and Combs reported that "we have more American staff than allowed."

Allowed by whom?

It appeared that a notional limit had been set for the Soviet embassy in Washington based on what the FBI and other agencies were recommending, and it would require a comparable limit in Moscow. No further explanation was provided, and it wasn't clear what kind of reductions would be made or when. Now we had something else to think about.

Liz flew to the United States to be with the children during their spring vacations. During her absence, I visited several theaters. I saw Chekhov's play *The Cherry Orchard* and the opera *Yevgeni Onegin*. With Mila's help, I secured a single ticket to the Taganka Theatre to see a four-hour play she had recommended, *Cerceau*, set on a stage with a mock dacha in the woods outside Moscow. It portrayed Russians of different generations conversing about themselves and their society.

My ears perked up when there seemed to be an allusion to the war in Afghanistan. An actor in a gas mask exclaimed:

> This is a war of lonely people. Everyone has his deep concrete foxhole on the side of a mountain. And from time to time, when our helicopters and airplanes direct fire from the mountain sides into the valley, we dart out and move to the next foxhole . . . How absurd and weird it is to see in this non-Christian country our nurses and their bright red crosses.

And on and on, against the din of off-stage "explosions."

During the intermission, I asked a young woman sitting next to me—a medical doctor—whether she thought the playwright was alluding to Afghanistan. She had been loquacious before the curtain went up, but now responded cautiously, "Let's see" (*"Posmotrim"*); and I couldn't restart the conversation.

Judging from what I saw on the Metro, Muscovites were more dispirited than usual. The long winter, the economy, and worsening reports from Afghanistan (Gorbachev's policy was encouraging more candid reporting) were taking a toll. Now and then a passenger would erupt in anger. A young male took a swing at me (and missed) as I pushed to the back of a crowded car. An old woman was shoved aside by a young woman pushing her way out. The old woman yelled "cow" to the woman, then unleashed a diatribe about the crudity of passengers. "Andropov wanted to exile two million people from Moscow. It's too bad he didn't."

In March 1986, the embassy library, which dated at least to the early 1940s, was dismantled. Word reached me that the space was urgently needed, and books were for the taking. I went downstairs and grabbed several from the few remaining, including one, *The Maritime History of Russia, 848-1948*, that bore Admiral Kirk's signature from his tour as ambassador from 1949 to 1952.

Kirk's successor, George Kennan, had written how Charles Bohlen had saved the Russian Division's library when the State Department moved to abolish it in the middle 1930s and how he (Kennan) had restored the books to their shelves after he became the Soviet desk officer.[475] But no Kennan or Bohlen was around in 1986 to save the embassy's library.

Mike Sellers, a CIA officer, was expelled by the Soviets for spying around the time the library was dismantled. Paul Stombaugh had been thrown out by the Soviets a year earlier; Paul had been working undercover in the economic section but had left before I met him.

The KGB was neutralizing the CIA's operations. This explained the mounting concern with security. Important officials back home had made up their mind that the embassy was to blame.

*   *   *

On April 9, 1986, the Soviet evening newscast *Vremya* showed me receiving a peace petition from representatives of a "committee to defend peace." They had wanted to deliver it to Hartman or Combs, but I was asked to accept it instead at the embassy's main entrance. Fred Mecke and a marine stood by to keep the Russians from entering.

The delegates, including a retired cosmonaut, made perfunctory complaints about being threatened with body searches and being denied entry. One of the representatives was the poet Rimma Kazakova. The television newscast, which claimed to have forty million viewers, carried a comment she made just after leaving the embassy that I knew her poetry. Actually, I had said that I was acquainted with the delegates' reputations; my Russian friends would be impressed, however, that I read poetry, even hers.

A week later, another officer received a similar delegation at the front entrance, and TASS criticized him for "having his hands in his pockets" when speaking with such distinguished callers.

Demonstrations against Tchaikovsky 19 were rare, but the Soviets organized three days of them beginning April 22 after U.S. Navy aircraft attacked Colonel Qaddafi's encampment in Libya. Several hundred Soviet and Arab students stood outside and chanted slogans ("Reagan is a murderer"). It was all quite controlled, but paint was hurled at the front façade, ink was thrown at a driver, and fists were shaken as we entered and left.

Just before the demonstration, Ambassador Hartman let Liz and I use his dacha for the weekend. Having a break at a time of tension was what we needed.

We read the books we brought out, wrote letters home ("We'll have a wood fire this evening and sip French wine"), and walked Tarasovka's tranquil paths.

Unknown to us, extraordinary events were lying in wait, not only at the embassy but elsewhere in the USSR.

13

One Explosion, Two Arrests, Reciprocity Runs Rampant

The fourth reactor of the Chernobyl nuclear power plant exploded at 1:23 AM on Saturday, April 26, 1986. I didn't become aware of it until the following Monday when a secretary in the front office showed me a telegram from Washington that reported, on the basis of satellite imagery, that a reactor was burning out of control.

There had been no Soviet announcement of the accident over the weekend, and the telegram, shown to section heads working on Tchaikovsky's top floors, generated no particular alarm. Chernobyl lay five hundred miles southwest of Moscow in the Soviet republic of Ukraine, and no one could say how the embassy would be affected, if indeed at all.

On Monday evening, Liz and I attended a dinner party hosted by a Belgian couple. During the *Vremya* television newscast at 9:00 PM, the announcer read a terse statement from TASS:

> An accident has occurred at the Chernobyl nuclear power station. One of its nuclear reactors was damaged. Measures are being taken to liquidate the consequences of the accident. Aid is being given to those affected. A government commission has been established.

Writing about Chernobyl on its twentieth anniversary, Serge Schmemann described the TASS announcement as "one of the great understatements of all time."[476]

Had the dinner party been at the home of an American diplomat, I am sure someone would have switched on a television set to hear the day's

351

top stories. Even then, however, we probably wouldn't have heard the announcement, for it was the twenty-second item, and few viewers watched *Vremya* for its full duration. Soviet television had given me better billing when the "peace delegation" visited the embassy.

Thanks to foreign broadcasts, reports of widespread contamination were soon circulating. Those who knew anything about radiation understood the explosion's possible ramifications for food and water.

For those in the embassy privy to satellite intelligence, the immediate concern was whether a second reactor, one closest to the fourth, would also explode. Fortunately it didn't.

At the country-team meeting on Tuesday morning, we learned that the Swedish embassy, alerted to abnormally high levels of radioactivity in Stockholm, had been informed by the Foreign Ministry that it had no information. A science section officer then gave us a briefing about the design and history of Soviet graphite reactors, but no one at the embassy could say what the accident would mean.

Liz and I attended five social events on the first three evenings of the week. By the time of Wednesday's reception—hosted by Pan American World Airways to mark its restoration of service—Chernobyl was the only topic of conversation.

The first guidance issued to the embassy community came in an administrative memorandum over the ambassador's name advising that "we are making no special recommendations regarding the use of water, fruits and vegetables, dairy products or meat products purchased and consumed in Moscow."[477] The memorandum noted, however, that the capital's water "comes from the east away from the area of the nuclear accident", that fruits and vegetables in Moscow's markets "are either last year's crops or those produced in greenhouses", and that fresh milk and dairy products consumed in Moscow "are produced in the Moscow region," not in areas proximate to Chernobyl. The memorandum carried no date but reached my desk on Tuesday. While it addressed the community's main concerns, others remained.

On Tuesday evening, Combs visited the Foreign Ministry under instructions from Washington and offered the Soviets U.S. technical and humanitarian help.

The embassy commissary was low on perishable goods, especially milk, due to a nationwide strike in Finland that had interrupted deliveries, and families with packaged dry milk were urged to share what they could with those with children. There were no American children in Krutitsky Val, but Liz established a rationing system for the four quarts of Finnish milk remaining in our freezer.

Pan Am let us know that one of its first flights to Leningrad carried only one passenger, and that half of the tour groups scheduled to visit the USSR from the United States had already cancelled.

We learned that the department had authorized women of childbearing age and children under sixteen to leave the embassy at Warsaw and the consulates at Krakow and Poznan. Ambassador Hartman noted that the traditional paddle tennis tournament in Warsaw, to which the embassy was planning to send a team, hadn't been called off; should we be piling into Poland while the posts there are letting women and children leave? After the meeting, we were told that the tournament had been cancelled.

NATO ambassadors were still boycotting official Soviet ceremonies, and Mark Ramee and I were again tapped to represent the embassy on Red Square, this time for the May Day parade. It turned out to be sunny and pleasant. Although the fourth reactor was still spewing radioactive dust over Belorussia, Ukraine, parts of Russia and the Baltics, some placards and banners targeted Reagan's Strategic Defense Initiative, "imperialism," and U.S. "state terrorism," with one showing Uncle Sam hurling a missile into space.

A Czechoslovak diplomat next to me complained that the Foreign Ministry was no longer serving wine at its stand near the diplomatic section. "It's giving us juice this year." A few weeks earlier, at a luncheon in the Palace of Congresses honoring Dante Fascell and other congressmen, Vadim Zagladin—first deputy head of the Central Committee's international department—and Georgi Arbatov, USA Institute director, had served only water and juice. Senior Soviet officials were observing the anti-alcohol campaign, at least in and around the Kremlin.

By Monday, May 5, a four-person health and radiation monitoring team from Washington was hard at work in a courtyard shack. They had brought along twelve trunks of equipment. Their preliminary measurements showed that radiation levels in Moscow were "normal," but they had no access to data about the city's background radiation and couldn't render a definitive opinion.

At the embassy, poisoning through the food chain—from milk obtained from cows eating radioactive grass and from products grown in radioactive soil around Chernobyl—remained on everyone's mind. Because the Soviet authorities weren't surveying the markets in Moscow for contaminated food, the administrative section began pouching food samples to Washington's Food and Drug Administration (FDA) for analysis. Two officers in my section, Mike Einik and Mike Mozur, had small children; and because the thyroid glands of children are more susceptible to radiation than those of adults, they would grab the administrative section's summary of the FDA findings as soon as they reached the office. According to the first one received in June, milk purchased ten days before showed 1395 Pico curies of iodine-131 per liter; ice cream, 1247 Pico curies of iodine-131 per kilo; and sour cream, 2480 Pico curies of iodine-131 per kilo. Readings for cesium-137 and 134 were also provided. The report concluded that "considering that there has been a one half life (approximately 8 days) reduction (50 percent) in the above I-131 levels, the levels at this time will be less than the FDA levels of concern for both adults and infants (less than one year)." Noting an omission, one of the Mikes scribbled an angry comment at the base of the memorandum: "What about the 137 and 134!?"[478]

Thyroid cancer turned out to be the most serious of Chernobyl's legacies, although no American was probably affected.[479]

Information also flowed into Tchaikovsky 19 from other embassies. We heard from the French that they had found a high level of radiation after testing veal bought in Moscow's main market. How much contamination were we ingesting when we ate or drank at receptions or dinner parties? Many in the diplomatic community simply hunkered down in their compounds.

Gorbachev proclaimed the need for openness, yet his policy had failed an important test. Not only did the Chernobyl accident go unreported for more than two days but the information being reported was usually incomplete. The regime kept millions in the dark about radiation poisoning. The report that received the widest distribution, through word of mouth, was never published; every Soviet citizen heard how Communist officials in Belorussia and Ukraine had rushed their families out of radioactive zones before May Day while ordinary citizens were encouraged to attend parades.

On Chernobyl's twentieth anniversary in 2006, the environmental organization Greenpeace (which makes no secret of its opposition to nuclear power) claimed that sixty thousand persons had died in Russia because of Chernobyl. A scientific study it released predicted that ninety-three thousand new deaths could be expected.[480] Reviewing the report, the *Economist* noted that Chernobyl's true cost may not be known "for decades."[481]

*   *   *

Toward the end of the country-team meeting on May 5, Ambassador Hartman mentioned that two of the embassy's six Russian-language teachers had been dismissed. Mila wasn't one of them.

The ambassador said that money was the problem, but obviously more was involved. The charwomen had been let go in December, and two young Americans had arrived in January to replace Svetlana and Lena at the embassy switchboard. Hartman, Combs and the administrative counselor were quietly thinning out the Russians according to the plan to which Hartman had earlier alluded.

The number of Americans at the embassy fluent or near-fluent in Russian was probably as low as it had ever been, yet we were dismantling the language program. Proficiency in Russian was essential for accomplishing the embassy's tasks: generating reporting, facilitating trade, aiding Americans, advancing human rights, etc. Good intelligence certainly couldn't be collected without strong Russian.

In a draft telegram from 1946 that he wrote but never sent, Kennan complained about Washington's neglect of the embassy. It should be "a guiding brain center of our policy toward Russia" but instead has become "the object of attacks by jealous self-seekers and discontented liberals, never enjoying the full backing or understanding of people in Washington, never properly staffed or properly housed." Nonetheless, it had "become a pioneering establishment in the American Foreign Service and the most respected diplomatic mission in Moscow."[482]

As the Cold War intensified, Washington had addressed the embassy's most pressing needs. Officers knowing Russian and trained in Soviet affairs had been assigned to Moscow, and language teachers had been hired locally to maintain their skills.

Now the government was backsliding.

A week after the teachers were dismissed, Hartman alluded to a "dilemma" that was looming: If the embassy required more Americans to do the work of the discharged Russians, and if the total number of Americans couldn't exceed a set number equaling the number of Soviets in Washington (a principle that the FBI and others were promoting), then the number of Americans doing the embassy's substantive reporting and analysis, including from its political and economic sections, would have to be reduced. The embassy would have to curtail the number of its language-proficient officers to make room for Americans skilled in the trades.

Left unsaid were the facts that Tchaikovsky 19 would require proportionally more blue-collar workers than the Soviet embassy in Washington due to the different working conditions in the two capitals, and that no American ambassador could dragoon nonworking spouses into unofficial service as a Soviet ambassador could.

Hartman seemed frustrated that no one in Washington seemed to be considering the dilemma. He mused aloud that if the embassy was to retain its historic *raison d'etre*, it might be forced to adjust its concept of acceptable security.

The Reagan administration liked to proclaim an absence of moral equivalency between the Soviet and American systems, yet it was taking its embassy down a path that presupposed total equivalency. Applying reciprocity in an absolute way ("You do it to us, so how can you complain if we do it to you?") works well if there is an equivalency in the way the governments and societies deal with their peoples, but not otherwise. I wasn't privy to the telegraphic back-and-forth on security, but I hoped our government wasn't taking us into a trap.

*   *   *

In early June 1986, the Foreign Ministry blocked my third attempt to travel to oil and gas fields in western Siberia. The rejection came after my requests for appointments at several economic ministries had been turned down. At the same time, correspondents at *Pravda* and *Izvestiya* declined to see me.

I vented my frustration in a letter home: "The Soviets are making it difficult for me to discuss economic issues with officials, journalists, and others."

Shortly thereafter, I learned that another Russian employee, Oleg Yuriev, had been removed. Oleg was the Russian to whom political and economic officers sometimes turned for assistance.

When I was running Pol/Int during my second tour, he had helped arrange appointments for me at various ministries, think tanks, and journals, not only in Moscow but sometimes in other cities. His English was more than adequate. If I had a problem translating a text, he would lend a hand. He was quiet, unassuming, and cautious; I once invited him to Leninsky 45, but he had declined. In retrospect, he was entitled to be cautious, working as he was with Americans while supporting a family. If he wasn't already reporting to the authorities, surely the UPDK and "others" were watching him closely.

I hadn't had much contact with the other dismissed Russians, but Oleg had been helpful, and I felt badly about his removal.

After encountering my second or third travel refusal, I had gone to his office—a dark, damp cubbyhole tucked away in the unfinished basement of the south wing—and asked for his help.

Once, at a country-team meeting, the administrative counselor had said that rats were running around Uncle Sam's; if rats had found their way into the compound's busiest site, then they were probably in Oleg's space. In any normal environment, it would have been shut down.

I asked him whether he could get me into Lenin Library. I had been eyeing its main building, which had been erected in the same Constructivist style as Lenin's Mausoleum in 1930, since my first assignment.

The "Library of the USSR in the name of V.I. Lenin," one of the world's largest repositories of books, journals, and newspapers, is described in the Soviet encyclopedia as both "central" and "public." Standing almost opposite the Kremlin's Borovitsky Tower, it is central but hardly public; no one without a reader's card (*chitatelsky bilet*) containing one's photograph under official seal could get by the *babushka* and militiaman guarding its main entrance.

Americans visiting the USSR as scholars under official exchanges agreements could secure a reader's card, but only two embassy officers—as far as I could determine—had qualified in more than a half a century.

Tom Whitney had used the library in 1944 when he was in the economic section; as he later recounted, however, gaining access was difficult once the Cold War began.[483] Several years later, according to the wife of Ambassador Kirk, "even by conforming to the rules, none of our officers has been able to get a card."[484]

In 1952, an embassy officer had passed himself off as a graduate student, but was only allowed to see two or three shelves of catalogues, and none of the eight books he ordered was ever delivered.[485] Harrison Salisbury, at the time, described the library as "a citadel of security."[486]

It was known that old Stalinists like Kaganovich and Molotov worked on their papers in the library, in prestigious Reading Room 1. Could this be why we were barred, or had no one thought to apply? The library has more than twenty different reading rooms; surely someone from the embassy could be given a spot in one.

If the Soviets blocked me from traveling outside the capital, I'd do my "exploring" within. The Leninka, as its patrons knew it, headed my list.

Oleg inquired and found that I would have to demonstrate "certain academic credentials." He filled out an application in which he cited my history and law degrees and delivered it to the library himself. We heard nothing for a few weeks, but this didn't surprise me: Russians have a somewhat different conception of time.

Then Oleg began following up. After repeated telephone calls produced no result, he paid another personal visit and was told that I should appear myself.

I talked my way past the front door and—after handing in several copies of my photograph, signing a few forms, and promising to behave—received the bright red, hard-covered, two-and-a-half-inch by three-and-a-half-inch booklet (*bilet*), my sealed photograph within, confirming my acceptance.

Thanks to Oleg, I had been admitted, and not to *any* reading room but to Reading Room 1.

The Foreign Ministry and the KGB must not have interfered. Had the library's security people slipped up? Or did the "competent organs" calculate that a library card would keep me off Moscow's streets?

I soon became a regular. Reading Room 1 was filled with numerous desks with green-shaded lamps. Most of them seemed to be unassigned. I'd look for one with a lamp that would light.

The library's stacks are closed, and its rules are strict. Even the dimensions of one's briefcase are controlled; it couldn't exceed ten by fourteen inches (twenty-five by thirty-five centimeters).

Each time I entered and displayed my booklet I'd receive a control card (*kontrolny listok*) I'd have to sign. Upon departing, the card would be checked by the *babushka* against my booklet and returned to me, to be handed by me to a militiaman standing a pace away.

On one of my first visits, I made a nearly fatal mistake. I left my control card with the woman in charge of Reading Room 1 with whom I had just placed an order for books. As no book would be available for several days, I showed the *babushka* my booklet but not my control card as I left. "So, young man (*molodoi chelovek*), you think you can leave without turning in your control card?" and she ripped the booklet out of my hand. I explained where I had left the card, and she ordered me to retrieve it, fill it out, and report back. Otherwise my booklet would be retained, and I'd be barred if I ever tried to return. I did as ordered and then received a tongue-lashing for having signed the card in pencil and not in ink. Grudgingly, she stamped and returned my booklet, and I was able to leave with it in hand.

Had I been suspended, my name might have been posted on a bulletin board on the third floor, "deprived of his *chitatelsky bilet* for one month for undisciplined behavior." Oleg told me his card had been permanently lifted, probably for having helped someone in the embassy.

On weekends and some weekdays, I'd visit the library, if only to study its catalogues that filled hundreds of drawers. The books I ordered (they couldn't be removed from the library[487]) would be delivered to a desk outside Reading Room 1. A sign on the desk warned users not to peruse books ordered by others.

Leninka gave me access to more than just books. Newspapers, journals, and pamphlets from every part of the Soviet Union, from places to which we couldn't travel and from government and academic institutions to which we had no access, were stacked up neatly in cubbyholes in two reading rooms.

The librarians were mostly women. A majority probably belonged to the Party, since announcements of its meetings were everywhere; if you wanted to keep a job at a prestigious institution, it was best to join the Party.

Physically, the building was in bad shape. Jammed in a corner of the basement near the main entrance were two foul-smelling bathrooms, a small area for smoking, and a primitive canteen. Bathrooms in Soviet offices and institutions rarely had toilet paper; the library's had no toilet seats. More often than not, the bathrooms on the second floor were awash in water from broken pipes.

But the library was a refreshing change from Tchaikovsky's eighth floor, and it wasn't long before I was digging into books and materials that threw light on Gorbachev's more interesting appointments.

*   *   *

Krutitsky Val continued to pose challenges. Hot water was cut off on May 10 and wasn't restored until June 1. Unlike the Leninsky District where the maintenance routine was carried out over summer, our district conducted its routine in the spring, and we were again forced to drag boiling water from the stove to the tub.

On June 1, just as hot water returned, Liz left for Washington to set up temporary quarters for the children. Because of the uncertainties related to Chernobyl, I was glad to have her go. She was away when the Angolan children carried out their second assault on the plate-glass entryway; shards of glass again littered the floor. The children were also dropping obscene drawings into the entryway mailboxes. Much worse from my perspective, they were pilfering the Soviet newspapers I subscribed to; I could get a head start by reading *Pravda* at breakfast.

But there was no *babushka* assigned to Krutitsky Val, as there had been at Leninsky Prospect. It appeared Moscow was running out of *babushkas*.

Because of concern about radiation poisoning, Americans were avoiding the peasant markets and were buying most of their food from the commissary. It, in turn, was struggling with shortages. Liz had thoughtfully stashed away a score of homemade dinners that would feed me through July 9, the date I planned to leave to join her.

When it was announced that a special flight from a base in West Germany would arrive with food on June 4, I nonetheless decided to secure what I was due.

Out of fear of a melee, the community association, which ran the commissary, issued a special instruction:

> A line should form in the courtyard . . . out of the area where the construction work is going on. The first fifteen people in line will be admitted to the Commissary as soon as we open; the next two in line may move to the top of the stairs [into the basement] and wait for a signal from a monitor who will be stationed at the Commissary door and will keep track of the number of people who exit and know when it's time to admit more shoppers. The two people waiting at the top of the stairs, upon receiving word from the monitor, should pass the word to the next person in

line in the courtyard, so that he/she can move forward to the top-of-the-stairs position.[488]

I waited and dutifully collected my allotment: a head of lettuce, three tomatoes, and three apples. However, what a contrast with the way things once had been done! Were we becoming like Russians with all their lines?

On Saturday, June 14, and Sunday, June 22, after visiting Leninka, I took in an exhibit of Ilya Glazunov's paintings at the Manege, the building near the library that Khrushchev had converted into an exhibition hall.

Manege exhibits typically featured socialist realist art. In 1962, Khrushchev had exploded when he saw seventy-five works by avant-garde artists in three of its rooms. "The people and the government have taken a lot of trouble with you, and you pay them back with this shit." In the same outburst he had excoriated jazz: "When I hear jazz, it's as if I had gas on the stomach."[489]

Thousands of Muscovites stood in line to see Glazunov's work. For the opening, there was a small VIP reception in the foyer where I met, for the first time in many years, Alexander Simchenko. Simchenko headed the protocol office at Intourist's headquarters, which occupied the old Mokhovaya embassy opposite Red Square. Although he was unctuous to an extreme, I had called on him for help when I ran the consular section; and more often than not he came through.

Simchenko wasn't pleased when I mentioned that Glazunov's art seemed to affront "the rules" of socialist realism. I learned from Alexander Wat's memoir a few years later that one shouldn't talk about socialist realism with educated Russians; it only embarrassed them.[490]

Word had gotten out that Glazunov's *Mystery of the Twentieth Century* would be on display. (During my second tour, the authorities had banned it from a Manege exhibit.) I found a large crowd gathered around it. Mother Russia was portrayed in the grimmest of ways: a desolate village, a devastated church, pigs and peasants vying for raw meat, etc. Khrushchev would have been livid. It also included caricatures of notable twentieth century figures, including, daringly, Solzhenitsyn, Stalin, Khrushchev, Kennedy, and Tsar Nicholas II.

While wandering other rooms and listening to the mournful music that Glazunov had arranged to be piped in (shortly before the exhibit, his wife had hurled herself to her death from the high-rise building where his studio was located), I heard a ruckus in the distance. Hastening to the source, I found a large crowd, four or five persons deep, around a table on which books lay for visitors' comments. The crowd was arguing, pushing, and shoving.

"You don't have to show the countryside this way," a middle-aged man shouted. "Show it the way Levitsky [a nineteenth century artist] had shown it, with optimism."

"This is an outrage," another said.

Others came to Glazunov's defense: "Russia is like this; you have to wait in line for meat."

Another cried out, "After all, he [Glazunov] gave money to the victims of Chernobyl."

Five militiamen suddenly appeared, one with a bullhorn: "Disperse, go look at the pictures." The crowd grudgingly melted away.

Public places in Moscow had once been tightly controlled; now disorders could break out anywhere, even in sight of the Kremlin. *If Gorbachev carries his openness campaign too far, he will have his hands full,* I thought as I returned to the library.

On Sunday, June 29, while wandering about the city, I noticed that more Metro riders than ever were wearing crosses. I sat opposite two teenage girls with small silver crucifixes hanging below the lace collars of their black satin dresses. As I disembarked at Barrikadnaya, a heavy-set young male wearing a wooden cross into which sparkling stones were embedded was boarding. When I mentioned my sightings to Igor, he said true believers don't display crosses in public. He was probably right, but fewer Russians seemed to care about what others might be thinking, and this was new.

Summer 1986 brought the usual staff turnover. The assignments of two officers in my section, Bob Bradtke and Mike Mozur, ended; and two officers new to the Soviet Union, Howard Clark and Mary Ann Peters, succeeded them. Mike Einik would stay. I nominated Bob and the two Mikes for a Superior Honor Award. Such was the disarray that months passed before the paperwork reached Washington; the award was made after my retirement.

I flew to the United States for a three-week vacation and returned with Liz at the end of July. As there was no embassy van to meet us at Sheremetyevo II, we hopped into a taxi.

The driver was as outspoken as any Russian I had met. He started by saying he and his friends were in mourning.

"What happened?" I asked.

"The price of vodka has gone up again."

Laughing at his joke, he said it cost twenty rubles to buy a bottle if you bought it from a middleman; otherwise, you waited in line for two or three hours.

"You should hear how they curse Gorbachev. Not even the militiamen controlling the lines care any more."

The pensioners, he went on, are taking advantage of the anti-vodka campaign. They stand in line for three rubles and get a bottle for a customer or sell it for their own account.

"Isn't there less drinking than before?"

"No, the situation under Gorbachev is worse. Most people in Moscow are drunk by eight in the evening." The driver rambled on and on, lambasting every aspect of the system.

His life, he said, consists of "work, television, and sleep." Yet the authorities demand, "give, give, give." As for Gorbachev, he is "hitting at the working class" when he should be "twisting the bureaucrats' necks."

Had it been 1981, I would have judged him a provocateur, but by 1986 he was speaking for many, and speaking out loud. *Glasnost* was loosening tongues.

A week after our return, the administrative section issued a memorandum announcing that the American-designed town houses and apartments would soon be ready for occupancy. "A good portion of the Embassy's staff will be able to be accommodated."[491] Liz and I were told that we could have one of the new town houses, designated for senior officers with representational responsibilities, in October. Some of the apartments had already been occupied, but the chancery at the center of the complex, the "new office building," remained in limbo, construction having come to a halt with the Russians' ouster the year before. The offices would stay at Tchaikovsky 19.

Liz and I had mixed feelings about the move, not because of any affection for Krutitsky Val but because we couldn't imagine our Russian friends, apart from Mila and Sergei, daring to visit us in the complex. Militiamen had already established posts at its two main entrances and had set up booths every twenty or so yards along the full length of its perimeter for later manning. We'd have to see our friends outside, at their places or somewhere else. Still, we decided we'd move.

Late in August, Combs told us to expect a deluge of temporary visitors from Washington. Gorbachev's proposal for the second summit in Reykjavik, Iceland, wouldn't reach the White House until September 19, yet most of us knew that a summit was looming.

Liz was now working as a "roving secretary," moving from office to office as different sections required extra assistance. She spent most of her time in the science section, which was still hosting U.S. experts helping the Soviets deal with Chernobyl's effects.

The process of replacing Russians with non-Russians, including third-country nationals with residence permits, continued apace. By summer's end, the budget and fiscal unit consisted of two Americans and nine persons from Great Britain, Canada, New Zealand, and other countries in Latin America and Asia. I wondered whether their backgrounds were being checked.

*   *   *

On August 23, 1986, the FBI arrested Gennadi Zakharov, a KGB officer working at the United Nations Secretariat. He was charged with recruiting an employee of a defense contractor to spy for the KGB. Because the American had been cooperating with the FBI from the start, Zakharov posed no immediate threat. As he was employed by the secretariat and not the Soviet Mission to the UN, he had no diplomatic immunity.

Zakharov's arrest would trigger tit-for-tat expulsions that would spin out of control.

According to Ambassador Matlock who was at the NSC, the department and CIA approved the FBI's proposal to make the arrest. Matlock writes that he had been surprised by State's acquiescence since "we could expect the KGB to arrest an American without diplomatic immunity in hope of forcing a trade."[492] But he didn't object, and Poindexter, the NSC advisor to whom he reported, gave his assent.

At the country-team meeting, Combs told us that the Soviets had informed the department that the United States would have to bear the consequences.

The "other shoe" fell on August 30 when the KGB arrested the journalist Nicholas Daniloff in Moscow and charged him with espionage. Daniloff was arrested just after accepting incriminating material from a Soviet citizen.

The Soviets had arrested innocent Americans in the past to recover their agents; I hadn't forgotten Jay Crawford's arrest in 1978.

My ears perked up when Combs let us know on September 3 that Daniloff had received photographs, including of Soviet troops in Afghanistan, from an acquaintance whom he knew as "Misha." He had met Misha in Frunze in 1982.

How interesting. I had also met a Russian by the name of Misha in Frunze. Returning to my office, I checked the index cards in my safe, on which I inscribed the names of Soviet citizens whom I knew, and found the name "Misha Kuznetsov." Elise and I had dined with him and his girlfriend Tanya in Frunze in 1980.

From Combs's subsequent comments, it emerged that Daniloff had met his "Misha" in the same restaurant in the same hotel.

A few days later, Combs added that there was an "embarrassing" twist to Daniloff's story that he wouldn't want to reveal other than to say that the Soviets "know what they are doing."

364 ROBERT F. OBER, JR.

I drafted a telegram reporting the similarities between the two Mishas (I had earlier telephoned Elise in Paris and refreshed my recollection of "ours") and sent it up to Combs. I wrote that Misha appeared to be a KGB plant.

Combs wasn't ready to question the White House's insistence (and Daniloff's too) that the KGB had forced an innocent Russian to cooperate, to become a co-opted agent; and he toned my telegram's conclusion down to an interesting hypothesis before approving and sending it.

Shortly thereafter, on September 11, Daniloff was released from Lefortovo Prison into the embassy's custody. I suggested to Combs that I meet with him to compare our Mishas, but Combs demurred. By this time, it was clear to most of us, however, that the KGB had engineered Daniloff's entrapment with one of its skilled professionals.

The full story, including the "embarrassing" twist, came out after Washington and Moscow traded their "spies," an exchange thinly camouflaged to uphold the White House's insistence that a journalist not be traded for a real spy. It emerged that the CIA officer whom the Soviets expelled from the economic section before I took charge had alluded to Daniloff in a telephone call to a second KGB plant, a Russian citizen masquerading as an Orthodox priest. The KGB had a recording of the conversation, including the "economic officer's" reference to the journalist as a friend. In fact, Daniloff and the economic officer had never met.

Therefore, the KGB had reason to suspect that Daniloff was either a spy or collaborating with a spy.

The bogus priest had earlier delivered a package to Daniloff that included a letter addressed to Hartman. Suspicious and prudent, Daniloff broke off contact with the "priest" and brought the package to the embassy. The CIA was sufficiently impressed by the material inside that it informed the "priest" through its economic officer that his communication by way of the journalist had been received.

Once Daniloff figured in an intercepted telephone call initiated by an Agency officer, he didn't stand a chance. "What idiocy," Shultz exclaimed when the screwup came to his attention.[493] The sloppy tradecraft would come back to haunt not only Daniloff but the embassy, the White House, and U.S-Soviet relations on the eve of a summit.

If the Soviet desk and the NSC itself had firmly said no to the FBI's proposal to arrest Zakharov, the developments that followed would have been averted or postponed. But the FBI needed a success; it had failed to prevent a string of Soviet *coups* through spies the KGB and GRU had run in the NSA and the navy (the Walker-Whitworth ring operated for seventeen years without detection), and it had more recently failed to prevent the flight to Moscow, in October 1985, of the CIA's agent-in-training Edward

Lee Howard. Howard's disclosures along with those of Ames and Hanssen would end up exposing at least ten Russians in the agency's employ.

So the FBI believed an arrest would redeem its reputation. As it turned out, however, the CIA officer in Moscow whose communication compromised Daniloff had started his own career with the FBI; the arrest of Zakharov opened up a Pandora's box of questions about the bureau's competency in recruiting, training, and deploying its personnel.[494]

My former deputy chief of mission in Athens, Alan Berlind, characterized the whole affair as a tragic "comedy," with the White House "pretending that a routine swap with winks was really a power showdown with blinks," and with an American journalist claiming the world's attention for two weeks "when real heroes suffer real deprivation for years in the dark, many of them in the Soviet Union."[495]

By becoming involved with someone eager to supply photographs and maps of war-torn Afghanistan, the Russian-speaking Daniloff had been uncharacteristically naïve. If it hadn't been Daniloff, however, the KGB would probably have found another American, someone without immunity, to use in a trade. It had likely pre-positioned a few. Washington's mistake was trying to make a general statement about Soviet espionage by arresting and convicting an agent instead of tossing him out.

Daniloff later recounted his adventure in a book.[496] He criticized both the FBI and CIA, the latter for "its use of obscure junior personnel in high-risk operations."[497] He also faulted the embassy. When meeting with a consular officer at Lefortovo, he hadn't been told he was not obligated to respond to the Soviet investigator's questions. The embassy "should improve its acquaintance with Soviet law, making sure it has a copy of the RSFSR [the Russian republic's] procedural code in its library."[498]

A copy of the procedural code had once been in the embassy's library. When I headed the consular section, I consulted it occasionally, and later, when summoned to Kabul and Prague to deal with the soldiers, I studied it carefully. By the time of Daniloff's arrest, however, the library and probably the code had disappeared. But still, couldn't the Soviet desk have alerted the embassy to the basics of Soviet criminal procedure as soon as Daniloff was arrested? Or was there no one on the desk who knew anything about Soviet law?

Daniloff had a further complaint. The embassy had become too inward looking, with "suspicion" often turning into "paranoia." "The embassy's security officers automatically assume that every Soviet who associates with a foreigner is a potential KGB agent; diplomats are instructed to venture out only in pairs and to report each contact with a citizen."[499]

Daniloff had probably seen the forms I found on my desk, the forms that had alerted me to the fact that the "embassy" where I had first served no longer existed. I ignored the forms without repercussions, but their very existence had left a bad taste. If Washington can't trust an FSO to use good judgment, what's the point of having a Foreign Service?

*   *   *

In early September, Ed and Nina Stevens invited us to dinner. Toward the end of the evening, one of their guests, an attractive woman in her fifties, was asked to sing a romantic Russian song, which she did with professional aplomb. Curious, Liz and I introduced ourselves and heard how Stalin had turned the life of one Soviet citizen, Valeriya Novikova, upside down.

Valeriya explained that she had once been married to someone at the embassy. The Stevens knew the full story, she said, but few others did. Within a week, she had invited us to her apartment, and in the months that remained we became good friends.

Valeriya had met Leon Patlach, a navy enlistee in the defense attaché's office, in early 1946. They fell in love and decided to marry, she said. After an interview that Ambassador Smith required, the wedding was held at Spaso House on July 4, 1946.

The Soviet regime only recognized those marriages it registered, so on the next day, July 5, she and Leon went to the Civil Registry Office (ZAGS) in Moscow. As Valeriya spoke, she extracted ZAGS certificate number 2125 dated July 5, 1946, from an antique chest of drawers and handed it to me.

I had seen such certificates as a consular officer, and didn't doubt the authenticity of hers. But could the ambassador have hosted a wedding on Independence Day, the day of the reception? At most, I thought, some symbolic ceremony might have occurred, before or after the traditional event. Smith's memoir, which I later read, makes no mention of any wedding.

Valeriya's mother had been a well-known actress before World War II, playing dramatic and comedic roles in theaters across the Soviet Union. As the member of an all-girl orchestra during the war, she had entertained Red Army troops. (The Soviets say that more than three thousand brigades performed more than four hundred thousand concerts at the front.)[500] Once, when her mother was performing on a flat-bed truck, three Messerschmitt aircraft appeared on the horizon for a strafing run. The soldiers scattered to dugouts, but the girls kept playing. According to Valeriya, her mother received a medal, Glory (*Slava*) First Class, for courage from Marshal Ivan Konev. This was the Konev whom Stalin threatened to shoot for failing to stop Hitler's advance in 1941; Marshal Zhukov talked him out of it, and in 1945, Konev led the Red Army across Poland and into Berlin.[501]

Valeriya's father had been a pianist but had died when she was twelve. She was often left with governesses while her mother pursued her career, and from one of them she had learned English. Apparently her family had been among the capital's privileged until Stalin decreed the devaluation of the ruble, from 10:1, in 1947, which wiped out most of its savings.

At war's end, Valeriya gained admission to Moscow's famed Institute of Foreign Languages. As veterans enjoyed preferences, it took influence to get in.

"How did you manage it?" I asked. "Through your mother?"

Yes and no. Her mother's sister Klavdia Novikova was an even more famous performer. She had studied music in Odessa and had made her debut at the opera there in 1912. Shortly after the Revolution, however, she followed her lover, a general in the anti-Bolshevik forces, to Shanghai. Altogether, there were over one hundred thousand Russians in Chinese cities in the early 1920s, most of them fleeing the Bolsheviks. One visitor discovered "an entire Russian city in Shanghai . . . sounds of Russian came from every corner, from stores and windows of the houses."[502]

Shanghai was already notorious for its nightlife, and the Russians contributed to it. Valeriya couldn't tell me whether her aunt had sung there professionally, but opera was important to the Chinese and to the foreign communities (opera "theaters opened as early as seven in the morning and did not close until after midnight"[503]). Most singers ended up working, however, in one of the city's several hundred cabarets.

Klavdia returned by herself to Moscow in 1926. At the time, Shanghai was becoming embroiled in the bloody conflict between Chiang Kai-shek's forces and the Communists.

"Was she arrested on her return?" I asked.

No, Stalin hadn't achieved full power, and she was able to reestablish her career. In 1927, she became a founding member of Moscow's Theatre of Operetta. Her voice had a three-octave range, and her career took off. (Liz and I have a recording of Klavdia's "laughing songs" from *The Geisha*, *Die Fledermaus*, and *La Percale*.)

The Soviet *Musical Encyclopedia* from 1976[504], which I later consulted, recounts Klavdia's career up to her death in 1968. It cites her service as "an actress on an agit-prop train" between 1918 and 1920. These were the trains "with live entertainers, phonograph recitals of Lenin's voice, and motion picture projectors" that the Bolsheviks sent around Russia to rally support for the Revolution.[505] The encyclopedia makes no mention of Klavdia's time in China (*glasnost* was a decade away when it was published), but it is likely that her early support of the Bolshevik cause helped ease her way past the OGPU (the NKVD's predecessor) and into her career.

Music was popular in the Kremlin in the 1930s. Stalin enjoyed Russian operas and ballets, Bulganin enjoyed operas (and opera divas), and Molotov liked playing the violin and mandolin. According to the diary of Ekaterina Voroshilova, the wife of the head of Stalin's defense ministry at the start of the war, the dictator "had a good tenor voice and loved songs and music."[506] At his dacha outside Moscow, he would preside over an American gramophone while his colleagues drank and danced.

Valeriya said her aunt soon came to the leaders' attention. She vividly recalls the limousine the leaders sent to bring her to the Kremlin to perform.

When the Germans threatened Moscow in 1941, Klavdia and the operetta company were evacuated to Novosibirsk behind the Ural Mountains, and she arranged for her sister and her niece Valeriya to join her. By the end of 1942, almost one million Soviet citizens, mostly women and children, had been relocated to Siberia from European Russia.

When the three returned to Moscow in 1943, victory was not far off, and it seemed to most Muscovites that the future would be better. On July 4, 1943, the conservatory mounted a concert devoted to American music. An American citizen returnee who had married a Russian before the war and had taught English at the same institute where Valeriya later studied recalls that American, British, and Soviet uniforms filled the lobby: "You could hear people discovering each other [who had] returned from evacuation." The State Symphony played "When Johnny Comes Marching Home Again," "My Old Kentucky Home," and "Rhapsody in Blue."[507]

When the news of Germany's capitulation reached Moscow on May 10, 1945, George Kennan, at the embassy for the third time, witnessed the "almost delirious friendship" ordinary Russians displayed for Americans. When Kennan hung the Soviet and American flags together outside the Mokhovaya embassy, there were "roars of approval and enthusiasm."[508]

Valeriya was introduced to Patlach in front of the institute. Having an American as a boyfriend, even one who worked at the embassy, posed no risk. However, as spring 1946 passed into summer and summer into fall, the atmosphere became thick with tension. It became intolerable in February 1947 when Stalin issued his decree forbidding marriages between his citizens and foreigners; for Russians, the Iron Curtain had unmistakably fallen.

Valeriya was ordered to dissolve the marriage; she avoided prison because she did. "I went to bed and never left the apartment," she told us.

Ambassador Smith had already sent Patlach home. For the young American, this was the end of the affair. Reprising a Soviet version of *Madame Butterfly*, Valeriya never heard from him again.

The American journalists who had married earlier were able to keep their marriages intact. Tom Whitney resigned from the embassy and joined the Associated Press in order to avoid transfer back to the United States. Ed and Nina Stevens had obtained their exit visas on the eve of the war; the other couples gained theirs upon Stalin's death.

At that time, Valeriya entered the conservatory and immersed herself in music. The authorities didn't forget the marriage, however, and she couldn't have a career.

Valeriya inherited her co-op apartment from her mother. Located two blocks from the conservatory, its three small rooms overflow today with antiques and family memorabilia. For our first dinner together, Valeriya served a seven-course meal, beginning with vodka and caviar and ending with liqueur. The plates had belonged to a tsar; we sat on chairs from a palace in St. Petersburg (the Yusupovs once owned it) and ate under a crystal chandelier from a second palace.

A photograph of Leon Patlach is fixed to the headboard of Valeriya's bed, and a Bulova watch he inscribed to his "wife" sits on the dresser. She keeps the apartment the way it was, she said, when she was happiest. The marriage papers she showed us during our first visit are probably no longer hidden.

We couldn't persuade Valeriya to visit us in the new compound, but by 1986 the fear that had consumed years of her life was finally lifting. She even detected a change in the country's leaders. "They no longer consider the intelligentsia their enemy. They may not be of the intelligentsia themselves, but some are Siberians and Siberians are more open."

As to the wedding at Spaso House, Valeriya didn't disagree when I surmised that Leon, and perhaps she (though it wouldn't have been necessary), had sworn an oath before a consular officer at Smith's reception, the oath I had taken from a score of prospective brides and grooms.[509] On the basis of the sworn statement, the Moscow ZAGS performed the marriage, the marriage that, because of Stalin, lasted less than a year.

*   *   *

On September 14, 1986, a week or so after the Stevens' dinner party, the promotion list came out, and my name wasn't on it. Expecting its absence, I had sold our car—this time to a Mexican diplomat—three days before.

I was disappointed but also understood. An editorial in the *Foreign Service Journal* that arrived the same week confirmed that "area and functional expertise can no longer preserve your career."[510] By specializing in Russian and Soviet affairs, I had cast my lot with a different career.

Liz and I had spent the prior weekend at the ambassador's dacha in Tarasovka. The temperature hovered in the 30s, but the woods were serene as always, and the telephone didn't ring. I used the time to write letters, and we played tennis. The court's surface contained treacherous icy spots and green algae; after an hour of hitting, the balls looked as if they had been soaked in grease.

During our absence, the building housing the embassy's commercial office, a half a block from Tchaikovsky 19, suffered heavy damage. Five stories of its brick and mortar facing had sheared off and dropped to the sidewalk. Fortunately no one was hurt, but a car belonging to a staff member was destroyed. The facades of Moscow buildings were known to collapse at times of winter thaws, but not in September.

Although we hadn't decided when to retire (in theory, we could remain a year), Liz and I took advantage of the embassy's "flea market" on the last weekend of September. In previous years, it had been held in the spring just before transfers occurred. Now it was a semiannual affair and held no longer at Spaso House or Uncle Sam's but on the grounds of the new dachas at Serebryanny Bor, forty minutes by Metro and trolley bus from Tchaikovsky 19.

The grounds were covered with an inch of snow when we arrived with several boxes of clothes. The administrative section had set up plywood tabletops on sawhorses outside the dachas. Reflecting the larger staff, many more Americans were now involved. Most of the buyers were third-world diplomats with unofficial rubles, those acquired outside official channels; a few Russians mingled among them.

Ron Kessler writes that "the Marines, because they did not have many goods to sell, generally did not participate," but for staff members who "could afford it," it was "a way of circumventing" Moscow's prohibitions on black marketeering.[511] In fact, there were marines present, and they and the Seabees marketed the costly items, mostly electronic and other equipment imported from abroad.

The flea market was no longer the small-scale event we recalled involving buyers most of us recognized by face if not by name. It was far more cumbersome to control, and struck me as more like a medieval village fair, something Bruegel might have painted, rather than a gathering of diplomats.

In the evening, Liz and I watched the first-ever telecast of Eisenstein's *Ivan the Terrible*. The film had been made in 1941 after Mosfilm was evacuated to Alma-Ata, and was first screened in Moscow in 1945 but had been rarely shown to the public. Another *glasnost* success! The announcer explained that, yes, Tsar Ivan had been cruel but he was also "linked with progressive aspects of Russian history," the strengthening of the state.

A week later, television highlighted the anniversary of Russia's victory over the Muslim horde at Kulikovo, somewhat surprising after it had ignored its 800th anniversary six years before, the celebration that the Foreign Ministry (and perhaps the KGB) had barred me from attending. After a filmed report about the victory, an Academy of Social Sciences official opined that "self-awareness" must be restored to Russia's youth. Apparently, the demoralization of Russia's young people would receive more attention.

Ambassador Hartman left on October 4, 1986, to attend the second Reagan-Gorbachev summit at Reykjavik, Iceland. Before leaving, he briefed us on Shevardnadze's letter to Reagan proposing the meeting. It seemed that Gorbachev needed the assurance of another meeting with the president before agreeing to attend a summit in Washington. The ambassador worried that Reykjavik might prove disappointing; he thought that some in the White House had concluded that Gorbachev had become the *demandeur*, ready to pay a high price for improved relations.

·On October 5, Liz and I visited the Costakis exhibit at the New Tretyakov Gallery opposite Gorky Park. This was the first showing of the avant-garde works that the collector had turned over to the regime to secure permission to export the bulk of his art. There were two Chagall's and three Malevich's on display, but no catalogue.

Moscow's new Party chief, Boris Yeltsin, figured in an increasing number of anecdotes. One described a surprise visit he made to the Yeliseyev *Gastronom*, the famous store which is mentioned in *War and Peace*. Yeltsin learned that it had received a shipment of four thousand kilograms of veal. So he decided to show up disguised as an ordinary Russian to find out whether it was being distributed honestly. He asked a Yeliseyev clerk about veal. "Who do you think you are!" she retorted. "We never get veal. Go to your local market."

Furious, he asked to see the director.

"Don't bother me" was the reply.

"May I use your telephone?" the local leader reportedly asked.

"Go out on the street and use your own two kopecks."

He did, reached the militia, and ordered it to surround the *Gastronom* and arrest its director. It turned out that the director had sold the veal to local markets on behalf of himself and corrupt assistants.

After Gorbachev selected Yeltsin and Council of Ministers chairman Nikolai Ryzhkov to join him in carrying out economic restructuring (*perestroika*), I had gone to Leninka and found several books that dealt with their careers in the closed city of Sverdlovsk, where Yeltsin had led the Party and Ryzhkov the industrial enterprise Uralmash. I extracted several nuggets and forwarded them to Washington. My digging wasn't always productive, but Leninka turned out to be another window into the system that Washington welcomed.

*   *   *

On his return on October 13, Ambassador Hartman summarized the summit at a country-team meeting. He said the two sides had discussed reducing strategic missiles by 50 percent and removing intermediate-range missiles from Europe. They also agreed to regular intergovernmental meetings on specific issues, including human rights. Although Hartman didn't foresee a third summit in the immediate future, he left no doubt that real progress was being made.

There hadn't been any discussion, however, of Washington's expulsion of officials from the Soviet Mission at the United Nations (SMUN), and this surprised me.

Just before the summit, on September 17, the administration had identified twenty-five officials whom it demanded Moscow remove from New York. Six months earlier, on March 7, 1986, it had ordered Moscow to reduce its staff at the SMUN (and at the Belorussian and Ukrainian Missions which it controlled) in increments of 25 over a two-year period, for a total reduction of 100 persons. The first 25 were supposed to be removed by October 1986 so the Soviets would meet a ceiling of 218 persons that Washington was imposing.

Although Hartman brought back no insights as to how the Soviets might react to the September 17 demand, speculation inside the embassy was rife. A new political officer suggested that the Soviets might limit themselves to increasing their harassment of reporting officers. She described how a Russian had approached her on a Moscow street and asked whether he could have the telephone number of an American journalist. I was amused that a political officer thought this was harassment; perhaps security had warned her to have nothing to do with Russians.

On October 16, Donna Hartman arranged a surprise party for the ambassador, with the Manhattan String Quartet visiting Moscow once again. In her welcoming remarks, she explained that it was the fifth anniversary of Art's taking the assignment; he had now fulfilled his "five-year plan." The ambassador claimed to be genuinely surprised. Eric Lewis and his group played compositions by Ravel, Ives, and Shostakovich—another memorable evening at Spaso House.

*   *   *

Three days later, the Foreign Ministry declared five American staff members *personae non gratae*, four at the embassy (including Bill Norville in my section) and one from the consulate in Leningrad. At first glance, this seemed like rather measured retaliation for the removal of twenty-five Soviet officials from New York.

Two days later, the State Department responded, ordering the expulsion of five Soviet officials, in retaliation for the five Americans who had been PNG'd, and another fifty Soviet officials in a forced reduction to a unilaterally set ceiling of Soviet officials, diplomatic and consular, in Washington and San Francisco. The reduction would bring the Soviet staff in the United States, in the aggregate, to 255 persons, to a level that the department would henceforth insist that Moscow maintain. Not surprisingly, the 255 matched the aggregate number of Americans accredited to work at the embassy in Moscow and the consulate in Leningrad.

Controlling the size of diplomatic and consular establishments was moving to center stage in the superpower relationship.

According to Ambassador Matlock, citing NSC Advisor Poindexter who heard the conversation, Reagan and Shultz had agreed that after Daniloff's arrest there would be no expulsions of Soviet officials until his release, but then "we can expel as many as we wish as soon as Daniloff is out."[512] In his memoir, Matlock explains that he alerted Poindexter to the danger of a strong Soviet reaction, and indicates that he personally favored expelling the Soviets in a step-by-step behind-the-scenes way—three a week as long as Daniloff was held—in order to avoid it.

None of us at the embassy was sure how the Foreign Ministry would react to the expulsion of fifty-five officials, but we knew it would react. Would it expel a comparable number of Americans? Would it stipulate a staff level that would force American reductions? Would there be some combination of the two?

"Couldn't we have a list of those being expelled from Washington so we could at least figure out who is vulnerable to retaliation?" The question was asked at the country-team meeting on October 22, but no answer was forthcoming. The embassy seemed to be in the dark, and we could only guess as to how Washington's application of reciprocity would play out. As I recall, no one mentioned the possibility that the Soviets would simply withdraw all their employees.

Liz and I had planned to go to Helsinki on October 22, leaving on the midnight train, but by early afternoon that day we knew that trouble was brewing. Without forewarning, the Soviets shut down the embassy's direct telephone line with Washington, an unusual occurrence. We decided to cancel the trip.

At 4:00 PM, TASS reported the execution of Adolf Tolkachev, a Soviet citizen who had spied for the United States, one of those whom Howard had exposed. When I passed by Barbara McRae's desk and mentioned that the Soviets had just "executed someone," she froze. Barbara was our new secretary, having been transferred to Moscow after a year in Paris.

"Executed?" she exclaimed, repeating the word.

"No," I assured her, "it wasn't any American, it wasn't anyone from the embassy."

But five hours later, the Soviets gave us a full dose of our own reciprocity.

14

The Breaking of an Embassy

Before leaving the embassy for the trip home, I learned that Gorbachev planned to deliver a speech on U.S.-Soviet relations at around 9:00 PM, when *Vremya* was usually broadcast. In view of the spy's execution, it wasn't a speech I could miss.

The Soviet leader unleashed a scathing attack on the Reagan administration, accusing it of using "half-truths" and "pure deceit" to describe the just-concluded summit. Gorbachev said he had hoped the president would consult with the American people after leaving Reykjavik and take the follow-up steps that were required. Instead, Reagan had distorted the summit and taken actions that, "to the normal human view, simply look wild." Citing the expulsion of the fifty-five Soviet officials, Gorbachev promised that the Soviet Union would "take reciprocal, very hard measures." He didn't say what they would be, but I went to bed believing that several of us would be ousted. In fact, Gennadi Gerasimov, the Foreign Ministry's press spokesman, revealed the measures shortly thereafter. Thanks to Washington, a word-by-word translation of his full statement was sitting on top of the economic section's telegrams when I arrived the very next morning.[513]

We were informed that all 260 Soviet employees were withdrawn from the embassy in Moscow and the consulate in Leningrad; that the number of official visitors to the embassy and consulate "on a so-called temporary basis for up to one year [TDY visitors] . . . would be brought firmly in line" with the number of such visitors to the Soviet embassy and consulate; and that five colleagues, including our neighbor Dick Naab, were ousted. In Gerasimov's words, "as a result of the measures . . . a complete balance is established in a quantitative sense as far as the personnel of the missions of the two countries are concerned."

That Gorbachev himself was personally involved in determining the "hard measures" is clear from the record of the Politburo meeting he chaired just before his speech. It was found in the Party's archives two years after the Soviet Union collapsed.[514] Because the Soviet embassy in Washington and consulate in San Francisco employed a mere six Americans, Gorbachev was in a position to disable the U.S.'s diplomatic and consular operations in the USSR without risking a commensurately telling counterblow in the United States.

On October 23, the next day, Charles Redman, the State Department's spokesman, accused Moscow of a "wholly unwarranted response," but went on to acknowledge in so many words that Washington had exhausted its reciprocity weapons. "We hope that this set of issues can now be put behind us," he allowed, and the two governments can "get on with the resolution of the larger issues affecting U.S.-Soviet relations and build on the progress made in the discussions at Reykjavik."[515]

The Reagan administration had set a numerical ceiling for the Soviet staff in Washington and San Francisco on the basis of the number of Americans who happened to be accredited at the posts in Moscow and Leningrad, without taking into account the 260 Russian employees who kept the posts operational. Had the department undertaken a modicum of planning, it would have been able to fill the more important vacated positions with a core of well-trained Americans, even if their arrival would necessitate a drawdown of substantive officers. Matlock confirms in his memoir that "there was no advance planning to help the embassy cope with the Soviet retaliation."[516]

Instead, two months would pass before the first workers, five drivers from the Defense Department, arrived at the embassy; and another month would pass before workers with other skills began trickling in.

Gerasimov noted that "up to 500 staff [members]" were staying every year on a temporary basis at the two American posts. When I read the number, I thought surely he must be exaggerating, yet the Foreign Ministry kept close tabs on the visas it issued, and the number was probably accurate. Because the Soviet embassy and consulate hosted comparatively few TDY visitors, Moscow could toughen its stance without risking meaningful retaliation. If there was something positive in Gerasimov's statement, it may have been this: The flood of TDY visitors to Tchaikovsky 19 would subside, and Washington agencies would begin to entrust those at the embassy on permanent assignment, those who knew something about the Soviet Union, with carrying out the tasks that were traditionally assigned to diplomats, the tasks performed by diplomats at other embassies. It was difficult not to conclude that a good many of the TDY'ers, particularly those who spent their mornings in Uncle Sam's, were visiting the embassy more to escape routines at home or have an adventure abroad than to conduct business only they could do.

At daybreak October 23, the militia guards at Tchaikovsky 19 began turning away the Russian employees who hadn't gotten the word. Galya, who radiated authority from thirty years in general services (and who some figured was KGB) argued her way in. She said she was determined to explain her files to whoever took them over. Believing she might damage vital U.S. interests from a courtyard shack, security had two officers watch her during her stay.

With the two Tanyas and the Russian kitchen staff gone, Uncle Sam's closed down. Alfredo told Serge Schmemann that he had been planning an unusual lunch—roasted quail, but the quail would have to stay in the freezer.[517] Later in the morning Pacific Architects and Engineering Co. (PAE), the firm involved in the new housing project, stepped in and prepared pizza. Payment was in dollars instead of the chits to which we were accustomed. Even before noon, the courtyard was filled with Seabees eating pizza and swilling beer as they moved equipment up scaffolding they had erected on the courtyard wall of Tchaikovsky's central wing.

The Hartmans' luncheon for Elie Wiesel, the Nobel Laureate visiting Moscow with the U.S. Holocaust delegation, went forward despite the absence of the residence's eleven Russians. Donna Hartman and Sarah Einik served and cleared the plates. But Spaso House's lights would essentially be "dimmed" for the next half year. Many Soviets were comfortable discussing policy and imparting information *only* at the residence, but this kind of interchange—along with Spaso House's role as the hub of American representational activity in the USSR, a role it had performed uninterruptedly since 1934—virtually came to a halt.

At 4:00 PM, the ambassador spoke to the community in Uncle Sam's. He said that no one should lose sight of why we are in Moscow: to support those in the embassy whose responsibility it is "to pierce the Soviet system." He said he was sorry to see good officers leave (he had delivered a toast to one of the expelled officers, Mike Matera, a guest at the luncheon), but he admitted he couldn't say whether the retaliatory cycle had finally ended.

*   *   *

Gerasimov's statement left numerous questions unanswered. Were spouses, working and nonworking, outside the ceiling? What about the third-country nationals already at the embassy, or the American teachers at the Anglo-American School? Or the clerics assigned to Moscow under the Roosevelt-Litvinov letters? For several weeks, discussions about the scope of the ceiling and the embassy's reorganization dominated meetings on the ninth floor. The larger issues in U.S.-Soviet relations, including those relating to the summit, were pushed aside.

At one meeting, the ambassador speculated that Dobrynin, in charge of the Party's international department after his reassignment to Moscow, had given Gorbachev the idea of pulling out the employees. While in Washington, Dobrynin had once asked Hartman how the American embassy would cope without its Russians.

Outside the meetings, most of us adopted a stiff upper lip. There was some talk that Secretary Shultz had opposed the expulsion of the fifty-five Soviet officials, which appeared to have triggered Gorbachev's reaction, but I don't recall serious finger-pointing. It was more a case of puzzlement about the rationale of such "flamboyant reciprocity"—the phrase the *New York Times* coined to describe it[518]—and the putative acquiescence of Matlock at the NSC and the Soviet desk in the department.

Within a few days, the administrative section had organized every staff member—except for Hartman, Combs, and their wives—into two different groups, All-Purpose Duty (APD) and Custodial. The APD group consisted of teams of seven or eight men who would perform the physically onerous tasks—loading and unloading the embassy trucks that hauled diplomatic pouches (packages and mail), garbage, and other supplies (including for the commissary); shoveling snow and chopping ice around Tchaikovsky 19 and Spaso House; and the like. The Custodial group, made up of teams of three or four women and one or two older men, assumed the lighter duties, such as cleaning Tchaikovsky's public areas and bathrooms, cleaning the apartments of departing personnel and making them ready for new arrivals, maintaining the "welcome kits" of basic kitchen and household items needed by both groups, and so forth. Usually no one on any one team worked for more than eight hours a day or for more than one day a week, except when large shipments arrived when we would all be deployed.

I was assigned to an APD, Liz to a Custodial group. I spent my first day loading a truck with the steel scaffolding that the Seabees had used in the courtyard and then unloading it at Spaso House's garage. We also moved two refrigerators and school furniture, and I swept out the now empty basement in Tchaikovsky's south wing. I managed well my first day, but the long winter was just beginning, and I knew that in time we'd pay a price. Liz fared less well; her hands were a mess after a daylong stint washing floors and scrubbing bathrooms, but she has always tackled assignments with zeal.

Amid confusion about the extent of the ceiling, compounded by the Foreign Ministry's reluctance or inability to answer the embassy's questions, Hartman sent Washington a proposed new configuration for 260 Americans, divided between 225 in Moscow and 35 in Leningrad. He recommended a combined political, economic, and science section of twenty-two persons, among whom would be several clerk-typists and CIA officers. Fewer than 10 percent of the 225 Americans would therefore be responsible for the embassy's traditional functions, conducting business with the Soviet regime and reporting and analyzing its domestic and foreign policies.

There was uproar in Washington when the proposal was circulated. The NSC and the CIA reportedly rejected it outright. A "senior Administration official" accused the ambassador of "doing what the KGB has been unable to do," squeezing the CIA out of Moscow. "He will have more maids in the embassy than CIA case officers," according to the official who spoke on background (anonymously) to the *Washington Times*, the administration's mouthpiece.[519]

Opposition took a milder form at a country-team meeting. The deputy head of the P&C section, seeing that the USIA staff might be reduced by half to seven, and the admiral in charge of the defense attaché office, seeing his contingent trimmed to nine (of whom only three would be officers), demanded of Combs that they be given the full picture—"the whole elephant" as one of them said, as if Hartman's plan contained concealed elements.

The problem was that 90 of the 225 positions in the newly configured embassy, if it was to function at all, would have to be occupied by support personnel. (It became ninety-five when the Soviets insisted that the embassy count the five Italian workers at Spaso House and Uncle Sam's within the ceiling). Among the ninety would be nineteen drivers, nine laborers, eight janitors, three plumbers, and two mechanics. Maids were never on any list.

Of course, the CIA, the defense department, and the other agencies that considered themselves aggrieved by the new configuration ought to have pondered the full implications of identical ceilings when the idea was first broached. Or didn't they and their representatives in the intelligence community understand how the American embassy operated; how its mundane, unclassified functions had always been shared among Americans *and* Russians? Matlock, of course, did understand, but he was disposed to having the embassy operate without Russians.

Hartman took the attacks in stride. "These are the same types," he said, "who have made trouble for us in the past."

The productivity of many of the Russians had been low, but I doubted that ninety workers from the United States—comprising less than half of the withdrawn complement and with minimal (if any) knowledge of Russian and the Moscow scene—could possibly cope. How could drivers with basic Russian talk their way past the barriers—cultural, bureaucratic, physical—that confronted us whenever we tried to execute even routine tasks at airports, hospitals, police stations, ministries, etc.? And how could Washington be sure that its new recruits would steer clear of the traps the KGB liked to lay, traps into which even seasoned officers had fallen? I liked the idea of a smaller embassy, but this wouldn't work.

*   *   *

Liz and I moved into the embassy compound, into town house number 4, on October 25, 1986, three days after the employees' withdrawal. We did the packing and unpacking ourselves; and a West German firm, accredited to do business in the USSR, loaded the boxes and trucked them to the town house.

It was spacious and splendidly furnished, a vast improvement over the Krutitsky apartment. However, maintaining a house on three floors with six bedrooms and baths while working days and some evenings would require outside assistance, even if only for the events we were expected to host. At the time of the town houses' construction, the assumption had been that we'd be able to hire domestic help.

Liz and I had employed a Russian maid during our first tour but hadn't found it worth the trouble and had let her go. Now no Russian could be hired in any capacity. With the ceiling in effect, the only domestic help in the community were the Italians working at Spaso House. The wives of those senior officers and military attachés used to having maids let out a collective complaint once they reached the town houses.

It took a few weeks before ours was running smoothly. Liz wrote home on November 4:

> The main problem with the house is that there is still no heat! Over a week now . . . and several people are working on it, but no results so far. It snowed this morning . . . luckily it has been unusually mild . . . . but one of these days the temperature is going to drop 20-30 degrees all at once. We were the first ones to move into one of the 11 town houses, which are on a different heating system—and they didn't know there was a problem.

The heating was ultimately fixed, and Liz tracked down some material with which to make curtains so we'd have some privacy.

But no one was able to fix the dumb waiter between the two kitchens, the one upstairs and the one downstairs. Given the state of relations, however, we couldn't imagine we'd have functions on a scale that would require it.

The two living rooms included handsome fireplaces, but there was no firewood. Would we have to apply to the diplomatic services branch, as Soviet diplomats in Washington were now required to do under the reciprocity rules?

To scrounge wood, Liz and I ventured into Morozov Park across the street from the compound. Pavlik Morozov was the "boy hero" who publicly denounced his father in 1931 for consorting with kulaks.

No sooner had I picked up a fallen log than two KGB plainclothesmen emerged from behind a bush and converged on me. I kept the log but Liz and I scurried out of the park. I had forgotten that the CIA had once used a fake stump to disguise a listening device near an ABM site; it hadn't fooled the KGB for long, but their people remained suspicious of Americans gleaning wood.

Soviet guards were already posted at the main entrance when we moved in. As the compound filled, others began taking up positions inside the booths pre-positioned around the perimeter. One morning I noticed a small sign in red Cyrillic letters hanging off their shack at the front gate—"Stop, We Shoot." I suggested to Combs that he mention it during one of his visits to the Foreign Ministry. The sign was subsequently rendered unreadable, twisted out of shape, either by a guard upon the ministry's instruction or by an irate American, one of the few who could read Cyrillic. Like most of the reporting officers, I watched Soviet television when evenings were free. The documentaries and news shows occasionally yielded interesting tidbits that we folded into our regular reporting. Once inside the compound, I found that the signal was weak and that one of the two channels couldn't be seen. Several of us raised the problem, but we were told that the embassy couldn't request an antenna. The intelligence community in Washington had already refused a request from the Soviets to install an antenna at their embassy. If we sought one, Washington would have to yield to the Soviets. Reciprocity would have to govern.

A few years later, I read that Shultz was once "strongly" advised by the Soviet desk not to receive the deputy head of the Soviet embassy, Oleg Sokolov, at a time when Dobrynin was ill because "it would undercut the effectiveness of our people in Moscow." Shultz called this kind of reciprocity "strained" and received Sokolov anyway.[520] This was in 1983, and reciprocity's grip on Washington's thinking had only grown stronger since.

On November 5, there was a bit of good news; the department awarded an "omnibus contract" to Pacific Architects and Engineers, the firm already at work in the new complex, so it could recruit the workers we urgently needed. We were told that the department, to accelerate the process, would permit PAE to recruit without security prescreening. The embassy would have the authority, however, to dismiss anyone so hired "for cause."

A few days later, the department reversed itself; prescreening would be required for everyone. This would delay the workers' arrival, perhaps until December.

Ambassador Hartman flew to Vienna on November 5 to meet with Secretary Shultz and Foreign Minister Shevardnadze. They were scheduled to have a two-day discussion about U.S.-Soviet relations on the margin of the foreign ministers participating in the Conference on Security and Cooperation in Europe (CSCE).

On his return, Hartman told us that the Shultz-Shevardnadze meetings had been "a bust." The Soviet side thought its negotiators could simply take the Reykjavik conversations, including Reagan's call for eliminating all nuclear weapons, and turn them into agreements without detailed discussion. Otherwise, the exchange had proceeded in good spirit, with both sides agreeing to pursue the work program set out in Reykjavik, including a bilateral meeting on human rights.

Before leaving for Vienna, Hartman had asked me whether I'd be willing to stay another year if he could find a loophole in the department's decision to retire me. The embassy needed to have a few officers around with experience.

Almost one hundred FSOs whose "window had closed" were in the same fix. I was skeptical there would be any loophole, but Hartman said he'd mention my situation to Shultz if I agreed. With Liz's concurrence, I had said, yes, we'd stay.

I wasn't surprised when he told me that his attempt had been in vain. Shultz couldn't do anything.

In fact, the secretary had more important things on his mind; the Iran-Contra affair was just breaking as he flew to Vienna, and it intruded on his meetings there. Ireland's foreign minister complained to him that NSC advisor McFarlane (who had replaced Poindexter) and four on his staff had used forged or stolen Irish passports to make a secret visit to Tehran. Shultz said that it was "as humiliating as any [meeting] I ever held as secretary of state."[521]

*   *   *

I did my best to stay focused on Soviet affairs. On November 11, 1986, *Izvestiya* reported that Molotov had died, quashing any hope I had of engaging Stalin's crony in Reading Room 1.

I was straying into other areas of the library, especially into special holdings (*spetskhran*) rooms closed to those without Soviet security clearances. I was taking a chance. The Foreign Ministry might complain if

I were caught, and I'd lose my library card; yet by confining me to Moscow, I felt it owed me something.

I'd arrive at Leninka looking like an indigent scholar from Eastern Europe—hair mussed, unshaven, ill-groomed. My shoes, scuffed from walking Moscow's streets, already looked the part. To heighten the effect, I'd wear a black turtleneck I had found in Paris three decades before. Although the station at the embassy had an expert on disguise, I had no intention of going this far.

In one of my first visits, I asked the young woman on duty in the *spetskhran* whether I could secure a copy of a speech Gorbachev had delivered to military officers in Minsk more than a year before, on July 10, 1985. It had aroused the interest of analysts during my consultations in Washington, in part because it wasn't published. What a *coup* if I could get my hands on it.

"Show me your card," she demanded. Glancing at it quickly before returning it, she ordered me back to Reading Room 1. I was sure she hadn't noted my name but had recognized me as no one from the Eastern bloc.

"Why, aren't foreigners allowed here," I countered with all the innocence I could muster.

"Go to your reading room immediately."

Concerned she might telephone her colleague at the desk outside my reading room who then might be prompted to investigate, I beat a retreat back to the embassy.

Thereafter, I limited myself to copying cards from the closed-area catalogues. I'd be careful to hide the fact I wrote left-handed; schooling had broken my Russian cohort of this.

The cards confirmed the library's vast collection of materials held back from ordinary Russians, materials ranging from Party documents from earlier eras to the entire output of émigré publishers.

Gorbachev might refer positively to Lenin's New Economic Policy, yet a thirty-two-page document from 1921 containing articles by "Comrades Lenin, Bukharin, and Preobrazhenski" on *The New Economic Policy and the Tasks of the Communist Party* was still being treated as classified. Even though Khrushchev had condemned Stalin for purging Lenin's coauthors (Preobrazhenski died in prison in 1937, Bukharin was executed a year later), the document was still "too hot" for the library's regular clientele.

The closed-room catalogues revealed extensive holdings of books published in Germany and Poland before World War II, books probably looted from libraries and collections during and after the war. "Trophy brigades" had confiscated seventeen important libraries and more than a million books from Germany alone.[522] Had I pressed my luck, I could have ordered *A Catalogue of German Trophy Material* published by the Bureau of New Technology in Moscow in 1947, *The Works of German Scientific-Research Institutes and Laboratories in Aviation* published in Moscow the same year, and *A History of Works Concerning the Creation of an Atomic Weapon in Germany, 1939-1945* published by Moscow's Central Scientific-Research Institute of Information and Technical Research on Atomic Science and Technology in 1971. The Soviet regime only acknowledged the brigades' existence in 1991.

From my stint in the department's exchanges office, I knew that Soviet visitors on academic and scientific exchanges would collect everything in sight at the American conferences they attended. The catalogues confirmed the scope of their activity; a single conference in Washington DC, the National Conference on Military Electronics, June 25-27, 1962, yielded 127 pages of material that the library held. But Andropov had since tightened the rules for the library's access to materials collected by Soviet scientists abroad, for there was a sharp falloff in the library's holdings after he became the KGB's chairman in 1967; or had the department and other Washington agencies become more effective in thwarting Soviet scientists and spies?

It was nearly impossible to make a copy in the library. A kiosk with several small openings was located in the so-called Hall of Reproductions, but the line of patrons was always long ("Heroes of Socialist Labor," war veterans, and other favored patrons were entitled to stand at the front); and the kiosk was manned only one hour a day. As soon as the kiosk fulfilled its daily plan of two thousand pages, it suspended work until the next day. If one succeeded in having a copy made (and each patron was limited to no more than twenty pages a day), it would only be available the following day. Library security reviewed every item copied (its clerks were inside the kiosk), and no copy could be removed from the library without an official stamp. An East European waiting in line told me that having articles copied from newspapers published in cities like Sverdlovsk and Omsk where defense industries were abundant was forbidden.

In summarizing my Leninka adventures to Washington, I noted that Marquis de Custine, the French traveler to Russia in the 1830s, had complained about finding "oppression disguised as love for order" everywhere.[523] Had de Custine visited Lenin Library a century and a half later, he wouldn't have found anything different. Looking back, one marvels at the quality of work Russian scholars still managed to do in the face of such controls.

*   *   *

On November 10, 1986, the Hartmans gamely hosted the marine ball, albeit without the traditional dinner.

It turned out to be our last formal event in the Foreign Service. Fancy-dress balls and black-tie dinners had once been commonplace, especially in the senior ranks, but they had largely disappeared in the course of our twenty-six years.

The Hartmans left for consultations at home on November 28. On December 1, we were told that thirty-six embassy positions were being abolished, including Mike Einik's in my section, so that workers from the United States could fit within the ceiling Washington instigated. To preserve as many substantive officers as long as possible, the embassy would keep the departure dates of Mike and the others open until the workers' travel dates were fixed.

On December 3, Combs circulated a memorandum congratulating everyone for carrying "an unprecedented load." "Please keep in mind", he added, "that we are now experiencing the worse of all times for embassy Moscow, the period between sudden withdrawal of all Soviet locals and the arrival of the U.S. support staff. Help is on the way."[524]

A few days later, the first workers—five drivers from the Pentagon—arrived.

Liz entertained several times, but it wasn't easy. Our first dinner party was for six young Americans studying in Moscow (we helped them usher two of their Russian friends surreptitiously past the guards), and Liz spent the full day preparing. My contribution was removing construction dust from the chandelier in the high-ceilinged dining room; in the absence of a step ladder, I polished its crystal while aloft on a chair on top of the table.

On December 13, Liz and I, along with other officers and wives in the economic section, hosted a more organized event, a reception to inaugurate town house number 4. It would be the first major event in any of the town houses. We invited thirty-seven diplomats, twenty-five Western businesspersons, eight officials from the Ministries of Foreign Affairs and Foreign Trade, five scholars from Soviet institutes, four Western journalists, and their spouses, in addition to embassy families. Ninety-one showed up. Many were curious about the compound and how we were faring without the Russians. Ed and Nina Stevens came with their daughter, Anastasia. Symptomatic of the sorry state of relations—and perhaps the intimidating militia presence—only one Soviet official and one Soviet scholar deigned to attend.

Back from Washington, Ambassador Hartman told us that not many officials seemed to be interested in the embassy's plight. I paraphrased his summary of the attitude he found in a note I wrote at the time: "Hurray, we've kicked out the spies and the affair is over."

Liz and I left for the United States to be with the children over Christmas. In five-degree below zero weather, we stood in a snowstorm in front of Tchaikovsky 19 and waited for a Soviet taxi we had ordered the previous day. We waited and waited; finally it arrived, and we reached Sheremetyevo II in the nick of time. At least the Russians who had made up the driver pool were punctual.

No sooner had we arrived in Washington than I read in the *Washington Post* that Hartman was retiring, and Matlock would succeed him. Hartman hadn't mentioned this before we left.

At lunch in Foggy Bottom on my first day, I gave George Vest, the Foreign Service's director general, a snapshot of life at the embassy without Russian workers. George heard me out politely but said that, frankly, not more than thirty people in the department understood the implications of what Gorbachev had done, and even fewer cared. Referring to the morning's press reports of rioting in Kazakhstan, I noted that travel outside Moscow had virtually ceased. Only a few at the embassy had figured out how to arrange their own Aeroflot ticketing and flights. As a result, effective coverage of the Soviet Union outside Moscow and Leningrad was disappearing.

I couldn't cite statistics but learned later that embassy officers traveled thirteen times outside Moscow in February 1987 while their counterparts at the Soviet embassy made 160 trips outside Washington. So much for the administration's brand of reciprocity!

Later I read of the CIA's satisfaction that satellite imagery had provided the White House "extraordinary photos of the riots" in Kazakhstan[525], the riots that cost some 200 lives and marked the start of Kazakhstan's drive to full independence. If the embassy hadn't been disrupted, the White House likely would have received eyewitness accounts. Indeed, had we been traveling at the rate we once did, the government would have received information about the unraveling of the Soviet Union not only from Kazakhstan but from elsewhere where it was beginning to occur. But Washington was more interested in satellite imagery than human intelligence in the 1980s.

I spent no other time at the department and set out to line up a second career. While at the ambassador's dacha, I had written a letter to the headmaster of Kent School, Fr. Richardson W. Schell, asking whether the school needed a history teacher. Kent had provided the academic preparation and perhaps the skills that helped me have a diplomatic career, and perhaps I could give something back. Father Schell responded by inviting me to meet him in New York. There he suggested a role that hadn't occurred to me, serving as the school's director of development; and I, with Liz's agreement, accepted. (Ironically, it would be our son who would become the history teacher at Kent.)

Schell said that I could begin when I wanted. This gave us the opportunity to return to the embassy for the full farewell that our friends deserved.

*   *   *

The weather was brutally cold—fifteen degrees below zero—when we landed at Sheremetyevo II on January 9, 1987. Two days earlier, it had been colder, twenty-six degrees below zero.

Tchaikovsky 19 was in a shambles. Pipes had burst and an expansion tank under the central wing's roof had malfunctioned, sending water cascading into the lower floors. A ceiling in the economic section had collapsed; a burst radiator had ruined two offices in the political section. The worse flooding occurred in the courtyard's wood-framed buildings; some of the American and third-country staff had to be relocated back to the central wing.

Among memoranda waiting for me was a notice from the administrative section that the commercial office in a building a half a block away had no heat: "You may want to consider this if you attend after-work activities there." Apparently late one evening, a militiaman guarding the building (it had lost much of its siding in September) had alerted the embassy that water was seeping out from under a front door.

The weather was so cold that icicles began forming inside Tchaikovsky 19's apartments.

The Seabees pitched in everywhere, but the fixes were temporary. The only workers who had arrived were the drivers—not any plumbers or electricians—though eleven weeks had already elapsed since Gorbachev's action.

On January 8, the administrative section distributed a memorandum entitled "Cold Weather Tips for Better Living":

> Soviet heating systems throughout the city are incomprehensible to the Western mind and in a general state of disrepair. The recent rash of burst radiators and hot water pipes in all Embassy leased buildings and apartments, and our inability to offer immediate repair in certain cases brings this point home in a manner all too costly and inconvenient for us to bear any longer. While we must expect a certain number of these catastrophes to occur throughout the winter, GSO has two suggestions to reduce our risk.

The tips were, "monitor the temperature occasionally" and "make occasional tours of all unused office and storage areas in your section to check for leaks or obvious signs of stress in radiators and all exposed plumbing."

Just before our return, the administrative section had vented its frustration in a telegram to Washington entitled "New Year's Greetings from the Titanic."

The All-Purpose Duty (APDs) and Custodial teams continued to do their jobs. Just after we left for Washington, they had unloaded 80,000 pounds of commissary dry goods, 15,000 pounds of lumber, and 7,000 pounds of mail and packages. The food sustained the community into January. The next big shipment—of rebar and concrete mix weighing 25,000 pounds—arrived January 8 and allowed the Seabees to push ahead with their projects. Another shipment, 13,000 pounds, was unloaded on the day we returned.

On our third day back, my APD group was mobilized in more temperate weather (fifteen degrees above zero) to clear snow around the embassy, load bricks into a truck (its frozen back gate couldn't be lowered so we tossed them over the sides one by one), and chop out two inches of ice from a Leninsky Prospect apartment. Its bathroom window had blown open, and a pipe had burst. An officer on my team attributed it to the KGB, but a typically loose-fitting window was more likely to blame. I knew the type from living in two Soviet compounds.

The bitter cold continued until mid-January before easing. Liz wrote a letter to my parents on January 15 saying that the sun had come out for a half hour and the temperature had risen to fifteen degrees above zero so "some people have gotten their cars started." She also wrote that "a lot of people are sick . . . and we are boiling water to guard against dysentery."

Beginning in December, giardiasis, a diarrhea-producing infection caused by a parasite, had begun contaminating the city's water because of pipe ruptures. On January 16, we were told that thirteen of our colleagues had tested positive for giardiasis. The medical unit encouraged anyone under the weather to submit stool samples, and it was soon overwhelmed with them. By the middle of February, thirty-seven persons from almost a fourth of the community's families were diagnosed with the infection.

On January 21, an administrative section memorandum advised that the motor pool, which now numbered six American drivers, was so "overwhelmed with transportation requests" that sections were instructed to limit their requests and/or to provide their own drivers. Could six Americans maintain an operation that normally required a score of experienced Russians? Even for them it hadn't been easy, dealing with the daily pile of diplomatic notes, letters, invitations, and tickets that needed to be picked up, collected, and delivered among the capital's numerous embassies, ministries, institutions, and transportation agencies. Chauffeuring diplomats to and from meetings, railroad stations, and airports was but a small part of the drivers' function, though I doubted this was understood in Washington.

One of the Pentagon drivers sent out a memorandum cautioning that anyone who borrowed a vehicle for official purposes would be held "responsible for [its] cleanliness," ensuring that it was "washed at a minimum of once a week . . . in accordance with Soviet law and to keep a good image of the U.S. community."

Keeping a vehicle clean in Moscow was always a challenge, and virtually impossible in winter. Soviet compounds provided no external faucets; one had to haul buckets of water down an elevator to the parking area. When the staff was smaller, one could use the Tchaikovsky courtyard and the garage's hose, but the courtyard was now filled with building materials and shipping crates, and entering it required special permission. But how could someone fresh from the United States know any of this? On January 23, the administrative section issued two more memoranda. In the first, the staff was faulted because it had left the carpentry shop in a mess ("plywood has been left in scraps . . . sawdust is ankle-deep, tools have been strewn about"); henceforth the shop would be kept under lock and key. That such a shop existed surprised me; it had probably arrived with the Seabee encampment.

As I was scanning this, Barbara dropped off a second memorandum claiming that the staff hadn't been heeding the embassy's guidelines on trash disposal and that "rodents and flying vermin" had resumed their depredations at the rear of the courtyard.

Rodents could survive in zero-degree weather, but "flying vermin"? Humor was always welcome, and I was finding plenty of it—even if inadvertent—in the embassy's output.

While administrative officers were doing their best to keep the embassy functioning, political and economic officers were pulling more and more reporting out of the Soviet media. Travel outside the capital had virtually ended, and visits even within it were difficult to arrange. I was glad I had been riding the Metro since 1972.

The community was awash in rumors. Two members of Congress gained the impression from talking with staff members that the Soviets had deliberately contaminated the embassy's water supply, and had "entered the residences of U.S. embassy employees while they were away and opened their windows in mid-winter, freezing radiator pipes that burst and caused heavy water damage."[526] If you were new at the embassy and suffering from the bitter cold and perhaps a parasite, it was easy to blame the Soviets for everything, including the weather.

*   *   *

While Liz and I were in Washington, Ambassador Hartman had informed the staff that he would retire and leave on February 20, 1987. Although everyone knew that Matlock would be Hartman's successor, the appointment wasn't officially announced until January 30.

On January 12, at the first country-team meeting after our return, Hartman told us that Marine Sergeant Clayton Lonetree had been arrested for espionage. The Marine Corps had announced Lonetree's arrest on January 2, but the press had ignored it initially. The *Washington Post* carried the first report on January 11.

The ambassador told us that Violetta Seina, the employee who had entrapped Lonetree, had been dismissed before the Soviet employees' withdrawal. I don't recall any extended discussion of Lonetree, but everyone was shocked.

Hartman suggested that the embassy would "likely run further such risks as we bring in more and more [untrained] people." Earlier in the meeting, he had said that a second contingent of workers would arrive in two weeks.

At a meeting on January 16, we were informed that thirteen of the twenty-eight marines were being disciplined for "indiscretions" unrelated to espionage. The marines were said to have arranged a "protection ring" so they could bring women in and out of their quarters. The second in command among the enlisted men, Sergeant Stufflebeam, who had the upper-floor cleaning contract, was among those disciplined.

During the few weeks that remained for Liz and me, allegations about the marines continued to swirl. Rumors about their misbehavior had circulated before Lonetree's arrest (the gang-rape of a British nanny who had been drinking in the Marine Bar was mentioned at a meeting in December), but no one had ever suggested espionage. When the Voice of America reported that a second marine, Arnold Bracy, was also being investigated for espionage, I was dumbfounded. The son of a minister, soft-spoken and polite, Bracy had impressed me as the best of the lot.

Assuming the worst, however, it was difficult to believe that the damage was serious. How could two marines, even working in concert, gain access to the communications center and its highly sensitive equipment, with the strict compartmentalization of functions and redundancy of controls that the embassy maintained?

We know today that the "Marine spy scandal" was "overblown"—the word used by David Wise, a sophisticated and longtime observer of U.S. intelligence and counterintelligence operations.[527]

Ambassador Matlock, who followed the story from the NSC (and from the embassy after his arrival in April 1987), needed but a few words to controvert the claim of "espionage":

> The marine guards did not have access to the most sensitive areas
> of the embassy, such as the communications center. They did
> not have combinations to the safes where classified material was

stored. About the only thing a single marine could do was extract some material of low classification from the burn bags he and his partner collected from offices at night.[528]

With regard to the allegation against Sergeant Bracy, Matlock pointed out that the embassy logs proved he had never been on duty together with Lonetree. After this and other discrepancies in the allegations were revealed, it became clear that "the Naval Investigative Service [that led the marine investigation] had extorted a confession from the second marine by methods just short of torture and had written his 'confession,' which he signed under duress and repudiated immediately." Matlock found the whole matter "a flagrant case of deceit for which nobody, to my knowledge, was punished."[529] As Matlock also wrote, before the truth finally emerged "a procession of lawmakers descended on the overworked and harassed embassy staff, eager to show the folks back home that, if it were not for their vigilance, the Republic would founder." Of course, they had been briefed by an administration "desperate to explain" the loss of its covert sources.[530]

David Major must have been pleased with Lonetree's arrest. After all, it was he who had provoked Reagan's interest in the embassy through a slideshow and challenged Hartman's management from his NSC perch.

Major left the NSC in September 1987 and returned to the FBI from where he had come. His new responsibilities included counterintelligence training. An acquaintance of Major's from previous assignments, Robert Hanssen, was working in the same office and, by Major's account, greeted him warmly upon his return.[531] This was the same Hanssen who had been spying for the GRU and the KGB since 1979, the Hannsen whose information helped lead the Soviets to Polyakov and other informants who were later executed.

The FBI only caught up with Hanssen in 2001.

How ironic that the NSC's counterintelligence expert ended up supervising Hanssen! No guard at Tchaikovsky 19, American or Soviet, could have done the damage that Hanssen did.

The CIA's Aldrich Ames was also delighted when Lonetree was arrested. Ames said in 1994 that the marine's arrest had enabled him to evade an early round of suspicion, to "get me off the hook.,"[532]

*   *   *

Liz and I tried to spend as much time as possible with our Russian friends. One of our first guests at the town house was Igor Palmin. I met Igor in Morozov Park on January 18 and conducted him past the militiamen without a hitch.

It turned out to be our last meeting before I left the Foreign Service. We gave Igor a bound collection of photographs of the United States. It was a modest gift in view of what his friendship had meant, but he wouldn't have understood anything grander, nor would have Moscow's "competent organs."

On January 22, we were informed that the compound's main gate would be locked and left unattended from 5:00 to 7:00 PM every evening. The embassy lacked the funds to recruit an American guard to cover these hours, so keys were issued to every family in the compound.

As more of the apartments and town houses became occupied, the militiamen became more aggressive. Twice I arrived at the gate to let in our guests only to find that they were being detained, their Soviet identification cards already in the hands of militiamen copying their data. I hadn't seen them act so blatantly at Leninsky Prospect or Krutitsky Val, although they undoubtedly interrogated some guests as they were leaving. It seemed to me that only the most intrepid Russian, or one already in the KGB's good graces, would dare enter the new compound.

On Monday evening, January 26, in the middle of a blizzard, I set out by myself to attend Moscow's first public showing of the film *Repentance* (*Pokayanie*), a Georgian film that had been completed three years before. As Gorbachev explains in his memoir:

> It had been produced under the personal "protection" of Shevardnadze [when he headed the Party in the Georgian Republic] and had been given a private screening at the House of Film and then shown in a few other closed halls [in Moscow]. The film was a real bombshell; it became both an artistic and a political phenomenon. The ideologists [probably Demichev] wanted a discussion in the Politburo about whether or not to release it for general viewing. I objected, saying that this matter should be resolved by the cinematographers' and artists' union, who had been waiting for this signal. Thus a precedent was set and soon censored works began to spill out.[533]

Mila had kept me informed of the controversy as it developed. In November, she had asked the director of the film, Tengiz Abuladze, whether I could attend a closed screening; he told her that it would be best if I didn't, since a debate about the film was still raging.

The fact that Gorbachev decided to entrust the union and not the Party's cultural watchdogs with responsibility for making a decision whether or not to release it was a turning point in his drive for "openness," as Gorbachev acknowledged. Elem Klimov, Sergei's good friend, had just become head of the union; Abuladze credits Klimov for the decision to release it but also thanks Shevardnadze for making Gorbachev aware of his film's existence.[534]

Mila told me that the first public showing would be far from the city center, at the small Tbilisi cinema theatre where Georgian films were sometimes shown. The closed showings had been downtown, easily accessible to the *nomenklatura*, but the authorities couldn't risk an outburst from the general public in the heart of the capital.

From Barrikadnaya, I traveled to the Profsoyuznaya station, which was four long blocks from the theater. When I approached it by foot an hour before the showing scheduled at 10:00 PM (a time that the authorities thought would discourage attendance), a crowd of about one hundred was milling about in front of wooden barricades, observed by six militiamen, one with a bullhorn. When the doors were finally flung open, about two hundred were in the crowd, including several diplomats from other embassies.

The film is a powerful indictment of Stalinism. A character wearing a black shirt and suspenders plays the part of a ruthless dictator. Abuladze had Lavrenti Beria in his sights, Stalin's security chief and a native Georgian who had started his murderous career in the Caucuses.

The film's sound track is in Georgian, but the audience heard a Russian language voice-over delivered in a chilling monotone. Everyone sat in rapt silence, motionless despite the theater's hard wooden chairs, thinly covered by cotton batting as in most theaters.

In the final dialogue, an old *babushka* asks whether the road down which she is walking leads to the church. No, she is told, it bears the name of the tyrant. The *babushka* replies, "What's the good of a road if it doesn't lead to the Church of the Virgin?" The Russian I heard omitted "of the Virgin", but the words were more effective just where they ended.

Everyone was subdued when exiting. If the authorities feared an outburst, they were mistaken. Making my way home, I knew that Gorbachev's openness had passed an important test. I didn't realize that the film would open the floodgates to works that had been forbidden for years.

*   *   *

My All-Purpose Duty crew had a difficult day on January 28. We started by supervising the pumping of sewage into a tank truck at the new Serebryanny Bor dachas. To keep them open for families' use during winter, faucets had been left open to ensure a continuous trickle, but this had overburdened the septic systems. None of us had prior experience with sewage issues.

From the dachas, we returned to the Tchaikovsky courtyard and dragged crates of food from the storeroom behind the garage into the commissary so a custodial team could replenish the shelves. Then we took a platform truck to Leningradsky Station and, talking our way past three checkpoints, reached the customs warehouse. There, we collected eighty-seven crates of milk, juice, and individual orders that had arrived on the overnight train from Helsinki. Two customs inspectors and a doctor examined each crate, requiring us to open three-fourths of them. They confiscated four exotic onions from one family's order; they had been "grown in Finnish soil." This prompted a member of our crew to recall customs' seizure of an avocado at Sheremetyevo a few weeks earlier. The greedy inspector had asked, "How does one cook this thing?" The quick-witted American replied, "Boil it for three and a half hours, and it should be fine." By the time I returned home at 6:00 PM, the temperature was retreating from the day's high of five degrees above zero.

At the end of January, the embassy managed to secure a load of scrap wood, which, when added to the "huge, wet, green tree trunks which UPDK facetiously wants to pass off to us as firewood" (to quote the administrative memorandum), enabled us to use our fireplaces. Along with the wood, we received the usual detailed advice:

> The wood comes in all shapes and sizes. Boards will be leaned against the wall and scraps will be deposited in a box . . . Unfortunately, the APD will not have the time to prepare the wood, so any imbedded nails must be removed by the user. An ax and claw hammer are hanging in the trash compactor control room . . . These may be used to chop the wood and pull unwanted metal bits . . . Cardboard boxes for hauling the wood may be found in the trash area, and a 'stump' for chopping will be placed near the wood.

The California architectural firm that designed the town houses hadn't provided overhangs above the front entrances or back balconies extending off the living rooms. Whenever it snowed, the granite staircases in front became dangerously slippery, and the French doors to the balconies wouldn't budge. So the administrative section gave us snow shovels.

Of course, we all welcomed the complex's proximity to Tchaikovsky 19. Even in snow and ice, it took Liz and me only a few seconds to reach the main gate, then a few minutes to go up the side street and past the beat-up box to Tchaikovsky's pedestrian entrance.

On February 9, I received a telegram from the department asking if I were interested in being the chief of the U.S. Interests Section, the *de facto* American embassy, in Havana, Cuba. My colleagues were amused that someone in the department didn't realize my days were numbered. "Take the job," they said, "For a few years Washington might not notice."

That evening, the Hartmans hosted their last social event at Spaso House, a concert at which Volodya Feltsman again performed.

A day later, Valeriya Novikova took Liz and me to a farewell lunch at the Praga restaurant. We brought along a new FSO to provide contact should she need it after our departure. In fact, Valeriya would come to know Ambassador Matlock and his wife Rebecca.

On February 14, Foreign Minister and Mrs. Shevardnadze hosted a luncheon for the Hartmans at the guest house on Alexei Tolstoi Street. Liz and I were included along with Deputy Chief of Mission Combs, Counselor for Administrative Affairs David Beall, and Counselor for Cultural Affairs Ray Benson, and their wives. Anatoli Dobrynin, Deputy Foreign Minister Alexander Bessmertnykh, and two others from the ministry joined Shevardnadze. Dobrynin and Bessmertnykh brought their wives. Although the Foreign Ministry (no less than the White House) had dealt Hartman a difficult year, it didn't stint on his farewell. There was caviar, salmon, and crabmeat to begin, crayfish and filet mignon for the main course. Despite the hostile words coming from the two capitals, those Shevardnadze addressed to Hartman were genuinely warm. The sour note was struck by the Dobrynins. Whenever Shevardnadze made a gracious comment, one of the Dobrynins would interrupt with a side remark. By the end of the luncheon, I understood why Gorbachev had selected Shevardnadze and not Dobrynin to be his foreign minister; the Georgian would project Soviet policy much more smoothly.

I don't recall that Gorbachev's decision to withdraw the employees was discussed, but Dobrynin's performance left me with no doubt he had been behind it.

On February 18, at the ambassador's final country-team meeting, I learned that only four of the thirteen contract workers who had been promised would arrive after all. Because of the marine scandal, security agencies were now vetting each worker's background with a fine-tooth comb. One worker had already been eliminated after a police check revealed two convictions for manslaughter. The Soviet embassy in Washington, for its part, was taking its time to process the workers' visa applications.

Delays weren't the only problem. Once in Moscow, a few of the workers turned out to be unsuitable. By the middle of March, eight of the first sixteen had been sent home. A plumber who had proved indispensable dealing with broken pipes was dismissed for "insubordination"; he refused to wear the Pacific Architect firm's official uniform (of "a cheap Hong Kong make," he claimed) because it made him itch. The security office, which oversaw the workers, had to caution several for evangelizing. One was hoarding food from the commissary in expectation of Christ's Second Coming.

*   *   *

On February 19, the Hartmans bade farewell to the community at a ceremony that also inaugurated the recreational facilities on the ground floor of the new chancery, the new office building, or the NOB as most now called it. The upper floors remained in limbo pending a decision whether to demolish and rebuild them or to add the usual safeguards to offset the KGB's listening devices. The ambassador cut a red ribbon at the entrance and, for the first time, Liz and I saw the basketball court, swimming pool, squash court, saunas, and other recreational amenities about which the Seabees had been raving.

There were cocktails, food, and music; and a few of the Hartmans' Russian friends participated along with the American community. Liz and I chatted with Mila and Sergei Vronski, Vladimir Feltsman and his wife, and Sergei Petrov, a refusenik photographer whose work the Hartmans admired.

The next morning, the ambassador and Donna flew back to the United States, ending forty years in the Foreign Service. Liz and I hadn't served with a more capable couple. Despite the pressure, they had remained sociable and warm, without a hint of the forced congeniality such as those at the mercy of relentless schedules often show.

From the beginning of his assignment, Hartman had foreseen the danger of applying a rigid code of reciprocity to U.S.-Soviet relations, of pursuing the ever-chimerical "total security" that could only end in deepening the embassy's isolation and reducing its effectiveness.

Hartman's approach had been based on years of experience—his own and that of hundreds of FSOs who had served in the Communist bloc—but it proved too sophisticated for those in the White House and in Washington's intelligence agencies, most of whom had zero experience working behind the Iron Curtain.

From the start of American diplomacy, heads of mission have had to wrestle with the problem of espionage. The first American minister to France[535] was Ben Franklin, and Franklin had a British spy in his midst, Edward Bancroft, the mission's Massachusetts-born secretary. (Bancroft's tradecraft was thoroughly professional; he used a chemical wash to make writing on his messages invisible and a "drop" in the hollow of a tree in Tuileries Park to transfer them to his British handler.[536]) Warned that he was surrounded by spies, Franklin refused to be diverted from the task at hand to marshal financial and military support from the French so the new republic would survive. As a recent biographer notes, "Without French funds the Revolution would have collapsed."[537]

Franklin would explain himself:

> I have long observed one rule which prevents any inconveniences from such [espionage] practices. It is simply this: to be concerned in no affairs I should blush to have made public, and to do nothing but what spies may see and welcome. When a man's actions are just and honorable, the more they are known, the more his reputation is increased and established. If I was sure, therefore, that my *valet de place* was a spy, as he probably is, I think I should probably not discharge him for that, if in other respects I liked him.[538]

I doubt that Hartman took guidance from Franklin, though he was in the line of those succeeding him as ambassador to Paris; but he knew what his tasks were in Moscow, and he didn't let himself be distracted from them.

Hartman also knew that the USSR was a police state and that Spaso House, Tchaikovsky 19, Soviet compounds, Soviet hotels, and many other places were bugged. He once explained that he held "most of my briefings with . . . [congressmen] in my house, because I knew that the system there was probably better than the one in my office. Ninety percent of what I did and said I wanted the Russians to hear." As for his driver, Hartman said, "I don't need an American driver . . . I'd rather have a Russian driver who knows where he is going in Moscow because I can't have a private conversation in my car anyway."[539]

It was an attitude that puzzled Americans who had never worked in Soviet conditions, or lacked the imagination to understand them. Alas, in the middle 1980s, these Americans included key members of Washington's intelligence community.

Visiting Spaso House in October 1986, Secretary Shultz was "surprised" when Hartman told him that "90 percent of what I want to say, I can say right here" because "we want our message to get across to the Soviets, and this is one of the few ways we can get them to listen to us."[540] Obviously, there were better ways to communicate with the Soviets, but Hartman wasn't unique when he spoke to walls.[541]

Kessler quotes from a statement that Hartman telegraphed to Washington in 1984, three years before the marine scandal broke. Hartman explained why those who were pressing for a mass expulsion of Soviet officials from the United States were mistaken: "The all-out assault (and that's what it is) on the Soviet official presence in the U.S., coupled with demands for an increase here, will lead to four years of Arctic solid-frozen relations." Proposals to remove Soviets from the United States "ignore the absolutely predictable Soviet reaction which will take the form of retaliation designed to hurt us most . . . They assume that we are so inept that we cannot combat the threat of a few hundred resident Soviet citizens [at their official establishments]."[542]

Hartman's advice was ignored, and the Reagan administration went ahead with its expulsions while failing to prepare for that "form of retaliation" calculated "to hurt us most."

Thanks to the emergence of Gorbachev and the break-up of the Soviet system, the United States was spared the "solid-frozen relations" that Hartman foresaw, or a Berlin, Cuban, or other crisis that would have required the embassy's peak performance, a performance that, in the circumstances, it couldn't have delivered.

A full year would pass before an adequate number of workers arrived at Tchaikovsky 19 and its operations returned to a semblance of normality.

Ambassador Matlock would write later that "by the end of the following year [1987], when Americans had been sent to Moscow to perform essential services, embassy operations ran more smoothly than they had with Soviet employees."[543]

If this had been so, why did Washington return the embassy to its historic configuration after Matlock's retirement and begin repopulating it with Russians in 1992? Did Washington decide that the Russians would no longer engage in spying after the collapse of Communism?

Far more likely, wiser heads understood by then that the Russians could help the Americans perform their tasks more effectively than rotations of workers from the United States. Perhaps Washington had also figured out—from the embassy's performance in the intervening period—that the Russians could also contribute something else, an opening of doors into their opaque society, at least for those Americans at the embassy having the interest and the skills.

The Russian contingent today of some four hundred employees is almost twice as large as it was during the Cold War. The KGB's successor organization undoubtedly has an effective presence among them. Undoubtedly too, embassy and consulate officers are aware of the problem and take account of it as they perform their duties.

*   *   *

Almost from the moment of my arrival as economic counselor, I tried to visit Soviet factories and meet managers who might help us better understand

Gorbachev's economic restructuring. Ten days before the Hartmans said farewell, I received my first invitation to see a factory—the ZIL factory in the district from which we had just moved. In my calendar I noted, "took one and a half years to get the Foreign Ministry's permission!"

Together with two officers from my section, I toured the floor where medium-weight trucks were assembled. Then we were hosted by ZIL's deputy director, a Comrade Buzhinski.

It was a huge operation spread over hundreds of acres, with more than sixty thousand of ZIL's one hundred thousand total workforce distributed among numerous buildings of which we were shown but one. Like other large-scale enterprises, it had its own hospital ("better than the Kremlin's"), sanatoria outside Moscow, and housing complexes.

Buzhinski spoke highly of ZIL's ventures with West German and Japanese companies, and wanted us to know that Americans were missing an opportunity. He was guarded, however, when responding to questions about Gorbachev's recommendations for improving quality control; and he flatly denied, in the face of what we knew to be true, that ZIL was manufacturing trucks for the military.

No sooner had this visit concluded than Hartman sent me an invitation that he and other Western ambassadors had received from the Foreign Ministry for a visit to a machine-tool factory. It may have been Hartman's first opportunity to roam a factory too, but he was ending his assignment the next day and passed the invitation to me. I accepted, toured an enterprise that employed five thousand workers, and took part in a two-hour question-and-answer period with the director general, Chikirev by name. He explained that he had been a "Stakhanovite" as a young man (Stakhanov was the coal miner who surpassed every production norm in 1935) and gained the factory's top position after forty-five years on the job. I took more than twenty pages of notes as he fielded questions from me and other diplomats. Upon reviewing his answers later, I found that I hadn't learned much, but at least the Soviets were opening a few sizeable factories to non-Communist diplomats.

*   *   *

On February 23, Dick Combs briefed the country team on Ambassador Matlock's arrival plans and expectations, as conveyed in a telegram sent by the Soviet desk. Matlock planned to arrive on April first or second. He wanted the staff to understand that protocol was important and he urged everyone to review the rules before he arrived. He expected officers' wives to call on Mrs. Matlock. Country-team meetings would begin on time ("late arrivals would find the door locked"), and none of his meetings would last more than thirty minutes. Everyone receiving an invitation to a Spaso House function should understand that a prompt response would be expected, and an attendee should consider himself or herself a "cohost."

Matlock also wanted it known he would not accept invitations to functions at officers' homes unless Soviet citizens were included. He would stress the importance of Russian language skills; ideally, everyone should be at the FSI's "limited professional level."

Listening to Matlock's list, I wondered whether he was aware that the language program had come to a halt with the disappearance of the Russian teachers. The administrative section was trying to revive it with two Americans who were ready to give part-time lessons but, according to the memorandum, "there are more prospective students out there than our present meager resources can handle."

Matlock had taught Russian at Dartmouth College before joining the Foreign Service in 1956. From three assignments in Moscow, including a stint as chargé d'affaires after Watson's retirement, he had brought his Russian to the highest level. He was known as a disciplinarian and stickler for etiquette but had never been harder on his staff than on himself. Anecdotes about his nervous intensity, especially when serving as the deputy chief of mission after Spike Dubs, were still circulating. Judging from what he asked Combs to relay, the White House hadn't mellowed him. A year after Matlock retired from the Foreign Service, a New Yorker writer would note that his relationship with President George H. W. Bush and Secretary James Baker hadn't been that warm.[544] I wasn't surprised. Matlock's career had moved forward "with its own furious inner propulsion,"[545] and careers like this don't allow for much relaxed socializing. However, no one doubted that Matlock was the right choice. The embassy's collective energy was depleted, its staff "demoralized," although the word is tiresomely used at almost every embassy. Moreover, the Soviet system and Gorbachev were facing intractable problems; where both were headed was still unclear. With his experience and his Russian, Matlock would not only open his own doors but would likely gain the ear and confidence of those with whom he met.

*   *   *

Liz and I set my retirement for March 31, 1987, and the officers in the economic section and their wives gave us a farewell dinner. For a gift, they presented a complete set of the second edition of the Large Soviet Encyclopedia, published between 1949 and 1958. Mike Einik had acquired it from a refusenik who had just received an exit visa. The encyclopedia's fifty-seven volumes stretched almost nine feet wide. Having lost our silver when we shipped out in 1981, I was skeptical it would reach Connecticut, but it did. Apparently, Soviet customs no longer attached importance to keeping this kind of artifact from the pre-Brezhnev era.

There were staff members at Spaso House to whom we needed to say good-bye. Piero, once a fixture at Uncle Sam's but now in the kitchen at Spaso House, drove me out to see Tang at his apartment. Tang's Russian wife had died, and his grandchildren were looking after him. His memory was failing (he had begun working at Spaso House in 1939), but there was a spark of recognition when I alluded to Beam's Independence Day reception in 1972 when we had first met.

Piero told me that Tang had fallen and had broken a hip in the basement of the residence just before retiring in 1984. He had lain there two days before his absence was discovered and help was summoned. I thought of the final scene in *The Cherry Orchard* when Firs, the eighty-seven-year-old valet, is left alone and abandoned in the manor house. Chekhov's Firs was probably no older than Tang and wore "a jacket and white waistcoat" such as Tang must have worn when he began his service: "They've gone . . . Forgot about me . . . Never mind . . . I'll sit here a spell . . . Not a bit o' strength left in you, nothing left, nothing."

The audience in the theater then hears, as the curtain descends, "the thud of an axe on a tree" far away and "the distant sound of a breaking [musical] string, dying away mournfully."[546]

On March 5, Clemente and Maria invited us to a farewell dinner at the carriage house behind the residence. Piero and his Russian wife Nadia, and Bob and Tatyana Berls (she of Russian ancestry) from the defense attaché's office were present.

I was astonished to see Clemente's collection of Russian icons and nineteenth-century paintings. I hadn't realized he was a serious collector. He told me he hoped to sell them all to Armand Hammer, Don Kendall, or another wealthy American who would then donate them back to Spaso House. This would enable him to buy a house for his and Maria's retirement in their native Pordenone north of Venice. He believed that the Soviet authorities would be agreeable. I wasn't so sure but kept my doubts to myself. Clemente was apprehensive about Ambassador Matlock's arrival. He said that the least favorite of the many Independence Day receptions he had organized occurred on Matlock's watch in 1981. Napkins were not put out on tables, and the appetizer was limited to popcorn. I suggested that perhaps Ambassador Watson had exhausted the embassy's representation allowance by the time of that year's celebration; Clemente shook his head, and we turned to other subjects.

Over May Day weekend 1991, Clemente was murdered. I was flabbergasted when Serge Schmemann, the *Times* correspondent, told me

402 ROBERT F. OBER, JR.

ROBERT F. OBER, JR.

while he was at Kent School attending his son's graduation. I immediately queried several former Moscow hands. One cited a Russian press report that two Soviet conscripts were implicated and that a homosexual affair had been involved. Ambassador Watson, retired in Connecticut, told me that he had seen Clemente during a visit to Moscow a few months earlier; gambling, he said, could have been involved. "In any case, he did not press caviar or icons on us this visit, and that's the first time."[547] Obviously, Clemente was still trying to sell his art when he died.

Had the crime occurred at the height of the Cold War, there would have been speculation about the KGB's role. When I read in 2003 that the CIA spy Tolkachev had established contact with the embassy by "approach[ing] the Italian majordomo of Spaso House" and handing him a note that then found its way to the CIA station chief, I wondered whether a rogue KGB element could have carried out a vendetta.[548] Tolkachev had cooperated with his interrogators, and the KGB had learned about the approach.

By 1991, however, a vendetta would have been unlikely. The Soviet regime didn't hesitate to impose death penalties on those Russians who spied for Washington, but Gorbachev was no Stalin, and no one in his right mind, not even from the KGB, would have executed a foreigner because of a chance encounter.

But it was a sad ending for the man who kept the residence running smoothly for a quarter century, who from behind the ambassador's chair heard some of the Cold War's most intriguing conversations.

* * *

On March 10, a State Department psychiatrist visited the embassy for a so-called "I'm Surviving Moscow Workshop." An unclassified memorandum from the administrative section explained:

> We will discuss the different aspects of our current life here in Moscow that produces stress: extended APD duty, freezing offices, steaming basements, giardiasis attacks, daily childcare emergencies, and other irritants. We look to Dr. Rigamer to help us identify possible patterns of behavior that would allow us to maintain sanity in the midst of all this.

The Soviet security types responsible for picking through the embassy's garbage must have been delighted to read the memo.

Two days later, disaster struck the recreational space that Hartman had just inaugurated. Apparently the architects had included sprinklers but no drains in their design of the women's sauna, and the FBO staff supervising the construction hadn't noticed. Late one night, the sprinklers had been triggered and 1,500 gallons of water swamped much of the ground floor, including the basketball court and the locker rooms.

On March 18, the administrative section announced that another contingent of workers would arrive from the United States, bringing the total to ten, and that a further ten would arrive at the end of March. The APD program would be phased out on April 15, two weeks after we left.

With a majority of the embassy's families housed in the new complex and with few officers venturing out into the city, there were signs that, as one colleague put it, "the community was turning in on itself." The stress of working long hours in uncomfortable and cold conditions, in a place beset by allegations of incompetence and disloyalty, was taking a toll.

The wife of a Foreign Service officer told us she had been summoned to the ninth floor and was asked by a security officer whether her husband was sexually involved with boys. The insinuation was appalling; she and her husband had been married fifteen years (and are married today). At a second meeting, she was asked whether she and her husband were furtively bringing Russians into their apartment through the back door off their balcony. The question was strange—no one could get into the compound except through one of the two gates or over the wall, and the gates and wall were guarded and patrolled by militiamen day and night. Did security suspect that an FSO was colluding with militiamen?

Against the background of spy talk in Washington, apparently no theory was too bizarre. With the decimation of the CIA's operations by the KGB and with the marine scandals, the pressure to find an enemy within must have been intense. "In such a climate, monstrous theories become daily fare," to borrow a phrase from John le Carré.[549]

An increase in petty theft was also reported. We were told that shoplifting had become a problem at the commissary. Also, a worker had taken a microwave oven from his new apartment and stashed it in his household effects hoping to ship it home. Uncle Sam's new management would no longer accept IOUs; customers had left Moscow leaving unpaid bills.

The administrative section announced on March 25 that only government-owned vehicles would henceforth be allowed in front of Tchaikovsky 19. The next day, a petition hung inside the elevator; seven families and eighteen single persons still living in Soviet apartments demanded an end to the restriction, complaining of "discrimination . . . due to the fact that we do not live" at the new compound.

Complaints about rules used to be made at meetings upstairs, but the staff had grown so large and the atmosphere so impersonal that they were now being posted publicly. So different had the community become!

Liz and I spent our last evening with Sergei and Mila and their family at the Vronski apartment. After dinner, Arisha, Anya's four-year-old daughter from her liaison with Andrei, recited stanzas from poems by Alexander Pushkin and Sergei Yesenin. As we said good-bye to our friends, it occurred to me that my career was ending as it had begun, amid the words of poets. Boris Pasternak had drawn me into the Foreign Service with his *Doctor Zhivago*. Now a precocious child who knew the poems of two other Russian poets was ushering me out.

15

Epilogue:
Area and Language Expertise in
Diplomacy's Service

L iz and I adapted to Connecticut, the state I knew from early childhood and school, but putting Moscow behind us wasn't so easy. No sooner had I arrived at Kent than an official from the CIA invited me to join an advisory group on Soviet affairs. He assured that I'd have to be in Washington only one or two days every few months. But from what he also said, I realized that security at the embassy would be on the agenda, and I wasn't ready for this.

On April 7, 1987, a week after we left Moscow, President Reagan held a news conference at which he expressed concern about the embassy. He announced that he had asked his secretaries of state and defense, his national security advisor, the chairman of the foreign advisory intelligence board as well as one former secretary of defense to conduct separate and independent studies of various aspects of the reported breach and its implications. "All the facts are not known," he said, but the "implications are widespread and . . . additional quick action is required to prevent further damage to our national security."[550]

Judging from Reagan's diaries, he didn't have any doubt that the allegations against the Marines were soundly based, and that these men had done "great damage." His public remarks added to the perception that disloyalty and bungling by Americans at the embassy were jeopardizing the country's security.[551]

By this time, two members of Congress had conducted their own on-site investigation. After talking with embassy staff members, Daniel Mica of

Florida and Olympia Snowe of Maine were quoted in the press saying that the embassy's equipment and practices were "fundamentally flawed" and its diplomats held "a negative attitude toward marines."[552]

On April 9, two days before Secretary Shultz's scheduled departure for meetings with Foreign Minister Shevardnadze, the U.S. Senate adopted a resolution—70 votes to 30—urging him not to go. Former Secretary Kissinger had earlier said that it would be humiliating for Shultz to meet with the Soviets after they had compromised the embassy. Shultz flew to the Soviet Union anyway, but not before arranging for a guaranteed-secure communications system housed in a huge Winnebago van to arrive ahead of him and to be stationed in Tchaikovsky 19's courtyard for his stay. Because of concern that the marines had let the KGB roam the ninth floor, the tank had already been dismantled and shipped back to Washington.

Ambassador Matlock reached Moscow just before Shultz. On April 6, he presented his credentials to Andrei Gromyko, who had been "kicked upstairs" as chairman of the Presidium of the Supreme Soviet to make room for Shevardnadze at the Foreign Ministry. According to Matlock, Shultz used the visit to set the stage for the Washington summit between Reagan and Gorbachev the following December.[553]

On May 4, 1987, the assistant secretary of state for diplomatic security let the *New York Times* know that the State Department and other agencies were investigating more than ten embassy staffers every year because of "unauthorized socializing with foreign employees and residents." He didn't explicitly cite the embassy, but this was the context. He assured readers that social contacts in Soviet-bloc and some Communist-dominated countries are severely limited. Another official quoted in the article said that "one-on-one social contacts are generally precluded in these places."[554] Concurrently, the FBI director informed Congress that the bureau was investigating State Department employees for security breaches.[555]

On May 8, Secretary of the Navy James Webb, a decorated ex-marine, accused Ambassador Hartman of displaying "a complete arrogance toward counterintelligence" and "indifference toward the environment which allowed the penetration by the KGB."[556]

Perhaps it was to be expected that the service secretary to whom the marine commandant reported would be embarrassed by the marines' indiscipline and try to shift blame elsewhere. But what did Webb know about the embassy or the Soviet Union? When I scanned a novel he later wrote (*Something to Die For*), the picture became clear. The villain in the piece turns out to be a secretary of defense who, as a devious Foreign Service officer, tried to convince the White House to triple the size of the marine contingent in Beirut just before terrorists blew 241 of them up.

Webb, who has since become a senator, had an ax to grind: as far as his world was concerned, Hartman was just another devious FSO.[557]

I wrote an op-ed article about the marine scandal, "The Demise of the Embassy Family," that the *Washington Post* published on May 12 and was carried in the *International Herald Tribune* a day later. The article described the "decomposition of once cohesive, family-based communities" at American embassies:

> During my first assignment in the Soviet capital in 1972-74, embassy employees generally were career officials and family members at one and the same time, with a deep commitment to the Soviet field. Spouses did not work, serving rather as a kind of "cement," binding the community together through their social activities and good works. Anchored in the family, the community effectively embraced all its members regardless of rank and responsibility. The Marine bar in the Tchaikovsky Street Chancery was as much a gathering place for married Foreign Service Officers as for unattached Marines.

The article pointed to the loosening of "the fabric of the community" during our second assignment, 1978-81, and its absence during our last. "Families were in a minority, and spouses, with few exceptions, worked." With the withdrawal of the Russian workers and the influx of unaccompanied Americans, "unattached personnel, intent upon a one-time Moscow 'adventure,' are setting the tone."

In conclusion, I cited a sentence from a contemporaneous best seller, *The Closing of the American Mind*: "Concern for the safety of one's family is a powerful reason for loyalty to the state . . . ."[558] I suggested that "the need for a cohesive community, a surrogate family, at our missions abroad is sufficiently compelling to require new approaches," including perhaps smaller embassies and incentives for nonworking spouses.

The article generated reactions pro and con from friends and strangers. Ray Benson, the embassy's counselor for cultural affairs, expressed approval and added that "the foreign service being what it is you are better off outside." A young FSO wrote from Moscow to say that "the situation is even more estranged [sic]: what the Soviets hadn't managed in years we've done to ourselves. Everyone is afraid to stand up to security, the Marines have been told not to socialize within the community, threats of lie detectors and new regulations mean that [the] two-thirds of the embassy leaving this summer [1987] have no incentive to leave the compound."

Ambassador Beam forwarded me a note saying that the problems were due to the fact that the embassy had become "overstaffed" since his retirement. I couldn't disagree with this.

Don Graves, a department officer who served at the embassy in the early 1970s, wrote that the article had sparked a debate at the FSI. A few dismissed me as an elitist, "a survivor of the old days when the Foreign Service was staffed by rich Ivy Leaguers" who had made "a commitment to the promotion path of language and regional expertise," when "the right career path is one of management at headquarters." Don labeled such critics as "converts to the MBA school of success." Others at FSI, he noted, had viewed the article as a realistic depiction of a real problem.[559]

*   *   *

In November 1987, six months after he assumed charge, Ambassador Matlock told Bill Keller of the *Times* that the embassy had largely recovered from its yearlong siege. According to Keller, the embassy now required that all contacts with Soviet citizens be reported either to the embassy's security office or to Washington. Any embassy officer planning to meet a Russian had to be accompanied by another American. "It is easier to be framed or set up if you're by yourself, it's a lot harder if somebody is along," Matlock explained.

With regard to staffers living inside the new compound, Matlock added, "There's no question that it makes it kind of cozy, and I suppose in a few cases if people are not sufficiently motivated, maybe it takes them off the street." It should be noted that Matlock acted on his observation; a senior officer at the embassy credited him with encouraging officers to "get out and engage the society."

Keller observed that "where before most employees lived in apartment buildings scattered about the city, a majority are now housed in the 134 brick-town house-style apartment blocks that resemble a miniature American suburb." His article bore the sub-headline, "Envoys, Distracted by Scandals, Lose Touch with Russians."[560]

Four months later, in February 1988, a blaze erupted at Tchaikovsky 19. It began on the fifth floor where the Seabees were welding. The alarm didn't go off, and the restricted sections on the upper floors, including the defense attachés' office, weren't alerted. Dense smoke forced everyone out, and one fire stairwell turned out to be locked. Russian firemen were allowed to enter and extinguish the fire. There were no casualties, and no classified information was compromised.

"Can you believe this?" a staff member was heard saying while standing on Tchaikovsky Street watching the flames. "The only thing we haven't had yet is a plague of locusts."[561]

A few weeks later, a former colleague, still in the economic section, wrote me that according to what she was hearing, the Soviets had resumed microwaving, that the water was not yet safe to drink, and that the security office was listening to staff telephone conversations, internal and external.

The following year, 1989, began with consequential events for Washington and Moscow. George H. W. Bush, who knew intelligence and counterintelligence matters from service as the director of the CIA in 1976-77, succeeded Reagan as president. In February, the last Soviet soldier left Afghanistan and, in the same month, Washington instructed the embassy in Moscow to suggest to the Foreign Ministry that the two governments increase the size of their diplomatic missions. To no one's surprise, the ministry agreed.[562]

It was around this time that I became acquainted with Ronald Kessler's book *Moscow Station*. Kessler, a former investigative reporter for the *Washington Post*, supplied plenty of fresh material, but his conclusions were far off the mark. He convinced himself that the KGB had compromised the embassy's communications center by putting bugging devices inside its cipher machines, and that Hartman and the staff were responsible for creating the kind of environment that enabled the marines to spy. The marine scandal, he said, is "one of the biggest scandals in U.S. history—a penetration that decapitated the CIA and its operations in the Soviet Union, that exceeded the damage done by [the navy's spy] Walker, that surpassed the Iran-Contra scandal as an example of government stupidity and culpability."[563]

On February 14, 1989, two days after Kessler promoted his theory on CBS's *60 Minutes*, the CIA issued an unusual public denial: The "intelligence community's review of the evidence does not substantiate" that the KGB planted eavesdropping equipment inside the communications center. Having his conclusion challenged, Kessler reacted as might be expected in Washington, saying the agency was engaged in a cover-up.[564]

Shortly thereafter, the marine commandant recommended to the new navy secretary (Webb had left the year before) that Lonetree's sentence be reduced from twenty-five to fifteen years. "The effect of Lonetree's action," he said, "was probably minimal," and his motivation had not been "treason or greed but rather the lovesick response of a naïve, young, immature, and lonely troop [sic] in a lonely and hostile environment."[565]

However, it would not be until the CIA's Aldrich Ames and the FBI's Robert Hanssen were arrested in 1994 and 2001, respectively, that the last skeptic understood it hadn't been the marines or others at the embassy, but rather disloyalty and incompetence back home, that had broken the back of the agency's Soviet operations. Ames and Hanssen along with Edward Lee

Howard, the ex-CIA trainee, wreaked havoc on U.S. intelligence operations and together accounted for the loss of no less than ten American agents.

In March 1991, yet another fire broke out at the embassy, destroying intelligence equipment in the area where the defense attachés and NSA officials worked. Had any embassy experienced such a calamitous run?[566]

On May 13, 1991, seven months before the Soviet Union collapsed, *Newsweek* headlined an article, "Out of Touch in Moscow, the U.S. Embassy Draws a Curtain Around Itself."[567] An American diplomat (asking that his name be withheld because "our security guys work a lot like the KGB") was quoted saying that, when he had reported meeting alone with a Soviet citizen in violation of the embassy's directives, he received "a long lecture and some insinuating questions about his loyalty." These and other anecdotes prompted *Newsweek*'s writers to conclude that, "when U.S. diplomats should be spending more time than ever with Soviet citizens, they are being wrapped in a cold-war cocoon."

To replace Ambassador Matlock, President Bush nominated Robert Strauss, a Washington insider and lawyer from his adopted state of Texas. Matlock met with Gorbachev on May 7, 1991, to tell him that he would soon be leaving, and urged the now-embattled leader to support a bill, then pending in the Supreme Soviet, to allow free emigration.[568]

At the end of July, President Bush arrived in Moscow for a summit meeting. Bilateral relations had improved to such an extent that the Soviet regime was on the threshold of being accorded most-favored-nation treatment; a new strategic arms agreement (after ten years of negotiation) was ready for signature; and the emigration bill had become law. On August 10, the evening before Ambassador and Mrs. Matlock ended their final assignment, Shevardnadze and his wife hosted them at a private dinner. For Matlock, it was "perhaps the most memorable" of all his evenings during eleven years in the Soviet capital. The highlight was the grace that Shevardnadze's five-year-old grandniece offered before dinner; with heads bowed, the adults listened as she prayed for several minutes in her native Georgian tongue. For the retiring ambassador, this was proof (although, by then, little was really needed) that the Communists, despite repressive measures over many years, had failed to replace their people's values with those of their own "Soviet man."[569]

One week later, Gorbachev's enemies tried to oust him. Yeltsin, then heading the Russian republic, rallied the people and the military; and the attempt failed. Ambassador Strauss arrived amid the turmoil.

At the beginning of December 1991, Lieutenant General Vadim Bakatin, the KGB head, invited Strauss to his office and presented him a map of the unfinished chancery that showed, astoundingly, where all the listening devices had been planted. According to Bakatin, his gesture of goodwill was sanctioned by Gorbachev and Yeltsin.[570]

At the end of the month, the Soviet system collapsed and, early in the New Year, Washington instructed the embassy to begin hiring Russians; but none who had any prior association with Tchaikovsky 19, including the language teachers. When I visited Moscow in March 1993, fifteen months after the collapse, 50 Russians were working as consular clerks and security guards (they hadn't been used in the latter capacity before) while 136 Americans under contract with Pacific Architects and Engineers were doing the balance of the work that 260 Russians had performed before their withdrawal eight years before.

I didn't spend much time at the embassy but was left with the impression that its "culture" had changed. This was confirmed a year later when I read that Sergei Kovalev, the chairman of the Russian republic's human rights commission, with whom I had worked to solve the Kudirka case, had picketed the embassy to complain about its refusal to issue a visa to Georgi Grigorenko, the son of a famous dissident, so he could visit his stepmother dying in the United States. "I spoke to two consular officers and neither had ever heard of Grigorenko," he said. They didn't recognize his own name, either.[571]

How strange, I thought. Only six years had passed since Reagan met Kovalev and other dissidents and refuseniks at Spaso House. Was there *no one* at the embassy who knew the names of two of the Soviet Union's most famous rights activists, Kovalev and Grigorenko? What had become of the embassy's once-renowned institutional memory?

The report reminded me that officers who were trained in Russian affairs were no longer doing consular work. Moreover, with most assignments made on the basis of management's four career tracks (today there are five), few political officers in Moscow come into contact with Russian citizens' everyday problems.

This is a loss for those who want to learn everything about a country, a loss for citizen-activists in countries like Russia where repression is often the rule, and a loss for Washington's coverage everywhere of political and human rights.

The same article took a swipe at the embassy's isolation: "Paradoxically, as Russian society grows more freewheeling and open, the suburban-style red-brick fortress America in central Moscow seems all the more impregnable." It reported that most employees are housed in "a kind of suburban American biosphere. Residents can easily avoid contact with Russian society, and many do."

A year later, in December 1995, I visited Moscow once again. After meeting Russian friends, I attended a reception at an apartment in the embassy compound.

The official community had grown to almost one thousand—Americans, third-country nationals, and Russians. Most worked in Tchaikovsky 19 or in a new Agency for International Development building that had gone up where a Soviet apartment house had once stood, between the garage in the courtyard and the compound. Some staff members had offices in the new chancery's underground garage, but no one was allowed on its "bugged" upper floors.

Thirteen officers now comprised my four-officer economic section. It was still situated on Tchaikovsky's eighth floor, in space expanded and refurbished following the 1991 fire. I was told that four of the thirteen officers could read Russian, but only one or two could speak it. The FSOs I met were surprised I had Russian friends; I was surprised they didn't, and wondered whether this was no longer allowed.

Back in Connecticut, in *The Tailor of Panama*, a new spy novel from John le Carré, I saw reference to a fictional embassy where "not a whisper of the real world penetrated."[572] Had le Carré read about my old embassy?

For more than a decade, the Congress had blocked the State Department from completing the chancery at the center of the compound: "The Senate refused to appropriate funds to use it at all but was willing to fund a different building . . . [and] the House . . . refused to authorize a different building unless the unfinished one could be used" (Ambassador Matlock's 1995 memoir[573]). In 1997, Congress, the State Department, and the intelligence community finally settled their differences and agreed on a solution. Three hundred American workers were sent to Moscow. They demolished the chancery's top two floors and, using materials shipped in from areas outside Communist control, replaced them with four new, secure floors. They also covered the "block of red brick" (that had made one critic think of a police headquarters) with an off-white limestone facade.

The project cost Washington a quarter of a billion dollars, on top of millions spent earlier to locate the listening devices. As Ambassador Matlock wrote in his second memoir, even if the Soviet technical systems had worked (they mostly didn't), the tried and true counter-system of having rooms within rooms would have provided security at a fraction of the cost.[574]

Thus, two decades after I witnessed Ambassador Toon's groundbreaking, the project came to an end.

*   *   *

The State Department began shifting resources away from Russian language and area training well before the collapse of the Soviet system. It first became obvious to me when Washington had to scramble to find

Russian-speaking officers to deal with potential defectors at the embassies in Kabul and Prague.

FSOs no longer receive the kind of intensive training in language, culture, and history that I received. They are sent neither to the Garmisch institute (that in 1992 became part of the George C. Marshall Center for European Security Studies) nor to comparable places where preparation lasts a year or more and approaches full immersion. Probably the last FSO to benefit from the U.S. Army's Russian Institute was Mary Ann Peters, who joined my economic section in 1986.

The fact I learned to read and write complex papers on Soviet affairs in Russian while being exposed to Russian culture made it easy to plunge confidently into my first Moscow assignment (and confidence counts for much in such settings), and to avoid problems of adjustment that the KGB would always be quick to exploit. The very existence of a specialized training center probably drew some FSOs without pre-Foreign Service exposure to the language into the field.

Today, it is the Foreign Service Institute (FSI) that prepares diplomats for assignments to posts in Russian-speaking areas. Language instruction at the FSI is good, but a five-day-a-week program of language-only lasting no more than ten months won't produce the same result as an almost seven-day-a week program lasting nearly a year (and preceded by several months at the FSI) in a setting that approximates "Russia." Of course, the results would be more impressive if FSOs were given the opportunity of studying for up to three years among émigrés, as Ambassadors Kennan and Bohlen did.

There are already signs that those ruling in Russia today won't hesitate to resort to their predecessors' lawless ways to advance their own or their country's interests. The State Department and other Washington agencies are mistaken if they believe that posts in the "new" Russia won't require officers steeped in Russian affairs, and that extended management experience will be more important for operating there than comprehensive area preparation.

It would be shortsighted if the department and the Foreign Service fail to maintain a cadre of knowledgeable Russian hands to serve in Russia and to contribute to policy making at home. Embassy sections and department desks led by amateurs or by professionals with little more than a tourist's knowledge won't do justice to our country's needs.

*   *   *

The FSI maintains four schools abroad that do teach foreign languages. Arabic is taught at Tunis, Chinese at Taipei, Japanese at Yokohama, and Korean at Seoul. These programs approximate full immersion training.

The State Department and the Foreign Service failed to train, however, a sufficient number of "Arab hands" despite repeated indications they'd be needed, from the time the first Bush waged a war to liberate Kuwait and the second Bush began to talk about "remaking" the Middle East. The fact that there are twenty-one American embassies and consulates to staff in the region was apparently overlooked.

In 2004, there were only twenty-seven persons in the Foreign Service Officer corps (of some 6,400 officer-generalists) who spoke Arabic at the professional and limited professional levels, the latter denoting the halfway mark to full fluency.[575] Eight of them (of whom one is an Iraqi-born junior officer who joined the career in 1999) had attained the highest level.

A quarter century earlier, in a much smaller Foreign Service (3,600 officer-generalists), there were sixty officers either at or at one step removed from these same levels of proficiency.[576]

I began to appreciate the Middle East's daunting complexity in 1998 after being appointed president of International College in Beirut, Lebanon, the largest American independent school (3,500 students, 350 faculty members) outside the United States. At the end of a memoir about the experience (completed as George W. Bush was preparing for war), I cited the skepticism of the historian Niall Ferguson that the United States would be able to mobilize "the right sort of people" with the needed staying power to help bring that region into the twenty-first century.[577] Little did I realize that the State Department itself was failing to draw the right sort of people from its own Foreign Service into the region.

By his own admission, Jerry Bremer, the retired FSO chosen by Bush in 2003 to head the Coalition Provisional Authority (CPA) in Iraq, knew little about the Middle East. He had reached the Foreign Service's top rank by becoming attached to Secretary Kissinger as a staff aide, making himself an expert on counterterrorism, and serving as ambassador to the Netherlands.[578]

Bremer would later claim that he had "more junior, mid-grade, and senior Foreign Service officers and retired ambassadors working in Iraq than anywhere but the State Department itself."[579] Yet the CPA's problem, as the writer George Packer observed in *The Assassins' Gate*, was that "many had never worked abroad, few knew anything about the Middle East, and that first summer [of 2003] only three or four of the Americans spoke Arabic."[580] Of the three officers who constituted Bremer's inner circle, none "had any prior experience in Arab affairs or any knowledge of Arabic."[581]

As the president's administrator, Bremer was able to recruit two Foreign Service retirees who did know the Middle East—Barbara Bodine who had served as ambassador to Yemen under President Clinton, and Hume Horan, ambassador to Saudi Arabia in the late 1980s. However, Bodine was "cut out of the loop" by the Pentagon's people before reaching Iraq[582], and Horan carried "baggage" that may have contributed to one of the administration's most egregious errors.[583].

Of course, the failure is not Bremer's but that of the department. And not only the department, it should be said; surveying Iraq in 2003, the investigative reporter James Risen wrote that "the CIA was flooding Iraq with officers on temporary assignment, drawn from all over the world, but few had experience in the Arab world, and even fewer could speak Arabic."[584]

How to account for the failure? Does it result from the fact that women fill almost half of the Foreign Service's officer positions and that women are naturally less inclined to embrace careers in this part of the world? Or is it because the department's Arabists have borne the brunt of outside criticism in recent years, including for alleged biases against Israel? In the 1940s and 1950s it had been the Asia hands who were targeted for having "lost China"; and few were available in the 1960s when their expertise was badly needed.[585]

Or is the department recruiting officers with different priorities?

When I joined the Foreign Service, it was axiomatic that we would specialize in one or two geographic areas and learn the appropriate languages. Thirteen years into our careers, my A-100 classmates and I had collectively attained "limited professional use" of the following languages: Arabic (three officers), Burmese, Indonesian, Korean, Russian (two), Serbo-Croatian, and Vietnamese. (My self-taught Polish didn't make the grade!) Virtually everyone in the class could cope in one or more other languages, acquired in college, the military, or at the FSI.

Language study has since fallen sharply in American schools and colleges[586], and, in the absence of conscription, fewer graduates acquire language training from the military.

But the failure is also due to the fact that the department and the Foreign Service have attached lower priority to language and area study. The Foreign Service reform of 1980 was designed to increase the proportion of "manager generalists" at the top of the career. The policy succeeded, but it also discouraged officers from specializing in areas and languages. The cohort whose careers abruptly ended in 1987 included six who spoke Arabic and twenty-seven who spoke Russian or an East European language. The lesson was clear: Don't waste time mastering a particular area when one's prospects are enhanced by moving around, as with Bohlen's proverbial "water bug."

There is a lack of forthrightness and a dearth of information about the number of FSOs embarking on hard-language training today.[587] The Foreign Service's director recently rejected the "myth" that the department "continues to fall short in Arabic language training"; in February 2007 he wrote that enrollments in Arabic at the FSI have "nearly quadrupled and the number of Arabic speakers at the level of 3/3 (general professional proficiency and above) has increased from 198 to more than 240."[588]

This is a bold assertion, and it seems to controvert the Iraq Study Group's finding, released in December 2006, that only six officers at the embassy in Baghdad's green zone were fluent in Arabic.

But the war in Iraq is already four years old, and the language capability wasn't there when it was most needed. Even a crash program can't undo the damage.

This failure will haunt American policy and reverberate and harm American interests in the Middle East for years to come. And there is no less potential for harm in other regions to which inadequately educated, ill-prepared Americans are sent. In 2006, the Congress's Government Accountability Office reported that nearly 30 percent of the State Department employees based overseas in language-designated posts fail to speak and write the local language to meet even the standard that the department requires.[589]

Bobby Inman, the former director of the National Security Agency and a former deputy at the CIA, was asked by a congressional commission what changes would strengthen American intelligence. "What is needed," he said "are observers with language ability [and] with understanding of the religions, cultures of the countries they're observing" in a State Department that's revived.[590]

*   *   *

If the past three decades be a guide, there is little certainty that even those senior FSOs equipped with language and area expertise will have the opportunity to influence policy making. It had been otherwise during most of the Cold War, at least before the department's influence began to wane with Kissinger's refashioning of the NSC.

Is the Foreign Service no longer producing officers of the caliber of Kennan who shaped the thinking of a generation of Cold Warriors, or of his colleague Bohlen who counseled Roosevelt from a White House office; who, with Kennan, took part in Truman's NSC meetings; and who advised three successor presidents from positions in the State Department and abroad?

Or has something else changed?

Lieutenant General (ret.) William Odom, a deputy national security advisor in the Carter administration (and later director of the National Security Agency), recently expressed skepticism about area experts, the kind exemplified by Kennan and Bohlen. Describing his reaction to Vice

President Mondale's lament that not a single Iranian affairs expert was present during the White House's discussion of the hostage crisis in Iran in 1979-80, Odom said:

> My private reaction was quite different: Thank God! If you include area experts in a high-level policy meeting, you'll discover that they're in love with the people from their area. They know a great many details about their area, but they are hopelessly inept at reaching sound recommendations for U.S. policy. They're the last people to ask what is the right thing to do. I'm a Russian expert, I know. You don't want a Russian expert near a policymaking discussion. You'll get in trouble. You should listen to the area experts before you go to the policymaking meeting.[591]

Odom was a military attaché at Tchaikovsky 19 during my first assignment and later studied at Columbia with Dr. Brzezinski. When Brzezinski was appointed the president's national security advisor, he asked Odom to join him as the NSC military advisor. Odom was no "shrinking violet" in Moscow and made contributions to the embassy's reporting. He shared Brzezinski's view of the USSR's expansionist appetite and probably improved his understanding of its military capabilities. In his memoir, Brzezinski praises "the relentless General Odom" for helping frame the Carter Doctrine, the administration's response to Moscow's invasion of Afghanistan.[592]

Since the early 1970s, skepticism about the government's area experts, particularly those from the State Department, has been the rule more than the exception in Washington and particularly the White House. It became more pronounced as the Cold War neared an end, as politically well-placed and more ideologically-inclined practitioners with little or no overseas experience came to monopolize the positions nearest the president.

In staffing the NSC, President Reagan and his aides drew upon the academic world (including Professor Pipes), the Pentagon, the CIA, and the FBI while excluding experts from the State Department. Only after the appointment of a pragmatic businessman with foreign-policy experience as secretary of state (Shultz), and of the Foreign Service's most experienced Russian hand (Matlock) as the White House's Soviet advisor did the administration develop the vocabulary and the policies that helped end the Cold War.

The administration of George W. Bush turned out to "surpass" even the first years of the Reagan administration in keeping government experts at bay. Anecdotes abound about the White House's avoidance of experts no matter from which agency they came; information and recommendations produced by those steeped in Middle Eastern affairs—if they reached

Bush's inside group (Vice President Dick Cheney, Defense Secretary Donald Rumsfeld, and his deputy Paul Wolfowitz)—were either reshaped to suit the group's preconceptions or cast aside.

General Odom cites the Iran affair of 1978-1980 in dismissing the importance of having "area experts" present at high-level policy making. In fact, American policy stumbled badly in Iran precisely because there was a dearth of expertise in the White House, the State Department, the Foreign Service, and other agencies:

1. *There were too few Foreign Service officers with Iranian language and area expertise to ensure that the White House received insightful reporting and analysis on which to base policy making.*

The political section at the embassy in Tehran comprised twenty-one officers in the 1960s. Because of BALPA and economies ordered by Washington, it had been reduced to six officers on the eve of the 1978 crisis, not all of whom spoke Persian (Farsi).[593] The then-acting head of the political section John Stempel summarized the result: "The diminished reporting presence contributed to decisions to spend less time on dissident contacts . . . [and] the possibility for broad gauge analyses was greatly reduced." Until March 1978, "there were no direct encounters between embassy officers and religious leaders."[594]

The CIA itself had no one in Tehran who could speak Farsi. To Brzezinski's amazement, CIA Director Stansfield Turner told the NSC's Iran Policy Review Committee—convened as soon as the diplomats were seized—that the agency had little information to share about the Iranians who opposed the shah.[595] (Did the agency draw the right lesson in the wake of the debacle? In 1998, a retired CIA officer reported that during the eight years that he worked in Iranian affairs not a single Near East Division chief knew Arabic, Farsi or Turkish—only one could get along in French—and no Iran-desk chief could speak or read Farsi.)[596]

The official in Washington knowing most about Iran, FSO Henry Precht, became head of the department's Iranian desk in June 1978, a year and a half before the embassy was occupied. Having been a political-military officer in Tehran from 1972 to 1976, he had seen the influence of the fundamentalists grow and the shah's power decline. But the deputy assistant secretary to whom he reported as desk officer was an Arabist who knew "little or nothing" about Iran; the assistant secretary overseeing the Near East Bureau was preoccupied by the Israeli-Egyptian talks; and the American ambassador to Iran hadn't served there before.[597]

Kenneth Pollack, a CIA and NSC alumnus, found that the volume of CIA reporting from Iran in the early 1970s "dropped below that of the late

1940s," and that White House advisors, beholden to the shah, discouraged embassy officers from talking with Iranians outside the Iranian Ministry of Foreign Affairs and SAVAK, the shah's secret police.[598]

2. *There was no interest in having State Department and Foreign Service area experts participate in White House deliberations.*

Before the radicals' first seizure of the embassy in February 1978 (they held it for two days), Precht recalls participating in a White House Situation Room meeting chaired either by Mondale or Brzezinski and finding no one there who knew anything about Iran.[599] Before long, Precht himself was excluded. (Mondale's comment that prompted Odom's observation must have been made after Precht's exclusion.) Had Secretary Vance not been occupied with negotiating SALT II and the Israeli-Egyptian rapprochement, he might have represented Precht's views, but Vance was often absent when Iran was being discussed. (He ultimately resigned because of his opposition to Brzezinski's proposal to rescue the hostages by military force.)

As the crisis developed, Precht didn't hesitate to point out that the administration's stream of pronouncements and actions supporting the shah were not only poisoning possibilities for dealing with the opposition but adding to the embassy's vulnerability. But Brzezinski made it clear that the shah would remain the administration's "man." He and the president even blocked the dispatch of an Iranian expert, a retired FSO and former ambassador to Afghanistan, to meet with Khomeini, a meeting that the American ambassador in Tehran had recommended and the reason for which the shah himself understood.[600]

3. *Iranian "experts" outside foreign-policy agencies filled the vacuum, acquiring the dominant influence on White House policy making.*

The White House pulled most of its information and advice from *everywhere but* the experts. Private persons—including emissaries dispatched to Tehran—and the shah's ambassador in Washington seemed to be those whom Brzezinski trusted most. Ten months before the embassy was finally lost, Carter and Brzezinski dispatched the deputy chief of the American military command in Europe (Air Force General Robert Huyser) to consult with Iran's military leaders ("for the express purpose of instigating a *coup d'etat* against the revolution," according to Pollack.) The general stayed a month until threats from Iranian radicals forced him to leave. It appears that, upon his return, he reinforced Brzezinski's erroneous belief that, if conditions worsened, the Iranian military would intervene in support of the shah.[601]

Brzezinski was also influenced by Ardeshir Zahedi, the Iranian ambassador in Washington who had initially expressed the view that the Communists were behind the turmoil.[602] After he returned to Tehran (his first trip "home" in seven years), he tried to rally the dispirited shah and the military, but in the process only stiffened the shah against yielding control of the army to moderates in the opposition. In the judgment of the political officer Stempel, Zahedi's "ultimate effect was extremely pernicious," disrupting a compromise that might have led to a "controlled transitional government" while failing "to unite the military to strong action."[603]

From his political-military work in Tehran, Precht knew the Iranian military and realized it had no leadership capable of executing a *coup*, but he and his opinions were no longer welcome.

4. *The White House persisted in viewing Iran through a Cold War lens.*

Just after the hostages were taken, Brzezinski adopted a theory propounded by a "professional anti-Communist polemicist" from Great Britain (the label used by another NSC official) that the Soviets were responsible. He sent an article elaborating the theory to Carter.[604] Area experts like Precht might have explained that it was "the religious network operating out of the mosques under the strategic control of Khomeini" and not the Soviets who were behind the turmoil.[605] In fact, there was never much evidence that Khomeini and the Islamists were interested in working with the USSR or local Communists (the Tudeh Party), either before or after the hostage taking.

Reflecting on Brzezinski a quarter century later, Precht judges that as "a Pole with terrible feelings about the Soviet Union," he didn't want to see "the Iranian part of our containment barrier weakened." The shah, in Brzezinski's view, was needed "to keep the Soviets from moving toward the Gulf."[606]

For a scholar drawn to doctrine like Brzezinski, it must have been difficult to conceive that the Kremlin's "plate" was full of far more serious concerns by the late 1970s, including an increasingly unstable Afghanistan bordering its Central Asia republics and a Poland made restive by the election of a Polish pope. Just before the hostage taking, Brzezinski wrote in his diary that "the Soviets no longer take us seriously and are asserting themselves in Iran and South Yemen and southern Africa [Angola] and Cuba."[607] As Ambassador Garthoff observes, the list is "rather odd," but "the important point is that it reflects Brzezinski's way of seeing the situation."[608]

Brzezinski writes of Iran that "for better or for worse . . . Carter was *his own* Secretary of State [Brzezinski's italics]."[609] He might have added that he, from 1978 through 1980, functioned as if he were running the department's Iranian desk. His memoir includes a calendar of a "typical" day; except for the senior rank of the officials with whom he dealt, it could have been the calendar of a busy FSO. Brzezinski later justified his control of the Iran portfolio with the accusation that Precht was "motivated by doctrinal dislike of the Shah" and that the State Department was "cheering the Shah's opponents." Brzezinski adduces no evidence; Precht rejects the charge, as does Vance in convoluted language.[610]

The outcome was that U.S. policy toward Iran was shaped by a small group of individuals at the National Security Council not one of whom had experience with that country. The policy proved disastrous (Khomeini's emergence as Iran's leader was not foreordained). The American electorate repudiated the Carter administration, but its failure goes a long way to explain Iran's current support of Hezbollah and drive to acquire nuclear weapons. Ambassador Stearns was thinking of American policy toward Greece and Turkey when he wrote that "the government may go in circles" when "policies are formulated without reference to the experts," but his words come to mind when one looks today at Iran and, indeed, the whole Middle East.

*   *   *

Every administration regardless of political affiliation sets out to "reform" the Foreign Service. Secretaries of state and their noncareer aides act out of frustration (as Kissinger acknowledged he did) or sincerely held beliefs ("there must be a better way"), but the outcome is usually the same, far reaching change imposed from the top. Because noncareer officials have four-year time-horizons (they usually "turn over" with a new administration or with the second term of a reelected administration), they aren't attracted to the idea of incremental change (change tested in one or two bureaus or on one or two officer-cohorts before full adoption) or change derived organically from time-consuming dialoguing.

Under the rubric "Transformational Diplomacy," Secretary of State Condoleezza Rice and the Bush administration are now embarking on a multiyear "global repositioning" of Foreign Service officers.[611] The repositioning has already involved the removal of one hundred FSOs from European embassies and consulates and their redeployment to India, China, Indonesia, Sudan, and less developed countries. Some FSOs are being assigned to cities outside foreign capitals where they will be responsible for administering programs instead of reporting and analyzing; others will be sent to war zones.

It is fortunate that Foreign Service veterans are raising questions about the "transformation." Undoubtedly, some officers have already been sidetracked from assignments for which they had been readying themselves through language and area study. In 2006, the president of the Foreign Service Association reminded administrators that the "distinguishing feature of the Foreign Service is its unparalleled foreign area expertise," and that "reducing this strength and shifting the focus of American diplomacy from preventing war to picking up the pieces afterward would be utterly profound." "Is that what transformational diplomacy is all about?" he asked.[612]

Another officer, now retired, writes:

> We have gone down this road before, of course. Those with longer memories will recall "GLOP"—Henry Kissinger's infamous Global Outlook and Programming shakeup of the mid-1970s. GLOP was supposed to move all of those infected with "localitis" (others might prefer the term "expertise") into new regions and stimulate fresh thinking. But all the exercise managed to do was eliminate a good part of the department's institutional wisdom on the Middle East, as many "Arabists" walked away into more lucrative pursuits rather than spend a couple of tours elsewhere.
>
> If we want to cultivate Arabists, China hands, a Republic of Korea group, or Amazon area experts, we will have to make a generation-long investment in officers who are essentially tagged for such regions.[613]

According to Ms. Rice, "Diplomats will be required to be expert in at least two regions and fluent in two languages in order to be promoted to senior ranks." By the double-area and double-language requirement, Rice probably believes her administration will foster the "global outlook" that Kissinger tried to achieve with his foray into personnel management, yet it will likely only lead to the watering-down of what is meant by "expert" and a further loss of the authentic expertise that Washington so badly needs. Although Bohlen and Kennan served their country outside the Communist bloc, they invested more than half their careers in Russian and Soviet affairs yet weren't accused of succumbing to the "localitis" that is on Rice's mind. Would they qualify today for the senior ranks under Rice's requirement?

There is also talk about revising the Foreign Service examination that some twenty thousand Americans take every year. The written test would be shortened and "structured resumes," references, and "team-building skills" would reportedly count for more. Ambassador Richard Holbrooke, who joined the Foreign Service directly out of Brown University in 1962, has expressed concern that this might betoken a lowering of the Foreign Service's standards for entry.[614] Others worry about political influences.

Several have suggested that race, ethnicity, and gender may become more important factors in recruiting.[615]

*   *   *

No matter what changes take place, talented Americans will surely continue to join the Foreign Service, and many of them will choose to become expert in one or more of the world's areas and languages. To the extent that Washington gives full support to those who pursue such careers—perhaps the worthiest careers a diplomatic service can offer, every citizen stands to gain.

Transliterating from the Russian

Foreign Service officers are supposed to observe a standard system of rules provided by the department. Some officers applied the rules more conscientiously than others. Because Washington agencies scrutinized every visa application submitted by Communist-bloc citizens with particular care, I always found that FSOs working in consular sections tended to observe them most closely.

There are always anomalies. The department's guidance would have required the street on which the embassy stood to be rendered as "Chaikovskiy," yet "Tchaikovsky" was the transliteration everyone seemed to use, and I don't recall the department suggesting otherwise.

This memoir takes a pragmatic approach. If a source uses a transliterated rendering most readers would recognize, I generally use it. In the department's guidance, the Latin letter *x* never occurs, yet readers will find that I render Kosygin's first name as "Alexei" instead of "Aleksei" or "Aleksey", which is the way the official's name appears in most English-language sources.

Two names suggest the cross-currents sometimes involved when making a choice:

In Russian "Igor Palmin" carries the soft sign after the "l", yet I generally omit the prime sign (so Igor's family name would read "Pal'min") that most systems would require.

"Sergei" Vronski could be rendered "Sergey", yet I have used the former, probably in deference to the calling card that Sergei handed me when we first met.

The same card carried Sergei's family name as "Vronsky." This is how the most recent translation of *Anna Karenina* (by Pevear and Volokhonsky) treats the name of Anna's lover, although the State Department's guidance would have the name rendered "Vronskiy."

I became accustomed, however, to Nabokov's usage of "Vronski", as in his essay on Tolstoy's novel. When I asked Mila about her preference, she agreed with "Vronski." I also like Nabokov's use of masculine endings in transliterating most Russian women's names (except in the case of female performers like "Pavlova").

With one or two exceptions, I have omitted patronymics. Sergei Vronsky's full name is Sergei Arkad'evich, but I didn't use his patronymic name when addressing him and wouldn't introduce it now simply for the sake of form.

Readers acquainted with Russian will note that I end many proper names with "i", although standard systems, including the department's, would often have me use "y", "iy", or "ii." If I do use "y", it is because the name has been popularized in English this way, as in "Tolstoy."

There will never be agreement about the optimal way of reducing each of the Russian language's thirty-one pronounceable letters to the English language's twenty-six.

Endnotes

Introduction

1. Monteagle Stearns, *Entangled Allies, U.S. Policy Toward Greece, Turkey, and Cyprus* (New York: Council on Foreign Relations Press, 1992), p. 15.

2. George Kennan, *Meet the Press* telecast, Vol. 11, No. 45, November 5, 1967.

3. I made cosmetic changes in some excerpts from my wife's and my letters, tightening a few sentences and eliminating redundancies. With regard to notes of conversations that I kept, the writer Mary McCarthy once alluded to the shame she felt taking notes while on a personal trip to Communist Vietnam: "you ought not to be two people, one downstairs listening and nodding, and the other scribbling in your room" (from McCarthy's *Vietnam* [1967], quoted in Carol Brightman, *Writing Dangerously, Mary McCarthy and Her World* [New York: Clarkson Potter Publishers, 1992], p. 540). But recording and reporting are what diplomats do, and this kind of scribbling never embarrassed me, nor surely McCarthy's husband who was a Foreign Service officer at the time

4. Solomon Volkov, trans. Marian Schwartz, *Conversations with Joseph Brodsky*, (New York: Free Press, 1998), p. 72.

5. KGB is the Russian acronym of *Komitet gosudarstvennoi bezopasnosti*, the Committee for State Security.

6. Leonard Woolf, *Growing: An Autobiography of the Years 1904 to 1911* (New York: H.B Jovanovich, 1961), p. 148.

7. Julia Briggs, *Virginia Woolf: An Inner Life* (Orlando: Harcourt, 2005), p. 351. Virginia, Leonard's wife, was troubled by the challenge of reconstructing the past, and never did complete a memoir.

8. I do not spell out the formal titles of each of the now-defunct republics, but occasionally use the English-language initials that correspond to them. The historically correct title of the Russian republic was the Russian Soviet Federative Socialist Republic, or RSFSR. It was "federative" because it encompassed 16 nominally "autonomous" republics. The titles of the other fourteen republics were similarly patterned: the Georgian Soviet Socialist Republic (SSR), the

Ukrainian Soviet Socialist Republic (SSR), etc. The Georgian republic included two "autonomous" republics and the Azerbaijan and Uzbek republics each included one, but only the RSFSR was considered to be "federative." The one republic I failed to visit was the Moldavian SSR.

9   George Kennan, "Reflections," *New Yorker*, February 25, 1985, p. 58.

Chapter 1

10   Robert Service, *Stalin: A Biography* (Cambridge: Harvard University Press, 2005), pp. 358–9; Simon Sebag Montefiore, *Stalin: The Court of the Red Tsar* (New York: Alfred A. Knopf, 2004), p. 257.

11   William Jay Smith, "Introduction," *Andrei Voznesensky: An Arrow in the Wall, Selected Poetry and Prose*, ed. William Jay Smith and F. D. Reeve, trans. Smith et al. (New York: Henry Holt and Company, 1987), p. xiii.

12   "A Russian Poet Finds a New Poetry In Collage," *New York Times*, June 30, 1991.

13   Yevgeny Yevtushenko, *Selections from the Bratsk Hydroelectric Station and other Poems*, trans. Bernard L. Koten (New York: New World Review, 1965), p. 10. Czeslaw Milosz, the Nobel-prize winning Polish poet, suggests the same idea in the *The Captive Mind* (London: Mercury Books, 1962), p. 175:

> In Central and Eastern Europe, the word "poet" has a somewhat different meaning from that which it has in the West. There a poet does not merely arrange words in beautiful order. Tradition demands that he be a "bard," that his songs linger on many lips, that he speak in his poems of subjects of interest to all the citizens.

14   See chapter 10 for English-language text and the corresponding note.

15   Olga Ivinskaya, *A Captive of Time: My Years with Pasternak*, trans. Max Hayward (New York: Doubleday & Company, 1978), p. 286.

16   Ada Louise Huxtable, *Architecture Anyone? Cautionary Tales of the Building Art* (New York: Random House, 1986), p. 295.

17   "The Moscow Blob," *New York Times*, September 18, 1988.

18   A Department of State publication (*State Magazine*, January 2004) reports that the "U.S. Embassy in Moscow and its three constituent posts, in St. Petersburg, Yekaterinburg and Vladivostok, have more than 1,500 employees." Perhaps the four hundred Americans and more than one thousand Russians cited by the FSOs are inclusive of those at the consulates. The same article indicated twenty-eight federal agencies "are permanently represented" in Moscow and the constituent posts," a number surpassing the sixteen that Ambassador Vershbow later mentioned.

19   Charles E. Bohlen, *Witness to History: 1929–1969* (New York: W. W. Norton & Company, 1973), p. 342.

20   Z.I. Pasternak, *Vospominaniya* (Moscow: Publisher GRIT, 1993), p. 295.

21   Ivinskaya, *Captive of Time*, p. 332.

[22] "This Muse Sang to the KGB," *New York Times*, November 30, 1997.

[23] Ibid.

[24] Ann Pasternak Slater, "Introduction," *A Vanished Present: The Memoirs of Alexander Pasternak*, ed. and trans. Ann Pasternak Slater (San Diego: Harcourt Brace Jovanovich, Publishers, 1985), p. xx.

[25] Galina Vishnevskaya, *Galina: A Russian Story*, trans. Guy Daniels (San Diego: Harcourt Brace Jovanovich, Publishers, 1984), p. 158.

[26] Nancy K. Anderson, *The Word That Causes Death's Defeat: Poems of Memory* (New Haven: Yale University Press, 2004); quoted in Aileen Kelly, *New York Review of Books*, November 3, 2005.

[27] Orlando Figes, *New York Review of Books*, June 22, 2006.

[28] Yevtushenko teaches Russian and European poetry as well as film at the University of Tulsa in Oklahoma.

[29] "New Times" (*Novoye Vremya*), as reported by an Associated Press dispatch, *New York Times*, August 25, 1950.

[30] Anthony Powell, *Memoirs: The Strangers All Are Gone* (New York: Holt, Rinehart & Winston, 1982), p. 182.

[31] Saul Bellow, *Humboldt's Gift* (New York: Viking Press, 1985), p. 120.

[32] Ronald Bergen, *Sergei Eisenstein: A Life in Conflict* (Woodstock, New York: Overlook Press, 1999), p. 124.

[33] Georgi Kostaki, *Moy Avangard, Vospominaniya Kolleksionera* (Moscow: Modus Graffiti, 1993).

[34] Thomas P. Whitney, *Russia in My Life* (New York: Reynal & Company, 1962), p. 90.

[35] Bohlen, *Witness to History*, p. 20.

[36] Ray Bearse and Anthony Read, *Conspirator: The Untold Story of Tyler Kent* (New York: Doubleday, 1991), p. 34.

[37] *Moscow News*, July 26–August 2, 1992.

[38] Robert L. Beisner, *Dean Acheson: A Life in the Cold War* (New York: Oxford University Press, 2006), p. 47.

[39] Forrest C. Pogue, *George C. Marshall: Statesman 1949–1959* (New York: Viking, 1987), p. 210.

[40] Eddy Gilmore, *Me and My Russian Wife* (Garden City, New York: Doubleday & Company, 1954), pp. 240–1.

[41] Ibid., p. 241.

[42] Stalin's daughter Svetlana Alliluyeva wrote about her relationship with Alexei Kapler in *Twenty Letters to a Friend*, trans. Priscilla Johnson McMillan (New York: Harper & Row, Publishers), 1967. Kapler subsequently taught at Moscow's Institute of Cinematography (GIK).

[43] Whitney, *Russia In My Life*, p. 146.

[44] "Leaks in Our Moscow Embassy Are Nothing New," *Wall Street Journal*, April 7, 1987. There were virtually no American women at the embassy during or

immediately after the war. According to Edmund Stevens, "Without enormous influence it was impossible to get one's wife—let alone one's daughter—past Mrs. Ruth Shipley, the adamant boss of the [State Department's] Passport Division": *Russia Is No Riddle* (New York: Greenburg Publisher, 1945), p. 146. Averell Harriman, who preceded Smith as ambassador, secured his daughter's presence by arranging for her to work as a volunteer for the embassy's Office of War Information.

[45]   "After 50 Years, Virginian Will Renew a Friendship Torn Apart by Soviets," *New York Times*, August 4, 1994, makes reference to this story. Several Soviet-American marriages that were registered during the Stalin era, including those of Gilmore and Whitney, are discussed in Lynn Visson, *Wedded Strangers: The Challenges of Russian-American Marriages* (New York: Hypocrene Press, 2001). Soviet women who married non-Soviet citizens from other countries fared no better. Between 1944 and 1946, thirty-three Soviet women married British men, including sailors on duty in Murmansk. They lost their jobs and two received prison sentences, one for ten and the other for twenty-five years. Only one saw her husband again; she had married a British diplomat, and he persevered from abroad until she received an exit visa, *Moscow News*, February 11–17, 1994.

[46]   Stevens, *Russia Is No Riddle*, p. 92.

[47]   "Art: Russia Through Six Centuries," *New York Times*, June 15, 1967.

Chapter 2

[48]   David E. Kyvig, *Daily Life in the United States, 1920–1940* (Chicago: Ivan R. Dee, 2002), pp. 69–70.

[49]   Rollin G. Osterweis, *Three Centuries of New Haven, 1638–1938* (New Haven: Yale University Press, 1953), pp. 429–30.

[50]   "Unions and Apprentices," *New York Times*, February 27, 1925. Francis identified himself as "trade analyst and supervisor of Apprentice Work, New York Building Congress."

[51]   Mary McCarthy, *The Company She Keeps* (New York: Harcourt, Brace and Company, 1942), pp. 167–246.

[52]   Robert Penn Warren, *Partisan Review*, November–December 1942, quoted in Frances Kiernan, *Seeing Mary Plain: A Life of Mary McCarthy* (New York: W.W. Norton & Company, 2000), pp. 186–87.

[53]   John Chamberlain, *A Life with the Printed Word* (Chicago: Regnery Gateway, 1982).

[54]   Brian Herbert, *Forgotten Heroes: The Heroic Story of the United States Merchant Marine* (New York: Forge Book, 2004), p. 92.

[55]   Captain Walter Karig, Lieutenant Earl Burton and Lieutenant Stephen L. Freeland, "Murmansk Run", *The United States Navy in World War II*, ed. S. E. Smith (New York: William Morrow & Company, 1966), p. 131.

[56] Circular telegram, "Poltava and Murmansk: Episodes in US-Soviet Military Relations in World War II" (Washington DC: Office of the Historian, Department of State, 1985). See also "50 Years Later, Russia Honors U.S. Saviors," *New York Times*, October 11, 1992.

[57] Stevens, *Russia Is No Riddle*, p. 167.

[58] Long after my retirement, Herb Kaiser, a Warsaw embassy colleague to whom I refer in chapter 3, encouraged me to read the book, available in a translation by Peter Constantine from a Russian text edited by Nathalie Babel (New York: W.W. Norton, 2002). Babel was one of the writers alluded to in chapter 1 who disappeared from Peredelkino during the Great Purge. As a regime-favored writer, he had received a dacha there in 1936. He was arrested in May 1939, charged with espionage, and executed in Lubyanka prison in January 1940.

[59] Alger Hiss, *Recollections of a Life* (New York: Henry Holt and Company, 1988), p. 188.

[60] Allan Bloom, *The Closing of the American Mind* (New York: Simon and Schuster, 1987), pp. 49–50.

[61] "L.B. Turkevich, First Woman To Be Teacher at Princeton, 85," *New York Times*, April 16, 1995.

[62] Entry, November 22, 1911, in *Tagebucher*, eds. Hans-Gerd Koch, Michael Muller, and Malcolm Pasley (Frankfurt: S. Fischer, 1990), cited in Reiner Stach, trans. Shelley Frisch, *Kafka: The Decisive Years* (Orlando: Harcourt Inc., 2005), p. 47.

[63] George F. Kennan, *Memoirs, 1925–1950* (Boston: Little, Brown and Company, 1967), p. 10.

[64] Sidney Hook, *Out of Step: An Unquiet Life in the 20th Century* (New York: Harper & Row, Publishers, 1987), pp. 54–55.

[65] A movie of the same title appeared in 1971 and popularized the novel.

[66] Robert Dallek, *An Unfinished Life: John F. Kennedy, 1917–1963* (Boston: Little, Brown and Company, 2003), pp. 493–94.

[67] Priscilla J. McMillan, *The Ruin of J. Robert Oppenheimer, And the Birth of the Modern Arms Race* (New York: Viking, 2005), p. 242.

[68] One of the textbooks in the course was Berman's own, *The Trial of the U 2* (Chicago: Translation World Publishers, 1960). Another professor whom I liked was Louis Sohn who taught law relating to the United Nations Organization and its work. Unknown to me at the time, Sohn had been born in Lvov (now Lviv) when it was a Polish city (Lwow), and escaped it just before World War II. Sohn, completely bald, looked much older than his years and I was startled when I saw his obituary in the *Times* on June 23, 2006, reporting his death at age ninety-two. Had I known he was alive when I visited Lvov in 1980, I surely would have corresponded with him.

Chapter 3

[69] John Lewis Gaddis, *The Cold War: A New History* (New York: Penguin Press, 2005), pp. 162–63; Peter Grose, *Gentleman Spy: The Life of Allen Dulles* (Boston: Houghton Mifflin Company, 1994), pp. 293–301; see also Frances Stoner Saunders, *The Cultural Cold War: The CIA and the World of Arts and Letters* (New York: New Press, 1999), chap. 2. The CIA released 702 pages of secret documents bearing on its activities, including some pertaining to Castro and Lumumba, on June 26, 2007.

[70] Grose, *Life of Allen Dulles,* pp. 328–29.

[71] In 2005, Alan Dale Diefenbach, an A-100 classmate, collected and painstakingly compiled information about the class and its members' careers, in the Foreign Service and thereafter. He has shared it with me and other classmates.

[72] "Talking with [Director General] George S. Vest," *Update from State* (Washington DC: State Department), January–February 1989.

[73] James A. Baker II with Thomas Defrank, *The Politics of Diplomacy* (New York: G.P Putnam's Sons, 1995), p. 28.

[74] David Brooks,"The Art of Intelligence," *New York Times,* April 2, 2005.

[75] Michael S. McPherson and Morton O. Schapiro, "Economic Challenges for Liberal Arts Colleges," in *Distinctively American: The Residential Liberal Arts College* (Transaction, 2000), quoted in Andrew Delbanco, *New York Review of Books,* March 10, 2005, p. 20.

[76] Cyrus Vance, *Hard Choices: Critical Years in America's Foreign Policy* (New York: Simon and Schuster, 1983), p. 41.

[77] Ronald I. Spiers, "The 'Budget Crunch' and the Foreign Service," *Current Policy* (Washington DC: State Department, Bureau of Public Affairs), May 6, 1988.

[78] *Update from State,* January–February 1989.

[79] Ambassador W. Robert Pearson, *State Magazine* (Washington, DC: State Department), February 2006.

[80] Ambassador Ruth Davis, *WWSNews,* Magazine of the Woodrow Wilson School of Public and International Affairs, Summer 2005, p. 4.

[81] Stephen Birmingham, *America's Secret Aristocracy* (Boston: Little, Brown and Company, 1987), p. 240.

[82] *Department of State News Letter,* undated, my files.

[83] Albert Speer, trans. Richard and Clara Winston, *Inside the Third Reich: Memoirs* (New York: Macmillan Company, 1970), p. 496.

[84] "That Which Befits a Profession," *Foreign Service Journal,* September 1965, p. 22.

[85] John Kenneth Galbraith, *A Life in Our Times: Memoirs* (Boston: Houghton Mifflin Company, 1981), p. 449.

[86] In fact, the Germans had already deported "more than three hundred thousand Jews from the Warsaw ghetto to the extermination camp in Treblinka" in 1942.

See Jan T. Gross, *Anti-Semitism in Poland after Auschwitz: An Essay in Historical Interpretation* (New York: Random House, 2006), p. 178 n.

[87]   Jos F. Baluta, *Practical Handbook: Polish Language* (New York: Polish Book Importing Co., 1915).

[88]   Graham Greene, *Ways of Escape: An Autobiography* (New York: Simon and Schuster, 1980), pp. 135–6; Norman Sherry, *The Life of Graham Greene* (New York: Viking, 1994), p. 246.

[89]   Greene, *Ways of Escape*, p. 230.

[90]   Norman Davies, *Rising '44: The Battle for Warsaw* (New York: Viking, 2003), p. 517.

[91]   Cleveland Amory, *The Proper Bostonians* (New York: E P Dutton & Co), pp. 42, 180.

[92]   David Fischer, a retired FSO who served in Warsaw, has refreshed my memory.

[93]   Davies, *Rising '44*, pp. 562-63.

[94]   Joseph Roth, trans. Joachim Neugroschel, *The Radetzky March* (Woodstock, New York: Overlook Press, 2002), p. 133.

[95]   "John Gronouski, 76, Kennedy-Era Postal Chief," *New York Times*, January 10, 1996.

[96]   James G. Hershberg, *Who Murdered "Marigold": New Evidence on the Mysterious Failure of Poland's Secret Initiative to Start U.S.-North Vietnamese Peace Talks, 1966"* (Washington DC: Woodrow Wilson International Center for Scholars, 2000). David Fischer called my attention to this study, conducted under the auspices of the Center's Cold War International History project

[97]   *An Unfinished Woman: A Memoir* (Boston: Little, Brown and Company, 1969, 1999), p. 200.

[98]   *Being Red: A Memoir* (Boston: Houghton Mifflin Company, 1990), p. 349.

[99]   In his previously cited *Fear: Anti-Semitism in Poland*, Jan T. Gross accepts, in a footnote on page 30, the 50–60,000 estimate that Paul Lendvai uses in *Anti-Semitism Without Jews: Communist Eastern Europe* (Garden City, NY: Doubleday, 1971). I recall that the embassy considered the total to be about half that number.

[100]   Gross, in his *Fear: Anti-Semitism in Poland after Auschwitz* (previously cited), attributes outbursts of anti-Semitism just after the war (including the pogrom in Kielce on July 4, 1946, which claimed up to eighty lives) to the perception of Polish Christians that the Jews represented "a threat to the [their] material status quo, security, and peaceful conscience," having taken the property of their Jewish neighbors and having assumed their roles "in tacit and often directly opportunistic complicity with Nazi-instigated institutional mass murder" during the war. Gross doesn't believe that anti-Semitic attitudes in prewar Poland and postwar Jewish collusion in the imposition of Communism account for the outbursts (pp. xiv, 226–31, 246–49). I can't argue with most of Gross's research

(although some evidence strikes me as too noncontemporaneous, too tainted, and too spotty to strengthen his argument), but I recall that during my time some Poles spoke harshly of the Jews who held important posts in the first postwar regime.

[101]   Davies, *Rising '44,* p. 558, citing a Soviet archival source.

[102]   I can't cite a source for this story, but Alexander Wat, in *My Century: The Odyssey of a Polish Intellectual* (Berkeley: University of California Press, 1987), p. 184, refers to the solidarity of Poles imprisoned in 1939, and one of his writings may have been my source. Wat served in more than a dozen Communist prisons during his "odyssey."

[103]   Lendvai, *Anti-Semitism Without Jews,* p. 139

[104]   The quotations are from Bogdan's letters and email correspondence, 2004–05.

[105]   Greene, *Ways of Escape,* p. 170.

[106]   Milosz, *Captive Mind,* p. ix.

[107]   "President Directs Agencies to Cut Overseas Personnel and Travel," Memorandum to the Secretary of State and Director, Bureau of the Budget, White House Press Release, January 18, 1968, published in *Department of State Bulletin,* February 12, 1968. President Johnson instructed his secretary of the Treasury (Henry Fowler) "to find short-term answers" to protect "the structure of world trade": Lyndon Baines Johnson, *The Vantage Point: Perspectives of the Presidency 1963–1969* (New York: Holt, Rinehart and Winston, 1971), p. 317. But the effects were long-term and sometimes harmful, as my chapter 15 suggests in discussing the undermanning of the political section at the embassy in Tehran in the 1970s.

Chapter 4

[108]   William Barnes and John Heath Morgan, *The Foreign Service of the United States: Origins, Development, and Functions* (Washington DC: Department of State, Historical Office, 1961), p. 203 et seq.

[109]   Bohlen, *Witness to History,* p. 133.

[110]   Kennan, *Memoirs, 1925–1950,* p. 10.

[111]   GRU derives from *Glavnoe razvedyvatel'noe upravlenie.*

[112]   Oleg Kalugin, with Fen Montaigne, *The First Directorate: My 32 Years in Intelligence and Espionage Against the West* (New York: St. Martin's Press, 1994), pp. 24–26.

[113]   Kennan, *Memoirs, 1925–1950,* p. 33.

[114]   Frank Round Jr., *A Window on Red Square* (Boston: Houghton Mifflin Company, 1952), p. 11.

[115]   Harrison E. Salisbury, *A Journey for Our Times: A Memoir* (New York: Harper & Row, Publishers, 1983), p. 272.

[116] Karig, Burton, and Freeland, *United States Navy*, p. 139.

[117] Edward Radzinsky, trans. Antonina W. Bouis, *Alexander II: The Last Great Tsar* (New York: Free Press, 2005), p. 38.

[118] Whitney, *Russia In My Life*, pp. 286–87.

[119] "U.S. Told To Move Offices in Moscow," *New York Times*, July 8, 1952.

[120] William L. Shirer, *Berlin Diary: The Journal of a Foreign Correspondent, 1934-1941* (New York: Alfred A. Knopf, 1941), pp. 83-84.

[121] Salisbury, *Journey for Our Times*, p. 180.

[122] Avraham Shifrin, *The First Guidebook to Prisons and Concentration Camps of the Soviet Union* (Toronto: Bantam Books, 1982), p. 49.

[123] Harold Nicolson, *Diplomacy* (London: Thornton Butterworth, 1939), p. 224.

[124] Dolgun wrote a full account of his life in the USSR, *An American in the Gulag* (New York: Alfred A. Knopf, 1975).

[125] UPDK is the acronym for *Upravelenie po Obsluzhivaniyu Diplomaticheskogo Korpusa*, or the Administration for Servicing the Diplomatic Corps, generally rendered in a shorter form in my text.

[126] Ambassador Vershbow signed a new forty-nine-year lease of Spaso House on October 12, 2004, so it will continue to be the residence of ambassadors until at least 2054. The previous lease, signed in 1985, was for twenty years, *Financial Times*, October 13, 2004.

[127] Walter Bedell Smith, *My Three Years in Moscow* (Philadelphia: J.B. Lippincott Company, 1950), p. 99.

[128] Edmund Stevens Jr., Nina and Ed's son, shared a copy of his mother's unpublished, unedited 138-page memoir, written with the help of the wife of a British embassy officer Jennifer Potter, in the early 1990s.

[129] Leslie C. Stevens, *Russian Assignment* (Boston: Little, Brown and Company, 1953), p. 46.

[130] Embassy press release, "Soviet Refusal To Grant Exit Permits To American Citizens In The U.S.S.R," no. 203, March 3, 1950, enclosing the text of the aide-mémoire.

[131] NKVD is the Russian acronym of *Narodniy komissariat vnutrennikh del*, or People's Commissariat of Internal Affairs. In 1934 it absorbed the Joint State Political Administration, the OGPU, or *Ob'yednynonnoye gosudarstvennoye politicheskoye upravleniye*.

[132] Pavel Sudoplatov and Anatoli Sudoplatov, with Jerrold L. and Leona P. Schechter, *Special Tasks: The Memoirs of an Unwanted Witness, A Soviet Spymaster* (Boston: Little, Brown and Company, 1994), pp. 281–82; *Moscow News*, August 9–16, 1992.

[133] The cover photograph was taken in April 1987, shortly after the embassy's main pedestrian entrance (which led to a passageway off of which there was a door to the north wing and a door to the central wing) had been sealed off. The gate in the one-story façade at the photograph's extreme right had become the only portal–by way of a short path–to the north-wing consular

section, as it still is. The photograph may have been taken on a Sunday when the embassy was closed because the normally ubiquitous militiamen standing in front are out of sight. The staircase barely visible at the extreme left leads to another entrance which, during most of my time, was kept locked. The vehicular entrance (through which one could walk) is just to the left of the central wing, and remains today as it was.

Chapter 5

[134] Stevens, *Russian Assignment*, p. 444.

[135] Ibid., p. 512. The Soviets informed the Turks that their courier had committed suicide, yet he had been found with a gunshot wound at "the base of his skull from behind, in the same way that people are executed in Russia."

[136] *Moscow News*, August 2–9, 1992

[137] Ibid.

[138] *Moscow News*, June 9–16, 1991.

[139] Letter of November 16, 1933, *Establishment of Diplomatic Relations with the Union of Soviet Socialist Republics* (Washington DC: Department of State, 1933), pp. 7–8.

[140] Salisbury, *American in Russia*, p. 111.

[141] William Taubman, *Khrushchev: The Man and His Era* (New York: W.W. Norton & Company, 2003), pp. 635–36.

[142] A Soviet doctor at the battle of Stalingrad is portrayed calling for cupping glasses to deal with a regimental commander lying in an underground bunker, his face "burning and his eyes . . . transparent and vacuous." Vasili Grossman, a correspondent at Stalingrad, based much of his great novel on real people and events. I have no doubt that he witnessed such an incident. Vasili Grossman, trans. Robert Chandler, *Life and Fate* (New York: New York Review Books, 2006), p. 419.

[143] Thomas J. Watson Jr. and Peter Petre, *Father, Son & Company: My Life at IBM and Beyond* (New York: Bantam Books, 1990), p. 99 et seq.

[144] Irina Yazykova, Hegumen [Father] Luka, and others, trans. Kate Cook, *A History of Icon Painting: Sources, Traditions, Present Day* (Moscow: Grand Holding Publishers, 2002, 2005 [English]), p. 240.

[145] Henry Kissinger, *White House Years* (Boston: Little, Brown and Company, 1979), p. 1270.

[146] Andrew Delbanco, *Melville: His World and Work* (New York: Alfred J. Knopf, 2005), p. 19.

[147] I have drawn on Nina's unpublished memoir that her son Edmund, as mentioned, kindly shared. Before I ended my final assignment in the USSR, Nina gave me a memorandum about the two Moscow houses in which she and Edmund had lived.

[148] Edmund Stevens, "Living the History of Modern Russia," *Architectural Digest*, February 1989.

[149]   Ibid.

[150]   Letter of Edmund Stevens Jr., *New York Times*, May 1, 1995.

[151]   Harvey Klehr, John Earl Haynes, and Fridrikh Igorevich Firsov, *The Secret World of American Communism* (New Haven: Yale University Press, 1995), pp. 299–302.

[152]   Kai Bird and Martin J. Sherwin, *American Prometheus: The Triumph and Tragedy of J. Robert Oppenheimer* (New York: Alfred J. Knopf, 2005), p. 115.

[153]   Patrick Marnham, *Dreaming with His Eyes Open: A Life of Diego Rivera* (New York: Alfred A. Knopf, 1998), pp. 248-60. See also Bertram D. Wolfe, *The Fabulous Life of Diego Rivera* (New York: Stein and Day, Publishers, 1963).

[154]   Thomas Merton, *The Seven Story Mountain* (New York: Harcourt Brace & Company, 1948, 1998), p. 157.

[155]   Malcolm Cowley, *Exile's Return: A Literary Saga of the Nineteen-Twenties* (New York: Viking Press, 1934, 1956), p. 11.

[156]   Malcolm Cowley, *The Dream of the Golden Mountains: Remembering the 1930's* (New York: Viking Press, 1980), p. 35.

[157]   Margaret Brenman-Gibson, *Clifford Odets, American Playwright: The Years from 1906 to 1940* (New York: Atheneum, 1981), p. 260 et seq.

[158]   As reported by Ed Stevens in the previously cited article in *Architectural Digest*, February 1989. One of those was arrested was Hu Hsiao, who edited Chinese translations of Marxist-Leninist classics at the cooperative. His death (probably execution) in 1938 was reported by a one-time Russian colleague, Vera Vladimirovna Vishnyakova-Akimova, trans. Steven I. Levine, *Two Years in Revolutionary China, 1925–1927* (Cambridge: Harvard University Press, East Asian Research Institute, 1971), p. 95.

[159]   Stevens, *Russian Assignment*, p. 213.

[160]   Gilbert A. Harrison, *The Enthusiast: A Life of Thornton Wilder* (New Haven: Ticknor & Fields, 1983), p. 307.

[161]   Masha Gessen, *Ester and Ruzya: How My Grandmothers Survived Hilter's War and Stalin's Peace* (New York: Random House, 2004), pp. 268, 274.

[162]   Whitman Bassow, *The Moscow Correspondents: Reporting on Russia from the Revolution to Glasnost* (New York: William Morris and Company, 1988), pp. 201–203.

[163]   Edmund Stevens, *This is Russia Un-censored* (New York: Eton Books, 1950), pp. 4, 26, 214.

[164]   Salisbury, *Journey of Our Times*, p. 292.

[165]   General Walter Bedell Smith, "Foreword," *Russia Un-censored*, p. 1.

[166]   Kennan, *Memoirs , 1925–1950*, pp. 82–83.

[167]   Davies, *Rising '44*, p. 161-62.

[168]   *"Drugoye iskusstvo,"* *Moskva 1956–76* (Moscow: Artistic Gallery, 1991), vol. 1, p. 173; vol., 2, p. 39 et seq.

[169] Op. cit., *New York Times*, June 15, 1967.

[170] Marnham, *Eyes Open*, p. 203.

[171] Michel Tatu, trans. Helen Katel *Power in the Kremlin: From Khrushchev to Kosygin* (New York: Viking Press, 1967, 1970), p. 461 et seq., especially p. 464 n 1.

[172] Bassow, *Moscow Correspondents*, p. 180.

[173] Kostaki, *Moy Avangard*, p. 92 et seq.

[174] Ibid., p. 102 (my translation).

[175] Ibid., p. 96. See also Peter Roberts, *George Costakis: A Russian Life in Art* (New York: George Brazillier, 1994), pp. 154–55.

[176] Leona and Jerrold Schecter, *An American Family in Moscow* (Boston: Little, Brown and Company, 1975), p. 164. They also reported that Nina didn't like Yevtushenko, yet it was at the Stevens' home that I first met Yevtushenko.

[177] *Russian Assignment*, p. 264.

[178] Jacob D. Beam, *Multiple Exposure: An American Ambassador's Unique Perspective on East-West Issues* (New York: W.W. Norton & Company, 1978), p. 227.

[179] Department of State Airgram 728, March 22, 1972.

[180] Anatoly Dobrynin, *In Confidence: Moscow's Ambassador to America's Six Cold War Presidents* (New York: Random House, 1995), p. 240.

[181] Raymond L. Garthoff, *Détente and Confrontation: American-Soviet Relations from Nixon to Reagan* (Washington DC: Brookings Institution, 1994 [revised edition]), pp. 78–79, 108–113; Kissinger, *White House Years*, pp. 26–30.

[182] Kissinger, *White House Years*, p. 1153.

[183] William H. Standley and Arthur A. Ageton, *Admiral Ambassador to Russia* (Chicago: Henry Regnery Company, 1955), pp. 119, 357–58.

[184] Garthoff, *Détente and Confrontation*, p. 372 n. 30.

[185] Kissinger, *White House Years*, p. 841.

[186] Garthoff, *Détente and Confrontation*, p. 349. The Yale historian Gaddis disagrees, writing that "to have attempted arms control negotiations with Moscow in the absence of a 'back channel' that allowed testing positions before taking them would probably have guaranteed failure" (*Cold War*, p. 172). However, Garthoff writes from the perspective of one who actually negotiated arms issues with the Soviets.

[187] Beam, *Multiple Exposure*, p. 234.

[188] Ibid., p. 235.

[189] "Slain Ambassador A Career Diplomat," *New York Times*, February 15, 1979

[190] Dobrynin, *In Confidence*, p. 436.

Chapter 6

[191] "Exit Permit Plea To Soviet Studied," *New York Times*, October 11, "Soviet Lets Four Emigrate to U.S.," *New York Times*, November 22, 1959.

[192] Kissinger, *White House Years*, pp. 138–41.

[193] Ibid, p. 1271.

[194] News Conference,May 29, 1972, reported in *Weekly Compilation of Presidential Documents* (Washington DC: Government Printing Office, June 5, 1972), p. 962.

[195] Dobrynin, *In Confidence*, p. 268.

[196] The three sentences in the transcript read: "On MFN, it was in this room, or a similar room, that we agreed on MFN and Lend-Lease together in 1972. I had never heard of the Jackson Amendment at the time. Nor had I ever mentioned Jewish emigration." William Burr, editor, *The Kissinger Transcripts: The Top Secret Talks with Beijing and Moscow* (New York: New Press, 1998), p. 340.

[197] Robert Dallek, *Nixon and Kissinger, Partners in Power* (New York:HarperCollins, 2007), pp. 413, 674.

[198] Kissinger, *White House Years*, p. 1271.

[199] Armand Hammer, with Neil Lyndon, *Hammer* (New York: Putnam Publishing Group, 1987), pp. 418–20.

[200] Marvin Kalb and Bernard Kalb, *Kissinger* (Boston: Little, Brown and Company, 1974), p. 188.

[201] Garthoff, *Détente and Confrontation*, p. 328.

[202] George Feifer, *Moscow Farewell* (New York: Viking Press, 1976), p. 63. Timothy Egan, in *The Worst Hard Time: The Untold Story of the Those Who Survived the Great American Dust Bowl* (Boston: Houghton Mifflin Company, 2006), summarizes the experiences of the many *Russlanddeutschen* who populated the Great Plains after arriving from Russia before World War I.

[203] Robert M. Gates, *From the Shadows: The Ultimate Insider's Story of Five Presidents and How They Won the Cold War* (New York: Simon & Schuster, 1996), p. 49.

[204] *The Reagan Diaries*, ed. Douglas Brinkley (New York: HarperCollins, 2007), p. 553.

[205] In recapitulating the events of 1973–74, I have drawn on Michael Scammell, *Solzhenitsyn: A Biography* (New York: W.W. Norton & Company, 1984), pp. 813–28.

[206] Richard Lourie, *Sakharov: A Biography* (Hanover: Brandeis University Press, 2002), pp. 256-57.

[207] Discussed in Vishnevskaya, *Galina*, pp. 126–30.

[208] Valery Panov, with George Feifer, *To Dance* (New York: Alfred A. Knopf, 1978), p. 168.

[209] "Kaleria Fedicheva, Ballerina and Ballet Teacher, Dies at 58," *New York Times*, October 28, 1994. Her travails in the USSR are recounted in the *Times*, February 18, 19, 25, 1975.

[210] *Department of State Bulletin*, January 7, 1974.

[211] The full story is recounted in Simas Kudirka and Larry Eichel, *For Those Still at Sea: The Defection of a Lithuanian Sailor* (New York: Dial Press, 1978), p. 180 et seq.

[212] Burr, *Kissinger Transcripts*, pp. 235 and 262 n. 31.

213   Ambassador Stoessel had his first meeting with Brezhnev on April 11. Against the background of a crisis between Israel and Syria (Golda Meir resigned her premiership the same day) and the meetings Kissinger was having with Gromyko at the same time at the State Department, this would not have been the moment for handing over a new representation list. During the meeting Brezhnev indicated his concern that Watergate might affect Nixon's ability to negotiate agreements at the forthcoming summit, as Nixon recounts in *The Memoirs of Richard Nixon* (New York: Grosset & Dunlap, 1978), p. 1026.

214   *Defection of a Lithuanian Sailor*, pp. 197–8.

215   Gerald R. Ford, *A Time To Heal: The Autobiography of Gerald R. Ford* (New York: Harper & Row, 1979), pp. 138–39.

216   Aryeh Neier, "Hero," *New York Review of Books*, January 13, 2005.

217   Rowland Evans and Robert Novak, *International Herald Tribune*, June 11, 1974. The headline might have been different in the *Washington Post*.

218   *Weekly Compilation of Presidential Documents* (Washington, D.C.: Government Printing Office, July 8, 1974), p. 763.

219   Nixon, *Memoirs*, p. 1024.

220   Ibid., p. 1034.

221   Henry Kissinger, *Years of Upheaval* (Boston: Little, Brown and Company, 1982), p. 995.

222   S. Frederick Starr, *Red and Hot: The Fate of Jazz in the Soviet Union* (New York: Oxford University Press, 1983).

223   Starr, *Fate of Jazz*, pp. 89–90.

224   Ibid., pp.109–10, 170.

225   "Willis Conover Is Dead at 75," *New York Times*, May 19, 1996.

226   Starr, *Fate of Jazz*, pp. 313–14; Hedrick Smith, *The Russians* (New York: Ballantine Books, 1976), pp. 228–31.

227   Diane Neumaier, ed., *Beyond Memory: Soviet Nonconformist Photography and Photo-Related Works of Art* (New Brunswick: Voorhees Zimmerli Art Museum and Rutgers University Press, 2004), p. 57.

228   "For the Orthodox Russian it was one of the highest expressions of his faith," as noted by Derek Hopwood, *The Russian Presence in Syria & Palestine 1843–1914: Church & Politics in the Near East* (London: Oxford University Press, 1969), p. 10. With World War I and the Revolution, the pilgrimage became impossible. With the collapse of the Soviet Union, Russian believers are again visiting Jerusalem in large numbers.

229   Lazar Fleishman, *Boris Pasternak: The Poet and His Politics* (Cambridge: Harvard University Press, 1990), p. 292, as quoted in Roberta Reeder, *Anna Akhmatova, Poet and Prophet* (New York: Picador USA, 1994), p. 359.

230   Ilf and Petrov, trans. John H.C. Richardson, *The Twelve Chairs* (Evanston: Northwestern University Press, 1961).

[231] Gleb Struve, *Soviet Russian Literature, 1917–50* (Norman: University of Oklahoma Press, 1951), p. 356.

Chapter 7

[232] Henry Kissinger, *Years of Renewal* (New York: Simon & Schuster, 1999), p. 799.

[233] Ibid., pp. 799–80.

[234] Barnes and Heath, *Foreign Service*, p. 212.

[235] Bohlen, *Witness to History*, p. 8.

[236] "New U.S. Embassy Praised by Nehru," *New York Times*, January 4, 1959.

[237] Conor Cruise O'Brien, *Memoir: My Life and Themes* (New York: Cooper Square Press, 1998), p. 274.

[238] Galbraith, *Memoirs*, p. 393.

[239] *Yojana*, January 26, 1975.

[240] Kissinger, *White House Years*, pp. 738–39; on the "tilt", *Years of Renewal*, pp. 82–83.

[241] Dallek, *Nixon and Kissinger*, p. 336.

[242] A report of White House transcripts of a Nixon and Kissinger exchange about Mrs. Gandhi appeared in *The Guardian* (London), June 29, 2005. The transcripts, based on Oval Office tapes, had been released the prior day. They have Kissinger referring to Indians as "bastards" and Nixon to them as "a slippery, treacherous people." See also Dallek, *Nixon and Kissinger*, pp. 338-40.

[243] *Compilation of Presidential Documents*, July 8, 1974, p. 762.

[244] John Kenneth Galbraith, *Ambassador's Journal: A Personal Account of the Kennedy Years* (Boston: Houghton Mifflin Company, 1969), p. 271.

[245] Watson, *Father, Son & Co.*, p. 430.

[246] Beam, *Multiple Exposure*, p. 219.

[247] Victor Cherkashin, with Gregory Feifer, *Spy Handler: Memoir of a KGB Officer* (New York: Basic Books, 2005), p. 110 et seq.

[248] This adage appears in Andrew Cook, *M, MI5's First Spymaster* (Stroud, Gloucestershire: Tempest Publishing Limited, 2004), p. 176.

[249] Lionel Trilling, *The Liberal Imagination: Essays on Literature and Society* (New York: Doubleday Anchor Books, 1950), p. 123.

[250] *New Wave*, January 5, 1975.

[251] Cited in "U.S. Challenged Over India Blast," *New York Times*, June 11, 1976.

[252] "U.S. Sees A Role in India's A-Blast," *New York Times*, August 11, 1976.

[253] The agreement reportedly restricts India's access to U.S. nuclear supplies should it again test a nuclear weapon. In order to obviate opposition in India to any foreign limits on its nuclear program, opposition that could doom the coalition government with which the U.S. made the agreement, the Bush

administration has agreed to assist India to "find alternative sources of nuclear fuel in the event of an American cutoff, skirting some of the provisions of the [U.S.] law," as reported in the "U.S. to Announce Nuclear Exception for India," *New York Times*, July 27, 2007.

[254] Galbraith, *Memoirs*, p. 407.

[255] Vance, *Hard Choices*, p. 24.

[256] Dobrynin, *In Confidence*, p. 377.

[257] Zbigniew Brzezinski, *Power and Principle, Memoirs of the National Security Adviser 1977-1981* (New York: Farrar Straus Giroux, 1983), pp. 297–8.

[258] Vance, *Hard Choices*, p. 34.

[259] Kissinger, *White House Years*, p. 887.

[260] Copy in my possession.

[261] Brzezinski, *Power*, p. 174.

[262] "Interagency Unit Under State Dept. To Coordinate Policy Toward Soviet," *New York Times*, July 19, 1977.

[263] Brzezinski, *Power*, p. 174.

[264] Rudy Abramson, *Spanning the Century: The Life of W. Averell Harriman, 1891–1986* (New York: William Morrow and Company, 1992), p. 692.

[265] Brzezinski, *Power*, p. 349.

[266] Gates, *Out of the Shadows*, p. 70.

[267] Brzezinski, *Power*, p. 174.

[268] Dobrynin, *In Confidence*, p. 356.

[269] John Barron, *KGB: The Secret Work of Soviet Secret Agents* (New York: Reader's Digest Press, 1974), pp. 3–4.

[270] Patrick Tyler, *A Great Wall: Six Presidents and China* (New York: Public Affairs, 1999), pp. 66-69.

[271] Stevens, *Russia Is No Riddle*, pp. 145–46.

[272] Dobrynin, *In Confidence*, p. 457.

Chapter 8

[273] Clint Willis, ed., *The Lawrence Durrell Travel Reader* (New York: Carroll & Graf Publishers, 2004), p. 366. The ballerina Maya Plisetskaya, writing about her years in the Soviet Union while living in Spain, claimed she always smelled "garbage in the streets" when arriving at the airport. *I, Maya Plisetskaya*, trans. Antonina W. Bouis (New Haven: Yale University Press, 2001), p. 289.

[274] "New Dimout Order Limits Cars In City To Parking Lights," *New York Times*, August 3, 1942.

[275] "U.S. Envoy Speaks on Soviet TV," *New York Times*, July 5, 1978.

[276] "President Is Withdrawing Ford Nomination of Toon As Ambassador to Soviet," *New York Times*, February 19, 1977 ; "Carter Retains Envoy in Moscow And Picks Career Man for Paris," *New York Times*, April 26, 1977.

[277] Beisner, *Dean Acheson*, p. 616

[278] Dobrynin, *In Confidence*, p. 454.

[279] "Some Looting at U.S. Fire in Moscow," *New York Times*, September 3, 1977

[280] Gates, *Out of the Shadows*, p. 101

[281] "Soviet Dissidents' Contacts Upset," *New York Times*, January 16, 1978.

[282] Gates, *Out of the Shadows*, p. 91.

[283] Strobe Talbott, *The Russians and Reagan* (New York: Vintage Books, 1984), p. 56.

[284] Dobrynin, *In Confidence*, p. 392.

[285] Brzezinski, *Power*, p. 164.

[286] Strobe Talbott, *Endgame: The Inside Story of SALT II* (New York: Harper & Row, 1979), p. 49.

[287] Vance, *Hard Choices*, p. 84.

[288] Ibid.

[289] Brzezinski, *Power*, pp. 206–19.

[290] Patrick Tyler, "The (Ab)normalization of U.S.-Chinese Relations", *Foreign Affairs*, September–October 1999, p. 104.

[291] Vance, *Hard Choices*, p. 116.

[292] David Rothkopf, *Running the World: The Inside Story of the National Security Council and the Architects of American Power* (New York: Public Affairs, 2004), p. 189. Rothkopf cites Tyler, *Foreign Affairs*, pp. 97–99, who details Brzezinski's methodical exclusion of Vance, assistant secretary for Asia Richard Holbrooke, and other department officers from the climactic discussions that led to normalization.

[293] Talbott, *Endgame*, pp. 153–54.

[294] Ibid., p. 154; Dobrynin, *In Confidence*, p. 413.

[295] Leo Tolstoy, trans. Richard Pevear and Larissa Volokhonsky, *Anna Karenina* (New York: Penguin, 2002), p. 254.

[296] Reagan hand-wrote a letter to Brezhnev in April 1981 appealing for the Pentecostalists' release, *Reagan Diaries*, p. 15. In 1983 they were finally allowed to emigrate.

[297] Plisetskaya, *I, Maya*, pp. 133–149.

[298] Today the State Department office is called the Office of Overseas Buildings Operations.

[299] Sociologists have an explanation: "But once the threshold of 'several hundred,' below which everyone can know everyone else, has been crossed, increasing numbers of dyads [two units treated as one] become pairs of unrelated strangers," at least as reported in Jared Diamond, *Guns, Germs, and Steel: The Fates of Human Societies* (New York: W.W. Norton & Company, 1999), p. 27, which refers to supporting studies. In short, the embassy community was becoming filled with an increasing number of members viewed as "strangers."

[300] Talbott, *Endgame*, p. 221.

[301] A day or so after being introduced to Dick, I misspelled his surname in an internal memorandum. For a deep-dyed Kremlinologist, misspelling a name was a serious offense (had I been working for *Pravda*, I would have been fired), and he reacted accordingly. Years later, I read that his father had been "so secretive" that "journalists routinely misspelled his name," Gregg Herken, *Brotherhood of the Bomb: The Tangled Lives and Loyalties of Robert Oppenheimer, Ernest Lawrence, and Edward Teller* (New York: Henry Holt and Company, 2002), p. 380 n. 100. Dick was private too but I was working on the same floor and didn't have an excuse.

[302] Mikhail Gorbachev, *Memoirs* (New York: Doubleday, 1995), p. 95.

[303] Boris Pasternak, trans. David Magarshack, *Letters to Georgian Friends* (London: Secker & Warburg, 1967), p. 80–81.

[304] Elliott Mossman ed., trans. with Margaret Wettlin, *The Correspondence of Boris Pasternak and Olga Freidenberg, 1910-1954* (New York: Harcourt Brace Jovanovich, Publishers, 1982), p. 183.

[305] Harold Schonberg, *New York Times*, November 20, 1966, quoted in Donald Spoto, *Lenya: A Life* (Boston: Little, Brown and Company, 1989), p. 286.

[306] M. Croydon, quoted in Leiter, a source not known to me but cited on-line at V.S. Vysotsky Foundation site (http://*www.kulichki.com*).

[307] T. J. Binyon, *Pushkin: A Biography* (New York: Vintage Books, 2002, 2003), p. 609.

[308] *Moscow News*, May 29–June 5, 1988.

[309] Kulagin, *First Directorate*, p. 197.

[310] Ibid., p. 198.

[311] Quoted in Nathaniel Davis, *A Long Walk to Church: A Contemporary History of Russian Orthodoxy* (Boulder: Westview Press, 1995), p. 96.

Chapter 9

[312] Talbott, *Endgame*, p. 270.

[313] Brzezinski, *Power*, pp. 196–206.

[314] Ibid., p. 403.

[315] See Strobe Talbott, *Deadly Gambits: The Reagan Administration and the Stalemate in Nuclear Arms Control* (New York: Alfred A. Knopf, 1984), p. 38: "The other reason was that the SS-20s in eastern regions of the U.S.S.R. also represented a threat to the U.S.'s chief Asian allies, Japan and Korea, and to the People's Republic of China, with which the Carter Administration was normalizing diplomatic relations and hoping to develop what Brzezinski sometimes called a 'strategic partnership,' a kind of unwritten alliance against the U.S.S.R."

[316] Brzezinski, *Power*, p. 211.

[317] Ibid. p. 216.

[318] Ibid., p. 220.

[319]   Ibid., p. 405.

[320]   Ibid., pp. 408–14.

[321]   Dobrynin, *In Confidence*, p. 418. Garthoff suggests that something close to "collusion" existed, evidenced by the sharing of U.S. intelligence about Soviet troop movements with the Chinese following their invasion, *Détente and Confrontation*, pp. 791–92. There was ample precedent for Brzezinski's action. At the time of the 1971 Indo-Pakistan conflict, Kissinger had shared intelligence with the Chinese about the disposition of Soviet troops, as recently noted in Dallek, *Nixon and Kissinger*, p. 345. Beginning in February 1972 Kissinger then turned over reams of classified material to the Chinese, as described in Margaret MacMillan, *Nixon and Mao, The Week That Changed The World* (New York:Random House, 2007), pp. 242-43. As soon as formal relations with the People's Republic were established, Brzezinski oversaw the establishment of CIA listening posts on Chinese territory to monitor Soviet missile tests. The State Department learned about this after the fact, as indicated by the exchanges reported in Ivo H. Daalder and I.M. Destler, moderators, *The National Security Council Project*, Oral History Roundtables, at the Center for International and Security Studies at Maryland and The Brookings Institute, November 4, 1999. See also Patrick Tyler, *A Great Wall*, pp. 278, 284–85. The monitoring equipment was shipped to the PRC beginning in August 1979, four months before the Soviet invasion of Afghanistan; undoubtedly the Soviets soon became aware of it.

[322]   Vance, *Hard Choices*, p. 122.

[323]   Trans. Strobe Talbott, *Khrushchev Remembers* (Boston: Little, Brown and Company, 1970), p. 507. Of course, "encirclement" is often voiced by statesmen to justify their pre-emptive actions. Wooing the Chinese Foreign Minister in Beijing, Brzezinski alleged a Soviet strategy "to encircle China" (Brzezinski, *Power*, p. 211).

[324]   Author's copy.

[325]   "Help After High-Stress Assignments," *Foreign Service Journal*, December 2006, p. 54.

[326]   Tyler, *Foreign Affairs*, September–October 1999, p. 109. The phrase "poisonous competition" is Tyler's, p. 94.

[327]   Joe Biden, Letter to Garrison, September 10, 1979.

[328]   Charles de Gaulle, trans. Jonathan Griffin and Richard Howard, *The Complete War Memoirs of Charles DeGaulle* (New York: Carroll & Graf Publishers, 1955, 1998), p. 227.

[329]   Brzezinski, *Power*, p. 340.

[330]   Vance, *Hard Choices*, p. 138.

[331]   Brzezinski, *Power*, p. 344.

[332]   Ibid., p. 343.

[333]   *Moscow News*, May 24–31, 1992.

[334] *In Confidence*, p. 425.

[335] *Hard Choices*, p. 390.

[336] John W. Parker, *Kremlin in Transition: From Brezhnev to Chernenko, 1978 to 1985*, vol. I (Boston: Unwin Hyman, 1991). I have drawn on John's work while refreshing my recollection of Pol/Int's reporting on Kulakov, Gorbachev, and Kirilenko.

[337] Gorbachev, *Memoirs*, p. 97.

[338] Joint Soviet-American Editorial Board, *The United States and Russia: The Beginning of Relations 1965–1815* (Washington DC: Department of State, 1980).

[339] Georgi Arbatov, *The System: An Insider's Life in Soviet Politics* (New York: Random House, 1992), pp. 290–91. *Moscow News*, August 1, 1998, reported that Kosolapov had "single handedly completed his labor of love," the publication of the final book in the sixteen-volume set. *Pravda*, August 22, 1986, carries the Central Committee resolution criticizing *Kommunist*. Arbatov accuses Kosolapov of being anti-Semitic.

[340] Alexander Werth, *Russia at War, 1941–1945* (New York: E.P.Dutton & Co., 1964), p. 1001.

[341] Menachem Begin, *White Nights: The Story of a Prisoner in Russia* (New York: Harper & Row, Publishers, 1977), p. 213.

[342] William Allen White, *The Autobiography of William Allen White* (New York: Macmillan Company, 1946), p. 244. Joseph Brodsky claimed that psychiatric hospitals in Leningrad where dissidents were sometimes incarcerated administered sulphur injections to calm unruly patients, causing "excruciating physical pain" (Volkov, *Conversations*, p. 68).

[343] *Literaturnaya gazeta*, September 26, 1979.

[344] Alfred Kazin, *New York Jew* (New York: Alfred A. Knopf, 1978), p. 273.

[345] Kalugin, *First Directorate*, p. 158.

[346] *Moscow News*, July 17, 1988.

[347] Zbigniew Brzezinski, in his *Second Chance, Three Presidents and the Crisis of American Superpower* (New York: Basic Books, 2007), p. 120, makes the startling comment that "upward of 25 percent of the Chechen population perished, with both sides resorting to terrorist tactics."

[348] "Rebels Attack Caucasus Area," *New York Times*, September 6, 1999. Interethnic incidents and killings in Dagestan and Buynaksk are also reported in "Bombs Hurt 8 in a Russian Republic," *New York Times*, June 26, 2005, and in more recent articles. See also "The language of bombs," the *Economist*, July 9, 2005.

[349] Garthoff, *Détente and Confrontation*, p. 1001 et seq.

[350] Ibid., pp. 804-05 n. 61.

[351] Watson, *Father, Son & Co.*, p. 421.

[352] Ibid., p. 416

[353] "1964: Thomas Watson Jr. Does a 360," *Fortune*, June 27, 2005. .

[354] Watson, *Father, Son & Co.*, p. 58.

[355] Garthoff, *Détente and Confrontation*, p. 1011.

Chapter 10

[356] Jimmy Carter, *Keeping Faith, Memoirs of a President* (New York: Bantam Books, 1982), p. 471.

[357] Dobrynin, *In Confidence*, p. 440.

[358] William Shirer points out that President Roosevelt "did not dare to insist on a boycott of the 1936 Games in Germany, despite his hatred of the Nazis," although there was more agitation in the United States against participating at that time than in 1980. The Berlin summer games came shortly after Hitler's march into the Rhineland in 1936. See *The Nightmare Years, 1930–1940* (Boston: Little, Brown and Company, 1984), p. 230 n.

[359] Watson, *Father, Son & Co.*, p. 55. The elder Watson's naiveté about prewar Germany is examined in Kevin Maney, *The Maverick and His Machine, Thomas Watson, Sr., and The Making of IBM* (Hoboken, NJ: John Wiley & Sons, 2003), pp. 202-223.

[360] *Newsweek*, February 11, 1980.

[361] Ibid.

[362] Davis, *Long Walk*, p. 81.

[363] President Reagan, who appointed Watson's successor, is said by Poindexter, the one-time national security advisor, to have "loved seeing the raw intelligence on the Soviet economy," as cited in Peter Schweizer, *Victory: The Reagan Administration's Secret Strategy That Hastened the Collapse of the Soviet Union* (New York: Atlantic Monthly Press, 1994), p. 5.

[364] Leonard Schapiro and Joseph Godson, eds., *The Soviet Worker: Illusions and Realities* (London: Macmillan Press, 1982), p. 129 n. 21.

[365] Geoffrey Hosking, *The Awakening of the Soviet Union* (Cambridge: Harvard University Press, 1991), p. 48.

[366] William O. Douglas, *Russian Journal* (Garden City: Doubleday & Company, 1956), pp. 155–56.

[367] Boris Schwarz, *Music and Musical Life in Soviet Russia, 1917–1970* (New York: W.W. Norton, 1972), pp. 138, 173.

[368] There were numerous press reports about the incident. George Griffin, retired from the Foreign Service and living in Blue Ridge Summit, Pennsylvania, shared his recollections, including the pertinent part of an oral history he provided Charles Stuart Kennedy, who heads the Foreign Affairs Oral History Project of the Association for Diplomatic Studies and Training in Washington DC.

[369] Cherkashin, *KGB Officer*, p. 173. Cherkashin wrote that the Soviets "forced" Kruglov out of the embassy with their actions, which is patent nonsense.

[370] When informing me of the new embassy's plan to honor Spike, Bernie was doing TDY duty at the old embassy. He said it had only suffered rocket hits from the Taliban.

[371] "Behind Disarray in U.S. Foreign Policy," *U.S. News & World Report*, September 29, 1980.

[372] Yevtushenko, *Bratsk Hydroelectric Station*, p. 23. The poem premiered as a play in 1967.

[373] William Taubman, *Khrushchev: The Man and His Era* (New York: W.W. Norton & Co., 2003), p. 382. Taubman estimates that 108 million people moved into new apartments between 1956 and 1965.

[374] "Building the Soviet Society: Housing and Planning," Harrison E. Salisbury, ed., *The Soviet Union: The Fifty Years* (New York: Signet Books, 1967, 1968), p. 319.

[375] Quoted in Stephen F. Cohen, "Introduction", p. x, in Yegor Ligachev, trans. Catherine A. Fitzpatrick, Michele A. Berdy, and Dobrochna Dyrcz-Freeman, *Inside Gorbachev's Kremlin: Memoirs of Yegor Ligachev* (New York: Pantheon Books, 1993). Ligachev completes his thought by saying, "[i]n Moscow they stab you in the back."

[376] Kennan, *Memoirs*, p. 262.

[377] Watson, *Father, Son & Co.*, p. 436.

[378] "Briefings" (The Watson Institute for International Studies), Fall 2005.

[379] Judging from a report entitled "Partner Adopted by an Heiress Stakes Her Claim," *New York Times* March 19, 2007, Mrs. Watson probably didn't have to worry about the marines. Her daughter is cited as having "married" another woman a few years later, a woman who sued the Watson family as a spouse for her share of an inheritance.

[380] Patrick Marnham, *Diego Rivera*, pp. 201–203; Bertram Wolfe, *Fabulous Life*, pp. 217–221.

[381] Watson, *Father, Son & Co.*, p. 436.

[382] "U.S. Army Attaché Called Target of Soviet Plot to Compromise Him," *New York Times*, February 16, 1981, and follow-up articles February 17, 21, and March 13, 1981.

[383] "President Sharply Assails Kremlin; Haig Warning on Poland Disclosed," *New York Times*, January 30, 1981.

[384] Gates, *From the Shadows*, p. 203 et seq. Of course, questions remain, including the possibility of yet undisclosed dealings between top Soviet and East German officials about the terrorists who were allowed to reside in East Germany. The memoir of East Germany's security chief doesn't answer every question: Marcus Wolf, with Anne McElvoy, *Man Without A Face: The Autobiography of Communism's Greatest Spymaster* (New York: Random House, 1997). Tim Wiener, examining Haig's allegation that "the Soviets were secretly directing the dirty work of the world's worst terrorists" (Wiener's language), while writing his *Legacy of Ashes,*

the History of the CIA (New York: Doubleday, 2007), concluded that, a quarter century later, Haig's "charge remains unproven" (pp. 288, 649-50 n.).

[385] "President Sharply Assails Kremlin; Haig Warning on Poland Disclosed," *New York Times*, January 30, 1981.

[386] "Door Diplomacy," *New York Times*, December 20, 1981.

[387] Alexander M. Haig, Jr, *Caveat: Realism, Reagan, And Foreign Policy* (New York: Macmillan Publishing, 1984), pp. 101-02.

[388] Jack F. Matlock, Jr., *Reagan and Gorbachev, How the Cold War Ended* (New York: Random House, 2004), p. 14.

[389] Stevens, *Russian Assignment.*

[390] As reported by Walter Graebner, *Round Trip to Russia* (Philadelphia: J.B. Lippincott Company, 1943), p. 108.

[391] Bohlen, *Witness to History*, p. 68. Maya Plisetskaya said she danced it "more than eight hundred times",*I, Maya*, p. 88.

[392] Andrea Lee, *Russian Journal* (New York: Vintage Press, 1984), pp. 100–101.

[393] Kessler, *Moscow Station*, p. 83.

[394] Mila gave me a copy of the poem as it appeared in a Russian collection of Voznesenski's poems, and I received her help in translating it. I do not have the date of the *LitGaz* issue in which it originally appeared.

[395] Kennan, *Memoirs*, pp. 97–99.

[396] John Derbyshire, *National Review*, January 30, 2005.

[397] Fearful of a leak, Secretary Haig, in commending the embassy and me telegraphically for resolving the incident, carefully avoided mentioning the fact that we had dealt with a Soviet soldier, but referred instead to our "recent visitor." Of course, there was nothing intrinsically sensitive about the incident to warrant treating it as secret. I sent two messages to Derbyshire at the *National Review* pointing to the comparable "cluelessness" (if one is use this word) of the Reagan administration in not assigning a Russian-speaking FSO to Prague, but didn't receive a response.

Chapter 11

[398] Rothkopf, *Running the World*, p. 164.

[399] Vance, *Hard Choices*, p. 41.

[400] "We *were* [underlined in original] told, however, both through the Foreign Service Act of 1980 and in the letter from the Director General to FS-1's in May, 1981, which initiated the 'window' system, that there would be 'regular and predictable flow upward through the ranks and into the senior foreign service.'" Source: Molineaux, Merrick, and Wallace [i.e., three affected officers] circular letter, May 8, 1987, to all Foreign Service Officers, Class 1.

[401] *New York Times*, April 23, 1986.

[402] Harold Nicolson, ed. Nigel Nicolson, *Diaries & Letters, 1930–1939* (New York: Atheneum, 1966), p. 53.

[403] Huxtable, *Architecture*, p. 271.

[404] Chris Simpson [former BBC correspondent in Angola], *BBC Africa*, February 25, 2002.

[405] President's Report, *Annual Report of the Council on Foreign Relations*, July 1, 1979–June 30, 1980, p. 15.

[406] Kissinger, *Years of Renewal*, p. 808.

[407] Garthoff, *Détente and Confrontation*, pp. 564-65.

[408] "Angolan Rebel Sees Top U.S. Officials," *New York Times*, January 30, 1986.

[409] Dobrynin, *In Confidence*, pp. 360-63.

[410] Kissinger, *Years of Renewal*, p. 816; also p. 786.

[411] Dobrynin, *In Confidence*, p. 407.

[412] George P. Shultz, *Turmoil and Triumph: My Years as Secretary of State* (New York: Charles Scribners' Sons, 1993), pp. 1112–18.

[413] A grand tour of Angola and the terrible damage wrought by Savimbi and his backers is provided by my neighbor, John Frederick Walker, *A Certain Curve of Horn: The Hundred-Year Quest for the Giant Sable Antelope of Angola* (New York: Grove Press, 2002, 2004). Walker writes as one who has spent time in Angola.

[414] Joseph Conrad, *Heart of Darkness* (New York: Alfred A. Knopf, [1902] 1993), p. 71.

[415] Kissinger, *White House Years*, p. 47.

[416] Haig, *Caveat*, pp. 84, 356.

[417] Vladimir Nabokov, ed. Fredson Bowers, *Lectures on Russian Literature* (New York: Harcourt Brace Jovanovich, 1981), p. 104.

[418] *Orbis*, Winter 1983, p. 849-867.

[419] Norman F. Cantor, *Antiquity, From the Birth of Sumerian Civilization to the Fall of the Roman Empire* (New York: HarperCollins Publisher, 2003), p. 10.

[420] Information about the architecture of various embassies, including the one in Athens, is found in Elizabeth Gill Lui, *Building Diplomacy: The Architecture of American Embassies* (Los Angeles: Four Stops Press, 2004).

[421] "Greek Ex-Leader Deplores Policy On Plane Downing and Missiles," *New York Times*, September 20, 1983.

[422] Monteagle Stearns, *Entangled Allies: U.S. Policy Toward Greece, Turkey, and Cyprus* (New York: Council on Foreign Relations Press, 1992), p. 143.

[423] Arthur Miller, *Timesbends: A Life* (New York: Grove Press, 1987), p. 143.

[424] Brzezinski, in his previously cited *Second Chance*, makes the comment: "One has to wonder what might have happened if, instead of sharing his concerns [about the course on which Bush was embarked with regard to Iraq] with a writer planning a book, he [Powell] had chosen to take a public stand on a matter so central to the national interest" (pp. 141-42).

[425] Susan Butler, ed., *My Dear Mr. Stalin: The Complete Correspondence of Franklin D. Roosevelt and Joseph V. Stalin* (New Haven: Yale University Press, 2005) p. 256,

citing Thomas M. Campbell and George C. Herring, eds., *The Diaries of Edward R. Stettinius, Jr., 1943-1946* (New York: New Viewpoints, 1975), pp. 128, 130.

[426] "Modest Hope for Soviet Trade Talks," *New York Times*, May 20, 1985; "Trade Gain In Soviet Talks Seen," *New York Times*, May 22, 1985.

[427] Service, *Stalin*, p. 561, citing A. Mgeladze, *Stalin, Kakim ya ego znal, Stranitsy nedavnego proshlogo* (2001), pp. 224–25.

Chapter 12

[428] *Reagan Diaries*, p. 348

[429] Gorbachev, *Memoirs*, p. 221.

[430] Lydia Kirk, *Postmarked Moscow* (New York: Charles Scribner's Sons, 1952), p. 273.

[431] Marie Brenner, "Mr. Ambassador! Bob Strauss Comes Home," *New Yorker*, December 28, 1992, p. 146. Brenner attributes the description to Strauss without using quotation marks.

[432] "Poetry in Motion on Capitol Hill," *New York Times*, July 23, 1985.

[433] Francine du Plessix Gray, *Them: A Memoir of Parents* (New York: Penguin Press, 2005), p. 51.

[434] Shultz, *Turmoil and Triumph*, pp. 583–84.

[435] Ibid., p. 585.

[436] Ibid., p. 171.

[437] Rothkopf, *Running the World*, p. 210

[438] Geoffrey A. Hosking, *Times Literary Supplement* (London), February 1, 1991, p. 4. Hosking writes that "the sentiment which permeates his [Pipes'] book is that the Russians must be written off as a primitive and boorish people capable of only dominant or submissive relationships."

[439] Shultz, *Turmoil and Triumph*, pp. 267–68.

[440] *Reagan Diaries*, p. 131. See also Shultz, *Turmoil and Triumph*, pp. 164-65.

[441] Richard Pipes, *Vixi, Memoirs of a Non-Belonger* (New Haven: Yale University Press, 2003).

[442] Ibid., p. 206, pp. 161–62.

[443] Lee, *Russian Journal*, p. 100.

[444] Kessler, *Moscow Station*, p. 11.

[445] Ibid., p. 117.

[446] Charlotte Y. Salisbury, *Russian Diary* (New York: Walker and Company, 1974), p. 70.

[447] L. N. Tolstoy, *Anna Karenina* (Moskva: "Khudozhestvennaya literatura", 1985), p. 718. See also pp. 361 and 752.

[448] Pipes, *Vixi*, p. 65.

[449] *Harvard University Alumni Gazette* (Cambridge), Winter/Spring 1993, p. 12. This is Hartman's paraphrase of what Kennan had said.

450 ROBERT F. OBER, JR.

450 Dobrynin, *In Confidence,* p. 585.

451 Matlock, *Reagan and Gorbachev,* p. 94.

452 Dobrynin, *In Confidence,* p. 575.

453 Ibid., p. 582.

454 Shultz, *Turmoil and Triumph,* p. 586 et seq.

455 Ibid., p. 597.

456 Ibid., p. 595.

457 Leo Tolstoy, trans. Ann Dunnigan *War and Peace* (New York: New American Library, 1968), pp. 233, 302.

458 Lillian Hellman, *An Unfinished Woman: A Memoir* (Boston: Little, Brown and Company, 1969, 1999), p. 164.

459 Shultz, *Turmoil and Triumph,* p. 603.

460 Kessler, *Moscow Station,* p. 134.

461 *Reagan Diaries,* p. 269.

462 Ibid., p. 151.

463 Statements made by Washington officials were routinely dispatched to the embassy in so-called "daily wireless files." Quotations in chapters 12 through 15 attributed to American officials often come from these dispatches, excerpts of which I have on file.

464 A senior CIA officer, now retired, affirmed his belief in the usefulness of these tests in a conversation with me in August 2006. He asserted that no more than 5 percent of test-takers are able to beat them, namely, those who are "sociopathic." To me, a 5 percent failure rate argues for their ineffectiveness as a tool to ferret out spies, some of whom probably are sociopathic. One possible way to beat a polygraph test is described in Martin L. Kaiser III and Robert S. Stokes, *Odyssey of an Eavesdropper: My Life in Electronic Countermeasures and My Battle Against the FBI* (New York: Carroll & Graf Publishers, 2005), p. 44.

465 Bohlen, *Witness to History,* pp. 320-31.

466 Fritz Stern, *Five Germanys I Have Known* (New York: Farrar, Straus and Giroux, 2006), p. 430.

467 Shultz, *Turmoil and Triumph,* p. 801. Shultz elaborated on polygraph evidence in testimony (which drew on a scientific study conducted by Congress's Office of Technology Assessment [OTA]) before the Senate Appropriations Committee in 1988, as quoted in a report delivered by Under Secretary of State Ronald I. Spiers on May 6, 1988:

> "In screening situations (where one in 1,000 may be guilty), OTA pointed out that even if one assumed that the polygraph is 99% accurate, the laws of probability indicate that one guilty person would be correctly identified as deceptive but 10 persons would be incorrectly identified as deceptive (false positives). An accuracy rate of something less than 100% may be acceptable in attempting

to forecast the weather. It should never be acceptable in matters affecting the reputations and the livelihoods of individuals."

[468] Ibid. pp. 885–86. In December 1987 Shultz urged Reagan to veto the Congressional authorization for the department because it called for administering the polygraph to State employees, *Reagan Diaries*, p. 560.

[469] Aleksandr I. Solzhenitsyn, trans. Harry Willetts, *The Oak and the Calf: Sketches of Literary Life in the Soviet Union* (New York: Harper & Row, Publishers, 1975), pp. 92-97, 174; Michael Scammell, *Solzhenitsyn, A Biography* (New York: W.W. Norton & Company, 1984), p. 514 et seq.

[470] My copy (in Russian)

[471] Kulagin, *First Directorate*, p. 217

[472] *Izvestiya*, August 21, 1986.

[473] *Journal of the US-USSR Trade and Economic Council*, vol. 11, no. 1, 1986.

[474] Spoof memorandum: as with other memoranda, in my files.

[475] Kennan, *Memoirs*, pp. 84–85.

Chapter 13

[476] "Remembering Chernobyl: Wet Rugs, Stonewalling Officials and a Run on Vodka," *New York Times*, April 27, 2006.

[477] My file.

[478] FDA report, my file.

[479] "In Throats of Emigres, Doctors Find Chernobyl's Toll," *New York Times*, April 20, 2006. The article states: "Thyroid cancers occurred most often in children, and those tended to appear in the first decade. But for adults exposed to radiation, thyroid cancer can take 20 years or more to develop."

[480] Press release, "Chernobyl Catastrophe Consequences on Human Health," April 21, 2006.

[481] *Economist*, April 22, 2006.

[482] *Memoirs*, pp. 290–92, 560–65.

[483] *Russia*, pp. 66, 140–41.

[484] Kirk, *Postmarked Moscow*, p. 74.

[485] Round, Window, pp. 132–33.

[486] Salisbury, *Journey of Our Times*, p. 39.

[487] But Molotov had special permission to do so as he mentions in *Molotov Remembers, Inside Kremlin Politics* (Chicago: Ivan Dee, 1993), p. 279.

[488] My file.

[489] Taubman, *Khrushchev*, pp. 589-90, citing Priscilla Johnson McMillan, *Khrushchev and the Arts:The Politics of Soviet Culture, 1962–1964* (Cambridge: MIT Press, 1965), pp. 101–05.

[490] Wat, *My Century*, p. 320.

[491] My file.

[492] *Reagan and Gorbachev*, pp. 197–98.

[493] Shultz, *Turmoil and Triumph*, p. 734.

[494] They had come to the public's attention in 1984 with publicity surrounding the arrest of an FBI special agent, Richard Miller, for selling classified documents to two Soviet KGB agents operating in Los Angeles.

[495] Letter, *International Herald Tribune*, October 25–26, 1986. At U.S. insistence, the Soviet authorities let a dissident and his wife emigrate after Daniloff's release so it would appear that more than a "trade" was involved.

[496] Nicholas Daniloff, *Two Lives, One Russia* (Boston: Houghton Mifflin Company, 1988).

[497] Ibid., p. 295

[498] Ibid., pp. 298, 260.

[499] Ibid., p. 4.

[500] Richard Stites, *Russian Popular Culture, Entertainment and Society Since 1900* (Cambridge: Cambridge University Press, 1992), p. 108.

[501] Rodric Braithwaite relates the story of Zhukov's intervention with Stalin to save Konev in his *Moscow 1941: A City and Its People at War* (New York: Alfred A. Knopf, 2006), pp. 203–04.

[502] Vera Vladimirovna Vishnyakova-Akimova, *Two Years in Revolutionary China*, p. 148.

[503] Stella Dong, *Shanghai, The Rise and Fall of a Decadent City* (New York: William Morrow, 2000), p. 38.

[504] I.M. Yampolski et al, *Musikalnaya Entsiklopediya* (Moscow: Izdatelstvo "*Sovetskaya entsiklopediya,*" 1976), vol. 3. p. 1003.

[505] Stites, *Russian Popular Culture*, p. 39.

[506] Diary, Ekaterina Voroshilova, Russian State Archive of Social and Political History, quoted in Montefiore, *Stalin*, p. 82. Jakub Berman, a Communist leader in Poland after World War II, described a typical evening with Stalin and his cronies at Stalin's dacha outside Moscow. After toasting, Stalin "would put on a record, generally Georgian music, which he adored. Once, in 1948, I think, I danced with Molotov . . . . I think it was a waltz, or at any rate something very simple, because I don't know the faintest thing about dancing, so I just moved my feet in rhythm." Teresa Toranska, trans. Agnieszka Kolakowska, "*Them*", *Stalin's Polish Puppets* (New York: Harper & Row, Publishers, 1988), p. 235.

[507] Margaret Wettlin, *Fifty Russian Winters: An American Woman's Life in the Soviet Union* (New York: Pharos Books, 1992), p. 240.

[508] Kennan, *Memoirs*, p. 240.

[509] Several officers, in addition to Ambassador Smith, resided at Spaso House at the time. At least two were FSOs. See Smith, *My Three Years,* pp. 86–88. Hellman writes of a "few foreign [service] career officers" living there in 1945, Hellman, *Unfinished Woman*, p. 180. One could have been a consular officer.

[510] "Will History Applaud?" *Foreign Service Journal,* September 1986.

[511] Kessler, *Moscow Station,* pp. 83, 263.

[512] Matlock, *Reagan and Gorbachev,* p. 201. The memoirs of Matlock and Shultz as well as pertinent issues of the *New York Times* were helpful in reconstructing this prolonged affair.

Chapter 14

[513] Articles in the *New York Times,* October 22–25, 1986, report on Gorbachev's and Gerasimov's statements, the tit-for-tat expulsions, and Washington's imposition of its ceiling.

[514] "Soviet Archives Provide Missing Pieces of History's Puzzles," *New York Times,* February 8, 1993.

[515] "Expulsion Rounds Now Appear Over," *New York Times,* October 24, 1986.

[516] Matlock, *Reagan and Gorbachev,* p. 207.

[517] "In Moscow, A Do-It-Yourself Embassy Copes," *New York Times,* October 24, 1986.

[518] "When Russia, Slyly, Expels Russians," *New York Times,* October 23, 1986.

[519] "NSC, State Lock Horns Over Staff in Moscow," *Washington Times,* November 18, 1986.

[520] Shultz, *Turmoil and Triumph,* p. 167.

[521] Ibid., p. 788.

[522] "Vibrant Birds of America, Via Germany," *New York Times,* June 25, 2004, and "In Moscow, a Proud Display of Spoils of War," *New York Times,* May 17, 2005.

[523] Marquis de Custine, ed. and trans. Phyllis Penn Kohler, *Journey for Our Time* (London: Arthur Barker, 1951), p. 232.

[524] This memorandum and others quoted in this chapter are from my files.

[525] Gates, *From the Shadows,* p. 385.

[526] From a Knight-Ridder news service dispatch summarizing a report by Representatives Daniel Mica of Florida and Olympia Snowe of Maine, based on their interviews with thirty-five embassy employees. My copy of the article, "Soviets reported harassing U.S. Embassy employees in Moscow" is from the *Hartford Courant,* May 14, 1987, which chose to include a comment from me, "I don't think anyone's made a credible case that the Soviets contaminated our drinking water." *The Foreign Service Journal,* May 2007, contains an article by Allan Mustard, "Recalling All-Purpose Duty in Russia," that describes conditions at Tchaikovsky 19 after the withdrawal of the Soviet employees. Allen was serving at the embassy at the time and recounts some of the stories then circulating:

> Hoses were slashed on washing machines, causing apartment floods. The lug nuts on DCM Combs' car were loosened, and the right front wheel fell off in traffic.

Diesel fuel was poured into gas tanks, and it jelled when the mercury dropped, plugging fuel lines. We later learned that the PNG'ed KGB and GRU officers had been unleashed against us.

I subsequently spoke with Dick Combs and he explained that the lug nuts on one wheel had become loose for reasons he couldn't explain, but the wheel never fell off and he dealt with the problem, which came to his attention because of the wheel's thumping sound. Dick had not heard the story about the unleashing of the PNG'ed Soviet officials.

I hadn't either. I find it improbable, although "free-lancing" by one or two such types could not be excluded. Allen later tracked me down to describe how his Volvo had been disabled by diesel fuel that jelled at seventeen below zero, forcing his wife to abandon their vehicle on a Moscow street.

[527] David Wise, *Nightmover: How Aldrich Ames Sold the CIA to the KGB for $4.6 Million* (New York: HarperCollins Publishers, 1995), p. 155. See also Wise's review of Kessler's book *Moscow Station*, "Once More Into the Embassy," *New York Times*, March 19, 1989.

[528] Matlock, *Reagan and Gorbachev*, p. 255.

[529] Ibid., p. 256.

[530] Ibid.

[531] Cherkashin, *Spy Handler*, pp. 231–39.

[532] Wise, *Nightmover*, p. 156.

[533] Gorbachev, *Memoirs*, pp. 206–07.

[534] Edward Shevardnadze, trans. Catherine A. Fitzpatrick, *The Future Belongs to Freedom* (New York: Maxwell Macmillan International, 1991), p. 200; "From Russia With Scorn," *New York Times*, November 29, 1987.

[535] The rank of ambassador was first granted to the senior American diplomat posted in Paris in 1893, and the grandfather of Charles Bohlen, interestingly, was the one to receive it.

[536] Walter Isaacson, *Benjamin Franklin: An American Life* (New York: Simon & Schuster, 2003), pp. 333-34.

[537] Stacy Schiff, *A Great Improvisation: Franklin, France, and The Birth of America* (New York: Henry Holt and Company, 2005), p. 5.

[538] Isaacson, *Franklin*, p. 336, pp. 44–45. See also Schiff, *Improvisation*, pp. 44–45.

[539] Harvard University *Alumni Gazette*, Winter/Spring 1993.

[540] Shultz, *Turmoil and Triumph*, p. 588.

[541] Graham Greene recounts a visit to the British ambassador's office in Warsaw (I used to visit Ambassador Thomas Brimelow there in 1966–67), and being "astonished by the freedom of his [ambassador's] speech between four walls." The ambassador explained to Greene that [Polish] "technicians came every

four weeks to check them." Greene said that it reminded him of a madam in a brothel who "assures the client that her girls are safe because they are 'inspected' by a doctor once a week," *Ways of Escape*, p. 234.

[542] Kessler, *Moscow Station*, p. 139.

[543] Jack F. Matlock, Jr., *Autopsy On An Empire: The American Ambassador's Account of the Collapse of the Soviet Union* (New York: Random House, 1995), p. 100.

[544] "Mr. Ambassador!" *New Yorker*, December 28, 1992, p. 151.

[545] Ron Chernow used the phrase to describe Alexander Hamilton as he pursued his career as an establishment outsider, *Alexander Hamilton* (New York: Penguin Press, 2004), p. 167.

[546] Anton Chekhov, trans. Laurence Senelick, *The Complete Plays* (New York: W.W. Norton & Company, 2006), p. 1043.

[547] Watson letter to author, July 12, 1991.

[548] Milt Bearden and James Risen, *The Main Enemy: The Inside Story of the CIA's Final Showdown with the KGB* (New York: Random House, 2003), p. 35. Cherkashin confirmed Tolkachev's approach at Spaso House, *KGB Officer*, p. 131.

[549] John le Carré, *The Secret Pilgrim* (New York: Alfred A. Knopf, 1990), p. 41. An observation of Justice Learned Hand that I recall from law school also comes to mind: "I believe that community is already in process of dissolution when each man begins to eye his neighbor as a possible enemy . . . where denunciation, without specification or backing, takes the place of evidence . . . ." Hand made the statement in New York at a time (October 24, 1952) when Senator McCarthy enjoyed considerable public support.

Epilogue

[550] "Transcript of Reagan's News Conference on Security at Moscow Embassy," *New York Times*, April 8, 1987.

[551] *Reagan Diaries*, p. 586.

[552] "Comment by Lawmakers," *New York Times*, April 8, 1987.

[553] Matlock, *Reagan and Gorbachev*, pp. 259–60.

[554] "U.S. Investigating Envoy Socializing," *New York Times*, May 5, 1987.

[555] "Webster Says F.B.I. Has the State Dept. Under Investigation," *New York Times*, May 9, 1987.

[556] Ibid.

[557] James Webb, *Something To Die For* (New York: William Morrow and Company, 1991). The only FSO who rose to become a secretary of defense was Frank C. Carlucci. According to the *Washington Post* (October 27, 2006), Webb quit as navy secretary after clashing with Carlucci. Reagan noted his departure in a diary entry February 22, 1988: "I don't think Navy was sorry to see him go" (*Reagan Diaries*, p. 580). Webb was elected to the U.S. Senate in 2006; during

the campaign, his opponent, Senator George Allen, raised questions about Webb based on passages from his other novels.

[558] Bloom, *Closing of the American Mind*, p. 112.

[559] Letters in my file.

[560] "Distractions Vex Envoys In the Soviet," *New York Times*, November 16, 1987.

[561] "Fire Hits U.S. Embassy in Moscow, Forcing Evacuation of Its Staff," *New York Times*, February 18, 1988.

[562] "U.S. and Soviets Agree to Increase Embassy Staffs," *New York Times*, March 4, 1989.

[563] Kessler, *Moscow Station*, p. 18.

[564] "C.I.A. Says Soviets Did Not Tap Codes," *New York Times*, February 15, 1989.

[565] Commandant's letter from 1989 is cited in "Top Military Court Hears Appeal of a Marine Convicted of Spying," *New York Times*, May 13, 1991.

[566] "American Embassy in Moscow Is Severely Damaged by Fire," *New York Times*, March 29 and "U.S. Asserts K.G.B. Entered Embassy, *New York Times*, May 1, 1991. There were other incidents, including the firing of a rocket-propelled grenade from Tchaikovsky Street into the chancery's sixth floor, without causing casualties, in 1995. Spaso House experienced its own mishaps; in 1988, Soviet fireman had to extinguish a fire there that caused property damage.

[567] *Newsweek*, May 13, 1991.

[568] Matlock, *Autopsy on an Empire*, pp. 525 et seq.

[569] Ibid. p. 576–77.

[570] A full report appeared in *Moscow News*, December 29, 1991-January 5, 1992 issue.

[571] "Russians Grouse (at U.S. Embassy)," *New York Times*, November 18, 1994. Andrei Sakharov had earlier commented on Kovalev's courage: "Kudirka had to enter the American embassy several times—this in a country where such visits by an ordinary citizen are viewed as near-treason—and on two occasions was stopped and searched after meeting with consular officials," *Memoirs* (New York, Vintage Books, 1992), p. 413.

[572] John le Carré, *The Tailor of Panama* (New York: Alfred A. Knopf, 1996), p. 95.

[573] Matlock, *Autopsy on an Empire*, p. 802 n. 21.

[574] Matlock, *Reagan and Gorbachev*, pp. 255–6.

[575] Jennifer Bremer, "Our Diplomats' Arabic Handicap," *Washington Post*, October 16, 2004.

[576] Information extracted from Barnes and Morgan, *Foreign Service of the United States*, pp. 370–72.

[577] Robert F. Ober, Jr, *Seeing Arabs Through an American School, A Beirut Memoir*, *1998-2001* (Philadelphia: Xlibris, 2003), p. 227, quoting Ferguson, *New York Times Magazine*, April 27, 2003, pp. 54, 56-57.

[578] L. Paul Bremer, *My Year in Iraq, The Struggle to Build a Future of Hope* (New York: Simon & Schuster, 2006), pp. 3–5 et seq. As Ambassador Peter Galbraith wrote in the *New York Review of Books*, March 9, 2006, "Bremer knew nothing about Iraq. He had never been there, did not speak Arabic, had no experience in dealing with a country emerging from war, and had never been involved in 'nation-building.'" Surely our country could have done better!

[579] Bremer, *My Year*, p. 187.

[580] George Packer, *The Assassins' Gate: America in Iraq* (New York: Farrar, Straus and Giroux, 2005), p. 184.

[581] Rajiv Chandrasekaran, *Imperial Life in the Emerald City: Inside Iraq's Green Zone* (New York: Alfred A. Knopf, 2006), p. 194. According to the author, Bremer considered the privatization of Iraq's state-owned enterprises his "third" highest priority (despite the fact these enterprises had been "ground down" by years of dictatorial rule and international sanctions), and brought to Baghdad, at the behest of President Bush, a Harvard Business School (HBS) graduate and Republican fundraiser, Tom Foley, to oversee the operation. Foley, a successful businessman, knew no Arabic and had no prior experience in the Middle East. After a few unproductive months, he left to become Bush's ambassador to Ireland. (Altogether, by 2007, Bush, an HBS graduate, had appointed eight of the school's alumni, including his own classmate and Foley's sister-in-law, to U.S. ambassadorships, according to *02138, The World of Harvard*, September-October 2007, p. 24.)

[582] Packer, *Assassins' Gate*, p. 132.

[583] According to Bremer's account (pp. 44, 137), Horan, the service's most accomplished Arabic speaker, was present when the notorious de-Baathification decree (CPA Order No. 1 of May 16, 2003) was signed. The decree deprived tens of thousands of Sunnis of their positions in the Iraqi military and government, and drove many into the resistance. The decree probably made sense to Horan. His mother was American but his father was an Iranian diplomat, a Shiite. Horan was being used by Bremer as an emissary to the Shiites. In *The Arabists: The Romance of an American Elite* (New York: Free Press, 1993), Robert D. Kaplan suggests that Horan's earlier mission to Saudi Arabia, where only Sunnis reign, had been cut short because of King Fahd's distaste for Horan's heritage (pp. 197–98, pp. 231–33). Horan took his own life after leaving Iraq, where his career had begun in the 1960s. Prime Minister Blair has conceded that de-Baathification was a mistake (White House Press Release, May 25, 2006); I am not aware that Bush has addressed the subject. Packer in *Assassins' Gate* and Thomas E. Ricks in *Fiasco: The American Military Adventure in Iraq* (New York: Penguin Press, 2006) examine the far-reaching effects of Bremer's first decisions. Bush's key policymakers began to distance themselves from Bremer and Bremer's decision as the insurgency grew. See Bob

Woodward, *State of Denial: Bush at War, Part III* (New York: Simon & Schuster, 2006), pp. 191–198, 219, 224.

[584] James Risen, *State of War: The Secret History of the CIA and the Bush Administration* (New York: Free Press, 2006), p. 143.

[585] See Kaplan, *The Arabists,* pp. 7–8. Kaplan notes Francis Fukuyama's charge that State Department Arabists have been more wrong than any other area specialists because they "not only take on the cause of the Arabs, but also the Arabs' tendency for self-delusion." (This purports to be a quotation from Fukuyama, but no source is cited in my edition of Kaplan's book). Fukuyama is the author of *The End of History*, proclaiming the final triumph of liberal democracy following the Soviet collapse. An account of the harassment of the service's China hands is provided by E. J. Kahn, Jr., *The China Hands, America's Foreign Service Officers and What Befell Them* (New York: Viking Press, 1972, 1975). A recent succinct account appears in a subparagraph entitled "Flogging the China Hands" in Beisner, *Dean Acheson*, pp. 299–303.

[586] It is declining in most Western countries. Jacques Barzun, a specialist in European culture and once Columbia University's dean and provost, has written that "[i]t is a noteworthy feature of 20C [twentieth century] culture that for the first time in over a thousand years its educated class is not expected to be at least bilingual." *From Dawn to Decadence: 1500 to the Present* (New York: HarperCollins Publishers, 2000), p. 45.

[587] Emails I forwarded to the State Department, following its web site's invitation to ask questions, have gone unanswered, despite automatic replies indicating responses would be forthcoming. (E.g., on February 14, 2006, I received the following reply: "[t]hank you for your question to the U.S. Department of State Web site. Your question has been received and we are working on an answer for you."). An official at the FSI, after confirming I wasn't a journalist and requesting anonymity, gave me a thumbnail sketch of the department's language field schools. He confirmed that there are no programs except those at the FSI to train diplomats for service in Russia.

[588] George Staples, "Setting the Record Straight," *State Magazine*, February 2007, p. 4.

[589] "Many In State Dept. Can't Talk the Talk," *Washington Post*, August 11, 2006.

[590] Malcolm Gladwell, "Open Secrets," *The New Yorker*, January 8, 2007, p 52.

[591] Rothkopf, *Running the World*, p. 203. Odom goes on to say that "[y]ou listen to area experts before you go to the policymaking meeting. Sort out what they have to say about realities, facts, etc. You really need to listen to them. They can tell you useful things. But you don't want them telling you what to do. So, the Carter NSC staff had a good process." If the process was so good, I wonder why are we where we are with Iran today.

[592] Brzezinski, *Power*, p. 450.

[593] John D. Stempel, *Inside the Iranian Revolution* (Bloomington: Indiana University Press, 1981), p. 70.

[594] Ibid., p. 71. The head of the Iranian desk, Henry Precht, has said that the "[t]he reporting from the embassy was generally terrible . . . ;" "The Iranian Revolution: An Oral History, *Middle East Journal*, Winter 2004 (vol. 58, no. 1), p. 15.

[595] Mark Bowden, *Guests of the Ayatollah: The First Battle in America's War with Militant Islam* (New York: Atlantiic Monthly Press, 2006), pp. 178, 122; Brzezinski, *Power*, p. 367.

[596] Edward G. Shirley, "Can't Anybody Here Play This Game?" *Atlantic Monthly*, February 1998, p. 48.

[597] Precht, "The Iranian Revolution," *Middle East Journal*, p. 12. As Precht and others acknowledge, there were differences inside the department about how to deal with Iran, including what posture to take toward the shah's opposition. Precht himself was blocked by department superiors from meeting with Ibrahim Yazdi, a close Khomeini aide, when he passed through Washington a year before the diplomats were seized; but these differences turned out to be minor compared to those which later developed between the department and the White House.

[598] Kenneth M. Pollack, *The Persian Puzzle: The Conflict Between Iran and America* (New York: Random House, 2004), pp. 95, 106, 163.

[599] Precht, "The Iranian Revolution," *Middle East Journal*, pp. 16–17. About his exclusion, Precht said: "There is a moment when the desk officer is listened to and then after that he is pushed into the background."

[600] Ibid, p. 23.

[601] Brzezinski, *Power*, p. 376 et seq.; Pollack, *Puzzle*, p. 172; Precht, *Middle East Journal*, p. 23; Stempel, *Inside the Revolution*, p. 160.

[602] Brzezinski, *Power*, p. 359 et seq.

[603] *Inside the Revolution*, pp. 148, 156–57. Gary Sick, a scholar and former Navy attaché in Egypt, who was involved with Iranian affairs at the NSC, discussed Brzezinski's relationship with Zahedi and Zahedi's ambitions in *All Fall Down, America's Tragic Encounter with Iran* (New York: Random House, 1985), p. 70 et seq.

[604] Sick, *All Fall Down*, p. 106. Various theories abounded in the NSC at the beginning, underscoring the absence of a steady hand with prior experience in Tehran. Brzezinski neglects to mention the Soviet "theory" in his memoir.

[605] Ibid. This, according to Sick, was Precht's view.

[606] Precht, *Middle East Journal*, p. 19.

[607] Brzezinski, *Power*, p. 520.

[608] *Détente and Confrontation*, p. 742 n. 174.

[609] Brzezinski, *Power*, p. 514.

[610] Brzezinski, ibid., pp. 355, 396. Precht rejects this characterization in *Middle East Journal*, p. 25. For Vance's reaction, see *Hard Choices*, p. 328.

[611] Secretary Condoleezza Rice, Remarks, Georgetown School of Foreign Service, U.S. Department of State *Fact Sheet*, January 18, 2006.

[612] J. Anthony Holmes, President's Views, *Foreign Service Journal*, May 2006, p. 5.

[613] David T. Jones, "Speaking Out," *Foreign Service Journal*, July-August 2006, p. 16.

[614] "Foreign Service Gets A Re-Exam," *Washington Post*, December 12, 2006.

[615] John K. Naland, "The New Foreign Service," *Foreign Service Journal*, February 2007, p. 46.

Index

Note: The following index does not give a range of pages if the subject is treated on more than one page. To the extent there are interruptions, however, a page number will be provided when discussion of a subject resumes.

O

P

Printed in the United States
116417LV00005B/52/P

9 781425 778460